National Welfare Benefits Handbook

24th edition

Lynn Webster
and
Geoff Tait
David Simmons
Gary Vaux
Martin Barnes
Emma Knights
Jim Read
Janet Gurney

[Handwritten annotations:]

✱ IS First — See if
qualifies, if Qualifies.
get 100% CT /HB.

If NO — HB/CTB/FC

FC — FT, Resp for child

FC, First the HB /CTB
FC is Taken o/b
A/c for both

Qualifying Conditions →

Child Poverty Action Group

Published by CPAG Ltd
1-5 Bath Street, London EC1V 9PY

© CPAG Ltd 1994

A CIP record for this book is available from the British Library

ISBN 0-946744-59-9

Cover and design by Devious Designs, 0742 755634
Typeset by Boldface, 071 253 2014
Printed by Bath Press, Avon

Contents

PART SEVEN: CALCULATING NEEDS AND RESOURCES

PART EIGHT: THE REGULATED SOCIAL FUND

PART NINE: THE DISCRETIONARY SOCIAL FUND

Acknowledgements

The present authors would like to thank the many contributors who have come before and, in particular, those who have worked on the post-1988 versions of this *Handbook*: Sarah Campling, Rob Good, John Hannam, Ian Hillier, Beth Lakhani, Jan Luba, Jim McKenny, Anna Ravetz, Marcus Revell, Jim Read, Mark Rowland, Penny Waterhouse and Penny Wood. We would also like to acknowledge the generous contributions made by DSS staff over the years; their co-operation has proved invaluable.

The Crown copyright material on pp102 and 103 was reproduced with the kind permission of the Controller of Her Majesty's Stationery Office.

We are especially grateful to Martin Barnes, Alison Garnham, Carolyn George, Jim Gray, Beth Lakhani, Lee Ogilvy-Webb, Jim Read and David Thomas for their meticulous checking and helpful suggestions. In particular, thanks to Jim McKenny for his contribution to the text and for agreeing to read and check the entire book at breakneck speed.

Thanks are also due to Debbie Licorish and Mary Shirley for their editorial and production work; to Katherine Dawson and Andrew Land for their swift and conscientious indexing; to Debbie Haynes and her team of packers for distributing the book; and to Peter Ridpath for marketing it.

Finally we would like to express our gratitude to the staff of Boldface Typesetters and the Bath Press for reliably meeting a very tight printing schedule.

Means-tested benefit rates

Income support applicable amounts

Personal allowances

under 18* (usual rate)	£27.50
under 18* (in certain circumstances)	£36.15
aged 18-24	£36.15
aged 25 or over	£45.70
Single parent	
under 18* (usual rate)	£27.50
under 18* (in certain circumstances)	£36.15
aged 18 or over	£45.70
Couple	
both under 18*	£54.55
one/both over 18*	£71.70
Dependent children	
under 11	£15.65
aged 11-15	£23.00
aged 16-17*	£27.50
aged 18	£36.15

*For eligibility of under-18s and calculating amounts, see pp67-76.

Premiums

Family	£10.05	
Lone parent	£ 5.10	/11·25 (HB, CTB)
Pensioner 60-74		
single	£18.25	
couple	£27.55	
Enhanced pensioner 75-79		
single	£20.35	
couple	£30.40	
Higher pensioner 80 +		
single	£24.70	
couple	£35.30	
Disability OR 60 ·		
single	£19.45	
couple	£27.80	
Severe disability		
single	£34.30	
couple (if one qualifies)	£34.30	
couple (if both qualify)	£68.60	
Disabled child	£19.45	

DLA
MA

Carer's   £12.40

Some claimants have their applicable amount calculated differently. This applies to the following groups:

Claimants who are only entitled to the urgent cases rate – see p44.
Claimants subject to a child support benefit penalty – p128.
Claimants who are voluntarily unemployed – see p58.
Claimants on government training schemes – see p61.
Claimants on strike – see p77.
Claimants in residential care or nursing homes – see p97.
Claimants in hospital – see p113.
Claimants who are prisoners – see p117.
Claimants without accommodation – see p119.

Housing benefit applicable amounts

Personal allowances and premiums as for income support,
except single person aged 16-24   £36.15
single parent under 18   £36.15
lone parent premium   £11.25

Council tax benefit

Personal allowances and premiums as for income support,
except lone parent premium   £11.25

Family credit

Adult credit   £44.30
Child credit
    under 11   £11.20
    aged 11-15   £18.55
    aged 16-17   £23.05
    aged 18   £32.20
Applicable amount (ie, threshold level)   £71.70

Disability working allowance

Adult credit
    single   £46.05
    couple/lone parent   £63.75
Child credit
    under 11   £11.20
    aged 11-15   £18.55
    aged 16-17   £23.05
    aged 18   £32.20
Applicable amount (ie, threshold level)
    single   £43.00
    couple/lone parent   £71.70

Social fund payments

Maternity expenses	£100.00
Cold weather payment	£7.00

Capital limits

Income support	£8,000.00
Family credit	£8,000.00
Housing benefit	£16,000.00
Council tax benefit	£16,000.00
Disability working allowance	£16,000.00

Non-means-tested benefit rates

Earnings replacement benefits

	Claimant £pw	Adult dependant £pw	Child dependant £pw
Unemployment benefit			
under pensionable age	45.45	28.05	
of or over pensionable age	57.60	34.50	11.00*
Sickness benefit			
under pensionable age	43.45	26.90	
of or over pensionable age	55.25	33.10	11.00*
Invalidity pension	57.60	34.50	11.00*
Invalidity allowance			
higher rate	12.15		
middle rate	7.60		
lower rate	3.80		
Statutory sick pay			
higher rate	52.50		
lower rate	47.80		
Severe disablement allowance	34.80	20.70	11.00*
Age-related addition –			
higher rate	12.15		
middle rate	7.60		
lower rate	3.80		
Statutory maternity pay (lower rate)	48.80		
Maternity allowance	44.55	26.90	
Invalid care allowance	34.50	20.65	11.00*
Widowed mother's allowance	57.60		11.00*
Widow's pension (55 or over)	57.60		
Widow's pension (45-54) from	17.28-52.17		11.00*
Retirement pension			
Category A	57.60	34.50	11.00*
Category B for a married woman	34.50		11.00*
Category B for a widow	57.60		11.00*
Category B for a widower	57.60		11.00*
Category C for a person not			
a married woman	34.50	20.65	11.00*

	Claimant £pw	Adult dependant £pw	Child dependant £pw
Category C for a married woman	20.65		11.00*
Category D	34.30		11.00*

Benefits for the severely disabled

£pw

Attendance allowance
  higher rate   45.70
  lower rate   30.55

Disability living allowance

Care component
  Higher   45.70
  Middle   30.55
  Lower   12.15
Mobility component
  Higher   31.95
  Lower   12.15

Industrial injuries benefits

Disablement benefit – variable, up to 100%   18.64-93.20

Industrial death benefit

Widow
  higher permanent rate   57.60
  lower permanent rate   17.28
Widower   57.60
Child   11.00*

Benefits for children

£pw

Child benefit (for only or eldest child)	10.20
(for other children)	8.25
One parent benefit	6.15
Guardian's allowance	11.00*
Child's special allowance	11.00*

*These are reduced by £1.20 for any child for whom you receive the higher rate of child benefit.

Income tax allowances

	pa	pw
Personal allowance	£3,445	£66.25
Married couple allowance	£1,720	£33.07

Additional personal allowance for
  caring for children   £1,720   £33.07
Blind person's allowance   £1,200

National insurance contributions

gross weekly earnings
Below £57   Nil
£57-£430   2% on the first £57 and
                                     10% on the rest, up to £430

This is the 'contracted-in' rate for Class 1 contributions. For other NI rates, see
CPAG's *Rights Guide to Non-Means-Tested Benefits*, Chapter 12.

Bands of taxable income (£)   *1994/95*

Lower rate – 20%   £0-£3,000
Basic rate – 25%   £3,001-£23,700
Upper rate – 40%   over £23,700

PART ONE

Introduction

CHAPTER ONE

An introduction to means tests

This *Handbook* covers only those benefits which are 'means-tested'. This chapter explains:

1. Which benefits are means-tested (below)
2. The administration of means-tested benefits (p4)
3. How means tests work (p8)

I. WHICH BENEFITS ARE MEANS-TESTED

Non-means-tested and means-tested benefits

Non-means-tested benefits are those paid with only limited considera-tion of how much money you have (your 'means' of support), provided you satisfy certain basic conditions such as being available for work, dis-abled or widowed.

The main earnings-replacement benefits are unemployment benefit, sickness benefit and invalidity benefit, severe disablement allowance, maternity allowance, invalid care allowance, widows' benefits and retire-ment pensions. Other non-means-tested benefits are intended to con-tribute towards the extra costs of bringing up children or of disability. They include child benefit, attendance allowance, industrial injuries benefits and disability living allowance.

To be entitled to some of the earnings-replacement benefits you have to have paid sufficient social security contributions; for other non-means-tested benefits there is a requirement that you should have lived in Great Britain for a certain length of time.

For information about non-means-tested benefits you should look at CPAG's *Rights Guide to Non-Means-Tested Benefits* (17th edn, 1994/5, £6.95 post-free from CPAG Ltd, £2.45 for claimants). However, the main benefit rates are included at the front of this book.

By contrast, to be entitled to **means-tested benefits** you do not have to satisfy any contribution conditions or conditions of past residence. Instead, you must satisfy certain basic conditions and your income and capital must be sufficiently low. The intention is to limit entitlement to those who are most in need. This involves quite detailed investigation of your means. The ways means tests work are outlined on p8 and there are different tests for the different benefits.

You may be entitled to a combination of non-means-tested and means-tested benefits. For example, you might receive unemployment benefit and child benefit topped up by income support. You would also qualify for help with your rent (housing benefit) and your council tax (council tax benefit).

The means-tested benefits covered in this *Handbook* are:

- income support (IS) (p12);
- family credit (FC) (p183);
- disability working allowance (DWA) (p198);
- housing benefit (HB) (p214);
- council tax benefit (CTB) (p296);
- social fund (SF) payments (p415);
- help with National Health Service charges (p470);
- free milk and vitamins (p481);
- free school meals and other education benefits (p484);
- housing renovation grants and other local authority grants and services (p487);
- discretionary payments for disabled people (p493).

To be entitled to some of these benefits you may have to be in full-time work, but this will not be the case for all benefits (see below).

Some benefits are administered by the Benefits Agency on behalf of the Department of Social Security (DSS) and others are administered by local authorities or other organisations (see below).

Working and entitlement to means-tested benefits

Income support is restricted to those who are not working 'full-time' (which usually means for 16 hours or more a week). Family credit and disability working allowance are restricted to those who are working full-time. Other benefits – including housing benefit – may be claimed whether you are working or not.

- **Benefits only for people *not* in full-time work:**
  - income support
  - social fund cold weather payments, community care grants and budgeting loans
  - free school meals
- **Benefits only for people in full-time work:**
  - family credit

- disability working allowance
- **Benefits for people both in and out of work:**
  - housing benefit
  - council tax benefit
  - social fund maternity payments, funeral payments and crisis loans
  - education benefits (other than free school meals)
  - housing renovation grants
  - all other benefits not listed

Some of the benefits listed above are only paid if you receive one of the main/basic means-tested benefits – ie, IS, FC or DWA. Other benefits you can get on low-income grounds alone – eg, health benefits.

2. THE ADMINISTRATION OF MEANS-TESTED BENEFITS

The benefit authorities

The administration of the various benefits described in this *Handbook* varies enormously depending on who is responsible for it.

- The Benefits Agency administers IS, FC, DWA and the SF on behalf of the DSS. Initial claims for IS should be made and dealt with locally but most London claims are dealt with centrally by large centres in Glasgow, Belfast and Wigan. All FC and DWA claims are sent to an office in Blackpool.
- Local authorities (usually district councils outside London) administer HB, CTB and housing renovation grants. HB and CTB are often administered by the same office.
- Local education authorities (county councils and metropolitan boroughs outside London) administer education benefits.
- The Health Benefits Unit administers health benefits.
- Various other organisations deal with the other benefits covered in Chapters 26 and 27 of this *Handbook*.

The Benefits Agency

The Benefits Agency was established in April 1991 as an 'executive agency' or 'next steps agency' of the Department of Social Security (DSS). Day-to-day running of the Agency has been delegated to a Chief Executive (Michael Bichard). The Agency is part of the DSS and is directly accountable to Ministers, but only indirectly accountable to MPs. Because the Agency has responsibility for the administration and delivery of benefits, questions from MPs on these matters are normally referred by Ministers to the Chief Executive. The answers are published in *Hansard*.

There is a separate policy section within the DSS, but the Agency also has the role of advising the Secretary of State for Social Security on policy matters as well as providing information for Ministers and the DSS. The responsibilities of the Agency are outlined in its *Framework Document*. The stated emphasis is on providing an efficient, accessible service for 'customers' and paying benefits promptly and accurately.

The Chief Executive is supported by a management team of six directors. Geographically the Agency is split into three territories covering south England, Wales and central England, and Scotland and north England. Each territory has a director who sits on the management team. There are 20 area directorates within the territories which are made up of 157 districts. Four other area directorates have responsibility for 'centralised' benefits such as child benefit, pensions, disability living allowance and family credit.

When the Agency was established considerable management and planning responsibility was delegated to district level with the intention that districts be given the 'freedom to manage' with little direct control from HQ. Each district has a district manager supported by a management team. Details of the local management structure may be included in a district guide to services or in the local business plan (see below).

Fraud officers are based in district offices but are accountable to an officer at area level and not the district manager.

Standards of service

The Secretary of State sets annual performance targets for the Agency covering benefit clearance times, accuracy, customer satisfaction and financial recovery (overpayments and fraud detection). The Agency also sets internal targets after consultation with Ministers. These are included in a national *Business Plan* which is published every March. The targets are important as they are intended to set minimum standards of service – for example, that IS claims should be dealt with within five working days. They also influence both national and local service priorities. The Agency is required to publish a *Customer Charter* setting out performance targets and service commitments as well as including information about the Agency, such as the procedure for complaints. Copies are available from your local office or from the Agency's HQ in Leeds.

Districts are also required to produce their own business plan setting out targets and objectives for the year. A local version of the *Customer Charter*, called a 'customer service statement', should be published containing service commitments to at least national standards. Benefit clearance time targets should be displayed in office waiting rooms.

Contacting benefit offices

Detailed advice about claiming and how decisions are made in the case of each benefit will be found elsewhere in this *Handbook*. However, there is some basic guidance about dealing with local Benefits Agency offices which may also apply, where appropriate, to other benefit offices.

Writing to your office is nearly always the best way to have your case dealt with. It is easier for the person dealing with your case and it ensures there is a permanent record of what you said. A letter enables you to cover all the relevant points clearly and systematically.

You should always put your name, address, the date and your national insurance number at the top of your letter. If possible, make a copy of it. You should also keep all letters and forms sent to you, even if the information is disappointing. Such a record may help you or your adviser later to work out whether any decision can be challenged.

The *Charter* states that the Agency will reply to all letters within ten working days (seven days if it is a letter of complaint). If you can only be sent a partial reply you should be told how long it will be before your letter can be fully answered. The person writing to you should give their name and telephone number.

If there is a delay in getting a reply, you can telephone to find out why, but it may be better to write a short reminder and only telephone if you still receive no response.

Nevertheless, on occasion, **telephoning your benefit office** may be necessary. If you are a London claimant, try your branch (or local) office first. If you have to ring the centre in Belfast, Glasgow or Wigan, you are only charged the local rate. Be ready to give your surname and national insurance number. Try to get the name, title and telephone extension number of the person you speak to as this may be useful in the future. Make a brief note of what is said together with the date. If the information is important, follow up the telephone call with a letter confirming the Agency's points that have been made so that any misunderstanding can be cleared up. You could ask the office to write to you but they are usually reluctant to do so merely to confirm a telephone conversation.

Visiting your office enables you to have a detailed conversation with an officer. However, check the opening times first. The *Charter* has set down standards of service – eg, you should expect the receptionist to see you within ten minutes. However, at busy times you should not have to wait more than 30 minutes. Be prepared to wait longer if you need to see someone else. The receptionist should tell you how long it is likely to take. If you want a private interview, this should be provided. Staff you see will wear name badges. An appointment can usually be arranged by telephone. Take with you any documents which may be relevant otherwise you may be asked to make a second visit to provide the additional information. Again, follow up any important meeting with a letter confirming the points you have made or ask the office to confirm in writing any advice to you. It is a good idea to take a friend or relative with you, not only for moral support, but also as a witness to what is said.

If you cannot get to the office, an officer may be able to visit you at home if your case cannot be dealt with by telephone. Ask if you need a visit. If you are refused and are not satisfied with the explanation, ask to speak to a supervisor or the customer care manager.

If you are a London claimant, you can go to your local branch office to discuss your claim. They will contact the social security centre in Belfast, Glasgow or Wigan if necessary.

Complaints

Ways of formally challenging decisions are explained elsewhere in this *Handbook*. However, you may want to complain about the way your case is dealt with to get a quicker decision or to have something properly taken into account.

If you are dissatisfied with the way someone is handling your case, you should contact a more senior official within the relevant department. Junior staff usually deal with most cases so it may be enough to contact a supervisor. Above the supervisors, there is an office manager and for each group of offices, a district manager. Benefits Agency offices also have a customer services manager, and you could try speaking to her/him.

Generally, complaints should be addressed to the customer services manager or district manager. If you complain to a supervisor make it clear that your letter is 'a complaint'.

Ultimately, there are government ministers including the Secretary of State for Social Security. Your local MP can take up a complaint of this sort for you. For more information about making a complaint, see p169.

Local authority offices are the responsibility of a senior officer (the Chief Executive, the Treasurer, the Director of Education or whoever – the relevant officer's name or title usually appears on letter-headings). In turn, those officers are responsible to councillors and you can write to one of your local councillors or the chair of the relevant council committee. Government departments also monitor local authorities so, if all else fails, you can write to the relevant minister – ie, the Secretary of State for Social Security for HB, the Secretary of State for Education for education benefits, and the Secretary of State for the Environment in other cases.

A similar approach can be taken in the case of NHS benefits which are ultimately the responsibility of the Secretary of State for Health.

Emergencies

If you have lost all your money or there has been a similar crisis, it is possible to get help at any time.

Any local police station should have a contact number for Benefits Agency staff on call outside normal office hours. In London there is a special Benefits Agency office open in the evenings and at weekends for emergencies. It is Keyworth House, Keyworth Street, London SE1 (tel: 071 407 2315 or, during the day, 071 620 1456).

There will also be a duty social worker who can be contacted via your local social services department or council, or the police.

3. HOW MEANS TESTS WORK

For most benefits there are complicated rules for assessing your needs and resources, and thus your entitlement. Some other benefits are payable once you have qualified for a different means-tested benefit (known as a 'passported' benefit). Other benefits are 'discretionary' – in other words, there are no set rules for deciding whether your means are sufficient or whether you should be paid, although your means are one consideration when it is being decided whether to award the benefit.

The main non-discretionary benefits

The following benefits have complicated rules for calculating your needs and resources:

- income support;
- family credit;
- disability working allowance;
- housing benefit;
- council tax benefit;
- health benefits (other than free milk and vitamins);
- housing renovation grants.

However, it is not always necessary to consider all the benefits separately because, except in the case of FC and DWA, you automatically satisfy the means test for the other benefits if you qualify for IS.

With the exception of FC and DWA, all the benefits have similar ways of taking account of your needs. These involve adding up personal allowances for each member of the family and then adding on extra amounts to take account of extra expenses you may have because of your circumstances. For IS, HB and CTB, these amounts are known as 'applicable amounts' and, where they are set figures, they are covered in Chapter 17. However, there are special rules for special groups of claimants, particularly for those claiming IS. Health benefits and housing renovation grants have similar rules.

All the benefits (including FC and DWA) also have similar ways of calculating resources to take into account both your income and your savings and other capital assets. Parts of your income and capital may be disregarded. If you have too much capital, you are not entitled to any benefit at all. If you have a lesser amount of capital, it may reduce the amount of benefit to which you are entitled because it is treated as producing an income. The main rules for calculating resources are set out in Chapters 18 and 19 although, again, there are variations for health benefits and housing renovation grants.

Once your needs and your income have been calculated, your benefit can be worked out. In the cases of IS and health benefits, that is simply done by deducting your income from your needs. In the cases of HB, CTB and housing renovation grants, there are more complicated formulae which take into account the amount of your rent, council tax or estimated cost of repairs, as well as your other needs and your income and which allow you to qualify even though your income is above IS level. These formulae are set out in the relevant chapters elsewhere in this *Handbook*. Each one produces the result that the higher your income, the less benefit you receive while, at the same time, those with incomes substantially above IS level may receive some help.

FC and DWA are also calculated on the basis of a complicated formula which is based on your maximum FC/DWA and takes into account your family's size but which is not intended directly to represent your needs. Again, the object of the formula is that you could be entitled to some benefit even though your income is substantially above IS level.

Passported benefits

Some benefits do not have their own means tests. Instead, to be entitled to such benefits, it is simply necessary that you are entitled to another 'passporting' benefit. These are:

Passporting benefit	Passported benefit
IS, FC, DWA	SF maternity expenses payments
IS, FC, DWA, HB, CTB	SF funeral expenses payments
IS, FC	Health benefits
IS	SF cold weather payments

IS	SF community care grants and budgeting loans
IS	Free school meals
IS	Housing renovation grants

In the case of all SF payments, it is a further condition of entitlement that your capital is not above a certain level. In the case of community care grants and budgeting loans, you must still persuade the social fund officer to exercise her/his discretion in your favour as these are also discretionary benefits.

For free school meals there are no other tests. If you are entitled to IS, your children are entitled to free school meals; if you are not, they are not.

Discretionary benefits

Where a benefit is discretionary, the means of the claimant are obviously crucial in deciding whether or not to award the benefit. SF crisis loans, budgeting loans and community care grants are paid on a discretionary basis, although certain rules also have to be followed. To get a budgeting loan or community care grant, a claimant must be entitled to IS.

Where local authorities have the power to make payments for things like school uniforms, they could do it on a purely discretionary basis but often have local means tests similar to the IS means test.

Many of the benefits covered in Part Ten of this *Handbook* are discretionary.

Passport To – MB, CTB, SF.
Health, free school meals
dental.

18+ not Working   Capital less than 8000 - available for worker

Not required to be available for work.

Applicable amount - Personal allowance + Premiums.

Family premium - Paid in addition to any other premium.
Disabled child premium   "   "   "   "

SDP = paid in addition to Disability Premium or Higher pensioner
Premium . Carers premium, in addition to any other.
            Must qualify for ICA

PART TWO

Income support
Non hanced 75-79
Higher 80 + or over 60 if DP.

Pensioner Premium - ~~Single~~ + Aged 60 - 74 Payable with.
Family premium - Disabled child premium , carers premium.

Non-dep - (look at non-dep)   /children up to 16
  18 + working FT - £72 under 5·00   or 19 in FT educ.
                     73 - 107·99   9·00   16+ Can-not claim
                    108· 138·99   13·00   IS, Must
                    139· ->   25·00   Sign on .
                                                   ___

disregard £15·00 - lone parent. - DP, HPP;.

all benefits full count except HB, CTB , DLA AA

£1·00 for ever 250 - 3000/8000

Net Earnings 15·00 disregard - Lone parents. - DP HPP.
Couple both u/e for 2yrs + I get IS for 2yrs - £5000
                                                any other

FT· 16hrs .

CHAPTER TWO

The basic rules of entitlement

This chapter covers:

1. Introduction to IS and basic rules (below)
2. Age (p14)
3. Full-time work (p14)
4. Full-time and part-time education (p17)
5. Availability for work (p21)
6. Presence in and temporary absence from Great Britain (p25)

1. INTRODUCTION

Income support (IS) is the main benefit for people with a low income. However, it is not paid to people in full-time work who may be able to claim family credit (see Chapter 9) or DWA (see Chapter 10) instead.

If you pay rent or council tax you may be entitled to housing benefit (see Chapter 11) and council tax benefit (see Chapter 15), as well as IS.

If you are entitled to IS you also qualify for:

- health service benefits such as free prescriptions (see Chapter 25); *and*
- education benefits such as free school meals (see Chapter 26).

You may also qualify for social fund payments (see Chapters 20-24).

The principal conditions

You can claim IS if you satisfy the following rules:

- Your income is less than your applicable amount (which is the amount, fixed by law, intended to cover your day-to-day living expenses – see p27). When calculating your benefit, some of your income may be ignored but you may also be treated as having income you do not really receive (see Chapter 18).
- Your savings and other capital must be worth £8,000 or less. Some capital (in particular, your home) may be ignored, but you may also be treated as having capital you do not really possess (see Chapter 19).

- Neither you nor your partner (see below) can be in full-time paid work (see p14). Note that you can claim if you are temporarily away from full-time work because, for example, you are sick.
- You are not in full-time education (although there are exceptions to this rule – see p17). However, if you are studying part-time, you may qualify (see p20).
- You are at least 16 (although 16- and 17-year-olds have to satisfy extra rules – see p67).
- You are signing on as available for work (see p52) and actively seeking employment (see p56), unless you are not required to do so because you are, for example, sick, aged 60 or more, a single parent, etc (see p22). If you cannot satisfy these rules you may be able to get a reduced rate of IS on hardship grounds (see p24).
- You are present in Great Britain (although there are exceptions to this rule – see p25).

There are some groups of claimants to whom special rules apply. Those rules are covered in Chapter 5.

You do not have to pay, or have paid, national insurance contributions to qualify for IS.

Who you claim for

You claim for your 'family' which consists of:

- you; *and*
- your partner (if any) who is
  either   your husband or wife, if you are living together,
  or   a person of the opposite sex to whom you are not married but with whom you are living as husband or wife (see p330); *and*
- any children for whom you are responsible (which may include children who have left school – see p335).

The amount of money you receive therefore takes account of the number of people in your 'family' (see p328). When calculating the amount of IS to which you are entitled, income and capital belonging to your partner are normally treated as yours. There are special rules for dealing with income and capital belonging to your children (see pp358 and 394).

How to claim

You must claim IS in writing, either on form A1 (SP1 for pensioners) which you can obtain free from your local Benefits Agency office or, if you are signing on as unemployed, on form B1 which you can obtain free from your local unemployment benefit office. If you get the form by telephoning or writing to the Benefits Agency office, your claim will generally be treated as having been made when you asked for the form. For more detailed advice about claims and how they are dealt with, see p142.

You are usually paid from the week of your claim, but your claim can be backdated for up to a year if you have good reason for claiming late (see p145). You are paid weekly or fortnightly by giro, order book or by credit transfer to a bank or building society account, and usually in arrears. For information about payments, see p151.

You may be able to get a crisis loan from the social fund to tide you over until your benefit is paid (see p449).

You will have to make a separate claim to your local authority for housing benefit (see p258) and for council tax benefit (see p318).

2. AGE

You have to be 16 or over to make a claim for IS.[1]

> If you are 16 or 17 you have to satisfy extra rules (see Chapter 5). You must also satisfy the basic rules described in the rest of this chapter.

If you are at school or college, see pp17-21. Once you are 18 or over you get IS in the normal way, provided you satisfy the basic rules of entitlement (described in this chapter).

3. FULL-TIME WORK

The rules below apply to claims made after 7 April 1992. Prior to this date full-time work was work for 24 hours or more a week. If you worked between 16-24 hours a week shortly before, and soon after, 7 April 1992, you may still be able to get IS under the old rules. See the rules on transitional provisions on p14 of the 23rd edition of the *National Welfare Benefits Handbook*.

The definition of full-time work

You cannot usually get IS if you or your partner are in full-time paid work. This means working 16 hours or more each week. Paid work includes work for which you expect payment.[2] You must have a real likelihood of getting payment for your work, not just a hope or desire to make money. A self-employed writer who has never sold a manuscript may well be working with no real expectation of payment and thus not be treated as in full-time work even if s/he spends a lot of time writing.[3] Paid lunch hours count towards the 16-hour total.[4]

Where your hours fluctuate, your weekly hours are worked out as follows:

- If you have a regular pattern of work, the average hours worked throughout each work 'cycle' or pattern is used. For example, if you regularly work three weeks on and one week off, your hours are the average over the four-week period.
- Where there is no pattern, the average over the five weeks before your claim is used, or a different period if this would be more accurate.
- If you have just started work and no pattern is yet established, the number of hours or average of hours you are expected to work each week is used.[5]

Appeal if you think the average was calculated unfairly, unless you are better off claiming FC/DWA instead (see Chapters 9 and 10).

Problems sometimes arise if you have an irregular work pattern. For example, many school workers work and are paid for term-time only. In this situation the normal work cycle is a whole year, including holidays, so if you work 20 hours a week in term-time only, your average hours may be less than 16 and you are eligible for IS.[6]

Exceptions to the 16-hour rule

You are treated as in full-time work and thus not entitled to IS even if you work less than 16 hours in that week, if:[7]

- you are off work because of a holiday. If you do not get any holiday pay – eg, because you have not worked for the company long enough – you could try for a social fund payment (see p449);
- you are away from work without a good reason;
- you are unemployed but have received pay in lieu of wages or in lieu of notice or holiday pay from your last job or an *ex gratia* payment in recognition of loss of employment (see p366);[8]
- you or your partner are involved in a trade dispute for seven days or less.[9]

You are not treated as in full-time work if you work 16 hours or more and:[10]

- you are off sick, or on maternity leave (but only if you have a right to go back to your job after your maternity leave ends);
- you are mentally or physically disabled and because of this
  - your earnings are 75 per cent or less of what a person without your disability would reasonably expect to earn, working the same hours

in that job, or in a comparable one;
- your hours of work are 75 per cent or less than a person without your disability would reasonably be expected to do in that or a comparable job;
- you work at home as a childminder (see p374);
- you are on a government training scheme (see p61);
- you are working for a charity or voluntary organisation or you are a volunteer and are giving your services free (except for your expenses). Where you receive any nominal payment (even one of £5 or less which would be ignored under the rule for disregarding part of your earnings), you could be counted as in full-time work. The only way round this is for the organisation to pay you for a specific number of hours a week and for you to be a volunteer for the remainder of the time (but see p392 on notional income);
- you or your partner are involved in a trade dispute and it is more than seven days since the dispute started (see p77). This will also apply for the first 15 days following your return to work after having been involved in a trade dispute;
- you are caring for a person (whether or not you receive invalid care allowance), who is either receiving or who has claimed attendance allowance or disability living allowance. In the latter case, you will only be treated as not in full-time work for 26 weeks after the claim or until the claim is decided, whichever is the earlier;
- you are working, while living in a residential care or nursing home, or a local authority home. This applies during temporary absences from the home too. It only covers people who are being paid at the special rates for people in homes (see pp104-113);
- you work as a part-time firefighter, auxiliary coastguard, member of the territorial or reserve forces, or running or launching a lifeboat;
- you are performing duties as a local authority councillor;
- you are a foster parent receiving an allowance for your caring responsibilities.

If you are working part-time or on short-time you may qualify for IS – for details, see pp55 and 57.

Self-employed people

The full-time work rule applies to self-employed as well as employed earners. Thus if you are working less than 16 hours in your self-employment you can claim IS. If you simply invest in a business and do not help to run it you are not treated as self-employed at all.[11]

A key problem for many self-employed people is that they work long hours for little financial reward, sometimes even making a loss.

Nevertheless, the work is done in expectation of payment and counts as full-time work. If you are in this position and you are not entitled to FC or DWA (see Chapters 9 and 10), or it is not enough for your needs, you will need to claim IS to supplement your income. However, you can only do this if you reduce your working hours to below 16 or abandon your self-employment altogether. This, of course, further reduces your income from self-employment and restricts your chances of increasing your profits in the future, and you may have to sign on as available for and actively seeking work. Nevertheless, it may be a necessary option if business is poor. You should seek specialist debt advice before pursuing this course.

Just being on Business Start-Up Allowance does not mean you should be treated as in full-time work if, in fact, you work less than 16 hours. However, the allowance is usually paid to enable you to work full-time so you should check that you can still qualify for it.[12]

4. FULL-TIME AND PART-TIME EDUCATION

People in full-time education cannot usually qualify for IS, but there are some exceptions. You may be able to claim if your course is part-time. The rules of entitlement depend partly on your age. **If you have a partner who is not studying, s/he could claim IS instead.**

Under 19 in full-time education

Relevant education

If you are under 19 and at school or college you are usually counted as being in relevant education. This means the course is 'non-advanced' (up to and including A-levels or higher level Scottish certificate of education) and lasts more than 12 hours a week not counting homework or other unsupervised study and meal breaks.[13] While you are in relevant education, your parents (or anyone acting as your parents) can get child benefit for you and claim for you if they get IS (see p335). You cannot get IS yourself[14] unless:[15]

- you have a child for whom you can claim (see p335);
- you are so handicapped that you are unlikely to get a job in the next 12 months;
- you are an orphan, and have no one acting as your parent;
- you have to live away from your parents and any person acting in place of your parents because you are estranged from them, or you are in physical or moral danger, or there is a serious risk to your physical or mental health.

A 'person acting in place of your parents' includes a local authority or voluntary organisation if you are in care, or foster parents.

'Estrangement' implies emotional disharmony,[16] where you have no desire to have any prolonged contact with your parents or they feel similarly towards you. It is possible to be estranged even though your parents are providing some financial support;

- you live apart from your parents and anyone acting as your parent(s) and, they are unable to support you and are in prison, or unable to come to Britain because of immigration laws, or chronically sick or mentally or physically disabled. This covers people who:
  - could get a disability premium or higher pensioner premium; *or*
  - have an armed forces grant for car costs because of disability; *or*
  - are substantially and permanently disabled;
- you are a refugee and have started a course to learn English in order to obtain employment during your first year in Britain. This will apply for up to nine months.

If any of the above apply you can get IS without having to sign on. 16- and 17-year-olds qualify in the same way as 18-year-olds. Check p74 for how much you get.

You continue to count as being in relevant education until the end of the holiday after the term in which you leave. If you leave school before the legal school-leaving date, you are treated as having stayed on until that date. The day on which you cease to be treated as in relevant education is called the **terminal date** but your parents continue to get benefit for you until the end of that week. You are able to get benefit in your own right from the Monday following your terminal date (and if you are 16 or 17, you must satisfy the extra rules described from p67). This Monday is also the first day of the **child benefit extension period** during which, if you cannot get IS, your parents can go on claiming child benefit and IS for you (see p337).

Time of leaving school	*Terminal date*
Christmas	First Monday in January
Easter	First Monday after Easter Monday
May/June	First Monday in September

You can claim earlier if you are 19 before the appropriate terminal date.[17]

If you return to school or college solely to take exams, you still count as in full-time relevant education. So if you leave school at Easter and return to take exams in the following term, you will not be able to claim IS until the first Monday in September.[18] If you are 16 or 17 you also have to fulfil extra conditions (see p67).

You can get benefit earlier if you were able to get IS while at school or college or if you come within one of the qualifying groups during the final vacation.

Advanced education

If your course is advanced you are treated as a student[19] and not usually entitled to IS (but see below). Advanced education means degree or post-graduate level qualifications, teaching courses, HND, diplomas of higher education, HND or HNC of the Business & Technology Education Council or the Scottish Vocational Education Council and all other courses above OND/ONC, A-levels or highers.

19 or over and in full-time education

If your course is full-time you are treated as a student regardless of the level of the course.[20] Most full-time students are debarred from claiming IS for the duration of the course, including vacations.

Whether a course counts as full-time depends on the college. Courses that appear part-time may be classed as full-time by the college authorities, but any course which is over 15 hours a week can be classified as full-time. There is no universally accepted definition of what constitutes a 'full-time' or 'part-time' course. Definitions are often based on local custom and practice within education authorities, or determined by the demands of course-validating bodies, or by the fact that full-time courses can attract more resources. The college or university's definition is not absolutely final, but if you want to challenge it you will have to produce a good argument showing why it should not be accepted.[21]

You cannot claim unless you are:[22]

- a single parent or foster parent; *or*
- getting a training allowance; *or*
- a student from abroad and entitled to an urgent cases payment because you are temporarily without funds (see p87); *or*
- a disabled student and you satisfy one of the following conditions:
  - you qualify for the disability premium or severe disability premium (see pp345 and 351);
  - you are unlikely to get a job within a reasonable period of time compared to other students because of your disability and you were getting IS immediately before 1 September 1990;
  - you made a claim for IS after 1 September 1990 and at some time in the 18 months before claiming you were getting IS as a disabled person under 19 in non-advanced education, or as a disabled student;
  - you qualify for a disabled student's allowance because you are deaf; *or*

- a couple who are both full-time students and who have a child, but only during the summer vacation, and provided they satisfy the normal rules for getting IS; *or*
- a pensioner.

If you stay on to finish a course of non-advanced education at school or college until after your 19th birthday, you only qualify for IS if you come into one of the groups listed above, even though – as long as you were under 19 – you would have received IS as a dependant or in your own right.

Giving up your course

If you abandon your course or are dismissed from it you can claim IS from that date. Thus, if you have to give up your studies (because, for example, you are in poor health, expecting a baby or in financial difficulties), you should cease to be treated as a student and can claim IS even if you hope eventually to resume your course.[23] This does not apply if you are still pursuing your studies by, for example, taking a year out to study for and resit exams, or spending an optional year abroad as part of a language course.[24]

Studying part-time

You may be able to get IS while studying part-time if you qualify under the 21-hour rule *or* by satisfying the availability for work test. Whether a course is counted as part-time depends on its actual length if you are under 19, or how it is described by the college if you are 19 or over (see above).

The 21-hour rule

You are still treated as available for work and thus entitled to benefit if:[25]

- you continue to actively seek work (see p56); *and*
- the course lasts 21 hours or less a week, not counting meal breaks and unsupervised study (work set by a supervisor, but carried out privately, is supervised study); *and*
- you are prepared to give up the course immediately a suitable job comes up; *and*

  either for the three months immediately before the course you were unemployed or sick and getting IS, unemployment benefit or sickness benefit, or you were on a Youth Training (YT) course;

  or in the last six months before the course, you were unemployed or sick and getting the above benefits for a total of three months altogether, or you were on a YT course for a total of three months and, sandwiched *between* these spells, you were working full-time or earning too much to qualify for benefit.

The three months on a YT course will only count if they are *after* the terminal date (see p18 for what this means).

The course must[26] be held at a recognised educational institution; *or* be similar to a course of training run by the Employment Service for which a training allowance would be paid.

It can be advanced (post A-level) or non-advanced.[27]

You cannot qualify under this rule if:

- you are 19 or over and your course is called full-time; *or*
- you are under 19 and your course is advanced.

Studying and available for work

If you cannot pass the test for the 21-hour rule you might still be able to claim IS provided you can convince the unemployment benefit office that you are willing and able to take a job, and they consider you are 'available for and actively seeking work' (see p50). You must be prepared to give up the course if a job comes up, but you can continue while you are looking for work.

When you sign on as available you may be asked to fill in a short questionnaire about your course. Your answers are considered to see whether you are truly seeking work and whether you are prepared to give up the course if a job arises.

You cannot qualify under the availability rule if you are under 19 and the course is non-advanced and over 12 hours a week.

5. AVAILABILITY FOR WORK

People who have to sign on

If you are under 60 you usually have to sign on at the unemployment benefit office as available for full-time work and show that you are actively seeking work in order to get benefit.[28] By signing on you are saying you are available to take up a full-time job of 24 hours or more a week. If you are physically or mentally disabled you will be expected to do as much as you can normally do given your health.[29] If you are working part-time you must be willing to make up your hours. Some people do not have to sign on in order to get benefit (see below). You can also get IS on hardship grounds (see p24).

For details about your IS entitlement if you have to sign on, see p48.

People who do not have to sign on[30]

You do not have to sign on if you come within one of the following groups:

Age

- You are aged 60 or more.
- You are aged 50 to 59 and have no prospect of getting full-time employment. You must not have had a full-time job in the last ten years, and not have been required to sign on during that time. This rule is aimed mainly at women who are widowed or divorced and whose children have grown up.

Sick and disabled people

- You are incapable of work because of illness or disability. You will be treated as incapable if:
  - you are receiving statutory sick pay;
  - you are entitled to sickness benefit, invalidity pension or severe disablement allowance;
  - you would be entitled to sickness benefit or invalidity benefit but for the fact that you have not paid enough contributions *or* you are disqualified from sickness benefit or invalidity pension *or* you have failed to make a claim or you have made a late claim but have no good cause *or* are claiming for a period more than 12 months before your actual date of claim.
- You are appealing a decision by the Benefits Agency not to treat you as incapable of work and your own GP continues to give you sick certificates. Until your appeal has been decided you continue to get IS without signing on.[31]
- You are mentally or physically disabled and because of this your earnings capacity or the number of hours you can work is reduced to 75 per cent or less of that for a person without your disability in the same job.
- You are registered blind. If you regain your sight you continue to be treated as blind for 28 weeks after you have been taken off the register.
- You work while living in a residential care or nursing home (see p16).

Carers and people with childcare responsibilities

- You are a single parent claiming for a child under 16. Once the child is 16 you have to sign on unless you are exempt from doing so on other grounds.

- You are a single person fostering a child under 16 through a local authority or voluntary organisation.
- You are looking after a child under 16 because their parent or the person who usually looks after them is temporarily away or ill.
- You are claiming for a child under 16 and your partner is temporarily out of the UK.
- You are taking a child abroad specifically for medical treatment.
- You are pregnant and unable to work; or there are 11 weeks or less before your baby is due, or your baby was born not more than seven weeks ago.
- You are looking after your partner, or a child under 19 for whom you are claiming, who is temporarily ill.
- You receive invalid care allowance, or the person for whom you care either receives or has claimed attendance allowance or the highest or middle rate care component of disability living allowance (DLA). In the latter case, you are entitled to IS without signing on for up to 26 weeks from the date of the claim for attendance allowance/DLA or until the claim is decided, whichever comes first. If you cease meeting these conditions you can claim IS without signing on for a further eight weeks. If you are now claiming IS, having ceased caring for a disabled person, you are also exempt from the need to sign on during the eight weeks after you stopped being a carer. See p335 to check when you can claim for a child.

Pupils, students and people on training courses

- You qualify for IS while in full-time non-advanced education (see p17).
- You are a disabled student and you satisfy one of the following conditions:
  - you qualify for the disability premium or severe disability premium (see pp345 and 351);
  - because of your disability you would be unlikely to get a job within a reasonable period compared to other students, and you were getting IS immediately before 1 September 1990;
  - you claimed IS on or after 1 September 1990 and at some time during the 18 months before claiming you were getting IS as a disabled person under 19 in full-time non-advanced education, or as a disabled student;
  - you qualify for a disabled student's allowance because you are deaf;
  - it is accepted and you have requested a supplementary requirement, allowance or bursary payable under education mandatory awards (in Scotland, allowances and bursaries) regulations.[32]
- You are a single parent student.

- You are on a government training scheme and receive a training allowance (see p61).
- You are attending a compulsory Open University residential course.

Others

- You have to go to court as a JP, juror, witness or party to the proceedings.
- You have been remanded in custody, or committed in custody for trial or to be sentenced.
- You have just come out of prison, or youth custody. You will not be required to sign on for seven days from the date of your discharge.
- You are a refugee who is learning English in order to obtain employment. You must be on a course for more than 15 hours a week and, at the time the course started, you must have been in Britain for a year or less. You will not be required to sign on for up to nine months.
- You are a 'person from abroad' and are entitled to the urgent cases rate of IS (see p87).
- You are involved in a trade dispute or have been back to work for 15 days or less following a trade dispute (see p77).

If you are not in one of the groups above, you have to sign on as available for work to get benefit, or apply on grounds of hardship (see below).

If you are claiming as a couple, and one of you does not have to sign on, this partner should probably be the claimant (see p143).

If your partner is the claimant, you do not have to sign on, but you may wish to do so voluntarily if you are unemployed and looking for work. Signing on gives you national insurance credits which help safeguard future entitlement to benefits. It also enables you to take advantage of any special concessions in your area for unemployed people. If you have been signing on for six months, you may be able to qualify for Training for Work (see p63).

Payments to avoid hardship[33]

You may get IS at a reduced rate if you would normally have to sign on as available for work to get benefit, but for some reason you do not satisfy the availability test (see p52) and you or a member of your family will suffer hardship if IS is not paid. You might come within this category if you are caring for someone who is not a member of your family and not entitled to attendance allowance, but you cannot continue to look after them unless you get IS; or if you are not allowed to sign on for religious or cultural reasons – eg, it is considered inappropriate for women to work outside the home. Hardship payments should always be considered if the adjudication officer has decided you must be available for work, but you do not or cannot make yourself available.[34]

Students cannot use the hardship provision to get benefit.

Under this rule you do not have to be available for work[35] but your benefit is reduced by the **voluntary unemployment deduction** (for how this is calculated, see p61).[36]

6. PRESENCE IN AND TEMPORARY ABSENCE FROM GREAT BRITAIN

Normally you can only get IS while you are living in GB. If you have recently come to this country from abroad you may get less benefit (see p87). If you go abroad temporarily, benefit can continue to be paid for up to four weeks, but if you are taking a child abroad for medical treatment it can be paid for up to eight weeks. To qualify for IS while abroad you must have been entitled to IS before you left the country, continue to satisfy the conditions for getting IS while away and not expect to be away for more than a year.[37]

Under the four-week rule you must also fall within one of the following groups:[38]

- you are going to Northern Ireland. (If you are going there long term, you should sign on at your local office in Northern Ireland and claim IS there);
- you and your partner are both abroad and your partner qualifies for a pensioner, higher pensioner, disability or severe disability premium;
- you are incapable of work and are not signing on on the day you go away and you have been continuously incapable for the previous 28 weeks;
- you are incapable of work because of illness or disability and you are going abroad specifically for treatment of your illness from an appropriately qualified person. Before you go you should check that the Benefits Agency accepts that this rule applies to you;
- you are not required to sign on. However, this does *not* apply to you if you do not have to sign on because you are:
  - at school;
  - involved in a trade dispute, or for the first 15 days after you have returned to work following the dispute;[39]
  - receiving an urgent cases payment of IS as a person from abroad (see p87);
  - a discharged prisoner;
  - incapable of work for less than 28 weeks.

Under the eight-week rule you must be taking a child abroad specifically for medical, physiotherapy or similar treatment from an 'appropriately qualified person'. The child must count as part of your family. If you were required to sign on as a condition of getting benefit before leaving Britain, this requirement automatically ceases while you are abroad[40] (see p23).

If you qualify for IS for up to four or eight weeks, your benefit is paid to you on your return, but if you are a member of a couple you can ask for it to be paid to your partner during your absence instead. If you are not entitled to IS while abroad or you have already used up your four or eight-week entitlement, your partner will have to make a claim in her/his own right (see p143). If it is your partner who goes abroad, your benefit is reduced after four weeks (eight weeks if your partner is taking a child abroad for medical treatment). You are then paid as if you were a single claimant or single parent but your joint income and capital counts.

While you are temporarily out of the country, you may be entitled to housing benefit to cover your rent, and council tax benefit towards your council tax (see p218 (HB) and p296 (CTB)). If your IS stops, you must make a fresh claim for these benefits.

CHAPTER THREE

How your benefit is calculated

This chapter covers:

1. The basic calculation (below)
2. Housing costs (p29)
3. Transitional protection (p43)
4. Urgent cases payments (p44)

I. THE BASIC CALCULATION

The amount of IS you get depends on your needs – called your 'applicable amount' – and on how much income and capital you have. If you have capital of more than £8,000 you will not qualify for IS at all, but remember, not all capital counts. Any capital you have over £3,000 is assumed to produce an income and will reduce the amount of benefit you get. For the rules on capital, see Chapter 19.

There are three stages involved in working out your IS – see below.

Calculate your 'applicable amount'

This is the amount you and your family are considered to need each week to live on. It is very low, so check whether you might be able to get a social fund payment to help with special expenses. Your applicable amount consists of:

- **personal allowances** for each member of your family; *plus*
- **premiums** for any special needs; *and*
- **housing costs**, principally for mortgage interest payments. (Some housing costs are not included in your IS applicable amount and are met separately by housing benefit, see p225.)

The detailed rules about how to calculate personal allowances and premiums are in Chapter 17. Housing costs met by IS are described on p29.

Your applicable amount can be reduced if you are:

- voluntarily unemployed (see p58);
- unwilling to apply for child support maintenance (see pp127-30).

Calculate your income

This is the amount you have coming in each week from other benefits, part-time earnings, maintenance etc. Most income counts in full, but some is ignored (see Chapter 18).

Deduct the income you have from the amount you need

The answer you get will normally be the amount paid as your IS.

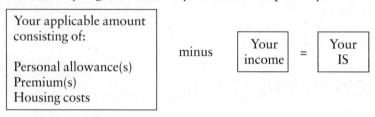

| Your applicable amount consisting of: | minus | Your income | = | Your IS |

Personal allowance(s)
Premium(s)
Housing costs

Example

Ms Hughes is a single parent aged **27** with a daughter aged **8**. She has no housing costs to be covered by IS. Her applicable amount is:

£45.70	personal allowance
£15.65	personal allowance for child under 11
£10.05	family premium
£5.10	lone parent premium
£76.50	Total

Her income is £10.20.
    Her IS is £76.50 (applicable amount) minus £10.20 (income) = £66.30.

Different rules for deciding how your benefit is calculated apply to you if you are:

- in local authority residential accommodation (p97);
- in a residential care home or nursing home (p100);
- in hospital (p113);
- a prisoner (p117);
- a person without accommodation (p119);
- 16- or 17-years-old (p67);
- a person from abroad (p81);

- affected by a trade dispute (p77).

People who are members of, and fully maintained by, a religious order do not get any IS at all.

You may get more than your normal IS entitlement because you are receiving transitional protection (see p43).

2. HOUSING COSTS

If you pay rent or live in board and lodging or a hostel you normally receive housing benefit to cover your housing costs (see p226). Other housing costs are met as part of your IS 'applicable amount'. These are:[1]

- mortgage interest payments (see p32);
- interest under a hire purchase agreement to buy your home (see p32);
- interest you pay on a loan for repairs and improvements to your home (see p36);
- rent or ground rent (in Scotland, feu duty) if you have a long lease of more than 21 years;
- rent if you are a Crown tenant (minus water charges);
- payments you make if you are part of a co-ownership scheme;
- service charges. This covers charges paid to your landlord for a service which s/he provides – for example, cleaning of common areas. Owner-occupiers can also be liable for such charges under the terms of their lease. A 'service' is something which is agreed and arranged on your behalf and for which you are required to pay. Thus if you own a flat, and your lessor arranges the exterior painting of the building every three years and you are required to meet your share of the cost, your IS includes this as a service charge. Such charges only count if they relate to the provision of adequate accommodation.[2] House insurance paid under the terms of your lease can be a service charge.[3] Service charges to cover minor repairs are not excluded, but the cost of major repairs and improvements is, and you must take out a loan to cover these on which you can claim interest (see p36). Charges made for services provided by an outside authority do not count, therefore charges for water and sewerage services paid to a water board are not covered.[4] However, you could argue that a bill for services provided by an outside authority counts if you are due to pay these as a condition of continuing to occupy your home, and they are necessary to ensure adequate accommodation;
- payments for a tent you live in and the site it is on;
- payments by way of rent charges.

Your IS does not include the following:

- housing costs which are covered by HB;[5]
- water rates. You are expected to pay for these from the rest of your IS. If you are a Crown tenant and your housing costs incorporate water charges, these will be deducted from your housing costs. If you do not know how much your water charges are, they are estimated as though you were not a Crown tenant and that amount is deducted;[6]
- the cost of heating, hot water, lighting and cooking where these are included in your housing costs.[7] The following amounts are deducted from your housing costs:

| heating | £8.60 | cooking | £1.05 |
| hot water | £1.05 | lighting | £0.70 |

  You are expected to meet these from the rest of your IS. However, if you can produce evidence of an actual or approximate charge for fuel, that amount is deducted instead;
- the cost of service charges that are listed on p228.[8] (But note that you can get help with certain service charges – see above);
- the costs of any repairs and improvements (of a similar kind to those listed on p36). However, if you take out a loan to pay for these items your housing costs include the interest on the loan;[9]
- the cost of any new or additional loans or second mortgage taken out while you are on IS (see p42).

When can housing costs be paid?

You must satisfy the following two conditions:

- The housing costs you pay are for the home in which you and your family normally live.[10] If you have to make payments on two properties, the Benefits Agency pay your housing costs for both in very limited circumstances (see below). Your home is defined as the building or part of the building in which you live and includes any garage, garden, outbuildings, and also other premises and land which it is not reasonable or practicable to sell separately.[11]
- You are responsible for paying these housing costs. This does not mean you have to be legally liable.[12] You are treated as liable if:
  - you have to pay them to someone who is not in your household (see p328-9 for meaning of 'household');
  - you share the responsibility to pay with other people in your household in practice (but not your partner or a 'close relative' – see p110 for meaning) and it is reasonable to treat you as sharing.[13] If you share, your proportion of the costs is covered;

– the person who is liable is not paying and you have to pay the housing costs instead in order to keep your home. This only applies if that person is your former partner or it is reasonable for you to pay.[14] For example, it can cover a situation where you are living in someone's home but they die and you need to pay the housing costs to remain in the home.[15]

You cannot get housing costs met if you are on IS and living rent-free in someone else's home but then take out a mortgage to buy your own home.[16]

If payments for housing costs have been waived because you have paid for repairs or redecoration, which are not normally your responsibility, you can still get IS for them for up to eight weeks.[17] However, if under the terms of your mortgage you are not required to pay any interest, you cannot receive IS for housing costs. This applies to special mortgage schemes for pensioners where the mortgage is repaid out of your estate when you die rather than by regular monthly payments.[18]

There are special rules if you and your partner are involved in a trade dispute (see p77).

Where you have to pay costs for two homes you get IS for both if:

• you left your old home through fear of violence and it is reasonable that you should get payments for two homes.[19] 'Violence' includes violence in your old home *or* from a former member of your family. Fear of a racial attack should be covered by this rule as long as the attack would take place *in* the old home; *or*
• your partner unavoidably has to live away from home as a student or while on a government training course (see p61), and it is reasonable to pay both costs.[20] A single person or single parent who is a student or on YT or TFW and who qualifies for IS, only gets housing costs for their normal or term-time home, but not both;[21] *or*
• you are moving and you have to make payments on both homes. Your housing costs are met for up to four weeks.[22] If you have had to move to temporary accommodation while repairs are done to your normal home, you only get help with the home for which you have to make payments.[23] If you have to pay for both you get the housing costs of your normal home.

If you became liable for housing costs before you moved in, your IS can include these costs for up to four weeks, if you could not move in because:[24]

• you were waiting for adaptations for a disability; *or*
• you were waiting for the result of a social fund application for help

with removal costs and expenses involved in setting up home (eg, furniture and bedding), and you have a child under six or your benefit includes a pensioner, higher pensioner, disability, severe disability or disabled child premium; *or*
• you became responsible for the housing costs while in hospital or in local authority residential accommodation (see p97).

You must have claimed IS before you moved in, or if you claimed and your IS did not include housing costs, you should re-claim within four weeks of moving in.[25]

If you are not covered by the above rules, you can only get your housing costs met when you 'normally occupy' the premises as your home. A person who has never actually lived in their home does not 'normally occupy' it.[26] It is arguable that moving in furniture and spending a night in the home could count as living there.

If you are away from home temporarily but are still entitled to IS and you do not let your home, your housing costs continue to be paid if you intend to return, and are unlikely to be away for longer than 52 weeks (the time limit is slightly relaxed if you cannot control when you will return – eg, you go into hospital). Payments will cease once you have been away for 52 weeks.[27]

Those **students** who qualify for IS, but who are away from their term-time home during the summer vacation, will not have the housing costs on that home met unless the reason they are away is because they are in hospital, or their term-time home is also their normal home.[28]

Mortgage payments

An amount for mortgage payments is included in your IS applicable amount under the rules described below. There are special rules about how this is paid (see p156), and there is a limit on the amount you can get (see p37).

Your applicable amount does not cover capital repayments, only the interest on a mortgage, hire purchase agreement or any other loan taken out in order to buy your home.[29] (We use the term 'mortgage' to refer to all such loans or agreements.) Special rules apply for the first 16 weeks that you claim IS (see p34). The cost of associated insurance premiums is not covered.[30] Thus, claimants with an endowment mortgage will not get the insurance element paid and should consider changing the terms of their mortgage. Most people pay mortgage interest after deduction of income tax but, if this does not apply, you are allowed the full amount of your payments. Otherwise, you get the net amount you pay.[31] Where interest is charged at more than one rate you receive the aggregated amount.[32] The amount actually charged by the lender is met as long as there is proof of the sum involved, even if that sum differs from the figure calculated by the Benefits Agency.[33]

You are only paid the interest where you have:[34]

- taken out the mortgage in order to buy a home. This includes buying an additional interest in the home – for example, converting a leasehold interest into a freehold one[35] or buying out your partner's share where s/he goes bankrupt and a trustee in bankruptcy takes over her/his assets.[36] Loans taken out to meet the cost of buying land and building a property on it are covered, as well as those used to buy an existing property;[37] *and/or*
- taken out a second mortgage or loan in order to repay the original mortgage, which was itself taken out in order to buy a home (sometimes called 're-mortgaging'). For example, if the amount outstanding on your first mortgage was £20,000 and you took out a second one of £25,000 to repay the first, you will only get the interest on £20,000 of the second loan met by IS; *and/or*
- taken out a loan for the cost of repairs or improvements (see p36).

If you have increased your mortgage or taken out a second loan while on IS, you may not be paid for the full amount (see p42).

Where a loan is taken out wholly or partly for other purposes (eg, to finance a business), the proportion of the interest payable on that part of the loan is not met except where the claim is made by a separated partner (see below). This applies even if the loan is secured on your home. If you later take out a mortgage on your home to pay off the secured loan, you will still not be paid housing costs because the purpose of the loan is to pay off the debt, not to acquire an interest in the home.[38]

Interest on arrears of a mortgage cannot be met[39] except where these arise:[40]

- during the 16 weeks after you first claim IS, when mortgage interest repayments are only covered partially (see p34); *or*
- from interest payments some or all of which are deferred for at least two years under the terms of your loan, and which you are liable to meet.

Separated couples

Where a couple separate and one partner buys out the other's share in the home, the additional repayment burden is met so long as this was taken out before you went on to IS, or you and your partner were getting IS immediately prior to your current claim and you are simply claiming for an equivalent amount.[41]

If your ex-partner is liable for but not paying the mortgage, you can have the mortgage interest met as part of your benefit.[42] You can also be paid interest on a loan which is not for house purchase (eg, it could be for a car), provided your partner has left and cannot or will not pay it, and it is secured on your home.[43] It does not matter whether the loan was taken out jointly with your partner or by her/him alone. This rule applies to you if your partner has died and there are outstanding loans which are not otherwise covered as part of your IS.

If you discover that your ex-partner has not been paying the mortgage as you assumed, you should ask for your benefit to be reviewed to include the arrears of mortgage interest that have not been paid.

The 16-week rule

You get only 50 per cent of the mortgage interest for the first 16 weeks of your IS claim. However, if you or your partner are 60 or over there is no reduction.[44] If either of you reach 60 during the first 16 weeks the restriction is removed. If you come off IS during this 16-week period, see below. After 16 weeks, you get the full amount of your mortgage interest.[45] The 16-week reduction applies again if you claim IS again at a later date, unless you are treated as entitled to IS even while not actually receiving it (see below).[46]

So that you can qualify for full mortgage interest more quickly, you are treated as being in receipt of IS for certain periods when you are not on IS, or you are not the person claiming (if you are, or were, a couple). You are treated as being in receipt of IS as follows:[47]

- during a gap of eight weeks or less between two IS claims;
- during the time when your partner was claiming on her/his own, provided you claim IS within eight weeks of becoming a couple;
- during the time when your ex-partner was claiming for you both, and you claim IS within eight weeks of separating;
- during the time when your partner was claiming for you both, if you take over the claiming role;
- during the time when someone else was claiming for you as a dependent child. But you must claim within eight weeks of this, and you must also be claiming for another child for whom s/he used to get benefit;
- for any period when you were not getting IS, but as a result of a review or appeal it was decided that you should have been receiving it.

Once you have qualified for the full mortgage interest as above:

- you or your partner can take a full-time job for 12 weeks or less, and you will be able to re-claim IS and get the mortgage interest paid in full.[48] But the normal eight-week break will apply (see above) if you or your partner leave the job voluntarily or are sacked and the voluntary unemployment deduction is applied (see p58), or if the person who took the job was, in the six months before that, in full-time work, in relevant education or a student;[49]

- you or your partner can attend a government training course (see p61), or attend an employment rehabilitation centre, and even though you may come off benefit as a result, you continue to be treated as though you are on IS while there. If you have to re-claim IS when the course is finished you get the mortgage interest paid in full immediately.[50]

If you do not qualify for IS because the 50 per cent rule means your income is higher than your applicable amount, but you would get IS if your mortgage interest was counted in full, make a second claim for IS between 16 and 20 weeks after the date of your original claim. Similarly, if your benefit was ended on review or appeal, re-claim between 16 and 20 weeks after the date of your claim that led to the original award. You will then be entitled to receive benefit (calculated on the basis that all your mortgage interest is included in your IS assessment) starting 16 weeks after the date of that original claim.[51]

If you use payments from a mortgage protection policy (taken out to insure against the risk of being unable to meet your mortgage payments) to cover the mortgage interest not met by IS, this money is ignored as your income[52] (see p389).

After 16 weeks you get 100 per cent of your mortgage interest payments so long as this is below the maximum[53] (see p37 – but see p42 for tenants who buy their own homes, and p40 for 'excessive' housing costs). You also receive the additional interest payable on the arrears of interest that have accumulated during this period.[54]

Capital repayments

Your IS does not include your mortgage capital repayments. Many lenders are prepared to accept interest-only payments for a while. If your loan is from a building society and your local branch are not prepared to do this, contact the head office of the society.

If you have to pay the capital, you may be able to increase your income by a small amount by taking in lodgers (see p384 for how this will affect your IS). Payment made direct to the lender from relatives, friends or a charity towards the capital repayments[55] is ignored (see pp392 and 409). There is a similar rule if the payment is made by a liable relative[56] (see p137).

If you use payments from a mortgage protection policy to meet your mortgage capital repayments these are ignored as your income.[57]

Loans for repairs and improvements

All claimants (not just owner-occupiers) are entitled to receive IS to cover the interest on loans taken out to pay for repairs and improvements to their home. The loan should be used for the repairs within six months of its receipt, or longer if such a delay is reasonable. The same 50 per cent restriction for the first 16 weeks on IS applies as in the case of loans to buy a home[58] (see pp34-5).

You cannot receive interest on a new loan for repairs and improvements taken out while you are on IS, unless it is to meet a service charge for such costs which you have to pay (see p43).[59]

Repairs and improvements are defined as:[60]

- major repairs necessary to maintain the fabric of the dwelling occupied as the home; *and also improvements like*:
- putting in bathroom fixtures – eg, a washbasin, bath, shower or toilet;
- damp-proofing;
- providing or improving ventilation or natural light;
- providing or improving drainage facilities;
- putting in electric lighting and sockets;
- putting in heating, including central heating;
- putting in storage facilities for fuel and refuse;
- improving the structural condition of the home;
- improving facilities for storing, preparing and cooking food;
- insulation;
- other improvements which are reasonable in the circumstances (eg, adaptations to the home for a disabled person[61]).

Improvements mean measures which improve the home's fitness for occupation. The individual needs of you and your family should be considered when deciding if this applies – eg, any special needs arising from a disability.[62] Account can also be taken of the needs of others in your home (eg, an elderly parent), but only if this is reasonable.[63]

If the loan included the cost of necessary redecoration following any of these works, the interest on that part of the loan should also be met by IS. External redecoration on its own could be an improvement or major repair.[64]

If you have to pay a service charge for repairs and improvements it may not be covered by IS (see p29), but under this rule you can take out a loan and be paid interest.

For information about housing renovation grants, see Chapter 26.

When your housing costs are not met in full

Your housing costs may not be met in full if:

- part of the loan was taken out for business purposes or to buy something other than your home (eg, a car);
- your home is used for both business and domestic purposes and neither part can be sold off separately. It is therefore classed as a 'mixed' or 'composite hereditament', and not just a private dwelling. Your housing costs are based on the proportion of the total value which relates to the part used for domestic purposes and you only get help with the interest payable on that part of the property.[65] Your local authority will have decided whether your property is a composite hereditament and you may need further advice from them;
- you have non-dependants living in your household (see below);
- the mortgage(s) on your home amount to more than £125,000. This includes all mortgages taken out to buy your home and also any loans for repairs and improvements (see p36). The restriction is applied proportionately to each loan. If a loan was for adaptations for a disabled person and that person qualifies for the disability, disabled child, enhanced pensioner or higher pensioner premium (see Chapter 17), that loan is ignored when calculating the maximum payable. It does not matter if the disabled person is you, one of your family or a non-dependant (see p38).

  If you can claim for two homes (see p31), you can be paid up to this limit for each. If, however, you used part of your mortgage on something other than housing costs, or your home is a composite hereditament (see above), the maximum is lower if the proportion of the loan covered by IS is less than £125,000.[66]

  Upper limits for mortgage loans have only existed since 2 August 1993. At that time the limit was £150,000. If you were entitled to IS on that date and have been continuously entitled since, the restriction does not apply;[67]
- your housing costs are less than £125,000 but nevertheless considered to be 'excessive' (see p40);
- you are a **tenant** and buy your own home (see p42);
- you have increased your mortgage, or taken out a second mortgage while on IS (see p42).

If your housing costs are restricted and you are left with insufficient money to pay your mortgage, you may be in danger of losing your home, particularly if you are on IS for a long time. You should inform your lender and let them know that you are trying to resolve the situation. You should also seek independent debt advice to explore the options.

Ultimately you may have to sell your home and buy somewhere cheaper, but you could try and make up the shortfall by:

- taking in a lodger (see p384);
- finding a part-time job and benefiting from the earnings disregard (see p369-71).

Alternatively you may be able to move to rented accommodation and let your home to cover your outgoings. If you do this the capital value of your home and any income is disregarded because it is regarded as a 'reversionary interest'.[68] The capital value may in any case be nil if you have negative equity in the property.

Another way around the problem is to put your house up for sale, which allows the capital value to be disregarded until it is sold.[69] If you can also rent it out while trying to sell, the income from any tenants can be disregarded up to the value of any mortgage outgoings which you have on that property.[70]

Deductions for non-dependants

A **non-dependant** is a person who normally lives with you and who is not part of your family for IS purposes (see p328) – eg, a grown-up son or daughter. A person is *not* a non-dependant if s/he:[71]

- is liable to pay you or your partner in order to live in your home – eg, a sub-tenant, licensee, or boarder. This also applies to other members of their household. The payment must be on a commercial basis. A low charge does not necessarily mean that the arrangement is not commercial; nor do you have to make a profit. An arrangement between friends can be commercial.[72] Close relatives (see p110) count as non-dependants even if they pay for their accommodation;
- is someone, other than a close relative (see p110), to whom you, or your partner, are liable to make payments on a commercial basis (ie, as a sub-tenant, licensee, boarder) in order to live in their property. Other members of their household do not count as non-dependants either;
- jointly occupies your home and is a co-owner or joint tenant with you or your partner. Your joint occupier's partner is not a non-dependant. Close relatives (see p110) are treated as non-dependants unless they had joint liability prior to 11 April 1988. Joint liability between close relatives which begins later only counts if it existed on or before you first lived in the property (or your partner did if s/he is the joint tenant/ owner);
- is employed by a charitable or voluntary body as a resident carer for you or your partner and you pay for that service (even if the charge is

only nominal). If the carer's partner also lives in your home, s/he does not count as a non-dependant.

A person can be treated as living with you only if they share any rooms except a bathroom or toilet or common access areas – eg, hall or landing or, in the case of sheltered accommodation, other common rooms.[73] Thus, this includes people who share the use of a kitchen. But a person who is separately liable to pay rent to a landlord is not counted as living with you.

If you have a non-dependant living with you, a set deduction is usually made from your housing costs whether or not s/he makes a contribution towards the cost of the accommodation. The amount varies according to the age and circumstances of the non-dependant.

No deduction is made from your benefit for a non-dependant who is:[74]

- 16- or 17-years-old;
- 18- to 24-years-old and on IS;
- getting a YT allowance;
- a full-time student. This also applies during the summer vacation unless s/he has a job during that time;
- currently staying in your household but whose normal home is else-where;
- a joint tenant or co-owner with you or your partner, even if that person is a close relative;
- not living with you because s/he is in prison or has been a hospital in-patient for over six weeks.

No deduction is made from your benefit if:[75]

- a deduction is already being made from your housing benefit;
- you or your partner are registered blind or treated as blind (see p345) or getting attendance allowance (or equivalent benefit paid because of injury at work or a war injury) or the care component of disability living allowance.

A deduction is made from your benefit for each non-dependant in your household unless exempted as above.[76]

Circumstances of non-dependant	*Deduction*
18 or over, in full-time work with gross weekly income of:	
– less than £72	£5.00
– between £72 and £107.99	£9.00
– between £108 and £138.99	£13.00

– £139 or more	£25.00
18 or over and not in full-time work	£5.00

For the meaning of 'full-time work', see p14. Remember that if you are off sick or on maternity leave you do not count as being in full-time work (even if you are on full pay).[77] Gross income includes wages before tax and national insurance are deducted plus any other income you have including benefits (but not attendance allowance or disability living allowance, payments from any of the Macfarlane Trusts, the Eileen Trust, the Fund, or the Independent Living Funds).

Couples and joint occupiers

• Only one deduction is made for a married or unmarried couple who are non-dependants.[78] Where each member of the couple would attract different deductions because of different circumstances the higher one is made. The total gross income of the couple is taken into account when deciding whether the lower deduction applies.
• Deductions for non-dependants are divided between joint occupiers, taking account of the number of joint occupiers and the proportion of living costs paid by each. Joint occupiers who are a couple count as one person.[79]

'Excessive' housing costs

You cannot have your full housing costs paid if it is decided that your housing costs are 'excessive'.[80] Account must be taken of the amount deducted from your housing costs for non-dependants living with you (see above).

The amount allowed for your housing costs can be restricted if:[81]

• your home, excluding any part that is let, is larger than is required by your family, any foster children and any non-dependants when compared to suitable alternative accommodation. The needs of everyone living in your accommodation must be considered. For example, if anyone needs additional space (ie, because of a disability), this should be taken into account. If you have a child in care, or an elderly or disabled relative who normally lives in a residential home but who regularly comes to stay with you, it is reasonable that you should have a spare room for this purpose; *or*
• the immediate area around your home is more expensive than other areas in which there is suitable accommodation; *or*
• your housing costs are higher than those of suitable alternative accommodation in the area. ('Area' here refers to the immediate locality – see below.)

No restriction should be made and your housing costs should be met in full if it is unreasonable for you to move. When deciding this, the Benefits Agency considers:[82]

- the availability of suitable accommodation ('availability' means it must actually exist, and it must be suitable for you);
- the level of housing costs in the area. An area is 'something more confined, restricted and compact than a locality or district . . . It might consist of . . . a number of roads, refer to a neighbourhood and even to a large block of flats. It is not capable of precise definition';[83]
- your circumstances and those of your family – in particular, your age, health, employment prospects and the possible upheaval in the education of any children living with you if you had to move.

Other circumstances may be worth pointing out – eg, particular difficulties you have in finding accommodation because of your family's size, your need to be near a relative to care for them or near members of your family or friends for support, the number of times you have had to move recently, the difficulty of selling your property, or the fact that you have negative equity and would be put into substantial debt if you sold now. It is also reasonable to argue that you should be able to remain in a home where you have lived for many years, but which is now larger than you need because, for example, there has been a death in the family, or you are now separated or divorced.

The fact that you have been told by the Benefits Agency that full mortgage interest would be paid is a factor that the adjudication officer should consider when deciding whether to limit housing costs.[84] Your inability to obtain another mortgage to buy another house is also relevant. Rented accommodation is not necessarily a satisfactory alternative if as a result you lose entitlement to IS or if you would be unable to find the deposit/rent in advance required to take on such accommodation. It would therefore not be reasonable to expect you to move unless you could be sure you could obtain a mortgage to buy an alternative property.[85]

There should be no restriction during the first six months you claim IS, provided you could afford the payments when you took them on. This should also cover a person who was a member of the family when the mortgage was taken on. So if the payments were affordable when taken on by a couple who later separated leaving one partner in the home, this rule should apply. Another six-month period is allowed if you are making every effort to find somewhere cheaper to live.[86] If full payment is made initially but then your benefit is reviewed, the six-month periods should run from the date of the review. Temporary breaks in entitlement to IS of up to eight weeks are included when calculating each of the six-month periods. In addition, if you have only recently become part of a couple or you have separated from your previous partner and you make a new claim within eight weeks, periods when your partner was entitled to IS also count towards the six-month period. This could mean that the restriction applies even before you have been on benefit in your own right for 12 months.

If restriction is appropriate your housing costs are limited to the cost of a home of suitable size or expense. You would get no housing costs if the equity in your home is sufficient to buy the alternative property outright.[87]

Tenants who buy their own homes

If you buy the home which you currently rent, and your housing costs go up, you may not get your new housing costs met in full.

If you sought advice from the Benefits Agency *before* buying and were told *wrongly* that your mortgage interest would be met in full, you are still caught by this rule. You will have to take legal action for wrong advice to recover any loss. It will help if the advice from the Benefits Agency was given to you in writing.

The amount for your housing costs is restricted to the amount of the rent used to calculate your HB before you bought your home.[88] If, subsequently, the cost of your mortgage or loan rises again, you are allowed the increase in the assessment of your housing costs. This does not later reduce when the mortgage interest rate goes down again.[89]

If you buy the home jointly with one or more non-dependants, you are treated as jointly responsible for the housing costs. Your allowance for housing costs is a proportionate share of the new housing costs.[90] If your share of the new housing costs is more than the rent used to calculate your HB, you only receive that lower amount.

If a member of the household who is a non-dependant buys your home, you are not treated as responsible for the housing costs.

For council tenants exercising their right to buy the restriction is removed if there is a major change in your family's circumstances which makes it inappropriate for there to be a limit on the amount allowed for your housing costs – eg, if you took on the loan because you were getting regular financial help from relatives and they can no longer pay.[91] The limit is also lifted once you have stopped getting IS for at least eight weeks and then claimed again (26 weeks in the case of tenants who did not have security of tenure).[92]

You are not caught by this provision if you were not claiming benefit during the week in which you became liable to complete the purchase – ie, when contracts were actually exchanged between buyer and seller.[93]

Remortgaging and second loans[94]

The government is proposing to change the rules from April 1994. The proposed changes are as follows. For the latest information, see the April 1994 issue of the *Welfare Rights Bulletin*.

If you increase your mortgage, or take out a second mortgage while you are on IS you cannot be paid for the additional cost. You are also excluded if you take out the additional loan while you are not on IS, but during a period of less than 26 weeks between two separate claims for IS. If you have a break of more than 26 weeks between your claims for IS you are paid the full cost of your mortgage when you re-claim, subject to any other restrictions noted above.

Additional mortgage costs *can* be met if they arise due to:

- changes in the mortgage interest rate;
- accumulated arrears of interest;
- adaptations to the property to meet the special needs of a disabled person;
- the need to buy a different home which is more suitable for a disabled person. 'Disabled person' means someone who fulfils the conditions for the disability, disabled child, higher pensioner or enhanced pensioner premium (see Chapter 17). Increases in mortgage commitments are allowed even if the disabled person was not previously living with you;
- loans taken out to pay for service charges to meet the cost of major repairs and improvements (but not other loans for repairs/improvements – see p36).

3. TRANSITIONAL PROTECTION

Introduction

Some claimants are paid more than their basic IS entitlement because they receive an amount of transitional protection. Transitional protection was created when IS replaced supplementary benefit in April 1988. Its purpose was to prevent those on supplementary benefit suffering a sudden drop in income because of the different way in which IS was calculated. Later changes to the IS rules have also caused some claimants to be worse off, and they too received transitional protection. It is a payment to cover the difference between the reduced benefit rate and the amount received prior to the change.

Payments were introduced at different stages and are as follows:

- **Transitional additions from 11 April 1988** for people claiming benefit immediately before and after this date.[95] If you have been receiving IS since its introduction you may still be entitled to a transitional addition. You could be getting a transitional addition on its own.

- **Transitional payments**[96] **from 30 May 1988** for those who were:
  - not entitled to IS between 11 April 1988 and 30 May 1988 because the capital rules were less generous than for supplementary benefit; *or*
  - temporarily absent from home at the changeover to IS.
- **Protected sums for people who were boarders on 10 April 1989**[97] (which is when boarders began to have their housing costs met by HB and not IS). You will only be getting this now if you are in supported lodgings. For all other boarders the protection was only temporary, lasting 13 weeks or 12 months. The protected sum was part of your applicable amount.
- **Protected sums for people living in hostels**[98] **on 9 October 1989** (which was when hostel residents began to have their housing costs met by HB and not IS). The protected sum was part of the applicable amount. It has been phased out gradually.

How transitional protection affects your current benefit

Although transitional protection is no longer relevant to most claimants, you may need to know about it to:

- check the amount you are currently receiving to see if it is correct; *or*
- calculate your IS for a past period.

For more details see the 19th edition of the *National Welfare Benefits Handbook*. The rules relating to protected sums for hostel dwellers were described in *Welfare Rights Bulletin 91*. If you do not have these items we can supply a photocopy of the relevant parts. Write to CPAG, 1-5 Bath Street, London EC1V 9PY.

4. URGENT CASES PAYMENTS

Who can claim

If you do not satisfy the normal rules for getting IS, you may nevertheless be able to get an urgent cases payment if you come within one of the following groups:[99]

- you are a 'person from abroad' and you meet certain conditions (see p87);

- you are treated as possessing income which was due to be paid to you but which has not been paid (see p391). If you were due to receive a social security benefit but it has not yet been paid you will not be treated as possessing it. The income you are treated as possessing must not be readily available to you and there must be a likelihood that if you do not get a payment, you or your family will suffer hardship.[100]

Even if your partner is entitled to ordinary IS you can claim urgent cases payments instead if the amount you receive would be higher.

It is important to note that an urgent cases payment is a payment of IS and thus you are automatically eligible for other benefits (see p9).

If you do not come within these rules but have no money, you may be able to get a crisis loan from the social fund (see p449).

If you are not entitled to IS because you cannot sign on, but you are likely to suffer hardship without help,[101] see p24.

How much you can get

Applicable amounts

Urgent cases payments of IS are paid at a reduced rate. Your applicable amount is:

- a personal allowance for you (and your partner). It is paid at 90 per cent of the personal allowance that would have been paid had you qualified for IS in the normal way; *plus*
- full personal allowances for any children; *plus*
- premiums and housing costs or residential allowance, if any, and any 'protected sum' paid because you were a boarder prior to 10 April 1989[102] (see p44).

If you are living in a residential or nursing home and have a preserved right (see p101), you receive 90 per cent of the personal allowance for you (and your partner) plus full personal allowances for any children plus the amount normally allowed for your accommodation.[103] You get 98 per cent of the amount paid if you are in local authority accommodation.

If your benefit is reduced because you are treated as voluntarily unemployed, the voluntary unemployment deduction (see p58) is applied before the 10 per cent urgent cases reduction.

Income and capital

Almost all of your capital and income is taken into account before an urgent cases payment is made.

Income

All your income counts, including income that is usually ignored, except the following:[104]

- assumed income from capital between £3,000 and £8,000 – ie, your 'tariff income' (see pp385-7);
- income you are treated as having if you are applying for an urgent cases payment for that reason;
- any housing benefit and/or council tax benefit;
- any payment made to compensate you for the loss of entitlement to housing benefit supplement or housing benefit;
- any payment from any the Macfarlane Trusts, the Eileen Trust, the Fund, or the Independent Living Funds;
- payments made by haemophilia sufferers to their partner, or children out of money originally provided by one of the Macfarlane Trusts. If the sufferer has no partner or children, payments made to a parent, step-parent or guardian are also disregarded, but only for two years. These payments are also disregarded if the sufferer dies and the money is paid out of the estate;
- payments arising from the Macfarlane Trusts which are paid by a person to a haemophiliac partner, or to their child(ren).

Certain income is treated as capital if you get IS under the normal rules (see p397).[105] However, if you apply for an urgent cases payment the following is treated as income:

- any lump sum paid to you not more than once a year for your work as a part-time firefighter, part-time member of a lifeboat crew, auxiliary coastguard or member of the Territorial Army;
- any refund of income tax;
- holiday pay which is not payable until more than four weeks after your job ended;
- any irregular charitable or voluntary payment.

Capital[106]

Your capital is calculated in the usual way but the following is also taken into account:

- money from the sale of your home which you intend to use to buy another;
- the liquid assets of a business (eg, cash in hand);
- arrears of the following: mobility supplement, disability living or disability working allowance, attendance allowance, IS, family credit, or any concessionary payments made to compensate for non-payment of any of these benefits;

- money which had been deposited with a housing association and which is now to be used to buy a home;
- up to £200 of a training bonus received after being on Training for Work (see p65);
- a refund of tax on a mortgage or loan taken out to buy, or to do repairs and/or improvements to your home.

CHAPTER FOUR

The unemployed and people on government training schemes

This chapter covers:

1. The claim procedures for unemployed people (below)
2. Availability for work (p52)
3. Actively seeking employment (p56)
4. Workers on short-time (p57)
5. The voluntary unemployment deduction (p58)
6. People on government training schemes (p61)

This chapter deals with people under 60 who are unemployed and required to sign on as a condition of receiving benefit and also those on government training schemes.

See p22 for circumstances in which people under 60 do not have to sign on to get benefit.

Even if you think you do not need IS, it is worth claiming in case you are not entitled to unemployment benefit, or if the latter takes time to come through.

If you have no money you should try for a crisis loan from the social fund (see p449).

1. THE CLAIM PROCEDURES FOR UNEMPLOYED PEOPLE

Signing on

If you are under 60, unemployed and not exempt from signing on (see p22), you must be available for and actively seeking work in order to get IS.[1] You claim by registering at an unemployment benefit office and normally you must then sign on once a fortnight in order to get benefit.[2] People under 18 who are eligible for IS and who have to sign on also have to register for employment at the JobCentre or Careers Office.[3]

If for any reason you have failed to sign on, but have now made a late claim (see p145), your failure to sign on does not mean that you were not available for work but you will need to tell the unemployment benefit office that you were looking for work and provide evidence of this.

When you sign on at the unemployment benefit office you are interviewed by a new client receptionist who makes an initial assessment of your situation and should give you the relevant forms on which to claim. S/he then makes an appointment for you to see a claimant adviser in order to discuss your availability and to formally take your claim. The new client receptionist may suggest claiming a different benefit – eg, sickness benefit if it seems you are too sick to work. The decision about which benefit to claim is yours and you should insist on making a claim as an unemployed person if that represents your true situation. If this is refused you should complain.

If your claim is successful, your IS is paid fortnightly in arrears two days after your signing-on day so you may have to wait up to 16 days.

Filling in the claim forms

Make sure you are given form B1 on which to claim IS as well as the unemployment benefit claim form (ES461). The two forms are quite different: form B1 is designed to find out about your personal circumstances and assess your financial needs; form ES461 is to check that you are genuinely available for and actively seeking work. The answers to both will be used when deciding if you are entitled to IS, even though the latter is technically a claim for unemployment benefit.

Form ES461 asks detailed questions about:

- your past work, experience and training;
- the type of work you are looking for and whether you are placing any restrictions on this;
- what steps you are taking to find work;
- any payments received from your last employer and any other benefits you are claiming.

When filling in the form it is important to remember that it aims to find out what you would accept as a minimum, not your ideal requirements.

The adjudication officer considers your answers on the ES461 and decides whether you have a reasonable chance of getting a job.[4] Your chances will depend partly on how long you have been out of work which affects the decision on whether to treat you as available for work.[5] The answers you give on form ES461 are not sufficient in themselves to justify a decision that you are not available for work, as the questions are leading questions. If you can show, for example, that, ideally you would like a job paying £200 a week and that was the amount you put on the form, but that in reality, you would accept less, you should not be refused benefit.[6]

A lot of weight is given to your answers and it is better to answer them realistically in the first place. The following tips should help:

- indicate both the type of job you would like and also what you would be prepared to accept. Be realistic. Do such jobs exist in your area and are you qualified to do them? If you are willing to take different types of work make this clear. Remember you are expected to take full-time work;
- do not restrict too much the distance you are willing to travel. The claimant adviser will expect you to be prepared to travel up to one hour each way unless there is a good reason why you cannot do this. You may be expected to look much further afield and even to move if you are seeking specialised work;
- where you are asked for the minimum wage or salary you will accept, you should put the going rate for that job.
  Try to check out current wage rates for the jobs you are seeking before you fill in the form;
- give clear examples of how you are going to try and find work (ie, using the JobCentre, an agency, newspaper advertisements, friends etc);
- state that you will be flexible about hours and days (but be sure you are willing to be this flexible);
- even if you have a child or adult dependant at home, you still have to show that you could take a job at a moments notice in order to be available. If you do not already have a childminder or carer lined up you should give the name of someone (eg, a friend or relative) who can provide care at least temporarily (but not someone who has to be available for work).

Checking you are available for and actively seeking work

Claimant advisers

Claimant advisers are based at the unemployment benefit offices and their function is to ensure that claimants signing on are both genuinely available for work and making suitable efforts to find work.

When you first sign on at the unemployment benefit office you are interviewed by a claimant adviser. However, a claimant adviser may check your availability at any time during your claim.

Interviews with claimant advisers can be difficult. You should take along any evidence which shows you have not restricted your efforts to find work. If you are unfit or have any particular problems (eg, a prison record) which make it hard for you to get a job, explain this too. You may be eligible for benefit due to incapacity for work without having to sign on as unemployed.

Keep a record of visits you make to JobCentres and agencies, and any other non-written enquiries you make about jobs, so that you can show what you have been doing to find work. Also keep advertisements you have followed up, copies of letters you write and any replies from employers and organisations about jobs.

If you cannot read or write you should tell the adviser at the JobCentre. The adviser may suggest you ask a friend or relative to help you keep a record of what is said, although a written record is not essential. The JobCentre may also suggest organisations able to help a person who speaks little or no English.

If the claimant adviser is dissatisfied with your efforts to find work, she passes your claim to an adjudication officer (AO) who then decides whether you did satisfy the test for actively seeking work and availability. If you disagree with the decision you should appeal.

You may be able to get IS paid on hardship grounds instead (see p24), but only if you are also found not to be available for work. If you are available but not actively seeking work you will not be paid. If you have been getting unemployment benefit only, you should make a new claim for IS on form A1.

Another role of claimant advisers is to make sure that you are getting the most appropriate benefit. If you are very disabled and it is particularly difficult for you to get a job, the claimant adviser might suggest that you should not sign on, but should get benefit as a person who is unfit for work. However, you should not be pushed to do this if you really want to go on looking for work. Nor should you take work which is unsuitable, given your health.

Restart

Under the Restart Scheme, if you have been unemployed for six months or more you are called for an interview by a claimant adviser at the local JobCentre in order to examine your attempts to find work, and any difficulties you have with a view to discussing retraining or job opportunities. You are allowed to take another person with you to the interview – eg, to interpret or to provide you with moral support.

It is important to attend such interviews – your benefit could be stopped if you don't (see p53). Prior to a Restart interview you are given form UB671R to fill in. This is very similar to the ES461 (see p49). Your answers are used to decide if you are still available for and actively seeking work. The claimant adviser will help you work out a plan of activities to get you back to work. S/he may even offer you a job vacancy which you should consider carefully. Alternatively you may be offered a place on a training scheme. You are not obliged to accept such offers, but if you refuse without a good reason you could be held to be not available for work.

Restart interviews take place approximately every six months and are an ongoing check that you are still looking for a job. After one year you can be required to attend a Job Plan workshop or a short Restart course to help you find work. This is compulsory and your IS is affected if you fail to attend (see p60).

Who decides whether you are available for work

The adjudication officer at the Benefits Agency office must decide on your IS claim but decisions about whether you are available for work are normally made by the unemployment benefit office, and the officer at the Benefits Agency which pays IS usually follows that decision. Where the question about your availability for work cannot be decided immediately by the unemployment benefit office, you are treated as not available in the meantime.[7] When this happens, the AO should automatically check whether:[8]

- you could be entitled to IS without signing on (see p22); *or*
- you should be paid IS to avoid hardship (see p24). You may have to remind the officer to do this.

If the AO at the unemployment benefit office decides at a later date that you *are and were* available, you should receive full IS backdated to the date of your claim.

2. AVAILABILITY FOR WORK

What 'available for work' means

You are treated as available for work if:[9]

- there is a reasonable prospect (in the foreseeable future[10]) of your obtaining the kind of work you say you are available to do but there are exceptions to this general condition (see below); *and*
- you are willing and able to accept (generally at once) any offer of work.

It must be work you can reasonably be expected to do, for which you expect to be paid and which is 24 hours or more a week, or as much as you can normally do given any mental or physical disability.[11]

If you can only be available within 24 hours because you are doing voluntary work, or within 14 days if you are attending a work camp organised by a local authority or charity for helping the community, or not immediately because you work part-time in emergency and rescue services, you are still treated as available.[12]

People treated as not available for work[13]

You are treated as not available for work and therefore do not qualify for IS if any one of the following apply to you:

(a) without good cause you have refused to apply for, or take a suitable job offered to you by the Employment Service/Careers Office, and the vacancy still exists;

(b) you have failed to take up any other reasonable opportunity of employment which is still open to you. This is wider than the condition above and would cover, for example, deliberately failing to attend an interview;

(c) you are aged 18-44 and single, or a member of a childless couple and your partner is also under 45 and you have failed to take up a reasonable offer of local short-term work. This does not apply to single parents, or if you or your partner is pregnant or mentally or physically disabled;

(d) without good cause you fail to attend a Restart interview, are invited to a second within 14 days of the original date set but you fail to attend a second interview (see p51);

(e) you have been refused unemployment benefit because you have not completed the part of the form dealing with availability for work properly;

(f) you are a student, unless you are disabled (see p19 for meaning), a single parent, or a single person looking after foster children, or you are receiving a training allowance, a refugee doing an English course and not required to sign on or you are a student from abroad who is entitled to an urgent cases payment because you are temporarily without funds (see p87). If you are one of a couple and both of you are students and you have a child, you can be treated as available during the summer vacation;

(g) you have a current work permit.[14] (If it has expired you will need advice about your position in the UK.);

(h) you place restrictions on the type of work you will do and where you will work, or the hours, pay, and conditions which you are prepared to accept and as a result you have no reasonable prospect of employment (but see below).

You continue to be treated as unavailable for work:[15]

- under (a), (b) and (c) above, for 26 weeks or until the vacancy is filled, whichever is shorter. When the vacancy is filled you are paid a reduced rate of IS – ie, with the voluntary unemployment deduction applied (see p58). In the case of (c) you are not treated as unavailable for work until 14 days after you were given written notice of the short-term work;
- under (d) above, until you attend an interview or are no longer required to do so;
- under (d), (e), (f) and (g) above, for as long as these paragraphs apply to you.

If you have been refused IS and you have a partner who could qualify for IS because s/he is signing on or is entitled to IS without signing on, you should swap the claiming role, and you will not lose benefit. If your IS includes a transitional addition (see p43), you need to calculate whether you are worse off by losing the transitional addition.

Restricting your prospects of employment

Your benefit should not be stopped if you have laid down conditions restricting your availability and:[16]

- the only reason you have no real chance of getting a job is because of temporary adverse industrial conditions in the area; *or*
- they are reasonable in view of your physical or mental condition; *or*
- they relate to the type of work you usually do – eg, you have always been an accounts clerk and this is the only work you are looking for. This rule applies only for a 'permitted period' of up to 13 weeks – it may be less depending on your skills, training and qualifications, how long you have been in this work and whether this type of work is available. The 13 weeks run from the first day you claimed unemployment benefit after last being in full-time work. If you have not been entitled to unemployment benefit at all since becoming unemployed, the 13 weeks run from the first day you claimed IS after leaving full-time work or vocational training in your usual line of work, or after ceasing to be incapable of work. If you have never worked, or do not have a 'usual occupation', you do not get a permitted period.[17]

Your benefit can be withheld when you first claim, or later when your case is reviewed. If you are willing and able to work and think you have a chance of getting a job within the conditions you have specified, you should appeal (see p170). You might also be able to get your benefit reinstated by widening the conditions under which you are prepared to take work.

Good cause for refusing a job

You are allowed to refuse a job if you have 'good cause'.[18] This is not defined for IS purposes but unemployment benefit legislation can be used where it is helpful.[19] For example, a person who has finished a training course within the last month can argue that s/he has good cause for turning down a job unrelated to the training.

Examples of good cause that are generally accepted are:

- the work might cause serious harm to your health, or cause excessive physical or mental stress;
- you have a religious or conscientious objection;
- you are responsible for looking after someone in your household, which would make it unreasonable for you to take a particular job;
- the time it would take to get to work and back is excessive – ie, over an hour each way, or less if your health would suffer or you are responsible for looking after another member of your household;
- the costs that would necessarily arise if you took the job, excluding childcare costs, are too high.[20]

Low pay does not, of itself, make a job unsuitable,[21] but you should argue that you have good cause for refusing a job if the pay (after travel expenses) would be less than IS.

Part-time work or study

If you are in part-time work or on a part-time course (see Chapter 2) you may still be treated as available for work and entitled to IS. Your earnings (and the part-time earnings of your partner) are taken into account when calculating the amount of IS you receive (see p357). If you are required to sign on for work to get benefit you must be able and willing to make up your hours to 24 or more.[22] If you are mentally or physically disabled, the required number of hours is the number you are capable of working.[23]

Even if you are not counted as unemployed for purposes of claiming unemployment benefit because your earnings are too high (ie, £57 a week or more, or more than £2 on a particular day), you can still claim IS if you satisfy the above rules.

3. ACTIVELY SEEKING EMPLOYMENT

What 'actively seeking employment' means

You must be taking active steps to find work each week in which you are unemployed.[24] These steps include:

- applying for jobs by letter or telephone in response to advertisements;
- getting information about possible jobs from employers, registered employment agencies, and advertisements in newspapers etc;
- registering with an employment agency.

To be treated as actively seeking work, the Employment Service would normally expect you to take at least two 'active steps' each week. For example, you could buy a newspaper to look through the job advertisements, *and* write to an employer asking for information about a job.

You are expected to take whichever steps are most likely to lead to an offer of a job. When deciding whether you have taken reasonable steps to find work the unemployment benefit office must take account of:[25]

- your skills, qualifications, any health and physical or mental limitations;
- the length of time since you were last in work;
- the attempts you have made to find work in previous weeks;
- any jobs which are available and where;
- whether you are on a training course or studying;
- whether you are doing voluntary work;
- the time spent helping in an emergency;
- whether you are homeless, and attempts you have made to find accommodation;
- any other circumstances that affect your ability to seek work.

You are **automatically treated as actively seeking work** in certain weeks including:[26]

- the first and last weeks for which you claim;
- two weeks in any period of 12 months while you are away from home (eg, on holiday) in the UK as long as you notify the unemployment benefit office in advance and can be contacted by them. You must fill in a form giving details of where you are staying;
- the first five weeks of an employment programme or training course that lasts at least three days a week and for which you are not paid a training allowance;
- if you are blind, for up to six weeks where you spend up to four weeks on a guide dog training course that you attend at least three days a week;

- up to eight weeks during which you are taking active steps to set yourself up in self-employment under the Business Start-Up Allowance Scheme;[27]
- up to three weeks of an Outward Bound Course that lasts at least three days a week;
- any week in which for three days you are treated as available for work because you are a lifeboatman, part-time fireman, or have helped in an emergency.

You do not have to be actively seeking employed earner's employment.

Who is not required to actively seek work[28]

You do not have to actively seek work to get IS if you are not available for work but are getting hardship payments (see p24), or if your incapacity for work is in dispute, you have appealed, and are continuing to submit evidence that your are incapable of work (see p22).

You are also exempt from the actively seeking work condition if:

- you (or your partner, if you are one of a couple) are pregnant and the pregnant woman would suffer hardship if IS was not paid;
- you or your partner have a dependent child and that child would suffer hardship if IS was not paid;
- your IS includes a disability premium (see p345) and you (or your partner if s/he is the one who qualifies for the premium) would suffer hardship if IS was not paid.

4. WORKERS ON SHORT-TIME

You may be entitled to IS when laid-off, if your hours of work (or, if your hours fluctuate, your average hours) have fallen below 16 hours a week.[29] When deciding the number of hours you work, the AO will have to decide whether to take into account the hours you work when you are not on short-time, or the hours you work now that you are on short-time. The question is whether your short-time working has become normal. You must sign on at the unemployment benefit office for the days you do not work and be accepted as available for, and actively seeking, work. If you receive a guarantee payment under the Employment Protection (Consolidation) Act 1978 or under a collective agreement or wages order, this counts as earnings and is taken into account accordingly.[30]

5. THE VOLUNTARY UNEMPLOYMENT DEDUCTION

If you are disqualified and your partner could claim IS, they should consider claiming instead to preserve your entitlement in full.

In certain circumstances you can be counted as 'voluntarily unemployed'. You are disqualified from receiving unemployment benefit and only paid a reduced rate of IS. The disqualification can last for up to 26 weeks and the reduced rate of IS lasts for the same length and period.[31] If you do not get unemployment benefit (eg, because you do not have sufficient contributions), you still get reduced IS.[32] The decision to disqualify is taken by the AO at the unemployment benefit office. The Benefits Agency assumes you are voluntarily unemployed in the meanwhile. The reduction only applies if you are required to be available for work in order to get benefit. If you do not have to sign on (see p22) you are paid as normal.

When the deduction applies

You are treated as voluntarily unemployed if you have:[33]

- lost your job because of misconduct; *or*
- left your job voluntarily without good cause; *or*
- without good cause refused to apply for, or take, a suitable job; *or*
- without good cause failed to take up a reasonable opportunity of employment; *or*
- without good cause failed to follow reasonable recommendations made to help you find suitable employment; *or*
- lost a place on Youth Training (YT) because of misconduct, or given up a place without good cause; *or*
- without good cause, refused or failed to take up training approved by the Employment Service. In practice this affects 18-year-olds who refuse to take up a YT place. The Training for Work Scheme is not compulsory (but see p63). Also, see p60 if you refuse to take a Restart course.

You should not be penalised if you had a good reason for leaving a job. Some examples of when your benefit should not be reduced are:[34]

- you have left one job to start another which fell through, through no fault of your own;
- you left your job because of bad working conditions, or because of difficulties over pay, such as a refusal of your employer to pay the accepted rate for the job;
- you left or refused a job because you could not manage it – eg, it

involved working at heights;
- you had to put up with racist abuse or sexist remarks and harassment;
- you left a new job between 6-12 weeks after starting it. This 'trial period' rule applies only where you have been out of work and not in full-time education or training for at least six months before trying the new job.

See CPAG's *Rights Guide to Non-Means-Tested Benefits* for more information about what misconduct means, and when a person has good cause for leaving a job.

Good cause includes the points noted on p58 but you should not be penalised if you have turned down a job because:[35]

- it is work of a kind you do not usually do and you are still within your 'permitted period' (see p54);
- it is a job that is available only because of a trade dispute;
- it is not related to the type of work for which you have just finished training for at least two months. You can only use this argument for four weeks after the course ends;
- the job is one you found out about yourself, unless you were also formally told about the job at the unemployment benefit office, or you worked for the same employer less than a year ago and your pay and conditions will only be as good as before.

If you refuse without good cause to apply for, or take, a job, or fail to take up a reasonable opportunity of employment and the vacancy is still open, you are treated as not available for work (see p53), and not entitled to IS at all, except on hardship grounds. As soon as the job is taken, you are no longer treated as 'not available' for work but you are still counted as voluntarily unemployed. You are paid IS[36] but it is reduced by the voluntary unemployment deduction.

The reduction can be made for up to 26 weeks.[37] Very often the maximum period is imposed automatically but each case should be examined on its merits. If you have been disqualified from unemployment benefit, your IS is reduced for as long as the unemployment benefit disqualification lasts.[38] You should appeal if you disagree with either the period of the reduction or the reduction itself, or both – eg, you think you had good cause for giving up or refusing a YT place; or you left your job because of bad working conditions; or you dispute that it was misconduct which lost you your job. In many cases appeals result in the 26-week period being reduced.

If you have lost unemployment benefit because of disqualification you should appeal that decision also. If you win, the reduction to your IS is reviewed and reinstated. Even if you know that you are not entitled to unemployment benefit (because, for example, you have not paid enough contributions), you should still press the unemployment benefit office to make a decision on disqualification, and appeal this if it goes against you. This is because the Benefits Agency have to follow the unemployment benefit office decision. There is no point challenging an IS decision alone.

Restart courses and the voluntary unemployment deduction[39]

This section only applies if you fail to take up the opportunity of a Job Plan Workshop or Restart course (see p52).

If you are unemployed you may be required to attend such a course to improve your chances of getting work by increasing motivation and self-confidence. If you fail to attend all or part of the course, your benefit may be reduced by the voluntary unemployment deduction.

The rule does *not* apply to a course which:

- is provided by, or on behalf of the Secretary of State; *and*
- *either* provides training for employment or is concerned with acquiring work experience;
- *or* is longer than five weeks.

Your benefit is reduced if you do not attend an appropriate course, *and*:

- you have been unemployed and entitled to unemployment benefit and/or IS for 12 months without a break, or during that time have been in work for periods of less than 57 days. (Periods when your benefit is reduced by the voluntary unemployment deduction do not count); *and*
- you have been notified of the course.

There are exceptions. Your benefit is not reduced if you fail to attend the course for one of the following reasons:

- you are ill or physically or mentally disabled and therefore not able to attend the course, or your attendance would put at risk other people on the course;
- the time it would take to travel to the course would normally be more than one hour each way;
- you are caring for someone else in your household who is unable to look after themselves and there is no one else to do this and it is not practical to make arrangements for another person to provide the care;
- you have to go to court including attending as a witness or a juror;
- you are arranging your partner's or relative's funeral;
- you are involved in a domestic emergency;

- you are providing help as part of an organised group to people in an emergency, including a fire, flood, explosion, railway or other accident or natural catastrophe;
- you are involved in an emergency as a lifeboatman or part-time fireman.

Calculating the reduction in benefit

Your IS is reduced by an amount equal to 40 per cent of the personal allowance for a single claimant; this is the voluntary unemployment deduction.[40] The amount is the same even if IS is for a couple.

A smaller reduction of 20 per cent is made where:[41]

- you, your partner or child is pregnant or seriously ill; *and*
- you have savings of no more than £200.

The following table shows the amount by which your benefit is reduced:

Claimant's personal allowance	40 per cent reduction	20 per cent reduction
£27.50	£11.00	£5.50
£36.15	£14.45	£7.25
£45.70	£18.30	£9.15

6. PEOPLE ON GOVERNMENT TRAINING SCHEMES

There are a variety of government-funded training schemes which are intended to help unemployed people back into work. These are:

- Youth training (YT) for 16- and 17-year-old school leavers who cannot find work;
- Training for Work (TFW), which is aimed mainly at people who have been out of work for six months or more and could benefit from additional job training;
- Community Action (CA), which allows long-term unemployed people to do part-time voluntary work of benefit to the community while also actively seeking work;
- the Learning for Work (LFW) scheme, which pays for vocational training for those unemployed for over a year;
- the Business Start-Up Allowance (BSUA), which provides financial help if you wish to take up self-employment.

This section explains your benefit entitlement while participating on a scheme – it does not deal with the rules for getting on to a scheme (see instead the *Unemployment and Training Rights Handbook* listed in Appendix 3).

Except in the case of YT allowances which are flat-rate payments, your training allowance is normally paid at the rate of the benefit you were getting before starting a training scheme. If your benefit was IS there is no need to make a fresh claim as your allowance is equal to your IS entitlement. Part of the training allowance is deemed to be IS to protect your entitlement to passported benefits (see below). If you were not entitled to benefit previously (eg, because you were not available for work), you should now claim IS.

You do not have to sign on in order to qualify for benefit.[42]

Youth training

Although most 16- and 17-year-olds cannot claim IS if they are unemployed, you can claim if you are doing a YT course.[43]

Young people aged 16/17 who have not been able to find a place on YT by the end of the child benefit extension period (see p69) and who would not be regarded as suitable for YT (eg, because of a disability or learning difficulties) may be given a placement of up to six months on initial training. The trainee is eligible for a training allowance and IS top-up if appropriate.

Youth Training allowance and IS top-up

The YT training allowance is £29.50 for 16-year-olds and £35 for those aged 17 and over. If you are single and living at home without housing costs to meet, your allowance usually exceeds your IS applicable amount and so you do not qualify for an IS top-up. Trainees who are likely to qualify for IS are young people with a dependent child and young people whose IS includes a disability premium. They include claimants whose severe disablement allowance ceased when they went on YT but who continue to receive the disability premium.[44] When calculating your IS entitlement, the training allowance counts in full except for:

- any reimbursement of travelling expenses;[45]
- any 'living away from home' allowance, but only to the extent that you are not getting housing benefit to cover the cost of your temporary accommodation.[46]

If you are a couple and one of you is away from home while doing the course, see p335 for how your benefit is calculated.

Some participants in YT schemes have the legal status of employees (and are normally given contracts of employment). They do not qualify for IS because they are in full-time work.

Training for Work, Community Action and Learning for Work

These schemes are not compulsory. Although you may be offered a place at a Restart interview (see p51), you are not obliged to take it. The government has stated that you will not be disqualified from getting benefit if you do not want to take part, or decide to leave early. But ministers have also said that 'if an unemployed person persistently refuses all offers of help, it may well raise doubts about their availability for work'. The benefit office therefore considers a refusal of a place within the general context of your history of trying to find work.

Training allowances and income support

You are paid a training allowance and training premium of £10 while on TFW/CA. If you are on a Learning for Work scheme, you get the training allowance only, without the premium. You get the premium on its own if you qualify as the partner of a person who is eligible for TFW/CA (eg, a married woman returning to work) or you have not been getting benefit in your own right. The premium is ignored when calculating your IS, FC, DWA, HB and CTB.[47] If you are only entitled to a training premium but not the allowance, you should claim IS as you may now be eligible.

Training allowances are paid at different rates according to your circumstances. In effect, you continue to receive the same amount as you received in benefit before you went on TFW/CA, plus the training premium.

If you were only getting unemployment benefit before you started TFW/CA, you receive a training allowance equal to that plus the training premium.

If you were getting IS you get the same amount as your previous IS, but only part of it is treated as the training allowance. The remainder is deemed to be IS and allows you to retain rights to passported benefits (eg, maximum housing benefit, free school meals, social fund payments, maximum council tax benefit etc – see p331). The basic training allowance is usually set at the level of whichever national insurance benefit you received, or would have received had you been entitled to a contributory benefit, before you joined TFW/CA. However, it can be lower so that your IS is enough to allow you to continue to have certain deductions made from it – eg, for fuel direct, social fund repayments. You also get the training premium.

If you were receiving reduced IS before joining TFW/CA because of voluntary unemployment (see p58) you receive an allowance equal to your *full* benefit plus the premium, once on the training course. When you finish you go back on to reduced benefit again only if the course lasted for a shorter time than the number of weeks your voluntary unemployment deduction was due to run. (For example, if your deduction was due to run for a further 20 weeks when you started TFW/CA and the place was for 15 weeks, your benefit would then be reduced for five weeks after you finished.)

If you are still receiving a transitional payment as part of your weekly benefit, you continue to receive this. However, you may lose all or part of your transitional protection if your circumstances change. The training premium does not affect your transitional payment.

If you have a mortgage you must persuade your lender to accept interest-only payments. Some lenders require regular statements confirming your unemployed status. Unemployment benefit office staff are told not to sign any statement which implies you are unemployed while you are on TFW/CA, but they can give you a letter stating that you are on TFW/CA and how much you get. The Building Societies Association has said that this should not be a problem and that interest-only payments will continue to be acceptable.

If you are one of a couple your partner's earnings affect the amount of benefit you receive if you get the full training allowance. Remember that your partner can earn £5 (or £15 if entitled to the higher disregard – see p369) without it affecting your benefit. If your partner gets a full-time job you lose your allowance and go on to the premium only. You may be able to claim family credit (see p184).

If you do extra work *on top* of the hours covered by your training plan, £5 (or £15) paid for that additional work is also ignored[48] under the earnings disregard rules (see p369).

If you receive only a small amount of IS, the impact of earnings and other payments which are not ignored could have the effect of pushing you off IS altogether. You would then not be entitled to full housing benefit, council tax benefit or 'passported' benefits (unless you qualified under the low-income rules – see p470) or free school meals.

If your circumstances change while on TFW/CA, you should tell the unemployment benefit office and your allowance is adjusted so that you receive an amount equal to the IS to which you are now entitled, plus the training premium. If you are not on IS and your circumstances change so that you qualify for IS while on TFW/CA (eg, you joined the scheme at 24, and are now 25) you must tell the unemployment benefit office and you will be given a claim form for IS. Your allowance is then adjusted accordingly.

Other payments made to TFW trainees

Certain expenses do not affect your IS (or FC) entitlement. These are:[49]

- the training premium;
- any reimbursement of travelling expenses. You may also get travelling expenses to take a child to nursery or the childminder etc;
- any 'living away from home' allowance, but only to the extent that you are not getting housing benefit to cover the cost of your temporary accommodation.

You should not have to pay for **protective clothing, books or equipment** etc, that you need. These expenses should be met by the training manager. However, if it is normal practice at your workplace for the trainee to buy these items, the Department of Employment can make a payment.

A training bonus can be paid if you complete your training action plan or get a recognised vocational qualification. How much you get is up to the organisation with which you are placed. The bonus is not taxed and will not count as weekly income for IS purposes.[50] Any bonus in excess of £200 counts as capital and could therefore make a difference to your benefit if you are near the capital limit or one of the tariff income limits (see p385).

If you are a single parent on TFW/CA you may be paid **childcare costs**, or a creche provided in lieu, subject to eligibility criteria.

Training managers have discretion to make **additional payments**. They can pay an extra £10 without IS being affected because the payments are treated as charitable or voluntary payments (see p382). They can also recompense you for other expenses, but these are taken into account for IS.

Your IS may not be affected if you receive payments in kind and/or the payments are made to a third party for you (see p392).

Business Start-Up Allowance

BSUA is paid if you take up full-time self-employment of at least 36 hours a week. You are thus not eligible for IS because you are in full-time work. If you find that you are not working over 16 hours, or that you have to give up your business because trade is poor, you could claim IS, but you should notify the organisation paying your BSUA as you will no longer be entitled to receive it. See p16 for how the full-time work rule affects self-employed people.

European Social Fund (ESF) training issues

If you are a trainee on an ESF course you are not covered by the above rules as your training is not funded under the Employment and Training Act 1973. Thus, you must sign on in order to obtain benefit, and there are no specific powers to disregard your training allowance, unless you can argue that it is 'earnings' or a 'voluntary payment' (see pp362 and 382). (If part of your allowance is a payment in kind it can be disregarded – see p392.) You may be entitled to IS under the 21-hour rule (see p20) or because you are in one of the groups who do not have to sign on (see p22).

CHAPTER FIVE

Special rules for special groups

This chapter covers:

1. 16/17-year-olds (below)
2. People affected by a trade dispute (p77)
3. People from abroad (p81)
4. Residential and nursing care (p97)
5. People in hospital (p113)
6. Prisoners (p117)
7. People without accommodation (p119)

1. 16/17-YEAR-OLDS

Income support (IS) is usually only paid if you are 18 or over. The Benefits Agency assumes that 16/17-year-olds who do not have jobs or Youth Training (YT) places are supported by parents or other adults (who can claim IS for young people who are still at school or college – see p335). If this does not apply to you, you can only get IS if you fulfil the special rules in this section.

16/17-year-olds who are still at school or following a non-advanced course at college are usually disqualified from claiming IS themselves because they are regarded as being in full-time education, but there are exceptions (see p17).

16/17-year-olds who have left school or college are also usually disqualified from IS. However, some can qualify until they are 18 (see below). Others can claim during the child benefit extension period (see p68), and those who are sick or who have recently been released from serving a custodial sentence may also claim for other short periods (see p70). For those who do not qualify under any of those rules, discretionary payments may be paid to avoid hardship (see p70). There are special rates of benefit for 16/17-year-olds (see p74).

Those between jobs or YT may qualify for bridging allowances (see p76).

Claiming until you are 18[1]

You can get IS at any time while you are under 18, if you satisfy the usual conditions and at least one of the following:[2]

- You are a single parent or single foster parent with a child under 16.
- You are one of a couple with a child for whom you can claim.[3]
- You are looking after a child under 16 while her/his parent or equivalent is temporarily away or ill.
- Your partner is temporarily out of the UK and you claim for a child under 16.
- You are taking a child abroad for treatment (see p25).
- You are caring for your partner or child who is temporarily ill.
- You receive invalid care allowance, or are caring for someone who has claimed or gets attendance allowance or disability living allowance (see p23).
- You are pregnant, and unable to work, or you are in that period starting 11 weeks before the baby is due and up to seven weeks after the birth.
- You are blind (see p22).
- You are incapable of work or training and a doctor says this is likely to last more than 12 months.[4] If less, see below. Remember, you have to make a claim for a sickness benefit even though you may not qualify, in order to get benefit without signing on (see p22).
- You are a disabled student who does not have to sign on (see p23).
- You are on a government training course and getting a training allowance.
- You are a refugee learning English for at least 15 hours a week – you can get IS for up to nine months. You must have been in Britain for a year or less when you started the course.
- You are a person from abroad entitled to urgent cases payments (see p87).
- You have been temporarily laid off but are available to return to your job.[5]

If you qualify as a member of a couple with a child, you have to sign on unless you are exempted (see p22). You also have to sign on if you qualify as temporarily laid off. In all other cases, people in the above groups do not have to sign on.

Claiming during the 'child benefit extension period'

If you are not entitled to claim under the above rules but it takes you some time to find a job or a YT place after leaving school, you may be able to claim IS for a period called the 'child benefit extension period'. It begins on the Monday after your 'terminal date' after you leave school or college (see p18) and ends three or four months later.

The child benefit extension periods for 1994/95 are:

First day	*Last day*[6]
Monday 10 January 1994	3 April 1994
Monday 18 April 1994	10 July 1994
Monday 12 September 1994	1 January 1995
Monday 9 January 1995	2 April 1995

You can get IS during this period if you register for work or YT at the Careers Office or JobCentre,[7] and are:

- a member of a married couple whose partner is 18 or over, or is registered for work or YT, or is eligible for IS until 18 (see above); *or*
- an orphan with no one acting as your parent (which includes a local authority or voluntary organisation if you are in care or are being looked after by them, or foster parents); *or*
- living away from parents and any person acting as your parent, and immediately before you were 16 you were in custody, or being looked after by the local authority (and not living with parents or a close relative while in care – see p110 for meaning of 'close relative'); *or*
- living away from parents and any person acting as your parent, and instead are living elsewhere:
  - under the supervision of the probation service or a local authority; *or*
  - to avoid physical or sexual abuse; *or*
  - because you need special accommodation due to mental or physical illness or handicap; *or*
- living away from parents and any person acting as your parent, where the parents or other person is unable to support you because they are:
  - in custody; *or*
  - unable to enter Great Britain because of the immigration laws; *or*
  - 'chronically sick or mentally or physically disabled' (for meaning, see p18);
- having to live away from parents and any person acting as your parent, because:
  - you are estranged from them; *or*
  - you are in physical or moral danger; *or*
  - there is a serious risk to your physical or mental health.

In practice this means if you live with an elder sister, for example, you will be entitled to claim under this provision as long as the Benefits Agency accepts that she is not acting as your parent. If you are refused, you can appeal.

See p17 for definition of 'parent'. If you are sick, see below.

Claiming for short periods after the child benefit extension period

You can claim after the end of the child benefit extension period if certain conditions apply.[8]

- **You are discharged from custody** after the child benefit extension period ends, and you are in one of the groups which qualify during that period (see above). You will be entitled to IS for up to eight weeks from the date of discharge provided you register for work or YT.
- **You have to live away from your parents** (and anyone acting as your parent) and you are living independently following a stay in local authority care. You will be entitled to IS for up to eight weeks from the date of leaving care provided you register for work or YT. If you leave care during the child benefit extension period you will be entitled to IS under the rules on p69.

Example

If the young person leaves care three weeks before the end of the child benefit extension period and has to live away from home and therefore qualifies during the child benefit extension period for IS, the person will get a further five weeks benefit at the end of that period.

- **You are incapable of work and training** under YT because of physical or mental illness or disability and your incapacity is likely to last less than a year. You will be entitled to IS until you recover (see p22 for how you prove you are incapable of work). (If you are sick **during** the child benefit extension period you will get benefit if you come within the groups listed on p69. If you don't come within these groups you may have to try for a severe hardship payment if you live at home, particularly if your YT allowance ceases – see below).

Discretionary payments to avoid hardship

If you do not come within the above groups you may still be able to make a claim for a discretionary payment of IS. The Secretary of State has the power to award a payment in order to prevent 'severe hardship'.[9] The responsibility for making decisions to award 'severe hardship' payments is now shared between staff at local offices and the staff of the Severe Hardship Claims Unit (SHCU) (see Appendix 1). Some local offices will continue to refer cases to SHCU until the end of May 1994. The decisions are made on behalf of the Secretary of State and therefore cannot be appealed. The general rule is that the local offices should refer every-thing to SHCU for decisions except straightforward 'yes' cases. All the following should be referred:[10]

- All 'no' decisions.
- Sensitive or borderline cases.
- Likely 'no' decisions.
- Likely revocations – where the young person is already in receipt of benefit but has, for example, not attended the Careers Office.
- Where social services still have a responsibility under the Children Act.
- 'Partner cases'.
- Where the office does not consider it appropriate to pay from the date of the claim.
- Where backdating a claim is possible because there is good cause (see p146) – eg, if the young person was misdirected by a Benefits Agency or Careers Office and told the wrong procedure.
- Where there is no officer in the local office who holds the Certificate of Authority, to be conferred by the local higher executive officer with responsibility for 16/17-year-olds.
- Where the young person or their representative wants a review of a local office decision.
- Where severe hardship payments have been made for a period of 16 weeks.

The SHCU will be monitoring the statistical returns which local offices will be obliged to send them. If your benefit decision is delayed because of the shared responsibility, you should ask your local advice agency to contact CPAG. Local Benefits Agency staff who interview 16/17-year-olds must undergo special training. They must give you a professional, sensitive and sympathetic hearing[11] and should offer you an interview in private.[12] Decisions on claims can be made only by an adjudication offi-cer holding a Certificate of Authority.[13]

The following factors should be taken into account when deciding whether to award IS.[14] They are:

- whether you would be entitled to IS without claiming a severe hard-ship payment;
- your financial and personal circumstances;
- your health and vulnerability;
- whether you have accommodation and whether it will be at risk if no benefit is paid;
- whether you have any income;
- whether you have friends or relatives who can help;
- whether you have any debts;

* whether you or your partner is pregnant;
* your attitude to seeking work or getting a YT place.

Arguably income that would not count for IS should not be taken into account. Where young people are homeless they are clearly not in a position to find work or a YT place, and would be at risk of turning to crime in order to survive. Where the young person is in the early stages of pregnancy an inadequate income will have repercussions for the health of the unborn child.

If the Benefits Agency staff want to know more about your home circumstances, they may want to contact your parents. They should do so only with your consent.[15] In general they should accept your account.[16]

The local authority may still be responsible for you. However, you may still be able to get benefit but your claim will be decided by SHCU.[17]

You should not be refused a severe hardship payment just because you live at home – 30 per cent of successful claims come from young people who are living with parents. The Benefits Agency must take into account the possibility of family hardship.[18]

It is accepted that in certain circumstances young people getting the bridging allowance (see p76) will qualify for a severe hardship payment. If you are a young couple only getting IS at the single person's rate (see p74), you may also be eligible in certain cases. Each case of low income should be considered on its merits.

The length of the award depends on the following:

* the time the Careers Service think it will take you to get a YT place;
* evidence that you are seeking a YT place;
* how near you are to your 18th birthday;
* whether you are living at a temporary address.

Directions to pay benefit are of varying length. You will normally be paid for eight weeks. You may be paid for only six weeks if you are homeless, pregnant, a young offender or have recently come out of local authority care. Alternatively you may be paid for up to 16 weeks if within that time you will become 18, start a youth training course or work, start a further education course or reach your 11th week of pregnancy.[19]

The Secretary of State has been willing to make severe hardship payments until a YT place is found for those who have been unable to find a place by the end of their child benefit extension period, or by the end of the eight-week period covered by the bridging allowance.

The Secretary of State has also taken note of the particular difficulties of people with behavioural problems, and Benefits Agency offices are instructed to refer cases to the Senior Medical Officer if the claimant has no GP, or if the information from the GP is inadequate or a certificate is refused, or if the medical evidence is contradictory.[20] The Senior Medical Officer will recommend whether the person should be treated as incapable of work and training and therefore paid under the rules described on p68, (for meaning of 'incapacity for work', see p22). Meanwhile a severe hardship payment should be considered.[21]

Getting a severe hardship payment

You should sign on at the Careers Office or unemployment benefit office in the normal way. The latter should not turn you away just because you are under 18. Complete form B1 (see p142 for information about claiming). On the form, under Part 12 'Other information', state that you are claiming on grounds of severe hardship. Take the form, together with any other information about your circumstances, to the local Benefits Agency office.

The Benefits Agency *must* interview you if you believe you are not entitled to IS under the normal rules for 16/17-year-olds (see above).[22] They should first decide whether you can get IS under the ordinary rules. **If you do not qualify under these rules, they must:**[23]

• obtain information about your circumstances;
• tell you what help is available;
• obtain your permission to contact another person about your situation – eg, the Careers Service;
• consider payment under the 'severe hardship' rules.

The local officer should allow another person to be present during the interview.[24]

There must be no delay in deciding these claims. The SHCU have to give a decision within 24 hours of receiving all necessary information from the local office. If possible the local officer should give you the decision in writing before you leave the office.[25]

Severe hardship payment awards are paid in arrears in the normal way, but if payment is due immediately, the officer can make a giro payment over the counter.[26] If you need money urgently you should apply for a social fund crisis loan (see p449). The local office may deal with the application for a crisis loan and the severe hardship claim in one interview.[27] If you have already applied for a loan and been turned down but have since been told you will get IS, you should re-apply for a crisis loan to tide you over.

If there is insufficient information to decide your claim, the Benefits Agency may either:

• make a provisional decision allowing benefit to be paid for one or two weeks – eg if they cannot contact the Careers Office; *or*

- refer the case to SHCU if the officer does not believe you are trying to get a YT place.[28]

When your benefit ends, the officer can issue a renewal direction so that you continue to get severe hardship payments. You do not have to complete a fresh B1; instead the local Benefits Agency office will go through a repeat claim form with you.[29] Only SHCU can revoke or refuse to review a direction. This can happen if, for example, you:

- refuse a suitable YT place; *or*
- put unreasonable restrictions on taking up YT; *or*
- fail to attend interviews with the Careers Office without good reason.[30]

Your local Benefits Agency office works out the amount of your benefit entitlement including a voluntary unemployment deduction if you have left work or YT without a good reason[31] (see p58).

If you need to claim a severe hardship payment, try to get as much evidence as you can to back up your case. **About 85 per cent of the claims made each week on hardship grounds are successful.** There is no right of appeal against a refusal because the decision is made on behalf of the Secretary of State, but you can ask the SHCU to review the local office decision if you think they did not know or failed to take proper account of an important fact.[32] You can also complain to your MP if you are refused and think you will suffer hardship and you could consider judicial review (see p182).

The Secretary of State has the power to stop your severe hardship payments at any time.[33] This will be done by referring your case to SHCU. The Secretary of State may revoke the direction allowing benefit to be paid if:

- your circumstances change and he believes the withdrawal of benefit need no longer result in severe hardship; *or*
- his (original) decision to award you a severe hardship payment was made as a result of a mistake about, or in ignorance of, the facts. If an adjudication officer then decides that you misrepresented or failed to disclose the material facts, then the Secretary of State has the power to recover the discretionary IS.[34] You can appeal against the adjudication officer's decision – see p170 on appeals.

Rates of benefit paid to 16/17-year-olds

Single people and single parents

There are two levels of payment:[35]

- lower rate £27.50

    – higher rate £36.15

You qualify for the higher rate if:[36]

(a) you qualify for the disability premium; *or*
(b) you come within one of the groups on pp68-70 who get IS during the child benefit extension period, or for a limited period after the child benefit extension period; *or*
(c) you come within one of the groups on p68 who can get IS until they are 18, and your situation is similar to a person who qualifies under (b) above apart from the requirement to register for YT or work. For example, a single parent living at home gets £27.50 (plus premiums and the allowance for her child etc); a single parent who has to live away from home because s/he is estranged from her/his parents and any other person acting as her/his parent gets £36.15 (plus the appropriate premiums and allowances for her/his child etc); *or*
(d) you come within one of the groups on p17 entitled to IS although in relevant education, and your situation is similar to a person who qualifies under (b) apart from the requirement to register for YT or work. For example, you live on your own because you have no parents and no one acting as your parent and you are still at school; *or*
(e) you get a discretionary payment of IS to prevent hardship (see p70) and your situation is similar to a person who qualifies under (b) whether or not you are required to register for YT or work. For example, you are living away from home to avoid physical abuse, the child benefit extension period is ended and you do not have a YT place and therefore get IS on hardship grounds.

The highest rate of IS is higher than the basic YT allowance, so you may be entitled to an IS 'top-up' to your YT money if you are living away from home or if you are a lone parent or disabled.

Couples[37]

The amount paid to couples depends on the age of the partners and whether one or both of them would be eligible for IS as a single person. We use the word 'eligible' to include eligibility for IS on hardship grounds.

    Benefit is paid at either the normal rate for couples or at a reduced couple rate or at the single person rate appropriate to the age of the other partner.

    The rates for couples are set out below:

• One aged 18 or over and the other under 18 and eligible for IS	£71.70
• Both under 18 and either both are eligible for IS, or one is responsible for a child, *or*	£54.55

they are married and each is either registered
for YT or eligible for IS
- One aged 25 or over and the other under   £45.70
  18 and not eligible for IS
- One is 18-24 and the other under 18 and   £36.15
  not eligible for IS
- Both under 18 and one is eligible for IS at   £36.15
  the higher rate for under 18s
- Both under 18 and one is eligible for IS at   £27.50
  the lower rate for under 18s

Bridging allowances between jobs or YT

Bridging allowances are paid at the discretion of the Secretary of State
for Employment while you are between jobs or YT places. They are not
social security payments.[38]

If you are registered disabled with the Department of Employment (ie,
you have a green card) you can also get a bridging allowance immediately after the end of the child benefit extension period (see p69). To get a
payment, you must[39] be under 18, not entitled to IS or unemployment
benefit and have left a job or YT. You must also have registered for work
or YT at a JobCentre or Careers Office.

The bridging allowance is £15 a week or £3 a day. It can be paid for up
to eight weeks (40 days) in a 52-week period, unless you are registered
disabled with the Department of Employment when no time limit
applies. If you do not use up eight weeks' worth of bridging allowance,
you can claim again within the 52-week period and get an allowance for
the rest of the eight weeks. If you are liable to pay rent you get maximum
housing benefit while receiving the bridging allowance. But it counts as
income for IS.

If you refuse a suitable YT place, the Department of Employment can
refuse to pay you a bridging allowance on the grounds that you are voluntarily unemployed. The unemployment benefit office will be asked to
decide whether this applies in your case.

You claim the bridging allowance on form BA1 which you can pick up
at the Careers Office (or JobCentre) where you register for YT. You must
fill in parts A to C (the staff complete part D), giving the date you registered. You must take the form to the unemployment benefit office within
the next two days. The allowance is paid fortnightly by giro. You have to
sign on fortnightly and register for YT.

2. PEOPLE AFFECTED BY A TRADE DISPUTE

If you are involved in a trade dispute your right to IS is affected. You either receive a reduced amount or nothing.

Involved in a trade dispute

You are treated as involved in a trade dispute if you have lost employment as a result of a stoppage of work due to a trade dispute at your place of work.[40] You are not treated as involved in a trade dispute if:

- your employer dismisses you during the course of a trade dispute and you can prove you are no longer directly interested in the dispute.[41] If this happens you have not lost your job due to a stoppage of work, but because you have been sacked (though you may still be disqualified if 'misconduct'[42] is involved);
- you can show that the stoppage of work is not at your own **place of work**, but in a separate section or department[43] – eg, in the case of a colliery canteen worker who lost her employment during the 1984 miners' strike, it was held that the trade dispute was not at her place of employment;[44]
- you can show that you are not 'directly interested' in the dispute.[45] You have to show that you have nothing to gain either financially or in connection with your conditions of work;
- you are dismissed due to redundancy during the stoppage. You are no longer treated as involved in a trade dispute and can claim unemployment benefit and/or IS in the normal way.[46]

If at any time during the trade dispute you:

- become incapable of work; *or*
- you are pregnant and your baby is due within six weeks; *or*
- you have had a baby less than seven weeks ago;

you do not count as involved in the dispute.[47] You get full IS until your incapacity ends or until seven weeks after the birth of your child.[48] (You usually cannot claim statutory maternity pay and statutory sick pay.)

The decision as to whether you are involved in a trade dispute for the purposes of IS is made by an adjudication officer at the Employment Service[49] and, until then, your IS is suspended (see p147).[50]

The amount of benefit

You are not entitled to any IS if you are involved in a trade dispute and you are single, or a couple without children and both of you are involved in a trade dispute.[51] A single parent, or a couple with children who are both involved in a trade dispute, are eligible for some IS. In the case of a couple where only one partner is involved in a trade dispute, the other partner and any children are eligible for IS (see below).

If you are involved in a trade dispute you do not have to sign on in order to get benefit (and cannot claim unemployment benefit).[52] You should therefore claim IS direct from your local Benefits Agency office, telling them that you are out of work because of a trade dispute.

You are not entitled to any IS immediately but are treated as in full-time work for a period of seven days following the stoppage of work, or, if there is no stoppage, from the date you or your partner withdrew your labour.[53] If you are getting IS and your part-time earnings stop because you are involved in a trade dispute, the seven-day exclusion period will not apply but your IS is reassessed according to the rules for people on strike (eg, if you are a single claimant you will not get any IS).[54]

Payment of IS is made weekly in trade dispute cases.[55]

Your applicable amount consists of the following:[56]

For a single parent who is involved in a trade dispute:	the normal personal allowances for the children, *plus* the family premium and lone parent premium, *plus* disabled child premium, *plus* housing costs, if appropriate.
For a couple without children where only one is involved in a trade dispute:	half the personal allowance for a couple, *plus* half the couple rate of any premium payable for the person not involved in the dispute, *plus* housing costs, if appropriate.
For a couple with children where only one is involved in a trade dispute:	half the personal allowance for a couple, *plus* half the couple rate of any premium payable for the person not involved in the dispute, *plus* the normal personal allowances for the children and the family premium, *plus* disabled child premium, *plus* housing costs, if appropriate.
For a couple with children where both are involved in the dispute:	the normal personal allowances for the children, *plus* the family premium, *plus* disabled child premium, *plus* housing costs, if appropriate.

Where the person involved in the trade dispute is normally responsible for paying the housing costs, other member(s) of the family are treated as responsible for these instead[57] (even if the only other member is a child), unless they too are involved in a trade dispute.

Your capital and income is calculated as follows:
A person involved in a trade dispute is assumed to receive £24.50 strike pay whether or not s/he in fact gets any.[58] If both members of a couple are involved in a trade dispute only one amount of £24.50 is deducted. Any actual payment from a trade union of up to £24.50 is ignored. If both members of a couple are involved in a trade dispute, only £24.50 in total is ignored.[59] Other capital and income is treated in the way described in Chapters 18 and 19 except that the following are taken into account in full as income:

- any tax refund due because of the stoppage of work;[60]
- any payment made under sections 17 or 24 of the Children Act 1989 (in Scotland, sections 12, 24 or 26 Social Work (Scotland) Act 1968);[61]
- all charitable or voluntary payments (whether regular or irregular, with no £10 disregard for regular payments) except any payment from the Macfarlane Trusts, the Eileen Trust or the Fund, or either of the Independent Living Funds;[62]
- any payment of income in kind except any payment from the Macfarlane Trusts, the Eileen Trust or the Fund, or either of the Independent Living Funds;[63]
- holiday pay which is not payable until more than four weeks after your employment ends or is interrupted[64] (this counts as earnings and therefore attracts an earnings disregard – see pp362-3);
- any advance of earnings or a loan made by your employer.[65] Where these payments are earnings, they attract an earnings disregard.

Any other payments that are obtained because the person involved in the trade dispute is currently unemployed are also treated as income and counted in full.[66]

Benefit loans on return to work

If you return to work with the same employer, whether or not the dispute has ended, you can receive IS for the first 15 days back at work, in the form of a loan.[67] You are not treated as in full-time work for this period[68] nor required to sign on[69] and you are no longer disqualified from getting benefit for yourself. If you are a member of a couple you are not entitled to IS if your partner is in full-time work.[70] Your income (including any earnings you receive from your employer) is calculated in the same way as if you were still involved in the dispute (see above) except that any payment in kind or income tax refunds are ignored, and there is no deduction from your benefit for assumed strike pay.

Any IS that you are awarded is paid in advance.[71] You may not get IS if you are entitled to less than £5.[72]

Repayment of the loan

Any IS paid during your first 15 days back at work can be recovered from your employer.[73] Your employer deducts the sum to be repaid from your earnings. If this is not practical (eg, because you are currently unemployed) it can be recovered directly from you.[74]

When awarding you IS on return to work, the Benefits Agency at the same time decides the amount of your **protected earnings** – ie, the level below which your earnings must not be reduced by repayment of your IS loan.[75] Your protected earnings level is equal to:[76]

- your applicable amount excluding housing costs; *plus*
- £27 (£8 if you live in a hostel); *less*
- child benefit and one parent benefit.

If your available earnings (see below) are less than £1 above your protected earnings level, there will be no deduction. If they are £1 or more above, your employer will deduct half of the excess above your protected earnings level. If you are paid monthly, you work out your weekly protected earnings level and multiply by five to get your monthly protected earnings level. If your monthly earnings are less than £5 above this level, no deduction is made. Otherwise, half the excess over your monthly protected earnings level is deducted. If your earnings are paid daily, the amount of your protected earnings and the £1 figure is divided by five to determine the amount (if any) of the deduction. The calculation can be adjusted as appropriate where your wages are paid at other intervals.[77]

Your '**available earnings**' are the whole of your earnings, including sick pay, after all 'lawful' deductions have been made.[78] These include tax and national insurance contributions, trade union subscriptions and any amount being deducted under a court order or, for instance, a child support deduction order. Any bonus or commission if paid on a different day is treated as paid on your next normal pay day.[79] If you are paid more than one lot of wages on one pay day, your protected earnings level and the £1 figure is multiplied to reflect this.[80]

A deduction notice is sent to your employer by the Benefits Agency setting out your protected earnings level and the amount of IS to be recovered.[81] If you have not actually received the IS and you can satisfy your employer that you have not, no deduction should be made.[82] Your employer *can* begin making the deductions from the first pay day after receiving the notice and *must* start doing so one month after getting it.[83]

A deduction notice ceases to have effect if:

- it is cancelled; *or*
- you stop working for that employer; *or*
- your IS loan has been repaid; *or*
- 26 weeks have passed since the date of the notice.[84]

If you stop work, another deduction notice can be sent if you get another job and part of your IS loan is still outstanding.[85]

You should tell the Benefits Agency within ten days if you leave a job or start another while part of your IS loan remains unpaid.[86] If you fail to do so you can be prosecuted.[87] It is a criminal offence for your employer to fail to keep records of deductions and supply the Benefits Agency with these.[88] If your employer fails to make a deduction which should have been made from your pay, the Benefits Agency can recover the amount from your employer instead.[89]

Other benefits during a trade dispute

- You can get a social fund payment for help with the cost of **baby things** (see p416), **funeral expenses** (see p418) and **travel expenses** to visit a close relative or a member of the same household who is ill[90] (see p432).
- A crisis loan can only be awarded in cases of **disaster** or for items needed for **cooking or space heating**.[91] Budgeting loans are not available to strikers.[92]
- Strikers and their families may be entitled to **free prescriptions, free dental treatment and free glasses** (see Chapter 25), even if they are not on IS.
- If you are on strike and your partner undergoes kidney dialysis, or has to follow a vital but expensive diet for other health reasons, it may be possible to argue that this should be covered under the NHS Act 1977 (see p496).

3. PEOPLE FROM ABROAD

In IS law the phrase 'person(s) from abroad' is used to describe certain people with limited leave or without leave who are not entitled to IS at the full rate. However, this Handbook *uses the phrase more broadly to describe any immigrant regardless of status or entitlement to IS. Where it is used in its technical sense it is in inverted commas.*

You do not have to be British to get IS. This section describes the special rules that apply to people from abroad.

This section covers:

- Immigration issues which affect entitlement (below)
- People entitled to full IS (p83)
- People not entitled to ordinary IS (p85)
- Couples who can get reduced IS (p86)
- Urgent cases payments for people from abroad (p87)
- Sponsorship and undertakings (p88)
- The rights of European Union (EU) citizens (p89)
- Foreign fiancé(e)s, spouses and children (p92)
- Applying for refugee status or political asylum (p93)
- Availability for work (p94)
- Investigation of entry status (p95)
- Divided families (p96)

Immigration issues which affect entitlement

Entitlement to IS depends on either immigration status or citizenship.

People with 'right of abode' are not subject to immigration control – ie, they can enter the United Kingdom freely at any time regardless of how long they have been away, and their passport is not stamped on entry. They are entitled to full IS in the normal way. People in this group are:

- British citizens; *and*
- some Commonwealth citizens if they have a parent born in the UK; *and*
- women who are Commonwealth citizens, and who were married before 1 January 1983 to men who were born in the UK, or who were registered or naturalised as British, or who are Commonwealth citizens with a parent born in the UK.

People subject to immigration control can be divided into two groups:

- People who are legally 'settled' in the UK – ie, here with indefinite 'leave' to remain, with no restrictions on taking employment. ('Leave' means permission to stay in the UK.) They are entitled to full benefit.
- People with 'limited leave'. This means your stay in the UK is subject to either a time limit or a restriction on your right to take employment or both. Many people who have limited leave are admitted to the UK subject to an additional restriction that they shall not have recourse to public funds and, if this applies, they will not be entitled to IS.

A list of who can claim IS is given on p83. People not able to claim because of immigration status may be able to get an urgent cases payment instead (see p87). If you are a couple and only one of you can claim, see p86.

The public funds test

Under the immigration rules some people are admitted to the UK on condition that they do not rely on public funds. The term 'public funds' covers IS, housing benefit, family credit and housing under Part III of the Housing Act 1985 (Housing the Homeless). It does not presently include council tax benefit nor any of the other benefits described in this book, although the government may extend its definition to include council tax benefit during 1994/95. Contact CPAG or the Joint Council for the Welfare of Immigrants (see below) to find out whether this change has been/will be made. Do **not** contact the DSS or the Home Office. Public funds do not include non-means-tested benefits.

If your terms of entry require that you should have no recourse to public funds, you may nevertheless have a right under social security law to certain benefits – ie, IS urgent cases payments in limited circumstances and family credit. However, a claim for either of these could affect your right to remain in the UK or obtain an extension of stay, so it may be unwise for you to claim. In August 1993, further restrictions based on immigration status were incorporated into the IS regulations and similar changes will apply to housing benefit and council tax benefit from April 1994.

See below on getting further advice.

There are close links between the DSS and the Home Office. Claims for benefit are often reported to the Home Office (see p95). If you are unsure about your right to claim public funds or whether it would be wise to claim, you should get advice first – from the Joint Council for the Welfare of Immigrants (tel: 071 251 8706) or a law centre or independent advice centre dealing with immigration problems – before making a claim for benefit.

For more details about immigration law and benefits see CPAG's *Ethnic Minorities' Benefits Handbook*.

People entitled to full IS [93]

You are entitled to full benefit if:

- you are not subject to immigration control; *or*
- you have no restrictions attached to your stay; *or*
- you have limited leave under the immigration rules, but the terms of your entry are not subject to there being 'no recourse to public funds'; *or*
- you have 'exceptional leave' – ie, you were admitted with the permission of the Secretary of State outside the terms of the immigration rules and your leave has not expired. In these circumstances, you have

a right to claim IS whether or not the terms of your entry refer to there being no recourse to public funds (see above). (This does not apply to immigrants given temporary admission while seeking asylum); *or*
- you satisfy the new 'habitual residence' test. This test applies to nationals of countries in the European Economic Area (see below).

In practice this means you will be entitled to claim IS if: [94]

- you are a British citizen;
- you are a British Overseas citizen with right of re-admission to the UK;
- you have right of abode, or a certificate of entitlement to right of abode, in the UK. This may include a certificate of patriality;
- you are here without any time limit on your stay or you have been granted indefinite leave to enter or remain in the UK (but if you are sponsored, see p88);
- you have exceptional leave to remain;
- you are a citizen of the Channel Islands or the Isle of Man;
- you are a British Dependent Territories citizen, British Overseas citizen, British Protected person or British subject with indefinite leave to remain;
- you have been granted refugee status or political asylum (but if you have applied for refugee status, see p93);
- you are a European Union (EU) national – ie, from Belgium, Denmark, Eire, France, Germany, Greece, Italy, Luxembourg, the Netherlands, Portugal or Spain (but see p89);
- you are a national of a country that signed the European Convention on Social and Medical Assistance (1953) – ie, Iceland, Malta, Norway, Sweden or Turkey (but, if you have applied to vary your leave or are appealing against a refusal of leave – see pp87-8, and if you have to be available for work – see p94);
- you are a national of Austria or Cyprus (but, if you have to be available for work, see p94);
- you hold a current work permit (but if you are unemployed and therefore have to be available for work, see p94).

Habitual residence

The government is proposing to introduce before summer 1994 a new test of 'habitual residence' which will deny IS, housing benefit and council tax benefit to those people who do not have 'habitual residence' in the UK. Some people in the groups listed above will fail this test. People affected by the new test are nationals of what is called the European Economic Area. That covers British and Irish nationals, plus other nationals of the European Union and nationals of the following states:

Austria, Cyprus, Finland, Iceland, Malta, Norway, Sweden and Turkey. 'Habitual residence' is not clearly defined but will have the same meaning as in EU law. For more information on this, see CPAG's *Ethnic Minorities' Benefits Handbook*. There are doubts about the legality of the new test and, since the definition is unclear, it is likely that many people will have valid arguments against decisions that they are not 'habitually resident'. For a more detailed explanation of 'habitual residence', see the April 1994 issue of the *Welfare Rights Bulletin*.

People not entitled to ordinary IS

You are not entitled to ordinary IS if you come into one of the following groups:[95]

(a) you have limited leave and your terms of entry are subject to there being no recourse to public funds. (This includes visitors, most students, fiancé(e)s, husbands/wives during the probationary 12 months, businessmen and self-employed persons, writers, artists, ministers of religion, persons of independent means and their dependants);

(b) you have been granted temporary admission to the UK because you are an asylum-seeker;

(c) you are waiting for the Secretary of State's decision on your immigration status;

(d) you are an EU national who has been required to leave the UK by the Secretary of State;

(e) you have applied for variation of leave. (But if you already have exceptional leave to remain you continue to be entitled while seeking variation of leave);

(f) you have remained in the UK beyond the period covered by your limited leave;*

(g) you are subject to a deportation order;*

(h) you are an illegal entrant;*

(i) you fail the new 'habitual residence' test (see above).

*There is close liaison between the DSS and the Home Office. If you have remained here after your limited leave has expired, or are subject to a deportation order, or are an alleged illegal entrant, neither you nor your partner should claim unless you have already contacted the Home Office in order to regularise your position. This advice should be followed even if your partner can claim.

If you do not qualify for IS, you will not get benefit for a child regardless of their status.

Couples or single parents who are not 'persons from abroad' and who qualify for IS, but who have children who come within the above groups, are paid benefit for themselves and any children and appropriate premiums, even if the children are 'persons from abroad'.[96]

If you are in one of the above groups, you may qualify for an urgent cases payment[97] (see p87). If you have a partner who is not excluded from claiming IS, s/he could claim instead. If both of you qualify you will have to decide who should claim.

Couples who can get reduced IS

If you are a couple with one partner who qualifies for IS, that partner should claim (but if either of you is an illegal entrant, overstayer or subject to a deportation order, a claim will jeopardise your right to stay here).

You get the applicable amount (personal allowance plus premiums as appropriate), for each member of the family who does not come within groups (a) to (i) listed above, provided the claim is made by a person who is entitled. Your housing costs are also met.[98] Although you do not get any benefit for the 'person from abroad' her/his income and capital nevertheless counts when IS is assessed. As no IS is paid for the 'person from abroad' they should not be treated as having recourse to public funds.

Example

Fatima and her 5-year-old son, Yunus, have British citizenship. Her husband, Salim, has come to the UK as a visitor. He has six months' leave. Salim has no income but he has capital of £4,200. Salim is not entitled to IS because his terms of entry require that he should not have recourse to public funds. Before Salim arrived in the UK, Fatima claimed IS as a single parent. Her IS was calculated as follows:

Personal allowances		Income	
Self	£45.70	Child benefit	£10.20
Yunus	£15.65		
Premiums			
Family premium	£10.05		
Lone parent premium	£5.10		
Net income support	£66.30		

After Salim's arrival, Fatima is no longer considered to be a single parent. As she does not come within a group exempted from signing on (see p22) she has to be available for employment. Her IS entitlement is actually reduced because she loses the lone parent premium and because of tariff income which is now taken into account. Her revised IS calculation is:

Personal allowances		Income	
Self	£45.70	Child benefit	£10.20
Yunus	£15.65	Tariff income	£5.00
Premiums			
Family premium	£10.05		
Net income support	£56.20		

If the partner who comes from abroad would qualify for an urgent cases payment (see below), financially it may be better if s/he claims this for her/himself and the other members of the family. But in so doing you will be having recourse to public funds so you should get immigration advice before claiming.

Urgent cases payments for people from abroad[99]

If you are not entitled to ordinary IS, you may be able to get an urgent cases payment. See p44 for how your urgent cases payment is calculated, and how your capital and income is treated. You may be able to claim an urgent cases payment if you fail the new 'habitual residence' test (see p84).

You are entitled to an urgent cases payment if:

• your terms of entry refer to there being no recourse to public funds, but your source of funding from abroad has temporarily stopped. Provided that you have been self-supporting during the period of limited leave, and there is a reasonable chance that your funds will be resumed, you can get an urgent cases payment for up to 42 days during any one period of limited leave. If your leave is extended, the extension is treated as part of the same period of limited leave. This will most commonly apply to overseas students;
• you are seeking asylum;
• you are waiting for the result of an appeal you have made under the Immigration Act. This includes appeals under the 1993 Asylum and Immigration Appeals Act;
• you have been served with a deportation order (under section 5(1) of the Immigration Act 1971), but your removal from the UK has been deferred *in writing*;
• you are not subject to a deportation order, but have been given permission to stay, pending the removal of another person who is subject to a deportation order but whose removal has been deferred *in writing*;
• you are an illegal entrant, but have been notified by the Home Office *in writing* that you can stay here;
• a direction has been made seeking your removal from the UK, but

your removal has been deferred *in writing*;
- you have exhausted all rights of appeal to remain here, but you have been allowed to stay while representations are made to the Home Secretary;
- you have been granted temporary admission or you are waiting for the Secretary of State to make a decision on your immigration status. The urgent cases payment lasts until leave is granted or you are removed from the UK, or until a decision is made on your immigration status.

In practice, where the regulation assumes the decision will be in writing, the Home Office does not put it in writing. If you have difficulty getting benefit as a result, seek advice from a local advice centre and ask them to contact CPAG.

If you are disputing your removal from the UK you are entitled to an urgent cases payment until removal from the UK or until leave to remain is granted.

Urgent cases payments are a type of IS and as a result help you to qualify for other benefits, but they are also 'public funds' so a claim might affect your immigration status (see p83 on public funds and further advice).

Transitional entitlement to urgent cases payments

The urgent cases provisions were amended with effect from 2 August 1993. The amendments have excluded people who are subject to the public funds test from entitlement to urgent cases payments where they were applying for variation of their leave to remain to a category that would not be subject to the public funds test. For details of the previous rules you should refer to the 23rd edition of the *National Welfare Benefits Handbook*.

If you were entitled to urgent cases payments under the old rules for the benefit week which included 2 August 1993, you can continue to get benefit as long as you continue to meet the conditions and you have not broken your claim.[100]

Sponsorship and undertakings

A person wishing to enter the UK may be sponsored by a relative or friend living in this country. The sponsor provides the British High Commissioner or Embassy with evidence of their ability to maintain and accommodate the person from abroad for the period of any leave granted. A sponsored entrant can nevertheless claim IS as long as they have indefinite leave to remain – ie, have been admitted for permanent settlement. If you claim, you may be asked questions about the sponsorship arrangements but payment of benefit should not be delayed. The Benefits Agency should not ask *you* to try to obtain the payments from your sponsor.

Sponsors who are liable to maintain

Sponsors *may* be asked to give an undertaking that commits them to a financial responsibility for support and accommodation. This is different from a sponsorship declaration which does not necessarily bind the sponsor. An undertaking is not mandatory and should only be given if the applicant from abroad or sponsor is specifically asked for one. In practice, few sponsors are asked.

An undertaking is only binding if the agreement was made under the terms of the Immigration Act 1971 on or after 23 May 1980.[101] A sponsor is not liable if the sponsorship was made outside the terms of the Immigration Act 1971 – eg, for a special voucher holder.

A sponsor who is liable remains financially responsible for as long as the sponsee remains in the UK, even if the person's immigration status is changed. However, if the sponsee becomes a British citizen, the sponsor ceases to be responsible. The payments made to maintain the sponsee are treated as liable relatives' payments (see p124).

Failure to maintain

If the person you are sponsoring claims IS and also gets a social fund loan, the Benefits Agency may recover the loan from you.

If you are liable but fail to maintain the sponsee, the Benefits Agency has the power to recover from you whatever amount of benefit has been paid to the person for whom you are responsible. Where a sponsor cannot afford to maintain the person from abroad, the Benefits Agency should not pursue the matter. This was confirmed in a parliamentary answer (15 February 1989), when Mr Peter Lloyd (the Parliamentary Under-Secretary of State for Social Security) stated that liability to maintain would be enforced 'wherever necessary' and '*where [the sponsor] has the means*'. The Benefits Agency works out how much the sponsor can pay in the same way as for liable relatives (see p123). They can take legal action to force the sponsor to pay in the same way as for liable relatives, although with one recent exception neither CPAG nor the Joint Council for the Welfare of Immigrants has heard of any prosecutions. If you are prosecuted, see Appendix 2 for details of who to contact.

The rights of European Union citizens

A list of EU countries is on p84. The EU was previously known as the European Community (EC). As from January 1995 there will be four new member states: Austria, Finland, Norway and Sweden. The Treaty of Rome allows for the free movement of people within the EU. An EU citizen may be admitted to the UK for the following reasons:

*   to take up employment ('workers');
*   to establish a business or be self-employed;
*   to provide or use a service – eg, education.

An EU citizen who is seeking work is also allowed to enter. A person wishing to provide or receive a service has a right of residence, which will last for the duration of the service provided or received. Those taking up employment or setting up a business also have a right of residence here.

EU citizens are admitted subject to the public funds requirement but they nevertheless have rights to claim full IS, unless they have been required to leave the UK by the Secretary of State. This will not be the case for most EU nationals who are exercising their rights as migrant workers. (See Work-seekers who are required to leave the UK, p91.) All EU citizens can claim IS for as long as they are exercising their right to be here under the Treaty. They must satisfy the normal rules of entitlement.

All EU citizens will become subject to the new 'habitual residence' test (see p84).

EU workers and IS

A 'worker' is a person who:

(a) is in employment, including part-time employment; *or*
(b) has become unemployed, not through choice, and is willing to take another job; *or*
(c) has been employed in the UK but has become permanently disabled through illness or injury; *or*
(d) has worked here and is now aged 60 (or 65 if a man);[102]
(e) has been admitted to the UK in order to seek work.[103]

It does not include a person who is unemployed, or a student (but see below). A person who has spent a very brief time in work as a proportion of their time in the UK may not count as a worker.[104]

You normally prove your right of residence with a residence permit which the Home Office grants once you take employment, but the permit itself does not give you right of residence.[105] You have that just by being an EU worker. If you do not have a permit the Benefits Agency should still pay you IS if you can show that you are exercising your Treaty rights as a worker.[106] If you come within groups (a), (b) and (e) above, you also have to be genuinely seeking work and not be voluntarily unemployed.[107]

The 1988 Immigration Act contains a section which brings UK law in line with the Treaty of Rome. Though this section has not been formally implemented, the rights of EU national workers are those prescribed by the Freedom of Movement provisions in the Treaty of Rome. Because of this, EU nationals who are workers do not require leave to enter or remain in the UK. This happens already as EU nationals do not have to show their passports or have them stamped on entering the UK. You cannot become an overstayer because you have no leave to overstay. You are therefore entitled to full IS.[108] If IS is refused you should appeal. If you are claiming as a part-time worker, you could also argue that refusal of IS discriminates against non-British EU nationals and is in breach of the Treaty of Rome and EC Regulations.[109] Benefit should be paid irrespective of any restrictions under UK law if these conflict with your rights under EU law.

Work-seekers who are required to leave the UK

If you have been seeking work for more than six months without success and have claimed IS throughout this period, the Department of Employment may decide that you have no 'genuine chances' of obtaining employment.[110] The Home Office may then advise you and the Benefits Agency that you are required to leave the UK. Your IS will be withdrawn because you will be treated as a 'person from abroad' who is not entitled to IS. If this happens and you believe you do have a reasonable chance of obtaining employment, you should appeal the decision not to pay benefit. You should also seek advice and ask an advice agency to contact CPAG. The Home Office cannot insist that you leave Britain just because you have no chance of getting employment. This rule also applies to housing benefit and council tax benefit. If your benefits are withdrawn you should consider asking for a review.

Other EU citizens with 'right of residence'

People with right of residence should have equal access to benefit in member states.[111] This covers people who are self-employed or in receipt of services. There may be a time limit on their residence.

EU citizens not covered by the Treaty

EU nationals not exercising their Treaty rights are subject to UK immigration law. They are also entitled to IS but must satisfy the normal rules of entitlement and the Home Office may ask them to leave if they claim. Students, retired people and others who have not worked in the UK, do not have the equal access to benefit rights that accrue to workers.[112] (Note that retired people who have worked here count as workers.)

Although they are allowed to enter the UK under EC Directives, they are required to be financially self-supporting. If this applies, or if you are subject to UK immigration law and claim IS, you may be asked to leave the UK. If this happens you will not be entitled to IS.[113] If you seek to return to the UK and have had recourse to public funds in the past, and not been in work since then, you could be refused entry if it is felt that you are not genuinely coming for an EU purpose (see p90).

Foreign fiancé(e)s, spouses and children

Wives entitled to claim IS on entry

Most foreign spouses are not able to claim benefit until they have been settled in the UK for over a year. Some women who have acquired right of abode in the UK by marriage (see p82) have a right of entry to the UK without being subject to the public funds test and can claim benefit immediately on entry if they satisfy the normal rules of entitlement (see p12).

Foreign fiancé(e)s and spouses admitted subject to the public funds test

The status of foreign fiancé(e)s and spouses changes up to four times in a period of 18 months. For most of that time they are not supposed to have recourse to public funds and another person (usually the spouse (to be) or another member of the family) is expected to maintain her/him. The chart below sets out the position. A person entering the UK as a foreign husband/wife enters the chart at stage 3.

	Status	Entitlement
Stage 1	Foreign fiancé(e) admitted to UK for a period of up to six months in order to marry a British citizen, or any other person settled in the UK. Her/his entry is subject to the condition that s/he does not take employment, and the requirement that s/he shall 'not have recourse to public funds'.	No IS or urgent cases payment payable.
Stage 2	Fiancé(e) marries and applies to the Home Office for variation of leave. S/he remains subject to the above conditions.	No IS or urgent cases payment payable.
Stage 3	Spouse is granted up to 12 months' stay normally from the date of that	No IS or urgent cases payment payable.

decision. A husband/wife entering
the country is given an initial 12
months' leave from the date of
entry. In each case s/he can work
but not draw public funds. S/he
applies for variation of leave before
the expiry of the 12 months.

Stage 4   S/he is granted indefinite leave to   Entitlement to full IS.
remain.

Home Office practice and the immigration rules differ on what should
happen during this 12-month period (see stage 3 above). The rules state
that the couple should maintain themselves and their dependants without recourse to public funds. In practice, the Home Office advises the
person from abroad by letter that there is no objection to the spouse
based in the UK claiming public funds to which s/he is entitled in her/his
own right. S/he can therefore claim IS for her/himself (and a child dependant), but nothing for the spouse from abroad. There would, of course,
be no difficulty if the partner were to claim a non-means-tested benefit –
eg, unemployment benefit – including the allowance for the adult dependant from abroad, as this does not count as public funds.

   Some fiancé(e)s and spouses are admitted as 'visitors'. Visitors are not
entitled to benefit and are subject to the public funds test. A fiancé(e)
or spouse may apply for variation of leave having entered the UK as a
visitor.

Children admitted for settlement

Children admitted to the UK to join parent(s) settled here are usually
given indefinite leave on entry and the parent is able to claim full benefit
for them. However, if they enter with a parent who is given 12 months'
leave, they are also granted 12 months' leave. During that time, they are
subject to the public funds test and the settled parent cannot claim for
them. After 12 months they are granted indefinite leave (along with the
parent) and benefit can be paid in the normal way.

Applying for refugee status or political asylum

If you apply for refugee status or political asylum at the port of entry you
are usually granted temporary admission. You are not entitled to full IS
but can claim an urgent cases payment while the Home Office is considering your application[114] (see p87). Citizens from countries which have
signed the European Convention (1953) who seek refugee status may be
admitted as visitors. They can apply for variation of leave (as an asylum-
seeker) and qualify for an urgent cases payment.[115] When claiming IS, an

asylum-seeker may be asked to produce a document issued by the Asylum Screening Unit (either an SAL or a GEN32) as evidence of identity. A GEN32 is an acknowledgement of contact with the Asylum Screening Unit. An SAL is an acknowledgement of a political asylum application.

Sometimes, a person applying for refugee status may be detained on entry and refused temporary admission. Her/his solicitor may then apply for bail. Once s/he is released on bail the person from abroad is entitled to an urgent cases payment while her/his case is being considered.

Immigrants already in the UK and who apply for refugee status are entitled to an urgent cases payment[116] (see p87). Asylum-seekers who do not formally apply for asylum, but instead apply for an extension of stay because of exceptional circumstances, qualify for urgent cases payments.

If you are entitled to urgent cases payments you do not have to be available for work. However, six months after you have applied for refugee status you can apply to have any restrictions on your right to take employment lifted and work instead of claiming IS.

You need a national insurance number (which can be issued purely for benefit purposes regardless of your immigration status – see p143). A person from abroad is expected to send her/his passport with the application for the national insurance number. As your passport is likely to be with the Home Office or you may not have one, you may have to supply the local Benefits Agency with alternative identification or to give a sworn affidavit regarding your identity.

Illegal entrants, overstayers or people subject to deportation orders do not usually have conditions attached to their stay and can therefore take up employment without getting special permission. Check your rights first with an agency with knowledge of immigration law (see p83).

Once you have been granted refugee status (or exceptional leave to remain) you are entitled to full IS subject to the normal rules.

Asylum-seekers may want help from the social fund. You can apply for help with the cost of buying basic necessities such as winter clothing etc, through the social fund (see Chapters 21-23).

You may find it helpful to contact the Refugee Council at Bondway House, 3 Bondway, London SW8 and the Joint Council for the Welfare of Immigrants for further advice about immigration issues.

Availability for work

Some people from abroad safely escape the restrictions on entitlement to IS which are linked to immigration issues, but fall foul of the general rule that you have to be 'available for work' to get benefit (see p21).

If you have a work permit, you are not considered to be available for work, because you are not immediately available for work.[117] The reason for this is that any prospective employer has to check with the Department of Employment and Home Office before being able to employ you. You can, however, get benefit when sick.

You are not treated as available for work if the terms of your entry do not allow you to work.

People from abroad who are claiming urgent cases payments do not need to be available for work.[118]

Investigation of entry status[119]

The claim forms (A1 and B1) for IS include the following questions:

- Have you or anyone you are claiming for come to live in the UK in the last five years?
- Have you come to live in the UK under a sponsorship agreement?

You are required to state on the form the nationality of the person who has come from abroad, and the Benefits Agency usually calls you for an interview unless you or the member of your family concerned:

- is British; *or*
- is from Eire, the Channel Islands or the Isle of Man; *or*
- is known to be sponsored; *or*
- has already had their immigration position investigated.

At the interview, you are asked about your immigration status and that of your family; passports, identity cards, travel documents and letters from the Home Office may be examined.

The Benefits Agency may notify the Home Office that you are getting IS if you are:

- an EU citizen (from Belgium, Denmark, France, Germany, Greece, Holland, Eire, Italy, Luxembourg, Portugal and Spain);
- a citizen of a European Convention country (from Iceland, Malta, Norway, Sweden and Turkey);
- any other person from abroad who is currently not entitled to ordinary IS on grounds of immigration status, and you have made an application to change your status or length of stay or appealed against a decision regarding your status.

If there is a dispute about your status – eg, the Benefits Agency says your leave to remain here has expired, while you say it has been extended – you should appeal (see p170). The adjudication officer has to produce, for the tribunal, documentary proof from the Immigration and Nationality Department of the Home Office to back up her/his statement about your status.[120] A tribunal must usually accept the immigration authority's rulings on a person's status.[121] However, it can look at the question of whether a person needs leave to be in the UK if the answer is not clear.[122] Thus, where a dispute concerns an EU citizen and entitlement to IS, the tribunal should not feel bound to accept the Home Office view. You should argue:

- that under EU law an EU worker does not require leave to enter the UK;
- that although changes to British law are included in the 1988 Immigration Act but not yet implemented, *the requirements of the Treaty of Rome override British law*. These require freedom of movement within the community, therefore leave is not necessary;
- that the requirements of the Treaty of Rome are recognised, in practice, as leave is not granted by the British immigration authorities to EU citizens. Instead they are admitted freely and their passports are not stamped on entry;
- that when considering the question of leave, the tribunal or commissioner should be willing to refer the matter to the European Court of Justice for a preliminary ruling on whether leave is required.

If the Benefits Agency delays payment of benefit while checking details about your identity and immigration status and, as a result, you suffer hardship, ask a local advice agency to contact CPAG.

Divided families

Where your spouse is living abroad, and unable to come to the UK (eg, because of the UK immigration laws or for practical reasons), you may be able to claim benefit in your own right. This will depend on whether you and your spouse are treated as one 'household' (see p328). If it is accepted that you form a separate household, you are treated either as a single claimant or as a single parent if your children are here.

If you are waiting for a husband or wife and/or children to join you here you are expected to be able to maintain and accommodate them without help from public funds (see p83). It would therefore be unwise for you to claim IS, housing benefit or family credit as your family may be refused entry clearance. For more details, see the *Ethnic Minorities' Benefits Handbook*.

If your partner was living here but has gone abroad for a short period – eg, because of a death in the family – see p333 on when you will still be treated as one household and p143 on swapping the claimant role. If your child has gone abroad, see p335 for the effect on your benefit.

4. RESIDENTIAL AND NURSING CARE

If you need to go into a home to be looked after, you can either find a private or voluntary home yourself or you can apply to the local authority to help you find one. If you use the local authority they can place you in one of their own homes, or make arrangements for you to go into a private or voluntary home. If they do this they will help to pay for the accommodation if you do not have enough money yourself, but you may be able to claim IS to meet some of the cost.

If you live in a home, your IS is worked out in a special way and the normal rules do not always apply. How much IS you get depends on whether you are living in a private or voluntary residential care or nursing home, or in local authority accommodation. In this *Handbook*, accommodation provided directly by a local authority is called 'residential accommodation'.

• To find out what counts as a residential care home – see p100.
• To find out what counts as a nursing home – see p101.
• To find out what counts as residential accommodation – see below.

The rules about how much IS you can get in a residential care or nursing home were changed in April 1993. Many people have 'preserved rights' to benefit under the old rules. To check which rules apply to you – see pp101-104.

To find out how much IS you can get,

• in a residential care home – see pp104-113;
• in a nursing home – see pp104-113;
• in residential accommodation – see pp98-100.

If you are in a residential care or nursing home, you might find that you do not get enough IS to pay all of your accommodation charges. To find out about other sources of help – see pp108 or 111-12.

Local authority residential homes

What counts as residential accommodation

It must be owned or managed by the local authority under the National Assistance Act 1948 (usually called Part III accommodation). Homes for the elderly are usually but not always established under the National Assistance Act. In Scotland, similar accommodation is provided under section 27 of the NHS (Scotland) Act 1947, section 59 of the Social Work (Scotland) Act 1968 and section 7 of the Mental Health (Scotland) Act 1984. If a local authority transferred ownership of a care home on or after 12 August 1991, and you were treated as being in residential accommodation prior to that date you continue to be treated as in residential accommodation.

Local authority residential accommodation is a means-tested service and the authority will assess you for a contribution according to your income and capital.[123] The capital rules changed in April 1993 and are being phased in over three years for people already in residential accommodation by that date.[124] Your social worker or local authority finance section will have the full details if you have savings over £3,000. If you have savings of over £8,000 you may eventually have to pay the full cost of your accommodation, so get advice. Any income you receive above the personal allowances listed on p99 may be taken as your contribution, as well as £44.50 of the personal allowance. You should be left with at least £13.10 for your own expenses.

You will not be treated as in residential accommodation if:[125]

- you are in a home for the rehabilitation of alcoholics or drug addicts that is registered under the Registered Homes Act 1984 (you will be paid on the basis that you are living in a residential care home – see p100); *or*
- you are in a home which does not provide board. You will be paid the ordinary rate of IS personal allowance and can claim housing benefit (see p230). Residents in local authority hostels who buy their own food or meals when they want, often known as 'pay as you eat' schemes, are not treated as being in residential accommodation;[126]
- you are in a private or voluntary home and getting IS but because of the maximum amounts (see pp105-107) you cannot meet the full charge, and the local authority is paying the balance. Such topping-up payments do not bring you within the definition of residential accommodation. However, if you are a pensioner, the local authority must have been topping you up for at least two years prior to your reaching pension age;
- you are under 18 and in local authority care in Scotland.

Income support for people in local authority residential accommodation

The amount of IS you get while in local authority residential accommodation depends on whether you go there temporarily or permanently and whether you are single or part of a couple. You should not be worse off than if the local authority were to offer you a place in a private sector home. You should always let the authority know if you are a temporary resident with continuing expenses in your permanent home. The prescribed means test does not have to be used for any placement of up to eight weeks, so the local authority can use its discretion as to what it charges you.[127]

Your benefit may include an extra amount if you were paid as a hostel-dweller before 9 October 1989. See p44 for more information on transitional protection.

Temporary stays in residential accommodation

- **If you are a single person** you will have an IS allowance of £57.60 plus housing costs for your normal home, if appropriate.[128]
- **If you are a single parent** you will have an IS allowance of £57.60 plus the personal allowance for each child for whom you were receiving benefit before going into the home, a family premium, a lone parent premium and housing costs for your normal home, if appropriate.[129]
- **Couples where both are in residential accommodation** will have an IS allowance of two lots of £57.60 plus their housing costs for their normal home, if appropriate.[130]
- **Couples where one member is temporarily in residential accommodation,** will receive £57.60 for the partner in the home and a single claimant's allowance for the other partner.[131]
- There were some gaps in **transitional protection** for people in residential accommodation which have been corrected – in particular, May 1988 payments and boarders' transitional protection (see p44) have been extended to single people, couples and single parents when they go into residential accommodation temporarily.[132]

Permanent stays in residential accommodation

- **If you are single or a single parent** you will get £57.60 of which £13.10 is a personal allowance.[133]
- You will receive double this amount if you are a **couple and both of you are living permanently in residential accommodation.**[134] If one of you goes into hospital, you will continue to get your normal benefit, but if you are single you will just get £13.10.[135]
- If you are a **couple and one partner has become permanently resident** in residential accommodation, you will no longer be treated as a couple.[136] The partner in the home will receive the residential accommodation allowance of £57.60 (see above), while the other partner will be assessed as a single person or single parent, as appropriate.
- If you are a **couple and normally live in residential accommodation but one of you is temporarily away,** you should get your benefit calculated in the normal way.

Other changes to your benefit
- If your child is living with you in the home you will receive the normal personal allowance for her/him.[137]
- If you are getting disability living allowance care component or attendance allowance when you go into residential accommodation, it will stop after four weeks.[138]
- If you are getting IS and you go into residential accommodation for eight weeks or less (eg, for a period of respite care) you will lose your ordinary IS and be paid at the above rates from the date you enter the home regardless of which day of the week you go into the home.[139]

Residential care and nursing homes

What counts as a residential care or nursing home

A home counts as a residential care home for IS if it is private or run by a voluntary organisation *and*:[140]

- it is registered under the Registered Homes Act 1984 (or deemed to be); *or*
- in Scotland, it is registered under the Social Work (Scotland) Act 1968 or run by a registered housing association and provides care similar to that given in a registered home; *or*
- it is managed by a body (other than a local authority) constituted by Act of Parliament, or incorporated by Royal Charter and provides board and personal care. You must be living there on a commercial basis.

Prior to April 1993, people living in Abbeyfield homes and some unregistered small homes were also treated as being in a residential care home. If this applied to you, you can continue to get IS at the old rate. Since April 1993, 'small homes' have also had to register with the local authority if they provide board and personal care. A small home is defined as one that has less than four residents, not counting any relatives of the owners or their employees or people who have lived in the home for more than five years.[141] This means that some 'supported lodgings' will have registered. Others however may *not* be registerable. This will depend on what care or board is provided and the attitude of the Council's registration officer. If you are in an unregistered home, you will get housing benefit instead of the residential allowance (see p231).

Personal care usually means the kind of care and assistance a relative would give to a disabled and elderly person – eg, help with washing, dressing and ensuring medicines are taken.

A home counts as a nursing home for IS if it:[142]

- is registered as such under the Registered Homes Act 1984, the Nursing Homes Registration (Scotland) Act 1938 or the Mental Health (Scotland) Act 1984; *or*
- provides nursing services and is managed by a body constituted by an Act of Parliament or incorporated by Royal Charter.

You are not treated as living in a nursing home if you are in a hospice whose primary function is to provide care for people with a progressive disease in its final stages.[143] The hospice must also be registered under Part II of the Registered Homes Act 1984 (England and Wales) or exempt under section 6 of the Nursing Homes Registration (Scotland) Act.

Where a residential or nursing home has already been registered, and a new person has taken over the management of the home, it will continue to count as registered, provided a new application to register has been made and not turned down.[144]

Which IS rules apply?

If you are living in a residential care or nursing home, you need to check which IS rules apply to you.

If you were living in a residential care or nursing home prior to April 1993, you have 'preserved rights' and your IS is calculated under the old rules which means that you get a higher amount of benefit. This special calculation applies if you were living in a residential care or nursing home on 31 March 1993, and one of the following applies:[145]

- you were getting IS at the residential care/nursing home rate; *or*
- you were not entitled to IS because you had sufficient money to pay for the cost of the home yourself, but you now need to claim IS; *or*
- you were not getting paid at the residential care/nursing home rate because the home in which you lived was run by a close relative, but the home now has a new proprietor who is not a close relative or you have moved to a different home. If you go back to living in a home run by a close relative you lose this right, but it can be restored if there is yet another change of proprietor.

You also have a preserved right if you were not actually living in the home on 31 March 1993 but were only temporarily absent on that date, so long as the absence did not exceed four weeks (if you were a temporary resident), 13 weeks (if you were permanently resident) or 52 weeks (if you were in hospital).

If you live in a home which caters for less than four people you only get the higher rate of IS if you were actually being paid at that rate

Preserved rights entitlement[1]

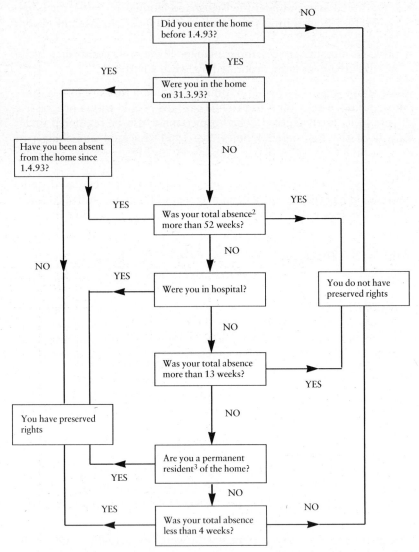

1. This flowchart does not apply to people who live in small homes (with fewer than four residents). See p103.
2. *Total absence* means the period between the day you left home up to and including the day before you returned.
3. You are a *permanent resident* if the home is your usual address. If you have another address where you spend as much or more time then you are classed as a temporary resident.

Preserved rights for people in small homes
(fewer than four residents)

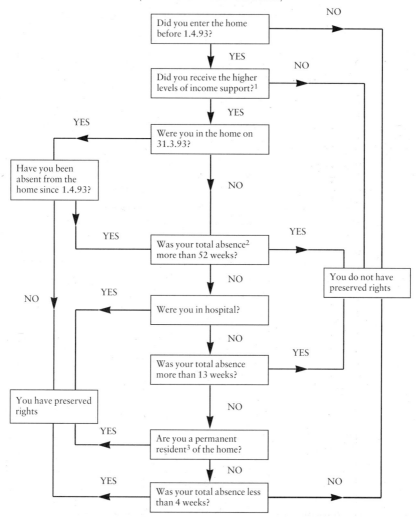

1. The higher levels are *not* payable if the home is run by someone related to you or if it did not meet the care criteria laid down before 1 April 1993.
2. *Total absence* means the period between the day you left home up to and including the day before you returned.
3. You are a *permanent resident* if the home is your usual address. If you have another address where you spend as much or more time then you are classed as a temporary resident.

immediately prior to April.[146] This is because not everyone in such small homes qualified for the residential care rate of IS. There are other special rules for these 'small homes' – see the flowchart on p103.

Note: From 4 October 1993, you will also have had preserved rights if you live in a small home that was not required to register because one or more of the residents there were relatives, or had lived there more than five years. This only applies if you were living in the home on 1 April 1993 and 4 October 1993 and were not absent from the home between those dates for more than 13 weeks.[147]

People who were in local authority-run residential accommodation on or before 31 March 1993 do *not* have preserved rights. Neither do people who were in hostel-type accommodation (usually defined as places where meals are not provided as part of the overall charge and housing benefit is paid to cover the rent).

If you have a preserved right to continue to be paid IS under the old rules, you lose this if you leave the home for longer than four weeks (temporary residents), 13 weeks (permanent residents) or 52 weeks (residents who go into hospital).[148]

If you have gone into a registered residential or nursing home since 1 April 1993, or have lost your preserved rights, your IS is worked out using the ordinary rules (see p27) with a few changes (see p111). Your accommodation must be provided on a commercial basis and you must be 16 or over.

Once you have decided which rules apply to you, check the amount of your IS entitlement (see below or p111).

IS for people with preserved rights who live in residential care or nursing homes

If you have preserved rights your IS will consist of an amount for **personal expenses** and an **accommodation allowance** to cover all or part of the charge made by the home. You are not entitled to any premiums.

Personal expenses[149]
These are as follows:

Single claimant	£13.10
Couple	£26.20
Dependent child aged	
18+	£13.10
16-17	£ 9.10
11-15	£ 7.85
0-10	£ 5.40

The accommodation allowance

The amount you receive will cover the weekly charge for your accommodation including meals and services where these are provided, but only up to a maximum or ceiling set by parliament.[150]

If you have to pay for some meals separately, your accommodation allowance will include for each person, either an amount to cover the actual cost of the meals if they can be provided by the home,[151] *or*, if not,

- £1.10 for breakfast
- £1.55 for lunch
- £1.55 for dinner

unless your meals taken outside the home cost less.

If you pay additional charges for heating, attendance needs, extra baths, laundry or a special diet you follow for medical reasons, these will be included in the accommodation allowance, so long as they are provided by the home and not by an outside agency.[152] You will not get the cost of these meals and/or extra services met in full if your accommodation charge plus the cost of meals or extra services is more than the maximum (see below).

If you receive housing benefit towards part of your accommodation charge this will be deducted from that charge and reduce your IS accordingly.[153]

Maximum accommodation allowances – ceilings[154]

Your accommodation charge (including any charges for additional services and meals) will usually only be met up to a 'ceiling'. This maximum varies depending on the type of home you are in and the type of care you receive.[155] You may find that the total amount you have to pay the home is not covered by your IS.

If you are in a residential care home the ceiling varies according to the level or type of care the home is registered to provide, or if the home is not registered, according to the care you receive.[156] The type of care depends on the health conditions and/or age of the residents. If more than one ceiling applies, the amount is decided as follows:[157]

- where the home is registered to provide the type of care you get, you will receive the amount that is allowed for that type of care;
- if the care you receive is different from the type the home is registered to provide, you will receive the allowance for the lower or lowest of the categories of care which the home is registered to provide;
- in any other case you will receive the amount appropriate to the care you receive.

Residential care homes

Health condition/age	Amount payable
Old age	£194.00
Past or present mental disorder but excluding mental handicap	£202.00
Past or present drug or alcohol dependence	£202.00
Mental handicap	£232.00
Physical disablement if under pension age, or, if over pension age, claimant had become disabled before reaching 60 (65 if a man)	£262.00
Physical disablement (over pension age and not disabled before reaching 60 (woman) or (65 man)	£194.00
Very dependent elderly (see definition below)	£224.00
Any other condition	£194.00

* These amounts are increased by £30 a week for homes in the Greater London area (see p111 for definition).

You will be considered to be 'very dependent elderly' if you are over pension age and *either*:

* registered or certified as blind; *or*
* entitled to attendance allowance or disability living allowance care component (AA/DLA care) at the highest rate (even if it is not payable because you have not met the qualifying period or because you are living in residential care); *or*
* getting war or industrial injury constant attendance allowance.[158]

Nursing homes

Health condition/age	Amount payable
Past or present mental disorder but excluding mental handicap	£290.00
Mental handicap	£295.00
Past or present drug or alcohol dependence	£290.00
Physical disablement, if under pension age, or if over pension age, claimant had become disabled before reaching 60 (65 if a man)	£325.00
Over pension age and had become physically disabled after reaching 60 (65 if a man)	£290.00
Terminal illness	£290.00
Any other condition (including elderly)	£290.00

* *These amounts are increased by £35 a week for homes in the Greater London area.*

The following definitions apply when deciding which maximum applies to you:

'Mental disorder' is defined as 'mental illness, arrested or incomplete development of mind, psychopathic disorder, and any other disorder or disability of mind'.[159]

'Mental handicap' is defined as 'a state of arrested or incomplete development of mind which includes impairment of intelligence and social functioning'.[160] 'Senility' is not mental handicap but can amount to a mental disorder.[161]

'Disablement' is defined as meaning that you are 'blind, deaf or dumb or substantially and permanently handicapped by illness, injury or congenital deformity or any other disability prescribed by the Secretary of State'.[162]

If you are in a nursing home the ceiling varies according to the type of care you receive there. If the home provides more than one type of care you will get the ceiling appropriate to the care you receive.[163] The type of care depends on the health conditions and age of the residents. You could, for example, get the 'terminal illness' rate if that is the level of care you receive even though you are not, in fact, terminally ill.[164]

Some homes may be registered both as a residential care and a nursing home. In these cases your maximum accommodation allowance will be decided according to whether you are receiving residential or nursing care.

Getting more than the ceiling

You can get more than the ceiling if one of the following applies:

- in the case of residential care homes, the home is in Greater London, in which case the allowance can be increased by up to £30 for each member of the family aged 11 or over (£35 extra in the case of nursing homes);[165]
- you have lived in the same accommodation for over 12 months and could afford it when you moved in. You will get your full accommodation charge for up to 13 weeks after you claim or after you apply for a review of your claim[166] if you are trying to move but need time to find somewhere else given the lack of availability of suitable accommodation and your and your family's personal circumstances (eg, your age, health, employment prospects and the effect on children of changing

schools). If you have any disregarded income you will have to put this towards the charge first.[167] The 13-week rule does not apply if you are being accommodated by the local authority because you are homeless or under the authority's duty to promote the welfare of children;

- you have been living in a residential care or nursing home since 28 April 1985 and your accommodation allowance under the present rules is lower than what you received then plus £10. (For further details on this see the 22nd edition of the *Handbook*, p78.)[168]

Money from other sources

Even if you have 'preserved rights' to IS under the old rules, you might find that you still need help in paying for your accommodation. The local authority might agree to pay the difference between your IS accommodation allowance and the charge you have to pay the home. This is what is known as a **'topping-up payment'**. If you are under pension age, topping-up payments can be paid in both residential care and nursing homes. If you are over pension age, they can only be paid in residential care homes and to qualify, the local authority must have been paying the 'topping-up payment' before you reach 60 (for women) or 65 (for men).[169] The payment will not affect your IS and you will not be counted as living in residential accommodation (see p98).

- The local authority is prevented from both 'topping-up' *and* taking over the full cost of the new placement. You would either have to find a home within the DSS limits or find an alternative source of funds.[170] The only exceptions to this rule are:[171]
  - people already getting a topping-up payment by 31 March 1993;
  - people without preserved rights or who have lost their preserved rights (see pp101-104);
  - people in residential care homes who face eviction, so long as the alternative home where topping-up is needed is not owned or managed by the same person or organisation. This final provision does not apply in the case of a home closure;
  - people under pension age who require nursing home care.
- Preserved rights are transferred with you if you move home. This also applies if you move from, for example, residential to nursing care – your new 'preserved right' would be to the nursing home ceiling.
- You may be receiving money from other sources – such as a charity or relatives – to help you pay for the part of your accommodation charge above the limit. This will also be ignored as income provided you do use it to pay the balance of the charge.[172]
- Where a health authority is providing top-up funding, you may find that the Benefits Agency still treat you as a hospital patient. This is a very complex area and you should get immediate advice.

The Department of Health has produced guidance for local authorities.[173]

Moving in or out of residential care or nursing homes

- If you are getting IS and you go into a home for eight weeks or less (eg, for respite care) you get IS for being in the home from the date you go in, whatever day of the week it is.[174]
- If you are in the home for only a few days but have to pay a full week's charge, your IS covers all of it.[175] Similarly, if you leave the home for less than a week, your claim is not reviewed and you continue to get full IS at the care home rate.[176]
- If you are in the home temporarily, you are also paid housing costs for which you are liable on your normal home.[177] If you pay rent you continue to get housing benefit while you are in the home.
- If someone in your family is temporarily away from the home the family still counts as being there as long as either you or your partner remain in it.[178]
- IS can cover a retaining fee payable while you are temporarily away from the home, but only up to 80 per cent of your normal accommodation allowance.[179] It is paid for up to four weeks if you normally live there, are away for at least a week and do not have to sign on (see p22) or for up to a year if you have temporarily gone into hospital or local authority residential accommodation. You are not covered by this rule if the residential accommodation does not provide board or it is for the rehabilitation of alcohol or drug users.[180]
- If you are a couple and one of you is temporarily in a residential care or nursing home and the other is living in the family home, or if the other one of you is also temporarily away from home (in hospital, or a residential care or nursing home, or residential accommodation), see pp330-33.
- If you are a couple, and one of you goes into a home permanently, you will cease to be treated as a couple.[181] The partner in the home will be paid benefit as a resident and the other partner will be assessed as a single claimant or single parent as appropriate. However, you are still treated as liable to maintain one another and may be asked to contribute to your partner's upkeep if you are not on benefit.

Remember that if you are moving out of a home to live in the community you may get a community care grant (see Chapter 22).

People with 'preserved rights' who do not count as living in a residential care or nursing home

You will not get IS at the residential care or nursing home rate if:

- the person who runs the home is a 'close relative'.[182] **Close relative** means a parent, parent-in-law, son, son-in-law, daughter, daughter-in-law, step-parent, stepson, stepdaughter, brother, sister or the partner of any of these. Sister or brother includes a half-sister or half-brother.[183] An adopted child ceases to be related to her/his natural family on adoption and becomes the relative of her/his adoptive family.[184] Where the home is run by a limited company of which the 'close relative' is a director, this rule does not apply;[185]
- the arrangement is not on a commercial basis.[186] Adjudication officers are advised to interpret broadly the meaning of 'on a commercial basis', and not just rely on whether or not a profit is being made. If the intention is to cover the cost of food plus a reasonable amount for accommodation, the arrangement should be considered to be a commercial one. A charity or individual might charge enough to make ends meet, but not necessarily to make a profit;[187]
- you are aged 16 or over but under 19, and are in care – except where you yourself are paying someone other than the local authority for your accommodation;[188]
- you are on holiday and have not been away from where you usually live for more than 13 weeks.[189] 'On holiday' would not include a period of respite care or convalescence;[190]
- you are going into a residential care or nursing home in order to take advantage of the allowances paid to residents of these homes;[191]
- you are in a home run by a body constituted by Act of Parliament (except a local authority) or by Royal Charter, and the personal care you receive is not because of old age, disablement, mental disorder, alcohol or drug dependency;[192]
- your home changed from being a local authority home to a residential care home while you were living there (or temporarily away). If the local authority is still obliged to provide accommodation for you and you stay in the same home, your IS is calculated as if you are in a local authority home (see p98). This rule applies from 12 August 1991.[193]

If any of the above apply, you will get IS at the ordinary rate, including premiums, but excluding the residential allowance (see p111).

If your local authority is sponsoring you in the home you will count as being in local authority residential accommodation and get benefit accordingly (see p98). But see also 'topping-up' payments (p108).

IS for people without preserved rights who live in residential care and nursing homes

If you do not have preserved rights, how much IS you get depends on whether you make the arrangements to go into a home yourself, or ask the local authority to help you. If you make the arrangements yourself and agree to meet the home's fees out of your savings, income or with help from a third party (relatives, a charity etc), you can claim IS in the ordinary manner (see below). If you ask your local authority social work department or social services authority for assistance, they will assess your need for residential or nursing care (see p112).

IS if you are making your own arrangements to go into a home
Your IS is calculated subject to the usual rules about capital (see p394). You will get:

- your personal allowance (see p340);
- premiums to which you are entitled (see p342);
- a residential allowance to cover your accommodation charges. This is paid at a flat-rate of £48 (or £53 if you live in the Greater London area).

    Greater London covers the 32 London Boroughs and the City of London, as well as part of Essex (the parishes of Chigwell and Waltham Cross), Hertfordshire (the parishes of Elstree, Ridge, Shenley and South Mimms and the southern part of Broxbourne Borough), and Surrey (the borough of Spelthorne and part of Elmbridge).

The premiums will be exactly the same as if you were living in your own home. However, if you are getting the severe disability premium, this may stop after four weeks if your AA/DLA care stops. This may mean you would also stop getting the higher pensioner premium and revert to the ordinary or enhanced rates.

If you are hoping to use AA/DLA care plus IS and other income to pay for your accommodation, you may find that AA/DLA care stops after four weeks in a home. This is because it was the DSS policy intention that people on IS whose accommodation *could* be funded by the local authority should not get AA/DLA care.[194] However, in practice, the Benefits Agency says that where someone has arranged accommodation themselves and the local authority therefore cannot help with its cost, AA/DLA care is payable.[195] If your AA/DLA care stops in this situation, you should seek advice. For more details about AA/DLA care for people in residential and nursing care, see CPAG's *Rights Guide to Non-Means-Tested Benefits*.

If you have been paying for your accommodation yourself from savings or other income, you could still approach the local authority if you are running short of funds, although the local authority would not be obliged to keep you in the same home if they agreed to help you financially.

Since 4 October 1993, payments from charities to people without preserved rights have been treated differently. Only some of the money paid by the charity will be treated as income. The Benefits Agency will disregard the difference between your applicable amount less personal expenses and the weekly charge for the accommodation.[196]

Example
Mrs B is a pensioner living in a home in London costing £300 a week. A charity is paying £250 towards the home fees. Her IS will be:

£ 45.70	Personal allowance
£ 18.25	Pensioner premiums
£ 53.00	Residential allowance
£116.95	Applicable amount
£ 13.10	Personal expenses
£103.85	

£300 weekly charge minus £103.85 = £196.15.
£53.85 of the payment from the charity is treated as income (£250 minus £196.15). The rest is ignored for IS purposes. Mrs B will get IS of £63.10 (£116.95 minus £53.85) plus £250 from the charity.

IS if you are getting help from the local authority
If you choose to ask the Social Services Department for help, they will assess your need for residential or nursing care. They may decide to offer you extra help to stay in your own home, or could involve the Independent Living Fund (see p495). However, if they offer residential or nursing care, you will be financially assessed according to the standard, national means test used by local authorities, although there is scope for some local discretion. Your benefit entitlement will depend on whether you are going to enter a residential care or nursing home or local authority accommodation. For yourself, there is really no difference, as the means test is the same and you will be left with a personal expenses figure of £13.10 a week either way. However, it is generally financially better for the local authority if you go into a non-local authority home. This is because you will get more IS if you live in a private or voluntary residential care or nursing home. Your IS applicable amount would be ordinary IS including the residential allowance in that type of home as opposed to just £57.60 in a local authority home (see pp98-100 and 111).

As the local authority takes any of your income over £13.10 a week as your contribution to the cost of the home, your contribution can be higher if you are in a private or voluntary home because your income is higher.

If you have savings of over £8,000, you will have to pay the full cost of the home, whichever type it is. Normal tariff income rules apply for savings below £8,000 (see pp385-7).

The local authority has some discretion with personal allowances. It can allow you a more generous figure than £13.10 a week.[197]

The local authority's rules on capital and deprivation of capital including property, are similar to the IS rules (see pp404-407).[198] The local authority has some discretion in their treatment of capital. It can choose to ignore the value of any property you own that is occupied by someone else.[199] This could mean that you are refused IS because the Benefits Agency takes the value of your property into account, while the local authority assesses you as not having capital. The local authority can, however, put a legal charge against your property and you would then have to pay for the cost of your care once the property is sold.[200]

There are special rules for couples, temporary stays, treatment of income from relatives etc. These are all contained in the *Charging for Residential Accommodation Guide*, issued by the Department of Health.

5. PEOPLE IN HOSPITAL

If you, your partner or child goes into hospital, your IS is reduced after a few weeks. Other benefits – eg, sickness benefit – are also reduced while you are in hospital so your IS may not go down as much as you expect, and you may even qualify for IS for the first time because of reduced income. Alternatively, you may lose your IS altogether if you have other income.

If you live in residential accommodation your benefit changes only if you are single (see p99). Special rules apply to people who normally live in residential care and nursing homes when they go into hospital (see p116).

If you are a member of a couple and one of you is in hospital and the other is also temporarily away from your normal home, check p334.

You are treated as being in hospital even if you spend part of the day outside it.[201]

Housing costs

You continue to get these until you have been in hospital for one year unless you are the claimant and the Benefits Agency believes that you are likely to be in hospital substantially longer than 52 weeks.[202] If you have a partner, son or daughter who is eligible for IS, they could claim instead and get the housing costs covered. For how your housing benefit is affected, see p247.

After 52 weeks you cease to get your housing costs met. If you are a couple, and one of you remains at home, you are treated as two separate people and the partner at home has her/his housing costs met.[203]

Single people in hospital

After four weeks any AA/DLA care you receive stops and you therefore lose your severe disability premium.[204] Otherwise your IS remains unchanged for your first six weeks in hospital.[205] A carer would also lose their carer's premium after ceasing to get invalid care allowance (ICA) for eight weeks.[206]

After six weeks your applicable amount is reduced to £14.40 personal allowance[207] plus any housing costs (see p113).

After 52 weeks you lose any IS housing costs and only get a personal allowance of £11.50.[208] You can be paid less than this if:[209]

- you are unable to look after your own affairs (eg, mentally ill or senile) and another person has been appointed to act on your behalf; *and*
- the IS is paid to the hospital at the request of the appointee, or to the hospital as the appointee; *and*
- a doctor who is treating you certifies that you cannot make use of all or part of your benefit, and that it cannot be used on your behalf.

This rule could leave you without any income at all, though your relatives and the hospital staff should be consulted about how much you should receive. Your appointee could refuse to allow the Benefits Agency to pay the hospital direct. S/he could receive payments on your behalf instead to make sure you get the money.

Single parents in hospital

After four weeks any AA/DLA care you receive stops and you therefore lose your severe disability premium.[210] Otherwise your IS remains unchanged for your first six weeks in hospital.[211] A carer also loses her/his carer's premium after ceasing to get ICA for eight weeks.[212]

After six weeks your applicable amount is £14.40 personal allowance *plus* your children's personal allowances, *plus* the family, lone parent and disabled child premiums,[213] plus housing costs (see p113).

If your child is also in hospital, see below.

After 52 weeks you continue to receive the same amount unless you are no longer treated as 'responsible' for your children (see pp335-6). In this case you just get the £11.50 personal allowance, and your children may be able to claim in their own right even if aged 16 or 17 and still at school (see p17-18).

Couples

The amount paid for a couple depends on whether they have children and whether one or both of them is in hospital.

After four weeks if the person who goes into hospital receives AA/DLA care, this stops. All premiums, including severe disability premium, continue to be paid. If you are a couple getting severe disability premium at the couple rate and one of you goes into hospital for more than four weeks and loses AA/DLA care, you will not lose the severe disability premium altogether but you will only be paid at the single person rate.[214] Any ICA paid to the carer stops after four weeks, but the carer's premium continues to be paid for a further eight weeks (a total of 12).[215] If it is the carer who goes into hospital they cease to qualify for ICA and therefore lose the carer's premium. If, as the carer, you qualified for ICA less than 22 weeks before going into hospital, the carer's premium could be withdrawn as soon as you go into hospital.[216]

After six weeks your usual applicable amount including all other premiums is reduced by £11.50 if only one adult is in hospital.[217] (This also applies if both of you are in hospital but only one of you has been there for over six weeks.)

If both of you are in hospital for over six weeks your applicable amount is £28.80 personal allowance for you both, plus personal allowances for your children, if any, plus family and disabled child (if any) premiums plus housing costs (see p113). You lose the severe disability premium.

After 52 weeks if one or both of a couple are in hospital, you count as separate claimants.[218]

If only one partner is in hospital s/he is paid a personal allowance of £11.50 and the other member is assessed as a single claimant or a single parent, as appropriate. If both members of a couple without children are in hospital they are each paid a personal allowance of £11.50 only.[219]

If both members of a couple with children are in hospital, one is treated as responsible for the children and receives £14.40 personal allowance for her/himself plus the children's personal allowances and disabled child premium, if any, plus the family premium.[220] The other is just paid the £11.50 personal allowance.

If a child is also in hospital, see below.

Children

If your child goes into hospital, your benefit stays the same for 12 weeks. After that the IS personal allowance you receive for the child reduces to £11.50.[221] Any premiums you receive in relation to the child remain in payment. Even if your child loses the care component of DLA because s/he has been in hospital for over 12 weeks, you still get a disabled child premium for her/him, as long as s/he continues to be treated as a member of your family (see p328).[222]

The rule about adjustment to IS for a child in hospital applies equally where both parent(s) and child are in hospital.

People in residential care or nursing homes

* If you have 'preserved rights' to the higher rate of IS (see p101) and you go into hospital for six weeks or less you will still get your personal allowance and your accommodation allowance as long as you still have to pay the charge for the home – or a reduced allowance if the charge is reduced.[223]
* If you do not have preserved rights, you will continue to receive your usual IS, including the residential allowance, for the first six weeks.[224]
* If you are single, do not have to pay the charge, and do not intend to return to the home, you will get IS as a hospital patient (see p114). If you do intend to return but do not have to pay the charge, you will get your personal allowance as a home resident, *plus* meals allowance, if any.

After six weeks in hospital (12 for a child), the following rules apply to people with preserved rights. For the rules for people without preserved rights, see p114.[225]

* The personal allowance for an adult in hospital is £14.40.
* The personal allowance for a child who has been in hospital for over 12 weeks will be £11.50.
* A single claimant, or a couple without children who are both in hospital, will receive £14.40 or £28.80 respectively *plus* either an amount for a retaining fee in respect of the home or an amount for housing costs, but not both.[226]
* For as long as another member of the family remains in the residential care or nursing home, an accommodation allowance will continue to be paid taking account of any reduction in the charge, and personal allowances at the residential care and nursing homes rate will continue for each member of the family still in the home or in hospital for six weeks or less (12 in the case of children).
* Where children do not live in the home while their parent(s) or only parent is in hospital, the benefit of the parent(s) is calculated in the usual way for patients (see p113) except it will include either an amount for a retaining fee in respect of the home or an amount for IS housing costs, but not both.[227]

Patients detained under the Mental Health Act

Single people detained under the Mental Health Act 1983 (in Scotland, Mental Health (Scotland) Act 1984), who were in prison immediately before their detention receive a weekly allowance of £11.50.[228]

Going in and out of hospital

- The date of the change to your IS applicable amount depends on whether your IS is paid in advance or arrears.[229] If you are paid in arrears, the first reduction takes place from the first day of the benefit week in which you have been in hospital for six weeks (not counting the day of admission). If your IS is paid in advance, the change takes effect from the first day of the benefit week which coincides with, or follows, the date when you have been in hospital for six weeks. In the first case you could *lose* up to six days' full benefit; in the second you could *gain* up to six days' full benefit.
- Separate stays in hospital less than 28 days apart are added together in calculating the length of time you have been in hospital.[230]
- Days at home: If you or a member of your family stop being a patient for any period of less than a week you should be paid your full IS for the days you are at home.[231]
- The days that you leave and return to hospital are not counted as days in hospital in the above circumstances.[232]
- Other benefits:
  - **Furniture and clothing:** You may be able to get a social fund payment for these when you come out of hospital, and for clothing if you are going into hospital (see Part Nine). You should apply before you are due to leave hospital to give the Benefits Agency time to deal with your application.
  - **Fares to hospital:** See p480 for patients' fares and p444 for visitors' hospital fares.
  - **Transitional payments** can be affected by a stay in hospital but may be reinstated on the person's return to their home, see p44.

6. PRISONERS

If you are a prisoner, you are not entitled to IS apart from housing costs in certain limited circumstances (see p118).[233] You count as a prisoner if you are in custody on remand, or are serving a custodial sentence.[234] If you are married or living as husband and wife, your partner can claim benefit as a single claimant or single parent as appropriate while you are in prison.[235]

If you are on remand in a bail hostel you are *not* in custody, so may be able to get IS in the usual way (see p12). However, if you have a partner, you may be treated as members of the same household even though you are not living in the same place (see p329 for meaning of 'household').[236] If this happens, neither of you can get IS if the other is working full-time. You or your partner can only get IS if you can show that you will not be returning home or are likely to be away for more than 52 weeks.[237]

If a dependent child becomes a prisoner, you do not get any benefit for them.[238] If you have no other children you no longer qualify for a family premium and/or a lone parent premium and you may also need to 'sign-on' as a condition of getting benefit (see p21).

Housing costs covered by IS (see p29) are paid while you are remanded in custody or committed in custody for trial or to be sentenced.[239] Benefit is paid direct to the person you are liable to pay. You are also entitled to housing benefit for rent or a lodging charge if you pay either of these.

If you are only likely to be in prison for about a year you can get housing benefit for up to 52 weeks (see p218).[240] However, you do not get help with IS housing costs such as mortgage interest, after sentence.

If you are granted home leave shortly before release, you are entitled to IS. This is because a commissioner has decided that someone who is on home leave is not a prisoner.[241] Any person with whom you are staying is also entitled to IS for you. If your claim for IS is refused, you should appeal. Seek advice from your probation officer and ask them to contact CPAG.

You may also be able to get a community care grant to help towards your living expenses (see p439). A community care grant may be awarded even if the amount is less than £30.

The Prison Department can make a payment for home leave where the prisoner's family is not getting IS, but does not have sufficient money to support the prisoner while on leave; they can also pay for board and lodging during a period of temporary release for a prisoner regarded as homeless.

When you are discharged you may receive a discharge grant which is treated as capital and does not generally affect your right to be paid IS.[242] For the first seven days after your discharge (including the day of your discharge) you are not required to sign on as a condition of getting benefit[243] (see p24). If you need help with the cost of basic essentials (eg, clothing, furniture, or rent in advance), you may be able to get a social fund payment (see p438).

Help with the cost of **visiting a close relative in prison** comes from the Home Office. For this purpose, 'close relative' means husband, wife (including an established unmarried partner), brother, sister, parent and child. Adopted and fostered children and adoptive and foster parents are included. If the close relative is too ill, or too young, to travel alone, the fares of an escort can also be paid. It is normal policy to cover the travel costs (including an overnight stay and meals allowance where necessary), of up to 13 visits in a 12-month period if you are receiving IS or family credit. If your income is low but above IS level, the Home Office may pay part of the cost. Your income is assessed in the same way as for health benefits (see p470). You apply for help with the cost of visits on form F2022 obtainable from your local Benefits Agency office, or from the Assisted Prison Visits Unit, PO Box 2152, Birmingham B16 8QU, tel: 021 455 9855. There is no right of appeal against a refusal by the Home Office of fares or a warrant for a visit but you could take up the matter with your MP.

7. PEOPLE WITHOUT ACCOMMODATION

Benefit should not be refused just because you do not have an address. You are entitled to the normal IS personal allowance (see p341) for your weekly living expenses. You are not paid an allowance for a child dependant. You do not get any premiums for yourself, your partner or children.[244] Claimants known to stay in the area should be paid their benefit by giro or order book in the normal way, but if you are 'likely to move on or misspend your money' you may be required to collect your benefit on a daily or part-week basis.[245]

The *Adjudication Officers' Guide* defines 'accommodation' to include anywhere that is habitable and capable of being heated, and where you can sit, lie, cook and eat.[246] People in tents etc may therefore not be 'without accommodation' and could get premiums.

If you can get accommodation – eg, in board and lodging or a hostel – you get your normal personal allowances and premiums (if any) and you should apply for housing benefit for the board and lodging or hostel charge. If you need help with travel costs to accommodation you have been offered, you may be able to get a social fund payment (see p445).

People with no fixed abode, and no income, may initially require a crisis loan (see p449). The Benefits Agency may decide the claimant has an unsettled way of life and refer her/him to a voluntary project centre as an alternative. This is the practice of some Benefits Agency offices but should only be used with the client's consent and if a place is available. IS should not be refused or delayed if the claimant is unwilling to take the 'advice' being offered, or is not interested in being resettled.[247]

CHAPTER SIX

Maintenance payments

This chapter is divided as follows:

1. Introduction (below)
2. Liability to maintain (p122)
3. The child support scheme (p125)
4. The effect of maintenance on income support (p135)

This chapter deals with the liability of a person to maintain others and the effect any maintenance payments have on income support (IS), but it covers only heterosexual couples who have separated and the parents of children. Some of the provisions also affect sponsors who have signed undertakings to maintain people from abroad; the implications for them are dealt with on p88.

The rules about maintenance for children under the Child Support Act 1991 are included where they affect your right to, or the amount of, your benefit. For further information about the child support scheme, see CPAG's *Child Support Handbook*.

Payments for yourself could be on a voluntary basis, or under a court order. Detailed advice about maintenance orders is beyond the scope of this *Handbook* and you should see a solicitor. If you are receiving IS you can apply for legal aid for court proceedings. In addition, you can get free advice from a solicitor under the Green Form scheme.

1. INTRODUCTION

Claiming after a relationship breakdown

It often happens that a marriage or other relationship breaks down and if this happens you can claim benefit in your own right as a single person or parent. If you both remain living under the same roof, but live separate lives you can make separate claims for IS (and other means-tested benefits) and should not be treated as a married or cohabiting couple, provided that you keep separate households (see p330). You may be entitled to maintenance from your ex-partner and this affects the amount of your benefit (see p135). You are required to apply for maintenance for your children if you are on IS/FC/DWA unless you are exempt (see p125).

Lone parents

If you are a single person responsible for a child or young person under 19 who is living in your household and for whom you can claim (see p336), you are entitled to have the **lone parent premium** included in your applicable amount (see p344) and are entitled to have £15 of your net earnings disregarded when calculating IS (see p369). It is not necessary for you to be a parent of the child or young person.

While you are claiming for a child under 16, you are not required to be available for work and to sign on. Nor can any voluntary unemployment deduction be made if you lose a job through misconduct, etc.

As a single parent, you are likely to be able to claim **one parent benefit** which is an increase of child benefit paid at the rate of £6.15 a week. Again, it is not necessary to be a parent of the child. For full details, see CPAG's *Rights Guide to Non-Means-Tested Benefits*. If you do claim one parent benefit, it is taken into account in full as income so you are no better off unless your total income is then sufficient to lift you off IS altogether. However, you should think carefully before claiming one parent benefit if this would lift you just above IS levels because, apart from losing IS, you would lose entitlement to free school meals and also access to community care grants or budgeting loans from the social fund. These payments all depend on your being entitled to IS. Your IS is not reduced if you choose not to claim the one parent benefit. On the other hand, it is a good idea to claim one parent benefit if you are soon going to take full-time work and will no longer be entitled to IS anyway. This is because you would then have the use of the one parent benefit as soon as your entitlement to IS ended. If you are already receiving one parent benefit when you claim IS, or you later make a claim, make sure that the Benefits Agency office dealing with your IS claim knows so that you are not overpaid. The IS authorities do not always find out automatically, and overpayments in those circumstances are generally recoverable (see p161).

If you claim IS within three months of the birth of a child, claim a maternity payment from the social fund (see p416).

You are entitled to maintenance payments for your child(ren) and possibly for yourself if you were married. You are required to apply for child maintenance if you claim IS/FC/DWA, unless exempt (see p125), and the money you get affects your benefit (see p135).

Young mothers

If you are under 16, you cannot claim IS but can claim child benefit and one parent benefit and also health benefits (see p470). If your parents (or someone else) are entitled to include you in their family (see p335), they can also include your baby in their family for the purpose of a claim for IS or other means-tested benefits and they can claim a maternity payment from the social fund (see p416) if they are entitled to IS or FC.

If you are 16- or 17-years-old and have left school, you may receive IS while you are pregnant (see p68). You are entitled to IS from 11 weeks before the baby is due. If you are over 16 but have not been entitled to IS because you are under 19 and still in relevant education, you can make a claim for IS as soon as your baby is born (see p17).

You can get maintenance for the child from the father, and will be required to do so if you are claiming IS/FC/DWA in your own right (see p125) unless exempt.[1]

Separation due to care needs

Sometimes a couple are forced to live apart because one of them needs care or treatment. If your partner is in hospital, or in a residential or nursing home you may be assessed and paid as separate individuals for benefit purposes (see p333). However, you still remain liable to support your partner and you may be asked to make a financial contribution towards her/his care if you are able.

The same applies if it is your child who is in care.

In either case, you should not be asked to pay more than you can afford and, if you are on IS, no contribution is required for a partner.

2. LIABILITY TO MAINTAIN

You are liable to maintain your spouse and your children for as long as IS is being paid for them.[2] You are not liable to maintain your ex-spouse after you have been divorced (unless you sponsored her/him when s/he came from abroad, see p88). Nor are you liable to maintain children over 16 who are claiming in their own right or any children over the age of 19.

A parent who does not live with the person who is looking after her/his child(ren) is expected to pay child maintenance on a regular basis to the parent or other person who is currently caring for the child. If you are the parent looking after the child(ren) and claiming IS/FC/DWA you are required to apply for this maintenance unless exempt (see p125). However, you can refuse to apply for maintenance and have a penalty deduction made from your benefit. Although the Benefits Agency could approach an absent parent using the liability to maintain provision if the person looking after her/his child(ren) had refused to authorise the Child Support Agency to pursue child maintenance, CPAG has been assured that this will not happen. If this happens to you, ask your adviser to contact the Citizens' Rights Office.

The Child Support Agency's formula for calculating child support maintenance is a rigid one and there is no scope for the liable relative to dispute the assessment unless the calculation is based on incorrect information. There is more flexibility about how much you are required to pay for your spouse on IS and you should negotiate with the Benefits Agency to pay an amount you can afford given your outgoings. However, if the Benefits Agency feel that you are not paying enough they have the right to take you to court.

Enforcing a claimant's maintenance order

If there is already an order in favour of, or for the benefit of, a claimant *who is a parent*, or an order in favour of the claimant's children, the Secretary of State may do anything to enforce or vary the order which the claimant could do.[3] (This includes applying to have the order registered in the magistrates' court.) This is unlikely to be necessary for children as by April 1994, the Child Support Agency hopes to have taken over all IS cases with previous court orders (see p125).

Furthermore, if the Secretary of State notifies the relevant court officer that he wishes to be informed of any application by either the claimant or the liable relative to vary the order, enforce it or have any arrears remitted, he will be given that information and is entitled to take part in the proceedings.[4] Nevertheless, any maintenance which then has to be paid is paid to the claimant (unless diverted – see below).

Collection by the Benefits Agency

If maintenance is payable through a magistrates' court (including orders made in the county court or High Court but registered in the magistrates' court) and it is paid irregularly, you can authorise the clerk to pay it to the Benefits Agency when it does arrive and, in return, the Benefits Agency gives you an order book for the amount of IS you would receive if no maintenance was being paid.[5] The Benefits Agency does not usually accept this sort of arrangement unless payments have actually been missed, but may if you have a good reason for wanting it done and you explain why. The Benefits Agency are likely to be even less willing to do this now that the specialist sections dealing with such arrangements have been disbanded. The Child Support Agency may collect other types of maintenance at the same time as child support.[6]

An order for the Secretary of State

The Secretary of State may obtain an order against any person who is liable to maintain a claimant or a member of the claimant's family (see p328). The application is heard in a magistrates' court.[7] Since 5 April 1993, the courts have not had the power to make new orders for maintenance for children.[8] As the liable relatives sections of the Benefits Agency are no longer staffed, it is possible that the number of these actions on behalf of spouses may decline.

For maintenance in respect of your spouse, the court is entitled to refuse an order if your spouse has been guilty of adultery (without your acceptance), cruelty or desertion.[9] The fact that there was an agreement that your former partner would not ask for maintenance is not a bar to an order being made,[10] although all the circumstances must be taken into account.[11]

Prosecution

As a last resort you can be prosecuted if IS is paid as a result of your persistently refusing or neglecting to maintain your spouse or children. This is uncommon. Although the power remains in respect of children, it is very unlikely to be used given that child maintenance is now being dealt with by the Child Support Agency (see p125).

You can even be prosecuted for failing to maintain yourself! This is even rarer.

In either case, the maximum penalty is three months' imprisonment or a fine of £1,000 or both.[12] If you are charged with such an offence, see a solicitor. Legal aid may be available to help meet the cost.

Liable relatives

The following people (together with sponsors of people from abroad – see p88) who may make maintenance payments to you if they have the means are known as 'liable relatives':[13]

- a husband or wife. This includes one from whom you are separated;
- a divorced man or woman;
- a parent of a child or young person under 19;
- a person who has been living with and maintaining a child or young person under 19 and can therefore reasonably be treated as the father.

There are special rules about how payments from a liable relative are taken into account (see p135).

The Secretary of State can take proceedings against some liable relatives to pay maintenance for an ex-partner or child if you cannot or do not wish to do so yourself (see above). It is important to note that not all liable relatives whose payments affect IS are legally 'liable to maintain' claimants so as to enable the Secretary of State to obtain maintenance from them.

3. THE CHILD SUPPORT SCHEME

Maintenance for children has been dealt with by the Child Support Agency since 5 April 1993. If you were already getting maintenance for a child under a voluntary agreement or court order before this date, this can continue until the Child Support Agency takes on your case. The Child Support Agency expects to have taken on all existing IS cases where maintenance was already in payment by April 1994. All other existing IS cases will be taken on by the Child Support Agency by April 1996.

If you make a new or repeat claim for IS/FC/DWA, you are required to apply to the Child Support Agency for a maintenance assessment unless exempt. Failure to do so could affect the amount of benefit you receive (see p127).

Any maintenance you receive counts as income when calculating your benefit. However, the processing of your benefit claim by the Benefits Agency should not be held up by the Child Support Agency actions.

The Child Support Agency assessment overrides any previous maintenance agreement, including a court order. The courts now only have limited powers to make maintenance orders for children – see the *Child Support Handbook* for details.

The requirement to co-operate

If you are claiming IS, FC or DWA you are required to authorise the Secretary of State to apply for child maintenance from your child's other parent where you are living apart. The only exception to this rule is where you or your child would be put at risk of **suffering harm or undue distress** if your partner were to be pursued (see below).[14] The child support officer will decide if your reasons are sufficient to justify exemption. If your reasons are not accepted, your benefit could be reduced (see p128).

This requirement applies not only to lone parents, but also to couples where one of the children in the family has a parent who is living elsewhere. It does not apply where a child lives with neither parent. In this case, an application for child maintenance from the person looking after the child is voluntary.

Providing authorisation

When you claim benefit you are asked to complete a maintenance application form. If you sign the form, you are giving your authorisation to the Child Support Agency to pursue child maintenance. By doing so, you are formally requesting the Child Support Agency to assess how much maintenance the child's other parent should pay and also permitting the Secretary of State to ensure that maintenance is, in fact, paid. Without your signature, the Child Support Agency cannot take any action to pursue maintenance, even if all the necessary information is known. **Do not sign the maintenance application form unless you are sure that you want to apply for child maintenance.** If you believe that you are exempt from having to apply, you should send information to the Child Support Agency explaining why you or your child(ren) would be put at risk of suffering harm or undue distress.

If you are looking after children who have different parents, you can authorise the Child Support Agency to pursue one of the parents, and argue for an exemption from pursuing the other.

Harm or undue distress

Harm or undue distress is not defined, so if you believe that you or any of the children living with you would be at risk of harm or unreasonable distress if you pursued the absent parent for child maintenance, you should explain to the Child Support Agency why this is so. The exemption certainly covers situations where there is a possibility of violence or where there has been rape, sexual abuse, threats or other harassment. There does not need to have been a history of actual violence.[15] A child support officer decides if a fear of violence is reasonably held.

There will be many other situations in which you would find it distressing to pursue maintenance – eg, where you have not had any contact with the other parent for many years, you had a clean-break divorce, the other parent is threatening to contest who the child lives with, you chose to have the child against the father's wishes, or you believe it would threaten the arrangement between the other parent and the children. Instead of signing the maintenance application form, you should **return the covering letter explaining the situation.**

Each case is decided on its merits. Your word should be accepted without any supporting evidence unless you contradict yourself or the child support officer thinks the information is improbable.[16] For example, where you have named a celebrity as the father of your child.

Withdrawing your authorisation

If you signed the maintenance application form and later find that you or your children are at risk as a result of the maintenance assessment, you can ask the Child Support Agency to stop pursuing maintenance.[17]

You should give reasons for the risk and the Child Support Agency will go through the same procedure as if you had refused to co-operate at the beginning. If the child support officer decides that there are reasonable grounds for believing a risk of harm or undue distress exists, you are no longer required to co-operate and as long as you have requested that all action cease, the Child Support Agency must stop pursuing the maintenance. However, if the child support officer decides there is no risk involved, the Child Support Agency continues to act on the original authorisation and pursues the maintenance. You do not have the option of the benefit penalty at this stage.

Refusal to co-operate with the Child Support Agency

If you refuse to authorise the Child Support Agency to seek maintenance for your child(ren) or to provide information to help them assess maintenance liability, your benefit (IS, FC or DWA) can be reduced.[18] However, your benefit claim must still be processed by the Benefits Agency. You do not need to withdraw your benefit claim to avoid child maintenance being pursued. If you do not want to apply for child maintenance, do not sign the maintenance application form.

If you fail to complete and return the maintenance application form or if you do not provide any additional information which is required, the Secretary of State considers any information you have sent about a risk of harm or undue distress. If he is not satisfied that you have good cause for refusing to co-operate, you are then called for an interview with a staff member of the Child Support Agency at the local Benefits Agency office. You do not have to attend this interview if you do not wish to, and can instead provide your reasons in writing.

At the interview you will be asked why you have not provided the authorisation and/or information, and you should give details about any risk of harm or undue distress. If the interviewing officer decides you are not required to apply for maintenance the matter will not be taken any further. However, if s/he is not convinced by your case you should be notified in writing that you have not complied with the requirement to provide the necessary authorisation or information and warned that your benefit could be reduced unless you do so. You must respond within six weeks. You can use this time to get supporting letters – eg, from friends and relatives, your doctor, child's school, or other helpful organisations – if you wish. If you still fail to comply, a child support officer will write to you asking you either to provide the authorisation or information requested, or to explain why you have not done so. You are given 14 days in which to respond.[19]

In order to avoid the benefit penalty it is important that you give an explanation of the harm or undue distress which could arise and make it clear that this is the reason why you do not wish to co-operate. You do not have to reply in writing – a telephone call is acceptable.[20] Nor do you have to provide evidence to prove that you would be under threat. Your word should be accepted[21] though it is always useful to point to specific examples of problems which have occurred in the past or reasons why you believe they might occur in the future, to help illustrate what effect your co-operation might have. If there are reasonable grounds for believing that you or your child would suffer harm or undue distress were authorisation to be given, no further action is taken and you are advised of this.[22]

If the child support officer does not accept that there is any risk s/he may direct that your IS/FC/DWA should be reduced. When deciding whether to issue a reduced benefit direction, the child support officer must consider the welfare of any child involved.[23] You have a right of appeal against a reduced benefit direction (see below), although the benefit penalty will be imposed in the meantime.[24]

The benefit penalty

The adjudication officer (AO) at the Benefits Agency must follow a reduced benefit direction issued by a child support officer. Your benefit should be paid in full until a direction is issued but will then be adjusted. A current award of FC/DWA can be changed if a reduced benefit direction is issued, cancelled or suspended (see p194).

Benefit can be reduced even if your benefit does not include an amount for the child(ren) for whom maintenance is being claimed.[25] However, no reduction is made if you are in hospital, a residential care or nursing home, or a local authority residential home.[26]

If a reduction is being made to your FC or DWA and you then go on to IS the deduction continues to be made.[27]

Only one reduction can be made from your benefit even if you refuse to co-operate in seeking maintenance for children from different relationships.[28] When this reduction ends you cannot be subjected to a further penalty for those same children even on a subsequent claim for benefit.[29] However, if another child is born or joins your household the question of giving authorisation and information in relation to that additional child arises, and a second reduced benefit direction could be issued if you again fail to co-operate. If a second direction is made, the original one ceases even if it would otherwise run for several more months.[30] See below for how long the benefit penalty applies in this situation.

The amount of the reduction and how long it lasts

The reduction lasts for 18 months and is £9.14 a week for the first 26 weeks and £4.57 for a further 52 weeks.[31] This period begins on the first day of the second benefit week after the AO has reviewed and revised your claim.[32] If the reduction takes your benefit to below 10 pence (IS) or 50 pence (FC or DWA), a lower deduction is made so that you are left with this minimum amount of benefit.[33] When benefit rates are increased in April the amount of the reduction also increases. For IS, this happens straightaway but with FC or DWA it is adjusted when your claim is next renewed.[34]

If a second reduced benefit direction has been made against you because you have refused to co-operate in relation to an additional child, the original direction lapses and the reduction under the new direction lasts for a fresh 18 months.[35] You are thus subject to the benefit penalty for longer than usual. For example, you may have already had your benefit reduced for seven months under the original direction for your first child, and although this ends early, you are penalised for a further 18 months under the new one after refusing to provide authorisation in respect of your new baby's absent parent.

When a benefit penalty ends early

Normally a reduced benefit direction lasts for 18 months. However, it will end earlier if you decide to provide the authorisation or information requested by the Child Support Agency.[36] It can also be terminated on review (see below).

The benefit penalty is also suspended or withdrawn where:

- you stop getting IS/FC/DWA. If you re-claim one of these benefits within 52 weeks, the benefit penalty is reinstated for the remainder of the 18-month period. You must be given 14 days notice of this. If your new claim is more than 52 weeks after you last received IS/FC/DWA the direction is no longer valid. However, the requirement to co-operate still applies and you will be asked to complete a maintenance application form. A new direction could be made, though it should only run for the balance of the 18 months which was not used up on the previous claim;[37]
- the child(ren) cease(s) to be eligible for maintenance because they are over 16 and have left non-advanced education, or are 19 or over. If they become eligible again (eg, because they return to full-time education) the penalty can be resumed;[38]
- you cease to live with and care for the child(ren). The benefit reduction can be reinstated if you resume your role as carer;[39]

- you go into hospital, a residential care or nursing home or a local authority residential home. Initially the direction is suspended, but if you stay there for more than 52 weeks it ceases completely;[40]
- your child(ren) (if in Scotland) or their absent parent successfully apply to the Child Support Agency for a maintenance assessment.[41]

Both you and the AO should be notified if a reduced benefit direction ceases and an explanation should be given as to why.[42]

A direction can also be cancelled if it was made in error, or not ended earlier due to an error (in this case the money will be repaid).[43]

Where a reduction under a second reduced benefit direction (see above) ends, the earlier direction may be resurrected if you have not co-operated in relation to that absent parent. In this case the reduction is for the balance of the 18-month period remaining, after taking account of how long your benefit has been reduced under both directions. If this period is 52 weeks or less, £4.57 a week is deducted. If longer, £9.14 a week is first deducted for the number of weeks remaining in excess of 52.[44]

Reviewing a reduced benefit direction

A reduced benefit direction must be reviewed if you, or someone on your behalf, provides additional reasons as to why:

- you failed to co-operate with the Child Support Agency;
- you are no longer obliged to co-operate;
- the child(ren)'s welfare is likely to be put in jeopardy by the continuing existence of a direction.[45]

The review is done by a child support officer (but not the one who made the direction). S/he may decide to end the direction from the date that the reasons were supplied. You should be given a full written decision and informed of your rights of appeal if the direction is not withdrawn.

Child support assessment procedure

This section gives an outline of the procedures that the Child Support Agency use to assess maintenance once you have given your authorisation. For full details of the scheme, see CPAG's *Child Support Handbook*.

Providing information

Unless you or your children would be at risk of harm or undue distress, as well as providing authorisation you must also provide information and evidence to help the Child Support Agency assess the amount of maintenance which must be paid.[46] You must provide any necessary information requested as soon as reasonably possible.[47] The first stage of providing the information is completion of the maintenance application form. The Child Support Agency request that this form be returned within 14 days. The information required includes details about yourself and your child(ren) which will enable the Agency to decide if you qualify for child maintenance, for example:[48]

- your names, address and whether you all normally live in the UK;
- your marital status and whether your child(ren) is married;
- the child(ren)'s full name, date of birth and details of any course of education s/he is doing;
- the full names of the child(ren)'s parents and your relationship to the child(ren);
- your income and that of your child(ren) (other than a child's earnings);
- whether you receive any disability benefits;
- your housing costs;
- details of your bank, building society or other accounts;
- evidence as to who has parental responsibility for the child(ren) (parental rights in Scotland) if more than one person cares for the child(ren);
- the time spent by the child(ren) with each carer where care is shared;
- whether any other people live in your home and, if so, your relationship to them.

The Child Support Agency also has the right to ask you for a lot of information about the absent parent and her/his new family (if s/he has one). The maintenance application form includes questions about:

- the absent parent's full name and any other name s/he is or was known by;
- the absent parent's date of birth or age;
- the absent parent's national insurance number;
- the absent parent's present or last known address and telephone number;
- the name, address and telephone number of the absent parent's employer, or business if self-employed;
- the absent parent's job title or department at work;
- whether the absent parent is unemployed and what benefits s/he may be claiming.

If you do not know the answer to any of these questions, just explain that. If you give as much information as you can, even if it is not enough to trace the absent parent, you have satisfied the requirement to co-operate and will not be subject to a benefit penalty.[49] If you return the application form incomplete and the Agency cannot trace the absent parent, you will probably be asked to attend an interview with the Child Support

Agency. At the interview you will be asked for the information you did not provide and may be asked for further information to help locate the absent parent – eg, about friends and family, other contacts s/he may have (such as a probation officer, an accountant), places s/he socialises, details of her/his car.[50] If you do not give the information to enable child maintenance to be pursued, you will be exempt from the requirement to co-operate if you or your child(ren) would be at risk of harm or undue distress (see p125).

You do not have to notify the Child Support Agency of every change of circumstances (unlike IS claimants who have to notify the Benefits Agency). However, you do have to let the Agency know if:[51]

• the absent parent or your child has died;
• you, the absent parent or the child(ren) are no longer living in the UK;
• you have been living with the absent parent for six months;
• you no longer provide care for the child(ren);
• you are no longer receiving child benefit for the child(ren) – eg, because s/he has left school.

The maintenance enquiry form

The Child Support Agency will send a maintenance enquiry form to the absent parent once you have supplied an address or the Agency manage to trace one. If you have indicated on the application form that the absent parent does not know of the existence of the child, and/or he is not registered on the birth certificate, he will be contacted first by the Agency to warn him that he has been named as the father.[52]

The maintenance enquiry form must be returned within 14 days.[53] If the absent parent fails to provide the required information, after a warning the Child Support Agency can impose a penalty assessment called an interim maintenance assessment (see the *Child Support Handbook*).[54]

The date the maintenance enquiry form is sent to the absent parent is the date at which liability to pay the assessment generally begins.[55] The assessment process is expected to take between six and 12 weeks and therefore arrears of child maintenance will have accrued by the time you are notified of the amount due.

Paternity disputes

If the man you have named as the father disputes paternity, you will be asked to attend an interview at the Child Support Agency office where very explicit and personal questions may be asked.[56] If the alleged absent parent continues to deny paternity, he may also be interviewed.[57] If the denials continue, you will be interviewed again and asked whether you would be prepared for you and your child(ren) to undertake DNA tests if the case was taken to court.[58] The Child Support Agency will decide whether or not to apply to court on your behalf for a declaration of parentage.[59] The maintenance assessment cannot continue until the question of paternity is resolved.[60]

The amount of child maintenance

The Child Support Agency use a complex and rigid formula to assess the amount that your ex-partner must pay towards the upkeep of your child(ren). It takes account of both the cost of bringing up the child(ren) and the needs of your ex-partner to maintain her/himself. A few absent parents on very low incomes are not required to pay any child(ren) maintenance.[61] For details of the formula, see the *Child Support Handbook*.

Once the calculation has been done you and the absent parent are told how much s/he has to pay and enforcement action can be taken if s/he fails to comply (see below).

Deductions from the absent parent's IS

Deductions of £2.30 a week can be made from an absent parent's IS as a contribution towards the maintenance of her/his child(ren).[62] This does not apply if the absent parent:[63]

- is aged under 18;
- qualifies for a family premium or has day-to-day care of any child;
- receives sickness or invalidity benefit, maternity allowance, statutory sick pay or maternity pay, severe disablement allowance, attendance allowance, disability living or working allowances, invalid care allowance, industrial disablement benefit, a war pension or a payment from either of the Independent Living Funds. If this benefit is not paid solely because of overlapping rules, or an inadequate contribution record, s/he is still exempt from deductions.

If you are an absent parent on IS and have children from two or more different relationships, only one deduction can be made and the £2.30 is apportioned between the parents who care for the child(ren).[64]

If you do not agree that deductions can be made from your IS, you can apply in writing to the Child Support Agency for a review. You should try to show that the decision was given in ignorance of relevant facts, was based on a mistake about the facts or was wrong in law. The case is then referred to a different child support officer, who must give you 14 days' notice of the review date and ask for any further reasons for disputing the decision. You can give these verbally or in writing. If you do not respond, the decision will be made on the available information. You then have the right of appeal to a child support appeal tribunal within 28 days (see below).[65] If you are on IS, decisions as to whether you have to pay £2.30 a week are reviewed by a child support officer annually, or sooner if your circumstances change. You can apply for the review yourself or the child support officer can initiate one.

If the absent parent is not exempt from the deductions, the Child Support Agency send a notification to the Benefits Agency. This request for deductions to be made is binding on the adjudication officer of the Benefits Agency, unless other deductions are being made from IS which take precedence (see p161). Deductions for child maintenance cannot be made from any benefit other than IS, unless unemployment benefit, sickness/invalidity benefit, severe disablement allowance or retirement pension are paid in the same girocheque or order book as IS. If you are an absent parent who is not exempt from the deductions but disagrees that the Benefits Agency can make the deductions because other deductions have a higher priority, you have a right of appeal to a social security appeal tribunal (see Chapter 8).

Reviews and appeals

Child Support Agency assessments are reviewed every year.[66] If there is a relevant change of circumstances in the meantime, you (the carer), the absent parent or the child support officer can initiate a review.[67] However, not all changes of circumstance are significant enough to trigger a new assessment (see the *Child Support Handbook* for details).[68]

Both original decisions and review decisions can be challenged by requesting a second-tier review, known as a section 18 review. Except when challenging a current assessment you should, unless unavoidable, request the section 18 review within 28 days of the child support officer's decision.[69]

If you disagree with a decision to give a reduced benefit direction or any decision on section 18 review, you can appeal to a child support appeal tribunal.[70] You must appeal within 28 days of the decision being sent to you.[71] Your appeal may be accepted late if you have special reasons.

The procedures at child support appeal tribunals are broadly the same as for social security appeal tribunals – see Chapter 8. For more detailed information about child support appeal tribunals refer to CPAG's *Child Support Handbook*.

Collection and enforcement

Payment of child maintenance can be made to you as the carer, to the Secretary of State or to a third party.[72] The Child Support Agency will stipulate the method and frequency of payments – eg, standing order, cheque, postal order, cash.[73]

Child maintenance can be paid to the Child Support Agency rather than direct to you as the carer, if the Secretary of State agrees.[74] If you want this to happen, ask the Child Support Agency. You can request this on the maintenance application form. This is useful where maintenance payments are likely to be irregular or unreliable or, where you do not want to be located by the other party. If the Child Support Agency is collecting the payments for you, enforcement action will begin automatically when a payment is missed. Where payment should be made direct to you, it is up to you to contact the Child Support Agency when a payment does not arrive.

If you as the carer are on IS and the child(ren)'s absent parent is making payments to the Child Support Agency, your child maintenance is paid in the same order book/giro cheque as your IS. The Child Support Agency retains the payments made by the absent parent. If the Agency does not receive your child maintenance payment, you can still cash the full amount as IS. This guarantee does not apply to FC/DWA claimants. Instead the maintenance payments actually made by the absent parent are passed on to you by the Child Support Agency.[75]

The Child Support Agency has considerable powers for enforcing child maintenance, including deductions from earnings, the use of bailiffs and, as a last resort, imprisonment. For details, see the *Child Support Handbook*.

4. THE EFFECT OF MAINTENANCE ON INCOME SUPPORT

Child support payments count in full when calculating IS. Other payments made by liable relatives (see p136) are treated as maintenance and are also taken into account when working out your benefit.

If you are entitled to payments under a court order you can either get regular periodical payments for yourself, or a lump sum to be paid in one go or by instalments. If you are receiving IS, it is not usually a good idea to have a lump sum instead of periodical payments because most lump sums are treated as income at a sufficiently high level to disqualify you from benefit altogether even if they are for amounts well below the usual capital limit of £8,000. However, some lump sums are treated as capital and are not affected by this rule.

If you are on FC/DWA, see p378.

Child support maintenance

All payments of child support maintenance are treated as income and are taken fully into account on a weekly basis.[76] Where payments are made monthly, multiply by 12 and divide by 52 to obtain a weekly amount. Where regular payments are made at intervals other than each week or month, the payments are spread over the period, including any part week. It is the actual payments made, and not the amount due under the Child Support Agency assessment, which are taken into account in this way.[77]

The Benefits Agency should not calculate IS on the assumption that maintenance payments due under the Child Support Agency assessment will be made where this has not been happening. For example, a parent who would be floated off IS if payments due under the assessment were made can continue to receive IS if the child maintenance is not received; the Child Support Agency should then take over the collection of the maintenance (see p134). If you are on IS and maintenance payments are not being made regularly, ask the Child Support Agency to collect the maintenance and the Benefits Agency to pay IS gross. There have been some delays in obtaining increased or reinstated IS. If this is a problem, ask an adviser to contact CPAG.

Arrears at the beginning of the child support assessment

There are always arrears accrued by the time the assessment is made. Usually these arrears will be paid to, and retained by, the Child Support Agency if you are on IS. However, if the payment is made to you, the IS which has been overpaid can be recovered by the Benefits Agency.[78]

Arrears due during a claim

The Child Support Agency is responsible for collecting arrears of child support maintenance if you are on IS. The Agency retains the amount of arrears equal to the overpayment of IS which has occurred because the maintenance was not paid on the due date.[79]

Arrears paid for a period before the claim

A payment due before the IS claim but paid late during the claim is treated as paid in the week in which it was due.[80] Therefore only child support both due for and received in the weeks of the claim can be taken into account by the Benefits Agency.

Periodical payments

The rules about treatment of periodical payments made by liable relatives do not cover payments of child support maintenance (see above).[81]

Periodical payments are:[82]

- any payment made, or due to be made, regularly whether voluntarily or under a court order or other formal agreement;
- any other small payment no higher than your weekly IS;
- any lump sum which is made instead of regular payments either as payment in advance or to cover arrears (but not including any arrears due before the beginning of your entitlement to IS).

All periodical payments are treated as income and are taken fully into account to reduce your IS except:[83]

- payments in kind (unless you or your partner is involved in a trade dispute);
- boarding school fees (but see p358);
- any payment to, or for, a child or young person who has left your household;
- payments made after the liable relative has died;
- any payments arising from disposing of property after divorce or separation (which would normally be capital – see below);
- payments made to someone else for the benefit of you or a member of your family (such as mortgage capital payments) provided that it is reasonable to ignore the payment and it is not used for food, ordinary clothing or footwear, fuel, your eligible rent (see p225), eligible council tax (see p311), or those housing costs that could be met through IS. It is well worth appealing in a case where a payment is not ignored on this ground because a tribunal may take a different view as to what is reasonable.

Periodical payments which are received on time are each spread over a period equal to the interval between them. Thus, monthly payments are spread over a month. They are multiplied by 12 and divided by 52 to produce a weekly income figure.[84]

Certain other amounts do not count as periodical payments, for example: money from a liable relative which has already been taken into account under a previous claim, or which has already been recovered out of overpaid IS; and amounts which have been used up before a decision is made (provided that the money has not been spent in order to increase or become entitled to IS).[85] See also, lump sums treated as capital, p139.

Arrears of periodical payments due during your claim

If payments are not received while you are claiming IS, they should not be treated as income. Then when a payment does arrive and it includes a lump sum for arrears (or in advance), the payment is spread over a period calculated by dividing it by the weekly amount of maintenance you should have received.[86]

Example

You should receive £80 a month. It is not paid for three months and then you receive £200.

£80 a month is treated as producing a weekly income of:

$$\frac{£80 \times 12}{52} = £18.45$$

The £200 is taken into account for:

$$\frac{200 \text{ weeks}}{18.45} = 10.85 \text{ weeks}$$

You are therefore assumed to have an income of £18.45 for the next ten weeks and six days. The maintenance payments due to you are still two weeks and one day in arrears (£40).

If a payment is specifically identified as being arrears for a particular period, it will, in practice, often be taken into account for a forward period from the week after you inform the Benefits Agency about it. However, it ought to be attributed to the past period which it was intended to cover, unless it is 'more practicable' to choose a later week.[87] In this case the Secretary of State can recover the full amount of extra benefit paid to you while maintenance was not being received.[88] (This can still be done when you receive a payment after your claim ends which is for arrears of maintenance that should have been paid while you were still claiming.) If the amount of benefit you were receiving then and are receiving now are both greater than the weekly amount of maintenance, it does not matter whether the adjudication officer spreads the payment over the period when payment should have been made or forwards from a date after the payment was received.

However, for some people it does make a difference and you should argue for the payment to be spread over whichever period is more advantageous to you. This will depend on the amount of IS you would otherwise receive, the amount of the payment and whether any other periodical payments are being made.

Example

You should have been receiving maintenance at the rate of £25 a week but eight weeks are missed and you have to claim IS at the rate of £15 a week to top-up your part-time earnings. You reduce the number of hours you are working and your entitlement to IS then increases to £30 a week. You then receive a payment of arrears of maintenance which includes £200 to make up the missing eight weeks from before your IS was increased. However, you do not receive any further maintenance payments.

If that payment were taken into account at the rate of £25 a week for eight weeks from the date it was made, you would lose all £200. However, if it were attributed to the period when the maintenance ought to have been paid in the first place, you would lose only £120 (£15 × 8) because that is all the benefit you were paid then. If you can pay £120 to the Benefits Agency, you have a very good argument that it is not 'more practicable' to spread the payment forwards rather than over the past period. You should appeal if it is not accepted.

On the other hand, if you started to receive regular maintenance payments from the date the arrears were received, you would be better off having the payment of arrears spread forwards. This is because the new maintenance payments would reduce your IS to £5 a week so that taking the arrears into account for eight weeks would cost you only £40 (£5 × 8).

Arrears of periodical payments due before your claim

If the arrears are for a period before your claim they are not treated as a periodical payment. Adjudication officers tend to treat the payment as a **lump sum** derived from a liable relative so that it is treated as income rather than capital except to the extent that you have already spent it. This means that it is spread over a future period (see below). You should argue that the regulations do not exclude arrears from the definition of periodical payments[89] just to have them brought back into the calculation as other liable relative payments. The regulations intend that they should be excluded from the liable relative provisions altogether and the payment is to be treated as capital (or as disregarded income if you are receiving current periodical payments). Any other interpretation is unfair and gives the Secretary of State an unwarranted windfall at your expense.[90] It is also contrary to the new rule for arrears of child support maintenance (see above).

Lump sums treated as capital

If you receive a lump sum from a liable relative which would, if it were capital, take your capital to no more than £8,000, it is better if it can be treated as capital rather than income. (If it is more than £8,000, you will not receive any benefit whether it is treated as capital or income, although you might be able to re-claim sooner if it were capital.)

However, only the following lump sums can be treated as capital:[91]

- any payment arising from a 'disposition of property' (see below) in consequence of your separation, divorce, etc;

- any gifts not exceeding £250 in any period of 52 weeks (and not so regular as to amount to periodical payments);
- any payment in kind (unless you or your partner is involved in a trade dispute – see p77);
- any payment made to someone else for the benefit of you or a member of your family (such as special tuition fees) which it is unreasonable to take into account – you can appeal to a tribunal who may take a different view from the adjudication officer about what is reasonable;
- any boarding school fees (but see p358);
- any payment to or for a child or young person who has left your household;
- any payment which you have used before the adjudication officer makes her/his decision provided that you did not use it for the purpose of gaining entitlement to IS – it should not be taken into account if you have used it to clear debts such as your solicitor's bill;
- any other payment if the liable relative is already making periodical payments equal to
  - your IS if the payments include payments for you;
  - your child's applicable amount and any family and lone parent premium if the payments are only for a child.

If the periodical payments stop or fall below that level, what is left of the lump sum is taken into account as income (see below).[92]

'Disposition of property'

It is vital to distinguish between payments arising from a disposition of property and those that are not. 'Property' is not confined to houses and land, but includes any asset such as the contents of your former home or a building society account. There is a 'disposition' when those contents are divided up or your former partner buys out your interest.[93] Therefore, any lump sum which is paid in settlement of a claim to a share in any property is treated as capital. It is only those lump sums which are paid instead of income which are liable to be treated as income.[94] It is important to take this into account in any negotiations with your former partner and you should make sure your solicitor knows about this rule.

It is best if any court order is drawn up so as to record that any lump sum is in settlement of a claim to an interest in property. However, this is not essential and the Benefits Agency should accept a letter from your solicitor explaining why a lump sum was asked for and agreed.

Note that the proceeds of sale of your former home may be disregarded altogether for a period of time (see p399). Other capital, such as the home itself and its contents, may also be disregarded (see p398). There is therefore an advantage, while you are on benefit, to ask for a greater share of the home and accept less in the way of capital or income which would be taken into account to reduce your benefit.

Lump sums treated as income

All other lump sums are treated as income and are spread over a period so as to disqualify you (or your child) from IS for as long as possible.

If you are not also receiving periodical payments, the lump sum is treated as producing a weekly income equal to:[95]

- if the lump sum is for you or for you and any children, your IS plus £2;
- if the lump sum is just for a child or children, the personal allowance for you and each child for whom you get maintenance, any disabled child premium, family premium or lone parent premium, and any carer's premium if it is paid because you are caring for a disabled child for whom you receive maintenance. However, if your IS entitlement plus £2 would be less than this amount (eg, because you had other income), the lower amount is used. This means that the lump sum disqualifies you from IS for a longer period.

If you are receiving periodical payments (see p136), the income is calculated as being the difference between the periodical payment and:[96]

- the amount of IS plus £2 which would be paid if you did not get the periodical payment when it is paid for you alone or you and your children;
- the child's personal allowance plus family premium and lone parent premium if the periodical payment is just for a child.

If the periodical payments are varied or stop, the calculation is done again taking the balance of the lump sum into account.[97]

The lump sum is treated as producing that weekly income for a period beginning on the first day of the benefit week in which the payment is received and lasting for a number of weeks calculated by dividing the amount of the payment by the weekly income. For example, if you receive a lump sum of £2,000 which the above rules treat as producing a weekly income of £50, your IS is reduced by £50 for 40 weeks. The period can start in a later week if that is more practical.[98]

If you are disqualified, and your circumstances change so that your entitlement to IS would be higher, or the benefit rates are altered, ask the Benefits Agency to recalculate the period of your disqualification using the new figures.

Arrears of periodical payments due before your claim are often treated as being a lump sum so as to disqualify you from benefit. However, you should argue that that is wrong (see p139).

CHAPTER SEVEN

Claims, reviews and getting paid

This chapter is about how income support (IS) is administered. It covers:

1. Claims (below)
2. Decisions and reviews (p147)
3. Payments of benefit (p151)
4. Overpayments and fraud (p161)
5. Complaints about administration (p168)

See Chapter 2 for who is entitled to claim. If you are in urgent financial need but your local Benefits Agency office is closed, see p8.

I. CLAIMS

DSS organisation

Law and policy on social security are made by government ministers and civil servants in the DSS but administration and decision-making has been delegated to the Benefits Agency. This Agency has offices up and down the country, called branch offices, where you can make a claim or discuss your case. Branch offices are grouped together and managed by a district office and for each group of districts there is a territory with its own director.

As a claimant you should only need to deal with your local branch office and this is where your claim should go. You can obtain leaflets and information and there are benefit advisers to give advice and help with claims, and who have access to your computerised records.

London claimants have their claims dealt with by social security centres set up to deal with work which does not require face-to-face contact with the public. There are three centres, in Glasgow, Belfast and Wigan. Although the benefit centres decide your claim, you should still use your branch office to make initial claims or if you have any queries about your claim. If you have to telephone such a centre, your call is charged at the local rate. Branch offices may have free numbers which you can use. If you have a national insurance number, it should speed up your query if you quote it.

How to make a claim

You need to have a national insurance number so that your claim can be computerised. If you do not have one you may experience some delay, because your claim is dealt with manually. You can get one by applying to the contributions agency. You need to provide evidence of your identity.

If you are a single person, a single parent or in a lesbian or gay couple, you claim on your own behalf. If you are counted as a couple (see p330) you must choose which one of you will claim for you both. If you cannot agree, the Secretary of State decides.[1] You can change which partner claims, provided the partner previously claiming is agreeable.[2] It can be worth swapping – eg, if it would entitle you to a disability premium (see p345), or if one partner is about to go abroad (see p25) or otherwise lose entitlement (eg, become a student), or, if one partner is exempt from signing on (see p22). But if you get transitional protection because you used to get supplementary benefit (see p43), you lose this if you swap.

The Secretary of State can authorise an 'appointee' to act on behalf of someone who cannot claim for themselves – eg, they are mentally ill or suffering from senile dementia.[3] If this happens, the appointee takes on all the responsibilities of the claimant. Normally this would only apply from the date the appointment is agreed, but if you act on someone's behalf before becoming their official appointee your actions can be validated in retrospect by your appointment.[4] You can become an appointee by applying in writing to the Benefits Agency. You must be over 18.

An executor under a will can also pursue an outstanding claim or appeal on behalf of the deceased claimant even if the decision was made before the formal grant of probate.[5]

The claim form

A claim for IS must be in writing and on the appropriate form,[6] which is obtainable, free of charge.[7] If you are unemployed get form B1 from the unemployment benefit office. All other claimants should get form SP1 (for pensioners) or A1 (other claimants) from their local Benefits Agency office, or by filling in the tear-off slip in leaflet IS1 available from your local post office. The form should tell you the address to which it must be sent, once completed.

If you just write a letter, or send in the wrong form, the Benefits Agency will send you an IS form. Similarly, if you do not fill in the IS form properly they will return it to you. If you get it back to them correctly filled in within a month, you count as having claimed on the date they got your first letter or form.[8] The Secretary of State can extend this one-month period if he thinks it reasonable[9] – eg, because you were ill.

If you want to change anything on your claim form you can usually do so at any time before they have made a decision on your claim.[10]

If you want to withdraw your claim, notify the office to which you sent it.[11]

Information to support your claim

If you have a mortgage, you are asked to fill in form MI12 and then give this to your lender, who adds in details about your mortgage and returns the form to the Benefits Agency. This gives the information needed to calculate your housing costs, namely:

- the amount of your original loan and the amount outstanding;
- the mortgage interest due;
- the purpose of the loan (ie, for house purchase, repairs etc).

Your lender is also required to notify the Benefits Agency of any changes to the outstanding amount or the interest payable during your claim.

You can be asked to supply any other 'certificates, documents, information or evidence' considered relevant to your claim or to an issue arising from your claim – eg, birth certificate, rent book, or bank statement.[12]

In some cases the Benefits Agency may refuse to accept evidence that you are who you say you are. Many travellers and Irish claimants find that the evidence they provide is simply not accepted as genuine – eg, there is suspicion about the validity of birth certificates. Asylum-seekers and black people may also face hostility and mistrust when claiming. Where, for example, you have had to use forged papers to flee from persecution, the Benefits Agency often assume that you are making a fraudulent claim. Sometimes evidence is required even though it is simply not available – ie, a national insurance number for someone newly arrived in the UK. Apart from the humiliation caused by such attitudes among Benefits Agency staff, unnecessary demands for extra evidence can cause delays in assessing entitlement. It is important to try to provide any evidence to support your claim. If you are asked to provide information which you do not have, ask why it is necessary and what other evidence would suffice. Press the Benefits Agency to be clear about what is required and why, and complain if you feel that any requests for information are unreasonable (see p169). You may also wish to approach your local community relations council if you feel that you are the victim of racial discrimination.

If you cannot or will not provide the information, the adjudication officer must go ahead and decide your claim within a reasonable length of time, on the basis of the details s/he already has;[13] if you think the Benefits Agency is delaying a decision unreasonably, see p148. If you are unable to provide information and the adjudication officer decides against you, you should appeal.

If you are one of a couple, the Benefits Agency can ask your partner to give written confirmation that s/he agrees to you making the claim and that the information you have given about her/him is true. This is usually done by your partner signing on the claim form where indicated.[14]

You may be on benefit for quite a long time, during which your circumstances may change. You must tell the benefit office, in writing, of any change which might affect the amount of, or right to, benefit. Keep a copy of the letter you send reporting such changes. The Benefits Agency can accept notification by some other method (ie, by telephone); but this is not always accepted so it is best to do it in writing.[15]

If you fail to report a change and, as a result, you receive too much benefit, the Benefits Agency may take steps to recover the overpayment (see p161) or even treat this as fraud (see p167).

The date of your claim

Your claim is usually treated as made on the day it reaches the Benefits Agency office.[16] This applies even if it is a day on which the office is closed.[17] (See p143 if your initial claim was incomplete or made on the wrong form.)

You can claim up to three months before you qualify,[18] thus giving the Benefits Agency time to ensure you receive benefit as soon as you are entitled. This can be useful if you know you are going to qualify – eg, you are due to come out of hospital or prison. Otherwise, you must usually claim on the first day you want benefit to start.[19] However, the Secretary of State can decide to accept a claim up to one month late.[20]

Your claim can be backdated if you can show that throughout the time between the date by which you should have claimed, and the date you actually claimed, you had 'good cause' for failing to claim.

The good cause must continue up to the date of claim. Although the odd day may be overlooked, a substantial break in the good cause for not claiming will result in only the later period counting.[21] Even if you show 'good cause', IS cannot be paid for more than 12 months before the date on which you actually claim.[22] You may be paid less than 12 months' arrears if your claim arose because of a new interpretation of the law[23] (see p151). If you want a claim to be backdated you must ask for this to happen – the Benefits Agency will not consider it unless you do.[24]

It has been held that **good cause** means 'some fact which, having regard to all the circumstances (including the claimant's state of health and the information which he had received and that which he might have obtained), would probably have caused a reasonable person of his age and experience to act (or fail to act) as the claimant did'.[25] So, there is a general duty to find out your rights, but your age and experience are taken into account in deciding whether you have acted 'reasonably'. If you claim late because you were ignorant of your rights, the first thing you need to explain is why.[26] You are expected to make enquiries by looking at the relevant Benefits Agency leaflets[27] or asking the Benefits Agency,[28] a solicitor[29] or a citizens advice bureau.[30] Relying solely upon the advice of friends,[31] or even a doctor,[32] is not enough.

If you *have* made enquiries, you will have good cause for a late claim if you were misinformed, or insufficiently informed of your rights or were accidentally misled.[33] The enquiries need not necessarily have been in connection with that particular claim, and people have succeeded in proving good cause where they have simply misunderstood the system. So, a person who had once made enquiries about the rights of the self-employed to unemployment benefit and who had thought that the answers applied equally to sickness benefit succeeded in showing 'good cause'.[34]

While language difficulties, illiteracy and unfamiliarity with technical documents do not in themselves amount to good cause for not claiming, they obviously increase the likelihood of confusion and are important matters to be taken into consideration.[35]

Ill-health, whether physical or mental, may also amount to good cause in other cases.[36]

If you have made no enquiries at all it is more difficult to show good cause. You must show that your ignorance was due to a mistaken belief *reasonably* held, so you must explain exactly how you came to be under the wrong impression.[37] The general rule is that you cannot be expected to claim something if you have no reason to suspect you have a right to claim it. You are likely to be excused ignorance of detailed changes in the law which give you new rights.[38]

If a person has been formally appointed by a court or the Secretary of State to act on your behalf, the question is whether the appointee has good cause for any late claim – not whether you have.[39] If someone is *informally* acting on your behalf, the question is whether you have good cause and you must show that the delegation of the claim was reasonable, and that reasonable supervision was exercised.[40]

If you are prevented from receiving benefit because your claim was more than 12 months late due to an error on the part of the Benefits Agency, you should try to persuade the Benefits Agency to meet its moral obligation and make an *ex gratia* payment to you, as compensation (see pp154-5). To do this, simply write to your Benefits Agency office and ask. The intervention of an MP or the Ombudsman (see p169) may help in these circumstances.

2. DECISIONS AND REVIEWS

Who decides your claim

It is important to know who makes the decision on any particular question in your claim because that determines how you challenge the decision.

Most decisions are made by an adjudication officer at the Benefits Agency office where you claimed IS.[41] Some questions may be referred to an adjudication officer at the unemployment benefit office. For example:

• whether you are involved in a trade dispute (see p77);
• whether it was your fault you lost your last job or left a training course (see p58);
• whether you are available for and/or actively seeking work (see p48);
• whether you have refused a suitable offer of a job without good reason (see p55).

An adjudication officer at the child benefit centre may advise:

• whether you are in full-time non-advanced education (see p17).

While an adjudication officer elsewhere is being consulted on your case, it counts as decided against you in the meantime.[42]

Some decisions are made by the **Secretary of State** rather than an adjudication officer. These are:

• whether to accept a claim made other than on the approved form;
• whether a claim for one benefit can be treated instead of, or in addition to, a claim for another benefit;
• whether to demand recovery of an overpayment, and the amount of weekly deductions (subject to the maximum, see p166);
• the suspension of benefit pending determination of a question on review or appeal;
• whether IS should be awarded to a 16- or 17-year-old on grounds of severe hardship;
• whether a person living in a residential care or nursing home should receive a higher allowance to prevent hardship;
• whether to take action against persons liable to maintain, including

those responsible for maintaining a person under the Immigration Act
1971;
- appointment of appointees;
- who should be the claimant when a couple are unable to decide;
- issue and replacement of giros and order books and how IS should be
paid;
- whether to pay an interim payment;
- whether a school or college is a 'recognised educational establishment';
- circumstances in which a claim is to be treated as withdrawn;
- how often you have to sign on.

You should be notified in writing of the decision on your claim unless the
decision is to pay you in cash, or your benefit is being stopped and it is
reasonable not to give you a written decision.[43] Sometimes the decision is
unclear or difficult to understand. To get an explanation, write to the
appropriate office within three months of that decision.[44] If you appeal
(see Chapter 8) the papers you receive will give the full background to
the decision made by the adjudication officer.

You should automatically receive a letter showing how your benefit
has been worked out.[45] You can ask for a more detailed breakdown.
Check the details on this form.

Delays

It is very unlikely that you will get an immediate decision on your claim
because the facts need to be checked and your benefit calculated.

An adjudication officer should decide a claim for IS within 14 days 'so
far as practicable'.[46] Your claim should be passed on to an adjudication
officer as soon as the basic information required to decide it is available
(which could well be as soon as your claim form containing the necessary
information reaches the Benefits Agency).[47]

If you have been waiting more than 14 days for a decision contact the
benefit office. First, check that your claim has been received. If it has not,
let the office have a copy of your claim or fill out a new form and refer
them to the claim form you sent in earlier.

If your claim has been received but not dealt with, ask for an explanation. If you are not satisfied with the explanation for the delay, make a
complaint (see p169). All Benefits Agency offices have a *Customer
Charter* which sets out the time limits for dealing with claims and you
can refer to this. The national *Customer Charter* has a target clearance
time of five working days, which sets a minimum standard for all local
offices.

In addition to taking the steps already described, you should ask the office to make interim payments to you while you wait for the decision (see p152). You may also be able to obtain a crisis loan (see p449).

Reviews

An adjudication officer can review a decision of an adjudication officer, social security appeal tribunal (SSAT), or Social Security Commissioner. Following the review, the decision may be revised either to increase or decrease the amount of your IS. You can ask for a review (in writing to your local Benefits Agency) or the adjudication officer may decide that one is necessary. A review can be done at any time, even if it is several years since the decision was made.

A decision may only be reviewed if:[48]

- **There was a mistake about the facts of your case or it was made in ignorance of relevant facts.** If a decision is reviewed on this ground, any revision takes effect from the beginning of the period covered by the original decision. If it is in your favour, you receive arrears. If not you may have been overpaid and the adjudication officer decides whether or not it can be recovered (see p161).
- The original decision was made by an adjudication officer (not a tribunal or commissioner) and was wrong in law.
- **Your circumstances have changed since the original decision** or it is anticipated that they will do so. If a decision is reviewed on this ground it takes effect from the first day of the week in which it occurs if you are paid in arrears, or the week following the change if you are paid in advance (unless the change occurs on the first day of your benefit week in which case it is that day).[49] An amendment to the law counts as a change of circumstances, but a decision of a court or commissioner that the law has been wrongly interpreted does not.[50] Some situations never count as a change of circumstance: staying in temporary accommodation for seven days or less while on an employment course; the repayment of a student loan, and your absence from a nursing or residential care home for less than a week.[51]

An adjudication officer may review your benefit but still not change the decision. Alternatively, s/he may decide that there are no grounds for a review. In either case, you can appeal against the decision, but in the latter you must show why there are grounds for review as well as giving your reasons for disputing the decision. On appeal the tribunal must identify which decision is to be reviewed, establish whether there are grounds for review and from what date, and then check if the limitations on backdating restrict the arrears which can be paid (see pp150-51).[52]

Although on appeal the tribunal is usually considering whether the adjudication officer had grounds to review a decision, it is possible for them to review a decision themselves if new facts come to light during the hearing of which the adjudication officer is unaware but which give grounds for review.[53] It is not necessary for them to adjourn the hearing and refer the matter back to the adjudication officer, though they may choose to do this instead.

A review can be a quicker and simpler way of getting a decision changed than an appeal. It can also be a way of getting round the three-month time limit for appeals.

If the adjudication officer agrees to change the decision, you can usually get arrears of benefit going back a year before the date of your request for a review, or if you did not request a review, from the date the review took place.[54] It is important to make it clear that you want payment for the past period.

You can get more than a year's backdating if[55] the ground for review was ignorance of, or mistake about the facts and you can show that the decision is being revised because:

- there is specific evidence which was before the adjudication officer (or SSAT) who originally decided the claim, but which they failed to take into account even though it was relevant. You should argue that this applies even if the evidence does not conclusively prove your entitlement. So long as it raised a strong possibility that you were entitled to (more) benefit, it should have been taken into account;[56]
- there is documentary or other written evidence of your entitlement which the DSS, DHSS or Department of Employment had, but failed to give to the adjudication officer (SSAT or commissioner), at the time of the earlier decision;
- new evidence has come to light which did not exist earlier and could not have been obtained. This will only apply if you provide this evidence as soon as possible after it is available to you.

If the ground for review was that the decision was wrong in law you can get more than 12 months' backdating if:

- the adjudication officer overlooked or misinterpreted part of an Act, Order, regulation or decision of a commissioner or court when deciding your claim.

If you are trying to get arrears going back several years, it may be difficult to identify the grounds for review, particularly where the Benefits Agency has destroyed old papers relating to your claim, which they do from time to time. The onus is on you to show that your claim should be reviewed and you cannot simply rely on the Benefits Agency's lack of evidence.[57]

You may get less than a year's backdating if your entitlement is reviewed following a new interpretation of the law by a Social Security Commissioner or court. In this case you only get arrears back to the date of the decision by the commissioner or court.[58] The only way to avoid this restriction is to apply for a late appeal rather than a review (see p171).

If you were underpaid benefit because of a clear error by the DSS/Benefits Agency you could apply for compensation as well as getting arrears owed to you (see p154).

3. PAYMENTS OF BENEFIT

How and when you should be paid

The Secretary of State decides how benefit is paid to you.[59] You are paid either by giro or benefit order book, but you can ask to have your IS paid directly into a bank or building society account.[60] It may be possible to be paid cash in certain circumstances.[61] If your IS includes mortgage costs these are paid direct to your lender rather than to you after the first 16 weeks or, if you are 60 or over and entitled to full mortgage interest during the first 16 weeks, from the start of your claim. Housing costs are paid direct if your lender is a member of the direct payments scheme (see p156).

Once you have been awarded benefit you must cash it within a year of it being due.[62] This period can be extended if you can show good cause for the delay.[63] However, a giro or order is only valid for three months – if you do not cash it within this period you will have to try to get a replacement.

If you are entitled to less than 10 pence a week you are not paid IS at all, unless you are receiving another social security benefit which IS can be paid with. If you have just returned to work after a trade dispute, the same rule applies if your IS entitlement is less than £5.[64] If you are entitled to less than £1 a week the Secretary of State can decide to pay you quarterly in arrears.[65] If your IS includes a fraction of a penny it is rounded-up to a full penny if it is more than a half penny. Otherwise the fraction is ignored.[66]

The date your payments start depends upon whether you are to be paid in advance or in arrears.

You are paid in advance if you are:[67]

- receiving retirement pension; *or*
- over pension age (60 for a woman, 65 for a man) *and* not receiving unemployment or sickness benefit, invalidity pension or severe dis-

ablement allowance nor involved in a trade dispute (unless you were receiving IS immediately before the dispute began); *or*
- receiving widows' benefits (but only if you are not required to sign on, nor signing on voluntarily nor providing or required to provide medical evidence of incapacity for work); *or*
- returning to work after a trade dispute.

If you are paid in advance, your entitlement begins on the first pay day of any other social security benefit to which you are entitled (or would be entitled if you had sufficient contributions) following the date of your claim for IS. For example, retirement pension is paid on a Monday. If you claim IS on a Wednesday you are entitled to IS in advance from the following Monday. But if you claim on a Monday you get it from that day.

You are paid in arrears, if you are not in one of the above groups.[68] Your entitlement to IS starts from the date of your claim.[69]

Once your entitlement has been worked out, the Secretary of State decides how often and on which day of the week you are paid[70] unless you are entitled to unemployment benefit; sickness benefit; invalidity pension; severe disablement allowance; retirement pension; or widows' benefits. If you are entitled to one of these (or would be if you satisfied the contribution conditions), you are paid IS on the same day of the week as that other benefit and at the same intervals.[71] This means that if you are unemployed and signing on you are paid fortnightly in arrears. When you first claim, you therefore have to wait two weeks before you get your first payment of IS. You may have to wait longer if you receive certain payments at the end of a job (see p366). You may be able to get a crisis loan if you would suffer severe hardship before your first payment of IS is due (see p449).

Giros should be cashed within one month, or three months if in an order book.

Interim payments

If payment of your IS is delayed you may be in urgent need of money. If this is the case, you can ask for what are known as 'interim payments'.

An interim payment can be made where it seems that you are or may be entitled to IS and where:[72]

- you have claimed IS but not in the correct way (eg, you have filled in the wrong form, or filled in the right form incorrectly or incompletely) and you cannot put in a correct claim immediately (eg, because the Benefits Agency office is closed); *or*
- you have claimed IS correctly, but it is not possible for the claim or for a review or appeal which relates to it to be dealt with immediately; *or*

- you have been awarded benefit, but it is not possible to pay you immediately other than by means of an interim payment.

Whether to award an interim payment is a Secretary of State's decision and therefore cannot be appealed to a tribunal though it may be possible to apply for judicial review (see p182). If you are refused an interim payment contact your MP and see Chapter 23 for whether you can get a crisis loan.

You could also try using the emergency service (see p8). An interim payment can be deducted from any later payment of IS and if it is more than your actual entitlement, the overpayment can be recovered.[73]

You should be notified of this in advance, unless the payment is made because you have not received child support maintenance when any overpayment is recovered from the arrears of maintenance rather than your benefit.

Suspension of payments

The Secretary of State can order that your IS be suspended if:[74]

- **A question has arisen about your entitlement to benefit:** In this case, all or part of what is due to you is suspended pending a decision on a review or appeal concerning your entitlement. For example, if you are being paid IS but it is thought that you are in full-time work, your benefit may be suspended while information is gathered about the true situation.
- **It looks as though your IS award should be revised.**
- **You are awarded benefit on appeal but the Benefits Agency wants to appeal against that decision:** If this happens, your award can only be suspended for a month while they consider an appeal to the Social Security Commissioner, or three months for other appeals, after the adjudication officer receives the decision unless the Benefits Agency decides to seek leave to appeal, in which case you will have to wait until the case is resolved.
- **You are due to be paid arrears of a benefit but you may have been overpaid some benefit yourself:** Your arrears may be withheld in whole or in part while the possible overpayment is investigated.
- **The Benefits Agency is appealing (or considering an appeal) to the courts about someone else's claim,** and the issue under appeal affects your claim. Your benefit can be suspended in whole or in part until the appeal is decided, or the time limit for appealing has expired.

The decision to suspend benefit is made by the Secretary of State and you cannot therefore appeal against it to a tribunal. You must negotiate to get your benefit reinstated and/or request an interim payment. You may be able to persuade the Secretary of State that suspension is unreasonable, particularly if hardship is caused.

Lost and missing payments

If you lose a benefit giro or order book after you have received it, report the loss immediately to the benefit office by telephone or by a personal visit and confirm the loss in writing, requesting a replacement at the same time. If your giro is lost or stolen before you have had a chance to cash it, the Secretary of State has a duty to replace it. This applies even if the giro is subsequently cashed by someone else.[75] You should also report the matter to the police, and note the investigating officer's name and number.

If you have lost your order book, the benefit office issues you with a replacement, but will probably want to make some enquiries to see how many payments had been cashed and how many were left.

If the benefit office refuses to issue a replacement, or takes too long considering your request, you can take legal action to get the benefit due to you. You cannot appeal to a tribunal if a payment goes missing, but you can sue the Secretary of State in the county court.[76] This can take time, so you may wish to claim a crisis loan to tide you over (see p449).

Before taking legal action, you should write to the local Benefits Agency requesting them to replace the giro within a reasonable time – eg, seven days. Explain that court action will be taken if they do not respond. Keep a copy of the letter.

If the Benefits Agency does not replace your giro, you need to begin proceedings in the local county court. The forms to do this are available from the county court. Complete these and return them to the court. You have to pay a court fee, calculated as a percentage of your unpaid giro. The fee is refundable if you win. The Benefits Agency is allowed time to respond to your summons, but you will almost certainly find that the local Benefits Agency office will replace your giro without the need to proceed to a court hearing. Your court fee is repaid separately by the Benefits Agency Solicitors (see Appendix 1 for address), and you should not withdraw the summons until you have received both a replacement giro, and your court fee.

Compensation payments

In line with the *Citizens' Charter* and the Benefits Agency's own *Customer Charter*, you should expect prompt and accurate service from staff dealing with your claim. If you are dissatisfied with the way your claim has been administered you can seek compensation.

Official errors

Sometimes the Benefits Agency makes mistakes about the amount of your benefit. Where possible they correct the mistake by carrying out a review and awarding you the correct benefit (see p149).

If the procedure for review does not apply or does not properly compensate you for the effects of the mistake that has occurred, you may claim a compensatory payment. This is called an **extra-statutory payment** because it is made outside the normal benefit rules. Another name for it is an *ex gratia* or 'concessionary' payment. You should ask for a payment equal to the money you have lost, but you could also ask for additional amounts to cover interest on arrears and to compensate you for any hardship suffered owing to the mistake. Payments are discretionary, so you should stress the Benefits Agency error and the fact that you have suffered as a consequence of official negligence, in order to ensure payment. If your loss was as a clear result of incorrect advice or negligence on the part of the Benefits Agency, you may be able to bring a court action for damages. You will need the help of an advice agency or solicitor to do this.

Delays

Benefits Agency offices have target times for dealing with claims, but they are not always able to meet these. If there is a long delay in assessing your entitlement, you are entitled to compensation if:[77]

- the delay was solely due to Benefits Agency error; *and*
- the underpayment was more than £50; *and*
- the delay in payment was more than six months after the end of the target time set.

You are not automatically awarded compensation. You must write to your local Benefits Agency office and ask. If you do not get a sympathetic response you could ask your MP to write on your behalf, or to take up your case with the Social Security Minister.

Payments to other people

Payment is usually made direct to you but there are some circumstances in which payments can be made to other people or organisations on your behalf.

- If you are unable to manage your own money, your benefit is paid to a person appointed to act on your behalf (see p143).[78]
- If it is in the interests of you, your partner or your children, the Secretary of State can pay your benefit to someone else.[79] For example, if you are neglecting your children even though benefit is being paid for them, it might be paid to another person to help look after them

(eg, a grandparent or other relative). If your partner is refusing to support you, all or part of her/his benefit can be paid to you.

Mortgage direct payments

If your IS includes an amount for mortgage interest, this is paid to you for the 16 weeks during which you are only allowed half of your interest payments (see p34), and you should pay your mortgage as usual.

Once you receive full eligible interest (minus any non-dependant deductions or restrictions – see pp38 and 40), payment of this part of your benefit is normally sent direct to your lender for each complete week that you are on benefit.[80] The only exceptions to this are where your lender is not covered by, or has opted out of, the mortgage payments scheme.[81] The Benefits Agency should tell you if this applies and you must continue to pay your own mortgage.

Payments to cover your mortgage interest are made to your lender by deducting your housing costs from your total IS entitlement and giving you the balance. If you get unemployment benefit, sickness benefit, invalidity benefit, severe disablement allowance or retirement pension paid on the same giro/order book as your IS, deductions can be made from these benefits too. If you do not have enough benefit to meet the full cost, all but 10 pence of your benefit is paid over and you must pay the rest yourself.[82]

Payments are made four-weekly in arrears[83] even if your payments are due on a calendar month basis, so you may appear to be in arrears even though your full mortgage is being met. This should not be a problem as your lender has agreed to this method of payment.

If you have more than one type of housing cost (eg, mortgage interest and service charges), or more than one mortgage, deductions for non-dependants (see p38) or excessive housing costs (see p40) are apportioned using the formula described on p160.

Payments are also reduced where you have a mortgage protection policy which meets your mortgage interest.

If you are in mortgage arrears an extra £2.30 a week can be deducted from your benefit and paid over to your lender, but this does not apply where the arrears arose during the 16-week period when you only received half of your mortgage interest. If you have more than one loan, and both or all are in arrears, £2.30 is paid over for each but only a total of £6.90 can be deducted altogether for arrears, so a lower amount is paid if you have more than three loans.

Other direct deductions

Amounts can also be deducted from your IS for other housing costs, fuel, water charges, the recovery of social fund loans (see p455), council tax arrears, community charge arrears, child maintenance, fines (see p159) and overpayments (see p166).[84]

Deductions are made at the Benefits Agency office before you receive your regular benefit payment, so you have less money to live on while they are being made. If you want to have deductions made to help you clear any arrears or debts you owe, ask at the Benefits Agency office dealing with your IS claim. If you disagree with a decision about deductions, you can appeal (see p170).

When can direct deductions be made?[85]

- **Rent arrears[86] (and any inclusive water, fuel and service charges):** If you are on IS you should be getting regular housing benefit to help pay any rent. If you are in debt with your rent while on benefit, an amount for arrears can be deducted from your IS and paid direct to your landlord.

  'Rent arrears' do not include non-dependant deductions.[87] However, deductions can cover any water charges or service charges payable with your rent and not covered by housing benefit.[88] Fuel charges cannot be covered by direct deductions if they change more than twice a year.[89]

  To qualify for direct deductions for rent arrears you must owe the equivalent of four times your full weekly rent.[90] Deductions are made if it is in the 'overriding interests' of your family to do so – eg, where you are threatened with eviction if you do not pay and you have not paid your full rent for a period of less than eight weeks.[91] If you have not paid your full rent for more than eight weeks, direct deductions can be made automatically if your landlord asks the Benefits Agency to make them.[92] Once your arrears are paid off, direct payments can continue to be met for any fuel and water charges inclusive in your rent.[93]

- **Housing costs:**[94] Mortgage payments are usually paid direct to your lender (see p156). If this applies to you (or would if your lender had not opted out of the scheme) then the deductions under this provision will only cover payments for other types of housing costs.[95] If your current IS includes money for housing costs (see p29) and you are in debt for these costs (excluding payments for a tent, but including other loans to buy your house[96]), direct deductions can be made from your benefit both to clear the debt and to meet current payments. Deductions are made if it would be 'in the interests' of you or your family to do so – eg, where you would face repossession proceedings or the prospect of even higher interest.

In the case of mortgage payments, you must have paid less than eight weeks' worth of full payments in the last 12 weeks. For other housing costs, you can only qualify for direct deductions if you owe more than half of the annual total of the relevant housing cost. Even these conditions can be waived if it is in the 'overriding interests' of you or your family that deductions start as soon as possible – eg, repossession is imminent.[97]

The amount of mortgage taken into account is the amount after deductions for non-dependants and restrictions for high housing costs (see pp38 and 40).

- **Residential accommodation charges:**[98] If you receive IS, the amount you are paid may cover charges for your accommodation if you live in a residential care or nursing home, or local authority residential accommodation.

  These charges can be met by direct deductions from your benefit if you have failed to budget for the charges from your benefit and it is in your own interests that deductions should be made. If you are in a home run by a voluntary organisation for alcoholics or drug addicts, direct payments can be made even if these conditions do not apply.[99]

- **Water charges:**[100] Your weekly IS is assumed to include money to pay any water charges you have to pay. If you get into debt with water charges direct deductions might be made – 'debt' includes any recon- nection charges. 'Water charges' means charges for water and sewer- age.[101] If you pay your landlord for water with your rent, deductions are made under the arrangements for rent arrears (see above).[102]

  Deductions can be made if you owe at least half the annual water charges. If you have a water meter, the Benefits Agency must estimate your annual charge and then decide if your arrears add up to at least half of this amount. If you owe less, it must be in the interests of your family to make deductions.[103] If you get into debt with water charges you should consider making an agreement for direct deductions because the water authority can cut off your water supply if you do not meet your debts and current charges. If you are in debt to two water companies you can only have a deduction for arrears made to one of them at a time. Your debts for water charges should be cleared before your debts for sewerage costs, but the amount paid for current consumption can include both water and sewerage charges.[104]

- **Fuel debts:**[105] Your weekly IS is supposed to cover gas and electricity bills. If you are in debt, an amount can be deducted from your benefit each week and paid over to the fuel board in instalments – usually once a quarter. In return, the fuel board will agree not to disconnect you. Deductions can be made where[106] the amount you owe is more than £45.70 (including reconnection charges if you have been disconnected); *and* you continue to need the fuel supply; *and* it is in your interest to have deductions – known as 'fuel direct'.

The amount deducted for current consumption is whatever is necessary to meet your current weekly fuel costs. This is adjusted if the cost increases or decreases and deductions for current payments can be continued after the debt has been cleared.[107]

- **Council tax and community charge arrears:**[108] Deductions can be made from IS if the local authority gets a liability order from a magistrates' court (in Scotland, a summary warrant or decree from a sheriff's court) and applies to the Benefits Agency for recovery to be made in this way. For community charge purposes, if they want to recover arrears from both partners in a couple the order must be against both of them. Deductions can be made for arrears, recoverable overpayments and any unpaid costs or penalties imposed. Deductions cannot be made for council tax arrears while community charge deductions are being made.

- **Hostel payments:**[109] If you (or your partner) live in a hostel *and* you have claimed housing benefit (HB) to meet your accommodation costs *and* your payments to the hostel cover fuel, meals, water charges, laundry and/or cleaning of your room, part of your benefit can be paid direct to the hostel. You do not have to be in arrears for this to apply. These costs are all items which cannot be covered by HB (see p226) and which you must meet from your IS. Fuel costs are not paid direct if the charge varies according to actual consumption, unless the charge is altered less than three times a year.

- **Fines, costs and compensation orders:**[110] Magistrates' courts (any court in Scotland) can apply to the Benefits Agency for a fine, costs or compensation order to be deducted from your IS. If an application is made the adjudication officer has to check that you have enough IS to meet the cost and whether direct deductions are being made for other items. The total deductions cannot exceed £6.90 and deductions for fines cannot be made if they add up to more than this. This is also the case if you would be left with less than 10 pence IS. You should be notified about the decision to make deductions. Only one court application can be dealt with at a time – if a second application is made it is not dealt with until the first debt is paid.

  Deductions can only be made if you are over 18, on IS, and you have defaulted on payments. Payments continue until the debt is paid off, or your IS ceases or is too low to cover the repayments.

- **Maintenance for children:** Where you do not live with your child(ren) deductions can be made from your benefit and paid over to the person who cares for them. For details of when this applies, see p133.

How much can be deducted?

Deductions are made to pay off the debt, or current weekly costs or both. The amount that can be deducted for **rent arrears** is £2.30 a week.[111] For **housing costs** covered by IS it is £2.30 a week for arrears plus the current weekly cost. If you have more than one debt for housing costs covered by IS they can only deduct for three of them at any one time (ie, three lots of £2.30).[112] If your housing costs are not met in full because of a restriction (see p40) or a non-dependant deduction (see p38) the direct payment to meet current weekly costs is reduced as follows: Multiply the amount of the restriction and/or deduction by the amount of the item of housing costs to be paid direct and then divide by the amount of total housing costs. This ensures that such reductions are shared proportionately between different items of housing costs.[113]

For **fuel arrears** they deduct £2.30 a week, for each fuel debt plus an estimated amount for current consumption. But they cannot deduct more than £4.60 altogether for arrears.[114]

The deduction for **community charge arrears** is £2.30 for a single person or £3.60 for a couple.[115] If a couple separate, the lower deduction normally applies. The deduction for **council tax arrears** is £2.30.

For **water charges** the deduction is £2.30 for arrears plus an amount for current costs. If you pay by meter this is estimated. Where the estimate proves to be too high or too low it should be adjusted over a period of 26 weeks (or a longer period if this is more reasonable). If a debt is paid off, deductions for current charges can continue.[116] £2.30 is deducted as a contribution towards **maintenance** and **fines**.

If you have debts for several items, the total deducted for all your arrears (excluding community charge arrears), cannot be more than £6.90 a week (plus current liabilities).[117]

In the case of fuel, rent arrears, water charges and direct payments for mortgage interest arrears (see p156), if the combined cost of deductions for arrears and current consumption is more than 25 per cent of your total applicable amount (excluding any amount for housing costs), the deductions cannot be made without your consent.[118]

The deduction made to meet **accommodation charges** in a residential care or nursing home is your IS accommodation allowance (see p97) but no amount for arrears.[119] If you are in a private or voluntary home and getting ordinary IS plus a residential allowance, all of your IS can be paid direct to meet your accommodation costs, except for £13.10 for your personal expenses (and any extra payment for meals which are not included in the charge). For **hostel charges**, the local authority should have assessed how much of your accommodation charge covers these costs when assessing your HB and this is the amount which is deducted from your benefit and paid direct. If the HB section have not yet decided the amounts, the Benefits Agency must estimate the cost.[120]

Deductions are made from your IS and from any unemployment, sickness, invalidity benefit, retirement pension or severe disablement allowance paid with it in the same giro or order book.[121] You must be left with at least 10 pence. Council tax and community charge arrears can be deducted from IS only.[122]

Priority between debts

If you have more debts or charges than can be met within the limits for direct deductions, they are paid in the following order of priority:[123]

1st   mortgage interest payments
2nd   other IS housing costs
3rd   rent arrears (and related charges)
4th   fuel charges
5th   water charges
6th   council tax and community charge arrears
7th   unpaid fines, costs and compensation orders
8th   payments for maintenance of children

If you owe both gas and electricity, the Benefits Agency chooses which one to pay first, depending on your circumstances. If you have been over-paid benefit or given a social fund loan, you may have to repay by having deductions from your IS.[124] You should argue that these deductions should take a lower priority. If you have arrears for both council tax and community charge, only one application can be dealt with at a time and the earliest debt should be dealt with first.[125]

4. OVERPAYMENTS AND FRAUD

Overpayments

Duplication

Sometimes you receive too much IS because money which is owing to you does not arrive on time. For example, if you claim child benefit but it is not paid for several weeks, your IS continues at the full rate while you are not actually receiving child benefit. However, if child benefit had been promptly paid, your IS would have been reduced (see p376).

When you get your arrears, you must repay the IS which you would not have received if the other income had been paid on time. The rule applies to all types of income which affect the amount of your IS, including other social security benefits and to arrears of child support maintenance for the period from your application to the date it is assessed by the Child Support Agency. It also applies to benefits paid by other EU states.[126] You always have to pay the money back, even though it was not your fault that the income was paid late.[127] This rule can in theory apply even where the income is paid late to someone else. But the Benefits Agency has issued internal guidance, following a commissioners' decision[128] that you should not have to repay severe disability premium where arrears of invalid care allowance have been paid to your carer.

Mortgage interest paid direct to a lender

Any overpayment of mortgage interest which is paid direct to your lender (see p156) must be sent back to the Benefits Agency by that lender if it arose because:

- there was a reduction in the amount of your outstanding loan or the mortgage interest rate, and your IS entitlement therefore reduced but the Benefits Agency did not adjust your mortgage direct payments; *or*
- you ceased to be entitled to IS, but only if the Benefits Agency asks for repayment within four weeks of you going off benefit.

In the former case your mortgage account should simply be corrected but where you come off IS and interest is recovered you will be in arrears unless you have started to make payments yourself.

In all other circumstances the Benefits Agency must recover from you as the claimant under the rules described below.

Other overpayments

For all other overpayments, repayment can only be required if you have misrepresented or failed to disclose a material fact and too much benefit has been paid as a result[129] (but see p167). You may have to repay even if you innocently misrepresented your situation or you failed to tell the local office certain facts because you did not understand how the benefit scheme works.

If you have been (or are being) overpaid, your benefit entitlement is reviewed.[130] If the adjudication officer does not conduct a proper review before asking you to repay any money, the decision that you have been overpaid is invalid and you can avoid having to repay.[131] However, it is likely that your entitlement will then be reviewed and benefit may be recoverable (see p163). Pending this review, some or all of your current benefit can be suspended (see p153).

Even if they decide you have been overpaid, and the duplication of payment rules do not apply, you will not have to repay if you told the Benefits Agency all about your circumstances, and the overpayment was due to their error. However, the Benefits Agency may argue that it can recover using common law (see p167).

If you do not agree that you owe the Benefits Agency money, you can appeal (see p170). Do not pay back any of the money until your appeal has been decided, as they may keep any money you voluntarily repay, even if you later win your case![132]

There are three questions to consider when deciding whether you have to repay benefit and, if so, how much. For all three of the following questions, the burden of proving the case lies with the adjudication officer.

(a) Did you misrepresent or fail to disclose a material fact?

The first thing to check is whether you have been accused of misrepresenting your circumstances or of failing to disclose a material fact. **Misrepresentation** can be completely innocent.[133] Thus, if you misrepresent your circumstances because you yourself were unaware of the true situation, it still counts – eg, where you did not know that your partner's earnings had changed. You would not be guilty of misrepresentation if you add the phrase 'not to my knowledge' to your statement.[134] It is what you do or say on your current claim that is important. If you have declared a fact on a previous claim but inadvertently give incorrect information on a later claim, you have to repay. The Benefits Agency are not required to check back for you.[135] However, if what you say on your claim form is obviously incorrect and the adjudication officer does not check this out, the overpayment will be due to DSS error not your misrepresentation. For example, if you say you pay ground rent, and are a freeholder, the adjudication officer should recognise that this must be incorrect and check before paying.[136] **Failure to disclose** is different. You cannot be said to have failed to disclose a fact you did not know about (because, for example, of your mental incapacity). Also, it must be reasonable to have expected you to notify the office of the particular facts. It is irrelevant that you did not personally realise the need to tell the Benefits Agency these facts; the test is whether a reasonable person would have realised that disclosure was required.[137] So if you were told that such facts were not relevant you could say it was not reasonable for you to disclose them.

You cannot assume that changes in your social security benefits, paid by one section of the Benefits Agency, are known to the other sections. You should give the IS section any information which might affect your IS.[138]

It is not necessary for you to show that you told the office in writing about your situation. It will do just as well if you give the information over the telephone, or in an office interview, either verbally or by presenting the relevant documents.[139] If you filled in a form while giving information, a tribunal should look at what you said in the form, but also consider whether you gave the necessary information in another way.[140] A claimant who fails to fill in a form correctly, but who gives the relevant information in the wrong place, has disclosed the material facts.[141]

If there is no record of a verbal statement a claimant only has a case to answer once the adjudication officer has shown, 'on the balance of probabilities', that there would be a record of the conversation at the local office if it had taken place. In order to do this, the adjudication officer must give a tribunal information on:[142]

- the instructions which should have applied for recording and attaching information to the claimant's file;
- whether there were the appropriate administrative arrangements to enable these instructions to be carried out;
- to what extent *in practice* these instructions are, or are not, carried out.

Where there is no record of what happened, other than the claimant's own statement, the Benefits Agency will be unable to prove that there has been a recoverable overpayment.[143] However, an admission by you that you did not tell the Benefits Agency relevant facts may be used as grounds for saying there has been an overpayment, even if there is no other evidence. You need not report a change direct to the Benefits Agency if you give the information in another way which might reasonably be expected to reach the relevant local office – eg, you tell the pensions section and ask them to inform the IS section too. However, if a claimant realises or should have realised that the information has not reached the IS section, s/he is under an obligation to take further steps to inform them.[144] Some time, if only a short time, may elapse before you can reasonably be expected to realise that the original information has not been acted on.[145] You could argue that the unemployment benefit office acts as 'agent' for the Benefits Agency in connection with IS for the unemployed. This would mean that information disclosed to the unemployment benefit office counts as though it had been disclosed to the Benefits Agency.[146] However, it is not good enough if the information is given to the unemployment benefit office in the course of a different transaction.

Which test applies?

Usually the distinction between misrepresentation and failure to disclose is clear; the former arises where you write or say something which is incorrect, and the latter is where you simply do not inform the Benefits Agency at all. Most overpayments arise due to a failure to disclose and it is easier to challenge such a decision than to show that you did not misrepresent. Because of this the Benefits Agency has in recent months begun to rely on general statements which you have signed to argue that a failure to disclose can also be a misrepresentation. For example, when you cash a giro or order you sign a declaration that you have correctly reported any facts which could affect the amount of payment. If you have actually failed to disclose a particular payment, you can be held to have thus misrepresented your circumstances and be liable to repay any overpayment.[147] This practice has been accepted as lawful by the Court of Appeal, CPAG is trying to take a further appeal on this point.

(b) Did an overpayment result?

Even if you admit that there is information you failed to give the Benefits Agency or that you did misrepresent your circumstances, you can still argue that this was not the cause of the overpayment. However, if it was a contributory factor you have to repay. If the Benefits Agency have been given the correct information to decide your claim by someone else, but fail to act upon it, you could argue that any overpayment did not arise because of your failure.[148]

(c) How much is repayable?

It is always worth checking how the overpayment has been calculated as you may be asked to repay too much by mistake. Do not be afraid to ask the office for more information if you need it.

The amount of the overpayment is the difference between what was paid and what should have been paid.[149] The Benefits Agency works out the latter using the information that you originally gave the office, plus any facts which you misrepresented or did not declare.[150] If you discover you have also been underpaid for a past period, you cannot offset this against the overpayment if additional facts are needed to prove the underpayment.[151] However, if your claim contained enough information to alert the adjudication officer to a potential need, and s/he did not investigate this fully, you can argue that an offset should be made. It does not matter if the overpayment was for a different period, so long as there was sufficient information to alert the adjudication officer to your need for extra benefit.[152]

If other facts come to light which suggest that you have also been underpaid you can ask the Benefits Agency to review your claim. They could then withhold any arrears owed to you to reduce the overpayment.[153]

If you were overpaid because you had too much capital, the overpayment is calculated taking account of the fact that, had you received no benefit, you would have had to use your capital to meet everyday expenses. For each 13-week period, the Benefits Agency assumes that your capital is reduced by the amount of overpaid benefit.[154] This is known as the 'diminishing capital rule'.

Recovery of overpayments

If an overpayment must be repaid, it can be done through deductions from[155] any national insurance benefit, family credit (FC), disability working allowance or IS.

No deduction for other benefit overpayments can be made from guardian's allowance, child benefit, housing benefit, or council tax benefit. An overpayment of one of these benefits can be recovered from future payments of the same benefit.

If the overpayment is due to late payment of another social security benefit, the Benefits Agency normally deducts any overpaid IS from the arrears owing to you.[156] However, if they omit to do so you must still repay even if you have spent the money (see pp161-2).

Other overpayments can also be recovered from arrears you are owed, except arrears where benefit has previously been suspended.[157]

When it comes to your current weekly benefit, the following are the maximum amounts which can be deducted:[158]

- £9.10 if you have admitted fraud or been found guilty of fraud; *or*
- £6.90 in any other case.

If you have any earnings or income subject to the £5 or £15 disregard, the deduction may be increased by half this amount.[159] Remember, the above are maximum amounts. The Benefits Agency might be persuaded to deduct less, especially if you have other direct deductions made from your benefit. As long as a couple are married or living together as husband and wife (see p330), the amount of overpaid benefit can be recovered from either partner's IS or FC.[160]

If a claimant has died by the time the overpayment is discovered, the money can be recovered from the estate.[161]

It is important to note that a tribunal cannot 'write off' part of the overpayment even if there are mitigating circumstances. It can only decide if it is recoverable and, if so, how much is repayable. In a case where you acted in all innocence and hardship is likely to be caused, the best tactic is to apply to the Secretary of State who has the discretion to decide whether or not to recover the overpayment. You can do this by writing to the local office where an adjudication officer makes a decision on behalf of the Secretary of State. It is sometimes more effective to write direct to the Secretary of State at the House of Commons. Although he does not deal with your case personally, it can ensure that local staff take your case seriously if they are asked to investigate by the Secretary of State himself. In either case you may wish to involve your MP.

Recovery using common law

In the drive to recoup money lost through overpayments the Benefits

Agency are increasingly using other powers to get money back. If an overpayment made to you is not recoverable under the social security rules described above, the Benefits Agency may try to recover under the common law. In such cases the Benefits Agency claims that there is no appeal right as this is not an adjudication officer's decision. There is some doubt about the validity of this action given that there is a clear legal code for social security which defines when payments are and are not recoverable. Nevertheless, court action is commonly threatened and has been pursued in at least one case. If this happens to you, argue that there is no power to recover and contact a local advice agency for help in challenging the decision.

Fraud

Sometimes overpayments of benefit are caused by deliberate fraud rather than error or oversight on your part. There is a lot of concern currently among government ministers and DSS officials about fraudulent benefit claims. As a result, a lot of resources are being put into fraud investigations and the number of prosecutions has risen.

Fraud involves a deliberate intention to obtain benefit to which you are not entitled. Thus if you work and continue to claim IS without telling the Benefits Agency, or deliberately fail to let them know that you have extra money coming in which reduces your right to benefit, you are guilty of fraud. Other cases are less clear cut: for example, you may be suspected of living with someone as husband and wife and fail to declare this. However, this may not be because of any fraudulent intent, but rather because you are not sure how the relationship will develop and whether it will last in the longer term. You may not even have realised that you had to claim as a couple rather than as separate individuals in such situations (see p330). Nevertheless, your claim could come under scrutiny by a fraud officer and any irregularities will be checked out.

The definition of fraud and the way in which it is investigated is broadly the same for all means-tested benefits, and a fuller explanation of this and what to do if you are under investigation can be found on p284. The footnotes to that section contain IS references where these differ.

Your benefit can be suspended while your claim is being investigated (see p153). However, you cannot have your benefit withdrawn solely because of fraud; only if the investigation reveals that you are no longer entitled. If your benefit is suspended, you should push for a decision to be made as speedily as possible, or for your benefit to be reinstated while the investigation is completed, if this is likely to take some time.

If your benefit is stopped, you can do three things:

- **Make a fresh claim for benefit.** Benefit should be paid regardless of what the situation was in the past, if the local office is satisfied your circumstances are now different. If you were suspected of full-time working while on IS, you should be prepared to sign a statement saying you are not working full-time at present.

- **Appeal to a tribunal** (see p169) against any alleged overpayment. If you dispute that you have claimed fraudulently, you should argue that there has been no overpayment. If you accept that you have been overpaid, you can still check the calculation of the overpayment – adjudication officers often forget the normal rules about earnings disregards, etc, when calculating the figure. It is best to appeal before any criminal proceedings have been decided.
- **Apply for a social fund payment** (see p449, Crisis loans) **or an interim payment** (see p152).

Being under suspicion of fraud is very distressing and it can be difficult re-establishing your entitlement once your claim is under investigation. Fraud officers often take your papers away from the section which normally deals with your claim and it can sometimes be difficult to find out what is happening or to persuade other Benefits Agency staff to reinstate payments. Remember that a fraud officer cannot make a decision on your entitlement. S/he can only provide the adjudication officer with evidence that you are no longer entitled. If a fraud officer tries to make you give up your order book or persuade you not to claim, you should insist on a proper decision from an adjudication officer. Never withdraw your claim unless you know you are not entitled.

Some claimants have found the attitude and behaviour of fraud officers to be intimidating. While such officers are clearly required to check any irregularities on your claim, they should not threaten you or force you to do or say anything with which you do not agree. If you feel you are under undue pressure, you should ask for the interview to be terminated and complain about the manner of the investigation.

Although a fraud investigator cannot make a decision on your claim, s/he can decide whether or not to prosecute you. See p286 for further details. Remember that you can be required to repay any overpayment as well as being prosecuted.

5. COMPLAINTS ABOUT ADMINISTRATION

The procedures for appeal and review allow you to challenge decisions about your benefit (including the refusal of benefit). If you simply want to make a complaint about the way in which your benefit claim was handled there are other procedures you can follow. The things you might want to complain about could include:

- delay in dealing with your claim;
- poor administration in the benefit office (eg, they keep losing your papers, or you can never get through on the telephone);
- the behaviour of members of staff. Most benefit staff do a good job and try to be helpful, but you should certainly complain about staff rudeness or any sexist or racist remarks.

You should check your local office *Customer Charter* which sets out the standards and level of service which you can expect. The Benefits Agency produces a form (BAL1 'Have your say') which explains your rights and contains a form which you can use to explain your complaint.

Complaining to the Benefits Agency

As a first step contact the supervisor or assistant manager. Alternatively, you can contact the customer services manager for your branch office. S/he will investigate your complaint and should respond to your complaint within seven days. If this does not solve the problem you should write to the manager of your district office with details of the complaint. (Keep a copy of your letter.)

Complaining to your MP

If you are not satisfied with the reply from the officers to whom you have written, the next step is to take up the matter with your MP.

Most MPs have 'surgeries' in their areas where they meet constituents to discuss problems. You can get the details from your local library or citizens advice bureau. You can either go to the surgery or write to them with details of your complaint.

Your MP will probably want to write to the benefit authorities for an explanation about what has happened. If you or they are not satisfied with the reply, the next stage is to complain to the Ombudsman, via your MP.

The Parliamentary Commissioner for Administration (commonly called the 'Ombudsman' – see Appendix 1) investigates complaints made by MPs against government departments. The Ombudsman's office will send you a leaflet providing further information. Many of the complaints are about benefits. If s/he investigates your case, your MP will be sent a full report. If the Ombudsman finds you were badly treated, s/he will recommend an apology and possibly compensation.

CHAPTER EIGHT

Appeals

This chapter explains what you can do if you disagree with the Benefits Agency decision on your IS claim. It covers:

1. Social security appeal tribunals (below)
2. How to prepare an appeal (p175)
3. Appealing to the Social Security Commissioner (p178)
4. Appealing to the courts (p181)

1. SOCIAL SECURITY APPEAL TRIBUNALS

When you can appeal

You can appeal to an independent social security appeal tribunal (SSAT) against any decision taken by an adjudication officer. Decisions made by the Secretary of State cannot be appealed (see p147); thus, if you are awarded IS but do not receive payments, you cannot appeal but must go to court to seek payment.[1] If you wish to challenge a decision taken by the Secretary of State, write to the manager of the local office asking for it to be looked at again. You could also ask your MP to intervene. The only legal remedy available to you is to apply to the High Court for judicial review (see p182).

Sometimes, benefit is refused on the grounds that you have not provided all the information required to decide your claim (see p144). If correct, this argument would prevent you from having the right to appeal. But an adjudication officer must make a decision on every claim, even those where, having allowed a reasonable amount of time, the information demanded by the Benefits Agency has not been provided.[2] It is then up to the tribunal to decide whether the decision is correct.

How to appeal

Before challenging a decision, it is useful to know why it was decided against you. You have a right to a written statement of reasons if you apply for it within three months of being given the decision in writing.[3]

In practice, you need to ask for this as soon as possible because you only have three months from the date of the adjudication officer's original decision in which to appeal. On receiving the statement of reasons, you may decide it is worth asking for a review of the decision rather than appealing straightaway (see p149).

You appeal by writing to the adjudication officer explaining which decision you wish to appeal against and giving the reasons why. The appeal letter must arrive within three months beginning with the date the written decision was sent to you.[4] If your appeal is late you should explain why. The chairperson of the appeal tribunal can accept a late appeal for 'special reasons'[5] – eg, if the adjudication officer delayed sending you the reasons for her/his original decision, or where sickness or a domestic crisis prevented you from making your appeal. Postal delays may be accepted, so long as you are diligent in checking that your appeal has been received where you do not get any response.[6]

You cannot appeal against the refusal of the chairperson to hear a late appeal,[7] but you can ask the chairperson to look at the decision again or you may be able to apply to the High Court for judicial review (see p182).

Your appeal letter must give some reason why you wish to appeal. It is helpful if you provide references to the law. If you do not have access to these, put in your appeal and provide more details after you have taken further advice. Refer the tribunal to the law and any commissioners' decisions which apply to your case. This *Handbook* explains the legal rules – see p176 for where to find the relevant law.

Include any evidence you can produce to support your case. Are there any documents it would be useful to show the tribunal? Are there any witnesses who could give helpful information? All correspondence with the Benefits Agency which is relevant to your appeal should be considered by a tribunal.[8]

Your appeal letter appears in the documents which go before the appeal tribunal, along with a submission from the adjudication officer. The tribunal members receive these documents beforehand so they will have some idea of your arguments.

If you want the tribunal to hear your appeal quickly, make this plain in your letter, explaining why. You could also telephone the clerk at the Independent Tribunal Service office (see Appendix 1 for address) to check they have received your letter and to ask her/him to deal with the matter quickly.

If you change your mind you can withdraw your appeal. You can only do this with the written consent of the adjudication officer. Once the appeal tribunal hearing has begun, you can withdraw the appeal only with the consent of the chairperson and provided the tribunal has not yet made a decision.[9] Once an appeal has been withdrawn it cannot be reinstated, but if you decide that you want to go ahead after all, you could make a late appeal against the original decision.[10]

The tribunal hearing

After your appeal is received at the local office, you should receive an acknowledgement from the clerk of the Independent Tribunal Service (together with information about appeals and how to find someone to represent you if required). It can take several months before the appeal is actually heard. During this period, the local office is supposed to look again at the decision to see if it ought to be revised.

Consider asking your local advice centre or citizens advice bureau to help you prepare your appeal. They may be able to send someone to represent you at the hearing. If you take someone with you to a tribunal your chances of winning are much higher. You can take a friend, relative, adviser or representative with you[11] – you can have more than one person if the chairperson of the tribunal agrees.[12]

The Benefits Agency have to prepare a detailed explanation of the reasons for their decision on your claim and this is sent to you on a form called an AT2. It comes with a form (AT6) advising you to let the tribunal know whether you still wish to continue with your appeal, and if so, when you can attend a hearing. Once you have replied, a hearing date is set. It is very important to reply – if you do not do so within 14 days your appeal is cancelled. You should be notified if this is to happen and you can ask for your appeal to be reinstated but it is best to avoid this happening by replying promptly to the letter sent to you.

You have to be given at least ten days' notice of the hearing. If not, the tribunal can only go ahead if you agree.[13] Make sure that you return the form to say whether you will be attending. If the hearing date is inconvenient or you want more time to prepare your case, you can ask for it to be put off until a later date. Telephone the clerk's office as soon as you decide that you want a postponement and confirm the request by letter the same day. If you do not attend and have not asked for a postponement, the tribunal can hear the case without you, and you are less likely to succeed. However, they should not go ahead if you have advised them that you cannot attend and have asked for another hearing date, especially if you have a good reason for not attending.[14]

Along with the letter telling you the date of the hearing, there will be a copy of the papers which have been sent to the tribunal members. Read these papers carefully, and check for any mistakes.

Hearings before a social security appeal tribunal are in public unless you request a private hearing, or the chairperson thinks it should be in private. In practice, it is extremely rare for members of the public to turn up. However, the rule does mean that you could sit in on the case before your own, or see what tribunals are like before you actually represent someone.[15]

The tribunal members

A tribunal usually consists of three people. There is a chairperson, who is a lawyer, and two 'wing members', who sit on either side of the chairperson. They are supposed to be people who have knowledge or experience of conditions in your area, and who are representative of people living or working there. Wherever possible, at least one member of the tribunal should be the same sex as the claimant.[16] Tribunals can sit with only one wing member, but only if you agree. In this case, the chairperson has the casting vote.[17] The chairperson has to record the tribunal's decision, and write down its findings on the relevant facts of the case and the grounds for its decision. If the decision is not unanimous, s/he has to note the reasons why a tribunal member disagreed with the decision.[18]

The standards of tribunals are the responsibility of the President of the Independent Tribunal Service. The President is in charge of training, monitoring and ensuring that tribunals have all the materials they need. He issues regular practice notes to guide tribunals on how they should conduct themselves.[19] The President is helped by six regional chairpersons and eight full-time chairpersons, all appointed by the Lord Chancellor and all of whom are legally qualified. There is also a President of Appeal Tribunals in Northern Ireland. If you have a complaint about a tribunal member, or the way a hearing was conducted, write to your regional chairperson or the President (see Appendix 1 for the addresses).

Other people present at the hearing

The clerk to the tribunal is there in an administrative capacity. S/he meets you when you arrive and pays your expenses. You, your representative, an interpreter if needed and any witnesses may be able to get travel expenses paid. You can also claim for meals, loss of earnings and childcare costs.[20] S/he also takes you into the tribunal room when they are ready to hear your case. The clerk should not express any views on the case.

The presenting officer represents the adjudication officer. S/he explains the reasons for the decision you are appealing about. Her/his role is to help the tribunal make a decision by giving information about your claim. S/he is not there to defend the Benefits Agency's decision at all costs and may sometimes provide information which helps your case.

Procedure at the hearing

When the tribunal is ready to hear your case, you are taken into their room with the presenting officer.

The three members of the tribunal sit on one side of a large table. The clerk sits either at one end or at a separate table to one side. You are shown where to sit. Usually you and the presenting officer both sit directly opposite the tribunal.

There are no strict rules of procedure. Usually the chairperson starts by introducing the members of the tribunal and everyone else who is present. The presenting officer then summarises the adjudication officer's written submission and you are asked to explain your reasons for disagreeing with it. Alternatively, you may be asked to explain your position first. You can call any witnesses and can ask questions of the presenting officer, and the tribunal members ask questions of you both.

Your case may be adjourned unfinished to be heard on another day because, for instance, more evidence is required. Failure to adjourn to allow you to get relevant evidence is an error of law and you can appeal to the commissioner to get the decision overturned (see p178).[21] A tribunal should not adjourn where there is a test case pending which deals with the same issues as your appeal unless the case is likely to be heard within the next few weeks.[22]

If your case is adjourned the new tribunal must rehear your case from the beginning unless it has the same three members as before or you agree to it being heard by two members of the previous tribunal without the third.[23]

The tribunal decision

Usually you are told of the tribunal's decision at the hearing and you may be given a note confirming whether you have won or lost your case (form AT3A). The full written notice of the decision is sent to you later by the clerk. It is on a standard form (AT3) and should include relevant findings of fact and reasons for the tribunal's decision.[24]

If you have won, the Benefits Agency ought to carry out the tribunal's decision straightaway. They can do this on the basis of the AT3A rather than waiting for the full decision. However, they have three months in which to appeal against the tribunal's decision to a Social Security Commissioner. If considering an appeal, you will not be paid for a month while they decide what to do. If they decide to appeal, you will not be paid until the commissioner hears the case. If you are left without any money meanwhile, you might be able to apply for an interim payment (see p152), or get a crisis loan (see p449).

A tribunal decision can be overturned in a number of ways: it can be reviewed in the normal way (see p149) *except* where the tribunal made a mistake about the law in which case you must **appeal to the Social Security Commissioners** (see p178). It may be quicker to apply to the chairperson of the tribunal to have the decision 'set aside'. This is appropriate where:[25]

- you or your representative did not receive the appeal papers, or did not receive them in sufficient time before the hearing; *or*
- you or your representative were not present at the hearing; *or*
- 'the interests of justice so require'. This applies where there has been a procedural irregularity.[26] A failure to produce sufficient evidence at the hearing is not a 'procedural irregularity'.

An adjudication officer may also ask for a decision to be set aside. 'Setting aside' means cancelling the decision and hearing the case again. You must apply within three months of the decision being sent to you. A late application is only accepted if there are special reasons. Applications are normally decided without a hearing, so make sure you give a full explanation of your reasons when you apply.[27]

If a decision is wrongly set aside, any subsequent rehearing is invalid. The second tribunal could thus refuse to rehear the case if there was an obvious mistake in allowing a previous decision to be set aside. However, normally it would be appropriate to refer this question to a commissioner so that s/he can decide whether the later tribunal has jurisdiction to hear the case.[28]

If the written decision contains an accidental error this can be corrected by the tribunal.[29]

2. HOW TO PREPARE AN APPEAL

Your case may concern a dispute about the **facts** or the **law**, or both. Always try, if possible, to link the facts of your case and your arguments to the rules laid down in the benefit regulations.

Sorting out the facts

The tribunal has to decide your appeal on the evidence given by you and the Benefits Agency. Check through the appeal papers carefully to work out where there are disagreements between you. This will help you decide what evidence you need to win your case. Evidence consists of what you (and any witnesses) actually say at the hearing and any documents which you produce to support your case. Written evidence would include letters of support, medical reports, wage slips, bank statements, birth certificates and anything else which helps to prove the facts. If, for example, the Benefits Agency say that you failed to disclose an increase in your earnings and you have been overpaid, you could explain to the tribunal how and when you told them, but you may also be able to produce a copy of the letter which you sent informing them of the change.

Proving your case with additional evidence is useful but not essential. A tribunal cannot dismiss your verbal evidence without a proper explanation of why it has done so.[30]

The presenting officer puts the adjudication officer's case at the tribunal but is not always the person who actually made the decision in your case. The presenting officer's submissions are not evidence,[31] nor are comments made by another adjudication officer if s/he did not decide your claim.[32] The presenting officer can report what other people have said. This is called hearsay evidence. Tribunals can accept hearsay evidence but they should carefully weigh up its value as proof, given that the person who originally made the statement is not present at the hearing. Most evidence relied on by adjudication officers is written and you can point out that you have not had the opportunity of cross-examining the witnesses. You are not entitled to insist on the presence of any par_ticular witness,[33] but you should argue that the tribunal should not place any weight on the written evidence of, say, an interviewing officer if you are disputing the interview.

Both you and the Benefits Agency can ask witnesses to come and give information to support your case. Chairpersons do have the power to refuse to hear witnesses who are not relevant, but they should always be fair to claimants and generally allow witnesses to speak, even if it looks as if they may have nothing useful to say.[34]

When presenting your case to the tribunal, it is therefore important to correct any mistakes in the appeal papers and bring up new facts or arguments which the adjudication officer did not know about when s/he took the original decision. There may be facts which have arisen since the officer's decision, which you consider relevant. Present the true facts as clearly as you can and use any written evidence or witnesses to back up what you are saying.

A tribunal hearing is a complete rehearing of your case, so fresh facts and arguments can be put by either side.[35] You or the presenting officer can also ask for an adjournment if you think you need time to prepare your response to the new evidence, or arguments. It is up to the tribunal whether to grant an adjournment or not.[36]

Checking the law

The adjudication officer often gets the law wrong so it is worth checking the benefit rules to see if they have been incorrectly applied in your case. This *Handbook* explains what the law says and also gives you the legal references if you want to look them up for yourself. The adjudication officer will also have quoted certain parts of the law which support their decision and you should check these. It is quite common for the adjudication officer to quote a large number of commissioners' decisions, but these are not always of direct relevance to your appeal so check them carefully.

The law consists of Acts of Parliament and regulations. You can ask to see the law concerning income support, disability working allowance and family credit at the local Benefits Agency office. It should be available for public inspection at all reasonable hours and without payment.[37] Benefit laws are collected together in a large looseleaf book called the *Law Relating to Social Security*. It is in several volumes and is known as the 'Blue Book'. It is kept up-to-date with regular supplements. You can look at a copy of the 'Blue Book' at your nearest major library as well as at the Benefits Agency. Most of the law you need is contained in *CPAG's Income Related Benefits: The Legislation* edited by John Mesher and Penny Wood. As well as giving the law it gives explanations of what each bit means and tells you about relevant case law (see below). Tribunal members have this textbook.

Law relating to benefit is complicated and the staff who administer benefits are issued with guidance manuals. The *Adjudication Officers' Guide* covers benefits administered by the Benefits Agency. It is written by the Chief Adjudication Officer who is responsible for advising local adjudication officers about the law.[38] The Chief Adjudication Officer also issues regular circulars to staff.

This manual is only guidance and not law but sometimes provides information which may help clarify any difficulty you have with the benefit office. The adjudicating authorities are bound by the regulations but not by the guidance.

Case law is made by the **Social Security Commissioners** who are part of the appeal system (see p178).[39] Rulings they make about the meaning of benefit law are binding and must be applied in similar cases by adjudication officers and tribunals. The most important commissioners' decisions are published by HMSO and are called 'reported decisions'. They are prefixed by the letter 'R'. Thus, R(IS) 1/90 was the first commissioner's decision on IS to be reported in 1990. IS decisions are reported as R(IS) and family credit as R(FC). Sometimes you will be referred to supplementary benefit decisions which are R(SB), and to decisions on other benefits. Only the most important decisions are reported. Decisions which are not reported are prefixed by the letter 'C', and the year is written out in full – for example, CIS/13/1989. They are available for £1 each from the Office of the Social Security Commissioners (see Appendix 1 for the address).

This *Handbook* gives references to commissioners' decisions and you can keep up-to-date with the latest commissioners' decisions by reading

CPAG's bi-monthly *Welfare Rights Bulletin*. The main library in your area may have copies of reported commissioners' decisions or you can ask to see them at any Benefits Agency office.

Always check the decisions referred to by the adjudication officer to see if they really go against you. Then see if you can find others which help your case. If you want to refer to an unreported commissioner's decision, it is best to circulate it to the SSAT and Benefits Agency in advance. If this is not possible take enough copies for them, to the hearing. Sometimes commissioners' decisions conflict. If so, the tribunal must follow a reported decision in preference to an unreported one, and a Tribunal of Commissioners' decision to that of a single commissioner.[40] If there is a decision on the same point by the High Court on judicial review, the Court of Appeal or the House of Lords, it must be followed in preference to a commissioner's decision.

3. APPEALING TO THE SOCIAL SECURITY COMMISSIONER

Both you and the Benefits Agency have a further right of appeal to a Social Security Commissioner, but only if the tribunal has made an error of law.[41]

The Social Security Commissioners are lawyers with at least ten years' experience. Their offices are in London for England and Wales; Edinburgh for Scotland; and Belfast for Northern Ireland (see Appendix 1 for addresses). Their job is to interpret the law. The decisions they make must be followed by adjudication officers and tribunals in all future cases.

An error of law

There is an error of law if:[42]

- the tribunal got the law wrong – eg, it misunderstood the particular benefit regulation concerned;
- there is no evidence to support the tribunal's decision;
- the facts found by the tribunal are such that, had it acted reasonably, and interpreted the law correctly, it could not have made the decision it did. This argument would be used where the facts are inconsistent with the decision – eg, a tribunal finds that a man and a woman live in separate households, but decides they are living together as husband and wife;
- there is a breach of the rules of natural justice. This is where the procedure followed by the tribunal leads to unfairness (eg, you are not

allowed to call witnesses to support you or the tribunal refuses a post-ponement, even though you cannot attend for a good reason and have told it so), and the result is that you lost without having a chance to put your case properly;

- the tribunal does not give proper findings of fact or provide adequate reasons for its decision. This is a very common fault of tribunals. The tribunal must not simply announce its conclusion. It must put down sufficient reasons so that you can see why, on the evidence, it reached the conclusion it did.

How to appeal

You must first obtain leave to appeal.[43] This means that you have to show that there has *possibly* been an error of law and that you have the beginnings of a case.

If you wish to appeal, you should first apply to the chairperson of the tribunal.[44] You may do this orally at the end of the hearing when you are told the decision, or by writing to the clerk of the tribunal at the regional office within three months of being sent the decision of the tribunal. The chairperson is usually the one who heard your case originally.[45]

If the chairperson refuses leave to appeal, you may make a fresh application for leave to appeal direct to a commissioner within 42 days of being sent the decision refusing you leave. This period begins on the day after the date on the notification that leave has been refused by the tribunal chairperson.[46]

If you miss the time limit, you may still apply for leave to appeal but any application must be made direct to a commissioner who will give you leave only if there are 'special reasons' for the delay.[47] Delays by the post office (but not other courier firms) in delivering your appeal can be disregarded, so long as your application was prepaid and properly addressed.

Once you have been given leave to appeal, you have six weeks in which to send in notice of the appeal itself.[48] You are sent a form on which to do this. The time may, again, be extended for 'special reasons'. You may have been told that your notice of application for leave has been treated as a notice of appeal, in which case you do not have to send in another.[49]

The written procedure

All cases are taken over by adjudication officers at the Office of the Chief Adjudication Officer (see Appendix 1 for the address). A bundle of documents is prepared by that office and is sent to the commissioners' office who add it to any submissions from you. The commissioners' office then sends copies of the bundle to each party.

You are given 30 days in which to reply to the submission of the adjudication officer, although the commissioner may extend the time limit. There is a right of reply, if required, within 30 days.[50] If you have nothing to add and do not want to reply at any stage, tell the commissioners' office. A commissioner has the power to strike out an appeal that appears to have been abandoned, although you can apply for it to be reinstated.[51]

When the commissioner has all the written submissions, s/he decides whether or not there should be an oral hearing of the appeal. If you ask for an oral hearing, the commissioner will hold one unless s/he feels that the case can properly be dealt with without one.[52] It is not usual for a commissioner to refuse a claimant's request for an oral hearing unless s/he is going to decide the case in the claimant's favour. Occasionally, the commissioner decides to hold an oral hearing even if you have not asked for one.

If there is no oral hearing, the commissioner reaches a decision on the basis of written submissions and other documents.

Because of the length of time you have to wait before your case is dealt with, you should consider making a fresh claim for benefit.

The hearing

If there is an oral hearing, it will be at the commissioners' offices in London, Edinburgh or Belfast, or at the law courts in Cardiff, Leeds or Liverpool. You are told the date in good time and your fares are paid in advance if you want to attend. At least half a day is set aside for each case.

Usually, one commissioner hears your case but, if there is a 'question of law of special difficulty', the hearing may be before a tribunal of three commissioners.[53] The procedure is still the same.

The hearing is more formal than those before social security appeal tribunals but the commissioner will let you say everything you want. Commissioners usually intervene a lot and ask questions so you need to be prepared to argue your case without your script. A full set of commissioners' decisions and the 'Blue Books' (see p177) are available for your use. The adjudication officer is usually represented by a lawyer, so you should consider trying to obtain representation as well. The commissioner may exclude members of the public if intimate personal or financial circumstances or matters of public security are involved.[54] This is not usually necessary because it is rare for anyone not involved in the case to attend.

The decision

The decision is always given in writing[55] – often at some length – and it may be a few weeks before it is sent to you.

After a successful appeal, the case is usually sent back to a differently constituted social security appeal tribunal with directions as to how the tribunal should go about reconsidering the issues.[56] However, if the commissioner feels that the record of the decision of the original tribunal contains all the material facts, or s/he feels that it is 'expedient' to make findings on any extra factual issues necessary to the decisions, the commissioner makes the final decision.[57] It is unusual for a commissioner not to send a case back to a tribunal if there is a dispute about facts not determined by the original tribunal, unless all the evidence points in one direction.[58]

A commissioner may correct or set aside her/his decision in the same way as a tribunal (see p175).[59]

In certain circumstances, an adjudication officer may review a commissioner's decision (see p149).

Decisions of commissioners establish precedents and so may affect many cases other than your own.

4. APPEALING TO THE COURTS

Appeals from Social Security Commissioners

You may appeal against a decision of a commissioner to the Court of Appeal (in Scotland, the Court of Session). Again, the appeal is only on a point of law and you must first obtain leave to appeal.[60] If you want to appeal you should seek help from a solicitor, but check that you qualify for help with legal costs.

The application for leave to appeal must first be made to a commissioner, in writing, within three months of the date when you were sent the commissioner's decision. The commissioner may extend the time limit for 'special reasons'.[61] If you do not apply to the commissioner within the time limit and the commissioner refuses to extend it, the Court of Appeal (or Court of Session) cannot hear your appeal and you can only proceed by applying to the High Court (in Scotland, the Court of Session) for judicial review of the refusal to extend the time allowed for the appeal (see below).[62]

Applications to a commissioner for leave to appeal are almost invariably considered without an oral hearing. If the commissioner refuses, you can apply to the court for leave.[63] Your notice of application should be lodged with the Civil Appeals Office within six weeks of notification

of the commissioner's refusal being sent to you.[64] The court may extend
the time but you must explain the reasons for your delay and file an affidavit in support of an application for an extension of time.[65] Generally,
the Court of Appeal considers your application without an oral hearing. If
leave is refused, you may renew your application in open court within
seven days. Similarly, if leave is granted, the Chief Adjudication Officer or
the Secretary of State has seven days in which to ask for an oral hearing.[66]

If leave to appeal was granted by a commissioner, you must serve a
notice of appeal on the relevant parties within six weeks of being sent
notification of the commissioner's grant of leave.[67] If leave was granted
by the Court of Appeal, the notice of appeal must be served within the
same six-week period or within seven days of the grant of leave
whichever is later (unless your notice of application for leave was lodged
outside the six-week time limit, in which case a time limit for lodging the
notice of appeal should be contained in the court's order).[68] The solicitor
to the Benefits Agency will accept service on behalf of the Chief Adjudication Officer (see Appendix 1 for address).

You cannot appeal to the Court of Appeal against a decision of a commissioner refusing you leave to appeal to a commissioner (against a decision of a tribunal), but you can apply to the High Court for judicial
review of such a decision.[69]

The procedures in Scotland are similar.

The Chief Adjudication Officer or the Secretary of State has the same
rights of appeal as you.

Applying for judicial review

Occasionally it is possible to challenge the Benefits Agency by going to
court for a **judicial review**. You will need the services of a solicitor, law
centre or legal advice centre.

You can apply for judicial review of a decision made by the Secretary
of State or of a tribunal chairperson or a Social Security Commissioner
who refuses to grant you leave to appeal. However, this procedure cannot be used if you have an independent right of appeal such as against the
decision of an adjudication officer or a social security appeal tribunal.

Legal aid is available for cases in the Court of Appeal, the High Court
and the Court of Session and you should certainly obtain legal advice
and representation (see Appendix 2). In the past, the legal aid authorities
have taken the view that an application to a commissioner for leave
to appeal to the Court of Appeal cannot be covered by legal aid. However, it is arguable that such an application is a step 'preliminary to'
proceedings in the Court of Appeal and is thus work for which legal aid
is available.[70]

Calculate first & cannot on full for HB/CTB.

Work 16 hrs or more - with child - Paid 26 wk Regardless of change.
Capital less than 8,000. - FT work ie 16 hrs Responsible for at
least one child - do not need to be a parent.
Capital - Same Rules IS. Tariff £100 for every 250 between 3000 +
8000. - Child under 16 - Young person under 19 in FT education.

PART THREE

Family credit

Check Capital - Work out max FC. Work out weekly income.
Applicable amount threshold figure.

Max FC = Adult Credit plus Credit for each child / young
person.
Adult Credit is the same for couples + single parent.

		Income - Net earnings
Adult	44·30 -	benefits.
Child	11·20 under 11	Other income
	18·55 11-15	Tariff.
	23·05 16-17.	

Benefits Completely ignored - child benefit / one parent benefit.
Housing Benefit, CTB, DLA, Mobility Supplement (Part of a war
disablement pension. AA for 65+, Christmas bonus, SF Payments
Compensatory payments for IS.

Partially Ignored - SSP, Statutory Maternity Pay - treated as earnings.
Partly taken into A/c - Rent from tenants / sub tenants. £4·00 - £8·60
if charge covers heating costs. - £20·00 for each boarder.
weekly charge is ignored + 1/2 of the remaining balance is taken into A/c.
Maintenance Payments - first £15·00 disregard.

Family credit

Income above Applicable amount 100% FC. — 70% of diff.

This chapter covers all the rules about family credit (FC). It contains:

1. Introduction (below)
2. The basic rules (p185)
3. The amount of benefit (p189)
4. Special rules for special groups (p191)
5. Claiming and getting paid (p191)
6. Challenging a family credit decision (p195)

1. INTRODUCTION

Family credit is a tax-free benefit for low-paid workers with children. It tops-up your wages if you are in full-time work (see p186). If you have a disability, you may be able to claim disability working allowance (DWA) instead and this is likely to give you more money than FC (see p198). Part-time workers should claim IS instead of FC. If you pay rent and/or council tax you may get housing benefit (HB) (see p214) and council tax benefit (CTB) (see p296) as well but your FC counts as income for these benefits. FC also helps you to qualify for certain health service benefits (see Chapter 25), and some education benefits but not free school meals (see Chapter 26). You may also qualify for some social fund payments (see Chapter 20), and you can qualify for a grant towards the cost of insulating your home from your local authority or under the Home Energy Efficiency Scheme (see Chapter 27).

FC is a weekly payment which normally continues at the same rate for 26 weeks, regardless of any changes in your circumstances.

You qualify for FC if:

- your savings and capital are not worth over £8,000. Some of your capital may be ignored, but you may also be treated as having capital you do not really possess (see Chapter 19);
- your income is low enough. This depends on your circumstances.

Some of your income may be ignored, but you may be treated as having income which you do not possess. Some of your childcare costs may be disregarded from October 1994 (see p375);
- you are in Great Britain (see below);
- you work full-time (usually for 16 hours or more a week) (see p186);
- you have at least one dependent child (see p188);
- you have made a proper claim (see p191);
- neither you nor your partner is entitled to DWA (see p188).

You can claim for your 'family' which consists of:

- you;
- your partner (if any) who is
  either   your husband or wife, if you are living together (see p330);
  or   a person of the opposite sex to whom you are not married, but with whom you are living together as husband and wife (see p330);
- any children for whom you are responsible (see p335).

You must claim in writing on the form in leaflet FC1 which you can get from your local post office or Benefits Agency office. The claim must be made by the woman in a couple unless the Secretary of State decides that it is reasonable to accept a claim from the man. Both members of the couple have to sign the claim form.

For more details about claims, see p191.

2. THE BASIC RULES

Residence in Great Britain

To be entitled you must be in Great Britain.[1] This means England, Scotland and Wales. You can be treated as being in Great Britain if:[2]

- you are present and ordinarily resident in Great Britain; *and*
- your partner (if any) is ordinarily resident in the United Kingdom (UK) (but see below); *and*
- at least part of your earnings (or your partner's earnings) are derived from paid work in the UK; *and*
- your earnings (or those of your partner) do not come wholly from paid work done outside the UK.

You are **ordinarily resident** here if you normally live in Great Britain (or, if relevant, the UK).[3] The **United Kingdom** includes Northern Ireland as well as Great Britain. If your husband or wife is living abroad and has never lived in this country, s/he is *not* counted as a partner under social security law because s/he cannot be treated as a member of your household.[4] If your spouse was living with you in this country and is now living abroad, s/he may continue to be treated as a member of your household and therefore count as your partner (see p328).

If you cannot meet these conditions you could argue that the conditions above are not exhaustive and that as you are actually in Great Britain, you do not have to satisfy the test for being treated as being in Great Britain.

You cannot be treated as being in Great Britain if you or your partner are entitled to FC or DWA in Northern Ireland.[5]

There is no requirement for a child who is a member of your household to be present in Great Britain.[6]

If you or your partner are 'persons from abroad', see p191.

Full-time work

To be entitled to FC, you or your partner must be 'engaged and normally engaged in remunerative work'.[7]

Work includes self-employment, but not a training course[8] nor a course of education as a student.[9] If you are studying *and* working you can claim FC. People who work at home (eg, childminders, writers or carers) are eligible for FC if they are paid.[10]

You are entitled if you:[11]

* work for not less than 16 hours, or, if your hours fluctuate, 16 hours on average, a week; *and*
* are employed at the date of claim; *and*
* are paid, or expect to be paid (eg, on a commission basis). Any expectation of payment must be realistic – a mere hope or desire that you will be paid is not enough to make your work count as 'remunerative' work.[12] Payment in kind counts (eg, where a farm worker is provided with free produce and accommodation[13]). Business Start-Up Allowance also counts as earnings so even if you are not yet making any additional money from your self-employment you are treated as being in 'paid work'.[14] Work done as a volunteer or for a charity or voluntary body does not count if only your expenses are paid.[15]

In addition[16] you must:

* actually work for 16 hours or more in either the week in which you claim or one of the two preceding weeks; *or*
* be expected by your employers (or yourself if you are self-employed) to work for 16 hours or more in the week after the week you claim (this applies if you have just started work); *or*

- if you are on holiday from work – be expected to, or expect to work 16 hours or more in the week after you return. You are not treated as on holiday if you are off sick or on maternity leave.

The work must be your normal work and you must be likely to continue in that job for at least five weeks after your claim.[17] What is 'normal' depends on your individual circumstances,[18] for example, the likely future pattern of work, the past pattern and all other relevant circumstances.[19] If you have only just started work, but are likely to continue working, this should be sufficient to enable you to qualify.[20]

If you do not do at least 16 hours' work in one of the three relevant weeks, your claim will be disallowed (unless you are starting or resuming work after a holiday and thus covered because you are expected to work more than 16 hours). This applies even if the reason you have not been working the necessary hours is because of sickness,[21] maternity leave, suspension, short-time working, lay-off or because you are only on call.[22] However, you should be treated as working if you are on duty and required to be available during a part of the day and/or night – eg, if you are a warden in sheltered housing.

If your claim is refused for this reason, claim again in the first week in which you work 16 or more hours. It often takes the Benefits Agency a long time to send you a decision on your first claim, so make sure that you ask for your new claim to be backdated to the first week in which you actually worked for 16 hours or more.

In calculating your hours, include all the hours for which you are paid. If you routinely need to work over your contractual hours, these extra hours can also count even if you are not paid for them.[23] Lunch-breaks (and for DWA, paid time off to attend a hospital or clinic in relation to your disability) should be included in the total if they are paid.[24] Your total hours can be made up from more than one job.[25] If you are self-employed, you can count not only the hours spent on services for which you are paid, but also other time which is essential to your business (eg, preparation time).[26]

If you are employed and you have not got a normal pattern of working hours (because you have just started a new job, or just changed your hours, or just returned to work after a break of more than four weeks – 13 for DWA), you qualify if it is expected that you will work 16 or more hours on average each week.[27] If you are self-employed and have not yet worked for five weeks, the average hours that you expect to work are used.[28]

Otherwise hours are calculated by looking at your normal cycle of work and assessing your weekly hours. If you always work the same number of hours a week this is straightforward. If your work pattern is different – eg, you work one week on and one week off – your hours are averaged out. Periods when you do not normally work (eg, the 'week off') are included when working out the average but other absences (eg, for sickness) do not.[29]

If you have no recognisable cycle of work, the average over the five-week period immediately before the week in which you claim is used, or over another period if this would more accurately reflect your average working hours.[30]

Sometimes it is difficult to show that you normally work at least 16 hours a week and the distinction between FC and IS is not absolute. You may be refused both FC and IS because adjudication officers (AOs) at the local Benefits Agency office and the Family Credit Unit interpret the rules differently. If this happens, appeal against both decisions and ask for them to be heard together so a tribunal can decide which benefit is appropriate. In the meantime you apply for interim payments (see p152).

If you are a school-worker who works over 16 hours during term-time but not at all in school holidays, and your contract continues throughout school holidays, you should be treated as in full-time work for the whole year, and eligible to claim FC if the average hours over both holidays and term-time are over 16. If less, you should claim IS instead.[31] This applies whether or not you receive any holiday pay or a retainer.

You may fall within *both* schemes and therefore have to choose which benefit to claim. If you are a childminder working for 16 hours or more a week, you are not treated as in full-time work for the purposes of IS, and so may be entitled to claim either IS or FC/DWA.

Responsibility for a child

To get FC, you or your partner must be responsible for at least one child who is a member of your household.[32] You do not have to be their parent. (For when you are responsible for a child, see p335.)

If you have a child(ren) by a previous relationship and you and the other parent now live apart, you are expected to claim child support maintenance from her/him. The rules are the same as for IS (see p125) and, as with IS, if you refuse to allow the Benefits Agency to ensure that maintenance is paid your FC can be reduced.

Overlap with disability working allowance

You cannot get FC if you or your partner have been awarded DWA. This does not apply if your DWA is due to expire within six weeks of the date you claim FC, *and* you fulfil all the other conditions of entitlement to FC, *and* you are claiming FC for the period immediately after your DWA ends.[33] In all other cases, you have to wait until your DWA award comes to an end before claiming FC (see p192).

3. THE AMOUNT OF BENEFIT

You cannot get FC if your capital is more than £8,000 (see p395). Your FC is calculated by taking account of the number and ages of your children and the income you and your family possess. If you are a single parent, you receive the same amount of FC as a two-parent family.

To work out your FC, you first of all calculate the **maximum FC** for your family. Then you compare your income (see Chapter 18) with a set figure of £71.70 (called the **applicable amount**).[34] If your income is £71.70 or less you receive the maximum FC for your family.[35] If it is more you get the maximum FC reduced by 70 per cent of the difference between your income and applicable amount.[36]

Remember that your FC can be reduced if you fail to apply for child support maintenance (see p125).

Maximum family credit

The maximum family credit is made up of an adult credit and a credit for each child.[37] The adult credit is the same whether you are a single parent or a couple. The credit for each child depends on her/his age. The current rates are as follows:[38]

Credit for adult (single parent or couple)	£44.30
Credit for child aged	
0-10	£11.20
11-15	£18.55
16-17	£23.05
18	£32.20

Example of maximum FC

For a couple and three children aged 5, 7 and 13 the maximum is:

£44.30	for the couple
£22.40	for the two children under 11
£18.55	for the eldest child
£85.25	is the total maximum FC for this family.

You do not receive a credit for any child who:[39]

- has more than £3,000 capital (savings etc) of their own (see p394); *or*
- has a higher weekly income (other than disregarded income or that from maintenance) than the appropriate credit for a child of that age; *or*
- has been in hospital or residential accommodation because of illness

or disability for 52 weeks before the date of claim.

If you have more than one husband or wife (ie, you are polygamously married), and they are all members of your household, you get an extra credit in addition to the usual £44.30 for a couple and the appropriate amounts for children.[40] The additional credit for each additional spouse is:

- £23.05 if they are under 18;
- £32.20 if they are 18 or over.

The family credit calculation

You now compare your income (see Chapter 18) with the applicable amount.

Example 1: Income below applicable amount

Mary is a single parent with two children aged 10 and 14. She works 10am-3pm five days a week (25 hours) as a school-helper. Her total weekly income taken into account for the purposes of FC is £67. Her savings are less than £3,000.

Her maximum FC is £44.30 for herself and £11.20 for the younger, and £18.55 for the older of the children. This totals £74.05.

She will receive the full maximum FC of £74.05 a week, as her income is less than the applicable amount (£71.70).

Example 2: Income higher than applicable amount

Shahida has a partner and two children aged 3 and 5. Her partner works 35 hours a week and the total family income taken into account for the purposes of FC is £107.60. Family savings are less than £3,000. The maximum FC in her case is £66.70 (£44.30 for the couple and £11.20 for each child).

Her income exceeds the applicable amount by £35.90 (£107.60 less £71.70). 70 per cent of the excess is £25.13.

Maximum FC	£66.70
less	£25.13 (70% of excess)
equals	£41.57 weekly FC.

Shahida will therefore receive £41.57 each week in FC. For every £10 by which her weekly income increases on any future claim, her FC will reduce by £7.

Any fractions produced at the end of the FC calculation are rounded up to a penny if they are more than a half-penny, and are ignored if less than a half-penny.[41]

The minimum amount of FC that will be paid is 50 pence a week.[42]

4. SPECIAL RULES FOR SPECIAL GROUPS

People from abroad

If you are a 'person from abroad' you can claim FC as long as your immigration status does not debar you from working. Check that you fulfil the residence conditions (see p185). Capital abroad which you own affects your entitlement to FC (see p413). However, claiming FC counts as having **recourse to public funds** (see p83). You should get immigration advice before claiming if you have been allowed to stay in the UK on condition that you do not have recourse to public funds.

If you have a partner and children who are British, or have settled status, they should be able to claim FC without jeopardising your immigration status. Technically, the amount awarded will cover your needs, but because the adult credit is the same for a single person or a couple you could argue that you are not *personally* having recourse to public funds.

People involved in a trade dispute

If you are involved in a trade dispute, you can still claim FC but your normal weekly earnings are taken as those prior to the dispute[43] and so do not reflect your actual income during the dispute. If you are already getting FC when you become involved in a trade dispute you continue to receive it at the same rate for the rest of the 26 weeks of your award.[44] However, you are not entitled to FC if, because of the dispute, you were not at work in any of the three set weeks around the date of your claim (see p186).

Since there are no other special rules under FC for the assessment of your capital and income if you or your partner are involved in a trade dispute, the normal rules apply.

5. CLAIMING AND GETTING PAID

Claims

Your claim should be on form FC1 and is usually considered to have been made on the day it reaches the Family Credit Unit (see Appendix 1 for address).[45] If you do not use the right form or fill it in incorrectly, the Benefits Agency ask you to correct this. If you then return the form within one month, the date of your first claim counts. This time limit can be extended.[46] If you are just starting work after being unemployed you can ask a claimant adviser at the unemployment benefit office/JobCentre to give you the form. Alternatively you can get it from your local Benefits Agency. Both will help you fill it in and, in either case, your claim is likely to be dealt with more speedily as the UBO/Benefits Agency should mark the FC1 to ensure that you get a quick decision. If you prefer, you can get the form from a post office or advice centre.

A claim for FC can be backdated,[47] but only for a maximum of one year. To get your claim backdated you must have 'good cause' for not having claimed earlier (see p145). A claim can be backdated for a month without good cause, but this is at the Secretary of State's discretion. On renewal claims, the month is in addition to the 14 days after your last award ran out (see below).

If you have made a claim but then your circumstances change (eg, your income suddenly drops), you can amend or withdraw your claim (see below). But you must act quickly. A claim can only be withdrawn or amended before a decision is made by the AO.[48]

If you are **renewing your claim**[49] after a period on FC you should be reminded that it is about to run out and invited to make a fresh claim. You can put your claim in up to 28 days before the current award expires or within 14 days of it running out. Your new claim then follows on immediately from your previous award. If you are changing from DWA to FC you can claim up to 42 days before your DWA award expires or 14 days afterwards and FC is paid from the date the DWA ends.

When to claim

It is worth thinking carefully about which day and week you should make your claim, bearing in mind the following points:

- Awards of FC run from a Tuesday so you should try to get your claim to the Benefits Agency on a Tuesday or on the day before. If your claim arrives on a Wednesday, your entitlement will not start until the following Tuesday and you lose benefit for that week.[50]
- Make sure your claim is made during a week in which you are eligible to claim (see p186).
- If you are thinking about making a claim in late February or March it might be to your advantage to consider delaying the claim until April. This is because the amounts for FC are uprated in April, but only those claiming after the increase get the higher amounts. If you claim before April, you only get the benefit of the increase when you come to renew your claim six months later.[51] You will need to work out whether it is worth losing three or four weeks' FC in order to receive the higher rate for the next 26 weeks. However, if you claim no more than 28 days

before benefits are increased and you do not qualify for FC at the old rates but would under the new ones, you can be treated as entitled and paid from the date the increases take effect.[52]

A claim for DWA can be treated as a claim for FC.[53] If you are refused DWA, you could ask for this to happen and thus have FC paid from the date of your DWA claim. If you are entitled to both you must choose which one to claim *before* a decision is made. Once you have been awarded FC you cannot change to DWA until 26 weeks have elapsed and vice versa.

• Consider whether your family circumstances are about to change in a way which might affect your FC. For example, if you are about to take a drop in income or have another child, it might be worth delaying your claim.

• If you are making a renewal claim after your 26 weeks' FC has ended, your claim can be made 28 days before or 14 days after the FC finishes (see p192).

Once you have made a decision about when to claim, apply as soon as possible. If you do not claim quickly you might lose money. Send off the form even if you cannot complete absolutely all the details. You can send those on later. Keep a copy of your claim in case queries arise later on.

How your claim is dealt with

When your claim is received by the Family Credit Unit, the information you have provided is checked and verification can be obtained from your employer about your wages or salary.[54] You could ask your employer to reply promptly. If you have claimed through a claimant adviser or local Benefits Agency, your wages are checked by telephone which speeds up your claim. On a renewal claim, if you are still working for the same employer, the Benefits Agency may accept your wage slips as evidence of your earnings and not contact your employer again.

Then your claim is referred to an AO for decision. It should be dealt with within 14 days 'so far as practicable'.[55]

If you have been waiting more than two weeks for the result of your claim, contact the Family Credit Unit. Always keep a copy of your letter or make a note of the date of your call, who you spoke to and what was said. Check that the Family Credit Unit has received your claim. If they have not, send them a copy or fill out a new form and ask them to pay from the date you sent in the first one.

If your claim has been received and you are not satisfied with the explanation for the delay, complain to the manager, and/or go and see your MP (see p167). If the delay is unreasonable, you could take legal action.

You should also ask for **interim payments** to be made to you while you wait for the decision on your claim. The rules are the same as for IS (see p152). The Family Credit Unit have a policy of not making such payments and you may need to ask your MP to help you get one.

Family credit decisions – getting paid

You are given the decision concerning your claim in writing. The letter from the Family Credit Unit gives the reasons for the decision and tells you about your right to appeal.[56] If you have been awarded FC you should be sent an order book 'as soon as reasonably practicable'.[57] You can choose to be paid by direct credit transfer into a bank or other account if you prefer.[58] If your weekly FC is £4 or less, you can be paid in a lump sum. However, if it is less than 50 pence a week, you cannot get FC at all.[59]

You can cash an FC order book at your local post office. The book lasts for 26 weeks starting on the Tuesday of the week following that in which your claim was treated as made. Payments by order book are made weekly in arrears.[60] Credit transfer payments are credited to your account every four weeks in arrears.

If your order book is lost or stolen or your FC is suspended, the rules are the same as for IS (see p153).

Change of circumstances

If your circumstances change during the 26 weeks (eg, your capital or income go up or down or you have another child), this does not usually affect the amount you are being paid.[61] However,

- if a child or young person leaves your household while FC is being paid and IS, DWA or FC is awarded to them or for them in a different household, your FC stops from the first day of any overlap.[62] This may happen, for example, if your family splits up;
- if a claimant dies during the 26-week period, FC stops if s/he was single. If s/he was one of a couple (see p330), the partner can take over the rest of the award provided that s/he was the partner when FC was claimed;[63]
- if a new award of FC is made on review or appeal, any award of FC with which it overlaps is reviewed;[64]
- if you fail to comply with the requirement to apply for child support maintenance and a reduced benefit direction is issued (see pp128-30), the amount of your FC is adjusted during your current award. This also applies where the reduced benefit direction ceases, is cancelled or suspended, or reinstated after a suspension.

Where your earnings are estimated and it transpires that the estimate was too high or low, this does not amount to a change of circumstances and your benefit cannot be reviewed.[65] However, if you appealed against the amount of FC, your award might nevertheless be revised to take account of your actual earnings.

Overpayments and fraud

The rules on overpayments and fraud are the same as for IS (see p161). The IS rules limiting the maximum amount that can be recovered from your weekly benefit do not apply to FC, but guidance suggests that this same maximum should apply.[66]

6. CHALLENGING A FAMILY CREDIT DECISION

It is always possible to apply for a review of the decision on your FC claim on the grounds that the Benefits Agency:[67]

- did not know or made a mistake about facts relevant to your claim;
- got the law wrong.

For instance, your employer may have provided incorrect information or a mistake may have been made in working out your FC. You cannot get a review because your circumstances have changed except in the situations described on p194.[68]

When an FC decision is reviewed, payment of arrears is not restricted *unless* the review was because of ignorance of, or a mistake about, the facts, and you were aware of these facts but failed to tell the Benefits Agency. In this case you can only get up to 12 months' arrears.[69]

If you feel that you have been wrongly refused FC or that your entitlement has been miscalculated, you can appeal to a social security appeal tribunal.[70] Chapter 8 explains how to appeal. The rules are the same as for IS. See also Chapter 8 for information about judicial review, and p169 if you want to complain about how your claim has been handled.

PART FOUR

Disability working allowance

CHAPTER TEN

Disability working allowance

This chapter deals with the rules about disability working allowance (DWA). It covers:

1. Introduction (below)
2. The basic rules (p200)
3. The amount of benefit (p203)
4. Claims, reviews and getting paid (p204)
5. Appeals (p209)
6. Giving up work because of sickness or disability (p210)

1. INTRODUCTION

Disability working allowance is a tax-free benefit for low-paid workers with a disability. It tops up your wages if you are in full-time work. Part-time workers can claim income support (IS) instead. If you are in low-paid work but do not have a disability you could claim family credit (FC) if you have children (see Chapter 9). If you pay rent and/or council tax you may get housing benefit (HB) (see p214) or council tax benefit (CTB) (see p296) as well, but your DWA counts as income for these benefits. Receipt of DWA helps you to qualify for a disability premium with IS/HB/CTB. You may qualify for certain health service benefits if your income is low enough (see Chapter 25), and some education benefits – but not free school meals (see Chapter 26). You can also qualify for grants towards the cost of insulating your home, from the Home Energy Efficiency Scheme (see Chapter 27). You may also qualify for some social fund payments (see Chapter 20). Disability working allowance is a weekly payment which normally continues at the same rate for 26 weeks regardless of changes in your circumstances. If your earnings are too low to pay national insurance you will get a credit for each week on DWA.[1]

Who can claim

You qualify for DWA if:

- you are 16 or over;
- your savings and capital are not worth more than £16,000. Some of your capital may be ignored but you may also be treated as having capital you do not really possess (see Chapter 19);
- your income is low enough. This depends on your circumstances. Some of your income is ignored but you may be treated as having income which you do not possess (see Chapter 18);
- you are in Great Britain (see p200);
- you work full-time (usually for 16 hours or more a week) (see p186);
- you have a physical or mental disability which puts you at a disadvantage in getting a job (see p200);
- you are, or have recently been getting, a sickness or disability benefit (see p202);
- you have made a proper claim (see p204);
- you are not getting FC (see p202).

Who you claim for

You claim for your 'family' which consists of:

- you;
- your partner (if any) who is
  either   your husband or wife, if you are living together (see p330);
  or   a person of the opposite sex to whom you are not married, but with whom you are living together as husband and wife (see p330);
- any children for whom you are responsible (see p335).

If you have a child(ren) from a previous relationship and the other parent now lives elsewhere, you are expected to claim child support maintenance from her/him and this may affect the amount of benefit you receive (see p125).

How to claim

You claim in writing using the DWA claim pack which you can get from your local post office, Benefits Agency office or JobCentre. Alternatively, you can ring the Benefits Enquiry Line and speak to someone who will complete a claim form for you (see p204).

If you become sick while on DWA

There are special rules to protect your entitlement to the incapacity benefits which you were claiming before you took up work (see p210). If your disability prevents you from continuing in work you should not lose benefit because you tried to work.

2. THE BASIC RULES

Residence in Great Britain[2]

The rules are the same as for FC[3] (see p185).

Full-time work

The rules are the same as for FC (see p186).

The disability and disadvantage test

To qualify for DWA you must have a disability which puts you at a disadvantage in getting a job. Both physical and mental disability count.[4] If you are claiming for the first time, or after a period of two years when you were not getting DWA, you simply have to sign a declaration that this applies to you. This will be accepted *unless* the information given on your claim form is contradictory, *or* the adjudication officer has other evidence about you which indicates that you do not fulfil that condition.[5] For all other claims, you fulfil this condition if one of the following applies:[6]

- you are paid one of the following benefits (or its Northern Ireland equivalent):
  - the higher or middle rate care component or the higher rate mobility component of the disability living allowance;
  - attendance allowance;
  - industrial disablement benefit or a war pension, where you are at least 80 per cent disabled;
  - mobility supplement;
- you have an invalid 'trike' or similar vehicle;
- you were paid severe disablement allowance (or Northern Ireland equivalent) for at least one day in the eight weeks prior to your 'initial claim'. **Initial claim** means your first successful claim for DWA, or a new claim where you have not been getting DWA during the last two years;
- you cannot keep your balance without holding on to something when standing;

- you cannot walk 100 metres on level ground without stopping or suffering severe pain. You are expected to use walking aids such as crutches, a stick, a frame or an artificial limb if you normally use these;
- you cannot use your hands behind your back (as you would when putting on a jacket or tucking your shirt in);
- you cannot extend your hands forwards in order to shake hands with someone without difficulty;
- you cannot put your hands up to your head without difficulty (as when putting on a hat);
- you cannot pick up with each hand a coin of 2½ cm diameter because of a lack of manual dexterity;
- you cannot pick up a full one-litre jug and pour into a cup from it without difficulty;
- you cannot turn either of your hands sideways through 180 degrees;
- you are registered blind or partially sighted;
- you cannot read 16-point print from more than 20 cm distance, even when wearing your normal glasses, if any;
- you cannot hear a telephone ring when in the same room, even with your hearing aid, if any;
- you cannot hear someone talking in a loud voice when the room is quiet and they are only two metres away from you even with your hearing aid, if any;
- people who know you well have difficulty understanding what you say;
- you have difficulty understanding a person you know well;
- you lose consciousness during a fit, or go into a coma at least once a year during working hours;
- you are mentally ill and are receiving regular medical treatment;
- you are often confused or forgetful due to mental disability;
- you cannot do simple addition and subtraction;
- you hit people, or damage property or cannot socialise because of your mental disability;
- you cannot manage an eight-hour working day or a five-day week because of your medical condition or because you suffer from severe pain;
- following illness or accident you are undergoing rehabilitation. You can only use this condition to qualify on an initial claim (see p200).

If you fulfil the disability test for DWA because you are paid one of the specified benefits, or have an invalid trike, you will nevertheless be refused DWA if there is evidence that none of the other disability conditions are fulfilled.[7]

Receipt of a sickness or disability benefit

To qualify for DWA you must also be, or have been receiving, a sickness or disability benefit.[8] You are entitled if, *when you claim*, you are receiving:

• disability living allowance;
• attendance allowance, or an increase of your industrial disablement benefit or war pension for attendance needs;
• a corresponding benefit from Northern Ireland.

Alternatively, you qualify if, for at least one day in the eight weeks prior to your claim, you were getting:

• invalidity benefit or severe disablement allowance;
• IS, HB or CTB, but only if your applicable amount included the disability or higher pensioner (on the ground of disability) premium (see pp345 and 348);
• a corresponding benefit from Northern Ireland.

You can also meet this condition if you have an invalid trike or similar vehicle when you claim DWA.

If you are renewing your DWA claim within eight weeks of a previous award running out, you are deemed to be receiving invalidity benefit, severe disablement allowance or a disability or higher pensioner premium paid with IS, HB or CTB (or a Northern Ireland equivalent) where your previous award was made on this basis.[9]

Some people have difficulty meeting the benefit condition and thus may not qualify for DWA. For example:

• people with disabilities who are already in low-paid employment;
• people who are temporarily off sick and getting statutory sick pay and whose DWA award ends while they are still sick. If they do not return to work within eight weeks they will not requalify for DWA *unless* they are getting disability living allowance or attendance allowance, *or* they complete 28 weeks on statutory sick pay and go back on to invalidity benefit/severe disablement allowance prior to re-claiming DWA;
• people who do not receive invalidity benefit/severe disablement allowance because they get another social security benefit instead – eg, widows' benefits.

Contact your MP if you do not qualify because of this rule and press for it to be less restrictive.

Entitlement to family credit

You are not entitled to DWA if, when you claim, you (or your partner) are entitled to FC.[10] However, this does not apply if:[11]

- your FC claim runs out within 28 days of your DWA claim;
- you are otherwise entitled to DWA;
- your DWA claim is for the period immediately after your FC runs out.

It is important to check whether you are better off claiming FC or DWA. If you make the wrong choice you could lose money. DWA is usually paid at a higher rate but this may reduce your HB/CTB entitlement. Remember also that DWA is not yet a 'passport benefit' for NHS charges, whereas FC is (see Chapter 25), though from April 1995 people who get DWA will get help with NHS charges.

3. THE AMOUNT OF BENEFIT

You cannot get DWA if your capital is worth more than £16,000[12] (see Chapter 19). Your DWA is calculated by first working out **your maximum disability working allowance.** You then compare your **income** (see Chapter 18) with your **applicable amount** which is a set figure of:

£43.00 (single claimants)
or   £71.70 (couples or single parents).

If your income is less than your applicable amount you receive maximum DWA. If it is more, you get the maximum DWA minus 70 per cent of the difference between your income and the applicable amount.[13]

Your benefit can be reduced if you fail to apply for child support maintenance (see p125).

Maximum DWA

This is made up of allowances for each member of your family (see p328). These are as follows:[14]

single claimant	£46.05
couple/lone parent	£63.75
child aged:	
0-10	£11.20
11-15	£18.55
16-17	£23.05
18	£32.20
additional partners in a polygamous marriage:	
under 18	£23.05
18 or over	£32.20

No allowance is given for a child who has:

- capital of over £3,000 (see p394); *or*
- weekly income (excluding maintenance or disregarded income) which is greater than their allowance; *or*
- been in hospital or local authority residential accommodation for the 52 weeks prior to your claim because of physical or mental illness/ disability.

Calculating DWA

Make sure that you have properly worked out your income (see Chapter 18). Now compare this to your applicable amount.

Example

Winston is 19 and single. He works 25 hours a week. His income for DWA is £65. He has no savings.

His maximum DWA is £46.05.

His income exceeds the applicable amount of £43 by £22. Thus his maximum DWA is reduced by £15.40 (70% x £22) and he is paid £30.65 a week.

If his income had been below £43 he would have received the maximum DWA.

---

4. CLAIMS, REVIEWS AND GETTING PAID

Claims

You claim DWA using the claim pack[15] which you can get from the Benefits Agency, a post office or JobCentre. This consists of information about DWA and two forms. Form DWA1 is for basic information about yourself, your family and your earnings. There is also a form EEF 200 on which your employer must confirm your hours/earnings if you have not yet worked for nine weeks. If you have already worked for this long you simply need to send in pay-slips.

If you prefer, you can ring the Benefits Enquiry Line free of charge on 0800 882200. Benefits Agency staff will discuss your claim and complete the appropriate forms for you. These are sent to you to sign and post.

Your claim goes to the DWA unit in Preston (see Appendix 1). Do not delay sending in the DWA1 just because you do not yet have your pay-slips or a completed form EEF 200 – these can be sent later.

If you are one of a couple the disabled partner should claim. If both of you are disabled you can choose who should be the claimant, but if you cannot agree the Secretary of State decides for you.[16]

If you do not use the proper form, but nevertheless claim in writing you will be sent the form and so long as you return it within a month, you will be paid from the date your original letter was received. This also applies **if you do not properly fill in the form** – it will be returned to you to correct, or provide additional information; if you do this within a month, you will not lose benefit. This period can be extended if you have a good reason but it is best to act promptly.[17] If you want to amend or withdraw your claim, write to the Benefits Agency immediately. Your letter must arrive before the adjudication officer has decided your claim.[18]

If you claim FC, this can be treated as a claim for DWA if you would be better off.[19] However, you must let both the FC and DWA units know that you want them to do this *before* your FC claim is assessed.

Your claim is normally treated as made on the date it is received at the DWA unit.[20] However, if you start work on a Monday or Tuesday and claim DWA in the same week your claim is treated as made on the Tuesday of that week.[21]

If you are claiming within three months of being turned down on an earlier claim, your second claim is treated as a review request[22] (see p207) though your claim date is still treated as that of your later claim.[23]

A claim can be backdated for up to 52 weeks[24] but only if you have good cause for a late claim[25] (see p145 – the rules are the same as for IS).

Renewal claims

If you are currently getting DWA, you should be sent a claim form eight weeks before your payments end. You can re-claim from six weeks before your award runs out and up to two weeks afterwards. It is best to claim as early as possible to ensure that your payments are not interrupted. On your renewal claim you have to fill in a fresh DWA1 and you will also be sent form DWA2 which asks you questions about the extent of your disability and how it affects you.

If you are currently getting FC, you can claim DWA up to four weeks before your FC expires or two weeks afterwards.[26]

In both cases, this period can be extended by a month, but claim as soon as you can.[27]

For practical advice on when to claim, see p192.

Claiming for children whose other parent does not live with you

If you have a child(ren) by a previous relationship and you and the other parent now live apart, you are expected to apply for child support maintenance. The rules are the same as for IS (see p125). As with IS, if you fail to authorise the Benefits Agency to obtain child support maintenance your benefit may be reduced.

How your claim is dealt with

When your claim is received in Preston, the information in it is checked to see if further details are needed. If so, you are asked to provide extra information or documents. You are obliged to provide this if requested and should do so *within a month*.[28] If there is a good reason this time limit can be extended, but if you reply quickly your DWA will be paid sooner. The Benefits Agency can also approach your employer for confirmation of your earnings and s/he must reply.[29]

Your claim is then passed to an adjudication officer for decision, and this should be made within 14 days if possible.[30]

If this is your first claim for DWA or you are re-claiming after two years of not getting DWA, it is usually accepted that your disability puts you at a disadvantage in getting a job if you say it does on form DWA1. You do not have to fill in form DWA2 to prove this unless there is other evidence to suggest that you do not qualify, in which case the adjudication officer will ask you to do so. In all other cases, the adjudication officer considers your answers to the disability questions to decide if you qualify. The DWA2 form asks you to give the names of two health professionals who know about your disability and the adjudication officer may contact them to confirm your answers to the questions. S/he can also ask for advice from DSS doctors about your condition and how it is likely to affect you but s/he must make the decision.[31] If necessary you can be asked to go for a medical, though this is unlikely.

You should be sent a written decision and informed that you can appeal if you disagree with it.[32]

Payment of benefit

DWA is normally paid on a Tuesday. If you claim on a different day of the week you are paid from the following Tuesday[33] (but see p205 if you have just started a job). If you are currently getting DWA or FC and you re-claim within the time limits (see p205) you are paid from the day after your last award runs out.[34] If you claim up to 28 days before the annual benefit increases (which happen each April) and you are not entitled at the old benefit rates, you can be paid from the date the new ones come in.[35]

You are not paid at all if your entitlement is less than 50 pence a week.[36]

If you are awarded DWA it is paid for 26 weeks.[37] You are normally paid by a book of orders which you cash each week at a post office but, if you choose, you can have the money paid into a bank or building society account.[38] To do this you should write to the Benefits Agency office giving details of your account number. There is a section on the DWA1 form on which you can ask for payment to be made in this way. Benefit is paid a week in arrears (by order book) or four-weekly in arrears (into a bank). If your weekly DWA is £4 or less, it can be paid in a lump sum for the whole 26 weeks.

Payment is usually made to the claimant but it can be paid to a partner instead.[39] You could apply to the Benefits Agency for this to happen if it is more convenient, but it is a Secretary of State's decision so there is no right of appeal if he refuses. If there is a delay in assessing your DWA, you can claim an interim payment (see p152).

Payment of your DWA can be suspended (see p153). If your order book is lost or stolen, see p154. Changes of circumstances do not usually affect your DWA (but see below).

Change of circumstances

Disability working allowance is normally paid for 26 weeks. The amount remains the same even if your circumstances change during this period (eg, your earnings go up or down or the rate of allowances or applicable amounts are increased, as they are each April).[40] However, entitlement ceases if:

- your DWA includes an amount for a child or young person (see p335), but s/he is no longer a member of your household and someone else is claiming for her/him as a dependant in their DWA/FC/IS;[41]
- the claimant dies. However, if there is a surviving partner and s/he is included in the claim, DWA continues to be paid for the remainder of the 26 weeks;[42]
- you fail to comply with the requirement to apply for child support maintenance and a reduced benefit direction is issued (see pp128-30), the amount of your DWA is adjusted during your current award. This also applies where the reduced benefit direction ceases, is cancelled or suspended, or reinstated after a suspension.

In addition, if you are getting DWA and, on review or appeal, another award of DWA is made covering all or part of the same period, this is treated as a change of circumstances and replaces the first award.[43]

Reviews

If you are unhappy with the decision made by the adjudication officer you can ask for a review. If you do, your claim is looked at by a different adjudication officer who may give a more favourable decision. If you apply within three months of the date the decision was sent, you do not have to have special grounds for review,[44] you can simply say why you disagree with the decision. (If you apply within three months but because of an industrial dispute your application is received after this deadline, it counts as if made within three months.)

If you apply outside this period you must show that:[45]

- there was **a mistake about or ignorance of a fact** which is relevant to your claim;
- you have **claimed in advance and been awarded DWA**, but then do not fulfil the conditions on the date it is due to be paid. The review is to stop payment being made;
- the adjudication officer **got the law wrong**.

You cannot usually apply for a review because your **circumstances have changed**. Only the changes listed on p207 will affect your right to DWA.

Decisions made by appeal tribunals and Social Security Commissioners can also be reviewed, but only where there was a mistake about, or ignorance of the facts, an award was made in advance or one of the limited changes of circumstances applies.[46] If you think a tribunal or commissioner's decision is wrong in law you can ask for permission to appeal. The rules are the same as for IS (see pp171 and 181).

The rules about review apply whether or not you are disputing the initial decision on your claim, or a decision which was itself made on review, including a refusal to review.[47] Thus you could have a series of reviews on your claim. However, once you have applied for a review on any grounds (ie, within three months of a decision) you then have a right to appeal to an independent tribunal if you are still dissatisfied (see below).

You can ask for a review by writing to your local Benefits Agency office.[48] If you are applying under the three-month rule you can simply say why you think you qualify. If you are applying for a review outside this time limit, you also have to explain your grounds for asking for a review.

If you were refused DWA, and applied for a review within three months of the decision, you are normally paid from the date you applied for the review.

If you were awarded DWA and apply for a review within three months about the amount of the award, the general rule that reviews take effect from the beginning of an award should operate. In addition, up to 12 months' arrears of DWA can be paid if:

- you apply for a review within three months *or* because there was a mistake about or ignorance of relevant facts; *and*

- the review arises because you provide some information which you knew (or should have known) but did not previously give to the Benefits Agency; *and*
- the review leads to an award of DWA or an increase in the amount you are getting.

The 12 months run from the date you first provided the information.[49]

The rules for getting more than 12 months' arrears are the same as for IS (see p149).

Overpayments and fraud

The rules on overpayments and fraud are the same as for IS[50] (see p161) except that the maximum rate of recovery does not apply to DWA. Nevertheless, you should argue for realistic repayments.

5. APPEALS

How to appeal

If you disagree with an adjudication officer's decision you must normally apply for a review (see p207). However, if you have applied for a review within three months on any grounds you then have a right to appeal to either a disability appeal tribunal (DAT) or a social security appeal tribunal (SSAT).[51] **Your appeal goes to a DAT** if it concerns whether or not you have a physical or mental disability which puts you at a disadvantage in getting a job. If you are appealing about both this disability question *and* the other conditions of entitlement, the DAT hears the whole case.[52] However, **the appeal goes to an SSAT** if you are appealing *only* about the other conditions. An SSAT cannot decide a question if there was a right of appeal to a DAT. The rules for appealing to both a DAT and an SSAT are the same as for IS (see pp170-78), but the DAT has a different membership (see below).

The tribunal hearing

A DAT is made up of a chairperson who is a lawyer, and two other members. One of these is a medical practitioner and the other is a person who has experience of dealing with people with disabilities, either in a professional or voluntary capacity or because they have a disability themselves. People with disabilities should be on the panels in preference to carers or professionals if at all possible. Ideally, at least one of the tribunal members should be the same sex as yourself.[53] The DAT is independent and the members must not have previously dealt with your claim.[54] The hearing cannot go ahead unless all three members are present. You have the right to attend to explain why you think you qualify for DWA. (See p175 for how to prepare your case.) The tribunal members cannot medically examine you but they can refer you to a doctor who will do an examination and prepare a report to help them decide your claim.[55] This should only happen in rare cases where the DAT do not feel able to make a decision without a medical report.

Once they have listened to all your points they make their decision. (See p174 as the rules are the same as for IS. The ways of overturning a DAT decision are also the same.)

6. GIVING UP WORK BECAUSE OF SICKNESS OR DISABILITY

Disability working allowance is intended to encourage disabled people to try to work. If you have to stop working and you are sick, there are special rules to ensure that you can go back on to the incapacity benefit which you were claiming before you took up a job and claimed DWA. The rules differ depending on whether you are temporarily off sick or whether you stop work altogether.

Temporary sickness

If you are sick and off work but expect to return when you are well, you should claim statutory sick pay from your employer (unless you were getting sickness/invalidity benefit or severe disablement allowance within the last eight weeks, in which case you go back on to that benefit). You continue to get your DWA and you may also be entitled to claim IS, HB and CTB if your income is low enough (see Chapters 2, 11 and 15 respectively).

Giving up work

If you were claiming invalidity benefit or severe disablement allowance prior to getting DWA and you stop working altogether within two years of your invalidity benefit/severe disablement allowance claim, you can go straight back on to that benefit from your first day of sickness.[56] This is because days on DWA count as days of incapacity for work (and also as days when you were disabled for severe disablement allowance purposes) and your two periods of sickness are linked together. As well as any basic invalidity benefit/severe disablement allowance you get increases for your partner or child (if any) under the rules which applied on your last claim.[57] Although this rule gives you an automatic right to requalify for invalidity benefit or severe disablement allowance, you must still show that you are now incapable of work. If you have been working for some time, your incapacity may be questioned by the adjudication officer. Make it clear that you have had to give up work due to ill-health or disability when you re-claim.

Periods on DWA do not help you to get the disability premium, higher pensioner premium or the severe disability premium with IS/HB/CTB. You must requalify for these in the normal way (see pp345, 348 and 351).

If your job ends after the two-year period but you are nevertheless incapable of work, claim sickness benefit when you stop working.

If you give up work for reasons other than sickness or disability you must claim unemployment benefit instead. You can also claim IS/HB/CTB (see Chapters 2, 11 and 15 respectively).

For details about claiming sickness/invalidity/unemployment benefit and severe disablement allowance, see the *Rights Guide to Non-Means-Tested Benefits*.

HB - Means - Tested — low income, Rent their Homes, Paid in Addition to IS, FC, DWA.

Rent - Rebates — Council Tenants, Rent allowance _ Private Tenants.
Max 100% - less any Non-dep.

Rent x50 ÷ 52, Council Tenants, get 2 free weeks. — Water Rates.
Saving less than 16,000.
IS = Max HB,

Weekly income is the same or less than Applicable amount 100% HB.
weekly income greater than Applicable amount 65% Taper. ∴ 65p in
every £100 by which income exceeds Applicable amount.

check Capital, Work out eligable housing costs, Work out applicable
amount, work out weekly income..

Lone parent premium £11.25.

Earnings,   £25.00 disregard - Lone parent not receiving IS.
               £15.00   "   disability premium, SDP, HPP.
               £10.00   "   Couples other than above.
               £5.00   "   any other.

All benefits Count in full except. — Mobility Supplement, A.A
Constant Attendance Allowance, SF Payments, Christmas bonus
IS, DLA.

Capital £1.00 for every £250. or part of between 3,000 + 16,000

NON-dep deductions — lives in home, but not dep. ie
Adult Relative, undep child, ie one for whom the claimant does
not receive child benefit.

Not-NON-dep— A member of the claimants family.
Share liability for payments.
Sub-Tenant, tenant, boarder, landlord.
Carers, engaged by a charitable or Voluntary body to live in claimants
home where a charge is made

No deductions will be made if non-dep - Registered blind - receives AA - or Care component of DLA - Currently stay but home elsewhere. - receiving YT Allowance - full-time student - under 25 receiving IS..

8+ who is in renumerative work - gross income under £72 = 5.00
Non-dep   "   72.00 - 107.99 - 9.00
                   108 - 138.99 = 13.00
                   139.00 → 25.00

PART FIVE IS over 25 = 5.00.

Housing benefit
Any other Non-dep @ PT Work, Pension   5.00.

£25.00 disregard earnings. lone parents Not on IS.

£15.00 - DP, SDP - HPP.

£10.00 Couples.

£5.00 any other.

RENT X 50 $\frac{0}{0}$ 52 - Water Rates

CHAPTER ELEVEN

The basic rules

This chapter covers:

1. Introduction (below)
2. 'Eligible rent' (p225)
3. 'Unreasonably high' rents (p231)

1. INTRODUCTION

Housing benefit (HB) is paid to people who have a low income and who rent their homes. It is paid whether or not the claimant is available for or in full-time work and may be paid as well as income support (IS), family credit (FC) or disability working allowance (DWA), or just by itself.

HB is paid by local authorities and not by the Benefits Agency, although it is a national scheme and the rules are mainly determined by DSS regulations.

If you are a council tenant, your rent account is credited with your benefit. This is known as a **rent rebate**.

If you are a private tenant, you are paid a cash allowance (although it is sometimes paid direct to your landlord, especially if you have rent arrears). This is known as a **rent allowance**.

Who can claim?

You can claim HB if the following conditions are satisfied:[1]

- Your income is low enough. How low it has to be depends on your circumstances (see p357). Some of your income may be ignored, but you may also be treated as having income you do not actually receive (see Chapter 18).
- Your savings and other capital are not worth more than £16,000. Again, some of your capital may be ignored, but you may also be treated as having capital you do not actually possess (see Chapter 19).
- You or your partner are liable, or treated as liable, to pay rent for

accommodation (see below). 'Rent' includes many payments not usually regarded as rent such as licensee payments. Payments for bed and breakfast accommodation and hostels also count as rent. It does not matter if you are in arrears, or if you have paid your rent in advance.

- You normally occupy that accommodation as your home (see p217), or are only temporarily absent from it (see p218).
- You are not excluded under the rules explained on p221.

You can claim HB if you live in any type of accommodation – private, local authority, housing association, board and lodging, hostels, bed and breakfast, sheltered accommodation. You can claim if you are a sub-tenant or a lodger in someone else's home or if you share housing costs.

The amount of benefit you receive depends on your income (see Chapter 18), the number of people in your 'family' (see below) and your 'eligible rent', which may be less than your actual rent (see p226). If there are people living in your home who are not members of your 'family', that, too, usually affects your entitlement (see p242). The full calculation is explained on p240.

Also note that:

- HB is non-taxable and is not dependent on you having paid national insurance contributions;
- unlike council tax benefit (CTB) and IS, there is no specific lower age limit for claiming HB;
- if you are someone from abroad you can claim HB if you satisfy certain extra conditions (see p223).

Who you claim for

As with IS, you claim for your 'family' which consists of:

- you; *and*
- your partner (if any) who is
  either your husband or wife, if you are living together (see p330),
  or a person of the opposite sex to whom you are not married but with whom you are living together as husband and wife (see p330); *and*
- any children for whom you are responsible (which may include children under 19 who have left non-advanced education – see p335).

Income and capital belonging to your partner are treated as yours. There are special rules for dealing with your children's income and capital (see pp358 and 394).

How to claim

You must claim in writing from your local authority. If you are claiming IS, you should have been given an HB and CTB claim form with your IS form. You should return this to the Benefits Agency who will forward it to the local authority. Otherwise get a form from the local authority. A claim may be backdated up to a year in certain circumstances. See p258 for more detailed advice about claims.

Liability to pay rent

To get HB, you must normally be either the person who is liable to pay the rent on your home, or the partner of the person who is liable. The partner of a student excluded from benefit can be treated as liable to pay rent. Your liability to pay rent does not have to be legally binding. If the person who is actually liable has left and you have had to start paying the rent on your home in order to remain living there (even though you are not yourself legally liable) the local authority *must* treat you as liable for the rent if you are the **former partner** of that liable person.[2] It does not matter whether or not the landlord is prepared to transfer the tenancy to you or wants to evict you. As long as you remain in the property and pay the equivalent of the rent you can claim HB. This applies equally in the case of council properties. However, some councils may refuse to accept your HB claim in this situation because they have allowed their own interests as landlords to override their duties under the HB scheme. This is wrong. You should point out that the eligibility rules for HB and for transferring council tenancies are quite separate.

In any case where you have taken over paying the rent but are not the former partner of the liable person who has left, the council still has the *discretion* to treat you as liable if it considers that it is reasonable to do so – eg, if the former tenant was your lesbian/gay 'partner' or your parent who has died or gone into long-term care etc.[3]

Joint liability

If you are a **married or unmarried couple** (see p330) and are jointly liable for the rent, only one of you can claim HB (see p257).[4]

If you are one of two or more **single people** who jointly occupy a home and have joint liability for the rent, you can all make separate claims for HB on your share (except in any case where the local authority thinks the joint tenancy has been 'contrived', see p222). The local authority apportions the eligible rent between you by considering:

- the number of jointly liable persons in the property; *and*
- the proportion of the rent actually paid by each liable person; *and*

- any other relevant factors – such as the number of rooms occupied by each jointly liable person and whether any formal or informal agreement exists between you regarding the use and occupation of the home.[5]

Where the rent includes any ineligible service charges etc, these will be apportioned between you on the same basis as the rent.[6] Note that the HB rules are different from those which apply in apportioning joint council tax liability for CTB purposes (see p302). If only one of you is responsible for the rent, s/he is treated as the tenant or occupier and the other as a non-dependant (see p242). In most cases, you get more benefit by arguing you are joint tenants.

The definition of 'unmarried couple' does not apply to lesbian or gay couples, so if you are living with someone as part of a lesbian or gay relationship you are regarded as two single people sharing accommodation.

Special circumstances

If you have already paid your **rent in advance** before claiming HB, this will not affect whether you are treated as liable for that payment – even though you have already met your liability.[7]

You can still get HB if your landlord has agreed to allow you a rent-free period as compensation for you undertaking reasonable repairs or re-decoration which s/he would otherwise have had to carry out. However, this only applies where you have actually carried out the work and then only for a maximum of eight benefit weeks in respect of any one single rent-free period.[8] As you cease to be entitled to benefit once a particular rent-free period has lasted more than eight benefit weeks, you should arrange with your landlord to schedule the work in periods of eight weeks or less separated by at least one complete benefit week where you resume paying rent.

Occupying accommodation as your home

HB can only be paid for accommodation which you normally occupy as your home.[9] In most cases, this means you are not entitled to benefit until you have actually moved in and that benefit cannot be paid on more than one home at the same time.

In deciding whether accommodation can be regarded as 'normally occupied' as your home, the local authority must take into account any other accommodation which you or your immediate family occupy both within Great Britain and abroad. Where you or your family have more than one home, benefit is only payable on the accommodation regarded as your main home – except in certain circumstances listed below. This rule cannot be used to exclude from entitlement people who have set up home in this country but whose family, who are no longer part of their household, remain living abroad.[10]

If your family is so large that the local authority have had to house you in two separate dwellings (whether adjacent or some way apart), you are treated as occupying both as your home and eligible for benefit on both.[11] Note that this rules does not apply if you have found two separate properties to rent for yourself and your family in the private rented sector.

Temporary absences from home

If you are temporarily absent from home (even if abroad) – for instance in hospital, in prison, working away or looking for work – you can get HB for up to 52 weeks.[12] The 52 weeks should run continuously from the date you leave the home. If you return during this period, even for relatively short spells, the 52 weeks begins again each time you leave.[13] However, if you spend a great deal of time away from home, this may lead the local authority to treat your normal home as elsewhere. You must intend to return to your home within 52 weeks, or, in exceptional circumstances, for not substantially longer (DSS guidance suggests that this means up to 15 months). While you are away, your accommodation must not be rented to anyone else. You will not get paid once it becomes clear that you do not intend to return. In all cases, the local authority has no power to pay you benefit for more than 52 weeks' absence. People in prison need to assess when they are likely to be able to return to their home. In practice, prisoners do not serve all of their sentence. With remission most prison sentences are reduced by half. Therefore prisoners serving two years or less should get HB. Prisoners with longer sentences could qualify on the basis of their earliest date of release. You do not need to have been getting HB before you went to prison. You can claim for the first time while you are away. If you do not claim HB, you may be able to claim HB backdated to cover the period in prison (see p260). If you are in hospital and are still entitled to HB under these rules, your benefit may be reduced after six weeks in hospital (see p247).

Students and trainees

If you are either a **single person or single parent** who is an eligible student (see p251) or a trainee on a government training course, and living away from home during your course, you are treated as follows:

- If you are only liable for payments (including mortgage interest) at one address, then that is treated as the one you occupy as your home, regardless of the proportion of time you actually live there. This would apply, for example, if you rent accommodation during term-time but return to live with your parents in the vacations.[14]

- If you are liable for payments at both addresses, you are only allowed to claim for the accommodation which is your *main* home.[15]

If one member of a **couple** is an eligible student or trainee who has unavoidably to live away from home in other accommodation during study-time, the claimant is regarded as occupying both dwellings as her/his home and can claim benefit for both.[16] Note that these rules only apply where the student is not excluded from benefit because of the full-time student restriction (see p251). Otherwise, just the partner can claim on the home address only.

Fear of violence

If you have left your previous home, and remain absent from it, through fear of violence in that home or from a former member of your family outside the home, your HB entitlement will depend on your circum-stances. Note that you only have to show you left your former home through *fear of*, rather than *actual*, violence. 'Violence' can cover any kind of violence that could take place within or at the home, even though it may originate from outside it (eg, racial violence).

- **If you have gone to live somewhere else on a temporary basis where you are also liable to pay rent (eg, in a women's refuge) and you intend to return to occupy your former home** – the local authority can con-tinue to pay you HB on your former home as well as on your current home for up to 52 weeks if they think it is reasonable to do so.[17]
- **If you have gone to live somewhere else on a temporary basis where you are not liable to pay rent (eg, with a friend) and you intend to return to occupy your former home** – the local authority can continue to pay you HB on your former home for up to 52 weeks under the nor-mal temporary absence rules (see p218).
- **If you have gone to live somewhere else permanently but remain unavoidably liable for the rent on your old home for a period after you have moved** – the local authority can continue to pay you HB on your old home for up to four weeks after you moved out.[18] If you are liable for rent on your new home, you will also be able to get HB for this from the time you move in.[19]
- **If you have gone to live somewhere else on a temporary basis (eg, in a women's refuge or with a friend) until you can get a tenancy transfer on your old home** – the local authority can pay you HB on your for-mer home for only up to four weeks after you moved out, if they con-sider that you remained unavoidably liable to pay rent there.[20] You are not covered under the rules which allow HB to be paid for up to 52 weeks on your old home, even though you remain liable for the rent, because you have no intention to return to occupy the property.[21] This

means that you will run into difficulties if your former landlord does not provide you with a tenancy transfer within four weeks of you having moved out. If you are also liable for rent on your temporary accommodation you should be able to get HB on this from the time you move in, so long as the local authority considers you are now occupying this accommodation as your home. If you are in this situation, you should ask the local authority to exercise its discretion to pay you the maximum possible additional benefit on top of any HB you do receive on the grounds that your circumstances are exceptional (see p246).

Temporary accommodation during repair work

If you have had to move into temporary accommodation to enable essential repairs to be carried out on your normal home and you are liable for payments on either (but not both) dwellings, you are treated as occupying, as your 'home', the accommodation on which you are liable to make payments.[22] If you are a private tenant you should not be liable for payments on your normal home while you are unable to live there – in which case you should only be liable (and eligible for benefit) on your temporary accommodation during this period. However, it is common practice for many local authorities not to make any charge for the temporary accommodation, but to continue to levy the rent on the home address. In this case, you are treated as still occupying your normal home and remain eligible for benefit in respect of it, even though you are not actually living there. In any circumstances where you do have a liability for both your normal and temporary homes, you are only regarded as occupying (and thus eligible for benefit on) the one you normally occupy.

Moving house

If you have moved into new accommodation and have no option but to pay rent on both your old and new home, you receive HB for both homes for up to four weeks. Under this rule, you only get HB for the new home once you have moved in and from the date that you move in.[23] However, in certain limited circumstances you can claim HB for a period of up to four weeks before moving into a new home, although you will not be paid until after the move.[24]

To qualify for this retrospective benefit you must have:

- moved into your new home;
- been liable to make payments before moving in;
- claimed benefit before moving in and either your claim was not decided until after you moved in or it was refused (because you had

not yet moved in) and you made a second claim within four weeks of moving in.

Furthermore, the delay in moving into your new home must have been reasonable and:

either a member of your family is aged five or under, or your applicable amount includes one of the pensioner or disability premiums, and your move was delayed while the Benefits Agency decided on a claim for a social fund payment for a need connected with the move (eg, removal expenses or a household item or furniture);

or the delay was necessary in order to adapt your new home to the disability needs of either you or a family member;

or you became liable to make payments on your new home while you were a hospital patient or in residential accommodation owned or managed by a local authority.

If this rule applies and you are eligible to get payments on a new home prior to moving in because you were waiting for adaptations for a disability to be made to it, you can also get HB for up to four weeks on any rented accommodation which you occupy in the meantime.[25]

Who cannot claim

There are some situations in which you cannot get HB even though you satisfy the other conditions. You are not entitled to HB if:

• you have more than £16,000 capital or savings;
• you are a full-time student.[26] There are some exceptions (see Chapter 13);
• you live in a residential care or nursing home[27] – with a few exceptions (see p230);
• you own your accommodation or have a lease of more than 21 years – unless you are a 'shared owner' (ie, buying part of your house or flat and renting the rest from a housing authority or association), in which case you can get HB on the part you rent.[28] You are treated as the owner of the property if you have the right to sell it – even though you may not be able to do this without the consent of other joint owners;[29]
• you pay rent to someone you live with and either it is not a commercial arrangement or s/he is a close relative.[30] A 'close relative' is a parent, son, daughter, step-parent, step-son, step-daughter, parent-in-law, son-in-law, daughter-in-law, brother, sister, and the partner of any of these.[31]

You are regarded as living with your landlord if you share some accommodation with them other than a bathroom, toilet or hall/

passageway – eg, you share a living-room or kitchen. However, you can argue that you do not live with your landlord unless you also share living arrangements such as cooking and financial arrangements.

DSS guidance suggests that local authorities should not assume you do not have a commercial arrangement just because you pay below a market rent or because the landlord does not rent for purely financial reasons, so long as s/he covers her/his expenses;[32]

• you have made an agreement to pay rent in order to take advantage of the HB scheme. This rule cannot be used if you have been liable to pay rent for the accommodation at any time during the eight weeks before you made the agreement.[33] Many local authorities assume that if you are living in accommodation owned by a friend or relative your rent liability must have been created to take advantage of the housing benefit scheme. You may, for example, be a single parent living in a property owned by your brother for a nominal rent.

Assumptions that relatives will allow you to live rent-free in their property should always be challenged on review. Press the local authority to explain why they think that the tenancy is contrived. Just because you are related to your landlord does not make a tenancy contrived! It may be useful to show that you were paying rent prior to claiming HB, if this is the case, or that your relative was renting out the property to someone else previously. You could also explain that they need to charge rent to cover outgoings on the property and that it was done for sound financial reasons, not just because HB was available to meet the rent. The High Court has criticised the common local authority argument that a tenancy must be contrived if the claimant could not afford to live there without getting HB, since it could be said that this would disqualify all HB claimants! Instead, the local authority should consider all the circumstances – eg, your means, circumstances and intentions and those of your landlord. They should consider what would happen if HB was not paid – eg, you might be evicted.[34]

Sometimes landlords try to take advantage of the HB rules by only letting properties to people who are eligible for benefit, and who can claim without any rent restriction (see p231), in order to be able to charge them inflated rents well above the true market level in the expectation that these will be met by HB. Tenancies created especially for this purpose were found to be 'contrived' by the High Court and HB is not payable in this situation. This would not apply, however, to housing associations and other landlords genuinely providing accommodation for people with special needs since, in these cases, the higher rents charged reflect the cost of the special facilities provided rather than any intention to take advantage of the HB scheme.[35]

- you became a joint tenant within eight weeks of having been a non-dependant of one of the other joint tenants, unless you can satisfy the local authority that you did not do this to take advantage of the HB scheme;[36]
- you are getting income support (IS) and housing costs are included in your IS applicable amount (see p29) – eg, rent for long leaseholders, charges for people in residential care. If you are now getting your housing costs met through IS but were previously getting HB for the same accommodation, your HB continues for your first four weeks on IS. This is deducted from your IS so you do not get any extra benefit; it is merely an administrative arrangement to help with the transfer of housing costs from HB to IS;[37]
- you are a Crown Tenant – there is a separate scheme for some Crown Tenants;[38]
- you make payments under a co-ownership scheme under which you will receive a payment related to the value of the accommodation when you leave;[39]
- you make payments under a hire purchase, credit sale or conditional sale agreement for, say, the purchase of a mobile home;[40]
- you are a member of, and are fully maintained by, a religious order.[41]

If you are excluded from benefit because of any of the rules above you may be treated as a non-dependant if someone else in your household claims HB (see p242).

Persons from abroad

If you are classified as a **person from abroad**[42] you are not entitled to HB and/or CTB after 1 April 1994, even though you are legally liable to pay rent and/or council tax. If you are affected by the new rules but were already receiving HB/CTB at the point of change, you are allowed to continue to receive your benefit until the end of your normal benefit period – see p265.

If you are one of a married or unmarried couple and your partner is not a **person from abroad,** s/he can claim for you both and you are paid the full amount for a couple. However, your immigration status could be jeopardised by a claim for HB, as this benefit counts as public funds. The government may extend its definition of public funds to include CTB in 1994/95. For further details, see p83. If you are here subject to the condition that you should not have recourse to public funds, you should seek independent immigration advice before claiming.

If both members of a couple are **persons from abroad**, there is no entitlement to HB/CTB.

You are treated as a **person from abroad** if:

- you have been granted limited leave to enter or remain in the UK on condition that you do not have **recourse to public funds**. The definition of public funds under the immigration rules includes HB and may eventually include CTB (see p83 for more details); *or*
- you entered the UK with limited leave but have overstayed beyond that period of leave; *or*
- you have been made subject to a deportation order (except where your removal from the UK has been deferred in writing by the Secretary of State); *or*
- you have been adjudged by the immigration authorities to be an illegal entrant and you have not been given subsequent leave to enter and remain in the UK under the immigration rules (except where you have been allowed to remain in the UK with the written consent of the Secretary of State).

Not everyone from overseas is classed as a 'person from abroad' for HB/CTB purposes. You are not classed as a 'person from abroad' and can still claim HB/CTB if:

- you have the right of abode in the UK or leave to stay here indefinitely. This includes all British citizens and Eire nationals; *or*
- you are a refugee, or have exceptional leave to remain; *or*
- you are an asylum-seeker (this applies from the date your application for asylum is made until the date it is formally decided or abandoned); *or*
- you have been given temporary admission; *or*
- you are from the Channel Islands or the Isle of Man; *or*
- you are an EU national (ie, from Belgium, Denmark, Eire, France, Germany, Greece, Italy, Luxembourg, the Netherlands, Portugal or Spain); *or*
- you are a national of a state which has signed the European Convention on Social and Medical Assistance (Iceland, Malta, Norway, Sweden and Turkey) or the Council of Europe Social Charter (Austria, Cyprus and Finland); *or*
- you have limited leave and would normally count as a **person from abroad** but your source of funding from abroad has temporarily stopped (eg, where an overseas student's grant has not come through). Provided that you have been self-sufficient during the period of limited leave and there is a reasonable chance that your funds will resume, you can claim for up to 42 days in any period of leave (including extensions). The 42 days relates to the period that you are without funds – if you delay claiming in the hope that the money will come through you

will be paid for a shorter period, so claim as soon as there is a problem; *or*
- you have not yet had your immigration status determined by the Secretary of State (eg, where the immigration officer doubts the validity of your entry documents and has not given you formal leave to enter but you have not yet been held to be an illegal entrant); *or*
- you are entitled to IS.

It is necessary for the local authority to identify claimants who have come from abroad and they are advised to do this by adding questions to the claim form for HB/CTB asking about your nationality and whether you have come to this country in the last five years. Detailed guidance has been issued to local authorities to help them decide if you are a **person from abroad**, but there will sometimes be liaison between them and the Immigration and Nationality Department to check your immigration status. You should be advised if they are intending to do this. There will also be liaison between the local authority and the Benefits Agency if you are claiming IS as well, and information which you give to one department could be passed to the other.[43]

You may be interviewed to check out whether you are entitled to claim and you will certainly be asked to produce proof of your identity and immigration status. It is likely that the local authority will ask to look at your passport. You do not have to produce this, but you will need some other way of verifying your status.

If you are unsure about how a claim for HB/CTB might affect your right to remain in the UK, you should get **independent advice** about this before making a claim. If you subsequently discover that you can claim with no problems, you should ask for your benefit to be backdated on the grounds you have 'good cause for a late claim' (see p261).

Note: The government are also proposing to introduce a new **'residence test'** which will apply *in addition* to the above rules from summer 1994. This will serve to further disqualify many persons from overseas who are not already excluded from claiming HB/CTB under the above rules (eg, many EU nationals). For more details, see p84 and the April 1994 issue of CPAG's *Welfare Rights Bulletin* .

2. 'ELIGIBLE RENT'

Your 'eligible rent' is the amount of your rent or other payments which are taken into account for the purpose of calculating your HB. It may be less than the actual amount of rent that you pay because your 'eligible rent' does not include payments such as water rates, charges for fuel or certain other services. If your rent is considered excessive, only part of it may be considered to be eligible for HB (see p231). If you are jointly liable you can claim HB on your 'share' (see p216).

What counts as 'eligible rent'

Most payments you make for the accommodation you occupy as your home (other than water rates and mortgage payments) can count as rent. The following charges are eligible rent for HB purposes:[44]

- Rent you pay in respect of a tenancy.
- Payments you make in respect of a licence or other permission to occupy premises.
- Mesne profits (in Scotland, violent profits) which include payments made if you remain in occupation when a tenancy has been ended.
- Other payments for use and occupation of premises.
- Payments of service charges required as a condition of occupation.
- Mooring charges for a houseboat.
- Site rent for a caravan or mobile home (but not a tent, although that might be met through IS – see p29).
- Rent paid on a garage or land attached to your home. Either you must be making a reasonable effort to end your liability for it, or you must have been unable to rent your home without it.[45]
- Contributions made by a resident of a charity's almshouse.
- Payments made under a rental purchase agreement under which the purchase price is paid in more than one instalment and you will not finally own your home until all, or an agreed part of, the purchase price has been paid.
- In Scotland, payments in respect of croft land.

Deductions are made if your rent includes any of the payments listed below.

Payments not counted as eligible rent

- Most fuel charges (see p227).
- Some service charges (see p228).
- Charges for meals (see p230).
- Water rates.[46]
- If you receive IS, any payment which can be met through IS[47] (see p29).
- Mortgage and other payments made by an owner-occupier.[48]
- Payments for any part of your accommodation which is used exclusively for business purposes.[49]
- Payments for most people living in registered residential care and nursing homes[50] (see p230).

- Payments made by a Crown Tenant[51] (because there is a separate rebate scheme for some Crown Tenants[52] – check with the Crown Agent).
- Payments made under a tenancy for over 21 years[53] (unless it is a shared ownership tenancy granted by a housing association or local authority under which you buy part of your home and rent the rest).
- Payments under a co-ownership scheme.[54]
- Payments under a hire purchase, credit sale or conditional sale agreement (eg, for the purchase of a mobile home).[55]
- Payments for living in local authority homes for elderly people (Part III accommodation) or other local authority accommodation (eg, a mother and baby home) where food is provided without any extra charge.[56] Even if board is not provided you cannot get HB for your accommodation costs if you were in the home on 31 March 1993 and excluded from benefit at that time.
- Rent supplements charged to clear your rent arrears.

Fuel charges

HB is not usually paid for fuel charges that are included as part of rent, such as for heating, lighting, hot water or cooking.[57] As a rule of thumb, if the charge is specified this amount is deducted from your rent. If the charge is not specified, a fixed amount is deducted.

- **If your fuel charge is specified on your rent book or is readily identifiable from your agreement with your landlord** – the full amount of the charge is deducted in arriving at your eligible rent.[58] Where your fuel charge is specified but the local authority considers it to be unrealistically low in relation to the fuel provided, the charge is treated as unspecified and a flat-rate deduction made instead (see below). This is also the case where your total fuel charge is specified but contains an unknown amount for communal areas.

    If you are a council tenant, the regulations assume your fuel charges are always specified or readily identifiable since the local authority is also your landlord.[59]
- **If your fuel charge is not readily identifiable** – a flat-rate deduction is made for fuel.[60] The flat-rate fuel deductions are:
  (a) **Where you and your family occupy more than one room:**
    - for heating (other than hot water)   £8.60
    - for hot water   £1.05
    - for lighting   £0.70
    - for cooking   £1.05
  (b) **Where you and your family occupy one room only:**

- for heating alone, or heating combined with
  either hot water or lighting or both   £5.18
- for cooking   £1.05

These amounts are added together where fuel is supplied for more than one purpose. If you are a joint tenant, all the deductions are apportioned according to your share of the rent.[61]

Where flat-rate fuel deductions have been made in calculating your HB, the local authority must notify you about this and explain that if you can produce evidence from which the actual or approximate amount of your fuel charge can be estimated, the flat-rate deductions may be varied accordingly.[62] This applies regardless of whether you occupy more than one room, or one room only. However, there is no point in providing such evidence unless it is likely to show that your charge is less than the flat-rate deductions (eg, where you live in a small bedsit).

Guidance suggests that the lower deduction for one room only should apply where you occupy one room exclusively – even if you share other rooms (such as a bathroom or kitchen, or communal lounge in a hotel).[63] You should also argue for the lower level of deductions to be made where you are forced to live in one room because the other room(s) in your accommodation are, in practice, unfit to live in (eg, because of severe mould/dampness etc).

Fuel for communal areas

If you pay a service charge for the use of fuel in communal areas, and that charge is *separately identified* from any other charge for fuel used within your accommodation, it may be included as part of your eligible rent.[64] Communal areas include access areas like halls and passageways, but *not* rooms in common use except those in sheltered accommodation (eg, a shared TV lounge or dining-room etc).[65] If you pay a charge for the provision of a heating system (eg, regular boiler maintenance etc), this is also eligible where the amount is separately identified from any other fuel charge you pay.[66]

Service charges

Most service charges are covered by HB but only if payment is a condition of occupying the accommodation rather than an optional extra.[67]

The following services are eligible for HB:

- Services for the provision of adequate accommodation including general management costs, gardens, children's play areas, lifts, entry phones, communal telephone costs, portering, rubbish removal, TV and radio relay (only relay for ordinary UK channels is covered – not satellite dishes or decoders. Cable TV is also excluded unless it is the only practicable way of providing you with ordinary domestic channels).[68]

- Laundry facilities (eg, a laundry room in an apartment block), but not charges for the provision of personal laundry.[69]
- Furniture and household equipment (as provided in a furnished tenancy), but not if there is an agreement in which the furniture will eventually become your property.[70]
- Cleaning of communal areas.[71]
- Cleaning within your own accommodation, but only if no one living in the household is able to do it.[72]
- Emergency alarm systems in accommodation designed or adapted for elderly, sick or disabled people, or which is otherwise suitable for them taking into account factors such as size, heating system or other facilities. In all other cases, emergency alarms are ineligible.[73]
- Counselling and support services, but only to the extent that they are necessary for the provision of adequate accommodation or are provided personally by the landlord. Where they are provided by someone other than the landlord (eg, a warden or caretaker), these charges will only be eligible where that person's main duty is to provide other eligible services.[74]

Deductions are made for the above charges only if the local authority regards the charges as excessive, in which case the authority will make an estimate of what it considers to be a reasonable amount given the cost of comparable services.[75]

The following services are not eligible for HB:[76]

- Food including prepared meals (see p230).
- Sports facilities.
- TV rental and licence fees (but TV and radio relay charges are eligible).
- Transport.
- Personal laundry service.
- Medical expenses.
- Nursing and personal care.
- Counselling and other support services not connected to the provision of adequate accommodation.
- Any other charge not connected with the provision of adequate accommodation and not specifically included in the list of eligible charges above.

Any ineligible service charge must be deducted in full from your rent.

Where the ineligible charge is specified, this amount is deducted from eligible rent. Authorities have the power to substitute their own estimate of the ineligible charge where the amount is considered by them to be unreasonably low for the services provided, and this higher estimated amount is deducted from your eligible rent.[77] Where the amount has not been specified in your rent agreement, the local authority must estimate how much is fairly attributable to the service, given the cost of comparable services.[78]

Charges for meals

Any charges for meals (including the preparation of meals or provision of unprepared food) cannot be covered by HB.[79] Where your housing costs include an amount for board, the local authority makes set deductions in arriving at your eligible rent. These standard deductions always apply, regardless of the actual cost of your meals.[80]

Where at least three meals a day are provided:
* for the claimant and for each additional member of the
  family aged 16 or over   £16.30
* for each additional member of the family aged under 16   £ 8.25

Where breakfast only is provided:
* for the claimant and each additional member of the
  family, regardless of age   £ 1.95

In all other cases (part-board):
* for the claimant and for each additional member of the
  family aged 16 or over   £10.80
* for each additional member of the family aged under 16   £ 5.45

Where no meals are provided within the rent for either you, or a member of your family, no meals deduction should be made for that person. Otherwise, standard deductions are made for everyone who has meals paid for by you – including meals for someone who is not part of your 'family' (eg, a non-dependant). [81]

Residential care or nursing homes

Payments for residential care and nursing homes (whether provided by the local authority or a private/voluntary organisation) are usually not covered by HB.[82] Instead, the cost is covered by IS if you are eligible. The social services/social work department may also help you with the cost.

If you are provided with accommodation by a local authority you can only get HB if:

* the local authority does not own or manage the home *and* it is not reg-

istered under the Registered Homes Act 1984; *or*

- the accommodation is owned or managed by the authority but your charge is not inclusive of cooked or prepared meals as well as accommodation.

If you were living in local authority accommodation with board on 31 March 1993 and thus excluded from HB, you continue to be excluded even if the provision of board is later withdrawn.[83]

If you live in a private or voluntary home you can claim if:

- you were entitled to, or became entitled to HB, before 30 October 1990.[84] This protection lasts for life;
- you lived there prior to 1 April 1993 and were either in full-time work, or making payments on a commercial basis in a home run by a close relative, or living in a home for less than four people. This protection applies until you leave the home (apart from temporary absences) or if you cease to qualify for HB;[85]
- you live in a Royal Charter or Act of Parliament residential home (eg, Salvation Army establishments). You can claim either IS or HB to cover your accommodation costs. This does not apply if you are in a nursing home;
- you live in a small home which is not required to be registered under the Registered Homes Act 1984 (eg, some adult placement or supported lodging schemes).

Residential care and nursing homes are those registered or mentioned under the Registered Homes Act 1984 and, in Scotland, under the Social Work Act 1968 and Nursing Homes Registration Act 1938.[86]

3. 'UNREASONABLY HIGH' RENTS

In some circumstances the local authority will not meet your full rent through HB. When assessing the amount of your eligible rent, the local authority must always consider whether your accommodation is unreasonably expensive or large in comparison with suitable alternative accommodation. If this is the case, it must reduce your eligible rent to a more reasonable amount, taking account of the cost of such cheaper accommodation. The comparison must be with accommodation which is suitable for your personal needs.

Even if it decides that your accommodation is too large or too expensive, you can avoid the reduction for either 13 weeks or 12 months in limited circumstances. The reduction will not apply at all if you, or someone in your home, fulfils certain conditions, *and either* there is no suitable accommodation actually available, *or* there is *but* it is unreasonable for you to move. In all other cases, your HB is restricted.

Local authorities are encouraged to restrict eligible rents through the central government subsidy system which penalises authorities who calculate benefit on rents above certain levels decided by the rent officer under the subsidy rules. The rent officer's figure does not impose any restriction on the amount of rent the landlord can charge, only on the amount of subsidy the authority can receive on HB paid out in that case. The role of the rent officer and the subsidy system is described in more detail on p236. In deciding whether the accommodation is too large or expensive for HB purposes, the authority can take into account the rent figure provided by the rent officer under the subsidy rules. However, authorities are not entitled to automatically equate this figure with the rent payable for suitable alternative accommodation. This is because the criteria used by the rent officer is *completely different* from that which authorities must apply under the HB rules. The rent officer's determination of a 'reasonable market rent' is about how much rent s/he thinks the landlord *would have been able to charge* if, in effect, the HB system did not exist. By contrast, under the HB rules the authority must consider the *real rent levels* which exist in order to establish the rents *actually payable* for suitable alternative accommodation. Furthermore in deciding whether the accommodation is too large for subsidy purposes, the rent officer must apply fixed criteria which do not take into account the individual needs of the claimant or other occupants (ie, whether anyone needs extra space because of a disability). The local authority, on the other hand, must do the very opposite when deciding whether the accommodation is too large for HB purposes – because it is required to take into account the *reasonable needs* of the claimant and other occupants in the process. Because of these important differences between the HB and subsidy rules, authorities cannot automatically impose a blanket 'rent stop' based on the rent officer's figure without considering your individual circumstances.[87] A blanket policy such as this can be challenged by way of judicial review (see p292). Authorities which impose such rent stops are also likely to be found guilty of maladministration by the Ombudsman (see p293).[88] Nevertheless, a large number of local authorities still appear to rely on illegal 'rent stops', rather than on a proper application of the law.

If the local authority decides to impose a rent restriction in your case, you should insist on a full explanation which gives you not only the reasons why this has been done, but also all the factors and evidence which the local authority took into account in arriving at that decision. If you suspect that the local authority has either failed to apply all the proper tests or has allowed itself to be influenced by irrelevant factors – such as

administrative convenience – you should ask for a review (see p287).
The various steps which local authorities must take are set out below.

Is your accommodation unsuitable?

The local authority can only consider your accommodation unsuitable if either of the following apply:[89]

- it is larger than is reasonably needed for you and anyone who also occupies the accommodation (including non-dependants and sub-tenants) – taking into account the sort of accommodation occupied by other households of the same size; *or*
- your rent is unreasonably high compared with that for suitable alternative accommodation elsewhere.

The local authority can take account of any assessment made by a rent officer (see p236), but is not bound by it.

Is it too large?

The needs of everyone living in your accommodation must be considered. For example, if anyone needs additional space (eg, because of a disability), this should be taken into account. If you have a child in care, or an elderly or disabled relative who normally lives in a residential home but who regularly comes to stay with you, it is reasonable that you should have a spare room for this purpose. You should also argue that it is reasonable to remain in a home where you have lived for many years but which is now larger than you need because you are widowed, separated or divorced, or because your children have now grown up and live away.

Is it too expensive?

It is not sufficient for the local authority just to show that cheaper alternative accommodation exists. It must be regarded as 'suitable' for you personally.[90] If you currently have security of tenure, any suitable alternative accommodation should offer you a reasonably equivalent degree of security. The local authority must also bear in mind your age and state of health, and that of your family or relatives described below.

Guidance suggests that your housing costs should only be compared with accommodation outside the local authority's own area if no valid comparisons exist locally. Local authorities should not 'make comparisons with other parts of the country where accommodation costs differ widely from those which apply locally'.[91]

Finally, it is not enough for the local authority to show that your rent is merely higher than that for suitable alternative accommodation. It must be 'unreasonably' higher. This means your rent must be shown to be more than might reasonably be expected for your dwelling in comparison with the alternative accommodation. In making this comparison, the local authority must consider the full spectrum of rents which could be paid for such accommodation and not just the cheapest.[92] Providing your rent falls somewhere within the band of rents one could reasonably expect to pay for such alternative accommodation, no restriction should be made – even though some cheaper accommodation may exist at the lower end of this rent band.

What are the personal circumstances of your household?

If the local authority has decided that your accommodation is unsuitable, it must then consider the personal circumstances of your family and relatives living in your accommodation before deciding whether or not to restrict your eligible rent.[93]

Your family and relatives include:

- the claimant and any partner (see p330);
- any child or young person (see p335);
- any relative of the claimant or partner (including non-dependants, sub-tenants and joint occupiers), who have no separate right to occupy the accommodation.[94] Your relatives are a parent/son/daughter, step-parent/son/daughter, parent/son/daughter-in-law, brother or sister; or a partner of any of these people; or a grandparent, grandchild, uncle, aunt, nephew or niece.[95]

If you or any of the above people living with you:

- are aged 60 or over; *or*
- satisfy any of the tests of being incapable of work for social security purposes (see p345); *or*
- have a child or young person living with you for whom you are responsible (see p335),

the local authority must consider whether cheaper suitable alternative accommodation is actually available to you *and* whether it is reasonable to expect you to move (see below).

If no one meets any of these conditions, the next step is ignored and the local authority go on to decide the reduced eligible rent (see p236).

Is it reasonable to expect you to move to a cheaper alternative?

There are two separate tests involved.

Is there cheaper suitable alternative accommodation?

If a local authority considers that suitable alternative accommodation is available, it should identify the type of accommodation it has in mind and show that it is available to you and those who live with you. They do not need to refer to specific properties which are available and cheaper, but they should identify an area or a class of properties which are suited to your particular needs. It is not sufficient to say that, in general, there are a lot of cheaper properties available in your town.[96] In addition, the DSS guidance states quite clearly that 'authorities should regard accommodation as not available if, in practice, there is little or no possibility of the claimant being able to obtain it – eg, because it could only be obtained on payment of a large deposit'.[97] This means that it is not enough for the local authority to reach a conclusion on this issue based only on general evidence of the state of the local housing market and the likely chance of someone in your circumstances being able to obtain something suitable. You should insist on being told exactly what accommodation is being referred to, why it is considered 'suitable' for you and those who live with you, and on what evidence it is considered to actually be available to you. Where the local authority is unable to provide a satisfactory reply to any of these questions you should ask for a review (see p287), but bear in mind that although the courts have accepted the need for this, there is one case in which it was held that detailed evidence was not required where the claimant had no special needs.[98] Even in this case, however, the authority/review board were criticised for failing to explain adequately why, on the basis of the evidence, they were able to conclude that suitable alternative accommodation was available and why they had rejected the claimant's counter-evidence that such accommodation was not available.

Is it reasonable to expect you to move?

The regulations compel local authorities to consider the adverse effects of a move on your job and on the education of any child or young person living with you.[99] The authority can also take account of any other relevant factors which could have a bearing on whether or not such a move could be considered reasonable in your case. For example, you should press the local authority to consider the impact of a move on any of the following:

- if you are unemployed, your chances of getting a job;

- if you are a single parent, your access to family support and adequate childcare facilities;
- the care and support you give to an elderly or disabled friend or relative who does not live in your accommodation but who lives nearby;
- the effect on your health of the move;
- the increased likelihood that you will suffer domestic or racial violence if you move into the area where the alternative accommodation is situated;
- your finances, if you are in debt and cannot afford the cost of moving home;
- if you require special medical treatment or counselling, your access to the facilities you need.

It must be reasonable to expect you to move.

If the local authority refuses to consider any relevant factor which you bring to its attention, you should request a review (see p286).

If the local authority finally considers that suitable cheaper alternative accommodation does not exist or, where it does exist, it is not reasonable to expect you to move – your HB entitlement will be based on your *full* eligible rent.

The amount of the eligible rent restriction

If you cannot satisfy the tests set out on pp233-6, the local authority must restrict your eligible rent to whatever amount it considers appropriate. However, the local authority must consider your individual circumstances and have regard to the cost of suitable alternative accommodation elsewhere. Although the local authority should not be influenced by the amount of subsidy payable when deciding whether or not to restrict rent, they could take this into account when deciding on a reasonable level at which to fix the eligible rent. The reduction cannot reduce the eligible rent below that payable for suitable alternative accommodation.[100]

No restriction can be made within 12 months of the death of anyone who used to live in your accommodation and whose circumstances would have been taken into account in deciding whether or not to impose a restriction[101] (see p234). Also, if you or someone else in your household were able to meet your housing costs when you first moved in, no restriction is made for the first 13 weeks of your benefit period[102] unless you were previously receiving HB within 52 weeks of the beginning of your current benefit period.[103]

The role of the rent officer and subsidies

Local authorities get a reduced subsidy from central government in certain cases where HB is paid for rents above a fixed threshold, set by the Secretary of State, for each area. They also get a reduced subsidy on individual claims for private rents if the rent officer decides that the claimant's accommodation is either too large for the number of occupants or above a 'notional' reasonable market rent. Where this happens, full subsidy is calculated on the basis of the lower rent figure considered by the rent officer to be appropriate in that particular case.

To assess the market rate for subsidy purposes, the local authority refers your case to the rent officer if you live in private accommodation and have a deregulated tenancy, licence or other agreement (including where you are a boarder). The local authority has the discretion to refer tenancies which have transferred to the private sector – eg, voluntary transfers, Tenants' Choice New Town Transfers and Housing Action Trusts. As a rule of thumb, this probably applies to you if your tenancy etc was either created or renewed on or after 2 January 1989 in Scotland, or 15 January 1989 in England and Wales. In some cases, it is necessary for the rent officer to visit you at home. While the rent officer has no right to demand entry into your home, if you refuse to co-operate with her/him the local authority can withhold your HB.[104]

The local authority cannot decide to restrict your eligible rent simply because the rent officer has decided that your rent is higher than what they consider is a market rent, or because reduced subsidy is payable in your case.[105] However, where the rent officer decides that your accommodation is either too large or expensive, the local authority can take the rent officer's view of these matters into account when assessing your eligible rent (see pp233-6). But the local authority is not bound by the rent officer's assessment. It must pay HB on your full rent if it considers that your rent is not unreasonable or you are protected by the legislation, despite the rent officer's decision and the subsidy implications.

The authority must consider your case individually against the steps described above. In particular, the criteria that the authority must consider in assessing unreasonably high rents and suitable alternative accommodation are quite different from those adopted by the rent officer in deciding market rents. Decisions by the rent officer can be, therefore, only one source of information used by an authority to assess eligible rents under HB legislation. If an authority automatically imposes a restriction based solely on the rent officer's decision, you should insist on a review (see p287) and consider making a complaint of maladministration to the Ombudsman (see p293).

Unreasonable rent increases

The starting point in the calculation of your rent rebate or allowance is 100 per cent of your eligible rent. Any increase in your rent is reflected by a corresponding increase in your HB. However, the local authority has the power not to meet the full amount of a rent increase in your benefit if it thinks that:

- the increase is unreasonably high compared with the increases in suitable alternative accommodation;
- the increase is unreasonable because a previous increase has occurred within the preceding 12 months.[106]

Where the local authority considers a rent increase to have been unreasonable, it may either refuse to meet all of that increase or only so much of it as it considers appropriate in the circumstances. However, if your rent has been increased for the second time in under 12 months but is still below the market level for suitable alternative accommodation, or the increase reflects improvements made to your accommodation, you should press for the full amount to be allowed.[107] If the local authority refuses, you should ask for a review (see p287).

CHAPTER TWELVE

The amount of benefit

This chapter covers:

1. The basic calculation (below)
2. Deductions for non-dependants (p242)
3. Extra benefit in exceptional circumstances (p246)
4. People in hospital (p247)
5. Transitional payments (p248)

I. THE BASIC CALCULATION

How your benefit is worked out

This depends on:

- your 'applicable amount' – which represents your family's needs (see p341);
- your 'eligible rent' (see p225);
- whether any deductions are to be made for non-dependants who live in your home (see p242);
- your income (see Chapter 18).

Remember that no benefit is paid if your capital is over £16,000.

The most HB you can get is called your **'maximum housing benefit'**. This is your 'eligible rent' less any deductions for non-dependants.[1] In some exceptional cases you can get extra HB (see p246).

Because entitlement to IS acts as an automatic passport to maximum HB (once you have made a claim for HB), the local authority does not need to work out applicable amounts, income or capital. However, if you are not on IS, you do need to work them out (see p240).

No HB is payable if the amount would be less than 50 pence a week.[2]

A local authority may round any figure used in working out your entitlement to the nearest penny (a half-penny is rounded upwards).

The steps below will help you to calculate HB.

If you are on income support

Step 1 Work out your **weekly eligible rent** (see p225).

Step 2 Work out whether there should be any **non-dependant deductions** from your rent (see p242).

Step 3 Deduct the amount in Step 2 from that in Step 1.

The result in Step 3 is the amount of HB to which you are entitled.

If you are not on income support

Step 1 Work out your **capital** (see Chapter 19). If you have more than £16,000 capital, you do not need to continue as you will not be entitled to any benefit.[3] If you have capital between £3,000 and £16,000, remember this will give you an assumed tariff income which will need to be included in Step 5 (see p385).

Step 2 Work out your weekly **eligible rent** (see p225).

Step 3 Work out whether there should be any **non-dependant deductions** from your rent (see p242).

Step 4 Work out your **maximum HB** (see p239).

Step 5 – Work out your applicable amount (see pp339-56).
  – Work out your income (see Chapter 18).
  – Compare your income with your applicable amount. *If your income is equal to, or less than, your applicable amount*, you are entitled to your maximum HB worked out in Step 4.[4] *If your income is more than your applicable amount*, work out the difference and carry on to Step 6.

Step 6 Work out your HB which is your maximum HB (worked out in Step 4) less 65 per cent of the difference between your income and applicable amount.

The percentage of 65 is known as a 'taper' because it determines the rate at which your HB is reduced (or tapers off) as your income rises above your applicable amount.[5] In practice, this means a reduction of 65 pence in your maximum HB for every pound of extra income.

Example I

Mr and Mrs Finestein and their adult son live together in a flat. Mrs Finestein is the sole tenant and pays rent of £65 a week, which includes all their fuel. Mr Finestein receives IS for himself and his wife while they are looking for work. Their son earns £110 a week gross. Mr Finestein claims HB.

His eligible rent is £53.60 a week (ie, £65 – £11.40 deducted because of the fuel charges – see p227).

His son counts as a non-dependant and the appropriate deduction for him is £13 a week (see p244).

Therefore, his maximum HB is £40.60 a week (£53.60 – £13).

Because he receives IS, his HB is £40.60 a week. The amount is lower than his actual rent because his fuel charge is not covered by HB and because his son is expected to make a contribution to the rent.

Example 2

Mrs Finestein then finds a job for which she is paid £120 a week after deductions of tax and national insurance contributions. There is no occupational pension scheme. Her husband ceases to be entitled to IS because she now works full-time and he makes a new claim for HB.

Mr Finestein's maximum HB is still £40.60 a week.

His applicable amount is £71.70 (the standard rate for a couple – see p341).

His income is £110 a week (because £10 of his wife's earnings is disregarded – see p371).

The difference between his income and his applicable amount is therefore £38.30 a week.

65 per cent of £38.30 a week is £24.90 a week.

Mr Finestein's HB is therefore £40.60 – £24.90 = £15.70 a week.

Calculating a weekly amount of HB

Entitlement to HB is always paid for a specific benefit week, a period of seven consecutive days beginning with a Monday and ending on a Sunday.[6] So if you pay rent at different intervals (eg, monthly) the amount has to be converted to a weekly figure before the benefit can be calculated.[7]

If your rent is paid in a multiple of weeks (eg, four-weekly), you simply divide the rent figure by the number of weeks it covers.[8]

If the rent period is not a whole number of weeks, you divide the figure by the number of days in the period. This 'daily rent' is then multiplied by seven to give the equivalent weekly figure to be used in the calculation.[9]

Rent-free periods

If you have a regular rent-free period (eg, you pay rent on a 48-week rent year) you get no benefit during your rent-free period, and different figures are used to calculate your benefit during the weeks you pay rent. The intention is that your income for the whole year is used to assess your HB for the weeks in which you actually do pay rent. This is achieved by adjusting your applicable amount, your weekly income, non-dependant deductions, the set deductions for meals and fuel charges and the minimum amount payable (but not your eligible rent).[10] The rules for doing this are as follows:

- **Where your rent is paid weekly or in a whole multiple of weeks**, you should multiply the figures to be converted by 52 (or 53 as appropriate) to give the annual amounts. These should then be divided by the number of weeks in the year in which you actually pay rent to give the converted amounts for use in the calculation. So, for a 48-week rent year, all the figures would need to be multiplied by 52 and the result divided by 48.[11]
- **Where your rent is paid on some other basis**, you should multiply all the figures to be converted by 365 (or 366 as appropriate) and divide the result by the number of days in the rent year for which rent is actually payable. So, if you pay rent every calendar month except December (31 days), all the figures would need to be multiplied by 365 and the result divided by 334 (365 – 31).[12]

You then calculate HB using these adjusted figures. This rule does not apply if your landlord has temporarily waived the rent in return for you doing repairs, see p217.

2. DEDUCTIONS FOR NON-DEPENDANTS

A deduction may be made from your HB where you live with someone who is not part of your 'family'.[13] These people are called 'non-dependants'. It is assumed that they contribute towards the costs of the accommodation – regardless of whether or not this actually happens.

Who is a non-dependant

A non-dependant is someone who normally lives in your household such as an adult son/daughter or other relative. If someone pays you to live in part of your accommodation on a commercial basis s/he is not a non-dependant but a tenant, sub-tenant or boarder – unless s/he does not count as paying rent under the HB rules, in which case s/he is counted as a non-dependant – eg, someone paying rent to a close relative (see p222). The definition of non-dependant is a negative one in that it includes everyone who 'resides' with you who does not fit into some other category. **The following people living with you are not counted as non-dependants** in your benefit assessment:[14]

- any member of your 'family' (see p328);

- any child or young person who lives with you but who does not count as a member of your 'household' (eg, a foster child – see p328);
- anyone who jointly occupies your accommodation and shares liability for 'payments in respect of occupation' – eg, a joint tenant. The intention of this rule is to restrict the definition of 'joint occupier' to people who share liability for mortgage or rent payments. However, the wording leaves open the possibility that 'payments in respect of occupation' could include joint responsibility for payments such as fuel costs and water rates;
- anyone who occupies part of your dwelling who is your tenant/ sub-tenant, boarder or your landlord and their family;
- any carer engaged by a charitable or voluntary body to live in your home and look after you or your partner – but only where a charge is made for doing so.

A non-dependant is only regarded as 'residing' with you if s/he is not separately liable for her/his own housing costs to the landlord and s/he shares some accommodation with you apart from a bathroom, lavatory, or a communal area such as a hall, passageway or a room in common use in sheltered accommodation.[15] For example, where part of your home has been converted to include a self-contained 'granny-flat', the person occupying it would not be a non-dependant even though s/he shares your bathroom and toilet. On the other hand, a grown-up son or daughter who lives in your home and shares the use of the kitchen as well as the bathroom and toilet would be classed as your non-dependant – even though they may have another room to themselves. However, it may be possible to argue that a person cannot be considered to be 'residing with' you unless s/he also shares living arrangements, such as cooking and paying the bills, as well as accommodation. Before advancing this argument it is important to check that you will be better off, because income from non-dependants is ignored but income from other people may be taken into account (see p384).

Deductions from your eligible rent

When no deduction is made

- No non-dependant deductions are made if either you or your partner are registered blind or have regained your eyesight within the last 28 weeks; or receive attendance allowance, or the care component of the disability living allowance. This is regardless of the number of non-dependants or their circumstances.[16]
- No deduction is made in respect of any non-dependant who is:[17]

- currently staying in your household but whose normal home is elsewhere;
- receiving Youth Training allowance;
- a full-time student. This only applies during the period of study (which includes the short vacations). It also applies during the summer vacation unless the student is in full-time work;
- in hospital for more than six weeks;
- in prison;
- under 18-years-old;[18]
- aged under 25 and receiving IS.[19]

The amount of deductions

Local authorities may be reluctant to investigate the circumstances of your non-dependants in too much detail and may make the highest deduction unless you tell them otherwise. Try to provide information to show which deduction applies, and if you cannot (because, for example, a non-dependant will not co-operate), ask the local authority to consider their circumstances – ie, are they doing a job which is normally very low paid.

Unless you or your non-dependant(s) are exempt, a deduction is made from your eligible rent for every non-dependant living in your household (except in the case of a couple – see below).

The non-dependant deductions are as follows:[20]

Circumstances of the non-dependant	*Deduction*
Aged 18 or over and in full-time work with a weekly gross income of	
£139 or more	£25.00
£108-£138.99	£13.00
£72-£107.99	£ 9.00
Aged 25 or over on IS	£ 5.00
All others aged 18 or over (including those in part-time work, on pensions or other benefits but excluding those on IS between 18-24)	£ 5.00

Full-time work is paid employment of 16 hours or more each week.[21] In estimating the number of hours worked, any recognised holidays or leave are ignored. The local authority also ignores any absences from work which, in its opinion, are without good cause[22] (this probably includes days lost through strikes and lay-offs). Where the number of hours worked fluctuates, the average is taken.[23] However, where a person is on IS for more than three days in any benefit week, they are not treated as being in full-time work for that week.[24]

Generally, non-dependants involved in Training for Work are not regarded as being in full-time work and the lowest deduction applies. If they were on IS prior to getting HB and thus their training allowance includes an amount of IS, no deduction should be made.[25]

A non-dependant who is sick or on maternity leave is not in full-time work and the lower deduction should apply, even if the employer is making up the non-dependant's full wages.[26]

The earnings amounts are gross figures (ie, in the case of wages the amount before tax and national insurance are deducted). They relate to the total income of the non-dependant, (apart from attendance allowance, disability living allowance and payments from any of the Macfarlane Trusts, the Eileen Trust, the Fund and the Independent Living Funds which are ignored as income) and not just income from employment. For example, where the non-dependant is a working single parent, any child benefit or maintenance received would be taken into account along with wages. In the case of a non-dependant couple, their joint income counts in deciding the level of deduction, even if only one of them is in full-time work.

The earnings bands only apply to non-dependants in full-time work. A non-dependant who works less than 16 hours will not attract the higher levels of rent deduction even if their weekly gross income exceeds £72.

The DSS guidance stresses that local authorities are not expected to investigate the income of non-dependants in every case.[27]

Non-dependant couples

Only one deduction is made for a married or unmarried couple (or the members of a polygamous marriage) who are non-dependants. Where the individual circumstances of each partner are different, the highest deduction is made.[28]

Non-dependants of joint occupiers

Where joint occupiers share a non-dependant, the deduction is divided between them. This should be done taking into account the number of joint occupiers and the proportion of housing costs paid by each one. But no apportionment should be made between the members of a couple.[29] Where the person is a non-dependant of only one of the joint occupiers (ie, a grown-up son or daughter), the full deduction will be made from that joint occupier's benefit only.

Capital and income of a non-dependant

Normally, the capital and income of any non-dependant living in your household is completely ignored when assessing your HB entitlement[30] (except for deciding which non-dependant deduction applies). However, if:

- you are not on IS, *and*
- the capital and income of the non-dependant are both greater than yours, *and*
- the local authority is satisfied you have made an arrangement with the non-dependant to take advantage of the HB scheme,

your benefit entitlement is assessed on the basis of the non-dependant's capital and income rather than your own.[31] Any capital and income normally treated as belonging to you is completely ignored (but the rest of the calculation proceeds as normal – ie, the non-dependant deduction is based on the non-dependant's circumstances and the applicable amount depends on the circumstances of you and your family).[32]

This would apply, for example, where a tenancy has been transferred to another household member with lower capital and income in order to qualify for, or increase the amount of, HB. In such cases, the local authority must notify both the claimant and non-dependant of what action it has taken and why, and must advise them of their right to ask for further information and a review of the decision.[33]

3. EXTRA BENEFIT IN EXCEPTIONAL CIRCUMSTANCES

If the local authority considers your circumstances to be 'exceptional', it can pay you extra HB over and above your normal entitlement.[34] The meaning of the term 'exceptional circumstances' is not defined and it is for local authorities to decide how to use their discretion in any individual case. You should argue for this to be used wherever hardship would otherwise arise. Examples are where you have additional expenses due to disability but do not meet the strict criteria for a disability premium; where you are in serious financial difficulties because some unexpected event has led to a dramatic drop in your income, such as a family bereavement, illness or redundancy; where there is some temporary increase in your commitments, such as removal expenses and deposits etc on moving home; where you are threatened with eviction or fuel disconnection because of arrears.

It is your individual circumstances which count and this power should not be used to pay extra benefit on the basis of predefined conditions. In any case where additional benefit is paid, it can either be paid on a weekly basis for as long as the exceptional circumstances warrant it, or can be made as a 'one-off award'.

You are unlikely to be considered for any additional benefit unless you specifically ask for it. Make sure you give clear reasons why you need the additional help. The local authority must consider your request on the merits of your individual case. If you are refused additional benefit, you should ask for a review.

The overall limit is your eligible rent[35] (see p225). This means additional benefit can compensate for any non-dependant deductions and the effect of the taper. If you need a lump sum you can ask for your additional benefit to be backdated or paid in advance. The local authority cannot use this power unless you are entitled to receive HB during the period of payment of the extra benefit. The power can only be used to pay benefit in addition to, and not as a substitute for, normal entitlement.[36]

The local authority also has the power to pay extra benefit to people getting either a war disablement pension or a war widow's pension including similar pensions paid by non-UK governments, by ignoring this as income in the HB calculation.[37] If the authority uses this power it must apply the income disregard to *all* people in receipt of these benefits. This arrangement is usually called a 'local scheme' because the authority must pay for the extra benefit. The authority also has to pay for extra benefit paid to individuals because of exceptional circumstances. The total annual amount they can pay under both conditions is limited.[38] However, this total annual limit does not apply to benefit awarded by review boards.

4. PEOPLE IN HOSPITAL

If you or your partner go into hospital your HB is affected as follows:

- **up to six weeks** – there is no change to your HB;
- **after six weeks** – benefit is reduced for adults in hospital;
- **after 52 weeks** – no HB is paid.

If you get IS the six-week rule does not apply to HB (but may to your IS) and your HB is paid in full for up to 52 weeks, as long as you intend to return home within the year, or not much more than a year[39] (see p218).

After six weeks in hospital

If you are on IS these rules do not apply and your HB is paid as normal. If you are not on IS, after six weeks your applicable amount (see p339) is reduced as follows:

- **Single claimant** – Your applicable amount is reduced to £14.40.[40]
- **Single parent** – Your applicable amount is reduced to £14.40 personal

allowance *plus* your children's personal allowances, *plus* the family, lone parent and disabled child premiums.[41]

- **Couple with one adult in hospital** – Your applicable amount is reduced by £11.50 (this also applies if you are both in hospital but only one of you has been there for over six weeks).[42]
- **Couple with both adults in hospital** – Your applicable amount is reduced to £28.80 personal allowance for you both, *plus* personal allowances for your children, if any, *plus* family and disabled child premiums, if any.[43]
- **Partners of polygamous marriages where not all partners have been in hospital for six weeks.** Your applicable amount is reduced by £11.50 for each adult in hospital for over six weeks.[44]
- **Partners of polygamous marriages where all adults are in hospital.** Your applicable amount reduces to £14.40 for each partner, *plus* allowances for children, *plus* family premiums or disabled child premium.[45]

The six weeks are calculated by adding together any separate stays in hospital less than 28 days apart.[46] The reduction takes effect from the beginning of the benefit week (see p265) *after* you have been in hospital for six weeks.

There are no reductions to your benefit if a dependent child goes into hospital.

5. TRANSITIONAL PAYMENTS

In April 1988, HB was changed. Some people who were worse off under the new scheme were made payments to compensate for their losses.

For more information, see the 19th edition of the *Handbook*, p209.

CHAPTER THIRTEEN

Special rules for students

This chapter covers:

Most full-time students cannot claim housing benefit (HB) during their course, including the summer vacations falling within it. However, there are some exceptions to this rule. Students who remain eligible for HB are subject to additional rules. There are special rules for the treatment of students' income, including grants and top-up loans (see p379). For the position of students claiming council tax benefit (CTB), see Chapter 15.

I. GENERAL RULES

Who counts as a student

A **student** is someone attending a course of study at an educational establishment.[1] This covers any full-time, part-time or sandwich course, either advanced or non-advanced, whether or not you get a grant for attending it. The term educational establishment is not defined in law, but DSS guidance suggests it should include private as well as state-funded institutions. Once you have started on your course you are treated as a student attending a course throughout all your term and vacation periods, until either the **last day of the course** or until you **abandon** it or are **dismissed** from it. 'Last day of the course' means the date on which the last day of the final academic year is officially scheduled to fall and not the date you actually leave if you do so just before then (eg, where you are able to leave a few weeks early after having taken final exams).[2]

You should be eligible to claim HB if you decide to take a year off from your studies because you will have *abandoned* your course for this period. Your local authority may refuse to accept this on the grounds that you clearly intend to resume your studies on the same course at some point in the future – ie, 'abandon' is often assumed to mean 'give up irrevocably'. The considerations are the same as for income support (IS) (see p20) and although IS case law is not binding on the local authority you should persuade them to accept the correct legal interpretation which it contains.

Full-time students

The law does not define 'full-time student', except to say that it includes someone on a sandwich course.[3] The local authority is expected to decide by looking at the nature of the course you are attending and, if in doubt, by consulting the educational establishment involved. Local authorities are advised that student grants are normally only payable for full-time courses. If you get a grant, and especially if the level of your grant seems appropriate to a full-time course, the local authority will probably decide to treat you as a full-time student.[4] If you disagree with a decision made by the local authority, you should request a review (see p287).

The period of study

If you are eligible, your entitlement in any week depends on whether that week falls either inside or outside a period of study. Your period of study[5] is *either*:

(a) where your course is for one year or less – the period from the first to the last day of the course; *or*

(b) where your course is for more than one year and a grant is paid, or would be paid, on the basis of you studying throughout the year (as in many post-graduate courses) – the period from the first day of the course until the day before the next year of the course. In the final year the period of study ends with the last day of your final academic term; *or*

(c) in any other case (ie, in most cases), where your course is for more than one year – from the first day of each academic year until the day before the start of the recognised summer vacation. In the final year the period of study ends with the last day of your final academic term.

In deciding whether or not your grant has been assessed on the basis of you studying throughout the whole year (as in (b) above), the local authority should ignore supplements to your grant (eg, dependants' allowances) which are paid for the full year, regardless of the length of the course.

Your period of study includes Christmas and Easter vacations and periods of practical experience outside the educational establishment for students on sandwich courses.[6]

2. STUDENTS WHO ARE ELIGIBLE

Full-time students

There are a number of exceptions to the general rule that full-time students are not entitled to HB. You can claim HB as a full-time student if:[7]

- you are on IS;
- you are under 19 and not following a course of higher education. Higher education includes degree courses, teachers' training, HND, HNC, post-graduate courses;
- you and your partner are both full-time students and have dependent children;
- you are a lone parent who satisfies the conditions for a lone parent premium;
- you are a lone foster parent where the child has been formally placed with you by a local authority or voluntary agency;
- you have a disability *and*:
  - meet the conditions for either the disability or severe disability premium, *or*
  - were getting IS immediately before 1 September 1990 as a disabled student on the grounds that you would be unable to get a job within a reasonable period of time compared to other students, *or*
  - claimed HB/IS after 1 September 1990 and for any period in the 18 months before you claimed HB/IS, were getting IS as a disabled student in both advanced or non-advanced education, *or*
  - satisfy the conditions for a grant supplement in the form of a disabled student's allowance award because of deafness;
- you are a pensioner who satisfies the conditions for one of the pensioner premiums.

Full-time students who can claim HB are subject to the special rules described in this chapter. If you are on a government training scheme (see p61) receiving a training allowance, you are not classed as a student and none of the special rules for students apply to you.

Partners of ineligible students

Partners who are not themselves ineligible as students can claim HB.[8] Where a partner makes a claim, her/his benefit is calculated according to the normal rules (ie, based on a couple's applicable amount and joint income/capital), except that the special rules for calculating a student's income (see p255) and for calculating eligible rent (see p254) are applied.

Part-time students

Part-time students can claim HB.

3. STUDENTS WHO ARE INELIGIBLE

Full-time students

You cannot get HB for the duration of the whole of your course (including vacations) if you are a full-time student (but for exceptions, see p251).[9] If you have a partner who is not a full-time student s/he may be able to get HB (see above). Part-time students can still claim HB.

Being away from your accommodation

If you are a **full-time student** (see p250) who is eligible for HB and you are absent from your accommodation for the whole of any benefit week outside your period of study, you are still not entitled to HB for your rent for that week unless:[10]

- your main purpose in occupying your accommodation is not because it makes it easier for you to attend your course – eg, it is where you normally live; *or*
- you have had to go into hospital for treatment – except where you would have been absent anyway, for some other reason.

The local authority may set your benefit period to end at the start of the summer vacation so that they can check that you are entitled.[11]

Full-time students are affected by this during the long summer vacation. But it only applies where it is the claimant who is a full-time student. If you are claiming HB, and you are the partner of a full-time student, this restriction will not apply unless you are also a full-time student.[12] Thus, if you are not a full-time student you should ask the local authority to treat you as the claimant instead (see p257). Where this restriction does not apply, any temporary absences are dealt with under the normal rules as for other claimants (see p218).[13]

Accommodation rented from an educational establishment

If you rent your accommodation from your educational establishment (ie, you live in a hall of residence), *regardless of whether you are a full-time student or not*, you are not eligible to claim HB during your period of study (see p250).[14]

However, this only applies where you pay rent to the same educational establishment as the one you attend for your studies. It does not apply where your educational establishment itself rents the accommodation from a third party, unless this is on a long lease or where the third party is an education authority providing the accommodation as part of its functions.[15] So you are eligible for benefit where your educational establishment has temporarily leased accommodation from a private landlord, housing association or housing authority and sub-lets it to students.

However, the local authority can still apply this rule if it decides that your educational establishment has arranged for your accommodation to be provided by a person or body other than itself in order to take advantage of the HB scheme.[16]

If you and your partner jointly occupy accommodation rented from your educational establishment, and your partner is not a student, the restriction which would have been applied to you also applies to her/him if s/he is the claimant.[17]

Regardless of any restrictions which may apply during your period of study, you can claim a rent allowance if you continue to rent your accommodation from your educational establishment outside that period.[18]

Living in different accommodation during term-time

The rules about claiming HB for two homes are explained on p219.

If you are a member of a couple and receive HB for two homes, the assessment of benefit for each home is based on your joint income, your couple's applicable amount and, in both cases, the rent deduction (see p254) and corresponding income 'disregard' (see p255) is applied.

4. STUDENTS FROM OVERSEAS

Most overseas students cannot claim HB because they are persons from abroad (see p223). Even if you are entitled, a successful claim for HB

254 *Housing benefit* 13: Special rules for students

could affect your right to stay in this country and it is best to get immigration advice before making a claim. To qualify for HB you must be an eligible overseas student and you must also fulfil the general rules for students.

Partners of ineligible overseas students

Where you are not eligible, but there are no restrictions on your partner, either as a student or as a person from abroad, s/he may be able to claim instead.[19] However, if s/he receives HB and *you* are a **person from abroad** (see p223) this may affect your right to remain in the UK under the immigration rules because a claim by one partner is a claim for both.

5. CALCULATING STUDENTS' BENEFIT

If you or your partner get IS or a training allowance, the fact that you are studying does not affect how your HB is calculated and none of the rules which follow apply to you. In all other cases where you and/ or your partner are students and eligible for HB, this is worked out in the same way as for other non-IS claimants (see p240), apart from some extra rules about assessing your income and eligible rent (see below).

Assessing your rent

The student rent deduction

If you are a **full-time student**, your weekly eligible rent (ie, the rent figure used in working out your HB – see p225) is, in most cases, reduced during your period of study by:

- £24.80 if you are attending a course in London; *or*
- £17.20 if you are studying elsewhere.[20]

Note that the level of deduction depends on the area where you study rather than the area where you live. When a deduction applies, it must be made every week during your period of study (see p250), even where a grant is not paid or is paid for term-time only. Where the deduction is more than your rent, your eligible rent is reduced to zero and you are not eligible for any HB regardless of your income level. However, you may be entitled to some HB outside your period of study when the rent deduction does not apply.

In any week in which your eligible rent is reduced, your income used for calculating your entitlement is reduced by the same amount (see p255). Nevertheless, the overall effect is to give you less benefit.

The rent deduction applies equally where it is the claimant's partner who is a full-time student,[21] but only one rent deduction and income disregard should be made where both partners are full-time students. Where several full-time students share accommodation as joint occupiers, the full rent deduction must be made from each individual student's share of the total rent.

When the student rent deduction does not apply

The student deduction is not made if:[22]

- you are only a part-time student;
- you or your partner are on IS;
- you or your partner receive a training allowance for your own maintenance or for that of your child;
- you are a student on a sandwich course during any period of work experience (industrial, professional or commercial);
- your income for HB purposes is less than the sum of your applicable amount and the amount of the rent deduction, and one of the following also applies:
  - you are a single parent; *or*
  - the disability premium applies; *or*
  - you have a partner and only one of you is a full-time student.

If none of these apply to you and the deductions result in hardship, you could ask the authority to make a discretionary addition to your benefit, see p246. The authority will not be able to increase your benefit above the eligible rent figure calculated under the *main* rules (see pp225-30) – for students this means your eligible rent *before* the student rent deduction has been applied.[23] This will enable the authority to compensate for the effects of the rent deduction where your circumstances are exceptional.

Assessing your income

These extra rules apply equally where a student's partner is the claimant.

In any week when the student rent deduction applies (see p254), an equivalent amount is also deducted from your income.

For rules about the treatment of grants, top-up loans and covenant income, for the purpose of calculating your income, see p379.

6. PAYMENTS

Students are covered by all the normal rules on the administration and payment of HB. However, there are two provisions which can apply specifically to students.

Firstly, the local authority has the discretion to decide how long your benefit period should last and, therefore, when you need to renew your claim. For most eligible students, there are two benefit periods a year – one during their period of study, and the other during the long summer vacation (see p250).

Secondly, the local authority may decide to pay a rent allowance once each term, subject to two conditions:[24]

- Rent allowance payments cannot be made more than two weeks before the end of the period to which they relate (this means that you would have to wait until two weeks before the end of term before being paid).
- Students have the same right as other claimants to insist on fortnightly payments if their rent allowance entitlement is more than £2 a week (see p267).

CHAPTER FOURTEEN

Claims, payments and reviews

This chapter covers:

1. CLAIMS

Who can make a claim

If you are a **single person** (including a single parent or a member of a gay or lesbian couple), you make a claim for housing benefit (HB) on your own behalf.

If you are a **member of a couple**, or a **partner in a polygamous marriage**, you can decide between you who should claim for your family. In most cases, the choice of claimant will not affect the level of benefit you receive as your needs and resources are combined (but see pp252 and 271 for some important exceptions). If you cannot agree who should be the claimant, the local authority can decide for you.[1]

If a person is either temporarily or permanently unable to manage her/his own affairs (eg, because of an accident or through mental or physical disability), the local authority must accept a claim made by someone formally appointed to act legally on that person's behalf – eg, someone appointed with power of attorney, a receiver appointed by the Court of Protection, or, in Scotland, a tutor, curator or other guardian administering the person's estate.[2]

Otherwise the local authority can decide to make someone an **appointee** who can act on the claimant's behalf. This may be someone who is already the appointee for DSS benefits or some other suitable person aged 18 or over (such as a relative, friend, neighbour or social worker).[3] For the purpose of the HB claim, an appointee has the responsibility of exercising all the rights (to make a claim, receive payment, request reviews etc) and duties (to provide information, report changes in circumstances etc) as though s/he were the claimant.[4] You can write in to ask to be an appointee, and can resign after giving four weeks' notice. The local authority may terminate any appointment it has made at any time.[5]

How to make a claim

All claims must be made in writing, either on an official claim form or otherwise in a way which is 'sufficient for the purpose' in your case, and accompanied by the information necessary to assess your claim.[6] Claim forms are available from your local authority – but if you are claiming income support (IS) you should find a special shortened HB and council tax benefit (CTB) claim forms (NHB1) folded into your IS claim form.[7]

DSS guidance suggests that a letter stating that you wish to claim could be regarded as an acceptable alternative to a claim form.[8] So you should not delay making a claim just because you do not have an official claim form, or you could lose benefit. Where a claim by letter is not accepted as sufficient, you will be sent an official claim form to fill in. If you return this within four weeks (or longer at the local authority's discretion), it is treated as if it had been received on the date of your original claim.[9] Similarly, if you do not complete the claim form properly it is sent back to you and, if you return it properly completed within four weeks (or longer, if the local authority allows more time), it is treated as though you had completed it properly in the first place.[10] Send your claim form immediately, as other information and evidence such as pay slips can be sent later (see p259).

As a claim must always be in writing, you cannot claim by telephone. However, if you telephone to ask for a claim form, ask on the form to have your claim backdated to the date of your phone call (or longer, if appropriate) because you have **good cause for a late claim** (see p260).

You may **amend or withdraw your claim** in writing at any time before it has been assessed. Amendments must be made in writing and are treated as though they were part of your original claim.[11] A notice to withdraw your claim takes effect from the day it is received.[12]

Usually, you claim HB and CTB together but in Scotland some claimants have to make a separate claim for a rent rebate or allowance and for CTB. This is because in Scotland, District Councils are responsible for HB and Regional Councils are responsible for CTB. In most cases, however, District Councils agree to operate the CTB scheme for Regional Councils on an agency basis so that only one claim is necessary.

Where to make your claim

Unless you are claiming IS, you should always send your claim to the local authority[13] (the address is on the claim form). If you pay rent to a New Town Corporation, the Development Board for Rural Wales or the Scottish Special Housing Association, you should apply to them for benefit.[14]

If you are claiming IS, you can either send your claim to your Benefits Agency office or to the local authority.[15] If you claim IS and send your HB/CTB claim to the Benefits Agency, it must be forwarded by the Benefits Agency to the local authority within two working days of either the date your IS claim was assessed, or the date your HB/CTB claim was received at the Benefits Agency, whichever is later, or as soon as possible after that.[16] One important implication of this is that a delay in assessing your IS claim also causes a delay in processing your HB/CTB claim. So, if you know there are significant delays at your local Benefits Agency office, it may be wise to send your HB/CTB form directly to the local authority. If you do this the local authority will want to verify your entitlement to IS before assessing your HB and usually does this by contacting the Benefits Agency direct, but should also accept a girobook as proof of IS. This may speed up your HB/CTB claim.

Information to support your claim

Your application for benefit should be accompanied by all the information and evidence needed to assess your claim, but you should not delay your claim just because you do not have all the evidence ready to send.[17] The local authority can require you to provide any further information it reasonably needs, before it assesses your claim. You must supply any information requested in connection with your claim within four weeks – or longer if the local authority thinks you need more time.[18] If you fail, without good reason, to provide information which it is reasonable for them to request within the time allowed, the local authority does not have to process your claim.[19] Contact the local authority as soon as possible with the information requested and ask them to extend the four-week period. You need to give a good reason for your delay – eg, you did not receive their letter requesting extra information, or the information was not available sooner. The local authority should not ask you to provide unnecessary proof or evidence which you cannot provide because it does not exist – eg, proof that you have no income. You do not need to declare receipt of payments from any of the Macfarlane Trusts, the

Eileen Trust, the Fund, nor income in kind,[20] nor do you have to tell the local authority that a non-dependant is receiving such payments.

The local authority must also remind you of your duty to report any relevant changes of circumstances which may take place both before and after your claim is assessed, and tell you exactly what sort of changes you must report[21] (see p271).

If you live in privately rented accommodation and have a deregulated tenancy or licence, your claim is usually referred to the rent officer (see p236) and so you may be visited by the rent officer in connection with your claim for HB. The main reason for the visit is to decide whether your rent is 'unreasonably high' or your accommodation is 'unreasonably large' for internal subsidy purposes (see pp233-6). If you refuse to co-operate with the rent officer, the local authority has the power to withhold your HB until you do.[22] Payment of HB may be delayed pending a decision of the rent officer and local authority over the level of your rent. If this happens you should make sure you get a payment on account (see p267).

Your date of claim

Your date of claim is important because it affects the date from which your HB begins (see p265). Usually, your claim is treated as made on the day it reaches the local authority.[23] The only exceptions are if:

- you have successfully claimed IS and your HB claim reached the Benefits Agency within four weeks of the date you claimed IS – in which case the HB claim is treated as having been made on the first day of entitlement to IS;[24]
- you have unsuccessfully claimed IS – in which case your HB claim is treated as having been made on the day it reached either the Benefits Agency or the local authority, whichever is the earlier;[25]
- you have made an advance claim (see p262);
- you are on IS and have just become liable to pay rent, and your HB claim form reaches the authority or Benefits Agency office within four weeks of you becoming responsible for the new rent – in which case the HB claim is treated as being made on the date that you first became liable for the new rent.[26]

Your HB normally starts from the Monday after the date of your claim.[27] This is called your date of entitlement (see p265). A claim may be backdated if you had good cause for the delay.

Backdating a claim

If you have been entitled to HB at some point over the past year, but failed to claim, you can make a late claim and receive backdated benefit. However, the local authority only accepts a late claim if you can prove you have continuous good cause for your failure to make that claim throughout the whole time for which you want to claim.[28] The maximum period for which a claim can be backdated is 52 weeks. Any backdated benefit is calculated on both your circumstances and the HB rules which applied over the backdating period.

What amounts to 'good cause' is not spelled out in the HB regulations. DSS guidance to local authorities, based on IS rules, suggests that the general test is where any reasonable person of your age, health and experience would probably have failed to claim in the same way as you did. While none of the social security case law is strictly binding on HB cases, the DSS guidance to local authorities does refer to the rules for IS – for more information, see p144. Although ignorance of your rights cannot normally, in itself, be regarded as good cause for a delay, the HB rules leave it open for you to argue your particular reasons for a late claim.[29]

Your local authority may be reluctant to backdate your claim because backdated benefit attracts a lower rate of government subsidy than would normally apply. However, the subsidy arrangements are not part of the 'good cause' test. So if you think your late claim has been turned down on any basis other than failure to prove good cause, you should insist on a review (see p287).

If you are not currently entitled to any HB, the local authority may refuse to backdate your claim because it mistakenly believes that it can only backdate an existing entitlement. This is wrong. If you satisfy the 'good cause' test, it is not your entitlement but the date from which you are treated as having made a claim which is backdated – whether you are actually entitled to any benefit from that date depends on what your circumstances were at that time, and not on your current circumstances. Regardless of whether you have any current entitlement, therefore, it is still possible to receive backdated HB in respect of an earlier period of entitlement that both began and ended before the date on which your current claim was actually made. You must, however, make a claim in order to have it backdated, even though you know you have no current entitlement.

As your claim cannot be backdated for more than 52 weeks, you lose any unclaimed HB in respect of any earlier period.[30] However, if you claimed late because you were given wrong information, or misled by the local authority, you should press for an *ex gratia* payment outside the HB rules, as compensation. Alternatively, you could ask for additional weekly benefit on the grounds of exceptional circumstances (see p246). Both of these possibilities also apply if you did receive some benefit but were underpaid more than 52 weeks ago (see Reviews, p288).

Advance claims

There are two situations where advance claims can be made.

- If you become liable for rent for the first time but cannot move into your new home until after your liability to make payments starts, it is important that you claim benefit *before* you move in (ie, as soon as you are due to pay). This is because, once you have moved in, you may be able to receive benefit retrospectively for up to four weeks prior to moving in (providing you satisfy the conditions set out on p220).[31]
- If you are not entitled to HB in the benefit week immediately following your date of claim, but will become entitled within 13 weeks of claiming (eg, because of a reduction in income or because a birthday will increase your 'applicable amount'), the local authority can treat your claim as having been made in the benefit week immediately before you are first entitled.[32] If this happens, you do not need to make a further claim later on. The effect of this rule is to treat your advance claim in the same way as if you made a claim when you became entitled.

Making a further claim when your HB runs out

Your HB is paid to you for a period up to 60 weeks, after which you have to re-apply. The length of this **benefit period** (see p265) depends on the circumstances of your case[33] and you must be told how long it will last.[34] Provided you make a repeat claim not more than 13 weeks before, and not less than four weeks after, your current benefit period ends, your new benefit period starts immediately your old one finishes.[35] If you have been granted benefit for more than 16 weeks and you have not made a further claim within eight weeks of when your existing benefit period is due to end, the local authority must send you an application form and remind you to re-claim.[36]

You also have to re-apply for HB if your entitlement to IS ends because that causes your benefit period to end (see p266).[37] Make sure you tell the local authority if you stop getting IS. A repeat claim form must be sent to you and, providing you return this within four weeks of the end of your previous benefit period, your new benefit period follows on without a break.[38]

If your partner or former partner was the original claimant but you are now making an HB claim for the same accommodation costs, the DSS guidance suggests that your claim will be treated as a repeat claim.[39]

2. DECISIONS

Delays

Once the local authority has received your claim, it must make a decision on that claim, tell you in writing what the decision is, and pay you any benefit you are entitled to within 14 days, or, if that is not reasonably practicable, as soon as possible after that.[40] However, the local authority is under no duty to deal with your claim if:

- your claim was not accepted because *either* you did not claim on an official application form, *or* your application form was not properly filled in and you did not re-submit your application within four weeks of being asked to do so (see p258); *or*
- you failed to provide information needed to assess your claim within four weeks of being asked to do so (see p259); *or*
- you have told the local authority you have withdrawn your claim (see p258); *or*
- you have re-claimed benefit more than 13 weeks before the end of your current benefit period (see p262).[41]

In practice, many local authorities take considerably longer than 14 days to deal with claims. If you are experiencing an unreasonably long delay in getting your HB sorted out, you should write to the HB manager and threaten a formal complaint of 'maladministration' to the Ombudsman (see p293), unless you are paid within 14 days. You should send a copy of the letter to your ward councillor and to the councillor who chairs the council committee responsible for HB, usually the Housing or Finance Committee (you can get their names and addresses from your local library). It might also be worth asking your local tenants' association for support. If this does not produce results, or if the delay is causing you severe hardship, you should consider court action.

If you are a private tenant and have not received your rent allowance within 14 days of your claim, you can get a payment on account (see p267).

Notification of the decision

Who should be notified

Written notification must be given to everyone affected by any decision taken on your HB, whose rights, duties or obligations are affected.[42] For example:

- the claimant;
- an appointee (see p257);

- your landlord, if your rent is paid direct (see p269);
- non-dependants whose capital and income are used instead of yours in calculating your benefit (see p245);
- your partner, if s/he is now the claimant and it is proposed to recover an overpayment made when you claimed (see p281).

Where a third party, such as a landlord, is notified as a 'person affected' it should *only* be about that particular aspect of your claim which affects her/him, such as a decision to pay rent direct. People taken into account in your benefit assessment but *not* directly involved in your claim, such as non-dependants (apart from the case mentioned above) are not notified. Nor are the members of your family whose income and capital are automatically combined with yours.[43]

Information a notification should contain

When the local authority writes to tell you what decisions it has made about your entitlement it must include in its notification a minimum amount of information.[44] In addition to this, it may also include other relevant information.[45]

All notifications must tell you:

- of your right to ask for a further written explanation of the local authority's decision, how you must do this and the time limit for doing so[46] (see below); *and*
- of your right to ask the local authority to reconsider its decision, how you can do this and the time limit for doing so[47] (see p286).

Other information that the local authority must provide varies with the particular circumstances of your case. All the following should be included where relevant:[48]

- the normal weekly amount of benefit you are entitled to;
- your weekly eligible rent;
- the amount of any notional fuel deductions, why they have been made, and that they can be varied if you can provide evidence of the actual amount involved;
- the amount and category of any non-dependant deductions;
- if you are a private tenant, the day your HB will be paid and whether payment will be made weekly, monthly etc;
- the date on which your entitlement starts and how long it will last (your benefit period);
- if you are not receiving IS, your applicable amount and how it is calculated;
- if you are not receiving IS, your assessed weekly earnings and other income;

- if your level of benefit is less than the minimum amount payable, that this is the reason why you have no entitlement;
- if your claim was successful, your duty to notify the local authority of any changes in circumstances which might affect your entitlement and what kinds of changes should be reported;
- if your claim was unsuccessful, a statement explaining exactly why you are not entitled to benefit;
- if it has been decided to pay your rent allowance direct to your landlord, additional information saying how much is to be paid to your landlord and when payments will start. (This is the only information, apart from a statement on the right to obtain a further written explanation and request a review, which is provided in a written notice to your landlord);
- if the income and capital of a non-dependant has been used instead of yours to calculate your HB (see p245), additional information saying that this has happened and why. (This is the only information, apart from a statement on the right to obtain a further written explanation and request a review, which is provided to the non-dependant concerned);
- if the local authority decides you have been overpaid, it must also provide you with detailed notification about this (see p282).

In addition to this information you have a right to ask the local authority for a more detailed explanation of how your benefit has been worked out. This must be sent to you within 14 days, or, if that is not reasonably practicable, as soon as possible after that.[49] Local authorities have also been recommended to tell you, in non-IS cases, if they think you are likely to be entitled to IS.[50]

3. PAYMENT OF BENEFIT

Benefit period

Your benefit period is the length of time for which your benefit is paid before you need to re-apply.[51]

When your entitlement starts

The date your entitlement starts depends on your date of claim (see p260). Normally, your benefit starts on the Monday after your date of claim.[52] This is because your entitlement to HB starts in the benefit week following your date of claim.[53] **A benefit week** is a period of seven days running from Monday to Sunday.[54]

However, if you take on a new tenancy (or otherwise become liable for housing costs which can be met by HB), your HB entitlement starts in the same benefit week as your new liability – provided your date of claim for HB occurs in that same benefit week.[55] This means that:

- if your rent is due weekly or at intervals of a multiple of a week, your HB starts at the beginning of the week in which liability starts (ie, you receive a full week's benefit for that first week – even if your tenancy did not start until part-way through that week);[56]
- if your rent is due at other intervals (eg, each calendar month) your HB starts on the same day your liability actually begins (ie, the benefit you receive in the first week is equivalent to one-seventh of your normal weekly benefit multiplied by the number of days in that week for which rent is due).[57]

When your entitlement ends

Your benefit period could last any number of complete benefit weeks at the local authority's discretion, usually up to a maximum of 60.[58] In deciding how long your benefit should last before you must renew your claim, account is taken of any likely future changes which could affect your entitlement.[59] In particular, the benefit period is often limited to a few months for boarders, self-employed people and students.

Your first week of entitlement normally marks the beginning of your benefit period.[60] But if your date of claim has been backdated (see p260), your benefit period begins in the benefit week in which your claim was actually received.[61] Any backdated benefit does not, therefore, form part of your benefit period. This enables your benefit period to end on the future date originally fixed by the local authority, irrespective of any benefit you may receive for a past period.

If you re-apply for benefit within four weeks after the end of your old benefit period, your new benefit period follows on immediately so that you continue to get benefit without a break.[62] If you have not renewed your claim by the last week of your current benefit period, and you are either on IS or your applicable amount includes the disability, severe disability or higher pensioner premium, the local authority can decide to extend your current benefit period by up to four weeks to give you a further reminder, and more time, to re-apply.[63]

Your benefit period *will* end early if your entitlement ceases because of a change of circumstances[64] and *may* end early if your entitlement is altered because of a change of circumstances.[65] In particular, your benefit period ends when you cease to be entitled to IS[66] – although you should be invited to re-apply and be reassessed.[67] In all cases, whatever the change in your situation, your benefit period ends with the last benefit week in which you have any entitlement.[68] This is determined by the date on which the relevant change of circumstances takes effect (see p272).

If there is a gap between two benefit periods, you can ask for the second period to be backdated if you have a good reason for the delay in your claim (see p260).

How your benefit is paid

If your landlord is the housing authority responsible for the payment of HB, you receive HB in the form of a reduction in your rent. This is called a **rent rebate**.[69]

If you are the sub-tenant of a council tenant, your landlord is the council tenant and not the council. Therefore, you receive a rent allowance and not a rebate.

If you are a private tenant, you receive HB in the form of a **rent allowance** which is usually paid to you as a cash payment[70] although, in some cases, it may be paid direct to your landlord or to someone acting on your behalf (see p269).

If you are entitled to a rent allowance it can be paid either weekly, two-weekly, four-weekly, or monthly, depending on when your rent is normally due. It can also be paid at longer intervals if you agree.[71] If rent is paid in arrears, your rent allowance may be paid in arrears. Otherwise, if you are paid two-weekly, you are paid in advance.[72]

If your rent allowance is less than £1 a week, the local authority can choose to pay your benefit up to six months in arrears.[73]

You can insist on two-weekly payments if your rent allowance is more than £2 a week.[74] The local authority can pay your rent allowance weekly either to avoid an overpayment or where you are liable to pay weekly and it is in your interests to be paid weekly.[75]

Although rent allowances are normally paid in cash, the local authority has the discretion to pay you by whatever method it chooses but, in doing so, it must have regard to your 'reasonable needs and convenience'.[76] It should not insist on payment into a bank account if you do not already have a bank or giro account, nor make you collect benefit if it involves a difficult journey.[77] If it does, you should ask for a review (see p287) and complain to your local councillor (see p293). If that has no effect, ask your MP to take the matter up with the local authority, and also complain to the Ombudsman (see p293).

Interim payments on account

Local authorities are required to deal with your claim and pay your benefit within 14 days as far as possible. If you are a private tenant and the local authority has not been able to assess your rent allowance within this period, you should receive a payment on account while your claim is being sorted out, whether or not you are also getting IS. The local authority should automatically consider this if there are delays in paying you and you do not need to make a separate claim.

Some local authorities treat these interim payments as though they are discretionary. However, the law says the local authority must pay you an amount which it considers reasonable, given what it knows about your circumstances – eg, your rent, the number of non-dependants, any income you have etc. DSS guidance reminds local authorities of their duty to pay.[78]

Interim payments can only be refused if it is clear that you will not be entitled or the reason for the delay is that they have asked you for information or evidence in support of your claim and you failed, without good cause, to provide it (see p259).[79] They should not refuse if you have not been asked for any information. If you are not responsible for the delay (eg, the local authority is awaiting confirmation of IS entitlement from the Benefits Agency), the only discretion the local authority has is in deciding how much it is reasonable to pay you – not whether or not you should be paid. If your local authority has not made adequate arrangements to make payments on account, you should complain. You could also argue that it is guilty of maladministration and apply to the Ombudsman (see p293).

If the local authority makes a payment on account, it should notify you of the amount and point out that it can recover any overpayment which occurs if your actual benefit entitlement is different from the interim amount.[80] If so, your future benefit payments are adjusted until the overpayment has been put right.[81] If it is found that you are not entitled to any HB, the overpayment may be recovered from you by other methods (see p281).

If your interim payment is less than your true entitlement, you should receive a cheque/giro for the arrears.

Lost and missing cheques and giros

The law says nothing specifically about the replacement of lost or missing giros. This is seen as an administrative matter. The DSS guidance advises that, before replacing a payment, local authorities must satisfy themselves that all reasonable steps have been taken to ensure the loss is genuine. Beyond that, the question of whether to replace a payment is left for local authorities to decide.[82] However, if the local authority refuses to replace a payment which has never arrived, you can either try appealing on the basis that the authority has not paid you[83] or threaten to sue them in the county court. The process is the same as for the Benefits Agency (see p153).

Payment of your benefit to someone else

The payment of any rent allowance should normally be made to you as the person entitled to benefit.[84] However, sometimes payment may be made to a third party such as an appointee, agent, your landlord or your next of kin.

Payment to a claimant's personal representative

Where an appointee, or some other person legally empowered to act for you, has claimed HB on your behalf, that person can also receive the payments[85] (see p257).

If you are able to claim benefit for yourself, you can still nominate an agent to receive, or collect, your benefit for you. To do this you must make a written request to the local authority. Anyone you nominate must be aged 18 or over.[86] This may be useful if you are temporarily away from home (eg, in hospital or prison) or you are housebound and need someone to collect your benefit from the post office etc (eg, a neighbour or home-help).

If a claimant dies, any unpaid benefit may be paid to their personal representative or, where there is none, to their next of kin aged 16 or over. For payment to be made, a written application must be received by the local authority within 12 months of the claimant's death. However, the time limit can be extended at the local authority's discretion.[87] Where HB was being paid to the landlord prior to the claimant's death, the local authority can pay any outstanding benefit to clear remaining rent due.

Payment direct to a landlord

The local authority *must* pay your HB including payments on account[88] directly to your landlord:

- if you or your partner are on IS and the Benefits Agency has decided to pay part of your benefit to your landlord for arrears;[89] *or*
- if you have rent arrears equivalent to eight weeks' rent or more, unless the local authority considers it to be in your overriding interest not to make direct payments[90] – in which case, your benefit is withheld (see p270). Once your arrears have been reduced to less than eight weeks' rent, compulsory direct payments will stop. The local authority can then choose to continue direct payments on a discretionary basis if it considers it to be in your best interests to do so (see below).

The local authority *may* pay your HB directly to your landlord:[91]

- if you have requested or agreed to direct payments; *or*
- without your agreement, if it decides that direct payments are in the best interests of yourself and your family; *or*

- without your agreement, if you have left the address for which you were getting HB and there are rent arrears. In this case, direct payments of any unpaid benefit due in respect of that accommodation can be made, up to the total of the outstanding arrears.

The local authority needs to be advised that these conditions are met, and your landlord could contact them about this.[92]

If the local authority implements direct payments, both you and your landlord should be notified accordingly. If it is not in your interests to have benefit paid directly to your landlord (eg, because you are deliberately withholding rent to force your landlord to carry out repairs) it is worth trying to persuade the authority to withhold benefit rather than paying it to your landlord where there are more than eight weeks' arrears. Landlords can sometimes place authorities under pressure to pay them direct and the authority may not use this alternative option as a result.

Withholding benefit

Your rent allowance **must** be withheld if you have rent arrears equivalent to eight weeks' rent or more but the local authority has decided it is in your overriding interest not to make direct payments to your landlord[93] (see p269).

HB should not be withheld if either you pay off your arrears or can satisfy the local authority that you will pay off your arrears once you have received your payments.[94] This could apply, for example, if you have recently been discharged from residential care and direct payments to your landlord could undermine a rehabilitation programme. In this case, the local authority could be asked to pay you your benefit if you can show you will be able to clear your rent arrears because you have regular support to get your finances under control (eg, through debt counselling).

If the local authority subsequently decides it is no longer in your overriding interest not to pay your landlord, the benefit withheld must be paid direct to your landlord unless your arrears have been reduced to less than eight weeks' rent (see above).

Your rent allowance *may* be withheld if:

- the authority believes you are not paying your rent regularly to your landlord;[95]
- you have claimed HB and have a deregulated tenancy, licence or other agreement, but have refused to co-operate with the rent officer in her/his assessment of your rent level[96] (see p237);

- a query has arisen about your entitlement to, or the payment of, your benefit;[97]
- the local authority thinks you may have been overpaid and that the overpayment is recoverable[98] (see p276).

Any HB suspended because you are not paying your rent regularly is paid to you if you *either* pay off your rent arrears, *or* satisfy the local authority that you will pay off your rent arrears once you have received the amount withheld.[99] Otherwise, you can ask for your benefit to be paid direct to your landlord (see p269).

If your HB has been withheld pending a review of your entitlement, payment or possible overpayment, any benefit withheld and to which you are subsequently found to have been entitled, is paid to you once the queries have been sorted out. If you have been overpaid HB, only those overpayments which are legally recoverable may be deducted from the benefit withheld (see p276).[100] If you die while benefit is being withheld the local authority must pay any outstanding arrears to your estate.

4. CHANGES IN YOUR CIRCUMSTANCES

Duty to report changes of circumstances

From the moment you claim HB, you have a duty to let the local authority know in writing of any changes in your circumstances which you might reasonably know are likely to affect your benefit in any way. If you do not, you may be overpaid benefit and might have to pay it back (see p276). This applies to changes which occur before your claim is assessed, as well as those which occur throughout your subsequent benefit period. If your benefit is paid to someone else on your behalf (eg, an appointee or landlord), the duty to report any relevant changes extends to her/him as well.[101] The local authority must tell you about the changes you have to report.[102]

You must always report the following changes, in writing, to the local authority:[103]

- any change to your rent if you are a private tenant;
- when entitlement to IS ends. Failure to notify the local authority that IS has ended is a common reason for overpayments arising. You should not assume that the Benefits Agency will do this on your behalf. They often do, but not until much later and in any case you are legally obliged to tell the local authority of this change.
    Make sure that you make a fresh claim for HB if you are still on a low income after coming off IS;

- any change in the number of, or circumstances of, any non-dependants that may affect the level of deductions made to your benefit (see p243).

If you do not receive IS you must also report:

- any change in family income or capital;
- any change in the number of boarders or sub-tenants or in the payments made by them;
- any change in your status (eg, marriage, cohabitation, separation or divorce).

Other changes

Whether or not you get IS, there may be other changes which the local authority requires you to report, depending on the particular circumstances of your case. The need to report these additional changes must be drawn to your attention at the time you are notified of your benefit entitlement.[104] This is important because you only have a duty to report changes which you 'might reasonably be expected to know' might affect your benefit.[105] This may affect whether or not you have to repay any overpayment resulting from your failure to report a change (see p276).

You do not have to report:[106]

- any changes in your rent if you are a local authority tenant;
- changes in the ages of members of your family, or of non-dependants, unless the change results in a young person ceasing to be a member of the family.

It is important that you should remember to report any changes to the right department. In theory, the Benefits Agency and the local authority should pass on information you give (eg, if you tell the Benefits Agency about a change regarding your non-dependants, it should be passed on to the local authority). But you must not rely on this; it is your responsibility to see that any changes relating to your rent, and non-dependants are reported by you in writing to the local authority. You also cannot assume that information you give to one part of the local authority (eg, a housing officer) will be passed to the HB section. Your duty to notify changes is to the HB department not to the local authority as a whole.[107]

When changes in circumstances take effect

If you have made an application for benefit and reported a change of circumstances before the local authority has assessed your claim, your application is assessed on the basis of the revised information you have provided.

If a change of circumstances takes place within your benefit period, the local authority must establish the date on which that change actually occurred.[108] Where you have ceased to be entitled to some other benefit (including IS and family credit (FC)), the date the change occurred must always be taken as the day after your last day of entitlement to that benefit.[109]

In most cases, the change takes effect from the start of the benefit week after the one in which the change actually occurred.[110] This means that, on whatever day of the week the change actually occurs, from Monday to Sunday, the change is implemented as from the following Monday. This includes cases where IS stops and HB ends, apart for the exceptions listed below.

- If IS ends because another benefit becomes payable, the HB benefit period ends at the end of the benefit week in which the **payment** of IS ceases (where IS ends in any other case, the HB benefit period ends at the end of the benefit week in which IS **entitlement** ceases – ie, the normal rule applies).[111]
- A change in rent is taken into account in the benefit week in which it actually occurs. If you pay your rent weekly, or in a multiple of weeks (ie, two-weekly, four-weekly etc), the change is taken into account for the whole of the week in which it occurs. This means that the change takes effect on the Monday, though your rent may not have changed until, say, the Thursday, of that week. If you pay rent monthly, the change is taken into account on the day it actually occurs.[112]
- A change in your income solely due to a change in tax and national insurance contributions can be disregarded for up to 30 weeks (see p362).[113]
- A change in the HB regulations takes effect from the date the amendment occurs.[114] If the change is the annual uprating of benefits, it takes effect from the first Monday in April if you pay rent weekly (or in multiples of weeks). If you pay at other intervals it counts from 1 April.
- A change in the regulations affecting other social security benefits at uprating in April can be taken into account up to two weeks before the uprating date.[115]
- A payment of income (other than benefits) for a past period counts retrospectively from the date it would have been paid. Your past entitlement thus falls to be reviewed and the resulting overpayment may be recoverable (see p276).

If two or more changes occurring in the same benefit week would, according to the above rules, normally take effect in different benefit weeks, they are treated as taking effect in the same benefit week in which they occur and take effect from the beginning of that benefit week (unless one of the changes relates to monthly rent, in which case all the changes take effect on the same day as the rent changes).[116] If you pay rent weekly (or in multiples of weeks) and the annual uprating occurs at the same time as another change (excluding a change to your rent or the HB regulations) they all count from the first Monday in April.[117]

Reassessment of your benefit

The local authority may deal with your change of circumstances by ending your benefit period early and inviting you to re-claim so that your entitlement can be completely reassessed.[118] This always happens if you have ceased to be entitled to IS (see p266).[119] Otherwise, it reviews your existing entitlement and either increases or reduces your existing benefit, as appropriate.[120] A review is likely to cause less disruption to your benefit payments than a fresh claim, so you may wish to ask for them to consider this option, particularly if your circumstances change quite frequently. Local authorities rarely use this option and may need to be persuaded to do so.

If you delay in reporting changes of circumstances, you could be underpaid or overpaid. If you have been underpaid, you can be paid the arrears, but *only* for up to one year (but see p288).[121] If you have been overpaid, the local authority can recover the overpayment.[122]

5. OVERPAYMENTS

If the information you give the local authority is wrong, or if you do not report a change in your circumstances (see p271), you could end up being paid too much benefit. You could also be overpaid as a result of an official error or delay which is not your fault. Not all overpayments are legally recoverable and have to be paid back although local authorities sometimes recover them illegally.

What is an overpayment

An overpayment is any amount of HB (including a 'payment on account' – see p267) which has been *paid* to you but to which you were not entitled under the regulations.[123] A 'payment' includes both a direct payment of benefit to you or your landlord and also benefit entitlement as a credit on your rent account.[124] The local authority must have actually paid you some benefit to which you were not entitled for an overpayment to have taken place. It does not matter whether you were overpaid by cash, a cheque, payment into your bank account, credits to your local authority rent account, or direct payment to your private landlord.

Dealing with overpayments

Local authorities should take the following steps in an overpayment case:

Step 1 Establish the cause, or causes, of the overpayment (see below).

Step 2 Determine whether any of the overpayment is recoverable by the local authority under the regulations (see p276).

Step 3 Decide, where the overpayment is recoverable, whether or not recovery should be sought (see p277).

Step 4 Work out the amount of the overpayment and the period over which it occurred (see p278).

Step 5 Decide from whom recovery should be made, by what method and at what rate (see p280).

Step 6 Notify you of all the above decisions regarding the overpayment and give you an opportunity to request further information or a review (see p282).

The rules and procedures regarding overpayments apply equally to all cases regardless of whether or not you get IS.

The cause of the overpayment

The reason why any overpayment has taken place determines whether, and from whom, it is legally recoverable. The local authority has a duty to tell you why it thinks the overpayment occurred (see p283).[125]

An overpayment may arise for a number of reasons.[126] These are:

- **Claimant error or fraud** if you or someone acting on your behalf (eg, an appointee) are responsible for the overpayment taking place. For example, perhaps you gave the wrong information on your application form or failed to report a change of circumstances. You may have caused the overpayment innocently (eg, through a genuine mistake, or forgetfulness) or fraudulently (eg, by knowingly making a false statement or deliberately not reporting a pay rise). If fraud has been committed, the local authority can prosecute you as well as recovering the overpayment (see p286).[127]

- **Official error** if the overpayment is due to a mistake made or something done, or not done, by the local authority, Benefits Agency or the Employment Service acting on behalf of the Benefits Agency. For example, the local authority may have delayed acting on information supplied by you, or miscalculated your weekly benefit, or the Benefits

Agency may have mistakenly awarded you IS. However, if you or someone acting on your behalf (eg, an appointee), or someone to whom the payment was made (eg, an agent or landlord), contributed to the overpayment it is classified as a *claimant error*. In particular, it is regarded as a claimant error if you report a change of circumstances to the Benefits Agency instead of the local authority and the information is not passed on or is forwarded late. This is because you have a duty to report changes, in writing, directly to the local authority (see p271).

- **'Payment on account'** if a private tenant has received an interim payment at the beginning of a claim which is subsequently found to exceed her/his actual benefit entitlement (see p267).
- **Other errors** including overpayments caused by a third party such as your landlord or employer, or which may not be anyone's fault. For example, you may have received a backdated pay rise, or social security benefit.

An overpayment may have **more than one cause**, in which case the local authority must separately identify the amount of the overpayment which has arisen as a result of each particular cause. The two most usual causes of overpayments are delays in notifying and acting on changes of circumstances. For example, if you delay notifying the local authority of a change in circumstances for three weeks and then the local authority subsequently fails to take any action for a further two weeks, two kinds of overpayment have taken place – a 'claimant error' overpayment for the first three weeks and an 'official error' overpayment for the last two weeks.

Overpayments which are recoverable

Most overpayments, including all HB 'payments on account' (see p267), are legally recoverable, which means that the local authority can make you pay them back. However, you do not have to pay back an overpayment if:[128]

- it was due to an official error (see above); *and*
- it was paid for a past period; *and*
- you or someone acting on your behalf (eg, an appointee) or someone to whom the payment was made (eg, an agent or landlord), could not have reasonably been expected to know that an overpayment was being made at the time that the payment was notified or received.

This rule does not apply where benefit has been credited to your rent account for a future period. In this case, the forward award of benefit can be withdrawn even if it arose due to official error. Benefit paid after the date your claim is reviewed is recoverable.

However, where too much benefit has been credited to your account for a *past* period you could argue that the overpayment cannot be recovered if you have not been notified of the credit.[129] This is because you cannot reasonably be expected to know that you have been overpaid until you have been told about your entitlement. For the same reason, if you are a private tenant you should argue that if official errors lead to the wrong payments being directly credited to your bank/giro account or that of your appointee, agent or landlord, the past overpayment is not recoverable unless you were notified of the payment.

The extent to which you can reasonably be expected to realise that an overpayment is being made to you depends on the extent to which the local authority has advised you about the scheme or your duties and obligations, particularly about your duty to notify changes of circumstances. It depends not on what you know, but on what you could have known at the time of the payment or the notification.

If, for example, you declared your full capital but the local authority took the wrong amount into account, you could argue that you could not reasonably have known that you were being overpaid because of the complexity of the tariff income rules, which makes it hard for a claimant to understand how their capital has been assessed. On the other hand if you have declared an increase in income and your benefit was not reduced it may be harder to argue that you could not have known that you were being overpaid, because the local authority may say that you should have expected a corresponding decrease in your benefit. However, the local authority is not entitled to simply assume that because you knew your benefit was *wrong* you must have known you were being *overpaid* (some changes of circumstances may increase your benefit and lead to you being *underpaid*). Remember that the local authority must show, not just that you could have reasonably been expected to know that you *might have been overpaid*, but that you *were overpaid*.[130] You should always argue that as a claimant, you cannot be expected to know the intricacies of the HB legislation and that unless it was glaringly obvious that a change of circumstances would reduce your benefit you should be given the benefit of the doubt.

Recovering overpayments

Any overpayment of a 'payment on account' **must** be recovered by the local authority in every case[131] (see p268). All other recoverable overpayments may be recovered at the local authority's discretion.[132] In practice, authorities operate a wide range of different policies towards the recovery of overpayments. Some recover all recoverable overpayments and others only recover those caused by claimant error.

The Benefits Agency guidance makes it clear that local authorities are expected to 'minimise overpayments' and to make recoveries 'wherever appropriate'. This is reinforced by the subsidy arrangements which have clearly been designed to offer local authorities a financial incentive to make recoveries, and which impose financial penalties where overpayments remain unrecovered.[133]

Nevertheless, local authorities have a legal duty to exercise their judgement on whether or not to make a recovery *on the merits of each and every individual case* (and the merits of the case do not include the subsidy arrangements!). While they may have general policy guidelines on how to approach the issue in a consistent manner, these must not be so rigid as to effectively decide the outcome of each case in advance. A policy of always recovering recoverable overpayments would, therefore, amount to an unlawful 'fettering' of the local authority's discretion which could be challenged by judicial review.

If you have been overpaid and this was either not your fault or the result of a genuine mistake or oversight on your part, you should ask the local authority not to recover the overpayment, especially if recovery causes you hardship. You should tell the authority about any existing financial difficulties you have which will be aggravated by recovery action – eg, where you already have serious debts or have to repay a loan from the social fund. Any illness, disability or other family problems may also be relevant. If the local authority still insists on proceeding with recovery action, you should ask for a review. The rules allow you to ask for a review on whether recovery should take place, the recovery method and the rate of recovery.[134] This is not the same as IS rules where you cannot appeal these decisions. If the overpayment was caused by some one else (eg, your landlord), you could suggest that recovery is made from her/him instead. You may be asked to repay an irrecoverable overpayment on a voluntary basis. You are under no legal obligation to do so.

The amount of overpayment which is recoverable

If you have been overpaid HB and the local authority considers that it is recoverable, it must tell you how it worked out the amount of the overpayment.[135] This should be the difference between what you were paid and what you should have been paid during the period of the overpayment.[136] The authority should distinguish between those overpayments it regards as recoverable and those it does not. Complications can arise where some of the overpayment is caused by claimant error and some by official error. You should also check that the authority has offset certain payments against the overpayment. These are:

- if you have been getting a rent rebate over the overpayment period and, for some reason, have paid more into your rent account than you should have paid according to your original (incorrect) benefit assessment, any overpayment arising over that period may be reduced by the amount of the excess payment. The authority will probably not apply this rule where the extra rent is to repay your rent arrears;[137]
- a recoverable overpayment has occurred because your capital has been incorrectly assessed – eg, because the local authority made a mistake, was misled, or not told, about how much capital you or your family have. If this overpayment is for a period of more than 13 benefit weeks, the local authority applies the 'diminishing capital rule' when calculating the amount of the overpayment.[138]

The logic behind the **diminishing capital rule** is that, had your unassessed capital been taken into account in the first place, and your benefit consequently reduced or withdrawn, you would have drawn on your capital in order to help meet your housing costs. The rule works in the following way:[139]

- The amount overpaid during the overpayment period is first calculated in the normal way.
- At the *end* of the first 13 benefit weeks the claimant's assessed capital is reduced by the amount of the overpaid benefit which occurred over that period.
- This reduced capital is then used to recalculate the claimant's entitlement, and hence, overpayment, from the beginning of the 14th benefit week onwards.
- This procedure is then repeated for each subsequent block of 13 weeks until either the claimant's capital is reduced to below £3,000 (so it has no effect on entitlement) or there are less than 14 weeks left before the end of the overpayment period.

The reduction in capital only takes place at the end of each complete block of 13 weeks in the overpayment period. This means the rule has no effect until the beginning of the 14th week of the overpayment period. It also means that capital cannot be regarded as reducing over any period of less than 13 weeks.[140]

If you are making voluntary repayments following an official error, make sure the local authority has taken the diminishing capital rule into account when calculating the amount of the overpayment. The diminishing capital rule is only relevant for calculating overpayments. Your current entitlement is based on your actual capital.

How overpayments are recovered

There are special rules that lay down who a local authority can recover an overpayment from and how they can recover it. There are no rules about the rate of recovery. Authorities have a lot of discretion in how they decide to recover an overpayment. You can challenge any decisions they take in recovering an overpayment from you (see p287).

From whom the overpayment is recovered

In all cases, the local authority has the power to recover a recoverable overpayment from either the claimant or the person to whom it was made (eg, a landlord).[141] However, where the overpayment arose as a result of a 'misrepresentation or failure to disclose a material fact' (either fraudulently or otherwise) by the claimant, someone acting on her/his behalf, or the person to whom benefit was paid, the local authority has the power to recover the overpaid HB from the person responsible. This could apply to an appointee, agent or landlord, even if they did not actually receive the benefit.[142] See p161 for information on what constitutes 'misrepresentation or failure to disclose a material fact'.

An overpayment may also be recovered from the partner of a claimant, but only where they were members of the same household both at the time of the overpayment, and when recovery is made.[143]

In the event of the death of the person from whom recovery is being sought, local authorities may consider recovering any outstanding overpayment from that person's estate.[144]

Where recovery is made from your landlord, this does not put you in rent arrears. The landlord may require you to pay her/him back, but cannot evict you for not doing so.[145]

How the overpayment is recovered

If an overpayment is recoverable, the local authority has the discretion to decide both how it will recover the money and at what rate.[146] It can make deductions from any future HB or from any arrears of HB owing to you. If you are no longer entitled to HB, you can be asked to repay the money directly through instalments or by a lump sum. In some cases, the local authority can ask the Benefits Agency to undertake recovery by making deductions from other social security benefits you are getting (see p281). As a last resort, the local authority can recover the money you owe through the county court if it thinks you could afford to make repayments.[147] You have six weeks to ask for a review of the decision that the overpayment is recoverable (see p287). This should be borne in mind when local authorities are deciding when to start proceedings.

If a local authority recovers overpaid HB by adjusting its own rent account, the overpayment should be separately identified and you should be informed that the amount being recovered does not represent rent arrears. Local authorities are reminded in guidance from the DSS that overpayments of HB in respect of their own tenants are not rent arrears and should not be treated as such.[148] Unfortunately, this advice seems frequently to be ignored. The practice of debiting overpayments to rent accounts to become rent 'arrears' can cause unnecessary difficulties for council tenants – such as being refused a housing transfer because they 'owe rent'. It can also lead to inappropriate methods of recovery, such as possession proceedings, because the local authority can no longer distinguish between the overpaid HB and genuine rent arrears. If you are a council tenant you should check that the authority has assessed the overpayment according to the steps outlined on p275.

The local authority cannot evict you for an overpayment of HB. If you are threatened with eviction for 'rent arrears', therefore, you should point out that the fact that these 'arrears' consist either solely or partly of overpaid HB is a defence in court.

Recoveries of overpayments made to your partner (see p280) may be recovered by deductions from your HB (although the actual rate of recovery is not specified).

If your landlord has been overpaid HB for another tenant the local authority *cannot* recover this from *your* HB (ie, by making deductions from direct payments of *your* benefit).[149]

Overpayments arising as a result of a 'payment on account' (see p267) can only be recovered through deductions from HB unless you no longer have any current entitlement.

Overpayments of HB cannot be recovered by deductions from CTB (and vice versa).[150] Unpaid council tax *cannot* be recovered through HB payments (although some local authorities may attempt to do this).

Recovery through the Benefits Agency

The primary responsibility for recovering overpaid HB lies with the local authority. However, it can ask the Benefits Agency to recover the overpayment through deductions from some other social security benefits if:[151]

- a recoverable overpayment has been made as a result of a misrepresentation or failure to disclose a material fact (whether innocently or fraudulently – see p161) by, or on behalf of, the claimant or some other person to whom HB has been paid; *and*
- the local authority is unable to recover that overpayment from any HB entitlement; *and*

- the person responsible for that overpayment is receiving at least one of the benefits from which a deduction can be made – providing that this benefit is payable at a sufficiently high rate for deductions to be possible.[152]

Sometimes the first you hear of an overpayment is when you get a letter from the Benefits Agency saying that they intend to recover from your benefit. This cannot happen until you have been properly notified of any overpayment and given the opportunity to dispute whether or not it is recoverable (see p283), and you should complain if the local authority have failed to follow the correct procedures.

Benefits from which deductions can be made are IS, FC, disability working allowance (DWA) and other social security benefits except child benefit and guardian's allowance. Benefits paid by other EU states count[153] but CTB is not included. The amount deducted each week is limited in the case of IS (see p165).

Deductions continue until the overpayment has been recovered. If deductions stop because the person ceases to be entitled to that social security benefit, or entitlement drops below the minimum for deductions, the Benefits Agency notifies the local authority which, once again, becomes responsible for any further recovery action.

How much is recovered

A local authority can decide how much of a recoverable overpayment it will actually recover. It can ask for the whole amount at once or recover it by instalments.

The DSS guidance suggests that, if you are getting IS, the **rate of recovery** should be limited to the maximum that could be recovered from IS itself (see p165) unless you agree to more. However, if you are already having deductions made from your IS (eg, for fuel debts), you should ask the local authority to deduct less to avoid causing you hardship.

If you are not on IS but your income is below or not much above your applicable amount, you can argue for the same weekly maximum to apply. You should also ask the local authority to take into account any other debts or financial commitments you may have. If you complain to the local authority that the rate of recovery is causing you hardship, it may consider reducing the amount of the repayments.

You should check that the methods used by the authority and the rates of recovery are consistent between groups of claimants. For example, council tenants should not be required to repay overpayments in a lump sum (ie, the whole overpayment is debited to their account) where private tenants can repay by instalment (ie, by weekly deductions made to their HB). If this is happening, you should ask for a review.

Notification of overpayments

If the local authority decides that a recoverable overpayment has occurred, it must write to the person from whom recovery is being sought (within 14 days, if possible) and notify them accordingly.[154] This notification must state:[155]

- the fact that there is an overpayment which is legally recoverable;
- the reason why there is a recoverable overpayment;
- the amount of the recoverable overpayment;
- how the amount of the overpayment was calculated;
- the benefit weeks to which the overpayment relates;
- if recovery is to be made from future benefit, how much the deduction will be;
- that you have a right to ask for a further written explanation of any of the decisions the local authority has made regarding the overpayment, how you can do this and the time limit for doing so;
- that you have a right to ask the local authority to reconsider any of the decisions it has made regarding the overpayment, how you can do this and the time limit for doing so.

It may also include any other relevant matters (eg, that you should tell the local authority about any hardship which will result from recovery action or, where recovery is to be made by a means other than deduction from your HB, what the recovery method will be).

If you write and ask the local authority for a more detailed written explanation of any of the decisions it has made regarding the overpayment, it must send you this within 14 days or, if this is not reasonably practicable, as soon as possible after that.[156] Notifications provided by many local authorities have been either inadequate or non-existent. Such authorities are in breach of their statutory duties. If your local authority does not give proper notification, you should write and point out that the decision to recover the overpayment is not valid until you are given proper notification. No recovery should be sought until after you have been notified and have had a chance to discuss your case or apply for a review.

6. FRAUD

Sometimes an overpayment arises due to deliberate fraud rather than an error or misunderstanding on your part. Local authorities have powers to investigate and, if appropriate, to prosecute you if you are guilty of fraud. Since April 1993, the government has encouraged authorities to do more fraud work by giving them extra subsidies where they successfully identify fraud and stop it occurring. These financial incentives have encouraged local authorities to expand their fraud work by employing more fraud staff and increasing the number of investigations into benefit claims.[157]

Local agreements have been developed between Benefits Agency and local authority staff to ensure that overpayments of other social security benefits are also identified, and the local authority has powers to investigate fraud relating to these benefits and liaise with the Benefits Agency to ensure that you do not get more than you are entitled to. By the same token, if the Benefits Agency discover that you are fraudulently claiming a benefit paid by them, they can notify the local authority and investigate whether you are getting the correct amount of HB/CTB.[158]

DSS guidance suggests that local authorities should ask you to sign a statement on the back of your giro before cashing it. The statement is a declaration that you are entitled to claim and that you have notified all changes in your circumstances. It is intended to make it easier to prosecute you for misrepresenting your circumstances. Landlords receiving payment direct may also be asked to sign such statements. There is no requirement to do so in order to get benefit.

As a result of these anti-fraud measures you may find that your claim for HB/CTB comes under scrutiny, particularly if you have been overpaid. You have nothing to fear if you have not done anything dishonest, though you may have to repay any overpaid benefit.

What is fraud?

You are guilty of fraud if, in order to get benefit (or more benefit), you deliberately make false statements or use false documents or information.[159] A deliberate failure to report a change of circumstances may constitute fraud.[160]

If a mistake arose through genuine error or oversight, you cannot be prosecuted for fraud and you should make sure that you do not say or sign anything which could give the authority the opportunity to accuse you of fraud.

Remember that there is a difference between overpayment and fraud and the local authority should distinguish clearly between your current entitlement, any past overpayments and deliberate fraud. Make sure that the following steps have been followed:

- **Establish the facts.** Ask what information they have on your claim and correct any inaccuracies. If they are relying on anonymous allegations against you, insist that they tell you who is making these so that you can comment. Check whether they have proof that you have committed fraud and whether their information is reliable. While the authority is establishing the facts they can withhold your benefit (see p270).

- **Reassess entitlement.** Any new information might not lead to a change in your benefit, but your entitlement could go down or even end. You can ask for a review of your entitlement if you disagree (see p287).
- **Calculate any overpayment.** This should be dealt with under the normal rules (see p278).
- **Decide whether fraud has been committed.** If the authority considers that your actions were deliberate and that you have gained benefit to which you were not entitled as a result they could prosecute you. The power to prosecute is in addition to the right to recover any overpayment so you may have to pay a court fine as well as repay the overpayment.

What happens if you are accused of fraud?

If you are suspected of fraud, your case is looked at by special fraud officers who will check whether you have given correct information in support of your claim and make sure that the information on your case file is fully up-to-date. If there is any irregularity, they may visit you or ask you to come to the office for an interview.

If you are asked to attend an interview, get advice and/or take a friend or adviser with you. Fraud staff are very aware of the need to make savings by identifying cases where benefit is being wrongly paid and sometimes claimants complain of being pressured into making statements that are not accurate. If you feel this is happening to you, make sure you do not agree to anything which is not true and ask for the interview to be terminated if necessary. If you feel that the behaviour of the interviewing officer was inappropriate, you should complain.

It can be very threatening to be suddenly accused of fraud and the important thing is to try to remain calm, listen to the allegations against you and then explain the true position. You do not have to say anything if you do not want to, but remember that if there is any doubt as to your entitlement, your benefit could be suspended while further enquiries are made (see p271).

Fraud staff have the power to do interviews under caution. If this happens they should advise you of your right to silence and explain that they will be taking a formal record of the interview which could be used as evidence in a court hearing. If you are interviewed under caution, try to make notes of what was said immediately afterwards. Prosecutions often take some time and it is easy to forget what was said, particularly if you were feeling flustered.

Do not forget that fraud officers can ask about other benefits too if they think you are fraudulently claiming more than one. However, if you are getting both IS and HB/CTB, the Benefits Agency investigates any allegations that you are living with someone as husband and wife, not the local authority.[161]

Prosecution[162]

If the local authority feel that they have strong enough evidence against you, they can prosecute you for fraud. This is normally done within three months of them obtaining sufficient evidence to justify a prosecution, or within 12 months of the offence being committed. You should seek advice if this happens and ideally get a solicitor to represent you in court. If you lose you face a fine of up to £2,000, or up to three months' imprisonment, or both. Remember that you may also have to repay any overpaid benefit on top of this.

You will not always be prosecuted even if you have committed fraud. The decision to prosecute takes account of a number of factors – eg, the amount of money involved, the reliability of the evidence against you, whether you have been guilty of fraud in the past, any social factors and your physical or mental condition, whether you voluntarily confessed, and whether there was any maladministration of your case or any shortcomings in the way the investigation was handled.[163]

A prosecution should not jeopardise any future claims for benefit so long as you are legitimately entitled. However, you may face difficulties in getting your claim assessed promptly because, for example, the local authority decide to check out your circumstances especially thoroughly given your past conviction. You should complain if they take an unreasonable amount of time to decide your claim.

7. REVIEWS

A review is the process by which a local authority or the housing benefit review board (see p288) looks again at a decision and decides whether it should be altered.

A decision may be reviewed by the local authority without any request from you to correct an error or to take account of a change of circumstances. Such a review may be in your favour or may reduce the amount of benefit you receive.

However, *you* also have the right to *ask* for a review. This is very important because there is no right of appeal to an independent tribunal in HB cases. If you wish to challenge a decision, you can do so only by asking for a review.

Local authority reviews

The local authority can review any of its own decisions, and those of the review board, at any time if:

- there has been a change of circumstances (see p271); *or*
- it is satisfied the decision was made in ignorance of, or based on a mistake as to, some material fact. In the case of a review board decision, this must be shown by fresh evidence that was not available to the board (and which could not have been put before the board at the time); *or*
- in the case of a local authority decision only, it is satisfied that it was based on a mistake as to the law. However, local authorities cannot decide that a regulation is invalid because the Secretary of State exceeded his powers in making it.[164]

If a decision is amended on a review initiated by a local authority, this counts as a fresh decision requiring notification in the normal way, so you can ask for yet another review (see p288) if it is unfavourable to you.[165] When notifying you of the review decision, the local authority need give details only of the part of your claim being reviewed, the reasons for the review and your right to ask for the new decision to be reviewed.

If as a result of the review you get more benefit, any arrears due to you can only be paid for a maximum of 52 weeks from the date of the review, unless the review concerns a decision to backdate your claim, in which case any arrears will be paid from the date your claim is treated as being made.[166]

Your right to a review

You can always ask a local authority to review its decision under the powers described above. This may be done at any time.

You can also ask for a review of any decision (including a local authority review decision) simply on the ground that you disagree with it. The right to a review also applies to other people affected by the decision – eg, a landlord where direct payments are refused.[167] Such an application must be received by the local authority within six weeks of the decision being notified to you,[168] although the local authority can allow a late application if there are special reasons.[169] The local authority must tell you of your right to apply for a review every time you are notified of a decision.[170] If it fails to do so, that will be a special reason for allowing a late application. An application for an extension must be made in writing, and, if it is refused, the local authority's decision is final[171] (although, in an exceptional case, it might be challenged by judicial review – see p292).

If you want a written explanation from the local authority (see p265) so that you can state your case more effectively, the period between your request reaching the local authority and the explanation being posted to you is ignored when calculating the six-week limit.[172] It is often worth asking the local authority for a written explanation before formally requesting a review, because the law is complicated and you will then know the basis on which the decision was taken. However, if the reasons for the decision are clear or your situation is urgent, you should not delay asking for a review. You can ask for a further written explanation at any time.[173]

Any written comments or observations you have made in support of your request for a review must be considered. There is no time limit laid down within which the authority must carry out the review. Some local authorities have a policy of carrying out the review within 14 days of receiving a request for a review.

You must be notified in writing of the outcome of the review. The information given to you following the review must conform to the normal rules about the notification of decisions (see p263). This means it should be sent to you within 14 days, if possible, and that it must include an explanation of your right to request a further written statement of reasons for the review decision.[174] It must also inform you of your right to ask for a further review by a review board (see below).[175]

If a decision is altered on review, the revised decision takes effect from the date of the original decision.[176] However, if the review results in an increase in your benefit, arrears cannot normally be paid for more than 52 weeks before the date the local authority first received your request for the review. The only exception is where the local authority has reversed a decision not to backdate your claim under the 'good cause for a late claim' provisions – in which case any arrears may be paid from the date your claim is now treated as having been made[177] (see p260).

The housing benefit review board

A hearing before a housing benefit review board is the nearest thing there is to an independent appeal for HB cases. Although review boards are not really independent, they must act as if they were independent. The review board is made up of local authority councillors.

Applying for a hearing

If you have exercised your right to a review (see p287), and remain dissatisfied with the local authority's decision, you can write and ask for a **further review**. It is this 'further review' that is carried out by a housing benefit review board.

When you apply, you must give your reasons. These need not be detailed or technical as long as it is clear what it is you disagree with. The request for the further review must reach the local authority within 28 days of the notification of the internal review being posted to you.[178] The review board may extend the deadline if there are special reasons for doing so. An application for an extension must be made to the local authority in writing, and, if it is refused, the review board's decision is final (although, in an exceptional case, it might be challenged by judicial review – see p292).[179]

The hearing

A hearing before a review board should take place within six weeks of your request reaching the local authority or, if that is not reasonably practicable, as soon as possible after that.[180] Some authorities make claimants wait months for a review board hearing. If this has happened in your case, write and threaten to make a complaint of maladministration to the Ombudsman (see p293). However, if you are challenging a decision to restrict your eligible rent (see p231) and the local authority has asked the rent officer to reconsider your case as a result, the review board may decide to defer your hearing pending the outcome.[181] You must be given at least ten days' notice of the time of the hearing and the place where it will be held, otherwise you have the right to insist on another date being set.[182] If you have been given adequate notice but would like the hearing to be postponed, or if you wish to withdraw your request for a hearing altogether, you must write to the review board chairperson who decides whether the hearing should still proceed.[183]

The review board consists of at least three local authority councillors (or members of the New Town Corporation, Development Board for Rural Wales or Scottish Special Housing Association) one of whom acts as chairperson.[184] But if there are only two members of the board present when you attend, the hearing can go ahead provided all parties consent.[185] DSS guidance suggests that the board should not consist of anyone who has had a previous involvement in your case.[186] If the issue to be considered by the review board affects your claim for HB *and/or* CTB *and/or* community charge benefit (CCB) (eg, the assessment of your income), the same review board can consider your claim for any combination of all three benefits at the same time, provided everyone concerned in the case agrees.[187]

The board chairperson decides how the hearing should be conducted.[188] If you want to provide a written statement to the review board, it must consider all the points you make.[189] You also have the right to attend the hearing and to present your case, call witnesses and question the local authority's witnesses. You can be accompanied to the hearing or be represented. During the hearing your representative has the same rights as you in presenting your case.[190] The local authority should pay your travelling expenses and those of one other person who accompanies or represents you, also anyone else affected (eg, witnesses).[191] The tactics for presenting a case before the review board are similar to those for social security appeal tribunals (see p174).

The review board has the right to ask people to give evidence, but it cannot compel anyone to appear before them who does not wish to.[192] If you fail to attend a hearing, the review board can proceed in your absence.[193] If you were unable to attend through circumstances beyond your control, and the review board has given an unfavourable decision, you may be able to have the decision 'set aside' (see p291).

You may apply to the chairperson in writing for the hearing to be adjourned, or for the case to be completely withdrawn, at any time before the review board has come to a decision (even during the hearing itself).

If the review board decides to adjourn a hearing and the case is subsequently heard by a board composed of any different members, the second board should hear your whole case again.[194]

The decision

After hearing your case, the review board either confirms or alters the decision of the local authority.[195] If the board is not unanimous, a majority decision is taken. If there are an even number of members, the chairperson has a second or casting vote if necessary.[196] The chairperson must record the board's decision and its finding on any material question of fact.[197]

In arriving at its decision, the review board is bound only by the law and not by any local authority or DSS policy. It may exercise any discretion open to the local authority under the regulations.[198] It is not bound by any of its own previous decisions, nor by any of the decisions made by social security appeal tribunals or Social Security Commissioners on similar cases and issues in other areas of the social security system, although it can take them into account. In particular, it should be slow to disagree with a commissioner's decision as commissioners are judges with considerable experience of this sort of law.

A copy of the decision must be sent to you within seven days or, if that is not practicable, as soon as possible after that, together with the reasons for the decision and the board's findings of fact.[199] These should give a clear explanation of why you have won or lost.[200] If the review board has altered the local authority's decision in any way, the local authority must implement the board's decision with effect from the date the original decision was made.[201] However, decisions of a review board are binding on the local authority only in the particular case in question.

If the board has awarded additional benefit, arrears may only be paid for up to 52 weeks before the date on which the local authority completed its initial internal review. The only exception is where the review board have overturned a previous local authority decision not to backdate a claim under the 'good cause for a late claim' provisions – in which case any arrears may be paid from the date your claim is now treated as having been made (see p261).[202]

A decision of a review board may be subsequently reviewed by a local authority in certain circumstances (see p287).

There is no right of appeal from a review board's decision but, if the decision was wrong in law, you can apply for judicial review (see p292).

Correcting a decision

Both local authorities and review boards can correct any accidental errors which have occurred in their decisions.[203] An accidental error is where the decision actually made is not the one recorded or notified because of a slip of the pen, a misprint, a mathematical error, or the omission of a word etc. Corrections may be made at any time and take effect as though they were part of the original decision, or record of a decision, being corrected. Every person affected must be informed of the correction. You cannot seek a review against the correction of a decision, but you can ask for a review of the decision itself.[204]

Setting aside a decision

Both local authorities and review boards also have the power to set aside their own decisions if the interests of justice warrant it.[205] 'Setting aside' means deleting the decision as though it had never been made in the first place. A new decision is then made.

The law allows a decision to be set aside if it appears just to do so because:[206]

- you, your representative, or some other person affected by the decision, were not sent, or did not receive, a document relating to the matters concerned in that decision, or the document arrived too late;
- in the case of a hearing before a review board, you, your representative, or some other person affected by the decision were not present;
- for some other reason, the interests of justice require it.

Any person affected by a decision may apply to have that decision set aside.[207] Applications must be in writing and must reach the local authority or review board concerned within 13 weeks of the notification of that decision being posted to the applicant.[208] The 13-week limit cannot be extended but does not include any period before the correction of (or refusal to correct) that decision, or the setting aside of a previous decision.[209] The local authority or review board must send copies of the application to any other persons affected by the decision and give them a reasonable opportunity to comment.[210]

The outcome of an application to have a decision set aside must be notified in writing to every person affected as soon as possible, and this must contain a statement explaining the reasons for meeting or rejecting that request.[211]

If your request to have a decision set aside is rejected, this cannot be challenged by means of a review,[212] but you may still request a review of the original decision itself. In applying the time limits for requesting a review, no account is taken of any period between the date when the notification of the decision, and the notification of the refusal to set it aside, were each posted to you.[213] If you have been denied a fair hearing before the review board and your request to have the board's decision set aside is turned down, you may be able to challenge this by way of a judicial review (see below).

Judicial review

Judicial review is a method of challenging a decision of any form of tribunal, government department or local authority.

Applications are to the High Court (in Scotland, the Court of Session), and should be made within three months.

In practice, it is not a procedure that can be used very much in social security cases except in HB and CTB cases against decisions of review boards. That is because there are two major restrictions on the power of the court to intervene. Firstly, the court very seldom intervenes if there is an alternative right of appeal. Secondly, the court can only intervene to correct an error of law. For these purposes, error of law has the same meaning as for appeals to a Social Security Commissioner in IS cases (see p177). In nearly all social security cases where there is no right of appeal to a tribunal, the person or authority making a decision is using a purely discretionary power and it is very difficult to show that an error of law has been made in such cases. Judicial review can, however, be used to compel a person or body to make a decision if there is excessive delay.

Review boards quite often make errors of law. If you consider that one has been made in your case, you should consult a solicitor. Legal aid is available in judicial review cases. CPAG's solicitor may be able to advise if you go through an advice agency.

8. COMPLAINTS

The review procedure enables you to challenge the way that a local authority has applied the law in your case. If you wish to challenge the manner in which your claim was dealt with rather than the actual decision itself, you should make use of the council's complaints procedure. Where there is no formal procedure, you should begin by writing to the supervisor of the person dealing with your claim, making it clear why you are dissatisfied. It is always best to put a complaint in writing so all the issues can be properly considered. Include details of everything that has gone wrong, and make it clear what you expect the council to do about it (eg, sort out the claim within seven days, make a formal apology, compensate you for any loss). If you do not receive a satisfactory reply, you should take the matter up with someone more senior in the department and ultimately the Principal Officer. You could also consider involving your local councillor.

Complaints to councillors

If you are not satisfied with the treatment of your case by the local authority you can ask a councillor to write or speak to the relevant officers on your behalf. S/he may be able to persuade them to respond more favourably. S/he can also pursue any necessary changes to local authority policy or procedure which may be required to ensure that other claimants do not suffer from the same problem. This is particularly useful where the authority has discretion in the way it implements the HB scheme. A councillor can also take up complaints about the way the authority has handled your case – eg, delays, discrimination and other ways in which the service is provided such as opening hours, getting hold of someone to talk to. To complain to a councillor you can either contact your local ward councillor, the Chair of the Committee that is responsible for HB – usually Housing or Finance Committees – or you can go straight to the Leader of the Council. The names of councillors are kept by local libraries.

The local government Ombudsman

If you have tried to sort out your complaint with the local authority but you are still not satisfied with the outcome, you can ask the Commissioner for Local Administration (more commonly known as the local government Ombudsman) to look at what has happened in your case. The Ombudsman can investigate any cases of maladministration by local authorities and make recommendations about what should be done to remedy matters. Although local authorities are not obliged to follow the recommendations, they almost invariably do so. In many cases the mere fact that you have applied to the Ombudsman is sufficient to persuade the local authority to sort out your claim.

The most common type of maladministration dealt with by the Ombudsman is delays in processing claims or applications for review. A delay of four weeks or more would usually be regarded as unacceptable. Failure to properly apply the procedure for dealing with claims or to give you proper notifications about your entitlement are also covered, as are blatant misapplications of the law (eg, where the local authority makes deductions from your benefit to recover an overpayment made to your landlord in respect of another tenant), though in most cases if there is a right of appeal against a decision the best remedy is to use that right. The Ombudsman can investigate the way a fraud allegation has been handled, or the procedures for replacing lost giros, though these are sensitive issues and it is sometimes difficult to show maladministration.

You apply to the Ombudsman by writing to the appropriate local office (see Appendix 1). You are given a form to complete, outlining your complaint and as long as they are satisfied that you have tried to resolve matters locally first and that this is a case of maladministration rather than a dispute about the law, your case is investigated. The Ombudsman has extensive powers to look at documents held by the local authority on your claim, and can use these to check out what happened and whether there was any fault on their part. You may be interviewed to check any facts. Straightforward cases can be dealt with in about three months, but some cases take much longer. However, the Ombudsman can recommend financial compensation if you have been unfairly treated or suffered a loss as a result of the maladministration, and local authorities usually agree to pay such compensation. A complaint may also make the authority review its procedures and practices, which could be of benefit to claimants other than you, so it is worth making a complaint.

Max = 100% , Capital below 16000.

only claiment per couple.   IS = 100%

Taper 20% -   20p every £1·00 - over Applicable amount.

weekly benefit . ∴ Amount ÷ 365 × 7.

Applicable amount - weekly income same as HB.

Non dep - 18 or over in renumerative work - gross income
£108 → ₽2·30
up to 107·99 - ~~HB~~ 1·15 , others Ag 18+ 1·15.

PART SIX

Council tax benefit

£25·00 disregard earnings,
lone parent .

CHAPTER FIFTEEN

Council tax benefit

This chapter covers:

1. The basic rules (below)
2. Liability to pay council tax (p298)
3. The amount of benefit (p309)
4. Claims, payments and reviews (p318)
5. Students (p323)
6. People in hospital (p324)

I. THE BASIC RULES

Council tax benefit (CTB) is paid by local authorities and not by the Benefits Agency, although it is a national scheme and the rules are mainly determined by DSS regulations. If you qualify for CTB, your liability for the tax is reduced.

There are two types of benefit: main CTB and alternative maximum CTB which is usually known as second adult rebate. Most people will only qualify for the former, but if you are eligible for both, you will be paid whichever is the higher.

Until April 1994, **persons from abroad** with entry restrictions placed on their stay in the UK could claim either type of CTB if they were liable to pay council tax, although there were restrictions on most overseas students. CTB was also not treated as 'public funds' under the immigration rules (although this may change sometime in 1994/95). Persons from abroad with entry restrictions are now also excluded from making new or repeat claims for CTB after April 1994. A new **'habitual residence'** test will also apply to all claimants from summer 1994. However, any person potentially affected by either of these new tests who is already receiving CTB at the point of change will remain legally entitled to benefit until the end of their normal benefit period. These new rules are the same as for housing benefit (HB) (see p223 for more details).

Who can claim

To claim main CTB or second adult rebates, you must be liable to pay council tax on a property which you normally occupy as your home. If you have more than one home it must be your main home. Full-time students are not usually able to claim main CTB but there are exceptions (see pp323-4).

You can claim **main CTB** if:

- your income is low enough. How low it has to be depends on your circumstances. Remember that some of your income may be ignored but you may also be treated as having income you do not really receive (see Chapter 18);
- your savings and other capital are not worth more than £16,000. Again, some of your capital may be ignored, but you may also be treated as having capital you do not really possess (see Chapter 19).

The amount of benefit you receive depends on your income, the number of people in your 'family' (see below) and the amount of your council tax. The full calculation is explained on p311.

You can claim a **second adult rebate** if:

- with certain exceptions you are the only person liable for the council tax on your home (see p314); *and*
- with certain exceptions no one living in your home pays you rent (see p314); *and*
- there are certain other adults living with you who are on low incomes. Your own income and capital are ignored.

Also note that:

- CTB is non-taxable and is not dependent on you having paid national insurance contributions;
- you must be aged 18 or more to qualify for CTB;
- you may claim CTB regardless of whether or not you or your partner are working or on income support (IS). There is no requirement that non-working claimants or partners must be available for work etc;
- you can still claim CTB if you have already paid your council tax bill in advance;
- if you are in arrears with your council tax bill this does not affect your right to claim CTB. You may even be able to get your claim backdated for up to one year (see p318);
- if you are temporarily absent from home you can continue to get CTB for as long as you are still treated as resident in, and remain liable for the council tax on your home while you are away. Unlike HB, there is no absolute time limit on how long benefit can be paid in this situation;

- you can claim a second adult rebate even if you are a full-time student and/or have capital in excess of £16,000.

Who you claim for

You claim for your 'family' which consists of:

- you; *and*
- your partner (if any) who is
  either   your husband or wife, if you are living together (see p330),
  or   a person of the opposite sex to whom you are not married but with whom you are living together as husband and wife (see p330); *and*
- any children for whom you are responsible (which may include children who have left school – see p335).

Income and capital belonging to your partner are treated as yours. There are special rules for dealing with income and capital belonging to your children (see pp358 and 395).

Claiming benefit

The rules for claiming benefit and for payment of benefit are very similar to those for HB. If you also intend to claim IS you can claim through your local Benefits Agency office by filling out HB and CTB forms supplied with your IS claim form. Other people, including *existing* IS claimants, should get a claim form from their local authority. In most cases, benefit is paid directly into your council tax account, reducing the amount of council tax you have to pay. Once you have claimed, you will be assessed for both main CTB and second adult rebate, if appropriate.

2. LIABILITY TO PAY COUNCIL TAX

The following paragraphs contain an overview of some of the rules used to decide who is liable to pay the council tax and how much the bill will be. For more details about these, and any other matters connected with the council tax, *including legal references*, you should refer to the *Council Tax Handbook* by Martin Ward, available from CPAG, which covers all the rules on the scheme, including the variations which apply in England, Wales and Scotland (see Appendix 3).

Which properties are subject to council tax

All dwellings (residential properties) are 'chargeable' to council tax unless they are treated as exempt. You may be liable to pay council tax to a local authority if you are solely or mainly resident in, or are the owner of, a chargeable property in that area. It is important, therefore, to check first of all whether your property is exempt.

Properties are **exempt indefinitely** from the council tax:

- where they have been left *unoccupied by a former resident* because that person is now:
  - in prison or detention (except, in England and Wales only, for non-payment of either the council tax or a fine imposed under it);
  - in hospital, a residential care home or nursing home;
  - living somewhere else in order to give or receive personal care;
  - a student (see p306 for definition of student) studying elsewhere;
- where they are *unoccupied* and:
  - have been repossessed by a mortgage lender;
  - are unfurnished (in Scotland) or substantially unfurnished (in England and Wales) and require, or are undergoing, major repairs or structural alterations to make them habitable;
  - are reserved for a minister of religion (ie, a vicarage in England and Wales, or a manse in Scotland);
  - occupation is prohibited by law (ie, because of a compulsory purchase order);
  - in Scotland only, owned by certain housing bodies and kept unoccupied pending demolition;
  - in Scotland only, form part of premises which includes another dwelling and are difficult to let separately (eg, a granny flat);
  - in Scotland only, were last occupied and used in connection with agricultural land;
  - in Scotland only, held by a trustee in a bankruptcy who would otherwise be liable;
- where they are *occupied* but are:
  - halls of residence predominantly occupied by **students** (see p306); *or*
  - any other dwellings where all the residents are **students** (see p306), including where that dwelling is occupied only during term-time;
  - armed forces (including visiting forces) accommodation;
  - in Scotland only, the sole or main residence of one or more persons under 18, *and no one else*;
  - in Scotland only, held by a housing association and used as trial properties for elderly or disabled persons who are likely to be rehoused permanently in other property provided by the association.

For council tax purposes you will still be treated as *resident* in a property during any absence which is only temporary. Any of the above exemptions which require the property to be unoccupied will, therefore, only be given where the former occupant has either left permanently or for a long period (many councils use as a rule of thumb, six months or more).

Properties are **exempt for up to six months** from the council tax where they are *unoccupied* and:

*   form part of the estate of someone who has died (the executor/administrator becomes liable six months after the grant of probate or letters of administration in England and Wales, or confirmation of executor in Scotland);
*   are unfurnished (in Scotland) or substantially unfurnished (in England and Wales) and are either newly built or have undergone major repairs or structural alterations (liability starts six months after the completion of works);
*   are owned by, and used for the purposes of, a charity. In establishing the last day on which any property was occupied, any periods of occupation of six weeks or less are ignored;
*   in any other case, are unfurnished (in Scotland) or substantially unfurnished (in England and Wales). In establishing the last day on which any property was occupied, any periods of occupation of six weeks or less are ignored.

You should check with your local authority if you think your property should be exempt. Exemptions apply on a daily basis and can be backdated to 1 April 1993 or the date the conditions for exemption were first met, whichever is the later. Unlike the backdating of many social security benefits, there is no need to show you have 'good cause' in order to backdate an exemption. Remember that if an exemption on your property is backdated, any CTB you received for the same period will have been overpaid (see p321). If you are liable for the council tax on an unoccupied property which is not exempt, you should be able to get a discount on your bill (see p305).

Who is liable to pay council tax

In most, but not all cases where a dwelling is occupied as someone's sole or main residence (ie, as their normal or main home), the council tax liability will fall on one or more of the **residents**. Otherwise, liability falls on the **owner** of the property.

Council tax payable by a resident

For both council tax and CTB purposes, a **resident** is someone who is:

- aged 18 or over; *and*
- solely or mainly resident in the dwelling.

Liability depends on your housing status. There is a 'liability hierarchy' when deciding who must pay if there is more than one resident in the property. The liable person is whichever resident falls into the highest of the following categories:

- an owner-occupier;
- a tenant;
- a statutory or secure tenant;
- a licensee in England and Wales or a sub-tenant in Scotland;
- any other resident not covered above (eg, a squatter in England and Wales).

Thus, if you own your own home and a friend lives with you and pays you rent, you alone would be liable as you are higher up the 'liability hierarchy'. If, on the other hand, you were both joint owners or were part of a married or unmarried couple, you would be treated as jointly and severally liable for the bill on that property (see p302 for who can be held jointly and severally liable).

Council tax payable by an owner

The **owner** of a dwelling is someone who is:

- a freeholder (in England and Wales) or a heritable proprietor (in Scotland); *or*
- in England and Wales only, a leaseholder (including someone with a sub-lease of six months or more).

Owners will be liable for the council tax on dwellings which:

- are **without any residents** (ie, unoccupied or where all the occupants are either under 18 or have their main home elsewhere). In Scotland, however, properties where all the occupants are under 18 are exempt (see p299);
- are in **multiple occupation**. (This only applies where the property was built or adapted for occupation by more than one household and where each resident is *either* only able to occupy part of the dwelling *or* is only liable to pay rent on part of the dwelling);
- are residential care homes, nursing homes and hostels providing care;
- are occupied by religious communities;
- have at least one resident, or member of their family, employed in domestic service – ie, stately homes with resident domestic staff;
- are occupied by a minister of religion and used for the performance of

her/his duties – ie, a vicarage in England and Wales, or a manse in Scotland.
• in Scotland, are provided as boarding school accommodation.

Any joint owners and/or the married or unmarried partners of owners will be treated as jointly and severally liable for the council tax on any of the above properties (see below for who can be held jointly and severally liable).

Liable owners are only eligible for CTB on the dwelling where they are solely or mainly resident (although they may be eligible for disability reductions (p304), discounts (p305) and transitional relief (p308) on properties where they do not reside but are liable for the bill). If you live in a property where the owner is liable for the council tax, you may be asked to pay an amount towards the tax as part of your rent. Where this happens, you will not be able to claim CTB for your 'share' of the bill because you will not be the person legally liable to pay it. However, if you qualify for HB, your share of the bill should be covered by treating it as part of your eligible rent (but see rent restrictions on p231).

Joint and several liability

Joint and several liability means that you share legal liability for the whole council tax bill with one or more other people – ie, you are not just liable for a 'share'. You also share liability for any arrears on that bill, even where these have been caused by someone else – eg, where one of the other jointly liable persons fails to pay their agreed share. There are two ways in which joint and several liability can arise. These are where:

• two or more persons satisfy the liability rules equally because they have the same legal interest in the dwelling. This applies as much to two owner-occupiers as it does to three joint tenants or two non-resident owners. In England and Wales, it would also apply to any number of persons who are squatters in the same property; *or*
• a person is the married or unmarried partner of any liable person with whom they are living as part of a heterosexual couple – even where the ownership or tenancy of the property is in the other partner's name only. There are no varying degrees of liability – ie, the partner of a liable owner is equally liable both with her/his own partner and with any other joint owners and their respective partners. The definition of 'couple' for council tax purposes is almost the same as the one which applies to HB and CTB (see p330). Under the council tax, it is only necessary that the members of a couple live in the same **dwelling**, rather than in the same **household** (see CPAG's *Council Tax Handbook* for more information on this point, including the situations

where the council tax and CTB definitions do not coincide in practice). Gay and lesbian couples will not be jointly and severally liable unless they are also joint owners/tenants/squatters etc.

There will only be one council tax bill for each chargeable dwelling, even where more than one person may be jointly and severally liable to pay it. Local authorities are not required to name every liable person on the bill, so it is important to know the rules on liability to ensure that you know whether you, or anyone else, ought to pay a share of it. You can only claim CTB if you are a liable person (see p300). Where you are jointly liable, except where this is only with your heterosexual partner, you can each claim separately on an equal share (see p310). If you have delayed making a claim because you were not named on the bill, and did not realise you were jointly liable, you should argue for your CTB to be backdated on the grounds you have 'good cause for a late claim' (see p318).

Joint liability and severely mentally impaired persons

An important exception to the general rule applies where a severely mentally impaired person would otherwise be held jointly and severally liable with one or more persons who are not severely mentally impaired (see p306 for who is classed as severely mentally impaired). This exception means that, where a severely mentally impaired person:

- shares the same degree of legal interest in the dwelling as one or more other persons (either as a resident or owner) any liability, or joint and several liability, will *only* fall on those persons who are *not* severely mentally impaired; *or*
- lives with a liable partner who is not severely mentally impaired, they cannot be held jointly and severally liable with their partner.

However, a severely mentally impaired person remains **liable and/or jointly and severally liable** where they:

- are the sole owner or tenant and there is no other liable person to whom the council tax bill could be sent; *or*
- share liability either as a resident, owner or partner and *all* the other liable persons concerned are also severely mentally impaired – in which case they all remain jointly and severally liable.

Note that the effect of this rule is to avoid granting exemption to dwellings owned or occupied by a severely mentally impaired person (the dwelling remains chargeable in the normal way, although a discount may apply – see p306). Severely mentally impaired persons are only excluded from liability in those cases where there is at least one other, non-impaired, liable person by whom the bill could be paid.

Ways to reduce a council tax bill

The local authority sets the overall amount of council tax each year and this varies from one area to another. Within any local authority's area, the level of council tax payable for any dwelling will depend on the **valuation band** to which it has been allocated (Band A properties pay the lowest bills, and Band H the highest). The valuation of a dwelling is based on a number of set 'valuation assumptions'. Your bill can be reduced, in certain cases, if you can show the valuation is too high (see CPAG's *Council Tax Handbook* for more details). Your bill can also be reduced in three other ways:

- disability reductions (see below);
- discounts (see p305);
- transitional relief (see p308).

The amount of your council tax is the figure set by your local authority minus any or all of these deductions, applied in the order listed above. In addition, you can claim CTB to further reduce the amount you pay if you are on a low income.

Disability reductions

For council tax purposes all properties are given an assumed value and put into one of eight bands on the basis of this valuation. These valuation bands are described by letters (A-H), with A being the lowest. The higher the band, the larger your council tax bill.

If you or someone living in your home is disabled, your council tax bill can be reduced to that payable on properties in the valuation band below the one allocated to your property. This is called the disability reduction. So if your property is in band G you pay council tax at the band F rate. If your property is in band A, no further reduction is possible. To get the reduction, you must apply in writing to the local authority each year. It is the person liable to pay council tax who has to apply, not the disabled person, if different. You may be asked to provide additional information to support your application and you should reply promptly to speed up the assessment and, at the latest, within 21 days of being asked for this. You must also tell the local authority if you think you no longer qualify.

For the purpose of this reduction, a person counts as disabled if s/he is **substantially and permanently disabled** irrespective of how the disability was caused. You can claim a reduction if:

- you are liable for the council tax (it does not matter if you share liability with someone else); *and*

- a disabled person has their sole or main residence in your home. This could be yourself or any other person, including a child; *and*
- your home has certain facilities required by the disabled person (whether or not these exist as a result of special adaptations having been made). These facilities must be essential for the disabled person's needs or be of major importance to them. Only the following facilities count:

either a **second** bathroom or kitchen with facilities appropriate to the person's disability. Adaptations to a **sole** bathroom or kitchen do not count;

or another room which is mainly used to meet that person's special needs (eg, a downstairs bedroom or a room specially set aside for physiotherapy or home dialysis);

or enough floor space to ensure that a wheelchair can be used indoors but only if the disabled person needs to use a wheel chair in the home.

Only one disability reduction can be awarded to any one dwelling, even where there is more than one qualifying disabled resident or where any disabled resident satisfies more than one of the qualifying criteria. The reduction is applied *before* discounts, transitional relief, or other benefits. If you disagree with the decision on your claim you can appeal to a valuation tribunal (see CPAG's *Council Tax Handbook* for more details).

Discounts

Council tax is based on the assumption that two residents live in each property. This does not include occupants aged under 18, or anyone not solely or mainly resident in the property, since they do not count as 'residents' for council tax purposes (see p300). If there are more than two residents, the bill remains the same. If there are less than two residents the bill is reduced. For example, if you live alone, your bill is reduced by 25 per cent. If your property is empty, the bill is reduced by 50 per cent (although Welsh authorities have the discretion to give you only a 25 per cent reduction, or no reduction at all, where the property is furnished and no one's sole or main residence for six months – ie, a second home). These reductions are called '**discounts**'.

Even if there are other residents living with you, a discount can still be made if they fall into one of the groups described below. This is because they have a '**status discount**' and are ignored when calculating your council tax bill. If all residents are ignored (including yourself), a 50 per cent reduction is made. If all but one of you is ignored, the 25 per cent reduction applies.

The following residents are ignored:

- 18-year-olds for whom child benefit is still payable (or would be if they were not in local authority care);
- school-leavers aged under 20 who left school or college after 30 April (but they are only ignored until 1 November of that year);
- students who are:
  - studying on a full-time university or college course. The course must last for at least one academic year of at least 24 weeks and involve a minimum of 21 hours tuition/study in term-time;
  - under 20 doing a further education course (up to A-level, ONC or OND) who study for 12 hours or more a week for at least three months;
  - student nurses on Project 2000 courses or academic courses at university (other student nurses *do not* count as 'students' – see below);
  - foreign language assistants registered with the Central Bureau for Educational Visits and Exchanges;
- student nurses on hospital-based training (not Project 2000) leading to initial inclusion on the register. Nurses already on the register doing further training, such as midwifery, do not have a status discount;
- people under 25 on Youth Training schemes;
- apprentices employed to learn a job and train for a recognised qualification (approved by the National Council for Vocational Qualifications/Scottish Vocational Education Council) who are paid less than £130 a week gross but who expect to earn substantially more on qualifying;
- patients solely or mainly resident in a hospital or in a residential care, nursing or mental nursing home (private hospital in Scotland), or bail or probation hostel which provides care and/or treatment. People in hostels catering for the elderly, disabled and mentally ill are also ignored, as are those in hostels dealing with alcohol or drug problems;
- people detained in prison or hospital under a court ruling. This includes those detained prior to deportation under the Immigration Act. Such people continue to be ignored even if they are temporarily released (in England and Wales, people in prison for non-payment of council tax, or a fine imposed under it, are not ignored);
- people who are severely mentally impaired, and certified as such by a doctor, and who are getting one of the following benefits: invalidity benefit, severe disablement allowance, attendance allowance, the higher or middle rate of the disability living allowance care component, disability working allowance, unemployability supplement or constant attendance allowance for an industrial or war injury. 'Severe

mental impairment' means permanent severe impairment of intelligence and social functioning;
- residential care workers who are employed by a public authority or charity, or by the person needing care (so long as they were introduced by such a body), and who provide care for at least 24 hours a week and earn £30 a week or less. The residential care worker must be living in accommodation provided by the employer. This covers community service volunteers;
- other carers, living with the person needing care and providing care for at least 35 hours a week. The person receiving care must be getting the higher rate of attendance allowance or the highest rate care component of disability living allowance or constant attendance allowance for an industrial or war injury. If the care is given to your partner (married or unmarried) or your own child under 18 you are not ignored. If you have left your old home unoccupied and gone to live somewhere else in order to give or receive care, your old home will be exempt (see p299);
- people in hostels or night shelters provided for those with no fixed abode;
- members of religious communities with no income or capital of their own;
- members of visiting armed forces, international headquarters and defence organisations (such as the United Nations or NATO).

If someone with a status discount is disregarded under the above rules, it does not necessarily mean that the council tax bill will be reduced. It is only if the number of adults residing in the property is less than two, not counting any that are disregarded, that a discount is awarded. The effect of a status discount is that the bill for the property will be the same as if that person were not living there.

A status discount does not mean that the person concerned is exempt from the council tax. The rules about status discounts are quite separate and do not affect liability (except in the case of some severely mentally impaired persons who would otherwise be held jointly and severally liable – see p303).

Example
A person under 25 on a Youth Training Scheme living alone as a sole tenant will, as a single resident with a status discount, be eligible for a 50 per cent discount on her bill. However, as the sole tenant she will also be the person *liable* to pay that reduced bill.

A discount applies on a daily basis and can be backdated to 1 April 1993 or the date the conditions for it were first met, whichever is the later. Unlike the backdating of many social security benefits, there is no need to show you have 'good cause' to backdate a discount. Discounts do not depend on a test of income or the submission of a formal claim. The council should automatically try to ascertain whether you qualify for one (they can also use the information on your CTB claim form for this purpose – see p310). However, it is your responsibility, as the liable person, to tell them if you think they have got it wrong and you are not entitled to a discount (your bill will be revised later if your discount was wrongly awarded). Remember that a future change in the composition of your household could affect both your entitlement to a discount and to CTB/HB.

If you disagree with a local authority's decision on discounts, you can appeal to a valuation tribunal. Remember that discounts are made after any disability reduction. For more information on both discounts and appeals, see CPAG's *Council Tax Handbook*.

Transitional reduction

Transitional reduction (TR) schemes apply in England and Scotland, but not in Wales. They are a form of transitional relief originally designed to limit the increases that some households faced when the council tax replaced the poll tax.

Transitional reduction was based on the circumstances of the residents occupying the property on 1 April 1993 (including any entitlement, on that day, to a disability reduction and/or a discount) and the valuation band to which the property was allocated. Once calculated, however, the amount of TR was not affected by any subsequent change of circumstances up to 1 April 1994. This is because TR was, and is, tied to the property rather than to the residents themselves. If the original residents move out they leave the TR behind. Any incoming residents automatically inherit the TR attached to the property (even though their circumstances may be quite different from those of the residents on whom the TR was originally calculated). TR is suspended for any day during which no one has their sole or main residence in the property, and is then re-applied at the original rate for that year when a new occupier moves in.

Transitional reduction will begin to be phased out from 1 April 1994. From that date, some properties will have their TR reduced, while others will lose it altogether. If you live in a property where TR still applies after 1 April 1994, it will continue to be paid at that new rate until 1 April 1995. All the other rules remain the same. If you subsequently qualify for a discount, remember that this will be calculated on your bill *after* any disability reduction has been applied but *before* deducting your TR.

Transitional reduction cannot apply to a property for the year beginning 1 April 1994 unless it was originally applied for the year beginning 1 April 1993. Transitional reduction should have been awarded automatically to all qualifying properties from 1 April 1993. There was no need to make a claim. However, if you think the local authority should have awarded TR in your case, but failed to do so, you can appeal. If you are successful TR will be granted from 1 April 1993 at the appropriate rate for that year, with a reduced rate for the current year, if applicable. Unlike the backdating of many social security benefits, there is no need to show you have 'good cause' in order to backdate TR. Remember that, if your TR is backdated for any period during which you received CTB, this will create a recoverable overpayment of benefit (see p321).

Appeals about transitional reduction are dealt with by a council tax benefit review board (see p323) not by a valuation tribunal. Prior to lodging an appeal you can make a written request to the local authority for a statement of reasons, and they must send you this within 14 days if possible. For more information on TR, including eligibility, calculation and appeals, see CPAG's *Council Tax Handbook*.

3. THE AMOUNT OF BENEFIT

Your entitlement to main CTB is worked out using a special formula. This is described below. If there are other adults living in your home, you may be entitled to a second adult rebate instead (see p313). Once you have claimed CTB the local authority should assess your entitlement to both types of benefit and pay you whichever is the higher. You cannot get both.[1]

Main council tax benefit

Council tax liability

The calculation of benefit is based on your net weekly liability for council tax – ie, your bill *after* any of the following reductions have been applied:[2]

- a disability reduction (see p304);
- a discount (see p305);
- transitional reduction (see p308).

Other special reductions awarded by the local authority because you pay your council tax in a lump sum at the beginning of the year are ignored and any benefit is calculated on the basis of your bill before this reduction is made.[3]

It is important that eligibility for any disability reduction, discount or transitional reduction is identified *before* your CTB is calculated, otherwise a recoverable overpayment will result (see p321). In order to help prevent this, local authorities can award you a discount on the basis of the information you put on your CTB claim form *before* they work out your CTB. In some cases this could result in your claim for CTB getting you a discount but no CTB (because the discount has reduced your liability). In other cases, where your income is low, you could end up being awarded both a discount and CTB together.

Joint liability

If you are jointly liable for the council tax with one or more other residents in the dwelling, the total net liability is divided equally by the number of liable persons in order to arrive at the share of the annual bill on which each of you can claim.[4] This does not need to happen where you only share joint liability with your heterosexual partner, as one of you makes a joint claim for both on the total bill.[5] However, where a couple are also jointly liable with one or more other residents, the couple can claim on a two-person share of the bill.

Example
Three residents are jointly liable for a net annual council tax bill of £600. They can each make a separate claim on £200 liability (an equal share). If two of the residents were a couple, however, either member of the couple could make a single claim on £400 liability (a two-person share), whereas the other resident could make a separate claim on £200 liability (a one-person share).

Note that this rule is different, and much simpler, than the rule relating to the apportionment of rent for HB purposes (see p216). With HB, the authority must decide each person's fair share of the rent taking into account the number of persons making payments, the proportion of rent *actually paid* by each, and any other relevant circumstances – such as the number of rooms each person occupies etc. For CTB, however, council tax liability is automatically divided on an equal basis in all cases.

Example
Two joint tenants (who are not a couple) share accommodation. One occupies two-thirds of the property and pays two-thirds of the rent/council tax, the other occupies, and accordingly pays rent/council tax for, the other third. The person occupying two-thirds of the property and paying two-thirds of the bills would be able to claim HB on two-thirds of the rent but CTB on only *half* of the total council tax bill.

The apportionment of liability for CTB purposes also gives rise to another particular problem. Under the council tax rules, a person who is jointly and severally liable can be held responsible for the full amount of the tax due on the property (see p302) while receiving CTB only on her/his 'share'.

Weekly council tax figure

Weekly net liability is assessed by dividing the annual charge by the number of days in the financial year and then multiplying this by seven.[6]

Example
Net liability £490
Divide this by 365 = £1.342466
Multiply this by 7 = £9.397262

DSS guidance recommends that the figures should not be rounded until the final annual amount of CTB is worked out, and that calculations should usually be done to six decimal places.[7] When notifying you of your benefit a rounded figure can be specified.[8]

Calculation of benefit

Once you have worked out your net liability you can assess your **maximum council tax benefit**.[9] This is your total liability minus any deductions for non-dependants (see below).

If you are on income support or have no income, you receive the maximum CTB.[10] If you have non-dependants, they are expected to contribute towards your council tax bill.

If you are not on income support, the calculation involves several steps:

Step 1   Check that your capital is not too high (see Chapter 19).
Step 2   Calculate your income (see Chapter 18).
Step 3   Work out your applicable amount (see Chapter 17).
Step 4   Compare the figures from Step 2 and Step 3. If your income is equal to, or less than, your applicable amount, you are entitled to maximum CTB. If it is higher, go on to Step 5.
Step 5   Calculate the difference between your income and applicable amount.
Step 6   Work out 20 per cent of this figure and deduct it from your maximum CTB. The result is the weekly amount of benefit to which you are entitled.[11]

Note that unlike HB, there is no minimum payment rule.

Non-dependant deductions

A non-dependant is someone who normally lives with you on a non-commercial basis[12] but who is not your partner or dependent child. It includes grown-up sons and daughters who remain at home. Only heterosexual couples are recognised in social security law so a lesbian or gay partner counts as a non-dependant unless s/he is a joint tenant or owner. Non-dependants have no liability to pay the tax themselves and are assumed to contribute towards your council tax. In most cases, a deduction is made from your CTB if you have non-dependants regardless of whether they do contribute,[13] and you should consider asking them to reimburse you for at least the amount of the deduction.

The following people *do not* count as non-dependants:

- someone who is jointly liable with you for the council tax.[14] However, if s/he was a non-dependant at some time in the eight weeks before becoming liable, the local authority can treat her/him as a non-dependant unless they are satisfied that the change was not made to take advantage of the CTB scheme (eg, to enable them to claim CTB on part of the council tax);[15]
- someone who pays rent to you or your partner.[16] However, if s/he is a close relative or the arrangement is not a commercial one s/he will count as a non-dependant.[17] 'Close relative' means a parent, parent-in-law, son, son-in-law, daughter, daughter-in-law, step-parent, step-son, stepdaughter, brother, sister or the spouse or cohabitee of any of these.[18] 'Commercial' does not necessarily mean profit-making but it does imply that you must at least break even. If the local authority thinks you are only charging rent in order to avoid a non-dependant deduction, it can treat your sub-tenant as a non-dependant unless s/he was otherwise liable to pay rent on the same property in the eight weeks before the current liability began;[19]
- someone who is employed by a charitable or voluntary body to live with, and provide care for you or your partner, if you have to pay for this service.[20]

Once it is established that you have one or more non-dependants, deductions are usually made for each non-dependant in your household. Only one deduction is made if the non-dependant is part of a couple, whether married or unmarried.[21] If you share liability for the council tax with others, the amount of the non-dependant deduction is shared equally between you, even if the other person is not claiming CTB. However, if the local authority thinks that the non-dependant only belongs to one resident, the whole deduction is made from that person's benefit.[22] If a couple share liability with a single person their CTB is reduced by two-thirds of the non-dependant deduction (ie, apportionment is made on the same basis as liability – see p310).

When no deduction is made[23]

The rules as to when a non-dependant deduction is *not* made are the same as for HB (see p243) except that *all* non-dependants on income support are ignored and not just those under 25. In addition, no deduction is made for non-dependants who are disregarded for discount purposes (ie, with status discounts – see p306) other than students who must count as full-time students for CTB purposes, if no deduction is to be made (see p323). Where the non-dependant is a student, no deduction is made during the summer vacation, even where s/he works.

The amount of the deduction[24]

Circumstances of the non-dependant	Deduction
18 or over and in full-time work with a weekly gross income of	
£108 or more	£2.30
up to £107.99	£1.15
Others aged 18 or over	£1.15

If the members of a non-dependant couple each qualify for a different rate, the higher amount is deducted.[25]

The definitions of **full-time work** and **earnings** are the same as for HB (see p244).

Income and capital of a non-dependant

As with HB, your main CTB can be assessed using the income and capital of a non-dependant, instead of your own, if it is felt you are trying to take advantage of the CTB scheme[26] (see p245-6).

Increasing the amount of your CTB

You can be awarded more than the normal amount of main CTB if your circumstances are exceptional. The rules are the same as for HB (see p246). Your CTB can be increased up to the total amount of council tax on which you are eligible to claim (see p309). The limit is your apportioned share if you are jointly liable (see p310).

The daily amount is assessed and then multiplied by seven to give your weekly increase.[27]

Second adult rebate

Second adult rebate is an alternative type of benefit which can be paid instead of, but not as well as, main CTB. Whenever you claim CTB the local authority must assess you for both types of benefit and award whichever is the greater.[28] Second adult rebate is designed to help you if you have certain other residents (referred to as 'second adults') in your home who do not share liability for council tax with you and who do not pay rent to you. Their presence in your home means you have to pay the full council tax without discount, but if their income is low they may not be able to contribute towards the cost. Second adult rebate compensates you for this. Remember that students can claim it even though they are excluded from main CTB.

Who is eligible to claim a second adult rebate?

You will be able to claim a second adult rebate where:[29]

- you are liable to pay the council tax on the dwelling you normally occupy as your home; *and*
- there is at least one other resident in the dwelling who is classed as a *second adult* (see below for who counts); *and*
- there is no other resident of the dwelling (apart from someone with a status discount – see p305) who is liable to pay you rent in order to live there. The DSS believe that where any resident pays you rent, you cannot get a second adult rebate. If the local authority follows this advice you should argue that this is not what the Act says, and that a specific exception is allowed where the person paying rent has a status discount.[30]

Note that the whole of your income and capital are ignored when you claim second adult rebate. So you can get it even if you have a high income and/or assets worth more than £16,000.[31] However, your income and capital will still count in the normal way for main CTB purposes if you are also being assessed for this as well.[32]

You cannot claim a second adult rebate if you live with another person who is **jointly liable** for the council tax with you (eg, your partner, or a joint owner or tenant) unless all, or all but one of you, are ignored for discount purposes (ie, have status discounts – see p305).[33] This is because with joint owners or tenants there is usually a full liability for council tax because there are at least two residents in the home and the presence of a third or fourth person is irrelevant in deciding whether a discount applies.

Who counts as a 'second adult'

A second adult is someone who lives with you on a non-commercial basis. It does *not* include anyone who:[34]

- is aged under 18 (they do not count as 'residents' and do *not* affect any possible discount);
- has a status discount (they are ignored for discount purposes and do *not* affect any possible discount);
- is your partner with whom you are jointly liable (they *do* affect discount entitlement but will be included in any claim for main CTB);
- is jointly liable to pay the council tax on the dwelling with you as a joint owner or tenant etc (they *do* affect discount entitlement but can claim main CTB for their own share of the bill – see p310).

Second adult rebates are intended to compensate you for the loss of a discount because one or more 'second adults' are living with you. The intention of the above rules is to ensure that anyone living with you will not be classed as a 'second adult' if their presence does not affect your likelihood of getting a discount (as in the first two cases) or where the potential loss of a discount can be compensated for in some other way (as in the second two cases). In practice, residents classified as second adults will tend to be the same persons as those treated as non-dependants for main council tax benefit purposes (see p312).

How much second adult rebate can you get?

Any second adult rebate is worked out on the basis of:

- the pre-discounted council tax liability for the whole dwelling[35] (see p316); *and*
- the total gross income of any second adult(s)[36] (see p316).

The amount of second adult rebate (as a percentage of pre-discounted council tax liability) awarded in different circumstances is set out below.[37]

Income of second adult(s)	*Second adult rebate*
2nd adult (or all 2nd adults) on income support	25%
2nd adult(s) total gross income:	
– up to £107.99 a week	15%
– £108 to £138.99 a week	7.5%
– £139 a week or more	Nil

Note that where the second adult, or where there is more than one *all* the second adults, are on IS you will get a second adult rebate equivalent to a discount (25 per cent of your council tax). This is because there is no allowance within IS to enable the second adult(s) to make any contribution towards your bill. On the other hand, the calculation assumes that, where the second adult, or adults, have a total gross income of £139 a week or more, they have sufficient income to fully compensate you for any consequent loss of discount and so no second adult rebate is necessary. Also note that the maximum benefit payable is always 25 per cent of liability, even in those cases where you would have received a 50 per cent discount, or would have been exempt altogether, were it not for the presence of two or more second adults in your home (eg, as in the case of a student nurse with two second adults on IS).

Council tax liability for a second adult rebate

The council tax figure used to work out your second adult rebate is:[38]

- the gross council tax liability for the dwelling as a whole; *less*
- any disability reduction (see p304); *and*
- transitional reduction (see p308).

Note that this is not the same figure as used for main CTB (see p309). However, the procedure for converting annual to weekly amounts is the same (see p311). Any reduction in council tax liability arising from the award of a discount is ignored for the purpose of a second adult rebate. In other words, where you have received a discount it must be added back on to the net amount of council tax payable to arrive at the figure used in the second adult rebate calculation. This is only done for the purposes of the benefit calculation – you will still receive your discount in practice. This will only apply in those cases where a discount has, in effect, been reduced from 50 per cent to 25 per cent by the presence of a second adult in your home.

Assessment of second adult income

To obtain a second adult rebate, you must give the local authority details of the gross income of any second adults living with you (see p315). Where there is more than one second adult, their combined gross income is used.[39]

Gross income[40] includes the second adult's:

- earnings;
- non-earned income, including social security benefits;
- actual income from capital (as opposed to tariff income) – eg, building society interest payments (the capital itself is ignored).

Gross income does not include:

- any income of a second adult on income support;
- any attendance allowance;
- any disability living allowance;
- the income of any person with a status discount (see p305), *except* where that person has a partner who is not ignored for discount

purposes (in which case the gross income of *both* partners, less disregarded income, is taken into account).[41]

A basic problem with second adult rebate is that it involves means-testing someone who is not the claimant and who may not always wish to co-operate (perhaps for reasons of confidentiality). If you have difficulty establishing the income of the second adults on whom your claim is based, you may find that the local authority automatically assumes total second adult income exceeds £139 a week and that you are not entitled to benefit (see p315). If you cannot persuade any second adults to give details of their income to you, they may be prepared to tell the local authority directly. Failing this, you could try finding out the going rate for the type of work they do, or social security benefits they receive, and ask the local authority to make a reasonable estimate based on that.

Second adult rebates and jointly liable claimants

In contrast to main CTB, where there is more than one resident liable for the council tax in your dwelling, any second adult rebate is always calculated on the (pre-discounted) liability for your *dwelling as a whole*. Any benefit arising is then split equally between all the jointly liable residents.[42] This does not need to happen where you are jointly liable with your heterosexual partner only since, in this case, one of you claims on behalf of both and receives all of the benefit.[43] Apart from this, every other jointly liable person must make their own separate claim in order to get their share of the benefit. For example, three eligible joint tenants would each be entitled to one-third of the total second adult rebate for the dwelling as a whole. If two of them were a couple, however, then they would be entitled to receive two-thirds, and the other single tenant, one-third, of the total benefit.

Extra benefit in exceptional circumstances

Where you are only entitled to a second adult rebate based on either the 7.5 per cent or 15 per cent figures , the local authority has the discretion to increase your existing benefit up to the maximum 25 per cent figure (or your share of it where you are jointly liable) if it considers your circumstances to be exceptional.[44] As with HB, it is left up to the local authority to decide what is meant by 'exceptional' in any case (see p246). In practice, the local authority is very unlikely to increase your second adult rebate unless you have a compelling reason and, even then, you will probably have to go to a CTB review board (see p323).

How to claim a second adult rebate

Second adult rebate is a type of CTB so the normal rules apply for claiming. You should be able to use the same claim form to claim both main CTB and second adult rebates. You do not need to say which type of CTB you are claiming. The local authority should automatically assess you for both and award whichever is the higher.[45]

If you cannot be paid main CTB because you are a **full-time student** or someone with **capital over £16,000**, you should still make a claim for second adult rebate if you share your home with one or more 'second adults' (see p314). If you are jointly liable with one or more other residents and you satisfy the special conditions for **jointly liable** claimants (see p314), remember that each of you (apart from your partner) must make your own separate claims in order to receive your share of second adult rebate. As benefit is calculated on the property as a whole and divided between you, if one of you qualifies for benefit then all the others will too, if they claim (unless they already are, or will be, entitled to main CTB paid at a higher rate).

4. CLAIMS, PAYMENTS AND REVIEWS

Claims

The rules for claiming CTB are the same as for HB. See p257 for full details, substituting CTB where it says HB. (The footnotes to that chapter give references to both HB and CTB legislation.)

The rules about advance claims for CTB are slightly different. You can claim up to eight weeks before you become liable for council tax and you are treated as having claimed on the day your liability begins.[46] If you make an unsuccessful claim for CTB but you are likely to become entitled within the next 13 weeks (because, for example, your income is going to reduce), your claim can be treated as made in the week before your entitlement begins.[47]

There is also a special rule when your local authority has not set its council tax rate by the beginning of the financial year. So long as you claim within four weeks of the council tax being agreed your claim is backdated to 1 April, or the date you first became entitled, if that is later.[48]

Late claims and backdating

The rules about late claims and backdated benefit are the same as for HB (see p260). A special case may arise for CTB where you are jointly liable for the council tax but did not claim because your name was not put on the bill (see p303). You could argue that you have good cause for a late claim because you did not realise you were liable as the council had failed (via the bill) to inform you of this.[49]

There are also two other special cases relating to council tax liability for the year beginning 1 April 1993. These are set out below.

- When CTB was introduced in April 1993, there were special transitional rules which allowed existing claims for HB and/or community charge benefit (CCB) to be treated as a claim for CTB. **If you were getting HB or CCB on 31 March 1993, you should have been transferred onto CTB without needing to make a claim.**[50] However, if you have missed out on benefit because the local authority failed to treat your claim for HB/CCB as a claim for CTB at that time, you should ask them to do so retrospectively, as the transitional rules are still in force. You should point out that, as this should have happened automatically, you are not making a late claim and do not have to show 'good cause' Any arrears should also be paid in full, without being subject to a 52-week limit, since they arise as result of a delay in processing a claim rather than through a review or backdating.
- **If you have only just received your council tax bill for 1993/94,** and are not covered by the above rule, the transitional rules still allow your claim for CTB to be treated as having been made on 1 April 1993. However, this only applies where you were liable for the council tax from 1 April 1993 (the start of the scheme) and did not contribute to the delay in issuing the bill. You must also make your claim for CTB within eight weeks of the bill being issued.[51] You should point out that as your claim automatically starts from 1 April 1993 under this rule you do not have to show 'good cause'. Any arrears should also be paid in full, without being subject to a 52-week limit, since this time limit applies backwards from your date of claim[52] which, in this case, is automatically taken as 1 April 1993.

If the local authority refuses to apply either of the above rules, or tries to impose a 52-week limit on any arrears you receive, you should request a formal review (see p323). If this is not successful you should ask for an '*ex gratia* payment' equivalent to the lost benefit since the situation is not your fault (see last year's edition of the *Handbook* for how your benefit should be calculated for this period). If the local authority refuses, you should threaten to complain to the Ombudsman since you have suffered 'maladministration causing injustice' (see p293).

Decisions and notifications

The rules about decisions are the same as for HB. See p263, substituting council tax and CTB for references to rent and HB. You will receive separate notifications for HB and CTB. The information which is to be included in a written notification is the same except that those items specifically relating to rent are, of course, excluded in a CTB notification and, instead, it is required that it includes notice of your weekly council tax liability rounded to the nearest penny.[53] The notification should also include the following, where relevant:

- if you have been assessed for, and are entitled to, both main CTB and second adult rebate, the amount of benefit entitlement in each case and the fact you can only be paid the higher amount;[54]
- if you have been assessed for a second adult rebate, the gross income of any second adult(s) used to determine the rate of benefit, including where any second adult is on IS;[55]
- details of how any of the figures supplied on the notification have been rounded (ie, to the nearest penny).[56]

Payment

As with HB, your CTB is paid for a benefit period, which usually runs from the Monday after your date of claim. If you have only just become liable for the council tax and you claim in the same week in which your liability begins, you will be paid from the Monday of that week.[57] The rules about when your benefit period ends are the same as for HB (see p266).

Payment of CTB is normally made by means of a reduction to your annual council tax bill. This is achieved by converting your weekly benefit to a daily figure by dividing by 7 and then multiplying the answer by the number of days between your first day of entitlement and the following 31 March. If your circumstances change before 31 March so that you become entitled to less benefit, or if you are overpaid for some other reason, any overpaid CTB credited to your council tax account for any period after the date your benefit is actually reviewed – ie, up to the following 31 March – will be legally recoverable.[58]

If you are jointly liable for the council tax with one or more other residents, apart from your partner, remember that any benefit they receive will also be credited to the same bill as your own. You will need to take this into account when agreeing with them how any remaining balance of council tax liability should be shared out between you.

Where your benefit cannot be used to reduce your bill – eg, because you have already paid the full amount in advance – payment can be made direct to you, for example by cheque.[59] Payment by this method is normally only made once you have paid your final instalment of council tax, and usually you must ask for the money to be sent to you. If you do not, your CTB is likely to be credited against your next year's council tax bill.[60]

However, if you are no longer liable for council tax in that authority's area, they should send you any outstanding CTB within 14 days if possible.[61] Payment is normally made to you as the claimant or to your appointee if you have one[62] (see p269).

Withholding of benefit[63]

The local authority can withhold all or part of your CTB if there is doubt about whether you are entitled or, it is thought that, they may be over-paying you. In this case, they can withhold your ongoing weekly benefit and/or any arrears owing to you until they have looked into this further. If your entitlement is established any benefit withheld should be paid to you by either of the methods referred to above.

Payments on death[64]

If a claimant dies, any outstanding CTB can be paid to the personal representative or, if there is none, to the next of kin aged 16 or over. A written application for this must be sent to the local authority within 12 months of the death.

Overpayments

An overpayment of CTB is called 'excess benefit'[65] but the rules about recovery are the same as for HB (see pp274-83).

As with all overpayments, the amount overpaid is the difference between what you were actually paid and what you should have received. However, there are two possible variations of what should have been paid – either a reduced amount of main CTB, or a second adult rebate if you are eligible for this and it would have been higher than the revised amount of main CTB. When assessing the amount overpaid the local authority should do both calculations, and can only recover the balance between the higher of the two figures and the amount which you, in fact, received. It is always worth checking that the second adult rebate calculation has been done and that the correct amount is being recovered.

You must always repay an overpayment which has arisen because you were paid CTB, but then your council tax liability was reduced because of a disability reduction, discount, transitional relief or charge-capping.[66] Unlike HB, recovery is always from the claimant or the person to whom benefit was paid (eg, an appointee) not from any other person, even if s/he caused the overpayment. However, the overpayment can be recovered by deductions from your partner's benefit if you were a couple at the time the overpayment was made, and still are when it is recovered.[67] If both HB and CTB have been overpaid they must be recovered separately. CTB overpayments cannot be recovered from HB.[68]

The rules on how the overpayment is recovered are also different from HB. The overpayment can be recovered by increasing your outstanding council tax liability.[69] In the case of jointly liable claimants remember that, if any one of you are overpaid, adding the overpayment back on to the bill creates arrears for which you will all be held jointly and severally liable under the council tax rules (see p302). If you wish, you can repay the overpayment instead.[70] This avoids you getting into arrears with your council tax. If the local authority cannot get the overpayment back by either of these methods, it can ask the Benefits Agency to make deductions from any other benefits which you receive[71] apart from guardian's allowance.[72] Deductions can be made from benefits paid by other EU countries. If the overpayment was caused by your failure to tell the local authority relevant information, or, because you misrepresented your circumstances, the Benefits Agency will pay part of your benefit over to the local authority, so long as you receive enough benefit for deductions to be made[73] Overpaid CTB can be recovered by court action but not until 21 days after you have been notified of the amount.[74]

Changes of circumstances

You must always notify the local authority of changes which affect your rights to, or the amount of, CTB.[75] The rules are the same as for HB (see p271) except that you do not need to notify any changes in rent for council tax purposes. Nor do you have to tell the local authority the amount of council tax you pay as they have this information already.[76]

If you are getting second adult rebate, you must write and tell the local authority of any changes in the number of adults living in your home and any changes to their gross income. If they are getting income support, you must notify the local authority when this ceases.[77] Remember that changes in the composition of your household could affect your entitlement to a discount too (see p305).

The rules about when changes of circumstances take effect are slightly different to those for HB. Normally, a change affects your CTB from the Monday after it occurs.[78] However, the following changes affect your benefit from the date they occur:[79]

- a change in the amount of your council tax;
- changes to the CTB regulations;
- the fact that you have become part of a couple;
- the death of, or separation from, your partner.

If two or more changes occur in the same week and each takes effect from a different date under the above rules, they are all taken into account from the date of the first change.[80]

If you stop getting another social security benefit, the change in circumstances is deemed to occur on the day after your entitlement ends
and your CTB is changed from the following Monday.[81]
    The rules for reassessing your benefit following a change of circum-
stances are the same as for HB (see p274), but remember that the local
authority should recalculate both main CTB and second adult rebate and
award whichever is currently the higher.

Reviews and complaints

The rules for CTB reviews are the same as those for HB (see pp286-92).
The notes to Chapter 14 include CTB legislation. It is always worth
applying for a review if you think the decision of the local authority is
wrong. If you are applying for a review on both your CTB and your HB,
one review board can deal with both claims if everyone agrees[82] (in
Scotland, HB is administered by district councils and CTB by regional
councils and this situation cannot arise). The local authority can also
consider an outstanding review on community charge benefit (CCB) at
the same time as your HB and/or CTB.
    If you are dissatisfied with the decision of a review board, judicial
review may be possible (see p292). If you wish to complain about the
way the local authority has dealt with your claim, see pp292-4.

5. STUDENTS

Students are liable for council tax but often do not have to pay the full
amount. Student halls of residence are usually exempt from council tax
as are properties where all the adults are students, so no payment is
required in these cases (see p299). In addition, many students liable for
the council tax qualify for a status discount (see pp305-306), and their
bill can be reduced by 25 or 50 per cent. Some students may be able to
reduce their bill further by claiming CTB.
    Most full-time students cannot get main CTB, though some may be
entitled to second adult rebate.[83] Part-time students can claim, as can the
partners of students who are not studying themselves. There are special
rules for calculating the income of students, which are the same as for
IS/HB (see p379).

Full-time students

For who counts as a full-time student, see p250. Note that the definition
is not exactly the same as the definition of 'student' which applies for
council tax purposes when awarding exemptions and discounts (see

p306). As with HB, most full-time students cannot get CTB, but you can claim if:[84]

- you are on income support;
- you are a pensioner who satisfies the conditions for one of the pensioner premiums;
- you are a lone parent who satisfies the conditions for a lone parent premium;
- you are a registered lone foster parent and a child has been placed with you by a local authority or voluntary agency;
- you and your partner are both full-time students and have one or more dependent children;
- you are under 19 and not following a course of higher education;
- you are disabled and eligible for the disability or severe disability premium;
- you satisfy the conditions for a grant supplement in the form of a disabled student's allowance awarded because of deafness;
- you are a Work Trainee on a training allowance.

If you do not qualify for main CTB as a full-time student, check to see if you qualify for second adult rate.

Overseas students

The rules on overseas students are the same as for HB. To qualify for CTB, overseas students must satisfy both the special rules which allow persons from abroad to claim (see p223) *and* the special rules for students (see p251). The footnotes covering these matters in Chapter 13 include references to CTB legislation.

Students and second adult rebate

Full-time students are not precluded from getting second adult rebate and should be assessed in the normal way (see p314).

6. PEOPLE IN HOSPITAL

You can continue to get CTB while in hospital – the rules are the same as for HB (see p247), except that benefit does not stop after 52 weeks but can continue to be paid at the reduced rate indefinitely, so long as your home remains your main residence. If you cease to be treated as residing in your home for council tax purposes because of a prolonged stay in hospital you cannot claim CTB. However, if your partner still lives in your former home they will now probably be treated as the liable person (see p300) and can put in their own claim for benefit. If they live there alone, they should also qualify for a discount (see p305). If, on the other hand, your former home is now unoccupied it should be exempt (see p299). Your benefit may also be adjusted if the local authority decides you are no longer part of a family and reassesses you as a single person (see p329).

PART SEVEN

Calculating needs and resources

*Income support (IS), family credit (FC), disability working allowance (DWA), housing benefit (HB) and council tax benefit (CTB) are all means-tested benefits. The amount you get depends on the **size of your family**, how much **capital** you have and how your **income** compares with your **needs** (called your applicable amount). The rules for all five benefits are the same or similar. This Part covers those rules which are common to all.*

CHAPTER SIXTEEN

Who counts as your family

This chapter explains who is included in your benefit claim. It covers:

1. Introduction (below)
2. Claiming as a couple (p330)
3. Claiming for children (p335)

I. INTRODUCTION

Who is a 'family'

You claim IS/FC/DWA/HB/CTB for yourself, your partner and any dependent children who are members of your household. This is your 'family' for benefit purposes.[1] A partner can include a wife, husband or cohabitee (of the opposite sex). When your benefit is worked out, the needs of your partner and any children are usually added to yours and so are your partner's income and capital. There are special rules for the treatment of the income and capital of dependent children (see pp358-9 and 394-5).

If one member of your family is claiming IS/FC/DWA/HB/CTB, no other member can claim the same benefit for the same period.[2] However, partners can choose which of them should be the claimant, except for FC when the woman must usually claim,[3] and DWA when the disabled partner should claim.[4] (If both of you are disabled, you can choose which one of you should be the claimant.[5]) For details about how to claim see p142 (IS), p191 (FC), p204 (DWA), p257 (HB) and p318 (CTB).

Membership of the same household

The idea of sharing a household is central to whether you can include a child or a partner in your claim. Your right to claim benefit for either ends if you cease to be treated as a member of the same household. This also means that their income and capital (and needs) are no longer taken into account when assessing your benefit.

However, the term 'household' is not defined. In many cases it will be obvious that you are members of the same household – eg, if you, your husband or wife and your children all live together in one house. There are also certain situations in which you will *not* be treated as members of the same household (see pp333-4 for couples and pp336-7 for children), though temporary absences from the home will not usually mean that you cease to share a household.[6]

Whether two people should be treated as members of the same household is very much a question of fact. Physical presence together will not in itself be conclusive. There must be a 'particular kind of tie' binding two people together in a domestic establishment (although this could, in appropriate circumstances, include a household within, for example, a hotel or boarding house[7]).

There will be some occasions where you are regarded as members of the same household, when you think you should not be – eg, if you are two friends of the opposite sex sharing a house (see p332). If this arises it will be important to try to show that although you both live in the same **house** you maintain separate **households.**

A separate household might exist if there are:

- independent arrangements for the storage and cooking of food;
- independent financial arrangements;
- separate eating arrangements;
- no evidence of family life;
- separate commitments for housing costs even if the liability is to another person in the same premises.[8]

You cannot be a member of more than one household at the same time.[9] If two people can be shown to be maintaining separate homes, they cannot be said to be sharing the same household.[10] A separate liability for housing costs could show that you are not part of someone else's household.[11] Even if you only have the right to occupy part of a room, you may have your own household.[12]

Where a child lives for part of the week with each parent, the rules for each benefit allow only one parent to claim for the child, and s/he is treated as a member of her/his household for the whole week (see p336).

Much of the case law on this issue relates to IS, but you should assume that it is also relevant for FC/DWA/HB/CTB.

2. CLAIMING AS A COUPLE

You claim as a couple if you and your partner are:[13]

- married, and living in the same household (see above for definition); *or*
- not married but 'living together as husband and wife'.

If you are lesbian or gay partners you do not count as a couple, and must claim as single people. A person under the age of 16 cannot be treated as a married or unmarried partner,[14] but will normally be treated as a dependent child (see p335).

You count as polygamously married if you are married to more than one person and your marriages took place in a country which permits polygamy.[15] There are special rules for the treatment of additional partners of polygamous marriages[16] – see pp340-41 and CPAG's *Ethnic Minorities' Benefits Handbook* (at p133).

Living together as husband and wife

If it is decided that you are 'living together as husband and wife' (cohabiting), only one of you will be able to claim benefit. Either partner (but see pp185 and 204 for special rules for FC and DWA) can be the claimant but s/he must claim for both partners. The amount of benefit for a couple is usually less than that for two single people, so it is important to dispute a decision that you are cohabiting if you believe you are not. However, in some cases you may have to prove that you are cohabiting to get benefit – eg, where you want to claim FC, you have children and you do not work, but your partner does. You must, of course, be consistent about your circumstances for each different benefit.

The criteria below are used to decide whether you are cohabiting.[17] All of these criteria may be relevant, but no single factor will in itself be conclusive.[18] Just as relationships between couples may often vary considerably, so each case will depend on all its own particular facts and circumstances.

These criteria relate to IS law, but as the principles for FC/DWA/HB/CTB are the same, you should argue that they apply to all benefits. If you are awarded IS, the local authority should not make a separate decision when considering your claim for HB/CTB.[19] However, if you have not been awarded IS, the local authority has a duty to give its own consideration to these criteria, and may reach a different conclusion from the Benefits Agency.

Do you live in the same household?

In all cases, you must be living and spending the major part of your free time not only under the same roof, but in the same **household** (see pp328-9 for a discussion of 'household'). If one of you has a separate address where you usually live, the cohabitation rule should not be applied. You cannot be a member of more than one household at the same time (see p329), so if you are a member of one couple, you cannot also be treated as part of another. However, being married to someone does not necessarily mean that you cannot be treated as part of a couple with someone else instead.[20]

Even if you *do* share a 'household', you may not be cohabiting. It is essential to look at *why* two people are in the same household.[21] For example, where a couple were living in the same household for reasons of 'care, companionship and mutual convenience' (one of them was disabled) they were not 'living together as husband and wife'.[22]

Separated or estranged couples living under the same roof should not be treated as couples if they are maintaining separate households.[23]

Is your relationship stable?

Marriage is expected to be stable and lasting. It follows that an occasional or brief association should not be regarded as 'living together as husband and wife'. However, the fact that a relationship is stable does not make it a 'husband/wife' relationship. You can have a stable landlord/lodger relationship but not be 'living together as husband and wife'.

What are your financial arrangements?

If one partner is supported by the other or household expenses are shared, this may be treated as evidence of a husband and wife relationship. However, it is important to consider how they are shared. There is a difference between, on the one hand, payment of a fixed weekly contribution or the rigid sharing of bills 50/50 and, on the other hand, a free common fund attributable to income and expenditure. The former does not imply 'living together as husband and wife', the latter might.

Do you have a sexual relationship?

Officers may not ask you about the existence of a sexual relationship, so they will only have the information if you volunteer it.[24] If you do not have a sexual relationship, you should tell the officer yourself – and perhaps offer to show her/him the separate sleeping arrangements.

A sexual relationship is a normal part of a marriage and therefore of living together as husband and wife. But just having a sexual relationship is not sufficient by itself to prove you are 'living together as husband and wife'.

A couple who abstain from a sexual relationship before marriage on grounds of principle (eg, religious reasons) should not be counted as living together as husband and wife until they are formally married.[25]

Do you have children?

If you have had a child together, there is a strong (but not conclusive) presumption of cohabitation.

How do you appear in public?

Officers may check the electoral roll and claims for national insurance benefits to see if you present yourselves as husband and wife. If the woman has adopted the man's name, this will be considered strong evidence of cohabitation. On the other hand, many couples retain their identity publicly as unmarried people. This does not mean they cannot be regarded as living together as husband and wife.

Challenging a 'living together' decision

Sometimes benefit is stopped or adjusted because a boyfriend/girlfriend regularly stays overnight, even though you might have none of the long-term commitments generally associated with marriage. But couples with no sexual relationship who live together (eg, as landlord/lodger, tenant or housekeeper, or as flat-sharers) also sometimes fall foul of the rule. People who provide mutual support and share household expenses are not necessarily living together as husband and wife, as this also happens where people of the same sex or friends of different sexes share a home.[26]

If you are at all unhappy with a decision that you are cohabiting, you should always appeal (see p170) or apply for a review (see pp149 and 286) and carefully consider what evidence to put before the tribunal/review board in relation to each of the six questions above and any other matters that you consider relevant. Possibilities include evidence of the other person having another address (eg, a rent book and other household bills), receipts for board and lodging, statements from friends and relatives or, where you have been married, evidence of a formal separation or divorce proceedings.

If the tribunal or review board does not wish to go into the question of whether or not there is a sexual relationship, you should argue that sex is an important part of marriage and that it is not possible to consider 'living together as husband and wife' properly in isolation from it. The burden of proof is on the Benefits Agency/local authority to prove that you are 'living together as husband and wife', because disqualification from benefit is involved.

If your benefit is withdrawn because you are living with someone as husband and wife, you should re-apply immediately if your circumstances change. You should also apply immediately for any other benefits for which you might qualify – eg, HB/CTB, where the local authority may reach a different decision to that of the Benefits Agency (see p330). You should apply on the basis of low income for other benefits for which you previously qualified automatically if you were on IS – eg, health benefits (see Chapter 25).

If you are still entitled to benefit you should be paid as a couple.

If your IS stops and you have diverted a maintenance order to the Benefits Agency (see p123), contact the magistrates' court immediately to get payments sent direct to you. Or, if the Child Support Agency is collecting a child maintenance assessment for you (see p135), ask them to start paying the money to you.

If you have no money at all, you may possibly be able to get a social fund payment (see Part Nine).

Couples living apart

If you separate *permanently* you can claim as single people immediately, but you continue to be treated as a couple while you and your partner are *temporarily* apart.[27] There is generally no specified period of time during which an absence counts as temporary, and each case is decided according to its particular circumstances. However, if any of the specific circumstances below apply, you will always be deemed no longer to count as a couple.

For FC/DWA

You no longer count as a couple if:[28]

- you and your partner are living apart and do not intend to resume living together; *or*
- you or your partner have been in hospital for 52 weeks or more; *or*
- you or your partner are a compulsory patient detained in hospital under the mental health provisions; *or*
- you or your partner are detained in custody serving a sentence of 52 weeks or more.

For CTB

You continue to be eligible as a couple as long as you both remain liable for the council tax at your address.[29] Note that the rules for establishing a couple's liability for council tax are not the same as the rules for establishing their entitlement to CTB (see CPAG's *Council Tax Handbook*).

For IS/HB

You no longer count as a couple if you or your partner are living away from your family *and*:[30]

- do not intend to resume living together; *or*
- are likely to be away for more than 52 weeks (or longer if there are exceptional circumstances such as a stay in hospital or if there is no control over the length of the absence, provided it is not 'substantially' more than 52 weeks. Guidance suggests that periods of absence of up to 15 months may be accepted in these circumstances[31]).

For IS

You will also no longer count as a couple if any of the following apply to either of you:[32]

- You are in custody.
- You are a compulsory patient detained in hospital under the mental health provisions.
- You are staying permanently in local authority residential accommodation, or a residential care or nursing home.
- The *claimant* is abroad and does not qualify for IS (see p25). However, where your *partner* is temporarily abroad you continue to be treated as a couple, but after four weeks (eight if s/he has taken a child abroad for medical treatment – see pp25-6) the amount of IS you receive is that for a single claimant or single parent.[33] You can get benefit without signing on if you have children under 16.[34] Your partner's income and capital continue to be treated as yours for as long as the absence is held to be temporary.

If you are no longer treated as a couple for the purposes of calculating your IS, you may still be liable to maintain your partner (see p124).

However, **you are still treated as a couple, and you can get more IS than usual,** if you are temporarily living apart and the following applies: one of you is at home or in hospital, or in local authority residential accommodation or in a residential care or nursing home, and the other is:[35]

- resident in a nursing home, but not counted as a patient; *or*
- staying in a residential care home; *or*
- in a home for the rehabilitation of alcoholics or drug addicts; *or*
- in Polish resettlement accommodation; *or*
- on a government training course and has to live away from home (see below for your right to housing costs for more than one home); *or*
- in a probation or bail hostel.

Although your income and capital are calculated in the normal way for a couple, your applicable amount is calculated as if each of you were single claimants, if this comes to more than your usual couple rate. If you have children, one of you is treated as a single parent. If you have housing costs, your applicable amount includes these as well as any costs of the temporary accommodation of the partner away from home. If you are both away from home, the costs of both sets of temporary accommodation and the family home are met.[36] If both homes are rented, see pp217-21 for when HB can be paid for more than one home at a time. If you own your home and your partner is staying in rented accommodation, board and lodging or a hostel you will get your housing costs met by IS and your partner will be able to claim HB.

Additional points

- See pp31 and 218-19 if one of you lives away from home as a student or on a government training course and you have to pay for two homes.
- See p444 if your child is in hospital and you have to stay in lodgings to be nearby.
- See p99 if one or both of you are temporarily in local authority residential accommodation.

3. CLAIMING FOR CHILDREN

You do not have to be a *parent* to receive benefit for a child, but you must be **'responsible'** for a child who is **living in your household**.[37] You claim for any child under 16; or under 19 if they are still in full-time 'relevant' education (up to and including A-level or its equivalent).[38] Full-time means more than 12 hours a week (see p17). See p337-8 for when a child no longer counts as your dependant.

'Responsibility' for a child

You claim IS, FC, DWA, HB or CTB for a child for whom you are 'responsible'. You will be treated as 'responsible' for a child if:

For FC/DWA/HB/CTB

- the child is 'normally living' with you.[39]

    It will usually be obvious whether the child is 'normally living' with you. However, where it is unclear whose household the child lives in (eg, because s/he spends an equal amount of time with two parents in different homes), you will be treated as having responsibility if:[40]
    – you get child benefit for the child;

- no one gets child benefit, but you have applied for it;
- no one has applied for child benefit, or both of you have applied, but you appear to have the most responsibility;

For IS

- you get child benefit for the child.[41]

  Where no one gets child benefit you will be 'responsible' if you are the only one who has applied for it. In all other cases the person 'responsible' will be the person with whom the child *usually lives*.[42]

  Where a child for whom you are 'responsible' gets child benefit for another child, you will also be 'responsible' for that child.[43]

Note: For FC/DWA/HB/CTB, it is only important to look at who gets child benefit where it is unclear whose household the child *normally* lives in. Yet for IS it is essential to look first at who gets child benefit, and only where this is not decisive is it relevant to look at where the child *usually* lives. So if you are claiming IS, you cannot be treated as responsible for a child for as long as someone else is getting child benefit for her/him even if the child spends all her/his time with you. If this means that you are no longer entitled to IS you may, however, be able to claim FC/DWA/HB/CTB for that child.

Curiously, the difference in the rules may mean that there are some situations where one parent may be able to claim IS for a child, and the other parent may be able to claim FC/DWA/HB/CTB for the same child at the same time.

However, where the same benefit is involved, a child can only be the responsibility of one person in any week.[44] There is no provision allowing benefit to be split between parents where a child divides her/his time equally between the homes of two parents (but see below for when a part award of IS may be paid where a child spends part of the week in local authority care or detained in custody). These rules can create problems if both parents sharing the care of a child are on benefit, but the parent who gets the extra benefit is unwilling to share it with the other.

Living in the same household[45]

If you are counted as responsible for a child, then that child is usually treated as a **member of your household** despite any temporary absence. (For the meaning of 'household', see p329.) However, s/he does not count as a member of your household if s/he:

IS/FC/DWA/HB/CTB

- is being fostered by you under a statutory provision. You can claim benefit for a child you are fostering privately;

- is living with you prior to adoption, and has been placed with you by social services or an adoption agency;

IS/HB/CTB

- is boarded out or has been placed with someone else prior to adoption;
- is in the care of, or being looked after by, the local authority and not living with you. You should receive IS for her/him for the days when s/he comes home – eg, for the weekend or a holiday.[46] Make sure you tell the Benefits Agency in good time so they can pay you the extra money. The local authority can also increase your applicable amount to include the child for HB/CTB for all of that week whether the child returns for all or only part of it;[47]

IS/FC/DWA

- has been in hospital or a local authority home for more than 12 weeks, and you or other members of your household have not been in regular contact with them (for FC/DWA this means 12 weeks prior to the claim; for IS the 12 weeks run from the date they went into the hospital or home or from the date you claimed IS, if later).

  Note: If a child has been in hospital or a local authority home for 52 weeks or more because of illness or disability, your FC/DWA will not include a credit/allowance for her/him even if you are still in regular contact;[48]
- is in custody. (For FC/DWA, being in custody on remand does not count.) You should receive IS for any periods your child spends at home;[49]

IS only[50]

- has been abroad for more than four weeks (the four weeks run from the day after they went abroad, or from the date you claimed IS, if later), or for more than eight weeks if the absence abroad is to get medical treatment for the child;
- is living with you and away from their parental or usual home in order to attend school. The child is not treated as a member of your family, but remains a member of her/his parent's household.

When you stop claiming for a child

For IS

You stop claiming for a child as soon as someone else starts receiving child benefit for her/him. You also stop claiming in the circumstances below.

For FC/DWA/HB/CTB

You stop claiming as soon as the child starts 'normally living' elsewhere (see pp335-6). You also stop claiming in the circumstances below.

For IS/HB/CTB

You claim for a child until s/he is 16, or 19 if s/he is in relevant education (see p17). Children count as in relevant education until the 'terminal date' (see p18), so you can claim for them until then, or until they get a full-time job if that is earlier. 'Full-time' work for dependent children means at least 24 hours a week. [51]

A 16/17-year-old who has left school or college may continue to be counted as part of your 'family' for a few months after the terminal date. You will get benefit for them during the **child benefit extension period** (see p68 for details and dates) provided the following apply:[52]

- you were entitled to child benefit for that child immediately before the child benefit extension period started; *and*
- you have made a fresh claim for child benefit in writing for the child benefit extension period; *and*
- they have registered for work/Youth Training (YT) at the JobCentre or Careers Office; *and*
- they are not in full-time work.

As soon as the child gets a full-time job or a YT place or becomes 18 s/he ceases to be your dependant. If s/he loses the job or leaves YT before the end of the child benefit extension period, s/he becomes your dependant again and you can claim for her/him as long as the above conditions are satisfied and you claim again in writing.

Some 16/17-year-olds can get IS in their own right before they are 18 (see pp67-8) and you will not be able to claim for them.[53]

You cannot claim for any child in advanced education (above A-level) even if they are under 19.[54]

For FC/DWA

A child only counts as your dependant for the purposes of your FC/DWA claim where, at the date of the claim, s/he is actually undergoing full-time non-advanced education.[55] Children do not count as dependants once they have actually left school even if you are still getting child benefit for them up to the terminal date, or in the child benefit extension period. This could be important if a claim for FC/DWA is not made before a young person actually leaves school but is submitted shortly afterwards during the following school holidays. They are also not counted as dependants if they become entitled to IS in their own right, or if they are in advanced education.[56]

CHAPTER SEVENTEEN

Applicable amounts

This chapter covers:

1. INTRODUCTION

For IS, HB and CTB, the 'applicable amount' is a figure representing your weekly needs for the purpose of calculating your benefit. For IS, your applicable amount is the amount you are expected to live on each week. For HB/CTB, it is the amount used to see how much help you need with your rent or council tax. This chapter explains how you work out your applicable amount for those benefits. For the way the amount of benefit is then calculated, see p27 for IS, p239 for HB and p309 for CTB.

The applicable amount for FC is always £71.70, and for DWA is £43 for single people and £71.70 for couples. The applicable amount for FC/DWA does not vary according to your personal circumstances. For the way FC/DWA are calculated, see pp189 and 203 respectively.

For IS, HB and CTB, your applicable amount is made up of:

- **personal allowances:** this is the amount the law says you need for living expenses (see p340);
- **premiums:** this is the amount given for certain extra needs you or your family may have (see p342);
- for IS only, **housing costs:** not all housing costs are met by IS and the applicable amount for these is covered on p29.

For IS, your applicable amount is different if you went to live in a residential care or nursing home before April 1993 (see p104) or if you are in local authority residential accommodation (see p98). If you have gone into a residential care or nursing home since 31 March 1993, it includes a residential allowance to cover your accommodation charges (see pp110-12). Your applicable amount is reduced if you are:

- voluntarily unemployed (see p58) or getting IS on hardship grounds (see p24);
- receiving an urgent cases payment (see p44);
- in hospital (see p113);
- involved in a trade dispute (see p77);
- a 16/17-year-old, in certain circumstances (see p67);
- a couple, one of whom is a person from abroad (see p81);
- without accommodation (see p119);
- a prisoner (see p117).

In addition, there are a number of other reasons why your benefit may otherwise be reduced, such as:

- you are subject to a benefit penalty for refusing to co-operate with the Child Support Agency (see p128);
- you are repaying an overpayment of benefit (see p166);
- you are repaying an SF loan (see p456);
- the Benefits Agency is making direct payments on your behalf in respect of housing costs, water charges, fuel debts, council tax and community charge arrears, fines or child support maintenance (see pp155-61).

Some IS/HB claimants get an amount of transitional protection on top of their ordinary IS/HB (see pp43 and 248).

2. PERSONAL ALLOWANCES

For IS, your personal allowance is an amount which is supposed to be sufficient – even if your applicable amount is reduced or deductions are being made from your benefit (see above) – to cover all your weekly needs such as food, heating, clothing, ineligible housing costs and water charges. You are also expected to be able to pay for any fines, maintenance charges and other debts, and save for one-off expenses such as a cooker or bedding (although you may be eligible for a social fund payment – see p424).

The amount of your personal allowance for IS, HB and CTB depends on your age and whether you are claiming as a single person or a couple. You also get an allowance for each dependent child. Note that you cannot get a personal allowance for a child who has more than £3,000 capital (see p394).

If you are polygamously married you usually receive an extra amount for each additional partner in your household.[1] For IS, where any additional partner is under the age of 18, you will only receive an extra amount if they are responsible for a child (see p335) or would otherwise meet the special conditions for qualifying for IS as a 16/17-year-old[2] (see p67). For the treatment of additional partners in polygamous marriages for FC and DWA, see pp190 and 203.

See Chapter 16 for who is included in your claim.

Rates of personal allowances[3]

Rates for children are the same for IS and HB/CTB. The rates are also the same for people over 18. However, your IS personal allowance is normally paid at a special rate if you, or your partner (if any), are under 18 (see pp74-76). No CTB is payable for a couple where both are under 18 because they are not liable to pay the tax (see p301). Where one partner is 18 or over then they get the couple rate for over-18s. Otherwise the personal allowances are the same for IS/HB/CTB.

Single claimant:
Aged under 18 (some IS cases (see p74) and all HB cases)		£36.15
Aged under 18 (other IS cases only (see p74))		£27.50
Other claimants aged under 25		£36.15
Aged 25 or over		£45.70

Single parents:
Aged under 18 (some IS cases (see p74) and all HB cases)		£36.15
Aged under 18 (other IS cases only (see p74))		£27.50
Aged 18 or over		£45.70

Couple:
Both aged under 18 (some IS cases (see p75) and all HB cases)		£54.55
Both aged under 18 (other IS cases only (see p75))	*either*	£36.15
	or	£27.50
One aged under 18 (some IS cases (see p75) and all HB and CTB cases)		£71.70
One aged under 18 (other IS cases only (see p75))	*either*	£45.70
	or	£36.15
Both aged 18 or over		£71.70

Polygamous marriages:
Each additional qualifying partner living in the same household[4]	£26.00

Children:
Under 11	£15.65
11-15	£23.00
16-17	£27.50
18	£36.15

3. PREMIUMS

Introduction

Premiums are added to your basic personal allowances and are intended to help with extra expenses caused by age, disability or the cost of children.

The eight premiums and their rates are:

Family premium	£10.05	
Severe disability premium		
Single	£34.30	
Couple	£68.60	These can be paid on top
Disabled child premium	£19.45	of any other premiums
(for each qualifying child)		(including disability or
Carer's premium		higher pensioner).
single, or one partner		
qualifying	£12.40	
both partners qualifying	£24.80	
Lone parent premium		
IS	£ 5.10	
HB/CTB	£11.25	
Disability premium		
Single	£19.45	
Couple	£27.80	Only one of these can
Pensioner premium		be paid: if you qualify
(i) if aged 60-74		for more than one you
Single	£18.25	get whichever is the
Couple	£27.55	highest.[5]
(ii) if aged 75-79		
Single	£20.35	
Couple	£30.40	
Higher pensioner premium		
Single	£24.70	
Couple	£35.30	

If you live in a **residential care or nursing home** and you are not entitled to IS but you claim HB (now only allowed in special cases – see p230), you are entitled to premiums. If you are on IS, see pp98, 104 and 110.

If you go into **hospital** your premiums may be affected (see pp113 and 247).

Entitlement to some premiums depends on receipt of other benefits.

Once you have qualified for a premium, if you or your partner are not getting one of these benefits (eg, invalidity benefit or severe disablement allowance) because of the overlapping benefit rules, or because you or your partner are on an employment training course or getting a training allowance, you will continue to receive the relevant premium for that time.[6]

Family premium[7]

You are entitled to this if your family includes a child (see p335), even if you do not receive a personal allowance for any child because they have capital over £3,000. However, only one family premium is payable regardless of the number of children you have. Where a child who is in the care of or being looked after by a local authority or who is in custody comes home for part of a week, your IS includes a proportion of the premium, according to the number of days the child is with you;[8] for HB and CTB you may be paid the full premium if your child who is in care or being looked after by a local authority is part of the household for any part of the week: how often and for how long the child visits will be taken into account in deciding whether they are or not.[9]

Disabled child premium[10]

You are entitled to a disabled child premium for each of your children who gets disability living allowance or who is blind.

A child is treated as blind if s/he is registered as blind and for the first 28 weeks after s/he has been taken off the register on regaining her/his sight.[11] If disability living allowance has been stopped only because the child is a patient in hospital, you will still get the disabled child premium for as long as s/he is treated as part of your family (see pp335-7). Note, however, that for IS the personal allowance you receive for the child will be reduced after 12 weeks in hospital (see p115). Where your child is in local authority care or in custody for part of the week, this premium will be affected in the same way as the family premium (see above). For how to qualify for disability living allowance, see CPAG's *Rights Guide to Non-Means-Tested Benefits*.

If the child has over £3,000 capital, you do not get this premium.[12]

Carer's premium[13]

You qualify for this if you or your partner are getting invalid care allowance, or would get it but for the overlapping benefit rules (ie, because you are receiving another benefit paid at the same or a higher rate). For example, a woman getting invalid care allowance who at 60 is awarded retirement pension at a higher rate than invalid care allowance, continues to qualify for the premium. To take advantage of the overlapping rule you must have claimed (or re-claimed) invalid care allowance on or after 1 October 1990, and the person you are caring for must continue to get the higher or middle rate care component of disability living allowance, or attendance allowance.

Under British legislation, you are not entitled to invalid care allowance after reaching 'pensionable age' (60 for women and 65 for men) unless you were entitled to it immediately before you reached that age (or you would have been but for the overlapping benefit rules).[14] If you continue to be entitled to invalid care allowance by the time you reach 'retiring age' (65 or 70), you will be entitled to invalid care allowance for life, even if you stop providing care and start full-time work.[15] Following a decision in the European Court,[16] 'pensionable age' could mean either 60 or 65, whichever is most favourable to you; and it is arguable that 'retiring age' means 65 for both men and women.

The upshot of all this is that you may be entitled to invalid care allowance after 60 (even if British legislation says you are not) and therefore entitled to a carer's premium.

If your invalid care allowance is overlapped, you can qualify for a carer's premium and this will not prevent the person you are caring for from being entitled to a severe disability premium (see p355).

If you stop getting, or being treated as getting, invalid care allowance, your entitlement to a carer's premium continues for a further eight weeks, even if you first claim IS/HB/CTB in this time.

An extra-statutory payment to compensate for non-payment of invalid care allowance also qualifies you for this premium.[17]

A double premium is awarded where both you and your partner satisfy the conditions for it.

Lone parent premium[18]

You are entitled to this if you are a single parent. You can continue to get it for as long as a child is treated as your dependant, which in some cases can be until s/he reaches 19 (see p338). You do not have to be the *parent* of the child, but you must be *responsible* for the child and s/he must be a member of your household (see p335).

A lone parent premium is paid even if you do not get a personal allowance for any child because s/he has capital over £3,000. Only one lone parent premium is payable regardless of the number of children you have. As with the family premium (see p343) and increases for dependent children (see p335), where your child is in local authority care or detained in custody, the lone parent premium may (for IS) be apportioned according to the number of days the child is with you; for HB/ CTB it will be paid in full or not at all, depending on the circumstances.[19]

Disability premium[20]

You can get a disability premium if you are under 60 and one of the following applies to you[21] (after you are 60 you may get the higher pensioner premium):

* You are getting a **qualifying benefit**. For the disability premium, these are **attendance allowance** (or an equivalent benefit paid to meet attendance needs because of an injury at work or a war injury[22]), **disability living allowance, disability working allowance, mobility supplement, invalidity benefit** or **severe disablement allowance**. Extra-statutory payments to compensate you for not getting one of these benefits also count.[23] You, or your partner, must be getting the benefit for yourself, not on behalf of someone else (eg, as an appointee).[24] See CPAG's *Rights Guide to Non-Means-Tested Benefits* for who can claim these benefits.

  If your attendance allowance or disability living allowance has stopped because you have been in hospital for more than four weeks (see CPAG's *Rights Guide to Non-Means-Tested Benefits*) you may well not lose your disability premium immediately, but you lose it after six weeks[25] (for the effect on your benefits on going into hospital, see p113 (IS) and pp247 and 324 (HB/CTB)).
* You are *registered as blind* with a local authority (England and Wales) or regional or Islands council (Scotland); if you regain your sight you still qualify for 28 weeks after you are taken off the register.[26]
* You have an **NHS invalid trike or private car allowance** because of disability.[27]
* You have been **incapable of work for at least 28 weeks**. To qualify under this rule you must have been getting statutory sick pay, or have claimed sickness benefit, severe disablement allowance or invalidity benefit and sent in medical certificates.[28] Note that, except for statutory sick pay, you do not have to be getting one of these benefits, as long as you have put in a claim for one of them and it is accepted that you are incapable of work (see below). It does not matter that you cannot be paid any of these benefits because you fail to satisfy other conditions for them (eg, you do not have good cause for a late claim or you do not satisfy the contribution conditions). In all cases you lose the disability premium as soon as you stop sending in medical certificates. But if you fall ill again within eight weeks you can get the disability premium again without having to wait 28 weeks.[29]

'**Incapable of work**' means incapable of any work which it is reasonable to expect you to do bearing in mind your age, health, education, experience and any other personal factors.[30] In practice, for the first six months of illness an adjudication officer is likely to take account only of your capacity to do your normal work. After that your capacity to do any type of work will be considered. You need to explain your disabilities – eg, that you cannot sit or stand for long periods or you get frequent serious headaches etc. 'Work' in this context means paid work (full- or part-time) for which an employer would be willing to pay a normal wage. See CPAG's *Rights Guide to Non-Means-Tested Benefits* for more details about 'incapacity for work'.

Couples will get the disability premium at the couple rate (£27.80) provided either one of you qualifies under the above rules. But if you qualify only because one of you has been incapable of work for 28 weeks, you will only get the premium if the person who qualifies is the claimant for the couple.[31] S/he does not have to have been the claimant during the 28-week qualifying period. You may, therefore, need to swap the claimant role (see pp143 and 257).

If you go on a Training for Work or Youth Training course, or for any period you receive a training allowance, you will keep the disability premium even though you may cease to receive one of the 'qualifying benefits', or cease to be incapable of work during the course, as long as you continue to be entitled to IS, HB or CTB. After the course, the premium continues if you are still incapable of work, or getting a qualifying benefit.[32]

Backdating

- Your 'qualifying benefit' (see p345) is not usually awarded until some time after you claim it, but it is then backdated to the date of your claim, or sometimes even earlier. If you are already getting IS/HB/CTB you should ask for your claim to be reviewed and for your disability premium to be backdated either to the same day, or to when you first got IS, HB or CTB if that is later.

    Note: For HB/CTB your disability premium can never be backdated for more than a year (see pp287 and 323). It may be possible for your IS disability premium to be backdated for more than a year in exceptional circumstances (see p150) – eg, if the Benefits Agency knew you were incapable of work but omitted to act on this knowledge.

Example
You apply for disability living allowance in May 1994. Disability living allowance is awarded in November 1994 backdated to May 1994. You request a review of your IS, HB and CTB to include a disability premium in December 1994. You have been getting IS from July 1994 and were getting HB and CTB throughout this period. The increase in your IS will be backdated to July 1994. You will anyway have received maximum HB and CTB between July and December because you were on IS during that period. However, your HB and CTB will be increased for the period May to July to take account of your entitlement to the premium.

- If as a result of getting a 'qualifying benefit' backdated you now qualify for IS, HB or CTB because your needs are greater with the disability premium included in your applicable amount, you should make a new claim and ask for it to be backdated for up to a year (see pp145, 260 and 318). In the above example you may be able to apply for a review (see p149) of your IS to backdate it to May 1994.
- If you have been incapable of work for 28 weeks or more, but not sending in medical certificates, you should immediately claim the premium and also ask for it to be backdated to when you could first have qualified for it. You will have to ask your doctor for backdated medical certificates (form MED5) and claim an incapacity benefit for that period (even if you know you will not qualify for it). Backdated certificates are acceptable provided there has been the opportunity for a decision to be made on the question of incapacity for work.[33] The test for getting the premium is that you have been incapable of work for 28 weeks, so if your claim for the incapacity benefit is refused because it is a late claim, this does not matter, as long as your medical certificate for the backdated period is accepted. Even if you have been incapable of work for less than 28 weeks you should not delay sending in medical certificates (and backdated certificates) and claiming an incapacity benefit so that you can qualify for the premium when you reach the 28-week point.
- If you are one of a couple where the person who is incapable of work is not the claimant, you can swap the claimant role and s/he can backdate a new claim if s/he has 'good cause' for her/his late claim (eg, ill-health, reasonable ignorance of the rules – see p145 (IS), pp260 and 318 (HB/CTB)). In this way you can get the disability premium backdated for up to 12 months.[34]

Similar considerations will apply to backdating the higher pensioner premium (see p348) and the severe disability premium (see p351).

Pensioner premium[35]

The pensioner premium is paid at two rates according to age:

- The lower rate is paid if you are aged 60-74 inclusive.
- The enhanced rate is paid if you are 75-79 inclusive. (This is not to be confused with the higher pensioner premium paid to certain disabled pensioners and those aged 80 or over.)

The couple rate for either is paid even if only one partner fulfils the condition. If you or your partner are **sick or disabled** check to see if you could get the higher pensioner premium instead (see below).

Higher pensioner premium

You can get this if one of the following applies:[36]

- You or your partner are 80 or over.
- You were getting a disability premium as part of your IS, HB or CTB before you were 60 and you have continued to claim that benefit. You must have been getting a disability premium at some time during the eight weeks before you were 60, and have received that benefit continuously since you reached 60.[37] (But you can have a period off that benefit of up to eight weeks and still qualify. For HB/CTB if you were entitled to a higher pensioner premium for one benefit in the previous eight weeks you will get a higher pensioner premium with the other if you then qualify or requalify for that benefit.)[38] In the case of couples, the person who was the claimant for that benefit before s/he was 60 must continue to claim after that, but it is not necessary for the claimant to have been the person who qualified for the disability premium.[39]
- You or your partner are aged 60-79 *and* either of you receive a qualifying benefit (as for the disability premium – see p345), are registered blind, or have an NHS trike or a private car allowance (see p345).

Receipt of a qualifying benefit

If you get **attendance allowance** or **disability living allowance** and you have been in hospital for more than four weeks, as with the disability premium (see p345) you will not usually lose your higher pensioner premium immediately (but see pp113-17 (IS) and pp247-8 (HB/CTB) for the effect on your benefits of going into hospital for six weeks or more).

If you get **severe disablement allowance** and go on claiming it until you reach 65 (woman) or 70 (man) (although arguably, under European Law, both men and women should be able to claim until the age of 70 – see Discrimination, p350), you will then be entitled to it for life and therefore continue to qualify for the higher pensioner premium.[40] Alternatively, if it ceases to be paid only because you get retirement pension at a higher rate, you also continue to qualify.[41] You do not have to claim a retirement pension when you reach 60 (woman), 65 (man). As severe disablement allowance entitles you to a higher pensioner premium, it is probably sensible to continue getting it (although it is possible that the adjudication officer may apply the notional income rules (see p391) if your retirement pension would have been worth more.

If you, or your partner, stop getting **invalidity benefit** because you change to retirement pension, you can still get a higher pensioner premium with your IS, HB or CTB, if you remain continuously entitled (apart from breaks of eight weeks or less) to the same benefit.[42] In the case of HB/CTB, if you were entitled to a higher pensioner premium for one of these benefits in the previous eight weeks, you will get a higher pensioner premium with the other if you then qualify or requalify for that benefit.[43] If it is your partner who has changed to a retirement pension, s/he must still be alive (IS), or still be a member of your family (HB/CTB).[44] In the case of IS, the higher pensioner premium or a disability premium must also have been 'applicable' to you or your partner.[45] So, if, up to the time your invalidity benefit ceased, your applicable amount was calculated by a method that did not include premiums (eg, because you were in a hostel prior to 9 October 1989, or you lived in a residential care or nursing home before 31 March 1993), you will not be able to qualify for an IS higher pensioner premium in this way.[46]

De-retiring

If you are incapable of work, it is possible if you have not reached the maximum age for invalidity benefit (65 (woman) and 70 (man))[47] for you to de-retire (ie, start claiming sickness benefit instead of retirement pension). After six months on sickness benefit you will receive invalidity benefit and requalify for the higher pensioner premium. The problem with this may be that unless your claim can be linked with a previous one[48] (ie, be part of the same 'period of interruption of employment' – see CPAG's *Rights Guide to Non-Means-Tested Benefits*), you will have to spend 28 weeks on sickness benefit which is payable at a lower rate than retirement pension or invalidity benefit. This may result in the notional income rules (see p391) being applied on the ground that you have chosen to claim sickness benefit payable at a lower rate. If so, the adjudication officer will treat you as having an additional amount of income equal to the difference between your sickness benefit and your retirement pension for 28 weeks.[49] You should, therefore, calculate whether you gain more in the long term by getting a higher pensioner premium to balance this loss of income for 28 weeks.

You will only be able to qualify for the higher pensioner premium in this way if you are more than six months under 65 (woman) or 70 (man). This is because these are the maximum ages for de-retiring and for entitlement to invalidity benefit.

If you decide to de-retire, you should not delay doing so as it is not usually possible to backdate an election to de-retire.[50]

Discrimination

The conditions of entitlement to the higher pensioner premium discriminate against women. This is a consequence of the different upper age limits applying to claims for invalidity benefit and first claims for severe disablement allowance, two of the qualifying benefits for the premium.

A number of challenges have been brought to the European Court of Justice (ECJ) alleging that UK legislation is in breach of the EC Directive on equal treatment for men and women in social security.[51]

The ECJ has said that neither HB[52] nor IS[53] is covered by the Directive. It is therefore not possible to argue that the premium itself is unlawful, even though it is discriminatory. However, it is possible to challenge the rules for the benefits which can qualify you for the premium so as to remove its discriminatory effect.

In 1993, the ECJ decided that the rules for a first claim for **severe disablement allowance** (and invalid care allowance), which discriminate against women between the ages of 60 and 65, were unlawful.[54] As a result, the government will have to bring in new regulations. However, in the meantime, if you are a woman aged between 60 and 65 you can rely on the European ruling and make a first claim for severe disablement allowance and in this way qualify for a higher pensioner premium.

As far as **invalidity benefit** is concerned, the Court of Appeal has very recently asked the ECJ whether the different age rules between men and women (as with severe disablement allowance and invalid care allowance resulting from the different pensionable ages) are lawful. The reference to the ECJ has been made in the course of appeals brought by the government against decisions by commissioners that the differential treatment is unlawful.[55] Invalidity benefit, unlike severe disablement allowance and invalid care allowance, is a contributory benefit, but if the ECJ decides that discrimination is not justifiable for the purposes of the contributory scheme, the government will have to amend these regulations as well.

If you are a woman and have been unable to qualify for the higher pensioner premium because the discriminatory age limits prevent you from claiming sickness or invalidity benefit or from de-retiring, you should immediately ask to de-retire and/or claim the appropriate benefit and ask for the higher pensioner premium to be included in your IS/HB/CTB.

Severe disability premium[56]

[handwritten: Couple Rate both get Qualifying benefit.]

You can get the severe disability premium if all of the following apply to you:

- **You receive a qualifying benefit.** For the severe disability premium this is either **attendance allowance** (or the equivalent war pension or industrial injury benefit), or the **middle or higher rate care component of disability living allowance** (or extra-statutory payments to compensate you for not receiving any of these[57]). If you are a couple (or polygamously married), whichever one of you is claiming IS/HB/CTB must be getting a qualifying benefit and your partner(s) must also either be getting a qualifying benefit or else s/he must be registered blind (or treated as blind).[58] The qualifying benefit must be paid in respect of yourself/selves, as receipt of benefit for someone else (eg, a child) does not count.[59]

- **No non-dependant aged 18 or over is living ('residing') with you** (see below). For IS/HB, someone is only counted as living with you if you share accommodation apart from a bathroom, lavatory or a communal area such as a hall, passageway or a room in common use in sheltered accommodation. If s/he is separately liable to make payments for the accommodation to the landlord, however, s/he will not count as living with you even if you do share, for example, a kitchen or even a bedroom.[60] For CTB, 'residing with' is not defined but presumably a similar test will apply.

- **No one gets invalid care allowance for looking after you,** or, if you are a couple (or polygamously married), no one gets invalid care allowance for both (or all) of you.

Couples will get the couple rate if both (or, in a polygamous marriage, all) of you are getting a qualifying benefit and no one gets invalid care allowance for either of you. However, if your partner does not get a qualifying benefit but is registered blind (or treated as blind), or if invalid care allowance is paid for one of you, you will only get the single rate.

Non-dependants[61]

The following people who live with you will *not* be counted as non-dependants when assessing your eligibility for the severe disability premium:

For IS/HB/CTB

- Anyone aged under 18 (including therefore any children, whether or not they are treated as part of your household).
- Your partner (but remember, s/he must be getting a qualifying benefit

or registered or treated as blind – see p351).
- Anyone else who receives attendance allowance or the higher or middle rate care component of disability living allowance.[62]
- Anyone who is registered blind (or treated as blind).[63]
- Anyone staying in your home who normally lives elsewhere (only people who normally live with you may count as non-dependants).
- Any person (and, for IS only, their partner) employed by a charitable or voluntary body as a resident carer for you or your partner if you pay a charge for that service (even if the charge is only nominal).

For IS only
- Any person (or their partner) who jointly occupies your home and is either the co-owner with you or your partner, or jointly liable with you or your partner to make payments to a landlord in respect of occupying it. If this person is a close relative, however, s/he *will* count as a non-dependant *unless* the co-ownership or joint liability to make payments to a landlord existed either before 11 April 1988 or by the time you or your partner first moved in (but see **transitional provisions** below).
- Any person (or any member of their household) who is liable to pay you or your partner on a commercial basis in respect of occupying the dwelling (eg, tenants or licensees), unless they are close relatives of you or your partner (but see **transitional provisions** below).
- Any person (or any member of their household) to whom you or your partner are liable to make such payments on a commercial basis, unless they are a close relative of you or your partner (but see **transitional provisions** below).
- **Transitional provisions.** In the three situations above, the presence of close relatives will *not* prevent you from continuing to get the severe disability premium if you fall within the scope of the transitional provisions which applied to claimants entitled to this premium before 21 October 1991. These were set out in the 22nd edition of the *National Welfare Benefits Handbook* (1992/3).
- If someone (other than those listed above) comes to live with you in order to look after you, or your partner, your severe disability premium will remain in payment for the first 12 weeks.[64] After that, you will lose the premium (or get a lower rate premium), although invalid care allowance may well be payable to the carer by then.
- In the case of a couple, a person will be treated as receiving attendance allowance (or the higher or middle rate care component of disability living allowance) – even though it has stopped because s/he has been in hospital for more than four weeks. Similarly, a person will be treated as receiving invalid care allowance – even if the attendance allowance (or disability living allowance) of the person for whom s/he is caring

has stopped because that person has been in hospital for more than four weeks.[65]

For HB only[66]

- Any person who jointly occupies your home and is either the co-owner with you or your partner, or liable with you or your partner to make payments in respect of occupying it. The Court of Appeal has recently said[67] that 'jointly occupies' has a technical legal meaning, and does not refer to the situation where people have equality of access to different parts of the premises. That is how the phrase has been interpreted in an IS case.[68] However, the Court of Appeal decision strictly speaking only applies to HB. A joint occupier who was a non-dependant at any time within the previous eight weeks will count as a non-dependant if the local authority thinks that the change of arrangements was created to take advantage of the HB scheme.
- Any person who is liable to pay you or your partner on a commercial basis in respect of occupying the dwelling unless they are a close relative of you or your partner.
- In these last two cases, the person will count as a non-dependant for HB if the local authority thinks that the rent agreement has been created to take advantage of the HB scheme. This cannot apply if the person has been liable to pay rent for the accommodation at any time during the eight weeks before the agreement is made.
- Any person, or any member of their household, to whom you or your partner are liable to make payments in respect of your accommodation on a commercial basis unless they are a close relative of you or your partner.

For CTB only[69]

- Any person who is jointly and severally liable (see p302) with you to pay council tax. If s/he was a non-dependant at any time within the eight weeks before s/he became liable for council tax, s/he will count as a non-dependant if the local authority thinks that the change of arrangements was created to take advantage of the CTB scheme.
- Any person who is liable to pay you or your partner on a commercial basis in respect of occupying the dwelling unless they are a close relative of you or your partner.
- In these last two cases, the person will count as a non-dependant for CTB if the local authority thinks that the liability to make payments in respect of the dwelling has been created to take advantage of the CTB scheme. This cannot apply if the person has been liable to pay rent for the accommodation at any time during the eight weeks before that liability arose.

Close relative means parent, parent-in-law, son, son-in-law, daughter, daughter-in-law, step-parent, step-son, step-daughter, brother, sister, or partners of any of these.[70] It does not include, for example, a grandparent or aunt or uncle.

Note: The conditions of entitlement to the severe disability premium are considerably more stringent than they used to be. In particular, the rules about 'joint occupiers' and those now relating to payments on a commercial basis (see above) have been the subject of considerable legal dispute as a result of which the law has changed regularly since it was first introduced in 1988 in order to limit the number of people able to avoid being classed as 'non-dependants'. The intention has been to prevent payment of the severe disability premium in family settings where, not uncommonly, a disabled person lives with her/his parent or adult son or daughter. Most notably, the changes introduced a 'commercial basis' test to the question of liability for accommodation costs on 1 October 1990, and have excluded most close relatives since 11 November 1991.

Many claimants are still awaiting the outcome of outstanding appeals relating to earlier periods where the rules were more flexible. For example, in the period 11 April 1988 to 8 October 1989, it has been established by a commissioner that the only test for 'joint occupiers' was that they had equal access to and use of the accommodation.[71] This enabled practically all adults to avoid being classed as non-dependants, although the reasoning behind this decision has subsequently been criticised by the Court of Appeal in an HB case.[72]

For the period **9 October 1989 to 30 September 1990** (ie, before the 'commercial basis' test), it has been confirmed that an adult could be a licensee of her/his parent(s) and therefore liable to them for the costs of their accommodation, in the sense that if no payment was made the licence could be terminated[73] (although there has been no suggestion that there need be any real sanction – eg, eviction – if the liability was not met).

Whether such a liability exists will depend upon the terms on which a claimant lives in her/his parent(s)' home; the purpose, amount and regularity of any payments; whether any costs have been incurred; and how any payments are used. It will be more significant if they are used, eg, for the rent or mortgage than if they are used just for the claimant's needs, and it will be easier to infer that a liability existed if hardship would result if payments were not made.[74] Although in many family settings it may not always be possible to establish how much of a person's benefits are set aside as a contribution to the specific costs of occupying the home, it may still be possible to infer that an indirect contribution to some general fund used for household costs will be sufficient to establish liability.[75]

An English commissioner has decided that payments towards gas, electricity, rates and water charges do not count,[76] but this decision has been rejected by a later decision of a commissioner in N Ireland who concluded that a liability for fuel charges does arise from occupying the home.[77]

In the case of people with severe learning difficulties who do not have the capacity to make a contract, there can be no **contractual liability**. A commissioner has suggested that, if there is no contract, they cannot satisfy the test of liability with or to someone else.[78] If this is right you cannot argue that, although there is no contract, there is something akin to one, on the basis that the person providing the accommodation should in fairness be reimbursed out of the claimant's money. However, on the particular facts in that case, it was found that the claimant, who had Down's Syndrome and an appointee taking responsibility for her claim, *did* have contractual capacity, and the commissioner's comments are therefore not binding. In any event, he expressed the hope that adjudicating authorities would adopt a consistent approach in England and Scotland, where the relevant law is different and contractual liability is not always necessary.[79]

The 'commercial basis' test introduced from 1 October 1990 has been held to apply a test similar to that which may be expected in arrangements with a paying lodger,[80] and it has been assumed that it would be unlikely (but not impossible) that such an arrangement could be said to exist between close family members. The exclusion of close relatives from 11 November 1991 has, however, left that question beyond doubt in all cases from that date.

If you think you could have qualified for the severe disability premium in an earlier period, you should get advice from a local advice agency and consider lodging a late appeal (see p171).

Severe disability premium and carer's premium

If someone gets invalid care allowance for looking after you, that excludes you from the severe disability premium. If your carer is not getting invalid care allowance, you can get the severe disability premium. But if your carer stops claiming invalid care allowance, the notional income rules could apply to her/him (see p391).

If your carer has claimed invalid care allowance but it is not being paid because of the overlapping benefit rules, s/he can get a carer's premium (see p343) and this will not prevent you from being entitled to the severe disability premium. Invalid care allowance is not in this case 'in payment' to your carer.[81]

If your carer receives any arrears of invalid care allowance when it is first paid, you may find (because the severe disability premium should not be paid for any period that invalid care allowance is paid for) that you will have to repay any overpayment from your own benefit.[82] If this happens to you, ask your local advice agency to contact CPAG for further help. In the course of an appeal to the Court of Appeal,[83] the DSS has indicated that it does not intend to recover overpayments in this way.

CHAPTER EIGHTEEN

Income

This chapter explains the rules for working out your weekly income for income support (IS), disability working allowance (DWA), housing benefit (HB), council tax benefit (CTB) and family credit (FC). It contains:

1. Introduction (below)
2. Earnings of employed earners (p362)
3. Earnings from self-employment (p371)
4. Other income (p375)
5. Notional income (p391)

1. INTRODUCTION

Your entitlement to IS/FC/DWA/HB/CTB and the amount you receive depends on how much income you have. Note that if you get IS you do not need to work out your income again for HB/CTB purposes because you receive your maximum HB (see p240) or CTB (see p311).

The rules for working out your income are very similar for each benefit. Where there are differences these are indicated.

When working out your IS/FC/DWA/HB/CTB your income may be completely ignored, *or* partially ignored, *or* counted in full.

Note: Some income is treated as capital (see p397), and some capital is treated as income (see p387).

Whose income counts

Income of a partner

If you are a member of a couple (see p330), your partner's income is added to your income and counts as if it belongs to you.[1]

If you receive a reduction of the normal personal allowance for a couple because your partner is under 18 and not eligible for IS (see p75), an amount of her/his income equivalent to the reduction is ignored.[2]

Similar rules apply to additional partners in polygamous marriages.[3]

Example
Kalid is 19. His partner, Kate, is 17 and is not able to claim IS. Kalid's personal allowance is £36.15 (the rate for a single person aged 18-24, see p341). If Kate was eligible for IS, their personal allowance would be £71.70. Up to £35.55 (£71.70-£36.15) of any income that Kate has is ignored.

Income of a dependent child

If your child has over £3,000 capital, you do not get benefit for her/him[4] (although for IS/HB/CTB, the lone parent and family premiums – but not the disabled child premium – may still be payable – see pp343-5) and their income is not counted as yours. However, maintenance paid to, or for a child, does count as yours.[5]

If your child has capital of £3,000 or less, any of their income (including earnings, see below) that is not disregarded is usually treated as yours.[6]

If that income comes to more than her/his personal allowance plus any disabled child premium for IS/HB/CTB, or the 'child credit/allowance' for FC/DWA, the extra will be ignored.[7] However, any maintenance that is not disregarded and which is paid to or for a child counts in full.[8]

Your child's **earnings** while they are *at school* do not normally count,[9] but if you are on IS/HB/CTB (not FC/DWA), and your child gets a *full-time* job *after leaving school* but while you are still claiming for them (eg, during the summer holiday), their earnings over £5 count as your income.[10] If the child qualifies for the disabled child premium (see p343) (or would, but for her/his being in a residential care or nursing home), and her/his earning capacity is not, as a result of the disability, less than 75 per cent of what it otherwise would be, £15 is ignored.[11] In either case, any income that exceeds their personal allowance and any disabled child premium is also ignored.[12] However, part-time earnings are still completely ignored. You should argue that 'part-time' here means less than 24 hours a week.[13] For more details, ask your local advice agency to contact CPAG.

School fees paid by someone other than you or your partner are dealt with differently for each benefit.

Your entitlement to IS is not affected if someone is paying school fees directly to the school,[14] except that the payments for the child's living expenses at the school count as the child's income for the period that the child is there.[15] If your child comes home for part of the week, s/he is treated as having income sufficient to wipe out her/his IS for the days s/he is at school that week and you receive benefit for the child for the days s/he is at home.[16] If your child spends a night with you s/he does not count as at school on that day.[17]

If your child goes away to school and this is paid for by the local education authority, the child is treated as having income equal to the amount of their IS for the days they are at school.[18] You are entitled to benefit for the child for the days they spend at home.

There are no special rules about school fees for FC/DWA. For HB/ CTB, the local authority is advised that boarding school fees met by, for example, a child's grandparents should be ignored unless they are already broken down into separate amounts for education and maintenance. In that case, the education element is disregarded and the living expenses part, if it is taken into account as the child's income under the rules for payments made to someone else on your behalf (see p392), is treated as a charitable or voluntary payment and qualifies for the £10 disregard (see p384).[19] (See above as to how a child's income is counted.) The education element of school fees paid by a former partner is also ignored, but the living expenses part, if taken into account as income under the rules for payments made to someone else on your behalf (see p392), counts as maintenance (see p358) and qualifies for the £15 disregard (see p379).[20]

Converting income into a weekly amount

IS, FC/DWA, HB and CTB are all calculated on a weekly basis so your income always has to be converted into a weekly amount if it is paid for a longer or shorter period. The following rules apply to income from employment (for the rules on averaging income from self-employment – see pp373-4) and other income (see p375):[21]

- If the payment is for less than a week it is treated as the weekly amount.
- If the payment is for a month, multiply the amount by 12 and divide by 52.
- For IS, FC and DWA, multiply a payment for three months by four and divide by 52.
- For IS, FC and DWA, divide a payment for a year by 52.
- For all benefits, multiply payments for other periods by seven and divide by the number of days in the period.

In the case of a person (eg, a supply teacher) who only works on certain days but is paid monthly, it is necessary to decide whether the payment is for the days worked or for the whole month. This depends on the terms of her/his contract of employment.[22]

For IS, where your income fluctuates or your earnings vary because you do not work every week, your weekly income may be averaged over the cycle, if there is an identifiable one; or, if there is not, over five weeks, or over another period if this would be more accurate.[23] If the cycle involves periods when you do no work, those periods are included in the cycle, but not other absences (eg, holidays, sickness).

Example

Ahmed works a cycle of two weeks 'on' and one week 'off'. He works 30 hours a week in the weeks he works for which he is paid £60. In the third week he is paid a retainer of £30. He claims IS in the third week. His average weekly earnings will be £50 a week (£60 + £60 + £30 = £150 divided by 3 = £50) which will be taken into account in calculating his IS entitlement.

For IS, there are a number of rules about the calculation of income for part-weeks. They are:

• Where income covering a period up to a week is paid before your first benefit week, and part of it is counted for that week; or, if, in any case, you are paid for a period of a week or more, and only part of it is counted in a particular benefit week: you multiply the whole payment by the number of days it covers in the benefit week, and then divide the result by the total number of days covered by the payment.[24]
• Where any payment of unemployment benefit, maternity allowance, sickness benefit, invalidity benefit, or severe disablement allowance falls partly into the benefit week, only the amount paid for those days is taken into account. For any payment of IS, that amount is the weekly amount multiplied by the number of days in the part-week and divided by seven.[25]

For IS, where you have regularly received a certain kind of payment of income from one source, and in a particular benefit week you receive that payment and another of the same kind from the same source, only the one paid first is taken into account.[26]

This does not apply if the second payment was due to be taken into account in another week, but the overlapping week is the first in which it could practically be counted (see p361).

See p361 for definition of IS benefit week.

The period covered by income for IS

If you are an employed earner, or getting 'other income' and claiming IS, your income counts for a future period. There are special rules for deciding the length of this period and the date from which payments count. This rule does not apply to self-employed earnings (see p371).

• Where a payment of income is made in respect of an identifiable period, it will be taken into account for a period of equal length.[27] For example, a week's part-time earnings will be taken into account for a week.

- If the payment does not relate to a particular period, the amount of the payment will be divided by the amount of the weekly IS to which you would otherwise be entitled. If part of the payment should be disregarded, the amount of IS will be increased by the appropriate disregard. The result of this calculation is the number of weeks that you will not be entitled to IS.[28]

Example

You receive £683.20 net earnings for work which cannot be attributed to any specific period of time. You are a single parent with one child aged 8, and your rent and your council tax are met by HB/CTB. Your IS is £66.30 (applicable amount of £76.50 less child benefit of £10.20). As a single parent you are entitled to a £15 earnings disregard.

£683.20 ÷ (£66.30 + £15) = 8 with £32.80 left over

This means that you are not entitled to IS for eight weeks and the remaining £32.80 (less a £15 earnings disregard, leaving £17.80) is taken into account in calculating your benefit for the following week.

- Payments made on leaving a job are taken into account for a forward period (see p366).

The date from which a payment is counted

The date from which a payment counts depends on when it was due to be paid. If it was due to be paid before you claimed IS, it counts from the date on which it was due to be paid.[29] Otherwise it is treated as paid on the first day of the benefit week in which it is due, or on the first day of the first benefit week after that in which it is practical to take it into account.[30] Payments of IS, unemployment benefit, maternity allowance, sickness benefit, invalidity benefit or severe disablement allowance are treated as paid on the day they are officially due.[31]

The **benefit week** for IS is the seven days running from the day of the week on which benefit is paid. It will often overlap two calendar weeks.[32]

The date that a payment is due may well be different from the date of actual payment. Earnings are due on the employee's normal pay day as set out in her/his contract of employment. Only if the contract does not reveal the date of due payment and there is no evidence pointing in another direction should the date the payment was received be taken as the date it was due.[33] If your contract of employment is terminated without proper notice, outstanding wages, wages in hand, holiday pay and any pay in lieu of notice are due on the last day of employment and are treated as paid on that day, even if this does not happen.[34] (If income due to you has not been paid you may be entitled to an urgent cases payment, see p44.) If an employee leaves without giving proper notice, the employer is not usually obliged to pay any outstanding wages etc until the date stated in the contract of employment. (For treatment of payments at the end of a job and how they affect your right to claim IS, see p366-8.)

2. EARNINGS OF EMPLOYED EARNERS

Calculating net earnings from employment

Only certain deductions are allowed from your gross earnings. These are income tax and class 1 national insurance contributions, plus half of any contribution you make towards a personal or occupational pension scheme.[35] The resulting net income will not always be the same as your weekly take-home pay – since, for example, you may have to pay the remaining half of the payment towards an occupational pension scheme from your net weekly income. There is no provision for the deduction of any other work expenses (eg, fares and most childcare costs, but see p375 for details about new rules). If you pay class 3 voluntary national insurance contributions no account is taken of these.[36]

If your earnings are estimated (as is sometimes necessary for FC/DWA or HB/CTB) the authorities estimate the amount of tax and national insurance you would expect to pay on those earnings, and deduct this plus half of any pension contribution you are paying.[37]

For HB/CTB, the local authority has the discretion to ignore **changes in tax or national insurance contributions** for up to 30 benefit weeks. This can be used, for example, where Budget changes are not reflected in your actual income until several months later. When the changes are eventually taken into account and your benefit entitlement is either increased or reduced accordingly, you are not treated as having been underpaid or overpaid benefit during the period of the delay.[38]

What counts as earnings

Earnings means 'any remuneration or profit derived[39] from . . . employment'.[40] As well as your wages, this includes:[41]

- Any bonus or commission (including tips).
- Holiday pay. But if it is not payable until more than four weeks after your job ends or is interrupted, it will be treated as capital.[42] **Note:** For IS, this rule does not apply if you are involved in, or returning to work after, a trade dispute (see p77). For more detail on payments at the end

of a job, see p366.

- Except for IS, any sick pay.[43] For IS this is treated as other income and counted in full less any tax, class 1 national insurance contributions and half of any pension contributions.[44]
- For HB/CTB, any maternity pay.[45] For FC/DWA, any statutory maternity pay and maternity allowance are ignored altogether,[46] although any additional non-statutory contributions that may be made by an employer should be treated as earnings. For IS, any maternity pay is treated as other income and counted in full less any tax, class 1 national insurance contributions and half of any pension contributions.[47]
- Any payments made by your employer for expenses not 'wholly, exclusively and necessarily' incurred in carrying out your job. This includes payments for fares to and from work.
- A retainer fee – eg, you may be paid this during the school holidays if you work for the school meals service.
- For DWA, any payment made by your employer towards your council tax or community charge.[48]
- Except in the case of FC/DWA,[49] payments in lieu of wages or in lieu of notice, but only insofar as they represent loss of income.[50]
- An award of compensation for unfair dismissal and certain other awards of pay made by an industrial tribunal, and for IS/HB/CTB, certain payments made directly by your employer as compensation for loss of employment.
- Certain other payments from your employer – eg, arrears of wages (but see below for payments from an employer which do not count).

See p366-9 for definitions of the last three.

The following are examples of payments not counted as earnings:

- Payments in kind (eg, petrol).[51] These are ignored[52] unless you are on IS and involved in a trade dispute (see pp77-81).
- An advance of earnings or a loan from your employer. This is treated as capital[53] (it will still be treated as earnings for IS if you or your partner are involved in a trade dispute, or have been back at work after a dispute for no longer than 15 days[54]).
- A job start allowance paid under the Employment and Training Act 1973.[55]
- Payments towards expenses that are 'wholly, exclusively and necessarily' incurred, such as travelling expenses during the course of your work.[56]
- If you are a local councillor, travelling expenses to and from council offices or constituents etc and home, and subsistence payments are

ignored as expenses 'wholly, exclusively and necessarily' incurred in your work. However, allowances for attending meetings etc are counted as earnings.[57]
• Earnings payable abroad which cannot be brought into Britain (eg, because of exchange control regulations).[58] If your earnings are paid in another currency, any bank charges for converting them into sterling is deducted before taking them into account.[59]
• Any occupational pension.[60] This counts as other income and the net amount is taken into account in full.[61]

The value of any **accommodation provided as part of your job** will be ignored for IS.[62] For FC/DWA, if it is free, the authorities will take account of its value by adding £12 to the calculation of your weekly earnings. If your employer charges you less than £12 rent, the difference between that amount and £12 is added instead. If the accommodation is worthless to you – eg, it is provided but you never use it,[63] no amount will be added.

For CTB, and for HB where job-related accommodation is in addition to the normal home, argue that this is payment in kind[64] and disregarded.

How earnings are assessed

All payments of earnings must be converted into a weekly amount (see p359). For IS it is also necessary to work out the period which these payments cover (see p360). However, for FC/DWA/HB/CTB a past period is usually used to assess your 'normal weekly earnings'. See p366 if you have just started a job.

For FC

Unless you are employed as a director (see below), the normal rule is to average your weekly earnings over an 'assessment period' of:

• six consecutive weeks or three consecutive fortnights in the last seven weeks if you are paid weekly or fortnightly; *or*
• three months or three four-week periods if you are paid monthly or four weekly; *or*
• six consecutive pay periods if you are paid at another interval that is less than a month (eg, daily); *or*
• one year if your pay period is longer than a month;

immediately before the week of your claim.[65]
Any weeks/months in the assessment period in which your earnings were reduced because you were involved in a trade dispute, are ignored and replaced by the next earliest 'normal' pay period.[66]
Any pay period in which your earnings are 20 per cent or more above

or below your average earnings are left out. If this applies to all the weeks/months in your assessment period, only those in which you received no pay or received pay for a longer period than usual (eg, two week's holiday pay in one week) are left out. If this still results in all the weeks/months in your assessment period being left out, your employer will be required to provide an estimate of your likely earnings for the period for which you are normally paid.[67]

Where your earnings vary widely (eg, seasonal workers) you may find that the figure arrived at using these rules can be based on just one wage slip which could be up to 20 per cent above or below your real average earnings. Therefore it may sometimes be sensible to delay your claim in order to allow for the lowest possible rate of pay to be taken into account and thus maximise the amount of FC you will receive for the next 26 weeks.

If you are employed as a **director** of a company, different rules apply. Your normal weekly earnings are worked out by looking at how much you received in the year immediately before the week of your claim. If you have been employed for less than a year, an estimate is made of what you are likely to earn in the first year, taking into account what you have in fact earned. Any week when you do no work and do not get paid is ignored in calculating your weekly earnings.[68]

For DWA

The normal rule is to take your weekly earnings over an 'assessment period' of:

* five consecutive weeks in the last six weeks if you are paid weekly; *or*
* two months if you are paid monthly;

immediately before the week of your claim.[69]

Any time in the assessment period during which your earnings were irregular or unusual does not count[70] – eg, any week in which you received, for instance, a one-off bonus or holiday pay, or in which large deductions were made from your wages.

If your earnings fluctuate, or your earnings in the five-week or two-month period before your claim do not represent your normal earnings (eg, because you are on unpaid maternity leave[71]), a different period can be used if this gives a more accurate picture of your normal weekly earnings.[72]

If there is a period of short-time working of not more than 13 weeks or a trade dispute at your place of work, your normal weekly earnings will be taken as those prior to the period of short-time working or dispute. Trade dispute includes a work-to-rule or overtime ban as well as a strike.[73]

For FC/DWA

A bonus or commission paid separately, or for a longer period than other earnings, and which is paid in the year prior to your claim, counts as earnings.[74] The net amount is divided by 52 before it is taken into account.[75]

If you have just started a job or have just returned to work after a break of more than, for FC four weeks, or, for DWA 13 weeks, or your hours have just changed, and the period since the start or resumption of your employment or the change in hours is less than, for FC your assessment period, or, for DWA nine weeks, your employer will be required to provide an estimate of your likely earnings for the period for which you are normally paid.[76] If your actual earnings turn out to be lower than the estimate, this will not result in your FC/DWA being reviewed and increased, so it is important that your employer does not overestimate your earnings.

For HB/CTB

Earnings as an employee are usually averaged out over:

* the previous five weeks if you are paid weekly; *or*
* two months if you are paid monthly.[77]

Where your earnings vary, or if there is likely to be or has recently been a change (eg, you usually do overtime but have not done so recently, or you are about to get a pay rise), the local authority may average them over a different period where this is likely to give a more accurate picture of what you are going to earn during the benefit period.[78]

If you are on strike, the local authority should not take into account your pre-strike earnings and average them out over the strike period.[79]

If you have only just started work and your earnings cannot be averaged over the normal period (ie, five weeks/two months), an estimate is made based on any earnings you have been paid so far if these are likely to reflect your future average wage.[80] Where you have not yet been paid or your initial earnings do not represent what you will normally earn over the benefit period, your employer must provide an estimate of your average weekly earnings.[81] Where your earnings change during your benefit period, your new weekly average figure is estimated on the basis of what you are likely to earn over the remainder of the benefit period.[82]

Payments at the end of a job

Redundancy payments are normally treated as capital (see below). If your payment, together with other capital that is not ignored (see pp398-404), comes to more than £8,000 (IS/FC) or £16,000 (HB/DWA/CTB), you are not eligible for benefit;[83] if the total comes to more than £3,000 you are treated as having a certain amount of income from your capital[84] (see p385).

In spending any redundancy money, it is worth bearing in mind that if you deliberately get rid of money in order to get benefit, you are treated as still having it (see p404).

Some redundancy schemes make periodic payments after leaving work: for IS/HB/CTB, these are treated as other income (see p375).[85]

Other payments can cause problems, and are dealt with separately for each benefit.

For IS

If you retire from a full-time job (16 hours or more) and you are aged at least 60 (women) or 65 (men), any payments counted as earnings (eg, final wages, holiday pay, etc) that you receive are disregarded in full.[86] You are not treated as in full-time work for any period covered by those earnings after the end of your job.

In all other cases, only the following final payments that you receive when you leave a full-time job affect your right to IS:[87]

- holiday pay which counts as earnings (see p362);
- pay in lieu of notice;
- pay in lieu of wages;
- a compensation payment in respect of employment (ie, where you do not get pay in lieu of notice, or only get part of your pay in lieu of notice, and receive a lump sum instead – ie, *ex gratia*). This is divided by the maximum payable under the statutory redundancy scheme (uprated yearly). The result is the number of weeks the payment will cover up to a maximum of your notice period whether statutory, contractual or customary.[88] If the amount is less than the statutory maximum for one week or if the calculation creates a fraction, these are treated as capital.[89] Compensation for part-time workers is taken into account for one week only.[90] If the *ex gratia* payment is not compensation but a gift – eg, a 'golden handshake' – it should be treated as capital, not income.

You are treated as in full-time work for the number of weeks covered by these payments after your employment ended.[91] These payments are taken into account consecutively and in the following order:

- first, any pay in lieu of wages or in lieu of notice;
- then payments of compensation for loss of employment;
- then holiday pay.[92]

The period for which you are treated as in full-time work starts on the earliest date that any of these payments are due to be paid.[93]

If you are paid a **retainer**, this will be taken into account as earnings in calculating the amount of your IS. If you later receive an award of compensation for unfair dismissal or certain other awards of pay from an industrial tribunal, these are taken into account as earnings in calculating the amount of your IS from when the award is made.

Example
Mary leaves her full-time job with a final week's wages, a week in hand and one week's holiday pay. All three amounts are due to be paid on 30 May. Only the holiday pay will be taken into account, starting from 30 May. Mary will not be entitled to IS for one week.

If your employment is interrupted (eg, you are laid off), any holiday pay that is paid to you affects your right to IS; all other payments are disregarded except that any retainer you are paid is taken into account as earnings in calculating the amount of your IS.[94] If you have been suspended, any payment you receive will be taken into account and affect your right to IS.

If you were working **part-time** (less than 16 hours a week) before you claimed IS, any payments you receive when the job ends or is interrupted, except any retainer, are ignored and do not affect your IS (unless you have been suspended).[95] If, however, you were claiming IS while you were in part-time work, any payments made to you when that job ends are taken into account as earnings in the normal way. Your wages, including any final wages, are counted first, then any pay in lieu of wages or notice, then any compensation paid by your employer for loss of employment (see p367) and then any holiday pay.[96]

Once the period covered by payments at the end of a job has ended, any money remaining will be treated as capital.[97]

For FC/DWA

There are no special FC/DWA rules for payments received at the end of a job. However, if, for example, your partner has just lost his job and you apply for FC because you are working full-time, any payments that s/he received at the end of the employment (and indeed the amount of previous wages) should not be included as part of your 'normal' weekly income, unless there is evidence that the job will resume while you are getting your current FC award.

For HB/CTB

If you retire from a full-time job (16 hours or more) and have reached the age of 65 (men) or 60 (women), any payments counted as earnings that you receive are disregarded.[98]

In all other cases, only the following final payments that you receive are taken into account as earnings:[99]

- holiday pay which counts as earnings (see p362);
- pay in lieu of notice;
- pay in lieu of wages;
- compensation for loss of employment, but only insofar as it represents loss of income (the detailed rules for IS do not apply);
- an award of compensation for unfair dismissal, or certain other awards of pay from an industrial tribunal;
- any statutory sick pay or statutory maternity pay;
- any retainer fee.

If your work is interrupted, your earnings are disregarded except for holiday pay which counts as earnings (see p362) and any retainer paid to you.

Where you have been in part-time work (ie, less than 16 hours a week) before claiming HB/CTB, any earnings paid when your job ends or is interrupted are disregarded, *except* where that payment is a retainer.[100]

Disregarded earnings

For FC/DWA, your earnings, worked out in the way described above, are taken into account in full.

For IS and HB/CTB, some of your earnings are disregarded and do not affect your benefit. The amount of the 'disregard' depends on your circumstances. There are three levels.

£25 disregard

Lone parents on HB/CTB but not receiving IS have £25 of their earnings ignored.[101] This does not apply to IS.

£15 disregard

£15 of your earnings (including those of your partner if any) is disregarded if:

- for IS, you qualify for a lone parent premium (see p344). You are treated as qualifying for the premium if you would do so but for getting a pensioner premium or for being in a local authority home, or because you are a person in a residential care or nursing home with preserved rights (see p101);[102]

- you or your partner (if any) qualifies for a disability premium (see p345).[103] For IS, you are treated as qualifying for the premium if you would do so but for being in hospital, or a local authority home or because you are a person in a residential care or nursing home with preserved rights (see p101);
- for HB/CTB only, you or your partner (if any) qualifies for a severe disability premium (see p351);[104]
- you, or your partner (if any) qualifies for the higher pensioner premium (see p348), you or your partner are over 60 *and*, immediately before reaching that age, you or your partner were in employment (part-time for IS) and you were entitled to a £15 disregard because of qualifying for a disability premium. For HB/CTB this includes where, in the case of a couple, you would have qualified for a disability premium but for the fact that a higher pensioner premium was payable. Since reaching 60, you or your partner must have continued in employment (part-time for IS), although breaks of up to eight* weeks when you were not getting IS (or HB/CTB where you claim either of these benefits) are ignored. Again, for IS, you are treated as qualifying for the higher pensioner premium even if you are in hospital etc;[105]
- you are a member of a couple, your benefit would include a disability premium but for the fact that one of you qualifies for the higher pensioner premium or the enhanced rate of pensioner premium (see p348), one of you is under 60 and either of you are in employment.

  For IS, you are treated as qualifying for the higher or enhanced pensioner premium if you would do so, but for being in hospital, etc (see above);[106]
- you are a member of a couple, one of you is aged 75-79 and the other over 60, and immediately before that person reached 60 either of you were in part-time employment and you were entitled to a £15 disregard because of qualifying, or being treated as qualifying for an enhanced pensioner premium (see above). Since then either of you must have continued in part-time employment, although breaks of up to eight* weeks when you were not getting IS (or HB/CTB where you claim either of these benefits) are ignored;[107]
- you, or your partner (if any) qualifies for a carer's premium (see p343). The disregard applies to the carer's earnings. For a couple, if the carer's earnings are less than £15, the remainder of the disregard can be used up on her/his partners earnings as an auxiliary coastguard, etc (see below), or up to £5 (for HB/CTB up to £10) of it can be used up on her/his partner's earnings from another job;[108]
- you or your partner (if any) are an auxiliary coastguard, part-time firefighter or a part-time member of a lifeboat crew, or a member of the

Territorial Army.[109] If you earn less than £15 for doing any of these services you can use up to £5 (for HB/CTB up to £10 if you have a partner) of the disregard on another job[110] or a partner's earnings from another job;[111]

- for IS only, you are a couple both under 60 and you have been receiving IS continuously for the last two years. It is sufficient if, throughout this time, either you or your partner has been getting IS for you both, or one of you has been the claimant for a couple (though not necessarily the same couple). Neither you nor your present partner must have been in full-time work or in full-time education for periods of more than eight consecutive weeks in the last two years. Breaks of eight* weeks or less when you were not a member of a couple or getting IS are ignored.[112]

*For IS, this is increased to 12 weeks if you stopped getting IS because you or your partner started full-time work (see p14 for the detailed rules on this). Any period when you were not entitled to IS because you or your partner went on a government training scheme is ignored. But it will count as a period that you were in receipt of IS if you qualify for the £15 disregard as a long-term claimant (see above).[113]

If you qualify under more than one category you still have a maximum of only £15 of your earnings disregarded.

Basic £10 or £5 disregard

If you do not qualify for a £25 or £15 disregard, the rules vary depending on the benefit you are claiming.

For IS, £5 of your earnings is disregarded and £5 of your partner's earnings.[114]

For HB/CTB, £5 of your earnings is disregarded if you are single. If you claim as a member of a couple, £10 of your total earnings is disregarded – whether or not you are both working.[115]

The government has announced its intention to introduce new rules relating to childcare costs for FC/DWA/HB/CTB from 1 October 1994 (see p375).

3. EARNINGS FROM SELF-EMPLOYMENT

Calculating net earnings

Your 'net profit' over the period before your claim must be worked out. This consists of your self-employed earnings, including any enterprise allowance,[116] minus:[117]

- reasonable expenses (see below); *and*
- income tax and national insurance contributions; *and*
- half of any premium paid in respect of a personal pension scheme or a retirement annuity contract which is eligible for tax relief.[118]

For FC/DWA, the enterprise allowance will not count if it already ended before you claimed – so it may be worthwhile delaying your claim.[119]

In calculating your earnings any capital grant to set up a business, or a loan of working capital, is excluded,[120] (an appeal against another decision which said loans were earnings was agreed to by the government[121]), and any capital (eg, a legacy) not generated by the business cannot be treated as earnings.[122]

For IS/HB/CTB, if you receive payments for fostering from a local authority or voluntary organisation, these do not count as earnings[123] but are ignored.[124] For IS, if you receive payments for board and lodging charges these do not count as earnings[125] but as other income (see p384). For FC/DWA, these are treated as earnings if, after discounting all the disregards on pp375-91 (other than the boarder's allowance on p384), they form a *major part* of your total income.[126] Otherwise they are treated as other income, as for IS.

Reasonable expenses

Expenses must be reasonable and 'wholly and exclusively' incurred for the purposes of your business.[127] Where a car, or telephone, for example, is used partly for business and partly for private purposes, the costs of it can be apportioned and the amount attributable to business use can be deducted.[128]

Reasonable expenses include:[129]

- repayments of capital on loans for replacing equipment and machinery;
- repayment of capital on loans for, and income spent on, the repair of a business asset except where this is covered by insurance;
- interest on a loan taken out for the purposes of the business;
- excess of VAT paid over VAT received.

Reasonable expenses do not include:[130]

- any capital expenditure;
- depreciation;
- money for setting up or expanding the business (eg, the cost of adapting the business premises);
- any loss incurred before the beginning of the current assessment period. If the business makes a loss, the net profit is nil. The losses of one business cannot be offset against the profit of any other business in

which you are engaged or against your earnings as an employee;[131]
- capital repayments on loans taken out for business purposes;
- business entertainment expenses;
- for HB/CTB only, debts (other than proven bad debts), but the expenses of recovering a debt can be deducted.

Working out your average

There are different rules for each benefit.

For IS

For IS, the weekly amount is the average of earnings:[132]

- over a period of one year (this does not have to be the year immediately before the claim – it will normally be the last year for which accounts are available);
- over a more appropriate period where you have recently taken up self-employment or there has been a change which will affect your business.

If your earnings are royalties or copyright payments, the amount of earnings is divided by the weekly amount of IS which would be payable if you had not received this income *plus* the amount which would be disregarded from those earnings. You will not be entitled to IS for the resulting number of weeks.

For FC/DWA

Your normal weekly earnings are worked out by looking at:[133]

- your profit and loss account (and your trading account and/or balance sheet if appropriate), if this covers a period of at least six but not more than 15 months, which ends within 12 months before the date of your claim; *or*
- if you do not provide such a profit and loss account, but do provide a statement of your earnings and expenses for the six calendar months up to and including the month before your claim, your earnings over that period of six months; *or*
- if you do not provide a profit and loss account or statement of earnings and expenses, the six calendar months up to and including the month preceding your claim; *or*
- a different past period, if this represents your normal weekly earnings more accurately (eg, if there has been a recent change in the circumstances of your business).

Your weekly earnings are worked out by averaging the earnings you have received or can expect to receive over the assessment period or, where you have provided a profit and loss account, by averaging the earnings relevant to the period covered by that account.[134]

Any complete week(s) in the assessment period when you are not actually working (eg, because you are sick or on holiday) are ignored.[135]

If you have just started being self-employed (ie, for less than seven calendar months), for FC your normal weekly earnings are worked out over six calendar months, beginning with the month after the one in which you started the business. If you provided a statement of earnings and expenses for those months, up to and including the last month before the month in which you claim, the earnings of those months are taken; if you do not provide such a statement, the earnings up to and including the month before the one preceding your claim are taken. In either case, the amount you can expect to earn for the remainder of the six-month period is added. Any week where you do not work for the business is ignored.[136] For DWA an estimate will be made of your likely weekly earnings over the next 26 weeks from the date of your claim.[137] If your actual earnings turn out to be lower than the estimate this will not result in your FC/DWA being reviewed and increased.[138] However, if you were not *awarded* FC/DWA because your estimated earnings were too high, but by the time your appeal is heard you would be entitled on the basis of your actual earnings, the tribunal should have regard to your earnings up to the date of the SSAT hearing in deciding what your income really was at the date of claim. In this case the tribunal is deciding whether you are entitled to an award, not dealing with a change of circumstances affecting an existing award.[139]

For HB/CTB

The amount of your weekly earnings is averaged out over an 'appropriate' period (usually based on your last year's trading accounts) which must not be longer than a year.[140]

Childminders

Childminders are always treated as self-employed. Your net profit is deemed to be a third of your earnings less income tax, your national insurance contributions and half of certain pension contributions[141] (see p372). The rest of your earnings are completely ignored.

Disregarded earnings[142]

The rules are the same as for employed earners (see p369).

Childcare costs

The government has announced[143] its intention to introduce **new rules** for claims for FC/DWA/HB/CTB from 1 October 1994 whereby childcare costs of up to £40 may be offset against the earnings of certain claimants (employed or self-employed). Legislation has not yet been drafted, but the intention appears to be that this extra help will apply if you are:

- in a couple where both of you are working; *or*
- in a couple where one of you is working and the other is incapable of work; *or*
- a lone parent.

In addition, you must have a child under 11 and must use formal childcare through registered childminders, day nurseries etc.

Note:

- These rules will *not* apply to IS.
- £40 will be the maximum sum that can be offset regardless of the number of children you may have.
- As FC claimants are not charged for using local authority day nurseries, it appears that this applies only to the use of registered childminders etc (see p490).

In a current case before a commissioner,[144] an FC claimant is arguing that the existing FC rules, which do not allow childcare costs to be taken into account at all when calculating your earnings, are indirectly discriminatory against women under an EC Directive prohibiting discrimination in access to employment.[145] The argument is that, unless childcare costs can be deducted, most lone parents in practice cannot work and therefore cannot claim FC; the vast majority of lone parents are women; and the FC rules therefore discriminate against women. The Commissioner has asked the European Court of Justice a preliminary question whether FC comes within the scope of the Directive (the government says it does not). If it does, and if the discrimination point is successful, the principle should apply equally to the new rules, because £40 will not cover the cost of most childcare. For more information, ask an adviser to contact CPAG.

4. OTHER INCOME

All other types of income are taken into account less any tax due on them.[146] For HB/CTB, changes in tax and national insurance rates may ignored for up to 30 weeks,[147] as for earnings (see p362).

Where you are receiving payments from a private sickness insurance scheme, any continuing contributions you have to make in order to secure this income may also be deducted from the income you receive.[148]

Payments from TFW and YT schemes are covered separately (see pp62-5).

All income is converted into a weekly amount (see p359). For IS, this amount is attributed to a forward period (see p360) and affects the benefit payable for that period.

For FC/DWA/HB/CTB, a past period is used where possible to assess normal weekly income, and this figure is used to calculate benefit.

For HB/CTB, an estimate of income is made by looking at an appropriate period (not exceeding one year). The period chosen must give an accurate assessment of your income.[149]

For FC/DWA, your income during the 26 weeks immediately before the week of your claim will be used, unless a different period immediately before your claim would produce a more accurate assessment.[150]

See pp120-41 and 378-9 for maintenance.

Benefits

Benefits that count in full:

* unemployment benefit;
* sickness benefit, invalidity benefit and severe disablement allowance;
* except for FC/DWA, maternity allowance;
* invalid care allowance;
* widows' benefits (including industrial death benefit);
* retirement pensions;
* industrial injuries benefits (except constant attendance allowance and exceptionally severe disablement allowance);
* except for FC/DWA, child benefit and one parent benefit;
* for IS only, guardian's allowance;
* child's special allowance and war orphan's pension;
* FC/DWA (for IS and HB/CTB);
* for IS only,[151] statutory sick pay and statutory maternity pay – less any class 1 national insurance contribution and half of any pension contribution and any tax. For HB/CTB, statutory sick pay and statutory maternity pay are treated as earnings (see p363) and you may, therefore, benefit from an earnings disregard. For FC/DWA, statutory sick pay is counted as earnings but statutory maternity pay is ignored (see p363).

Problems can arise where, for example, the Benefits Agency takes into account a benefit you are *not* receiving, such as child benefit that has been delayed. In such a case, the benefit should not be treated as income possessed by you. For IS, you should get your full benefit and leave the Benefits Agency to recover the difference from arrears of the delayed benefit when it is eventually paid.[152] HB/CTB guidance makes a similar point. It says that if you have applied for FC, but not received it, it should be ignored when your income is being assessed (the same principle should apply to other benefits claimed but not yet paid).[153] For IS/FC/DWA/HB/CTB, any arrears of any means-tested benefits should be treated as capital and ignored for 52 weeks.[154]

Benefits that are ignored completely:

- attendance allowance (or constant attendance allowance, exceptionally severe disablement allowance or severe disablement occupational allowance paid because of an injury at work or a war injury) or any care component of disability living allowance. For IS only, it is taken into account in full up to a maximum of £45.70 a week if you went to live in a residential care or nursing home before 31 March 1993 and you are a person with preserved rights (see p101);[155]
- pensioner's Christmas bonus;[156]
- mobility allowance or either of the mobility components of disability living allowance;[157]
- mobility supplement under the War Pensions Scheme;[158]
- any extra-statutory payment made to you to compensate for non-payment of IS, mobility allowance, mobility supplement, attendance allowance or disability living allowance;[159]
- for FC, disability working allowance.[160] For DWA, family credit;[161]
- social fund payments.[162] For FC/DWA, they are not specifically disregarded, but they should not count as part of your 'normal weekly' income. For IS/FC/DWA/HB/CTB, social fund payments are disregarded as capital indefinitely;[163]
- except for DWA, resettlement benefit paid to certain patients who are discharged from hospital and who had been in hospital for more than a year before 11 April 1988;[164]
- any transitional payment made to compensate you for loss of benefit due to the changes in benefit rules in April 1988;[165]
- HB, CCB, CTB and refunds on community charge/council tax liability;[166]
- IS is ignored for FC/DWA and HB/CTB.[167] There are special HB/CTB rules for IS claimants (see p240 and 311);
- educational maintenance allowances[168] (see p485);
- certain special war widows' payments;[169]

- for FC/DWA/HB/CTB, guardian's allowance;[170]
- for FC/DWA, child benefit (including one parent benefit);[171]
- for FC/DWA, maternity allowance and statutory maternity pay.[172]
- where you are getting unemployment benefit, sickness benefit, invalidity benefit, maternity allowance, widowed mother's allowance, retirement pension, industrial injuries benefits (including unemployability supplement) or invalid care allowance, any increase for adult or child dependants, provided the dependant in question is not a member of your family (see p328).[173]

For the treatment of payments of arrears of benefits, see p403.

Benefits that have £10 ignored:

- war disablement pension;
- war widow's pension;
- an extra-statutory payment made instead of the above pensions;
- similar payments made by another country;
- a pension from Germany or Austria paid to the victims of Nazi persecution.[174]

Only £10 in all can be ignored, even if you have more than one payment which attracts a £10 disregard.[175] However, the £10 disregard allowed on these war pensions is additional to the total disregard of any mobility supplement or attendance allowance (ie, constant attendance allowance, exceptionally severe disablement allowance and severe disablement occupational allowance) paid as part of a war disablement pension (see p377).

Local authorities are given very limited discretion to increase the £10 disregard on war disablement and war widows' pensions when assessing income for HB/CTB.[176] Check your local authority's policy on this issue.

Maintenance payments

If you are responsible for and the parent of a child and you do not live with a parent of the child and you claim IS/FC/DWA, you will normally be required to apply to the Child Support Agency for a maintenance assessment (see pp125-35).

If you are claiming **IS** and receiving maintenance payments, or child support maintenance payments (see p125), from a former partner for yourself or any children, the rules on how this money is treated are considered on pp135-41.

If you claim **FC/DWA** and regular amounts of maintenance payments, or child support maintenance payments, are being made at regular intervals (eg, weekly or monthly) before you claim, the normal weekly amount counts as income.[177] If any child support maintenance payments made are more than the amount due under a maintenance assessment, only the amount due under the assessment is taken into account. If maintenance payments are due to be paid regularly but are not being so, the average of the payments made in the 13 weeks up to the week of your claim counts as income. With child support maintenance payments not paid regularly, you take the average of the payments made over the last 13 weeks, or, if the maintenance assessed was notified to you within the last 13 weeks, over the period since the notification. However, if that average is more than the maintenance assessment, it is that sum which is taken into account.[178] Other payments of maintenance are treated as capital.[179] Maintenance payments to or for a child in your family (see p335) should be treated as yours but only if the payments are actually made.

For **HB** and **CTB**, periodical payments simply count as income and lump sums as capital.[180] Maintenance paid to or for your dependent child counts as yours.[181]

If you are a single parent, or a couple with a child, for FC/DWA, HB and CTB, £15 of any maintenance payment made by your former partner, or your partner's former partner, or the parent of any child in your family is disregarded. If you receive maintenance from more than one person, only £15 of the total is disregarded.[182]

If you *pay* maintenance to a former partner or a child not living with you, your payments are not disregarded for the purpose of calculating your income for IS/FC/DWA/HB/CTB.

Grants and covenants to students

The term **grant** includes bursaries, scholarships and exhibitions as well as grants or awards from education authorities.[183] An educational award which is paid by way of a loan counts as a grant for IS.[184] You are treated as having the parental or partner's contribution to your grant whether or not it has been paid to you.[185] However, if you are a single parent, a single foster parent or a disabled student, only the amount of any contribution that you actually receive counts for IS.[186] Grant income is taken into account for the academic year, excluding the summer vacation, unless the grant expressly covers the whole year (eg, postgraduate students), or a different period. In each case, it is divided equally over the weeks in the period.[187] In the case of a sandwich course, grant income is averaged out over the period of study excluding the periods of experience (ie, in industry or commerce).[188] Any grant income paid under the Education (Mandatory Awards) Regulations that is intended for the maintenance of a student's dependants or which is an allowance for mature students is spread over 52 or 53 weeks.[189] (Benefit weeks and academic years sometimes run to 53 weeks, including part-weeks.) However, for other grants the normal rule (period of study or period for which grant payable) applies. So where a student on a sandwich course received a grant from the Department of Health, the element for his dependants was spread over the period of study only.[190]

The following grant income is ignored:[191]

- A fixed amount of £273 or whatever you get in your grant towards the cost of books and equipment.
- Any amount for travelling expenses. Where you are in receipt of a mandatory grant, and living away from your parents' home, this will usually be £143. If you are living at your parents' home it will usually be £222.
- Tuition and examination fees.
- Except for DWA, any allowance to meet the cost of special equipment for certain courses which began before 1 September 1986.
- Any allowance to meet extra expenses because you are a disabled student.
- Any allowance to meet the cost of attending a residential course away from your normal student accommodation during term-time.
- Any allowance for the costs of your normal home (away from college) but, for IS, only if your rent is not met by HB.
- Any amount for a partner or children abroad is ignored for IS and HB/CTB, but not FC/DWA.

Covenant income

Prior to 1988, there was provision for students to be paid under a deed of covenant whereby the payer could deduct the appropriate rate of tax from the gross amount of any contribution due, and pay the student only the net amount. The student could then claim a refund of the tax deducted.

There are special rules for the treatment of covenant income.[192] Very broadly, their intended effect is that if your grant and covenant income exceed the amount of the standard maintenance grant[193] the excess is taken into account. It is then spread over the whole year, and a £5 disregard applied to the weekly figure arrived at.

Any tax refund received by the student is ignored as income, but treated as capital for IS/HB/CTB (and ignored altogether for FC/DWA).

There has been no tax relief available on covenants since April 1988. Further details of these rules were set out in the 23rd edition of the *National Welfare Benefits Handbook* (1993/4).

General points about grant income

- If you have other income (eg, a regular charitable or voluntary payment) that attracts a £10 disregard, only £10 a week in total can be ignored.[194]
- Any payments, apart from your grant, coventant or top-up loan, you receive to help you with expenses referred to on p380, which exceed the amounts for these purposes included in your grant or disregarded from your covenant income, are ignored.[195]
- In the case of a couple, the amount of any contribution that one member has been assessed to pay to her/his partner who is a student, does not count as her/his income for IS/FC/DWA/HB or CTB purposes.[196]
- For HB only, if your eligible rent is subject to a flat-rate deduction (see p254), the same amount is disregarded from your income. If your income does not cover the deduction, the balance is ignored from your partners income.[197]

For information about student grants, contact your student welfare officer.

Student loans[198] under the statutory scheme are treated as income. Weekly income is calculated by dividing the loan over the 52 (or 53) weeks of the academic year. In the final year of the course, or for a one-year course, the loan is divided by the number of weeks from the start of the academic year to when the course ends. The end of the course is the last day of the last term.[199]

There is a £10 disregard on loan income, but it will overlap with any other £10 disregard on other income.[200]

If you give up your course before it finishes, your loan continues to be counted in the same way, but without any disregard.[201]

If you fail to apply for a loan to which you are entitled, the maximum amount payable to you is counted as weekly income, calculated as if you actually received it.[202] This does not apply if you have given up your course early (see above), since you are no longer a 'student'.

Access Fund payments[203] made to students by educational establishments to prevent hardship will be treated as voluntary or charitable payments (see below).

Adoption, fostering and residence order (in Scotland custody) payments

An **adoption allowance** counts in full for IS and HB/CTB up to the amount of the adopted child's personal allowance and disabled child premium, if any. Above that level it is ignored completely.[204]

For FC/DWA, anything above the level of the child's credit/allowance is ignored.[205]

If the child has capital over £3,000, you are not entitled to any benefit for the child[206] and the entire adoption allowance is ignored.[207]

The way that a **fostering allowance** is treated depends on whether the arrangement is an official one or a private one. If a child is placed or boarded out with you by the local authority or a voluntary organisation under legal provisions, any fostering allowances you receive are ignored altogether.[208]

If the fostering arrangement is a private one, any money you receive from the child's parents is counted as maintenance (see p378). If the money you receive is not from the child's parents, you should probably be treated as a childminder (see p374).

If you are paid a **residence order allowance** (in Scotland custody allowance) by the local authority, this is treated in the same way as an adoption allowance[209] (see above). Arrears of residence order (in Scotland custody) allowances are treated as capital for IS.[210] Any payments made by the natural parents count as maintenance (see p378).

If the local authority makes a lump-sum payment to enable you to make adaptations to your home for a handicapped child, this is treated as capital and ignored (see p399).[211]

Charitable and voluntary payments

Any payments including payments in kind from the Macfarlane Trust, the Macfarlane (Special Payments) Trust, the Macfarlane (Special Payments) (No. 2) Trust, the Fund, the Eileen Trust (see p494) or either of the Independent Living Funds (see p495) are disregarded in full.[212]

The Macfarlane Trusts make payments to haemophiliacs. The Fund was set up on 24 April 1992 for people who are not haemophiliacs who have contracted HIV through blood or tissue transfusions.

If you are, or were, a haemophiliac, or have received a payment from the Fund or the Eileen Trust, the following payments from money that originally came from any of the three Macfarlane Trusts, the Fund or the Eileen Trust are also disregarded in full:[213]

- any payment made by you, or on your behalf, to, or for the benefit of:
  - your partner, or former partner from whom you are not estranged or divorced;
  - any child (see p335) who is a member of your family, or who was but is now a member of another family; *or*
- if you have no partner or former partner (other than one from whom you are estranged or divorced), or children, any payment made by you, or from your estate if you have died, to:
  - your parent or step-parent; *or*

– your guardian if you have no parent or step-parent and were a child (see p335) or student at the date of the payment, or, if you have died, at the date of your death.

In the case of a payment to a parent, step-parent or guardian, this is only disregarded until two years after your death.

- any payment made by your partner, or former partner from whom you are not estranged or divorced, or on her/his behalf, to, or for the benefit of:
  – you;
  – any child who is a member of your family, or who was and is now a member of another family.

Any income or capital that derives from any such payment is also disregarded.

Any other charitable or voluntary payment that is made irregularly and is intended to be made irregularly is treated as capital.[214] However, if you are on IS it will count as income:

- if you are involved in a trade dispute and for the first 15 days following your return to work after a dispute[215] (see pp77-81); *or*
- where payments made to a child's boarding school are treated as the child's notional income[216] (see pp358-9).

An irregular charitable or voluntary payment will therefore normally only affect your benefit if the payment takes your capital over £3,000, or over £8,000, or over £16,000 (see p394).

If you receive a capital payment from a charity to repair or improve your home, this should be disregarded in full[217] (see p399). Any capital payment in kind made by a charity is ignored.[218]

Charitable or voluntary payments made, or due to be made regularly, are completely ignored if:[219]

- for IS/HB/CTB, they are intended, and used, for anything *except* food, ordinary clothing or footwear, household fuel, council tax, water rates and rent (less any non-dependant deductions) for which HB is payable; and for IS only, housing costs met by IS and residential care or nursing home accommodation charges for people with preserved rights (see p101) met by IS or by a local authority. Where you do not have a preserved right (see p101) and the local authority has placed you in a residential care or nursing home that is more expensive than normal for a person of your needs because you preferred that home, a charitable or voluntary payment towards the *extra* cost will be ignored for IS;[220]

- for FC/DWA, they are intended, and used, for anything *except* food, ordinary clothing or footwear, household fuel, council tax, community charge (but not standard community charge) and any housing costs.

School uniform and sportswear are examples of clothing and footwear that is not ordinary.

If not ignored altogether, charitable or voluntary payments have a £10 disregard. This is subject to a maximum of £10 in all on any payments made in the same week as other income which attracts the £10 disregard.[221]

For IS, these rules do not apply where you are involved in a trade dispute, and for the first 15 days following your return to work after a trade dispute. For IS/FC/DWA/HB/CTB, payments from a former partner, or the parent of your child are dealt with as maintenance (see p378).

(See also, payments made to someone else on your behalf, p392, and payments disregarded under miscellaneous income, p389-91.)

Concessionary coal or cash in lieu

Coal that is provided free by British Coal to a former employee or her/his widow is ignored as income in kind (for IS, if you or your partner are involved in a trade dispute, see p79).[222] Cash in lieu of coal is not a voluntary payment[223] but counts in full as income, or as earnings if paid to a current employee.[224]

Income from tenants and lodgers

Lettings without board

If you let out room(s) in your home to tenants/sub-tenants/licensees, £4 of your weekly charge for each tenant is ignored, and an extra £8.60 for each tenant if the charge covers heating costs.[225] The balance counts as income.

Boarders

If you have a boarder(s) on a commercial basis in your own home, the first £20 and half of any balance of each boarder's weekly charge is ignored and half of any balance remaining is then taken into account as your income.[226] The charge must normally include at least some meals.[227]

If another member of your household makes payments to you which include something for meals, but *not* on a commercial basis, s/he is treated as a non-dependant rather than as a boarder (see pp38 and 242). Payments from non-dependants are ignored altogether.[228]

Tenants in other properties

If you have a freehold interest in another property which is subject to a lease or tenancy, any net income you receive from rents is treated as capital[229] (see Reversionary interests, p401).

Income from capital

Actual income generated from capital (eg, interest on savings) of £8,000 or less (£16,000 for DWA/HB/CTB) is ignored as income[230] but counts as *capital*[231] from the date you are due to receive it, except income derived from the following items of *disregarded* capital[232] (see p398):

- your home;
- your former home if you are estranged or divorced;
- property which you have acquired for occupation as your home but which you have not yet been able to move into;
- property which you intend to occupy as your home but which needs essential repairs or alterations;
- property occupied wholly or partly by a partner or relative of any member of your family who is 60 or over or incapacitated;
- property occupied by your former partner, but not if you are estranged or divorced – unless (for HB/CTB) s/he is a single parent;
- property up for sale;
- property which you are taking legal steps to obtain to occupy as your home;
- your business assets;
- a trust of personal injury compensation.

Except in the case of your current home, income up to the amount of the total mortgage repayments (capital and interest), council tax and water rates paid in respect of such property for the same period as you receive the income is ignored.[233]

Tariff income from capital over £3,000[234]

If your capital is over £3,000, you are treated as having an assumed income from it, called your **tariff income**. You are assumed to have an income of £1 for every £250, or part of £250, by which your capital exceeds £3,000 but does not exceed £8,000 (IS and FC) or £16,000 (DWA/HB/CTB). If your capital does exceed £8,000 (IS and FC) or £16,000 (DWA/HB/CTB), no benefit is payable at all (see p394).

The following is the full table for tariff income:

Capital	Tariff income
£3000.01 to £3250	£1
£3250.01 to £3500	£2
£3500.01 to £3750	£3
£3750.01 to £4000	£4
£4000.01 to £4250	£5
£4250.01 to £4500	£6
£4500.01 to £4750	£7
£4750.01 to £5000	£8
£5000.01 to £5250	£9
£5250.01 to £5500	£10
£5500.01 to £5750	£11
£5750.01 to £6000	£12
£6000.01 to £6250	£13
£6250.01 to £6500	£14
£6500.01 to £6750	£15
£6750.01 to £7000	£16
£7000.01 to £7250	£17
£7250.01 to £7500	£18
£7500.01 to £7750	£19
£7750.01 to £8000	£20

(Capital limit cut-off for IS and FC)

Capital	Tariff income
£8000.01 to £8250	£21
£8250.01 to £8500	£22
£8500.01 to £8750	£23
£8750.01 to £9000	£24
£9000.01 to £9250	£25
£9250.01 to £9500	£26
£9500.01 to £9750	£27
£9750.01 to £10000	£28
£10000.01 to £10250	£29
£10250.01 to £10500	£30
£10500.01 to £10750	£31
£10750.01 to £11000	£32
£11000.01 to £11250	£33
£11250.01 to £11500	£34
£11500.01 to £11750	£35
£11750.01 to £12000	£36
£12000.01 to £12250	£37
£12250.01 to £12500	£38
£12500.01 to £12750	£39
£12750.01 to £13000	£40

Capital	Tariff income
£13000.01 to £13250	£41
£13250.01 to £13500	£42
£13500.01 to £13750	£43
£13750.01 to £14000	£44
£14000.01 to £14250	£45
£14250.01 to £14500	£46
£14500.01 to £14750	£47
£14750.01 to £15000	£48
£15000.01 to £15250	£49
£15250.01 to £15500	£50
£15500.01 to £15750	£51
£15750.01 to £16000	£52

(Capital limit cut-off for DWA/HB/CTB)

If you are underpaid because of a change in your capital affecting your tariff income, you should ask for a review (see p149 for IS, p195 for FC, p207 for DWA, p286 for HB and p323 for CTB). If there is a change in your capital increasing the amount of your tariff income as a result of which you are overpaid, see pp161-7, 195 and 209 for IS/FC/DWA, and pp274-83 for HB and pp321-2 for CTB on recovery of overpayments.

Capital which counts as income

The following will count as income:

- Instalments of capital outstanding when you claim benefit if they would bring your capital over the limit (ie, £8,000 or £16,000 see p394). For IS, the instalments to be counted are any outstanding either when your benefit claim is decided, or when you are first due to be paid benefit, whichever is earlier, or at the date of any subsequent review.[235] For FC/DWA it is any instalments outstanding at the date of your claim.[236] For HB/CTB it is any instalments outstanding when your claim is made or treated as made, or when your benefit is reviewed.[237] Any balance over the capital limit will be counted as income, by spreading it over the number of weeks between each instalment.[238]

  For IS/FC/DWA/HB/CTB, if instalments are outstanding in this way on your child's capital, a similar rule applies. If the total of these instalments and your child's existing savings come to more than £3,000, the outstanding instalments will count as your child's income, and be spread over the period between each instalment.[239]

- Any payment from an annuity[240] (see below for when this is disregarded).

- For IS, a tax refund if you or your partner have returned to work after a trade dispute[241] (see pp77-81).
- For IS, a 'section 17' payment from a social services department or, in Scotland, a 'section 12' payment from a social work department (see pp490-91), or payments from social services to young people who have previously been in care or been looked after by them, if you or your partner are involved in or have returned to work after a trade dispute (see p77-81).[242]
- For HB/CTB, a local authority will sometimes treat withdrawals from a capital sum as income.[243] This is most likely where a sum was intended to help cover living expenses over a particular period – eg, a bank loan taken out by a mature student. If this is not the intended use of any capital sum, you should dispute the decision.

  Even where the sum is intended for living expenses, you should argue that unless it is actually paid in instalments it should be treated as capital.[244]

  Any payments of capital, or any irregular withdrawals from a capital sum, which are clearly for one-off items of expenditure and not regular living expenses, should be treated as capital. Further, whatever the intention behind the sum, if no withdrawals are in fact made, it should be treated as capital.[245]
- Some lump sums from liable relatives (see p141).

Capital which is counted as income cannot also be treated as producing a tariff income (see p385).[246]

Income tax refunds

PAYE income tax refunds are not payable to unemployed people receiving unemployment benefit or IS until the end of the tax year, or until they obtain a job, whichever comes first. Strikers can only get a tax refund on return to work. Other people who are not counted as unemployed (eg, the sick or retired), or who are not entitled to unemployment benefit or IS (eg, married women who pay a reduced 'stamp'), can still get tax refunds when they fall due.

- Tax refunds under schedule D (self-employed people) are treated as capital.[247]
- PAYE refunds are treated as capital.[248]
- For IS only, if you or your partner have returned to work after a trade dispute (see pp77-81), tax refunds will be treated as income and are taken into account in full.[249]

For treatment of income tax refunds on mortgage interest or loans for repairs and improvements, see below; and on covenant income in the case of students, see pp379-81.

Miscellaneous income

Count in full:

- An occupational pension (except any discretionary payment from a hardship fund).[250]
- Payments from an annuity. *Except* that in the case of 'home income plans', income from the annuity equal to the interest payable on the loan with which the annuity was bought is ignored if the following conditions are met:
  - you used at least 90 per cent of the loan made to you to buy the annuity; *and*
  - the annuity will end when you and your partner die; *and*
  - you or your partner are responsible for paying the interest on the loan; *and*
  - you, or both your partner and yourself, were at least 65 at the time the loan was made; *and*
  - the loan is secured on a property which you or your partner owns or has an interest in, and the property on which the loan is secured is your home, or that of your partner.

If the interest on the loan is payable after income tax has been deducted, it is an amount equal to the net interest payment that will be disregarded, otherwise it is the gross amount of the interest payment.[251]

The following are ignored:

- For IS only, payments you receive under a mortgage protection policy which you use to pay 50 per cent of the interest on your mortgage or loan for repairs and improvements to your home while the Benefits Agency is meeting only 50 per cent of your payments. Insurance payments which you use to repay the capital due on your mortgage or loan and the premiums on the policy are also ignored,[252] but not those intended to cover your other mortgage or loan interest.
- For IS only, and as long as you have not already used insurance payments for the same purpose, any money you receive which is given and used to pay:
  - 50 per cent of the interest on your mortgage, or loan for repairs and improvements while the Benefits Agency is only meeting part of the interest on such mortgage or loan;[253]
  - the capital repayments;[254]
  - any of your other eligible housing costs which are not being met by IS[255] (see pp37-42) – eg, your house is considered too expensive and

the Benefits Agency is not, therefore, paying the whole of your mortgage interest payments;
- any rent that is not covered by HB[256] (see pp225-38);
- the part of your accommodation charge that is above the maximum payable by IS if you live in a nursing home or residential care home and you are a person with preserved rights (see p101) or above that payable by a local authority.[257]
- For HB/CTB, payments you receive under a mortgage protection policy are ignored up to the level of your repayments.[258]
- Educational maintenance allowances[259] (see p485).
- Any payment to cover expenses if you are working as a volunteer – eg, for a charity or voluntary organisation.[260]
- Payments in kind (for IS, if you or your partner are involved in a trade dispute, see p79).[261]
- A job start allowance paid under the Employment and Training Act 1973 and a payment (other than a training allowance) to a disabled person under that Act or the Disabled Persons (Employment) Act 1944 to assist them to obtain or retain employment.[262]
- Any payments, other than for loss of earnings or of a benefit, made to jurors or witnesses for attending at court.[263]
- A 'section 17' payment from a social services department, or, in Scotland, a 'section 12' payment from a social work department (see p490-91), and payments from social services to young people who have been in care or been looked after by them.[264] For IS, such payments are not ignored if you or your partner are involved in or have returned to work after a trade dispute (see pp77-81).
- Any payment you receive from a health authority, local council or voluntary organisation for looking after a person temporarily in your care.[265]
- Victoria Cross or George Cross payments or similar awards.[266]
- Income paid outside the UK which cannot be transferred here.[267]
- If income is paid in another currency, any bank charges for converting the payment into sterling.[268]
- Fares to hospital.[269]
- Payments instead of milk tokens and vitamins.[270]
- Payments to assist prison visits.[271]
- For HB/CTB, if you make a parental contribution to a student's grant, an equal amount of any 'unearned' income you have for the period the grant is paid, is ignored.[272] If your 'unearned' income does not cover the contribution the balance can be disregarded from your earnings.[273]
If you are a parent of a student under 25 who does not get a grant (or who only gets a smaller discretionary award) and you contribute to her/his living expenses, the amount of your 'unearned' income that is

ignored is the amount equal to your contribution up to a maximum of £36.15 (less the weekly amount of any discretionary award the student has).[274] This is only ignored during the student's term. Again, any balance can be disregarded from your earnings.[275]

5. NOTIONAL INCOME

In certain circumstances you will be treated as having income although you do not possess it, or have used it up.

Deprivation of income in order to claim or increase benefit

If you deliberately get rid of income in order to claim or increase your benefit, you are treated as though you are still in receipt of the income.[276] The basic issues involved are the same as those for the deprivation of capital (see pp404-407).

Failing to apply for income[277]

If you fail to apply for income to which you are entitled without having to fulfil further conditions – eg, statutory sick pay – you will be deemed to have received it.

This does not include income from a discretionary trust or trust set up from money paid as a result of a personal injury. For IS only, one parent benefit, unemployment benefit (if you do not have to be available for work) FC and DWA are also exempted.

You will be treated as having such income from the date you could have obtained it.

DSS guidance for HB/CTB now says FC (and presumably other benefits as well) should only count as notional income if you have not applied for it, but would stand a good chance of getting it. If you have applied for FC/DWA but have not yet been paid, it does not count as notional income and should be ignored until you actually receive it.[278] Remember that arrears of IS/FC/DWA/HB/CTB are treated as capital and not income (see p403).[279]

Income due to you that has not been paid

This applies to IS only.[280] You will be treated as possessing any income owing to you. Examples could be wages legally due but not paid, or an occupational pension payment that is due but has not been received.

However, this does not apply where an occupational pension has not been paid, or fully paid, because the pension scheme has insufficient funds.[281] The rule also does not apply if any social security benefit has been delayed, or you are waiting for a late payment of a pension under the Job Release Scheme, a government training allowance or a benefit from a European Union country. Nor does it apply in the case of money due to you from a discretionary trust, or a trust set up from money paid as a result of a personal injury.

If this rule is applied, an urgent cases payment should be considered (see pp44-6).[282]

Unpaid wages

This applies to IS only: if you have wages due to you, but you do not yet know the exact amount or you have no proof of what they will be, you are treated as having a wage similar to that normally paid for that type of work in that area.[283] If your wages cannot be estimated you might qualify for an interim payment[284] (see p152).

Income payments made to someone else on your behalf [285]

If money is paid to someone on your behalf – eg, the landlord for your rent – this can count as notional income. The rules are the same as for notional capital (see p409). For IS, payments of income in kind are ignored, unless you or your partner are involved in a trade dispute (but even then they are ignored if they are from the Macfarlane Trusts, the Fund, the Eileen Trust or either of the Independent Living Funds, see pp494-6).[286]

Income payments paid to you for someone else[287]

If you or a member of your family get a payment for somebody not in the 'family' (see p328) – eg, a relative living with you – it will count as your income if you keep any of it yourself or spend it on your family. This does not apply if the payment is from the Macfarlane Trusts, the Fund, the Eileen Trust or either of the Independent Living Funds. Note that the same exception for payments in kind applies for IS as for income payments made to someone else on your behalf.

Cheap or unpaid labour

If you are helping another person or an organisation by doing work of a kind which would normally command a wage, or a higher wage, you are deemed to receive a wage similar to that normally paid for that kind of job in that area.[288] The burden of proving that the kind of work you do is something for which an employer would pay, and what the comparable wages are, lies with the adjudication officer.[289]

The rule does not apply if:

Either you can show that the person ('person' in this context includes a limited company[290]) cannot, in fact, afford to pay, or pay more;

or you are doing voluntary work and it is accepted that it is reasonable for you to give your services free of charge.[291]

If you are caring for a sick or disabled person it may be reasonable for them to pay you from their benefits, unless you can bring yourself within these exceptions.[292] It may, for example, be more reasonable for a close relative to provide services free of charge.[293]

Capital

In this chapter we cover:

I. INTRODUCTION

The capital limit

This chapter explains how capital affects your entitlement to means-tested benefits and what counts as capital for IS, FC, DWA, HB and CTB. If you get IS, you do not need to work out your capital again for HB/CTB purposes because you receive your maximum HB (see p240) or CTB (see p311),[1] less any deductions for non-dependants.

If you have over £8,000 (IS and FC)[2] or £16,000 (DWA, HB and CTB)[3] you are not entitled to benefit (but for CTB, see p313 for second adult rebate). Some capital is disregarded (see p398), but you may also be treated as having some capital which you do not actually possess (see p404). If you have up to £3,000 it is completely ignored and does not affect your weekly benefit at all.[4] If you have between £3,000.01 and £8,000 (IS and FC)/£16,000 (DWA, HB and CTB) you may be entitled to benefit but some income will be assumed[5] (see p386).

Whose capital counts

Your partner's capital is added to yours.[6] Your child's capital does not count as belonging to you,[7] but if it is over £3,000 you will not get benefit for that child[8] (although, for IS/HB/CTB, the lone parent and family premiums are still payable – see pp344 and 343), in which case any income of the child will not be counted as yours either.[9] However, maintenance paid to, or for, a child does count as yours.[10] The rules used to work out your child's capital are the same ones that apply to you.[11]

2. WHAT COUNTS AS CAPITAL

The term 'capital' is not defined. In general, it is used to apply to a lump sum or one-off payment rather than a series of payments.[12] It includes savings, property and lump-sum payments like redundancy payments.

A payment of capital can normally be distinguished from income because it is made without being tied to a period; it is not related to a past payment; and not intended to form part of a series of payments[13] (although capital can be paid by instalments).

However, some capital is treated as income (see pp387-8), and some income is treated as capital (see p397).

Savings

Your savings generally count as capital, and include, for instance, cash you have at home, premium bonds, stocks and shares, unit trusts, money in a bank account, building society and the like.

Your savings from past earnings can only be treated as capital when all relevant debts, including tax liabilities, have been deducted.[14] Savings from other past income (including social security benefits) will be treated as capital (see p403). There is no provision for disregarding money put aside to pay bills.[15] If you have savings just below the capital limit, it may be best to pay bills for gas, electricity, telephone etc by monthly standing order, or by use of a budget account to prevent your capital going above this limit.

Fixed-term investments

Capital held in fixed-term investments counts unless you can show that the money is unobtainable. If you can convert the investment into a realisable form or sell your interest, or even raise a loan through a reputable bank using the asset as security, its value counts. If it takes time to produce evidence about the nature and value of the investment, you may be able to get an interim payment for IS, FC, DWA or HB[16] (see pp152, 193, 207 and 267) or, if you would be without any money immediately, a crisis loan from the social fund (see p449).

Property and land

Any property or land which you own counts as capital and you are not entitled to benefit if it is worth more than £8,000 (IS and FC)/£16,000

(DWA/HB and CTB). Many types of property are disregarded (see p398). See also proprietary estoppel – p397.

Loans

A loan usually counts as money you possess. However, a loan granted on condition that you only use the interest but do not touch the capital should not be counted as part of your capital because the capital element has never been at your disposal.[17] Where you have been paid money to be used for a particular purpose (eg, a holiday in India) on condition that the money must be returned if not used in that way, it should not be treated as part of your capital.[18] Where you have bought a property on behalf of someone else who is paying the mortgage;[19] or where you are holding money in your bank account on behalf of another person which is to be returned to them at a future date,[20] the capital should not count as yours.

For HB/CTB some loans might be treated as income even though paid as a lump sum (see p388).

Trusts

A trust is a way of owning an asset. In theory, the asset is split into two notional parts: the legal title owned by the trustee, and the beneficial interest owned by the beneficiary. A trustee can never have use of the asset, only the responsibility of looking after it. An adult beneficiary, on the other hand, can ask for the asset at any time. Anything can be held on trust – eg, money, houses, shares etc.

If you are the adult beneficiary of:

- **a non-discretionary trust:** You can obtain the asset from the trustee at any time. You effectively own the asset, and so its market value will count as your capital;
- **a discretionary trust:** You cannot insist on receiving payments from the trust. Payments are at the discretion of the trustee within the terms of the trust. Any payments made will be treated in full as income or capital depending on the nature of the payment. The trust asset itself would not normally count as your capital because you cannot demand payment (of either capital or income);
- **a trust which gives you the right to receive payments in the future** (eg, on reaching 25): This is a right that has a present capital value (see p402), unless disregarded (see pp401-402).

If you have a life interest only in an asset, the value of your right to receive income is disregarded[21] (see p402).

If the beneficiary is under 18, even with a non-discretionary trust s/he has no right to payment until s/he is 18 (or later if that is what the trust stipulates). Her/his interest may nevertheless have a present value.[22]

If you hold an asset as a trustee, it is not part of your capital. You are only a trustee either if someone gives you an asset on the express condition that you hold it for someone else (or use it for their benefit), or if you have expressed the clearest intention that your own asset is for someone else's benefit, and renounced its use for yourself[23] (assets other than money may need to be transferred in a particular way to the trust).

It is not enough to only *intend* to give someone an asset. However, in the case of property and land, **proprietary estoppel** may apply. This means that if you lead someone to believe that you are transferring your interest in some property to them, but fail to do so (eg, it is never properly conveyed), and they act on the belief that they have ownership (eg, they improve or repair it, or take on a mortgage), it would then be unfair on them were they to lose out if you insisted that you were still the owner.[24] In this case, you can argue the capital asset has been transferred to them, and you are like a bare trustee. Thus you can insist that it is not your capital asset, but theirs, when claiming benefit.

If money (or another asset) is given to you to be used for a special purpose, it may be possible to argue that it should not count as your capital. This is called a **purpose trust**.[25]

Trust funds of personal injury compensation are always disregarded (see p402).

Income treated as capital

Certain payments which appear to be income are nevertheless treated as capital. These are:[26]

- an advance of earnings or loan from your employer;*
- holiday pay which is not payable until more than four weeks after your employment ends or is interrupted;*
- income tax refunds;*
- income from capital (eg, interest on a building society account) but not income from certain disregarded property, business assets and trusts of personal injury compensation (see p385);
- for IS/HB/CTB, a lump sum or 'bounty' paid to you not more than once a year as a part-time firefighter or part-time member of a lifeboat crew, or as an auxiliary coastguard or member of the Territorial Army – for FC/DWA this counts as earnings;[27]
- irregular (one-off) charitable payments;*
- for FC/DWA only, irregular maintenance payments (see p379);[28]
- for IS only, the part, or the whole, of a compensation payment for loss of employment that is treated as capital under the IS rules (see p369);

- for IS only, a discharge grant paid on release from prison;
- for IS only, arrears of residence order (in Scotland, custody) payments from a local authority (see p381).

*Except, for IS, in the case of people involved in, or returning to work after, a trade dispute (see pp77-81).

Any income treated as capital is disregarded as income.[29]

3. DISREGARDED CAPITAL

Your home

If you own the home you normally live in, its value is ignored altogether when calculating your benefit.[30] Your home includes any garage, garden and outbuildings together with any premises (including land) that you do not occupy as your home but which it is impractical or unreasonable to sell separately (eg, croft land).[31] If you own more than one property, only the value of the one normally occupied is disregarded under this rule.[32] A holiday home would not be disregarded, as it is not your normal home.[33]

The value of other property can be disregarded even if you do not live in it, in the following circumstances:

- **If you have left your former home following a marriage or relationship breakdown,** the value of the property is ignored for six months from the date you left. It is also disregarded for longer if any of the steps below are taken. For HB/CTB, if it is occupied by your former partner who is a single parent its value is ignored as long as s/he lives there.[34]
- **If you have sought legal advice or have started legal proceedings in order to occupy property** as your home, its value is ignored for six months from the date you first took either of these steps.[35] The six months can be extended, if it is reasonable to do so, where you need longer to move into the property.
- **If you are taking reasonable steps to dispose of any property,** its value is ignored for six months from the date you first took such steps.[36] Putting the property in the hands of an estate agent or getting in touch with a prospective purchaser should constitute 'reasonable steps'.[37] If you need longer to dispose of the property, the disregard can continue if it is reasonable – eg, where a husband or wife attempts to realise their share in a former matrimonial home but the court orders that it should not be sold until the youngest child reaches a certain age.[38]
- **If you are carrying out essential repairs or alterations** which are needed so that you can occupy a property as your home (eg, the instal-lation of a bathroom on the ground floor for a person unable to climb stairs), for IS/FC/DWA/HB, the value of the property is ignored for six

months from the date you first began to carry them out.[39] If you cannot finish the work and move into the property within that period, its value can be disregarded for as long as is reasonable. For CTB, the value of the property is ignored for as long as is necessary for the work to be carried out.[40]

- **If you sell your home** and intend to use the proceeds of sale to buy another home, the capital is ignored for six months from the date of the sale.[41] If you need longer to complete a purchase, the authorities can continue to ignore the capital if it is reasonable to do so. You do not have to have decided within the six months to buy a *particular* property. It is sufficient if you intend to use the proceeds to buy *some* other home. If you do, you are entitled to a disregard of at least six months (and possibly longer).[42] If you intend to use only part of the proceeds of sale to buy another home, only that part is disregarded even if, for example, you have put the rest of the money aside to renovate your new home.[43] If you sell up and move to rented property with no intention of purchasing another home, all the capital from the sale of your former home is taken into account.

- **If you have acquired a house or flat for occupation** as your home but have not yet moved in, its value is ignored if you intend to live there within six months.[44] If you cannot move in by then the value of the property can be ignored for as long as seems reasonable.

- **If your home is damaged or you lose it altogether**, any payment, including compensation, which you intend to use for its repair, or for acquiring another home, is ignored for a period of six months, or longer if it is reasonable to do so.[45]

- **If you have taken out a loan or been given money for the express purpose of essential repairs and improvements** to your home, it is ignored for six months, or longer if it is reasonable to do so.[46] If it is a condition of the loan that the loan must be returned if the improvements are not carried out, you should argue that it should be ignored altogether.[47]

- **If you have deposited money with a housing association as a condition of occupying your home**, this is ignored indefinitely.[48] If money which was deposited for this purpose is now to be used to buy another home, this is ignored for six months, or longer if reasonable, in order to allow you to complete the purchase.[49]

- **Grants made to local authority tenants to buy a home or do repairs/ alterations** to it can be ignored for up to 26 weeks, or longer if reasonable, to allow completion.[50]

When considering whether to increase the period of any disregard, all the relevant circumstances must be considered – particularly your and your family's personal circumstances, any efforts made by you to use or dispose of the asset (if relevant) and the general state of the market (if relevant).[51]

It is possible for property to be ignored under more than one of the above paragraphs in succession.

Some income generated from property which is disregarded is ignored (see p385).

The home of a partner or relative

The value of a house will also be ignored if it is occupied wholly or partly as their home by:[52]

- *either* 'your partner'[53] – ie, your husband/wife, provided you are both still treated as living in the same household (see p328), or your cohabitee, provided you are still treated as living together as husband and wife (see p330);
  or   a relative of yours, or any member of your family;
  who in either case, is aged 60 or over or is incapacitated;
- your former partner from whom you are not estranged or divorced. This means your husband/wife where you are not still treated as living in the same household or your former cohabitee where you are not still treated as living together as husband and wife (in each case provided you are not estranged);
- for HB/CTB only, your former partner from whom you are estranged or divorced if s/he is a lone parent.[54]

A person should be accepted as 'incapacitated' if s/he is in receipt of a sickness or disability benefit, or if s/he is sufficiently incapacitated to qualify for one of those benefits.[55] For FC/DWA, the relative must have been incapacitated throughout the 13 weeks before you claim.[56] Relative includes: a parent, son, daughter, step-parent/son/daughter, or parent/son/daughter-in-law; brother or sister; or a partner of any of these people; or a grandparent or grandchild, uncle, aunt, nephew or niece.[57] It also includes half-brothers and sisters and adopted children.[58]

Note: Even where the value of the home cannot be disregarded – eg, because a partner or relative is not 60 or over or incapacitated, the value of your interest in any property may still be significantly diminished (see pp410-13). This will be particularly relevant where, for example, one partner has to go into residential care (see pp97-113) or following the breakdown of a relationship (see p412).

Personal possessions

All personal possessions, including items such as jewellery, furniture, or a car, are ignored unless you have bought them in order to be able to claim or get more benefit[59] (in which case the sale value, rather than the purchase price is counted as actual capital, and the difference is treated as notional capital[60] – see pp404-10).

Compensation for damage to, or the loss of, any personal possessions, which is to be used for their repair or replacement is ignored for six months, or longer if reasonable.[61]

Business assets

If you are self-employed, your business assets are ignored for as long as you continue to work in that business. For IS/FC/DWA, as little as half an hour's work a week is sufficient.[62] If you cannot work because of physical or mental illness, but intend to work in the business when you are able, the disregard operates for 26 weeks, or for longer if reasonable in the circumstances.[63] If you stop working in the business, you are allowed a reasonable time to sell these assets without their value affecting your benefit. For FC/DWA, if you have sold a business asset but intend to reinvest the proceeds in that business within 13 weeks (or longer if reasonable) the money is ignored.[64] It will sometimes be difficult to distinguish between personal and business assets. The test is whether the assets are 'part of the fund employed and risked in the business'.[65] Note that a house will not be disregarded as a business asset simply because it has been let to tenants[66] (but see Reversionary interests below).

Tax rebates

Tax rebates for the tax relief on interest on a mortgage or loan obtained for buying your home or carrying out repairs or improvements are ignored.[67]

Insurance policies and annuities

The surrender value of any life assurance or endowment policy is ignored.[68] So also is the surrender value of any annuity.[69] Any payment under the annuity counts as income[70] (but see p387 for when this is disregarded).

Reversionary interests

A reversionary interest – which is an interest in property that will only revert to you, or become yours for the first time, when some event occurs – is ignored.[71] An example of a reversionary interest is where someone else has a life interest in a fund and you are only entitled after that person has died.

It will also include an interest in a home that has been let to tenants.[72]

Note that the value of the right to receive future payments of rent is also disregarded (see below) and the net income of any rents will be treated as capital[73] (see p397).

Trust funds from personal injury compensation

Where a trust fund has been set up out of money paid because of a personal injury to you, your partner or a child, the value of the trust fund is ignored.[74]

In this context, 'personal injury' includes not only accidental and criminal injuries, but also any disease and injury suffered as a result of a disease. Thus a trust fund for a child who had both legs amputated following meningitis and septicaemia could be disregarded for the purposes of the parent's claim.[75]

Any payments actually made to you from these trusts may count in full as income or capital depending on the nature of the payment.[76] However, trustees may have a discretion to use such funds to purchase items that would normally be disregarded as capital such as personal possessions (see p400) – eg, a wheelchair, car, new furniture – or to arrange payments that would normally be disregarded as income – eg, for IS/HB/CTB, ineligible housing costs – or, for example, to clear debts or pay for a holiday, leisure items or educational or medical needs. See p382 for the treatment of voluntary payments and pp392 and 404 for the treatment of payments made to third parties. Note that the notional income and capital rules (see pp391 and 409) cannot apply to personal injury trusts while the money remains there.

If there is no trust, the whole of the compensation payment counts as capital even if the money is held by your solicitor.[77]

The right to receive a payment in the future

If you know you will receive a payment in the future from, say, a trust fund or a pension scheme, you could sell that future right at any time so it has a market value and thus constitutes an actual capital resource. The regulations provide that the value of this will be disregarded where it is a right to receive:

- income under a life interest or, in Scotland, a liferent.[78] When the income is actually paid, it will count in full (see p396);
- any earnings or income which are ignored because they are frozen abroad[79] (see pp364 and 390);
- any outstanding instalments where capital is being paid by instalments[80] (see p387);
- an occupational pension;[81]
- a personal pension;[82]
- any rent;[83]

- any payment under an annuity (see p389);[84]
- any payment under a trust fund that is disregarded[85] (see p402).

Benefits and other payments

Arrears of certain benefits are ignored for 52 weeks after they are paid.[86] These are mobility allowance, attendance allowance (or an equivalent benefit paid because of a war or work injury), mobility supplement, disability living allowance, DWA, IS, supplementary benefit, FC, family income supplement, HB/CTB, or concessionary payments made instead of any of these, certain war widows' payments,[87] and refunds on community charge and council tax liability.[88]

Compensation for loss of housing benefit supplement, IS or HB at the changeover to IS in April 1988 will be completely ignored, as will community charge benefit (CCB) and HB for CTB, and CTB and CCB for HB.[89]

The following payments are ignored for 52 weeks from receipt:

- Fares to hospital.[90]
- Payments in place of milk tokens or vitamins.[91]
- Payments to assist prison visits.[92]

Social fund payments are also ignored indefinitely.[93]

A payment to a disabled person under the Disabled Persons (Employment) Act 1944 or the Employment and Training Act 1973 (other than a training allowance or training bonus) to assist with employment, or a local authority payment to assist blind homeworkers will be ignored.[94]

Payments by social services

A 'section 17' payment from a social services department or, in Scotland, a 'section 12' payment from a social work department (see p490), is ignored. Payments made by local authorities to young people who have previously been in care or been looked after by social services are also ignored. But if you or your partner are involved in a trade dispute or it is paid during the first 15 days following your return to work after the dispute, it counts as income for IS.[95]

Charitable payments

Any payment in kind by a charity is ignored.[96] All payments from the Macfarlane Trusts, the Fund, the Eileen Trust and either of the Independent Living Funds (see p493) are ignored.[97] Payments from the Macfarlane Trusts, the Fund or the Eileen Trust do not have to be declared for HB/CTB at all, or to the Benefits Agency, if they are kept separately from the claimant's other capital and income.[98] Certain payments from money that originally came from any of the three Macfarlane Trusts, the Fund or the Eileen Trust are also ignored – the rules are the same as for income (see p382).

Payments to jurors and witnesses

Any payments made to jurors or witnesses for attending at court are ignored, except for payments for loss of earnings or of benefit.[99]

Training bonus

A training bonus of up to £200 is disregarded,[100] but only for a year for HB/CTB, FC and DWA. For IS only, this disregard does not apply to trainees in Scotland.

Payments in other currencies

Any payment in a currency other than sterling is only taken into account after disregarding banking charges or commission payable on conversion to sterling.[101]

Capital treated as income

Some payments which appear to be capital are treated as income. These are:

- certain instalments of capital which you are owed;
- payments from annuities;
- for strikers, tax refunds or certain local authority payments;
- some lump sums from liable relatives (see p141);
- for HB/CTB certain lump-sum loans may be treated as income.

See p387 for the detailed rules.

Any capital treated as income is disregarded as capital.[102]

4. NOTIONAL CAPITAL

In certain circumstances, you are treated as having capital which you do not, in fact, possess. This is called 'notional capital' and it counts in the same way as capital you actually possess.[103] There is a similar rule for notional income (see p391).

Deprivation of capital in order to claim or increase benefit

If you deliberately get rid of capital in order to claim or increase your benefit, you are treated as still possessing it.[104] You are likely to be affected by this rule if, at the time of using up your money, you know that you may qualify for benefit as a result, or qualify more quickly. It should not be used if you know nothing about the effect of using up your capital (eg, you do not know about the capital limit for claiming benefit),[105] or if you have been using up your capital at a rate which is reasonable in the circumstances. Knowledge of capital limits can be inferred from a reasonable familiarity with the benefit system as a claimant,[106] but if you fail to make enquiries about the capital limit, this does not constitute an intention to secure benefit. This is because you cannot form the required intention if you do not know about the capital rules.[107] Even if you do know about the capital limits (see p394), it still has to be shown that you intended to obtain, retain or increase your benefit.[108] For example, where a claimant, facing repossession of his home, transferred ownership to his daughter (who, he feared, would otherwise be made homeless), in spite of having been warned by Benefits Agency staff that he would be disqualified from benefit if he did so, it was held that, under the circumstances, he could not be said to have disposed of the property with the intention of gaining benefit.[109] The longer the period that has elapsed since the disposal of the capital, the less likely it will be that it was for the purpose of obtaining benefit.[110]

A person who uses up her/his resources may have more than one motive for doing so. Even where qualifying for benefit as a result is only a subsidiary motive for actions, and the predominant motive is something quite different (eg, ensuring your home is in good condition by spending capital to do necessary repairs and improvements) you are still counted as having deprived yourself of a resource in order to gain benefit.[111] Local authorities tend to apply this test less stringently in the case of HB and CTB. Examples of the kinds of expenditure that could be caught by the rule are an expensive holiday and putting money in trust.[112] (For IS/FC/DWA, putting money in trust for yourself does not constitute deprivation if the capital being put in trust came from compensation paid for any personal injury.[113]) But the essential test is not the kind of item that the money has been spent on but the *intention* behind the expenditure.

In practice, arguing successfully that you have not deprived yourself of capital to get or increase benefit may boil down to whether you can show that you would have spent the money in the way you did (eg, to pay off debts or reduce your mortgage), regardless of the effect on your benefit entitlement. Where this is unclear, the burden of proving that you did it in order to get benefit lies with the Benefits Agency (IS, FC and DWA) or local authority (HB/CTB). In one case a man lost over £60,000 speculating on the stock market. Due to his wife's serious illness which affected his own health and judgement, he did not act to avoid losses when the stock market crashed. It was held that the adjudication officer had not discharged the burden of proving that this had been done for the purpose of obtaining IS.[114]

For IS, FC and DWA, you can only be treated as having notional capital under this rule if the capital of which you have deprived yourself is *actual* capital.[115] So if you are counted as owning half a joint bank account under the rule about jointly held capital (see p411), but your real share is only a quarter, you are not caught by the deprivation rule if the other quarter is disposed of; and if the whole of your deemed half share is disposed of, you can only be held to have deprived yourself of the value of the actual quarter share. This is not spelt out in HB/CTB law, but you should try arguing that the same principle applies. Note that where a disposal of capital is not effective (eg, where a disposal between the serving of a bankruptcy notice and the appointment of a trustee in bankruptcy may be declared void) the actual capital rules, rather than the notional capital rules, will still apply.[116]

If you are treated as possessing notional capital, it is calculated in the same way as if it were actual capital[117] and the same disregards apply. Suppose it is decided that by giving your former home to your children you have deprived yourself of it. If the house is then put up for sale by your children, its value will be ignored for six months, or longer if reasonable (see p398), in calculating your notional capital.[118]

Other points on deprivation of capital

* Any deprivation must be found to have been for the purposes of claiming or increasing your entitlement to *that* benefit.

  It has been held[119] that a deprivation for the purposes of obtaining supplementary benefit could not be said to have been deprivation for the purposes of obtaining IS. This is because IS did not even exist at that time. It could also, therefore, be argued that there could have been no deprivation for the purposes of obtaining FC prior to April 1988, DWA prior to April 1992, and CTB prior to April 1993, as those benefits did not come into existence until those dates.

  And where an intentional deprivation has been found for the purposes of obtaining IS, for example, it does not necessarily follow that there has also been any intention to gain HB/CTB. Where your circumstances change – eg, you start work and claim FC – any finding of intentional deprivation for IS will not necessarily be relevant to your claim for FC.

* Each adjudicating authority must reach their own decision on each benefit. Even decisions on deprivation for HB must be made independently of decisions for CTB.[120] This may result in different conclusions being drawn on any disposal for each benefit. And even where intent is

found in two different benefits, there may be different views about the amount of benefit that has been intentionally disposed of.[121]

However, where you are held to have deprived yourself of capital for the purposes of claiming HB/CTB, and you then submit a successful claim for IS, the notional capital rules for HB/CTB will be put in abeyance for as long as IS remains in payment.[122]

The diminishing notional capital rule

Since 1 October 1990, there has been a 'diminishing notional capital rule' which provides a calculation for working out how your notional capital may be treated as *spent*.[123] The rule starts to operate from the first week (or, for IS/CTB only, part-week) after the week in which it is first decided that the notional capital will be taken into account. The rule provides that:

- where your benefit has been refused altogether because of your notional capital, the amount of your notional capital will be reduced by the weekly aggregate of any of the following benefits (or the additional amounts of the benefits, unless it is IS) that you would have been entitled to but for the notional capital rule:
  - for IS   – IS/HB/CCB/CTB
  - for FC   – FC/HB/CCB/CTB
  - for DWA   – DWA/HB/CCB/CTB
  - for HB   – IS/FC/DWA/HB/CCB/CTB
  - for CTB   – IS/FC/DWA/HB/CTB

  In order to ensure that account is taken of as many other benefits as possible, it is important (where you are not already doing so) to make a claim for any of the other benefits (where appropriate) as soon as the notional capital rule has been applied. Any notice you are then given of any amounts of benefits you have 'lost' can then be supplied as evidence of the total weekly aggregate that should be taken into account;
- where your IS/FC/DWA/HB/CTB is reduced because of tariff income from your notional capital, that capital is diminished by the amount of that reduction each week (or part-week). For example, if your notional capital is £3,750, giving a tariff income of £3 a week, the reduction is £3 a week until it reaches £3,500 when it will be £2 and so on. Account should be taken of any anticipated reduction in your tariff income band during any 26-week assessment period;[124]

  For FC/DWA/HB/CTB, the amount of your notional capital will also be reduced by the weekly aggregate of the following benefits (or any additional amounts of these benefits, unless it is IS) which you would have been entitled to but for the notional capital rule:
  - for FC   – HB/CCB/CTB

    – for DWA   – HB/CCB/CTB
    – for HB   – IS/FC/DWA/CCB/CTB
    – for CTB   – IS/FC/DWA/HB;

- the reduction in your notional capital is calculated on a weekly basis. However, where your benefit has been stopped altogether because of the notional capital rule, the amount is fixed for a period of 26 weeks. Even if the amount you would have been entitled to increases during this period, there will be no change in the amount by which the capital is reduced (except for HB/CTB where guidance[125] states that if circumstances not related to capital – eg, you have married or a baby has been born – a new assessment can be made). The aggregate of your benefit entitlement can, however, be recalculated from the end of this 26-week period when you re-claim benefit, and will be increased if it is more than it was before, but it will stay the same as in the earlier assessment if it is unchanged or less. You do not have to re-claim at the end of every 26-week period but there can be no recalculation unless and until you do. However, you cannot renew a claim until at least 26 weeks (IS/HB/CTB), 22 weeks (FC) or 20 weeks (DWA) have passed since the last assessment. Once the amount of reduction has been recalculated in this way, it is again fixed for the same period. For IS, you should be issued with a forecast of when your notional capital will reduce to a point where a further claim might succeed,[126] but the onus will be on you to re-claim when it is to your advantage to do so[127] (ie, when you may qualify for an increased assessment, or because you have requalified for benefit). Timing will be important. If you delay you may lose out as new assessments cannot take effect before you re-claim. However, if you re-claim too soon you will have to wait until the fixed periods have lapsed before you can apply for a fresh determination;
- where you have both actual and notional capital, you may have to draw on your actual capital to meet your living expenses, which may include (and will probably exceed) amounts equivalent to benefits you have 'lost'. There is no reason why this should affect the amount by which your notional capital is diminished, even if this effectively results in double-counting. Any reduction in your actual capital should be taken into account in calculating any tariff income arising from your combined actual and notional capital, unless, of course, you have spent it at such a rate and in such a way that it raises questions of intent, when you may find that the notional capital rules are applied all over again.

Note, however, that it has been decided that these rules on how your capital was *spent* only apply from 1 October 1990. Instead, prior to that date, any reasonable living and other sensible expenditure was counted, which could be far more generous than the rules now are.[128] Any notional capital you have been held to possess until 30 September 1990 will be reduced under the earlier rules, and any notional capital carried forward to 1 October 1990 and onwards will be reduced under the new rules.[129] Note that the new rules apply to deprivation of capital only; the earlier rules will still apply to other forms of notional capital.

For IS or FC, where the new and more restrictive rules have been applied to you for any period before 1 October 1990, you should consider submitting a late appeal (see p171) to take advantage of the more generous treatment. For HB, the position on how the rules should have applied in earlier periods is less clear, although you should argue that as the law was essentially the same, the more generous rules should apply.

Failing to apply for capital[130]

Examples of failure to apply could be where money is held in court which would be released on application or even an unclaimed premium bond win! It does not include capital from a discretionary trust or a trust set up from money paid as a result of a personal injury or a loan which you could only get if you gave your home or other disregarded capital (see pp398-404), as security. For IS, HB and CTB, you are only treated as having such capital from the date you could obtain it.

Capital payments made to a 'third party' on your behalf

If someone else pays an amount to a 'third party' – eg, the electricity board or building society – for you, this may count as your capital.[131] It counts if the payment is to cover your family's food, household fuel, council tax or ordinary clothing or footwear. (School uniforms and sports wear are not ordinary clothing;[132] nor are, for example, special shoes because of a disability.[133])

It also counts if it is to cover:

- **for IS, HB and CTB,** rent for which HB is payable (less any non-dependant deductions) or water charges;
- **for IS alone,** housing costs met by IS or a residential care or nursing home accommodation charge for a person with preserved rights (see p101) met by IS;
- **for FC/DWA,** any housing costs (or any outstanding community charge, but not any standard community charge).

If the payment is for other kinds of expenses – eg, children's school fees (see p358), a TV licence, accommodation charges above the IS limit, or (except for FC/DWA) mortgage capital repayments – it does not count.

Also remember that payments from the Macfarlane Trusts, the Fund, the Eileen Trust or either of the Independent Living Funds do not count, whatever they are for.

Payments made for the food etc, of any member of the family, count as the capital of the member of the family in respect of whom they are paid. Since a child's capital is not counted as belonging to the claimant, a payment to, for example, a clothes shop for your child, should count as the child's notional capital and not yours.

For IS, there are different rules if you could be liable to pay maintenance as a liable relative (see p135).

Capital payments paid to you for a 'third party'[134]

If you or a member of your family get a payment for someone not in your family – eg, a relative who does not have a bank account – it only counts as yours if it is kept or used by you. Payments from the Macfarlane Trusts, the Fund, the Eileen Trust or either of the Independent Living Funds do not count at all.

Companies run by sole traders or a few partners

This applies if, as a sole trader or a small partnership, you have registered your business as a limited company. The value of your shareholding is ignored but you *will* for IS/FC/DWA, *may* for HB/CTB, be treated as possessing a proportionate share of the capital of the company.[135] This does not apply while you are working for the company.[136] Even if you only work for the company for, say, half an hour a week, this will suffice.[137] DSS guidance for FC/DWA indicates that it is not necessary for the work to be paid.[138]

5. HOW CAPITAL IS VALUED

Market value

Apart from national savings certificates (see below), your capital is valued at its current market or surrender value.[139] This means the amount of money you could raise by selling it, raising a loan against it etc. The test is the price that would be paid by a willing buyer to a willing seller on a particular date.[140] So if an asset is difficult, or impossible, to realise, its market value should be very heavily discounted or even nil.[141]

In the case of a house, an estate agent's figure for a quick sale is a more appropriate valuation than the District Valuer's figure for a sale within three months.[142]

If you own part of an asset (eg, half of a house), it is your interest in the property that has to be valued, as this may be quite different from (and a lot less than) your proportionate share of the overall value.[143]

Appeal if you disagree with the valuation of your capital (see p170).

Debts

Deductions are made from the 'gross' value of your capital for any debt or mortgage secured on it.[144] If a creditor, (eg, a bank) holds the land certificate to your property as security for a loan and has registered notice of deposit of the land certificate at the Land Registry, this counts as a debt secured on your property.[145] Where a single mortgage is secured on a house and land and the value of the house is disregarded for benefit purposes, the whole of the mortgage can be deducted when calculating the value of the land.[146]

If you have debts which are not secured against your capital (eg, tax liabilities), these cannot be offset against the value of your capital.[147] However, once you have paid off your debts, your capital may well be reduced. You can be penalised if you deliberately get rid of capital in order to get benefit (see p404), but that should not happen if you are paying off genuine debts.[148]

Expenses of sale

If there would be expenses involved in selling your capital, 10 per cent is deducted from its value for the cost of sale.[149]

National savings

For IS, a certificate bought from an issue which ceased before the 1 July before your claim is decided, or your benefit is first payable (whichever is earlier), or the date of any subsequent review, has the value it would have had on that 1 July if purchased on the last day of the issue. For FC/DWA, it is the 1 July before the date of your claim; for HB/CTB, it is the 1 July before your claim is made or treated as made or when your benefit is reviewed. In any other case, the value is the purchase price.[150] DSS guidance contains a convenient valuation table for each issue.[151]

Capital that is jointly owned with someone other than your partner

This is treated as being shared equally between you regardless of your actual shares.[152] For example, if you own 70 per cent of an asset, and your brother 30 per cent, each of you are treated as having a 50 per cent share. The value of the remaining 20 per cent that you actually own does not count as your capital. Similarly, if you actually own only 10 per cent of an asset and one other person owns the other 90 per cent, you are nevertheless treated as owning a 50 per cent share.

However, it is only your deemed share looked at in isolation that is to be valued, which may well be considerably less than half the value of the whole property. If the asset is, for example, a house, the market value of any share may even be nil, particularly where it is occupied and the other owner(s) are unwilling to sell their share(s) and there is a possibility that the sale of the property cannot be forced.[153] However, the decisions of the commissioners which have recently restated this approach are currently being challenged in the Court of Appeal.[154]

If you are caught by this rule you should consider, where possible, selling your share as, once sold, only the proceeds of your actual share can be treated as capital. In the meantime, you may be able to apply for a crisis loan from the social fund (see p449).

Treatment of assets following the breakdown of a relationship

When partners separate, assets such as their former home or a building society account may be in joint or sole names. For example, if a building society account is in joint names, under the rule about jointly owned capital, you and your former partner are treated as having a 50 per cent share each.[155] But if your former partner is claiming sole ownership of the account, DSS guidance says that your interest in the account should count as having a nil value until the question of ownership is settled.[156] The guidance deals only with a marriage breakdown, but there is no reason why the same should not apply if you were not married. If your former partner puts a stop on the account, in effect freezing it, the account should be disregarded until its ownership is resolved. As you do not have any access to that account, it should not count as yours.

On the other hand, a former partner may have a right to some or all of an asset that is in your sole name (for example, s/he may have deposited most of the money in a building society account in your name). It was held in one case concerning a married couple that, until the matrimonial proceedings were completed, the partner in whose name the account was should be treated as not entitled to the whole of the account but as holding part of it as trustee for her former partner.[157] In this situation the rule about jointly owned capital has the effect of treating you as owning half of the amount in the account.

In valuing a former home (or a share in it – see p411) following a marriage breakdown, account must be taken of any statutory rights of occupation of a former partner[158] (see also p398 for when this is disregarded).

Shares

Shares are valued at their current market value less 10 per cent for the cost of sale.[159] Fluctuations in price between routine reviews of your case are normally ignored. Where a claimant has a minority holding of shares in a company, the value of the shares should be based on what the claimant could realise on them, and not by valuing the entire share capital of the company and attributing to the claimant an amount calculated according to the proportion of shares held.[160]

Unit trusts

These are valued on the basis of the 'bid' price quoted in newspapers. No deduction is allowed for the cost of sale because, unlike shares, this is already included in the 'bid' price.[161]

The right to receive a payment in the future

The value of any such right that is not disregarded (see p402) is its market value: what a willing buyer will pay to a willing seller.[162] This may be very small.

Overseas assets

If you have assets abroad, and there are no exchange controls or other prohibitions that would prevent you transferring your capital to this country, your assets are valued at their current market or surrender value in that country.[163] If, as a result of this rule, there are problems and delays in getting benefit because it is difficult to get the assets valued, you may be able to get an interim payment of IS (see p152), FC (see p193) or DWA (see p207), or a 'payment on account' of HB/CTB (see p267).

If you are not allowed to transfer the full value of your capital to this country, you are treated as having capital equal to the amount that a willing buyer in this country would give for those assets.[164] It seems likely that the price such a person (if there is one) would be willing to pay may bear little relation to the actual value of the assets.

The same deductions for any debts or mortgage secured on the assets abroad are made together with 10 per cent if there are expenses of sale. If the capital is realised in a currency other than sterling, charges payable for converting the payment into sterling are also deducted.[165]

PART EIGHT

The regulated social fund

CHAPTER TWENTY

The regulated social fund

This chapter covers:

1. Maternity expenses payments (below)
2. Funeral expenses payments (p418)
3. Cold weather payments (p421)
4. Reviews and appeals (p422)

The social fund (SF) is a government fund which makes payments to people in need. There are two types of payments available from the social fund:

- **Discretionary grants and loans** to meet a variety of needs. These are covered in Part Nine – see p424.
- **Grants available by right** for maternity expenses, funeral expenses and periods of cold weather. Unlike the discretionary payments, you are *legally entitled* to these grants if you satisfy the eligibility conditions, which are laid down in regulations.

1. MATERNITY EXPENSES PAYMENTS

The basic rules[1]

You are entitled to a payment for help with maternity expenses if:

- you or a member of your family are expecting a child within the next 11 weeks or have recently given birth (or have adopted a child – see p417); *and*
- you or your partner have been awarded income support (IS), family credit (FC) or disability working allowance (DWA) at the date of your claim; *and*
- you do not have too much capital (see p417); *and*
- you claim within the time limits (see p418).

The words 'family' and 'partner' are defined as for IS purposes (see p328).

You cannot claim FC until your first child is born. Even if your FC claim has not been decided, you should claim a maternity expenses payment within the time limits (see below). You will be paid when your FC is awarded.

If you are under 19 and not able to claim IS, FC or DWA in your own right, an adult getting IS, FC or DWA can claim a maternity expenses payment for you if you count as a member of their family (see p328).

If you or your partner are involved in a trade dispute (see p77), and either one of you is getting IS, you will qualify for the payment if the dispute has been going on for six weeks or more at the date of claim. If either of you is getting FC or DWA, you will qualify for a payment if the claim for FC or DWA was made before the beginning of the dispute.[2]

The amount of the payment

The maternity expenses payment is £100 for each child.[3] If this is insufficient to meet your needs, you could apply to the discretionary social fund for the extra amount you need (see p432).

The £100 is reduced by the amount of any capital you have in excess of £500 (£1,000 if you or your partner is 60 or over).[4] Capital is calculated in the same way as for IS,[5] except that lump-sum widow's payment (£1,000 – see CPAG's *Rights Guide to Non-Means-Tested Benefits*) is ignored for 12 months from the date of your husband's death.[6] Capital belonging to you and your partner counts.

Stillbirths

You are entitled to a payment for a stillborn child if your pregnancy has lasted 24 weeks.[7]

Adopted babies

You are entitled to a payment for a baby adopted by you or your partner if the baby is no more than 12-months-old at the date of claim.[8] You will receive a payment even if one has already been made to the natural mother or a member of her family.[9]

Claiming and getting paid

You should claim on form SF100 which you can get from your local Benefits Agency. The date of claim is the date the form is received by the Benefits Agency. If you make a written claim in some other way, you should be sent the form to complete. If you return it within a month, the date of claim will be the date the Benefits Agency received your initial application.[10] The Benefits Agency can treat an initial claim by letter as sufficient and will then not ask you to complete a form as well.

You can claim at any time from the 11th week before your expected week of confinement (your 29th week of pregnancy) until three months after your actual date of confinement. If you adopt a baby, you can claim up to three months following the date of the adoption order. If you claim late, you will only be paid if you can show 'good cause' for not claiming in time (see p145). However, you cannot be paid if you claim more than 12 months after the date of confinement or adoption.[11]

If you claim before confinement, you will need to submit a maternity certificate (form MAT B1) or note from your doctor or midwife. If you claim after the child is born, you will usually be asked for a maternity, birth or adoption certificate.

The rules for getting paid and the recovery of overpayments are the same as for IS (see pp151 and 161).

2. FUNERAL EXPENSES PAYMENTS

The basic rules[12]

You are entitled to a funeral expenses payment if:

- you accept responsibility for the costs of the funeral (the Benefits Agency should accept you are responsible if you have obtained a funeral director's estimate or bill[13]) *and either*
  - you were the partner of the deceased; *or*
  - you or your partner were a close relative of the deceased and there were no other equally close or closer relatives who can reasonably be expected to pay for the funeral, taking into account their income, capital and contact with the deceased. (**Note:** At the time of writing it was unclear what enquiries the Benefits Agency intend to make to obtain this information. In some families, for religious or cultural reasons, a specific member of the family may be expected to take responsibility for the funeral. The Benefits Agency should take this into account when deciding whether to award a payment); *or*
  - neither of the above applies but it is reasonable for you to accept responsibility for the funeral costs, given your or your partner's acquaintanceship with the deceased.

    The words partner and 'close relative' are defined as for IS purposes (see p328 and 354); *and*
- the funeral (ie, burial or cremation) takes place in the UK (this restriction is currently being challenged under the Race Relations Act); *and*

- you or your partner have been awarded IS, FC, DWA, housing benefit (HB) or council tax benefit (CTB) (either main or second adult rebate – see p296) at the date of your claim (if you have claimed any of these benefits but not received a decision, you should still claim a funeral payment within the time limits – see p420); *and*
- you do not have too much capital (see p420); *and*
- you claim within the time limits (see p420).

Involvement in a trade dispute has no effect on a claim.

The amount of the payment

The payment is calculated by first adding up the reasonable costs of the following items:[14]

- any necessary documentation (eg, death and cremation certificates);
- an ordinary coffin and, in the case of cremation, an ordinary urn;
- transport for the coffin and bearers, and one additional car;
- the reasonable cost of flowers from you;
- undertaker's fees and gratuities for a simple funeral;
- chaplain's, organist's and cemetery or crematorium fees for a simple funeral;
- any additional expenses other than the above arising from the religious faith of the deceased but not in excess of £75;[15]
- where the death occurred away from the deceased's home (ie, where s/he normally lived prior to death[16]), the costs of transporting the body within the UK to that home, or to the undertaker's premises or a chapel of rest;
- your reasonable travelling costs of one return journey within the UK in connection with the arrangement of, or attendance at, the funeral. Others, who are relatives of the deceased, may be eligible for a community care grant for travelling costs (see p444).

Expenses other than the above could be met by a payment from the discretionary social fund (see p432).

The following amounts are then deducted to arrive at the amount payable:[17]

- the value of the deceased person's assets which are or will be available to you without a grant of probate or letters of administration (the assets which existed at the time of death can count even if you have used them for other purposes[18]);
- any payment legally due to you, or a member of your family, from an insurance policy, occupational pension scheme, burial club or similar source on the death of the deceased;

- any contribution from a charity or a relative of your family (see p328) or the deceased's family, after offsetting any funeral expenses other than those specified above;
- a funeral grant paid by the government to a war disablement pensioner.

The funeral expenses payment is also reduced by the amount of any capital you have in excess of £500 (£1,000 if you or your partner is 60 or over).[19] Capital is calculated in the same way as for IS[20] except that the lump-sum widow's payment (£1,000) is ignored for 12 months from the date of your husband's death.[21] Capital belonging to you and your partner counts.

Any money you have been given or borrowed on the express condition that it be used to meet the costs of the funeral does not count as your capital.[22] However, if you have used any of your own capital (apart from disregarded capital) to pay for the funeral you are treated as though you still possessed it.[23]

Claiming and getting paid

You should claim on form SF200 which you can get from your local Benefits Agency. Send the funeral director's bill or estimate, made out to you, with the application. If possible, get the bill or estimate broken down with the cost of each component listed on p419. The date of claim is the date the form is received by the Benefits Agency. If you make a written claim in some other way, you should be sent the form to complete. If you return it within a month, the date of claim will be the date the Benefits Agency received your first claim.[24] The Benefits Agency can treat an initial claim by letter as sufficient and will then not ask you to complete a form as well.

You must claim within three months of the funeral. If you claim late you will only be paid if you can show 'good cause' for not claiming in time (see p145). You cannot be paid, however, if you claim more than 12 months after the funeral.[25]

The Benefits Agency can pay the funeral expenses payment direct to the funeral director, if the bill has not been paid.[26] Other than this, the rules for getting paid and the recovery of overpayments are the same as for IS (see pp151 and 161).

Recovery from the deceased's estate

The Secretary of State is entitled to recover funeral expenses payments from the deceased's estate and will normally seek to do so.[27] Funeral expenses are legally a first charge on the estate although there may, of course, be insufficient assets to meet full repayment.[28] Personal possessions left to relatives and the value of a house occupied by a surviving partner should not count as the deceased's estate.

3. COLD WEATHER PAYMENTS

The basic rules

You are entitled to a cold weather payment if:
- a 'period of cold weather' has been forecasted or recorded for the area in which your normal home is situated (see below);[29] *and*
- you have been awarded IS for at least one day during the period of cold weather; *and*
- *either*   your IS includes one or more of the following premiums: pensioner; disability; higher pensioner; severe disability; disabled child (see p342);
- *or*   you have a child under five.[30]

Note: *The amount of capital you have does not affect the payment.*

A 'period of cold weather'

This is a period of seven consecutive days during which the average of the mean daily temperature forecasted or recorded for that period is equal to or below 0° Celsius. The 'mean daily temperature' is the average of the maximum and minimum temperatures recorded for that day.[31] The regulations divide the country into 63 areas, each covered by a weather station at which temperatures are forecasted or recorded.[32] The area your home is in is determined by your postcode.

The amount of the payment

The sum of £7 is paid for each week of cold weather.[33]

Claiming and getting paid

You do *not* need to make a claim for a cold weather payment. The Benefits Agency should automatically send you a giro if you qualify.[34] Your district Benefits Agency should publicise when there are periods of cold weather in your area by placing advertisements in local newspapers, by radio broadcasts, and by distributing posters and leaflets – eg, to doctors' surgeries and local advice centres.[35] If you do not receive a giro and you think you are entitled, contact your local Benefits Agency. If you do not receive a payment or are told you are not entitled, submit a written claim and ask for a written decision. You can then appeal against an unfavourable decision.[36]

The rules for getting paid and the recovery of overpayments are the same as for IS.

4. REVIEWS AND APPEALS

The rules relating to reviews and appeals are the same as for IS – see pp149 and 170. Decisions are made by adjudication officers and you can appeal against the refusal of a payment (see above).

PART NINE

The discretionary social fund

CHAPTER TWENTY-ONE

General principles

Reviewle:

This chapter covers:

1. INTRODUCTION

In addition to the grants available by right for maternity expenses, funeral expenses and periods of cold weather described in Part Eight, the social fund (SF) also provides **discretionary grants and loans** to meet a variety of other needs. This part of the SF is very different in character to all other social security provision:

- It is strictly **budget-limited**. Each district office of the Benefits Agency is given an annual budget which it must not exceed.
- Payments are **discretionary**. There is no legal entitlement to a payment. The rules are only concerned with eligibility and how discretion is to be exercised.
- Many payments are in the form of **loans**. These have to be repaid to the Benefits Agency, usually by deductions from weekly benefit.
- Decisions are made by **social fund officers** (SFOs).
- There is **no right of appeal** to an independent tribunal. Instead there is a system of **review by SFOs** and further review by quasi-independent **social fund inspectors** (SFIs).

Despite the unpopularity and inherent problems of the discretionary SF, its wide remit makes it an important and valuable source of help and you should *always apply* if you have a need which can be met by the fund.

2. THE LAW AND THE GUIDANCE

The law

Primary legislation

The SF exists by Act of Parliament.[1] The Act empowers SFOs to make payments from the fund. In deciding whether to make a discretionary payment, the Act requires SFOs to take into account all the circumstances of each case and, in particular:[2]

- the nature, extent and urgency of the need;
- the existence of resources which could meet the need;
- whether any other person or body could meet the need;
- whether a loan is likely to be repaid;
- the amount of the Benefits Agency district office budget (see p426);
- SF directions and guidance (see below).

The Act also empowers the Secretary of State to issue directions to SFOs which are legally binding.[3]

The directions

The directions establish three types of discretionary payment available from the SF:

- **community care grants** (CCGs) (see p434);
- **budgeting loans** (see p446);
- **crisis loans** (see p449).

The directions set out the eligibility conditions for each type of payment. They also exclude payments for certain expenses (see p430) and cover reviews (see p461).

The regulations[4]

These deal with procedures. They cover:

- applications for grants and loans;
- applications for reviews;
- the acceptance and recovery of loans.

The Act, directions and regulations are included in *CPAG's Income Related Benefits: The Legislation* (see Appendix 3).

The guidance

National guidance

The Secretary of State issues guidance on how to interpret the directions and administer the SF. The guidance and directions are published in the *Social Fund Guide* and *Social Fund Administration Guide* (see Appendix 3). The guidance suggests the circumstances in which a payment should be made, for what items and services and which applications should be given priority.

SFOs must take account of the guidance,[5] but it is *not* legally binding. The guidance repeatedly reminds SFOs that they must exercise discretion according to the individual circumstances of each case.[6]

Local guidance

In addition to the national guidance, SFOs must also take account of local guidance issued by SF managers in Benefits Agency district offices.[7] Copies of this guidance should be available from your local office. It suggests which groups of clients and which needs should normally be regarded as priority for awards. The local guidance must not conflict with the principles laid down in the directions and the national guidance.[8]

It must also not impinge on the duty of SFOs to exercise individual discretion. In particular, local guidance which lists client groups in a rigid order of priority or suggests that certain groups or needs should always be accorded low priority or never be considered for a grant, is likely to be unlawful.

Local guidance tends to be the major determinant of decision-making by SFOs (see p427).

Social fund inspectors' decisions

SFI decisions (see p465) can be useful guidance because they indicate how discretion should be exercised by SFOs. However, they apply only to the case under review and do not create precedents.

SFIs have consistently criticised SFOs for failing to exercise their discretion properly and, in particular, for making decisions based rigidly on local guidance about priority groups. They have also questioned the legality of local guidance which is unduly restrictive.

SFIs have also stressed that most of the terms in the directions and guidance are not defined. Where terms are not given special definitions, SFIs have said they should be given their normal everyday meaning.

3. THE BUDGET AND PRIORITIES

Budget allocations

The government sets the total budget for the discretionary SF each year.

Each Benefits Agency district office is then allocated a fixed sum for grants and another for loans.[9] The amount allocated to each district is based on their previous levels of expenditure, their refusals on priority grounds (see below), and their income support caseloads.[10]

The district SF manager is responsible for planning and monitoring expenditure on a monthly basis. Any under or overspend in a particular month should lead to a revision of planned monthly expenditure for the rest of the year.[11] However, there is no monthly limit on expenditure and it would be unlawful to refuse a payment solely because planned expenditure for a particular month had been exceeded.[12] SFOs are instructed not to postpone decisions until subsequent months on budgetary grounds – ie, not to establish 'a waiting list of needs'.[13] However, they are advised to postpone decisions on 'borderline applications' to 'assist better decision-making'.[14]

The only limit on district expenditure is the total budget allocated for the year. The directions prohibit SFOs from spending more than their annual district budget.[15] Nevertheless, it is possible for the Secretary of State to allocate additional funds to a district in the course of the year.[16] The guidance suggests this could apply in an emergency or disaster,[17] but there is nothing to stop a district manager asking for more funds if the budget is being overspent to meet genuine need (see p429 – Tactics).

SFOs must have regard to the budget when deciding whether to make a payment and how much to award.[18] However, the state of the budget is only one factor they must take into account when making decisions (see p428). Refusal of an application on budgetary grounds alone is unlawful, unless the budget is exhausted. Always ask for a review if an application is refused on budgetary grounds.

Details of national and district office budgets are publicly available, including planned and actual levels of monthly expenditure on the grants and loans budgets.

Priorities

The directions require SFOs to manage the budget so as to give priority to high-priority needs throughout the year.[19] There is no definition of what constitutes a high-priority need. SFOs must decide what priority to give each application by considering all the circumstances of the case concerned.

The *SF Guide* gives suggestions and examples of priority claimant groups and circumstances. These are referred to in the chapters which follow about CCGs and loans.

Local guidance also lists priority groups of clients and needs and indicates which levels of priority will usually be met at any particular time.

SFOs are told to try and meet a broadly similar level of need throughout the year.[20] SF managers must review their guidance on priorities at least once a month.[21]

The key point to remember is that the guidance about priorities is not legally binding. If an application is refused on the basis of insufficient priority, it can be <u>challenged by review (see p461)</u>.

4. HOW DECISIONS ARE MADE

The theory

The demands placed on SFOs when making decisions are onerous and, in some respects, contradictory.

- They must carefully consider all the circumstances of each case including the nature, extent and urgency of the need and use their discretion and judgement to decide whether to award a payment.
- They must follow the law and the directions (see p425).
- They must take account of the Secretary of State's guidance and their district manager's local guidance (see p426), but must not be rigidly bound by either.
- They must have regard to the budget (see p426).
- They must give priority to high-priority needs (see p427).
- They are expected to exercise discretion flexibly but consistently so that all applicants are treated fairly and equally.[22]
- They should ensure their decisions are not in any way affected by bias or prejudice on such grounds as the race, colour, religion, gender or sexual orientation of applicants.[23]
- They are encouraged to liaise with local social services departments and other welfare rights and voluntary bodies about general matters (such as priority groups) and about individual applications, subject to normal confidentiality rules.[24]

The practice

Not surprisingly, the practice rarely matches the theory. Many people would argue that there is a basic conflict between meeting need and having regard to the budget; or between exercising discretion flexibly and taking account of the guidance. Also, most SFOs have neither the training nor the time to achieve the standard of decision-making imposed by all the above requirements.

In practice, decisions are largely determined by local guidance on priority groups rather than the needs and circumstances of each applicant (see p428). Applications which do not fall within the priority categories which the guidance says the local budget can meet, tend to be automatically rejected.

The SF has been likened to a lottery by many critics because your chances of success can depend on when you apply (ie, the state of the budget at that time) and where you live (there is little consistency between local priority lists).

5. TACTICS

Despite the inherent problems of the SF, its wide remit makes it an important and valuable source of help. Perseverance is the key to getting a payment. The following general tactical points may help.

Applying for a payment

- Remember, you can apply as long as you meet the basic eligibility rules (see pp434, 446, 449). You can apply for help with anything other than excluded items (see p430). Do not be put off by what the Benefits Agency or their leaflets say.
- Always ask for a grant, rather than a loan, if you satisfy the conditions on p434.
- Tips on completing the application forms are on p459. Always give full details of your needs and circumstances, explaining how your application fits the eligibility rules and why it should be given high priority. Obtain a copy of the local guidance on priorities from your district office.

Challenging decisions

If you are unhappy about a decision, *always ask for a review and, if necessary, a further review by the SFI* (see p465). This could apply if you have been refused a payment, been given less than you asked for, or been offered a loan rather than a grant. Social fund officers' decisions are regularly flawed because they are based on local priority groups rather than the merits of each case. Social fund inspectors regularly overturn such decisions.

Getting the local budget increased

If applications are consistently being refused on budgetary grounds, it is important for individuals and groups to come together to pressurise the district SF manager to ask the government for more money. SF managers can, and should, ask for more money if they are unable to meet basic needs because of lack of funds. They may be reluctant to do so because of the stigma of 'bad management'. Nevertheless, a local campaign involving MPs, councillors, advice agencies and the local press could pressurise a manager to take action. Moreover, there is nothing to stop a local advice agency making an open application to the Benefits Agency to increase the budget if the district manager refuses to do so.

If additional funds are secured, the district office should reconsider all the applications refused on budgetary grounds earlier in the year (see p427).

6. EXCLUDED ITEMS

Help with the items listed below is excluded by the directions.[25] If you ask for help for an excluded item you will be refused.

The general list of exclusions

- A need which occurs outside the UK.
- An educational or training need, including clothing and tools.
- 'Distinctive' school uniform, sports clothes or equipment (see p484 for clothing grants from local education authorities).
- Travelling expenses to and from school (but see p485).
- School meals and meals taken during the holidays by children on IS (but see p484).
- Expenses in connection with court proceedings (including a community service order) – eg, legal fees, court fees, fines, costs, damages, travelling and other expenses.
- Removal charges where you are permanently rehoused following a compulsory purchase order, a redevelopment or closing order, or where there is a compulsory exchange of tenancies or you are permanently rehoused as homeless under the Housing Acts. (In all these circumstances your local authority *may* help you.)
- The cost of domestic assistance or respite care. Domestic assistance includes local authority home-helps. Respite care could include a short-term break in residential care.[26]
- Repairs to property owned by public sector housing bodies including Councils, most housing associations, housing co-operatives and housing trusts.[27]
- Medical, surgical, optical, aural or dental items or services. A medical item does not include an ordinary everyday item needed because of a

medical condition – eg, cotton sheets when a person is allergic to synthetics.[28] SFOs are told to find out if there is help available from the NHS.[29] Some medical items may be available under the NHS Act (see p496).

- Work-related expenses. The guidance says this includes fares when seeking work and the cost of work clothes.[30]
- Debts to government departments. These could include national insurance arrears, income tax liabilities and customs charges.[31]
- Investments.
- Community charges (including collective community charge contributions) and community water charges.
- Most housing costs, including major repairs, deposits to secure accommodation, mortgage payments, water rates, rent, service charges, hostel charges and board and lodging charges. You can get a *loan*, however, for rent in advance where the landlord is not a local authority (see p449); for hostel or board and lodging charges payable in advance (see p449); and for minor repairs.[32] The *SF Guide* also says that owner-occupiers can get a budgeting loan for essential repairs and maintenance[33] (see p447). It also says you can get a grant for minor structural repairs, maintenance costs, survey fees and internal redecoration and refurbishment for which you are responsible[34] (see p440). You can also get a grant for accommodation costs if you are visiting a child away from home[35] (see p444).

Additional items excluded from community care grants[36]

- Telephone costs, including installation, call and rental charges (see p491 if you are chronically sick or disabled and need a telephone).
- Any expenses which the local authority has a *statutory duty* to meet.
- The cost of *any* fuel and standing charges.

Additional item excluded from budgeting loans[37]

- The cost of 'mains' fuel and standing charges. This exclusion does not apply to help with liquid gas, paraffin and coal.

Additional items excluded from crisis loans[38]

- Telephone costs including installation, call and rental charges (see p491 if you are chronically sick or disabled and need a telephone).
- Mobility needs.
- Holidays.
- Television or radio, TV licence, aerial, TV rental.

- Garaging, parking, purchase and running costs of any motor vehicle – except where payment is being considered for emergency travel expenses.

Maternity and funeral expenses

The discretionary SF covers needs other than maternity and funeral expenses, which are catered for by the regulated SF (see p416).[39]

Payments for items such as clothes, a cot, a pram and bedding for a young child can be distinguished from 'maternity expenses' and are not excluded from the discretionary SF. Other needs, which cannot be met out of the £100 maternity expenses payment, could also be applied for.

Payments for ceremonies or religious services on death should not be excluded as they are not funeral (ie, burial or cremation) expenses.[40] Expenses which cannot be met by a funeral grant (see p418) are also not excluded. CCGs are available for travelling expenses to attend a relative's funeral[41] (see p444).

7. PEOPLE INVOLVED IN TRADE DISPUTES

There are special rules affecting people involved in trade disputes (see p77).

Community care grants

If you or your partner are involved in a trade dispute you are not eligible for a grant other than for travelling expenses to visit somebody who is ill and then only in the following circumstances.[42]

- **You are involved in a trade dispute and are visiting:**
  - your partner in hospital or a similar institution;
  - a dependant in hospital or similar institution, but only if you have no partner living with you who could get a grant, or your partner is also in hospital or a similar institution;
  - a close relative or member of your household who is critically ill (whether or not in hospital or a similar institution).
- **You are not involved in a trade dispute but you are the partner or dependant of somebody who is, and you are visiting:**
  - a close relative or member of your household who is a patient in a hospital or similar institution or who is critically ill (whether or not in hospital or a similar institution).

To get a CCG you must be receiving IS or would be but for the trade dispute.

You will normally be paid public transport fares (excluding air fares), the cost of petrol or taxi fares if necessary.[43] Overnight accommodation costs can be met if necessary.[44] You can get fares for an escort if you cannot travel alone, even if the escort is the person involved in the trade dispute. However, the guidance says that the person involved in the trade dispute should not normally get fares for an escort.[45]

Budgeting loans

You are not eligible for a budgeting loan if you or your partner are involved in a trade dispute.[46]

Crisis loans

If you or your partner are involved in a trade dispute, you are only entitled to a crisis loan for:[47]

- expenses arising from a disaster (see p451);
- the cost of items needed for cooking or space heating (including fire-guards). This could include cooking utensils as well as a cooker.

Applied for Crisis loan for bedding etc. Because of recognised medical problem

CHAPTER TWENTY-TWO

Community care grants

This chapter covers:

1. INTRODUCTION

Community care grants (CCGs) are intended to promote community care by helping people to move out of, or stay out of, institutional or residential care and by assisting families under exceptional pressure.

There is no legal entitlement to a CCG. Payments are discretionary. However, you can ask for a review if you are not paid what you ask for (see p461). CCGs are a particularly valuable source of help because, unlike loans, they do not have to be paid back.[1]

The basic rules

You must satisfy *all* the following rules in order to be considered for a CCG. The rules are laid down in directions issued by the Secretary of State, which are legally binding. None of the words used are defined in the directions but some have been legally defined in case law. Words like 'partner' and 'family' are not restricted to their income support (IS) meanings.

- You must be in receipt of IS when you apply for a CCG.[2] The only exception to this rule is if you are due to leave institutional or residential care (see p437) within six weeks of your application for a CCG and you are likely to get IS when you leave.[3]
- You must not have too much capital. Capital of £500 or less (£1,000 if you or your partner is 60 or over) has no effect. Any CCG awarded is

reduced by £1 for every £1 of capital you have in excess of these amounts.[4] Capital is calculated as for IS (see p394) except that any payments from the Family Fund (see p493) are disregarded.[5] Capital held by you and your partner count. Capital held by your children should be disregarded.[6]

- You or your partner must not be involved in a trade dispute unless your claim is for travelling expenses to visit a sick person (see p432).
- You cannot get a CCG for an excluded item (see p430).
- You must be awarded a CCG of at least £30 (unless you are applying for travelling expenses or living expenses for a prisoner on home leave – see p439).[7]
- You must need a CCG for one or more of the following purposes:[8]
  - to help you, or a member of your family, re-establish yourselves in the community following a stay in institutional or residential care (see p437);
  - to help you, or a member of your family, remain in the community rather than enter institutional or residential care (see p439);
  - to ease exceptional pressures on you and your family (see p441);
  - to allow you, or your partner, to care for a prisoner or young offender on home leave (see p439);
  - to help you, or one or more members of your family, with travel expenses within the UK in certain circumstances (see p443).

Although at least one of the above purposes must apply you may be able to argue that a CCG will help in more than one way – eg, it will help you to stay in the community *and* ease exceptional pressures on your family.

The guidance and priorities

Introduction

The Secretary of State issues guidance to SFOs to help them decide who should get a CCG. Guidance is also issued by district office managers about local priority groups. This is fully discussed on pp426-8.

The important point about the guidance is that it is *not legally binding*. SFOs are told to use their discretion flexibly, sensitively and imaginatively, avoiding a rigid interpretation of the guidance.[9] They are particularly reminded that the object of the scheme is to promote community care and that the absence of guidance applying to a particular circumstance, item or service does not mean that help should be refused.[10] They must take into account the nature, extent and urgency of the need in each case.

In spite of this, SFOs tend to stick rigidly to the guidance, particularly the local guidance on priorities (see p427). If your application is refused, always consider asking for a review (see p461).

Priority groups

The *SF Guide* gives a general list of priority groups. It stresses, however, that *the list is not exhaustive and the groups are not given in any order of priority*.[11] The list is as follows:[12]

- elderly people, particularly those with restricted mobility or those who have difficulty performing personal care tasks;
- mentally handicapped people;
- mentally ill people;
- physically disabled (including sensorily impaired) people;
- chronically sick people, especially the terminally ill;
- people who have 'misused' alcohol or drugs;
- ex-offenders requiring resettlement;
- people without a settled way of life undergoing resettlement;
- families under stress;
- young people leaving care;
- young people unable to live with their parents due to moral or physical danger, insufficient parental accommodation, unavoidable separation, not having parents or an irrevocable breakdown of relationship with them.

Local guidance often accords varying priorities to the above groups or the circumstances they find themselves in. If the local guidance says you should get a CCG, you should point this out in your application. If it does not, but you fall within the above general list, you could point out that the national guidance regards you as priority.

Do not be put off from making an application if you do not fall within a priority category. Remember, the only legal requirement for eligibility is that you satisfy the basic rules set out on pp434-5. Always give *your* reasons why your needs are high priority.

Items and amounts

The *SF Guide* suggests what expenses should be met by a CCG. Remember, however, that you can ask for anything which is not excluded by law (see p430).

There are no suggested amounts for items. The minimum that can be awarded in most cases is £30 (see p435).[13] There is no legal maximum. The guidance states that the amount requested should normally be allowed unless it is unreasonable.[14] You should always cost each of the items you need on the application form (see p459).

2. MOVING OUT OF INSTITUTIONAL OR RESIDENTIAL CARE

Interpretation

A CCG can be paid to help you, or a member of your family, to re-establish yourself in the community following a stay in institutional or residential care.[15] The SF directions do not define the meaning of 'family', 're-establish', 'the community', 'stay' or 'institutional and residential care' but they have been interpreted in case law (see below). SFOs are instructed to adopt a flexible approach and avoid rigid interpretations.[16]

Re-establishment in the community

The term 're-establish' (rather than 'establish') would appear to exclude those moving into the community for the first time (eg, those who have been in institutional or residential care since birth). A recent High Court decision ruled that a refugee coming to the UK for the first time following a stay in a refugee camp in Somalia could not be re-establishing herself in the community. 'The community' was restricted to Great Britain rather than anywhere outside care.[17] Another case said you must be actually or imminently in the community to qualify.[18]

'A stay in' care

The *SF Guide* suggests that 'a stay in' care should normally mean at least three months, or a pattern of frequent or regular admission.[19] However, the High Court has ruled that undue importance should not be attached to the reference to three months.[20] The word 'stay' is not defined in the law and could refer to any length of time, depending on the circumstances of the case.

'Institutional or residential care'

The *SF Guide* says this means 'accommodation where a resident receives a significant amount of care or supervision because they are unable to live independently in the community'. Examples given are hospitals, residential care homes and nursing homes.[21] The High Court has ruled that only accommodation in an institution specifically set up to provide care for those unable to live independently is 'institutional or residential care'.[22]

Although there is a wide range of living arrangements which could be institutional or residential care including various types of hostels and temporary accommodation, group homes, therapeutic homes, supported lodgings, resettlement units, local authority care, prison and detention centres, the key factor is whether their purpose is to provide care rather than just accommodation. The boundary between 'community care' and 'institutional or residential care', however, is very unclear.

If you cannot establish that your previous accommodation was institutional or residential care, you could still qualify for a grant under section 3 (Staying out of care – see p439).

What to claim for

You can claim for help with any expenses which are necessary to help re-establish yourself or your family in the community. The *SF Guide* gives the following examples:

Furniture, household equipment, bedding etc [23]

The *SF Guide* says you can be awarded a CCG for specific items or be given an amount sufficient to meet your need where the application cannot be itemised accurately. It is best to supply a detailed costed list of everything you need in part 6 of the application form (see p459). This could include a cooker, beds, mattresses, bedding, kitchen and cleaning equipment, fridge, floor-covering, curtains, storage units, tables, chairs etc. You should be paid the amount you ask for unless it is unreasonable.[24] SFOs often restrict an award to cover 'essential' or 'priority' items such as a cooker, bed and bedding. However, there is no restriction in the law and if you are given less than you need, you should ask for a review (see p461), and explain why you need all the items you listed.

Clothing and footwear [25]

The *SF Guide* says you can be awarded a CCG if you have few suitable clothes, including protective clothing. Always supply a detailed costed list of what you need in part 6 of the application form (see p459). You should be paid the amount you ask for unless it is unreasonable.[26]

Moving expenses [27]

The *SF Guide* says you should normally be asked to supply two estimates of removal costs. If you use a self-hire van and have to pay a refundable deposit, you could be given a budgeting loan (see p446). A CCG could be paid to meet furniture storage charges, fares when moving home and connection charges. You can get a crisis loan for rent in advance (see p449). You should apply to the office which covers the area from which you are moving, if you are only asking for removal costs and fares. If you are also asking for a CCG to furnish a new home, your whole application becomes the responsibility of the office which covers the area into which you are moving.[28]

Circumstances covered in the *SF Guide*

- People discharged from hospital or nursing homes.[29]
- People leaving homes and hostels as part of a planned programme of rehabilitation or resettlement.[30] Examples given include hostels for homeless people, refugees and alcohol or drug misusers (but see p437 for the meaning of 'institutional or residential care').
- Children and young people leaving local authority or foster care.[31]
- People moving house to look after somebody coming out of care who will be living with them.[32]
- Prisoners being released and resettled.[33] If you need a CCG to care for a prisoner or young offender on home leave (see p435) the *SF Guide* suggests you are paid one-seventh of their IS personal allowance (one-seventh of the difference between the single and couple rate if the person is your partner) for each day of their leave.[34]

3. STAYING OUT OF INSTITUTIONAL OR RESIDENTIAL CARE

Interpretation

A CCG can be paid to help you or a member of your family to remain in the community, rather than enter institutional or residential care.[35] None of these terms are defined in the SF directions and SFOs are instructed to adopt a flexible and imaginative approach.[36] See p437 for the meaning of 'institutional or residential care'.

The sole legal test is whether a CCG will help somebody remain in the community rather than enter care. There is no requirement that a CCG must be able to 'prevent' entry into care. Nor does the threat of care have to be immediate.[37] SFOs are told to consider whether a CCG, 'would improve the applicant's independent life in the community and therefore lessen the risk of admission into care'.[38] Actual or potential risk to physical or mental health because of the lack of such items as basic furniture and cooking facilities, protective clothing, bedding and heating can be used to argue for a CCG on the basis that an award will lessen the risk of entry into hospital or other care. Special needs such as an orthopaedic mattress or firm upright armchair could be covered on the same basis.

The guidance is written as though the law only applies to you and your partner whereas it, in fact, applies to any member of the family.[39] The possibility of a *child* having to go into hospital or care because of inadequate facilities, clothing etc, is often a strong argument for the award of a CCG.

Circumstances covered in the *SF Guide*[40]

Improving living conditions[41]

CCGs for the following are suggested if they will help a person remain in their home and lessen the risk of care:

- **Minor structural repairs and maintenance costs**[42] for which you are responsible, where your home is not Council, Housing Association etc owned. You will normally have to supply an estimate, which should be met unless it is unreasonable.[43] The interest on a loan to pay for major structural repairs can be paid for by IS (see p36). A CCG can be awarded for any survey fee incurred.
- **Internal redecoration and refurbishment**[44] for which you are responsible including, for example, worn out floor-covering. SFOs are reminded that 'although furnishings may be serviceable they might still need replacing'.[45] Items damaged by behavioural disturbances could be replaced (the guidance fails to mention damage by children, but there is no reason why this should not also apply). Single rooms could be redecorated if you are mainly confined to one room during the day. The award should cover the cost of materials and labour costs if the work cannot be done by relatives, friends, neighbours, charities or employment trainees.[46]
- **Bedding**[47] if you have an exceptional need because you or your partner is bedridden or incontinent. This guidance is unduly restrictive. There is no reason why you should not get a CCG for bedding whatever your circumstances if you can show that a grant will improve your living conditions and reduce any health risk and admission to care.
- **Fuel costs and heaters:**[48] You cannot get a CCG for fuel bills (see p431), but you could get a CCG for reconnection charges if you are going on to fuel direct (see p158); for re-siting meters for easier access; for installation of a pre-payment meter; *and* for heaters.
- **Laundry needs:**[49] If you are bedridden, incontinent or disabled and no one else can do your washing, you should be given a CCG for a washing machine and/or tumble dryer. There is no reason why this should not also apply if you have an incontinent child, or a washing machine could help you to remain in your home for any other reason.

Moving to more suitable accommodation[50]

A CCG should be awarded if a move from unsuitable accommodation would help a person remain in the community. Accommodation could be unsuitable because of its size, structural defects, insanitary condition, difficult access or because your housing costs are not being met in

full. Suggested awards are for moving expenses and furniture etc
(see p438), but only for items you cannot transfer from your previous
accommodation.

Moving to provide or obtain support

The guidance says you can get a CCG if you are moving nearer to or
into the house of a vulnerable person to provide daily attention or
supervision.[51] Alternatively, you can get a CCG to help you move nearer
relatives or close friends who will be looking after you.[52] Suggested
awards are for moving expenses and any furniture etc you need (see
p438).

Setting-up home for the first time[53]

This covers CCGs for setting-up home if you have been living with relatives or in lodgings, cannot continue to do so and might otherwise end
up in care. If you would be homeless, you could argue you might end
up in institutional or residential care. Suggested awards are for moving
expenses and furniture etc (see p438).

4. EASING EXCEPTIONAL PRESSURES ON FAMILIES

Interpretation

You can get a CCG to ease exceptional pressures on you and your family.[54] The scope for applications is very wide. The term 'exceptional pressures' is not defined in the SF directions and SFOs are instructed to use
their discretion flexibly, sensitively and imaginatively.[55]

Despite this, families under exceptional stress tend to be classified as
'low or medium priority' in local office guidance. The national guidance,
however, suggests families under stress are a priority group (see p436)
and gives equal weight to CCGs for all purposes for which they can be
paid.

When making your application, always fully explain all the pressures
your family is experiencing and how a CCG will ease those pressures.

If your application is refused on the grounds of insufficient priority,
consider asking for a review (see p461).

'Exceptional pressures'

The *SF Guide* says that all families, especially those on low incomes, face
pressure at times, so that in itself is not a reason to award a CCG.[56]
However, a CCG may be appropriate where circumstances put a family

under greater stress than is normally associated with low income or single parenthood.[57]

SFIs have made some useful comments in their decisions regarding exceptional pressures. These and some of our own comments are noted below:

- The cumulative impact of pressures should be considered. (You should always, therefore, list all the different pressures which are affecting your family.)
- Whether the pressures are foreseeable, expected or common is irrelevant.
- Low income can add to pressures as can single parenthood.
- Pressures that arise from a sudden event (eg, a disaster) can be exceptional and traumatic. Pressures which have existed for a long time do not necessarily become easier to handle.
- There does not have to be any risk of a person going into care for exceptional pressures to exist.
- Mental stress, anxiety, depression, illness etc are all sources and symptoms of exceptional pressures. The fact that an applicant does not appear stressed at an interview does not mean that exceptional pressures do not exist.
- Exceptional pressures experienced by children are entirely valid – eg, shame, discomfort, health risk from lack of clothes.

'Family'

The law refers to 'easing exceptional pressures on a person and his family'. This implies that people not living in a family are excluded. This interpretation was endorsed in a High Court case.[58] A Social Security Commissioner, however, recently decided that the identical language which appears in IS legislation means 'a person and his family (if he has one)'.[59] However, this interpretation is only binding on IS law.

The word 'family' is not defined. The guidance says it should generally be taken to mean couples with children or single parents. SFIs, however, have frequently rejected this narrow interpretation. 'Family' could include:

- a couple without children;
- a household with grown-up children;
- adult brothers and sisters or relatives living together;
- a parent living with children for part of the week only.

It may also be possible to argue that a pregnant woman constitutes a family, particularly in later pregnancy when the baby is increasingly capable of independent existence.

Circumstances covered in the *SF Guide*

The guidance on families under stress is very limited and restrictive. *If it covers your circumstances, you could refer to it. Otherwise ignore it.* Always explain why *you* consider your family to be under exceptional pressure.

Breakdown of a relationship[60]

The *SF Guide* suggests a CCG should be awarded to help you move after the recent breakdown of a long-standing relationship (if you have no children) or a breakdown after you have been living with a partner for at least three months (if you have children). Priority should be given to domestic violence cases. Suggested awards are for moving expenses, furniture etc, and clothing and footwear (see p438).

Reconciliation of a relationship[61]

A CCG for removal expenses is suggested as appropriate if you are returning to a shared home after a period of separation following the breakdown of an established relationship.

Moving house[62]

A CCG for moving expenses and furniture etc is suggested as appropriate (see p438) if you are moving house to ease exceptional pressures – eg, if your home was overcrowded.

Disabled and other children

The *SF Guide* only covers:

- a washing machine and dryer if there are high washing costs because of a disabled child;[63]
- clothes and footwear needed due to excessive wear and tear of clothes or rapid weight change because of a child's condition;[64]
- minor structural repairs to keep the home safe and habitable for children;[65]
- repair/replacement of items damaged by behavioural problems;[66]
- short-term boarding-out fees pending adoption;[67]
- fuel reconnection charges if you are going on to 'fuel direct' (see p156), or the cost of installing a pre-payment meter, if you have a disabled child or child under five.[68]

5. TRAVELLING EXPENSES

Travelling expenses within the UK are specifically allowed for in SF directions.[69] Listed below are the five situations covered, and the guidance on each one. For the amount of payments, see p445.

Visiting someone who is ill

The law merely states that a CCG can be paid to assist you or one or more members of your family with travel expenses in the UK to visit someone who is ill.[70] The *SF Guide* is much more restrictive.[71] *Ignore it, if it does not apply to you.*

It suggests the person you are visiting should be a relative, partner or someone (a close friend if in hospital or care), who has no relatives or whose relatives have lost touch. The person could be at home, in hospital, in a care home or in staff-intensive, sheltered housing. SFOs are told to take account of any IS paid to the family for the patient which exceeds the hospital personal expenses allowance (see p113) and to offset it against travel expenses. You can claim the costs of overnight accommodation if you need to stay with a child in hospital.[72]

Attending a relative's funeral

You, or one or more members of your family, can get a CCG to attend a relative's funeral in the UK. If you are responsible for arranging the funeral you may instead be eligible for a funeral expenses payment (see p418), which includes travel expenses.

Easing domestic crises

You can get a CCG for travel costs to ease a domestic crisis.[73] The *SF Guide* suggests that priority should be given to those 'whose needs are most acute' – eg, a single parent who is going into hospital or is too ill to look after her/his child. Fares will not normally be paid for a holiday or short break. However, you can argue that a short break may be very necessary for a parent of a disabled child who needs a rest. An SFI accepted that it would be reasonable to pay a grant for fares to enable a person to take regular advantage of respite care.

Visiting a child pending a court decision

You can get a CCG for travel costs to visit a child who is with the other parent pending a court decision on who is to have responsibility for the child. This is 'to ensure that neither parent is seen by the court to be in a less advantageous position simply because s/he cannot afford the fares'.[74]

Where the child is staying some distance away, you may need to pay for accommodation as well and the guidance does say that the cost of reasonable overnight accommodation may be met as part of the grant where the distance is too far to make a return journey in one day.[75]

The *SF Guide* says you cannot get a CCG once responsibility has been decided.

Fares when moving home

You can get a CCG for fares to move to suitable accommodation.

The amount of the payment

The *SF Guide* suggests that grants for travelling expenses should be calculated as follows:[76]

- the cost of 'standard' rate public transport (excluding air fares); *or*
- the cost of petrol, either up to the cost of public transport if available or in full if public transport is not available; *or*
- taxi fares, if public transport is unavailable or you or your partner cannot use public transport because of physical disability or because you are frail or elderly and you cannot use private transport.

The reasonable cost of overnight accommodation may be paid if it is necessary, and the cost of an escort's fare if the person travelling is incapable of travelling alone – eg, they are a child, elderly, ill or disabled. CCGs for fares may be awarded in advance, or in instalments if the SFO considers it to be in your interest.

CHAPTER TWENTY-THREE

Loans

This chapter covers:

1. Budgeting loans (below)
2. Crisis loans (p449)
3. Repayments (p454)

The two types of loans covered in this chapter are very different from each other. Budgeting loans are intended to help people who have been receiving income support (IS) for at least 26 weeks to meet one-off expenses. They are not just for people with special problems. By contrast, crisis loans are not restricted to those receiving IS, but are only available to deal with special problems.

There is no legal entitlement to a loan. Payments are discretionary. You can, however, ask for a review if you are not paid what you ask for (see p461).

Loans are obviously far less attractive than grants because they must be repaid to the Benefits Agency although they are, at least, interest-free.[1] Another problem with loans is that they cannot exceed what the Benefits Agency think you can afford to repay.

It is always better, therefore, to ask for a grant if you are eligible to do so (see Chapter 22). There is nothing to stop you asking for a grant and a loan for the same item at the same time (see p459). Legally, your application is to the fund as a whole and should be automatically considered for a grant and a loan. If you are awarded a loan, you can request a review to get it changed to a grant (see p461).

I. BUDGETING LOANS

The basic rules

You must satisfy all the following rules in order to be eligible for a budgeting loan. The rules are laid down in directions issued by the Secretary of State, which are legally binding. None of the words used are defined in the directions (eg, 'partner' which is not necessarily restricted to its IS meaning).

- you must be in receipt of IS when your application for a budgeting loan is decided by the Benefits Agency;[2] *and*
- you, or your partner, between you must have been receiving IS throughout the 26 weeks before the date on which your application is decided.[3] One break of 14 days or less when IS was not being paid can be included in the 26 weeks.[4] The guidance says that you can have had more than one partner during the 26 weeks;[5] *and*
- you must not have too much capital. The rules are the same as for CCGs (see p434 for details); *and*
- you, or your partner, must not be involved in a trade dispute (see p77); *and*
- the loan must be to assist you to meet important intermittent expenses for which it may be difficult to budget;[6] *and*
- the loan must not be for an excluded item (see p430); *and*
- the loan must be at least £30; and at most £1,000 less any outstanding SF loan(s);[7] *and*
- the loan must not exceed an amount which you are likely to be able to repay[8] (see p448).

The guidance

The Secretary of State issues guidance to SFOs to help them decide who should get a budgeting loan. Guidance is also issued by district office managers. This is fully discussed on pp426-9.

The guidance is *not* legally binding. SFOs must consider each application on its merits, taking into account the nature, extent and urgency of the need.

National guidance

The *SF Guide* gives examples of high, medium and low priority expenses. It stresses, however, that the examples are not exhaustive and should only be used as a guide.[9] SFOs are reminded that ' . . . the absence of directions or guidance applying to a particular item requested . . . does not mean that help should be refused'.[10] They are also told that the particular circumstances of the applicant could raise the priority normally given to particular items.[11]

High priority:[12]
- essential (unspecified) items of furniture and household equipment;
- bedclothes, if you do not have sufficient;
- essential home repairs and maintenance if you are an owner-occupier

and you cannot get a bank loan or mortgage or home improvement grant;
- removal charges if it is essential for you to move;
- fuel meter installation and reconnection charges;
- non-mains fuel costs (eg, oil, bottled gas or coal).

Medium priority:[13]
- 'non-essential' items of furniture and household equipment;
- redecoration costs, if you are responsible for these;
- hire purchase and other debts;
- clothing, if you do not have sufficient.

Low priority:[14]
- rent in advance if you already have secure accommodation and a move is not necessary (SFOs are advised not to award rent for more than a month);
- removal charges if it is not essential for you to move;
- leisure items.

Local guidance

Local guidance also usually categorises needs into high, medium and low priority, which may or may not mirror the national guidance. If the local guidance says you should get a loan, you should point this out in your application.

Do not be put off from making an application if you do not fall within a priority category. Always give *your* reasons why your needs are high priority.

The amount of the loan

The amount awarded must be between £30 and £1,000 (see p447).[15] If, however, the item you need costs less than £30, you can still apply and should be awarded £30.

There is no guidance on how much should be paid for specific items or services. SFOs are told to accept your estimate of the cost if it is 'within the broad range of prices that would be considered reasonable for an item of serviceable quality'.[16] It is usually unnecessary to submit estimates from suppliers.[17] SFOs are told to consider whether an item could be repaired.

You cannot be awarded more than you can afford to repay. The amount you can afford to repay is usually calculated by multiplying your weekly repayment rate by 78 (see p455). If you already have one or more loans, you may also find you are offered less than you ask for. If you are unhappy about the amount awarded to you, you can ask for a review (see p461).

SFOs are told not to concern themselves with exactly what you should spend the award on (eg, what standard of items).[18]

2. CRISIS LOANS

The basic rules

You must satisfy all the following rules in order to be eligible for a crisis loan. The rules are laid down in directions issued by the Secretary of State which are legally binding. None of the words used are defined in the directions (eg, 'family' is not restricted to its IS meaning).

- you must be 16 or over;[19] *and*
- you must not be an 'excluded person';[20] *and*
- the loan must not be for an excluded item (see p430); *and*
- the loan must not exceed an amount which you are likely to be able to repay.[21] There are maximum awards (see p454), but no minimum amount is laid down in law;[22] *and*
- you must be without sufficient resources to meet the immediate short-term needs of yourself and/or your family[23] (see p451); *and*
- the loan must be for expenses in an emergency, or as a consequence of a disaster, and be the only means by which serious damage or serious risk to the health or safety of yourself or a member of your family may be prevented[24] (see p451); *or* the loan must be for rent in advance payable to a non-local authority landlord and a CCG is being awarded to help you, or a member of your family, re-establish yourself in the community following a stay in care[25] (see p453).

Excluded persons

The following people are excluded by the directions from getting a crisis loan, **in all circumstances**.[26]

- People in hospital, nursing homes or residential care homes (private or local authority), *unless* their discharge is planned to take place within the next two weeks.
- Prisoners and people in custody.
- Members of religious orders who are fully maintained by the order.
- People in 'full-time relevant education' who are not entitled to IS (see p17).

The following people are excluded by the directions from getting a crisis loan except **in very limited circumstances**:

- Full-time students not on IS, can only claim a crisis loan for expenses arising out of a disaster.[27] Those on IS have no restrictions on their eligibility.
- People from abroad who, because of their immigration status, would not be entitled to IS either at the ordinary or the urgent cases rate (see p82) can also only claim a crisis loan for expenses arising out of a disaster.[28] This rule, however, does not apply to people not entitled to IS because of the new habitual residence test (see p84).

  Note: If you are an overstayer, subject to a deportation order, or an illegal entrant, you should not apply for a crisis loan before getting advice about regularising your status here. People from abroad who are entitled to IS, can claim a crisis loan in the normal way. SFOs are advised to pay particular attention to the clothing needs of refugees and asylum-seekers.
- People involved in a trade dispute (see p432 for details).

The guidance

Introduction

The Secretary of State issues guidance to SFOs to help them decide who should get a crisis loan. Guidance is also issued by district office managers. This is fully discussed on pp426-9. The important point about the guidance is that it is *not* legally binding. Remember, you are eligible for a crisis loan as long as you satisfy the basic rules above.

SFOs must consider each application on its merits, taking into account the nature, extent and urgency of the need.

The *SF Guide* reminds SFOs to use their discretion flexibly, to consider the individual circumstances of each application and to decide whether a need requires immediate relief.[29]

When applying for a crisis loan, make sure you complete the application form SF400 or the self-completion form (see p459). Do not be put off by Benefits Agency counter staff who say you cannot get a payment. It is common for counter staff to advise potential applicants (particularly the homeless and young people) that they cannot get a crisis loan or that it is a waste of time applying. If you need a loan, you should *always* insist on applying and being given a formal decision by an SFO. If you are refused a crisis loan and you satisfy the basic rules, you can ask for a review (see p461).

Crisis loans should normally be given more priority than budgeting loans.[30]

Emergencies and disasters

Most crisis loans can only be awarded in an emergency or following a disaster (see basic rules, p449). Neither of these terms is defined. The guidance recognises that 'individual people may be affected differently by the same situation . . . so it is not intended to give a precise definition of terms'.[31] You should always explain, therefore, why a particular situation constitutes an emergency or disaster for you or your family.

The *SF Guide* gives fire or flood resulting in significant damage or loss, as an example of a disaster.[32] A Social Security Commissioner has defined 'disaster' as something of 'a ruinous or distressing nature; a sudden or great mishap or misadventure; a calamity'.[33] Whether a payment is appropriate following a disaster depends on your resources (see below) and ability to cope.[34]

Serious damage/risk to health or safety

A crisis loan has to be the only means of preventing serious damage or risk to health or safety. You will have to show there are no other resources or ways of meeting your need. This is often interpreted very strictly by SFOs. If an SFO suggests other means which are impractical or unavailable to you, ask for a review.

The potential serious risk to your health or safety might be obvious – eg, you have no money for food. Supporting evidence from your doctor, social worker etc will usually help your case.

Resources

You must be without sufficient resources to meet the immediate short-term needs of yourself and/or your family. 'Resources' are not defined in the SF directions. The *SF Guide* says all resources which ' . . . are actually available to the applicant or could be obtained in time to meet the need' should be taken into account.[35]

Resources that could count include:[36]

- cash, earnings, other income;
- capital, savings accessible with a cash card or cheque;
- credit but only if you are not on IS and if you could afford the repayments.[37]

Resources that should be disregarded:

The *SF Guide* lists the following:[38]

- other SF payments, housing benefit, disability living allowance (mobility component);

- the value of your home; premises acquired for occupation within the next six months; and premises occupied by a relative, or your ex-partner;
- the value of any reversionary interest (see p401);
- your business assets;
- any sum paid to you because of damage to, or loss of, your home or personal possessions and intended for their repair or replacement;
- any sum acquired on the express condition that it is used for essential repairs or improvements to your home;
- any personal possessions, except those acquired for the purpose of qualifying for a crisis loan;
- any payments from the Independent Living Funds, and the Macfarlane Trusts (see p494).

SFOs are advised to take into account help from other sources, 'if there is a realistic expectation that it would be available in time'.[39] They are told not to routinely refer applicants to employers, relatives or close friends 'unless there is reason to believe their help will be forthcoming'.[40] They are reminded that social services do not normally meet financial needs.[41] Emergency payments for children should be disregarded unless they meet the need for which the crisis loan is requested.[42]

The *SF Guide* suggests it may be reasonable to disregard other resources at least for a temporary period.[43] You could argue that money set aside to meet forthcoming bills (eg, council tax, fuel bills) is not available.

Guidance on crisis loan situations

The *SF Guide* gives a few examples of situations where a crisis loan may be appropriate but stresses that 'a situation not mentioned is not automatically excluded' and that the list is not definitive.[44]

Local guidance will usually specify when a crisis loan can be paid. If the local or national guidance suggests you should get a loan, you should point this out in your application.

Living expenses for a short period

The *SF Guide* suggests a crisis loan could be awarded to meet day-to-day living expenses in the following situations:

- You are waiting for your first benefit payment or wages (and your employer will not give you an advance).[45]
- You are suffering hardship because your employer has imposed a compulsory unpaid holiday.[46]
- You have lost money or you have lost a giro and replacement (see p154 on lost giros) is delayed.[47]

- You have been refused IS because your capital is over £8,000 but you cannot realise your assets immediately. A crisis loan can be paid to tide you over until you have raised money against your assets. SFOs are told that a crisis loan is not appropriate where you are making no attempt to realise the asset or arrange alternative credit facilities.[48]
- You are homeless and need living expenses. The guidance stresses the risk to physical and mental health brought about by sleeping rough and prolonged homelessness. In particular, the threat of assault and the vulnerability of young people to the risk of drug dependency, alcohol misuse, prostitution and offending is mentioned.[49] Homeless people could also get a crisis loan for items or services needed and for board and lodging charges in advance (see below).

The guidance suggests a crisis loan should only cover living expenses for more than 14 days in exceptional circumstances – eg, a continuing crisis; loss of money which would normally cover you until your next income is due; or no money because of misfortune or mismanagement.[50]

Travelling expenses

The *SF Guide* covers the following situations:

- You are stranded away from home, without access to your regular means of support.[51]
- You are a 16/17-year-old who needs the cost of a journey home after looking unsuccessfully for work or a Youth Training (YT) place elsewhere.[52] When deciding your ability to repay the loan, the SFO should take account of the fact that you should get a YT place and be paid a training allowance.
- The SFO will consider payment for hospital fares for you and, if necessary, an escort, where you or a member of your family need treatment and are unable to get help with fares to hospital (see p480) because, for example:
  - transport by ambulance or the hospital car scheme has been refused; *and*
  - your condition or that of a member of your family is serious; *and*
  - you cannot get the fare in advance from the hospital.[53]

Accommodation expenses

A crisis loan is payable for rent in advance to a non-local authority landlord if you are also awarded a CCG on leaving care (see p437). The rules about serious risk to health or safety do not apply.

The guidance suggests a maximum of four weeks' rent is met at a weekly rate limited to the amount of HB likely to be awarded.[54] The CCG and any capital should be disregarded.[55]

If your fuel supply has been disconnected but fuel direct has been arranged (see p159), you may get a crisis loan to meet the cost of reconnection.[56] Where fuel direct arrangements have broken down but this was not your fault, the DSS may consider making an *ex gratia* payment.

The amount of the loan

There is no legal minimum. There is a general legal maximum of £1,000 less any outstanding SF loan(s).[57] You also cannot be awarded more than you can afford to repay.[58] SFOs usually calculate the amount you can afford to repay by multiplying your weekly repayment rate by 78 (see below). If you already have one or more loans you may also find you are offered less than you asked for.

There are also more specific legal maximums for items, services and living expenses.

Items and services:[59] The maximum you can get is the reasonable cost of purchase (including delivery and installation) or the cost of repair, if cheaper.

Living expenses:[60] The maximum you can get is 75 per cent of the appropriate IS personal allowance for you and any partner (see p328), plus £15.65 for each child. If your applicable amount is reduced because of 'voluntary unemployment' (see p58) the maximum crisis loan is the total amount of IS payable, if less than the above formula.[61]

Subject to the above rules, you should be given the minimum you need to tide you over or remove the crisis.[62] For items or services, you should be paid what is reasonable. You do not normally need to supply written estimates.[63]

If you are unhappy about the amount offered, you can ask for a review (see p461).

3. REPAYMENTS

All loans must be repaid to the Benefits Agency. The rate of repayment, the repayment period and the method of recovery are technically decided by the Secretary of State and not by SFOs.[64] In practice, decisions are made on his behalf at the local Benefits Agency office by SFOs wearing a different hat.

Unlike SFO decisions (eg, the amount of loan awarded), which can be challenged by review, Secretary of State decisions are not subject to review. You can request that a Secretary of State's decision is reconsidered, however, by 'making a complaint' (see p457).

There is no legislation covering how repayment rates or periods should be calculated. The information below is based on the *SF Guide* alone.[65]

The repayment period

The period over which a loan is expected to be repaid is determined by the size of the loan and the weekly repayment rate. The *SF Guide* says loans should normally be recovered within 78 weeks, or exceptionally, 104 weeks (eg, if a further loan is awarded).[66] The amount of a loan will usually be restricted to what you can repay within these periods.

The rate of repayment

The *SF Guide* says repayment rates should take account of what you can afford.[67] It suggests three possible weekly rates of repayment:

- 15 per cent of your IS applicable amount (see p341), excluding housing costs, if you have no 'continuing commitments' (unspecified).[68]
- 10 per cent of your IS applicable amount, excluding housing costs, if you have continuing commitments of up to £6.85 a week.[69]
- 5 per cent of your IS applicable amount, excluding housing costs, if you have continuing commitments of more than £6.85 a week.[70]

A maximum repayment rate of 25 per cent of your IS applicable amount is suggested.[71]

Repayment of a crisis loan for living expenses should not begin until the end of the period covered by the loan.[72] The guidance says you should not repay more than one loan at a time.[73] Recovery of a new loan should be deferred until all other loans are repaid but all loans are expected to be repaid within a 'reasonable period' (usually 78 weeks).[74] This may mean increasing the normal weekly repayment rates for existing and new loans.[75] It may also mean an additional loan is refused or restricted on the grounds of your inability to repay it.

Repayment terms are notified to you with the decision offering a loan. If you accept them, you should sign and return the offer form within 14 days.[76] This period can be extended.[77] If you disagree with the terms, you can make a 'complaint' (see p457).

How loans are recovered

Methods of recovery

Loans can be repaid in cash or by cheque, postal order or banker's standing order. You can make a lump-sum payment any time to partially or wholly repay a loan.[78] The DSS can tell you how much you owe at any time.

Loans are, in fact, nearly always recovered by direct deductions from benefit. The Secretary of State is legally entitled to make deductions to recover loans from the following benefits:[79]

- income support;
- family credit;
- unemployment benefit;
- sickness and invalidity benefit;
- severe disablement allowance;
- invalid care allowance;
- disability working allowance;
- disablement benefit, reduced earnings allowance and industrial death benefit;
- widows' benefits (excluding the lump-sum widow's payment);
- retirement pensions (all types);
- war pensions;
- maternity allowance.

Increases of benefit for dependants and additional benefit under SERPS are also subject to deduction.

Deductions from FC, ICA, DWA or war pensions can only commence from the start of an award of these benefits (eg, the beginning of a 26-week FC award).

Deductions are put into effect by the office responsible for payment on instruction from SF sections, who decide the rate of repayment.

Note that deductions cannot be made from child benefit, statutory sick pay, statutory maternity pay or disability living allowance, attendance allowance, HB or CTB.

From whom recoverable

A loan can be legally recovered from:

- you (the applicant) or the person who the loan was for;[80]
- your partner, if you are living together as a married or unmarried couple as defined for IS purposes (see p330);[81]
- a 'liable relative' (see p124) or a 'sponsor' (see p88) of yours if you have claimed a crisis loan because they have stopped maintaining you.[82] If you claim IS, the crisis loan will be recovered from you. If you cannot claim IS because maintenance recommences, the crisis loan can be recovered from your liable relative or sponsor.[83]

Challenging the rate of repayment

There is no right of review or appeal against a decision about the rate of repayment of a loan.

If you are unhappy about the repayment terms when a loan is offered, you should write to the Benefits Agency and explain why. This is technically known as 'making a complaint'.[84] You should justify asking for a lower weekly repayment by referring to your financial circumstances and commitments. You could refer to the guidance on repayment rates if it helps your case (see p455).

You should receive a written decision in response to your complaint.[85] If new terms are offered, you will be given 14 days to accept them. The Benefits Agency may want to interview you before making a decision and may offer money advice.[86] If there are doubts about your ability to repay a loan, your award could be reduced or withdrawn. You can, of course, ask for a review in these circumstances. The Benefits Agency are only likely to agree to a lower repayment rate if the loan will still be repaid within 78 (or exceptionally 104) weeks.

If you are finding it difficult to repay a loan at the agreed rate, you can write to the Benefits Agency at any time and ask for 'rescheduling' – ie, lower repayments over a longer period.[87] You will need to show your current repayment rates are causing hardship.[88] The Benefits Agency can also reschedule a loan by increasing your weekly repayments if they think you can afford to pay more.[89] Rescheduling is also common when you take out a second loan.[90] The Benefits Agency often increase weekly repayments on the first loan so that both loans can be recovered within 78 weeks (exceptionally 104 weeks).

If you are having real difficulties and the Benefits Agency refuse to reduce your weekly repayments you could take the matter to your MP.

CHAPTER TWENTY-FOUR

Applications, payments and reviews

This chapter covers:

1. APPLICATIONS

Making an application

General matters

Applications for an SF payment must be made in writing, either on a standard application form obtainable from the Benefits Agency or in some other way which is acceptable to the Secretary of State (eg, a letter with all the necessary details).[1] If your application is incomplete, the Benefits Agency can ask you to provide additional information either in writing, or by calling in at your local office.[2]

An application can be made on your behalf by somebody else, as long as you give your written consent (this is not necessary if an appointee is acting for you – see p143).[3]

Your application is treated as having been made on the day it is received at a Benefits Agency office.[4] If your application was incomplete and you comply with a request for additional information, your application will be treated as made on the day it was originally received.[5]

Where to apply

You should normally apply to the Benefits Agency office which covers the area in which you live.[6] If you are applying for a crisis loan, however, you can apply to the office where your need arises.[7] In an emergency, social services or other agencies can contact the Benefits Agency 'out of hours' service on your behalf (see p8).[8]

If you are moving out of care and claiming a CCG, you should apply to the office which covers the area you are moving to unless you are only claiming removal expenses and/or fares.[9]

CCGs and budgeting loans

You should apply on form SF300, which is in an application pack available from the Benefits Agency and advice centres. The form is for both CCGs and budgeting loans.

Tips on completing the application form:

- In part 4 of the form, you are asked whether you want a grant or loan. Always ask for a grant if you satisfy the eligibility rules (see p434). You can ask for a grant and a loan. If you do, the SFO should decide whether to award a CCG first.[10] *Legally, your application is to the fund as a whole*[11] and each application should automatically be considered for a grant and loan.[12]
- You should complete part 6 of the form with full details of what you need. Be as specific as possible (do not just write 'furniture' or 'clothes' – list each item needed). Write down the actual cost or a reasonable estimate for each item. It is not usually necessary to supply written estimates from a supplier (unless you are asking for removal expenses, when two written estimates are usually required).
- Part 6 also asks why the items are needed. Part 7 asks more specific questions about why you need help. It is important to establish that you satisfy the rules of eligibility for a CCG or budgeting loan (see Chapters 22 and 23), including the purposes for which a CCG can be awarded. It is also important to show why your application should be given high priority. Refer to the local or national guidance if it helps your case (you can obtain a copy of the local guidance from your local Benefits Agency office). Use the space in Part 11 of the form and continue in a letter, if necessary.
- Submit any supporting evidence with your application – eg, a letter from your doctor or social worker.

Crisis loans

You apply for a crisis loan on either a form SF400 at the Benefits Agency or by submitting a self-completion form available from the Benefits Agency or advice centres. Make sure the form fully records your needs and circumstances and confirms that you satisfy the rules (see p449). Do not be put off if you are 'advised' by counter staff or the Benefits Agency that you cannot get a loan. Always insist on making an application and receiving a formal, written decision. You will usually be interviewed in connection with your application. Crisis loan decisions should be based on your circumstances at the date of decision and SFOs are instructed never to deliberately delay a decision until the need has passed.[13]

Repeat applications

If you have been awarded or refused a payment for an item or service, you cannot get a payment for the same item or service within 26 weeks of a previous application unless:

either there has been a relevant change of circumstances;
or   you are applying for a budgeting loan for which you were ineligible when you made your first application because neither you nor your partner had been on IS for 26 weeks.[14]

If your previous application was incomplete (see p458); or you withdrew it before a decision was made; or you declined or did not respond to a loan offer, the 26-week rule about repeat applications should not apply.[15]

A relevant change of circumstances could include any additional allocations made to the district office budget during the year (see p463).

2. DECISIONS AND PAYMENTS

Decisions

You should receive a written decision on your application. If a payment is wholly or partly refused, the decision should explain why and state that you have the right to request a review. The reasons given are usually very general and sketchy (eg, your application is not high enough priority or is not for one of the purposes for which a payment can be made). If you are not satisfied you should always ask for a review.

There are no legal time limits within which the Benefits Agency must make decisions. The guidance, however, says that 'All decisions should normally be made within 28 days of the date of the application.'[16] Decisions on urgent applications – for example, crisis loans – should be made within one working day.[17]

If there are unreasonable delays in getting a decision, you should complain to the SF manager in your district office. If this does not help, you should ask your MP to take up your case with the manager, the Secretary of State or the Ombudsman. The Benefits Agency has published a *Customer Charter* for claimants. This gives target times for processing crisis loans (the day the need arises or the application is made) and community care grants (an average of seven days). There are no targets for dealing with budgeting loans.

Payments

You will normally be paid by giro made out to you.[18] The Benefits Agency can, however, choose to pay a supplier directly.[19] Payment can also be made in the form of travel warrants, food vouchers or cash. They can also pay you in instalments. You can ask for a review of any decision to pay a supplier rather than you, or to pay in instalments.[20]

3. REVIEW BY A SOCIAL FUND OFFICER

Introduction

There is no right of appeal to an independent body against decisions regarding the discretionary SF. There is instead a review system, which is divided into two distinct stages.

First, when you ask for a review of a decision, the Benefits Agency reconsider the decision by conducting an internal review.

Second, if you are dissatisfied with the outcome of the review, you can ask for a further review by a social fund inspector (SFI) who reconsiders the case independently of the Benefits Agency.

You should always ask for a review if you are unhappy about a decision. Although decisions are not often changed as a result of the internal review, there is a better chance of a successful outcome after an SFI review. It is crucial, therefore, to pursue your review application through to the inspector stage, if necessary.

The law regarding reviews is set out in legislation and the SF directions.

Decisions subject to review

All SFO decisions are subject to review.[21] Decisions about the repayment of loans are made by the Secretary of State and not by SFOs and are, therefore, not subject to review.

The following decisions can be challenged by asking for a review:

- the refusal of a grant or loan;
- the amount awarded as a grant or loan;
- the award of a loan rather than a grant;
- the refusal to decide a repeat application (see p460);
- payment in instalments or to a third party (see above).

Applying for a review

Basic rules

You must apply for a review of a decision in writing to the Benefits Agency within 28 days of the date the decision was issued to you.[22] Your application must include your grounds for requesting a review (see below – Tactics).[23] If somebody is making an application on your behalf, it must be accompanied by your written authority (unless the person is your appointee).[24]

Late applications can be accepted for 'special reasons'.[25] 'Special reasons' are not defined – they could cover late applications due to ill-health, domestic crises, wrong advice or any other reasons. If your application is late, you should explain why it has been delayed. If the Benefits Agency do not accept there are special reasons, get advice. You may have to threaten judicial review if their refusal is unreasonable (see p182), and they are not prepared to review their decision.

The SFO can ask you to submit further information in connection with your application if reasonably required.[26]

You can withdraw your application in writing at any time.[27]

Tactics

- Your application must be in writing. Keep a copy if possible. Begin your letter by stating that you request a review and identify the decision you are unhappy about. Always quote your Benefits Agency reference number at the top of your letter. If your application is late (see above), explain in full why this is the case.
- Explain, as fully as possible, why you disagree with the SFO's decision.
- CCGs are often refused on the grounds that your application was not for one of the purposes for which CCGs can be given. You can challenge such decisions by stating that you are not satisfied that your needs and circumstances have been properly looked at by the SFO. You should then explain how your application *is* for one of the purposes for which a CCG can be given – ie, moving out of care, staying out of care or easing exceptional pressures (see p434).
- CCGs and loans are often refused on the grounds of 'insufficient priority', based on local guidance (see Chapter 21). You can challenge such decisions by stating you are not satisfied your particular needs and circumstances have been properly looked at. You should then explain why your application should merit high priority with reference to information already given and any further evidence or information you have.
- If you are unhappy about the amount you have been awarded, you

should state that you are not satisfied that the SFO has assessed your needs properly. Explain why you need the amount you asked for, giving any further evidence or information which was not in your original application.

- If you are awarded a loan rather than a CCG, you can refuse or accept the loan and also ask for a review explaining why you think you should be awarded a CCG instead.

Review without an application

An SFO can review a decision at any time without an application.[28]
   An SFO *must* review a decision which appears:

either   to have been based on a mistake about the law or directions;
or   to have been made in ignorance of a material fact or based on a mistake about a material fact;
or   where there has been a relevant change of circumstances since the decision was given.[29]

A relevant change in circumstances could include any additional allocation to a district office budget during the year (see p429). When this occurs, there is a strong argument that the Benefits Agency must review all previous decisions made during the year to refuse or restrict payments wholly or partially on budgetary grounds and issue fresh decisions. You should insist that the Benefits Agency reconsider your case if this applies to you. If they refuse, get advice (see Appendix 2).

Deciding reviews

The theory

SFOs are responsible for conducting reviews.[30] The *SF Guide* says wherever practicable the SFO who made the decision being challenged should also conduct the review[31] (but not if this involves delays[32]).
   When conducting a review, an SFO must have full regard to the following matters:

- All the circumstances of the case under review and, in particular, all the matters which have to be considered when making original decisions (see p428), including the nature, extent and urgency of the need and the size of the district budget.[33]
- The SF directions, the Secretary of State's national guidance and local guidance[34] (see Chapter 21).
- Whether the law was applied correctly when the decision under review was made. In particular, whether:
  - the decision was consistent with the evidence;

- all relevant and no irrelevant considerations were taken into account;
- the law and directions were interpreted correctly.[35]
- Whether the SFO who made the original decision acted fairly, without bias and exercised discretion reasonably, following the required procedural steps and giving you sufficient opportunity to put your case.[36]
- All the circumstances which existed at the time of the original decision, any new evidence which has since been produced and any relevant changes of circumstances.[37]

The practice

Not surprisingly, SFOs rarely conduct reviews with the thoroughness demanded by the above legal requirements. They have neither the time nor the training. In practice, budget considerations and local guidance on priorities tend to be the major determinants in reviews. Also there is a tendency for SFOs only to change their original decisions in the light of new evidence.

Review interviews

Procedure

If an SFO does not revise a decision wholly in your favour you must be given the opportunity to attend an interview.[38] You have the legal right to be accompanied by a friend or representative.[39] At the interview, you must be given an explanation of the reasons for the SFO decision and an opportunity to put your case, including any additional evidence you have.[40]

The guidance says that 'whenever possible, the interview should take place in a private interviewing room'.[41] The interview can be held in your home if, for example, you are severely disabled or ill.[42] The *SF Guide* says the interview should be with the SFO who made the original decision, unless they are unavailable.[43] The SFO must make an accurate written record of your representations, to be agreed and signed by you.[44]

Tactics

- Always ask to be interviewed in a private room and complain if one is not offered.
- Do not sign the written record unless you agree with it and everything you want to say has been recorded. You could ask to write the record yourself or provide a written statement and insist it is included in the record. If you have been told something by the SFO with which you

disagree, you could refer to it in the record. It is particularly important to include any new evidence, previously unknown to the SFO.

• If you do not wish to attend an interview (eg, you have nothing further to add to your application), tell the Benefits Agency. The review will then automatically proceed to the next stage (see below).

After the interview

If the SFO does not revise a decision wholly in your favour following the interview, your case must be looked at again by an SFO not below the rank of higher executive officer (HEO).[45] This is usually the SF assistant manager. S/he should check that the SFO has conducted a review properly and impartially in accordance with the law, obtaining all relevant evidence.[46] S/he should then record a decision fully explaining the circumstances of the application and applicant, and how the decision was arrived at.[47]

Getting a decision

You will be notified of the review decision in writing. There are no legal time limits for issuing decisions. If there are unreasonable delays you should complain to the SF manager. If that does not help, you could ask your MP to take up your case.

4. REVIEW BY A SOCIAL FUND INSPECTOR

Introduction

If you are dissatisfied with a decision of an SFO which has been reviewed, you have a right to request a further review by a social fund inspector (SFI).[48]

SFIs are based in an office in Birmingham (see Appendix 1) and conduct their reviews independently of the Benefits Agency. SFIs tend to produce a much higher standard of decision-making than SFOs. They are generally better trained and have more time. They tend to be less influenced by local guidance and budgets than SFOs.

You should always, therefore, ask for a further review, if necessary, as your chances of success are higher than at the first review.

The law regarding SFI reviews is set out in legislation and SFI directions.

Applying for a further review

Basic rules

You must apply for a further review in writing within 28 days of the date the review decision was issued to you.[49] Your application must include your grounds for requesting a further review (see below – Tactics).[50] If somebody is applying on your behalf, you must send your written authority[51] (unless the person is your appointee). A generalised authority for somebody to act on your behalf may not be sufficient. You should specifically authorise the person to make an application for further review by an SFI on your behalf. You will need to do this even if you supplied written authority when you applied for the first review by an SFO.

Late applications can be accepted for 'special reasons'[52] (see p462). Social fund inspectors usually interpret this widely including 'good cause' for lateness and any other reason why it is important for your review to go ahead. You must send your application to your local Benefits Agency office and *not* directly to the SFI office in Birmingham. The local office will send your application together with all relevant papers (including copies of your original application, the review decision and details of the local budget and guidance) to Birmingham. Decisions about late or incomplete applications must be made by the SFI and not the local office. The SFI will write to you direct for further information or evidence.

Tactics

- Submit your application in writing to your local Benefits Agency office, quoting your Benefits Agency reference number. Begin your letter by stating you request a further review by an SFI and identify the SFO review decision you are unhappy about. If your application is late, explain in full why this is the case.
- Your grounds for review are likely to be similar to the grounds for the initial review (see p462). Explain as fully as possible why you are unhappy with the SFO's review decision.
- It is a good idea to contact the SFI office a few days after submitting your application to make sure they have received it. Local Benefits Agency offices are told to send applications on to Birmingham by courier on the day they are received if possible.[53] Complain to the SF manager and, if necessary, your MP, if there are delays.
- If your case is urgent, state this and explain why.

Deciding further reviews

The law

When conducting a review, an SFI is legally bound to take into account the same matters which apply to SFO reviews (see p461).[54]

An SFI review is not quite a complete rehearing of a case. It does involve, however, a thorough consideration of whether the decision under review was arrived at properly and reasonably, taking into account the law, directions, guidance and all the evidence which was before the SFO. If an SFI is satisfied a decision was reached correctly, s/he must then decide whether the decision should be changed in the light of the original circumstances and any new evidence or relevant changes in circumstances. If the need has been met or the local budget is under pressure, a payment may not be awarded as these are relevant changes in circumstances. The need, however, may exist in a different form (eg, money was borrowed to meet the need giving rise to debt) and in those circumstances a payment can still be awarded.

The procedure

Reviews are almost always conducted on the basis of written information. You have no right to an oral hearing although an SFI can interview you, if necessary, 'at a mutually convenient location'.[55]

You will be sent copies of all the papers which the SFI has about your case before the review takes place. You should look through the papers and send any written comments you have to the SFI on the form provided. You are given two weeks to send in your comments but if you need longer, contact the SFI office and request an extension. The papers will include the full written decision of the HEO (see p465). You should read it carefully and comment on anything which is wrong, irrelevant or with which you disagree.

SFI decisions

SFIs can:[56]

either confirm the SFO's decision;
or substitute their own decision;
or refer the case back to an SFO for determination.

You will receive a detailed written decision. There are long delays (often several weeks) with SFI reviews and you could complain to your MP about these. Crisis loan reviews should be done urgently. If you are unhappy about an SFI decision, get advice. There is no right of appeal, but if the decision is unreasonable or wrong in law, you could ask the SFI to reconsider it,[57] or apply for judicial review in the High Court (you will need legal advice to do this and even if you win the legal argument you may not end up with a payment if the local budget cannot afford it).

If the SFI disagrees with the SFO decision, the case will usually be referred back to the local Benefits Agency office for redetermination. The SFI decision will give details of why the Benefits Agency decision is unacceptable. Common examples are that local guidance has been followed too rigidly or that the evidence does not support the decision given. The Benefits Agency must redetermine the case in the light of the SFI's comments.[58] You will then be issued with a fresh decision which should include full reasons, with reference to the SFI's comments, on form SF614.[59]

Second SFI reviews

If the Benefits Agency do not change a decision wholly in your favour after referral back by an SFI, you can request a second further review by an SFI. You should *always* do this if you are not satisfied that the Benefits Agency has properly taken into account the SFI's decision.

To apply for a second SFI review, you must write to your local Benefits Agency office within 28 days of being issued their last review decision. The rules and procedures are identical to first SFI reviews. Your grounds are likely to be that you are not satisfied the Benefits Agency took proper account of the SFI decision. SFIs seem generally willing to accept second applications, even if you apply late. They also commonly substitute their own decision rather than refer the case back to the Benefits Agency again. They will often find in your favour if it is clear the Benefits Agency has still failed to deal with your case properly. It is always, therefore, worth asking for a second (or even third!) SFI review, if necessary.

PART TEN

Other benefits

Health service benefits

This chapter covers:

I. INTRODUCTION

Although the National Health Service (NHS) generally provides free health care for everybody, charges are made for prescriptions and certain treatment and appliances.

Income support (IS) and family credit (FC) claimants and their dependants are 'passported', so that they do not have to pay charges. Some people do not have to pay these charges whatever their income or savings. Other people do not have to pay the charges, or only have to pay reduced charges, if their income is low. The precise rules for each type of charge are set out in the other parts of this chapter, but the way that low income is calculated is explained here.

How low income is worked out

If you receive IS or FC, you are automatically exempt from charges. If you have over £8,000 capital, you must pay them in full unless exempted on other grounds.

Otherwise, the DSS decides if your income is low enough by comparing your 'requirements' to your 'resources'. If your 'resources' are less than, or the same as, your 'requirements' you do not have to pay anything. If they are more than your 'requirements' you may still qualify for partial help with dental costs (see p476), sight tests (see p477), glasses (see p478), wigs and fabric supports (see p480) and fares to hospital (see p481). You cannot get partial help with prescriptions. You may be better off using a pre-payment certificate (see p474).

'Requirements' and 'resources' are calculated as at the date on which you claim free or reduced dental costs, glasses, fares to hospital etc, unless, having already paid, you are claiming a refund, in which case it is the date you paid.[1]

Requirements[2]

Your requirements are based on the rules for calculating entitlement to IS, but more housing costs are included and some of the restrictions do not apply.

Your requirements are:

- your personal allowances (see p341);
- your premiums (see p342);
- rent *minus* any housing benefit you receive;
- 100 per cent of your council tax *minus* any council tax benefit you receive;
- your repayments (both capital and interest and including insurance payments on endowment mortgages) on mortgages and other loans secured on your home (with no reduction for the first 16 weeks and including second mortgages and regardless of the purpose for which the mortgage or loan was taken out);
- accommodation charges for people in residential care or nursing homes, *plus* an amount for meals (see p97).

The reductions which apply to IS because of voluntary unemployment or involvement in a trade dispute do not apply. Nor do the special rules for people from abroad or members of religious orders, whose requirements are calculated in the usual way.

Resources

If you have **capital** over £8,000, calculated as for IS (see Chapter 19), you will not qualify on low-income grounds.[3]

Your **income** is calculated as for IS (see Chapter 18), with the following modifications.[4]

Liable relative payments

The complicated rules for calculating liable relative payments (see p133) do not apply. Instead, **maintenance payments** are treated as follows:

- If you are due to receive regular payments, your normal weekly income will be:

- the weekly amount of those payments if they are made regularly; *or*
- the average weekly amount you have actually received in the 13 weeks immediately before you claimed, if the payments were not made regularly.
- Payments which are not part of a regular series (ie, lump sums), are simply treated as capital.

Earnings

- The rule for deciding the *period* for which income is paid (see p360) does not apply. If you receive a payment of income which does not relate to a particular period, it is likely that it will be counted as income in the week in which it is paid.
- The rule about *when* income is treated as paid (see p361) also does not apply, so payments will only be taken into account as your resources when they are actually paid to you.
- If you are affected by a trade dispute, your earnings are taken to be those you would have received had there been no dispute.[5] None of the modifications to treatment of income under IS which apply to people affected by a trade dispute apply for the purpose of calculating your resources.

Disregards

- There is no £15 disregard for couples who have been unemployed for two years (see p371). Instead, if you are one of a couple not entitled to a £15 disregard on other grounds, you will have £10 of your earnings disregarded. If one partner's earnings are less than £10, the remainder of the disregard can be used on any earnings of the other partner.
- There is no disregard of payments you receive and intend to use towards housing costs not met under the IS regulations. Of course, most of the housing costs not eligible for IS are added into the calculation on the requirements side.
- There is no provision for dealing with the situation in which you receive two payments of earnings or income of the same kind from the same source in the same week. Your normal income or earnings for one week should be counted in calculating your resources.
- The £10 disregard from student loans only applies to student claimants who are eligible for a premium or who are deaf (in certain circumstances), and to non-student claimants with a student partner.

Low-income certificates

If your income is low enough to qualify for free services you get certificate AG2. If your income is not that low, you may still qualify for partial remission of charges and get certificate AG3. You get these certificates by completing form AG1, obtainable from your doctor, dentist, optician, hospital or Benefits Agency office.

Certificates last for six months. You should make a repeat claim on form AG1 shortly before the expiry date. If your circumstances change, write to the Health Benefits Unit. The form AG1 should be sent to the Health Benefits Unit, Sandyford House, Newcastle-upon-Tyne NE2 1DB who will issue a fresh certificate if necessary. The Prescription Pricing Authority took over responsibility for the administration of the low-income scheme in April 1993. There is no right of appeal against a decision made by the Authority, but if you feel they have made a mistake, ask them to reconsider their decision (see Appendix 1 for address).

2. PRESCRIPTIONS

Usually, prescriptions cost £4.75, but some people do not have to pay. Those who need a lot of prescriptions can limit the cost by obtaining a pre-payment certificate (see p474).

Free prescriptions

You qualify if:[6]

- you receive IS or FC (or you are a member of the family of someone who does – see p328); *or*
- your income is low enough (see p470); *or*
- you are under 16 or under 19 and in full-time education; *or*
- you are over pensionable age (65 for men, 60 for women)*; *or*
- you are pregnant; *or*
- you have given birth within the last 12 months (even if the child was stillborn or has since died); *or*
- you are a war disablement pensioner and you need the prescription for your war disability (in which case you claim from your War Pensions Office); *or*
- you suffer from one or more of the following conditions:
  - a continuing physical disability which prevents you leaving your home except with the help of another person;
  - epilepsy requiring continuous anti-convulsive therapy;
  - a permanent fistula, including a caecostomy, ileostomy, laryngostomy or colostomy, needing continuous surgical dressing or an appliance;
  - diabetes mellitus, except where treatment is for diet alone;
  - myxoedema;

- hypoparathyroidism;
- diabetes insipidus and other forms of hypopituitarism;
- forms of hypoadrenalism (including Addison's disease) for which specific substitution therapy is essential;
- myasthenia gravis.

* The different pensionable ages for men and women may be in breach of European Union equal treatment rules. Leave has been given to challenge the legality of the different ages in the High Court.

Claims

You claim by ticking a box on the back of the prescription but, unless you are claiming on grounds of age or because you are receiving IS or FC, you must already have a certificate.

If you are a pregnant woman, you should obtain a form from your doctor, midwife or health visitor (or, in Scotland, the Primary Care Division of the Health Board) and send it to the Family Health Services Authority (in Scotland, the Health Board). You will be sent an exemption certificate which lasts until a year after it is expected you will give birth.

If you are claiming on the ground that you have given birth within the last year (and do not already have an exemption certificate) or you are suffering from one of the conditions listed above, you should complete the form in DSS leaflet P11 which you can obtain from your doctor's surgery, a chemist or a Benefits Agency office.

If you are claiming on the ground of low income, obtain form AG1 from your doctor, dentist, optician, hospital or a Benefits Agency office and send it off. You will be sent certificate AG2 which you can use to get free prescriptions for the six months during which it is valid.

Refunds[7]

If you think you may be entitled to free prescriptions but do not have a certificate, ask the chemist for a special receipt – form FP57 (in Scotland, EC57) – when you pay the charge. The form explains how you claim a refund. You must apply within three months. These periods can be extended for as long as you can show good cause.[8]

Pre-payment certificates[9]

If you need a lot of prescriptions, but are not entitled to them free, you can still reduce the cost by buying a pre-payment certificate (sometimes called a 'season ticket'). This costs £24.60 for four months, or £67.70 for one year. It saves money if you need more than five items on prescription in four months or 14 items in a year. To get one, obtain form FP95 (EC95 in Scotland) from the Benefits Agency, a post office, or chemist. This should be sent to your Family Health Services Authority (Health Board in Scotland). A refund can be given if someone buys a pre-payment certificate and then, within a month, qualifies for free prescriptions, or dies.

3. DENTAL TREATMENT AND DENTURES

In this section, 'dental treatment' includes dental check-ups. NHS check-ups cost £3.92. The cost of subsequent treatment varies depending on what needs to be done. However, many people are entitled to free treatment and appliances such as dentures and bridges.[10] Others need pay only reduced charges.

Free dental treatment and dentures

You qualify if:[11]

- you receive IS or FC (or you are a member of the family of someone who does – see p328); or
- your income is low enough (see p470); or
- you are under:
  - 16 (for treatment, dentures or bridges),
  - 18 (for treatment),
  - 19 (for treatment, dentures, or bridges if you are still in full-time education); or
- you are pregnant and were pregnant when the dentist accepted you for treatment or you have given birth within the last 12 months (even if the child was stillborn or has since died); or
- you are a war disablement pensioner and need the treatment or appliances because of your war disability (in which case you claim a refund from the War Pensions Directorate).

Claims

You claim by ticking a box on a form provided by the dentist, so tell the receptionist that you think you qualify for free treatment *before* you have it.

A woman who is pregnant or has a child under the age of one may be asked to show her Family Health Services Authority Exemption Certificate, so it is best to get one before you go for the treatment (see p474).

If you are claiming on the ground of low income, you again need certificate AG2. This is the same one as is used for free prescriptions. See p472 for how to get it.

Refunds[12]

If you paid a charge when you could have had appliances or treatment free because you receive IS or FC or you have a low income, you can obtain a refund. You should get a receipt for the items or treatment you have paid for. You must apply, within three months of paying the charge, using form AG5 and form AG1 (obtainable from a Benefits Agency office) if you are claiming on low-income grounds and you do not have a current AG2 or AG3 certificate. This period will be extended for as long as you can show good cause for a late application.

Reduced charges

If you do not qualify for *free* treatment on low-income grounds, but your income is nevertheless low, you may get partial help with charges for dental treatment and appliances. Your 'resources' must exceed your 'requirements' (see pp470-72 for how these are calculated) by less than one-third of the charge, and you must have less than £8,000 capital. You will be entitled to the difference between the charge for one course of treatment, including any appliances, and three times the amount by which your income resources exceed your requirements.[13] To claim, you need certificate AG3 which you obtain in the same way as certificate AG2 (see p472). If you paid the full charge when you need not have done, you can obtain a refund (see above).

4. SIGHT TESTS AND GLASSES

Treatment for eye problems is free under the NHS, but sight tests are not; nor are glasses or contact lenses. However, certain people are entitled to free or reduced-cost sight tests and to vouchers which will cover all or part of the cost of glasses or contact lenses.

Free sight tests

There is no set charge for sight tests so it may be worth shopping around for them. Some opticians do not charge at all.
  You qualify for a free (NHS) test if:[14]

- you receive IS or FC (or you are a member of the family of someone who does – see p328); *or*
- your income is low enough (see p470); *or*
- you are under 16 or under 19 and in full-time education; *or*
- you are registered blind or partially sighted; *or*
- you have been prescribed complex lenses; *or*

- you have been diagnosed as suffering from diabetes or glaucoma; *or*
- you are aged 40 or over and are the parent, brother, sister or child of someone suffering from glaucoma; *or*
- you are a war disablement pensioner and require the sight test because of your war disability (in which case you claim from your War Pensions Office);
- you are a patient of the Hospital Eye Service.

To claim, tell the optician before you have the test. If you are claiming on the ground of low income, you need certificate AG2 – ie, the same certificate that entitles you to free prescriptions (see p472 for how to obtain one). If you do not have certificate AG2 before the test, you must apply for one within two weeks of the test and then apply for a refund (see below).

Reduced-cost sight tests

If your income is low but not low enough for you to qualify for free sight tests, you may be entitled to have a private sight test at a reduced charge.[15] To claim, you need certificate AG3 which you obtain in the same way as certificate AG2 (see p472). You will qualify only if your 'resources' exceed your 'requirements' (see pp470-72 for how these are calculated) by less than £12.92. You will have to pay three times the amount by which your 'resources' exceed your 'requirements'. If you do not have certificate AG3 before the test, you must apply within two weeks of the test and then apply for a refund (see p479).

'Full-value' vouchers for glasses and contact lenses

If your sight test shows you need glasses, you are given a prescription by the optician which is valid for two years.

You will qualify for a 'full-value' voucher to meet the cost of glasses or contact lenses if:[16]

- you receive IS or FC (or you are a member of the family of someone who does – see p328); *or*
- your income is low enough (see p470); *or*
- you are under 16 or under 19 and in full-time education; *or*
- you are a Hospital Eye Service patient needing frequent changes of glasses or contact lenses; *or*
- you have been prescribed complex lenses.

Certain war pensioners can obtain refunds of charges for glasses or contact lenses, even though they do not qualify for vouchers (see p479).

If you qualify for a voucher, the optician will give you one if:[17]

- you require the glasses or contact lenses for the first time; *or*
- your new prescription differs from your old one; *or*
- your old glasses have worn out through fair wear and tear; *or*
- you are under 16 and have lost or damaged your old glasses or contact lenses and the cost of repair or replacement is not covered by insurance or warranty; *or*
- you are ill and, as a result of your illness, have lost or damaged your glasses or contact lenses and the cost of repair or replacement is not covered by insurance or warranty *and*
  - you receive IS or FC (or you are a member of the family of someone who does – see p328); *or*
  - your income is low enough (see p470); *or*
  - you have been prescribed complex lenses.

The voucher is valid for six months.[18] Its value depends on the type of lenses you need, and each type of voucher is at a fixed amount.[19] It does not, therefore, automatically cover the value of your glasses. Although it should enable you to buy glasses or contact lenses (or have your existing ones repaired) without having to pay anything yourself (except in the case of complex lenses when you are expected to contribute to the cost unless you would qualify for a voucher on other grounds), you may have to shop around to find a cheap enough pair. If you cannot find a cheap enough pair, or if you choose to buy a more expensive pair, you will have to make up the difference yourself.

You must have the voucher *before* you buy the glasses or contact lenses. The circumstances in which refunds can be made are very limited (see below). This means applying for certificate AG2 if you wish to claim on grounds of low income (see p472).

There are eight different bands of value for the vouchers ranging from £25.50 to £157. A Benefits Agency booklet called *NHS sight tests and vouchers for glass* (G11) lists the vouchers available.

Reduced-value vouchers

If your income is low but not low enough to qualify for a full-value voucher, you may qualify for a voucher for a lower amount. The value of the voucher will be the value of a full-value one *less* three times the amount by which your 'resources' exceed your 'requirements' (see p470). You must apply for certificate AG3 (in the same way as for certificate AG2 – see p472) *before* you pay for the glasses or contact lenses.

Refunds

Sight tests

Refunds can only be made if you are entitled to free or reduced-cost sight tests on the ground of low income and apply for certificate AG2 or AG3 within two weeks of having the test, using form AG1 (see p472). You will get a refund if you then send certificate AG2 or AG3 with a receipt from the optician to the Family Health Services Authority within three months of having the test.

Glasses and contact lenses

Refunds will only be made if the glasses or contact lenses were prescribed through the Hospital Eye Service *and* you would have had a voucher on the ground of low income if you had had certificate AG2 or AG3, or you are getting IS or FC. Ask the hospital or Benefits Agency for form AG5 (and form AG1 if you want to claim on low-income grounds and you do not hold a current AG2 or AG3 certificate). You must submit your claim within one month of the date of the receipt.

War pensioners

If you qualify for a free sight test or free glasses or contact lenses only because you are a war pensioner, you must pay the charges and then claim a refund from Treatment Group, War Pensions Directorate, DSS, Norcross, Blackpool FY5 3TA.

Home visits

If you have certificate AG2 and you want to have your eyes tested at home, you can be visited free of charge. If you have certificate AG3, you can put this towards the cost of the visit.

Repairs and replacement

Children can get help with the repair of their glasses. It is advisable to take them back to the optician who sold them. Adults can get help with the cost of repair and replacement if, at the time it is required, they are entitled to help under the voucher scheme and the repair or replacement is required because the loss or damage has occurred as a result of illness.

5. WIGS AND FABRIC SUPPORTS[20]

NHS wigs cost between £40 and £151 and fabric supports cost either £18.50 or £24.50. Some people are entitled to them free or at reduced cost.

Free wigs and fabric supports

You qualify for free wigs and fabric supports if:

- you receive IS or FC (or you are a member of the family of someone who does – see p328); *or*
- your income is low enough (see p470); *or*
- you are under 16 or under 19 and in full-time education; *or*
- you are a hospital in-patient when the wig or fabric support is supplied; *or*
- you are a war disablement pensioner and need the wig or fabric support for your war injury.

You claim when you go to the hospital to have the wig or fabric support fitted. You may have to show some proof that you are entitled to free provision. If you are claiming on the ground of low income, you need certificate AG3 which you can get by filling in form AG1 (see p472).

Refunds

The rules are the same as for dental treatment (see p476).

Reduced charges

The rules are the same as for dental treatment (see p476).

6. FARES TO HOSPITAL[21]

Who can get help

You qualify for help if you are attending an NHS hospital or clinic for treatment or a disablement services centre *and*:

- you receive IS or FC (or you are a member of the family of someone who does – see p328); *or*
- your income is low enough (see p470); *or*
- you are a patient at a sexually transmitted disease clinic more than 15 miles from your home; *or*
- you are a war disablement pensioner and the treatment is for your war injury.

You may also get help if you live in the Highlands and Islands of Scotland or the Isles of Scilly.

Payment is made at the hospital each time you visit.

You usually have to get yourself to hospital, but once you are there you are paid the cost of the return trip. However, you can ask the hospital to send you the money in advance. If you cannot get this in time you may be able to get a crisis loan from your local Benefits Agency office (see p449).

If you are claiming on the ground of low income, you will need certificate AG3 which you can get by filling in form AG1 (see p472).

What costs can be paid

You can claim for:

- normal public transport fares;
- estimated petrol costs;
- a reasonable contribution to a local voluntary car scheme;
- taxi fares, but only if there is no alternative for all or part of the journey.

The travelling costs of a companion will also be paid if it is necessary for you to be accompanied.

Refunds

If you have already paid your travel costs and you want to claim a refund after your visit you must apply on form AG5. The rules are the same as for dental treatment (see p476).

Partial help

If your 'resources' exceed your 'requirements' and you have savings of less than £8,000, you will get the difference between your excess income and your weekly fares.

Visiting patients

If you are receiving IS and are visiting a close relative or partner, you may be entitled to help from the social fund (see p453).

If you are visiting a war pensioner who is being treated for her/his war injury, you may also be entitled to help.

7. FREE MILK AND VITAMINS[22]

Free milk tokens

The following people qualify for free milk tokens:

- Disabled children aged 5 to 16 who cannot go to school because of their disability (claim on form FW20 available from your Benefits Agency Office).

- Expectant mothers who are receiving IS (or who are a member of the family of someone who is – see p328). You do not have to wait for the Certificate of Expected Date of Confinement. A note from your doctor or midwife will entitle you to free milk tokens at once.
- Children under 5 whose family receives IS.

Note that expectant mothers and children under 5 also qualify for free vitamins (see p483).

The milk tokens for each person entitled can be exchanged for 7 pints/ 8 half litres of liquid milk a week, but if they are for a child under one they can be exchanged for 900 grammes of dried milk a week instead. You can use milk tokens at a clinic to buy dried milk or they can be exchanged for fresh milk from suppliers who are then reimbursed by the Secretary of State. Tokens cannot be used to purchase soya milk. Suppliers can accept milk tokens as part-payment if the milk you buy is more expensive than the basic-cost milk.[23] Otherwise you should not have to pay towards the cost of your milk, even though the Benefits Agency does not always reimburse your milk supplier for the full amount.[24] If you cannot find a supplier who will accept your tokens you can apply to the Benefits Agency to cash them.[25]

If you lose your milk tokens, the Benefits Agency may replace them, but it does not have to do so.[26] If you are turned down, you should try to negotiate, perhaps with the support of a social worker, health visitor, or your MP.

If you do not receive milk tokens to which you are entitled, they should be replaced by the Benefits Agency if 'the Secretary of State is satisfied . . . that some act or omission on his part was responsible'[27] for your failure to receive milk tokens. Again, there is no right of appeal if you are turned down, but you should try negotiating.

If you are absent from home for less than a week, with the result that you miss some of the milk covered by your token, your supplier can give you a refund for the pints you have missed. You have to ask the supplier to do this during the period within which the token is valid.[28]

Free milk for children in day-care

Children, whether with a registered childminder, a registered day nursery or a day nursery which is not required to register, can get one-third of a pint of milk free for each day that they are in such day-care.[29] This entitlement is in addition to any entitlement you get from being in a family on IS, or having a disabled child (see above). It is the childminder or organiser of the nursery who applies to the Benefits Agency. They are then reimbursed for money spent on milk, normally every four months in arrears. Children under one are allowed one-third of a pint, or dried milk made up to one-third of a pint.

Reduced-cost milk

Anyone attending a maternity or childcare clinic can buy dried milk at a reduced price.

Families on **family credit** with children under one can get dried milk at an even lower price from maternity and child health clinics.[30] You are allowed to buy up to 900 grammes of dried milk a week for each child under one, at a cost of £3.40. You can buy it for up to four weeks in arrears and up to four weeks in advance. You need evidence that you get family credit to buy dried milk at reduced prices from clinics, and that you get IS to get free vitamins (see below). If you do not have this evidence through 'some act or omission' on the part of the Secretary of State, you can get a refund.[31]

Free vitamins

The following qualify for free vitamins:[32]

- Expectant mothers who are receiving IS (or who are a member of the family of someone who is – see p328).
- Nursing mothers (ie, those breastfeeding a child(ren) under 30- weeks- old) who are receiving IS (or who are a member of the family of some- one who is – see p328).
- Children under 5 whose family receives IS.

Entitlement to free vitamins provides two bottles of children's vitamin drops every 13 weeks for children, five 45-tablet containers of vitamins to nursing mothers and two 45-tablet containers of vitamins every 13 weeks while the pregnancy lasts, to expectant mothers.[33] Vitamins are available from child health and maternity clinics.

If you are not entitled to free vitamins, you can still buy cheap ones if you are attending a maternity or childcare clinic.

CHAPTER TWENTY-SIX

Local authority benefits and services

This chapter covers:
1. Education benefits (below)
2. Housing renovation grants (p487)
3. Social services (p490)

I. EDUCATION BENEFITS

Free school meals

Education authorities must make such provision for meals 'as appears to be requisite' in the middle of the day,[1] but they have no responsibility to provide a suitable main meal of the day. All pupils must be charged the same price for meals, milk or other refreshments that are provided unless entitled to free meals. Education authorities have to provide such facilities as are considered 'appropriate'[2] for pupils to eat meals which they bring to the school. These do not have to be on the school premises.[3]

The only children entitled to free school meals are those who are members of the family (see p328) of a person receiving income support (IS). (This includes 16/17/18-year-olds receiving IS in their own right.[4]) Free meals should be available for nursery children, and to young people still in education up to their 19th birthday.

Clothing grants

Education authorities may only give grants for:

- school uniforms;
- 'necessitous' clothing which is not actually school uniform. This could include sports kit.[5]

They are free to determine the level of income at which grants (if any) will be paid, and to make their own eligibility rules. Grants may be in the form of either cash or vouchers.[6] There may be rules about the number of times you can claim. It is often best to apply in the summer term for the school year commencing in September.

Educational maintenance allowances

These weekly allowances are paid to those children who stay on at school after the school-leaving age.[7] They can be paid whether or not the child has stayed on to take exams. There is considerable variation between authorities as to how much is paid and even what they are called, but these allowances are always paid on income grounds, and are disregarded in full in calculating IS, family credit (FC), disability working allowance (DWA) or housing benefit (HB).[8]

A child who leaves school to go to a technical college full-time might be eligible for a minor award.[9] You can find out from your education authority.

There is a scheme for giving children free places at independent, fee-paying schools if they would not otherwise be able to go there. The school fees are reimbursed by the government.[10] For more information, contact the Department of Education, Schools 4, A.P.S., Mowden Hall, Staindrop Road, Darlington, Co. Durham DL3 9BG, tel: 0325 392163.

Free transport to school

Education authorities *must* provide free transport to school where it is not within walking distance of the child's home.[11] 'Walking distance' is defined as less than two miles for a child under 8, and less than three miles for older children.[12] The distance between home and school is measured by the 'nearest available route',[13] which is not necessarily the shortest.[14]

Education authorities must look at the age of the pupil, the nature of the route, and alternative routes s/he could reasonably be expected to take.[15] They can also look at the distance involved and do not necessarily have to provide free transport if there is a suitable school nearer to the child's home.[16]

Education authorities *may* meet any pupil's 'reasonable travelling expenses' even where there is no duty to provide free transport.[17] However, it is rare for authorities to use this power except to reduce the walking distances required to qualify for free transport.

Students attending a college of further education may get help with the cost of fares. You can get the form from the college.

Fares to visit boarders

If your child is at boarding school in order to receive special education and you cannot afford to visit her/him, the education authority has the power to meet all or part of your fares and any other expenses involved. The Department of Education and Science has told education authorities that they can provide this help if your child's education would suffer as a result of you not being able to visit.[18] A letter from a doctor, social worker or teacher supporting your case might be helpful. If your child is being looked after by social services, and is away at school or a children's home, the social services department (in Scotland, the social work department) can help you with fares.[19]

Charges for educational services

Although education authorities may charge for some educational services, the law makes it quite clear that there must be **no charge** for the following:

- an activity that occurs during school hours (with the exception of individual music tuition – but see below);[20]
- individual music tuition where the child is preparing for a public examination;[21]
- activities partly outside school hours where more than half, including travel, are in school hours;[22]
- activities wholly or partly outside school hours which are part of the national curriculum or part of the exam syllabus.[23]

Thus, transport, entrance fees and equipment must be free as long as they arise as part of the school curriculum.

The only exceptions are that parents **may be required to pay** for:

- board and lodging on field trips;
- examination fees if the child fails, without good reason, to meet any examination requirement. This will be decided by the education authority.[24]

However, *charging is optional*. No charge may be made until the governors and the education authority have decided a charging policy and a policy setting out when they will reduce charges or meet them in full. Charges must not exceed the actual cost. If the pupil's parent(s) receives IS or FC at the time of a school trip,[25] any charge for board and lodging must be met.

Any other charge *may* be met or reduced if it is appropriate, whether or not the parent(s) receives IS or FC.

Under the Children Act, a local authority *must* provide supervised activities for children in need outside of school hours or during school holidays,[26] and *can* provide it for all other children.[27] Any such service provided under the Children Act must be free to any family on IS, FC and DWA, whether classed as 'children in need' or not.[28] In any other case, the charge cannot be more than the client can reasonably be expected to pay.[29]

Pupils who are boarding

Education authorities may charge fees if they provide board and lodging; but they cannot charge if the board and lodging is provided because education suitable to the pupil's ability, age and aptitude cannot otherwise be provided. This applies whether it is a maintained or grant-maintained school.

Fees for board and lodging may also be met or reduced in cases of financial hardship.[30]

Student grants

These are beyond the scope of this *Handbook*. You can get information from your education authority or careers service, or from a welfare officer for the National Union of Students (NUS) at your college or university. The NUS provides information sheets on student grants. Write (enclosing a stamped addressed envelope) to the Student Financial Support Unit, NUS, Nelson Mandela House, 461 Holloway Road, London, N7 6LJ.

Claiming education benefits

To find out about any of the benefits mentioned above (other than student grants), ask an education welfare officer who can be contacted via the local school or college.

2. HOUSING RENOVATION GRANTS

A local housing authority has the power to provide help with the cost of improving your home.[31] This section describes the scheme as it applies to England and Wales. For Scotland, see the leaflet *Improve your home with a grant*, available from your local authority. The amount of financial help that you will receive depends on a means test, very similar to that for HB.

Types of grant

The following grants are available:

- Renovation – for works of improvement, repair or conversion.
- Common parts – for work to common parts of a building let as flats.
- Houses in multiple occupation – for improvement or repair to a house in multiple occupation (only available to landlords).
- Disabled facilities – to make a property suitable for a disabled occupant.
- Group repair – external repairs to groups of houses which are not in reasonable repair.
- Minor works assistance.

Who can apply for which grants – a rough guide

	Renovation	Common parts	HMO	Disabled facilities	Minor works
owner-occupier	yes	no	no	yes	yes
long leaseholder	yes	maybe	no	yes	yes
tenant	maybe	maybe	no	yes	maybe
landlord	yes	yes	yes	yes	no

Exclusions

You cannot apply for a grant unless the property is at least ten years old.[32] The property must not be owned by a local authority, a new town corporation, an urban development council, a housing action trust, or the Development Board for Rural Wales. None of these restrictions apply to disabled facilities grants.[33]

Restrictions are imposed which, in broad terms, require you or a family member to live in the dwelling. The exact rules vary depending on whether you are an owner-occupier, tenant or landlord applying for the grant.[34] Various other restrictions may apply related to the state of the property. The effect of these is that you are not eligible for a grant if the property is in such a poor state of repair that even when you have carried out the improvements it will still not be considered habitable.[35]

Minor works assistance grants can only be paid if you are in receipt of IS, FC, DWA, HB or council tax benefit (CTB), and are limited to a maximum payment of £1,080 an application and £3,240 in any three-year period.[36] Only people aged 60 or older can apply for some types of minor works assistance. Check with your local authority.

The grant is limited to £50,000 if it is in respect of a mandatory grant – ie, if the dwelling is unfit for human habitation.

Claiming

You must apply for a grant on the form supplied by the local housing authority,[37] and include two estimates for the works that are to be carried out. The local authority may agree to waive the requirement to supply two estimates. Grants are only available for work which has been approved by the local authority. If you have completed work before applying for a grant, or before a grant was approved, you get no help unless these works were necessary to comply with a statutory notice.

It may also be worth contacting the social services/social work department for the area in which you live if you need work doing because of ill-health or disability. They might be able to help with adaptations – eg, installing a downstairs bathroom (see p491).

The means test

If you are awarded a grant, you may still have to pay something towards the total cost of the work. The local authority calculates the amount you have to pay (if any) by comparing your income with your 'needs' (called your applicable amount). These are calculated in the same way as for HB (see p339 and Chapter 18), with the following main exceptions:

General

- The means test applies not just to you and your family, but to anyone else who has an interest in the dwelling as a joint owner or joint tenant and who lives in the property, or intends to do so, and any disabled person for whom a disabled facilities grant has been awarded.[38] This means that if you are applying with someone else who has an interest in the dwelling, but is not on IS, you may have to contribute towards the cost, even though you are on IS.

All references to legislation in this section are subject to change because the regulations are to be consolidated in 1994/95. The substance of the legislation will, however, remain the same.

Applicable amounts

- This always includes a renovation grant premium of £40.[39]
- There is no reduction in the applicable amount if someone is in hospital.
- If you are on IS your applicable amount is £1.[40]

Income

- Your income is normally based on the 52 weeks prior to the application, but if another period more accurately reflects your current finan-

cial situation this period should be used instead.[41]
- If you are on IS, you are counted as having no income.[42]
- Capital over £5,000 is assumed to produce an income at the rate of £1 for every £250 (or part of £250).[43]

Capital

- There is no upper capital limit which will bar you from making a claim but, of course, the tariff income may bar you instead.
- You receive a personal allowance for a child unless s/he has more than £5,000 capital.[44]

You receive the full cost of the work if *either* you are in receipt of IS *or* your income is the same or less than your applicable amount under the grants means test.[45]

If your income is greater than your applicable amount then the grant will be reduced using a formula. For details of this formula, contact your local council office who administers these grants.

3. SOCIAL SERVICES

Help for children and young people

Social services departments can give financial assistance, or assistance in kind, to safeguard and promote the welfare of children in need.[46] A wide variety of needs may be met and can include things like food, clothing, nappies, fuel bills, contributions towards the cost of a holiday and help in the home. The definition of 'children in need' is contained within the 1989 Children Act.[47]

Local authority social services departments can also provide help to young people who have left, or are leaving, 'care' (this includes young people who are 'accommodated' by the local authority). This help can include financial assistance – eg, to set up the young person in independent accommodation or to subsidise a young person who is in training, education, employment or seeking employment.[48]

Policy on how families and young people can be helped varies widely between different authorities. However, each local authority has to have a means by which representations and complaints can be made,[49] and must also publicise the services they provide under the Children Act for families, children and care-leavers.[50]

If a local authority provides a service for a child or young person in need, such as a day nursery or a home-help, no charge can be levied on the family if they are getting IS, FC or DWA.[51]

In Scotland, the power to give financial help to children and families is provided under section 12 of the Social Work (Scotland) Act.

Help for sick and disabled people

A local authority has the power to provide for chronically sick and disabled people:[52]

- practical assistance in the home – eg, a home-help;
- a radio, TV, library or 'similar recreational facilities', or help in obtaining them;
- lectures, games, outings or 'other recreational facilities' outside the home;
- help in taking advantage of educational opportunities;
- help with travelling to work or recreational facilities;
- help in carrying out adaptations to the home, or in providing extra facilities designed to give 'greater safety, comfort or convenience' (eg, a ramp or building an extra room on the ground floor);
- help in taking holidays (not necessarily at holiday homes or under official holiday schemes);
- meals, at home or elsewhere;
- a telephone, and any special equipment needed in using it, and/or financial help with getting one;
- residential or nursing care (see p97).

A local authority sets its own criteria for deciding whether you are in need of help. But once it has admitted that the need for a service under the Act exists, it has a duty to meet it.[53]

It may decide to charge you for that service. However, the charge must be 'reasonable' and no more than you can be reasonably expected to pay, taking your income into account.[54] This means, for example, that a local authority cannot charge everyone a flat rate for a service unless there is also some procedure for lowering or abolishing the charge for an individual. Although it may seem very unfair, it is not unlawful for a local authority to ask for a higher charge for a service, such as home care, from people getting attendance allowance or disability living allowance care component. However, a local authority cannot charge more for a service for people getting disability living allowance mobility component than it does for people who are not.[55]

It would also be unlawful to impose a charge that defeats the purpose of the Act. Local authorities cannot refuse or withdraw a service on the grounds of non-payment, but they can take debt enforcement proceedings for the arrears.

If you need any of the items or services listed above, you should apply to the local authority social services department. If they refuse to help, ask for a reason. If you are refused on the ground that, although it recognises the need exists it does not have the resources to help you, obtain legal advice about judicial review or suing the council.[56] You could also complain to the Minister for the Disabled at the DSS, Richmond House, 79 Whitehall, London SW1A 2NS. Give full details of your needs and circumstances and, if possible, evidence of the local authority's acknowledgement that you need the service requested. The Minister can declare the local authority in default of its duty and issue instructions as to how it should carry out that duty.[57]

Alternatively, you could use the local authorities' complaints procedure, which it has to have as part of its community care responsibilities.[58] If you are not satisfied with the outcome, you could then approach the local government Ombudsman.

CHAPTER TWENTY-SEVEN

Other sources of help

This chapter covers:

1. Special funds for people with disabilities (below)
2. Help from charities (p496)
3. Home insulation grant aid (p497)

I. SPECIAL FUNDS FOR PEOPLE WITH DISABILITIES

The Family Fund

This is a government fund administered by the Joseph Rowntree Memorial Trust. It exists to provide help in the form of goods, services or a grant of money to the families of children with severe disabilities.

Who can apply

Families with a child with a very severe disability can apply to this fund. The child must live in the UK and be under 16. There is a discretion to extend this age limit in some circumstances. Examples of very severe disabilities are the loss of two or more limbs and other serious deformities, severe mental retardation, the most serious forms of visual handicap or deafness and some multiple handicaps. If your child lives permanently in a residential home or hospital, help is limited to specific provision for existing expenses which have been refused by other sources of help.

What sort of help can be provided

The fund has wide discretion to provide help that would relieve stress arising from the day-to-day care of the child. In general, it can only help with certain needs which are not met by statutory services. You cannot get help for a foster child who is in the care of the local authority. The following are *examples* of items it has helped with:

- hire cars, taxi fares, cars and driving lessons, so that a family can go on outings;
- washing machines and dryers;
- clothing, bedding and furnishings;
- aids and adaptations (but only in very limited circumstances);
- family holidays;
- recreation equipment.

These are only some examples and parents are encouraged to ask for any items that they feel they need.

How to apply

Application forms are available from the Family Fund, PO Box 50, York YO1 1UY. When you have returned the form, you will be visited by a representative of the fund.

General family circumstances are taken into account, but there is no income test. If your application is refused you can re-apply, and if it is refused again you can apply to the Management Committee of the fund.

Help for people with HIV infection

For many people with HIV infection, the benefits system is inadequate and insensitive to their needs. For this reason, there are a number of local and national charities that may be able to help people with HIV infection. For more details, contact your local AIDS Helpline. Your local Lesbian and Gay Switchboard may also have details. Their phone numbers will be in your local phone book. For more detailed information about benefits and charities, contact the Terrence Higgins Trust, 52-54 Grays Inn Road, London WC1X 8JU, tel: 071 831 0330.

The Macfarlane Trust administers three government funds established to help people with haemophilia and HIV infection. Payments are made in the form of both grants and regular payments for living expenses (particularly for diet and heating needs). The payments do not affect tax or social security benefits, nor do you have to declare the payments to the Benefits Agency or local authorities for the purpose of a claim for any means-tested benefit. You apply by writing to: The Macfarlane Trust, PO Box 627, London SW1H OQG, or by telephoning 071 233 0342.

The Eileen Trust was set up on 29 March 1993. It operates in the same way for people who do *not* have haemophilia but who were infected by blood transfusions, organ transplants etc, during NHS treatment. Applications are made via the Macfarlane Trust.

There is also a scheme known as the Fund, run directly by the Department of Health. This provides lump-sum payments for people who do not have haemophilia but who were infected during NHS treatment.

The Independent Living Fund

The Independent Living Fund – a special trust financed by the government – was established to provide extra help for people with very severe physical or mental disabilities, on low incomes, who had to pay for personal care or domestic assistance in order to live in the community.

It did not take any new applications after November 1992. People who were already in receipt of payments, or who were waiting for assessment, will continue to receive money from a successor body, the Independent Living (Extension) Fund. If a person ceases to get payments for more than 26 weeks (eg, because they temporarily go into hospital), they lose their protection and will have to apply to the new fund on the same basis as other applicants (see below).

The care needs of individual beneficiaries may still be reviewed and payments adjusted to meet changes of circumstances, subject to the budget being sufficient.

The Independent Living (1993) Fund

This is the new fund set up by the government to replace the Independent Living Fund. However, its rules are more restrictive.

You must be aged 16 to 65 (inclusive), getting the highest rate of disability living allowance (care), be living alone or with people who cannot meet your care needs in full and be on a low income (income support or equivalent).

To get money from the fund, you will have to contact your local social services or social work department and ask them to assess your need for residential or nursing care. If the social worker thinks that you *could* remain in your own home given enough support, *and* you want to remain there, s/he can then involve the fund.

In conjunction with the social worker and yourself, the fund representative will estimate the cost of all the support services you need (home-help, day-centre places, live-in helpers etc). If the cost is less than £500 a week, you may get help from the fund. This depends on whether the fund has sufficient resources (it has an annual budget which the trustees cannot overspend), and whether the local authority is prepared to provide the first £200 worth of services a week. The trustees of the new fund have also indicated that help will not normally be given to people who are terminally ill.

If payment can be made (and the government estimate that around 1,500 disabled people a year will qualify), it will be a cash payment paid to you to purchase the services you need. The maximum amount that can be paid is £300 a week. However, this will be reduced by the financial contribution that you will be required to make, such as 50 per cent of your disability living allowance care component.

Problems will occur if the Independent Living (1993) Fund runs out of money during the year or if the cost of the services needed comes to more than £500. Local authorities should not be deciding to arrange residential care just because it is cheaper. You may be able to argue that the local authority should meet the needs it has assessed you as having, in order for you to remain in your own home. See Chapter 26, section 3.

Nationally, local authorities have been given an extra £64 million for 1994/95 in recognition of the additional costs following the closure of the Independent Living Fund and the introduction of the Independent Living (1993) Fund. The fund itself has a budget for 1994/95 of £11 million.

Further information about the Independent Living (1993) Fund is available from PO Box 183, Nottingham NG8 3RD, tel: 0602 290423 or 290427.

Help from health authorities

Health authorities can provide facilities needed to prevent illness, or to care for people who are or have been ill, if the Secretary of State considers it appropriate as part of the health service.[1] Under this provision, the health authority has the power, for example, to provide a fridge if you do not have one and your consultant says you need one in which to store drugs.

2. HELP FROM CHARITIES

If you cannot get help from the state schemes, you could apply to a charity. Your local reference library should have details of charities.

Charities are extremely varied. But *all* charities have to adhere to the terms of their trust, and so there is no point in applying if you fall outside of these terms.

It is suggested that you approach charities in the following order:

- Local charities.
- Charities connected with specific illnesses or disabilities, with specific trades or occupations, or charities for ex-servicemen and women (this may include anyone who has done National Service).
- National or general charities.

Some charities have to be approached via a social worker. They usually ask people to submit a statement of their problems, and sometimes this has to be on a special form.

There are two groups of charities about which little information is available to the public. These are the religious charities and charities incorporated in the National Health Service. It may be worth asking a minister of religion or a hospital-based social worker if they know of any charity which could help you.

3. HOME INSULATION GRANT AID

The Home Energy Efficiency Scheme (HEES) package of measures includes loft insulation, draught-proofing and energy advice. It is run by the Energy Action Grants Agency (EAGA) (Freepost, PO Box 1NG, Newcastle-upon-Tyne NE99 2RP – freephone 0800 181 667 or Minicom 091 233 1054).

You may apply for an HEES grant if:

- you get income support, family credit, disability working allowance, housing benefit or council tax benefit; *and*
- you (or the person you live with as husband or wife) own or rent your home;
- as from 1 April 1994, if you get disability living allowance or you are aged 60 or over.

You will not have to pay any money towards the cost of having the work done, so long as the total cost does not exceed the amount the government will pay (see below).

You do *not* have to pay the grant back.

If the work is going to cost more than the government grant allows for (eg, if your house is very large) you can agree in advance to pay the extra. The work is carried out by organisations registered with EAGA.

	The government pays up to:
Loft insulation	£198.70
Draught-proofing	£128.50
Loft insulation and draught-proofing	£305.00
Energy advice	£10.00
(You can only get this if you also have draught-proofing or loft insulation)	

The government grant is not paid direct to you unless you choose to do the work yourself.

Useful addresses

The President of the Independent Tribunal Service and regional chairpersons

The President
HH Judge A. Thorpe,
City Centre House,
39-45 Finsbury Square,
London EC2A 1UU
Tel: 071 814 6500

The President (Northern Ireland)
Mr C.G. MacLynn,
6th Floor,
3 Donegal Square North,
Belfast BT1 5GA
Tel: 0232 539900

Social Security Appeal Tribunals

National Chairperson
Mr R. Huggins,
City Centre House,
39-45 Finsbury Square,
London EC2A 1UU
Tel: 071 814 6500

Regional Chairpersons

North East
Mr J.W. Tinnion,
3rd Flr, York House,
York Place,
Leeds LS1 2ED
Tel: 0532 451246

Midlands
Mr I.G. Harrison,
Albion House,
5-13 Canal Street,
Nottingham NG1 7EG
Tel: 0602 472869

South East
Mr R.G. Smithson,
19-30 Alfred Place,
London WC1E 7LW
Tel: 071 580 3941

North West
Mr R.S. Sim,
36 Dale Street,
Liverpool L2 5UZ
Tel: 051 236 4334

Wales and South West
Mr C.B. Stephens,
Oxford House,
Hills Street,
Cardiff CF1 2DR
Tel: 0222 378071

Scotland
Ms L.T. Parker,
Wellington House,
134-36 Wellington Street,
Glasgow G2 2XL
Tel: 041 353 1441

Child Support Appeal Tribunals

CSATs Central Office,
8th Floor,
Anchorage 2,
Anchorage Quay,
Salford M5 2YN
Tel: 0345 626311

Disability Appeal Tribunals

DATs Central Office,
PO Box 168,
Nottingham NG1 5JX
Tel: 0602 472942

Offices of the Social Security Commissioners

England and Wales
Harp House,
83 Farringdon Street,
London EC4A 4DH
Tel: 071 353 5145

Scotland
23 Melville Street,
Edinburgh EH3 7PW
Tel: 031 225 2201

Northern Ireland
Lancashire House,
5 Linenhall Street,
Belfast BT2 8AA
Tel: 0232 332344

Benefits Agency Chief Executive
Mr Michael Bichard,
Quarry House,
Quarry Hill,
Leeds LS2 7UA
Tel: 0532 324000

Income support – 16/17-year-olds
Severe Hardship Claims Unit,
39 Cadogan Street,
Glasgow G2 7AQ
Tel: 041 204 4717

DSS Solicitor
New Court,
48 Carey Street,
London WC2A 2LS
Tel: 071 412 1421

Contributions Agency Benefits Unit
Longbenton,
Newcastle-upon-Tyne
NE98 1YX
Tel: 091 213 5000

Disability Working Allowance Unit
Diadem House,
2 The Pavilion
Preston PR2 2GN
Tel 0772 883300

Family Credit Unit
Government Buildings,
Warbreck Hill Road,
Blackpool FY2 OAX
Tel: 0253 500050

Independent Review Service for the Social Fund
4th Floor,
Centre City Podium,
5 Hill Street,
Birmingham B5 4UB
Tel: 021 631 4000

Central Adjudication Services
Quarry House,
Quarry Hill,
Leeds LS2 7UA
Tel: 0532 324000

Local authority Ombudsman

England
21 Queen Anne's Gate,
London SW1H 9BU
Tel: 071 222 5622

Scotland
23 Waller Street,
Edinburgh EH3 7HX
Tel: 031 225 5300

Wales
Derwen House,
Court Road,
Bridgend CF31 1BN
Tel: 0656 661325

Northern Ireland
Progressive House,
33 Wellington Place,
Belfast BT1 6HN
Tel: 0232 233821

Getting information and advice

Independent advice and representation

It is often difficult for unsupported individuals to get a positive response from the Benefits Agency. You may be taken more seriously if it is clear you have taken advice about your entitlement or have an adviser assisting you.

If you want advice or help with a benefit problem the following agencies may be able to assist:

- Citizens Advice Bureaux (CABx) and other local advice centres provide information and advice about benefits and may be able to represent you.
- Law Centres who can often help in a similar way to CABx/advice centres.
- Local authority welfare rights workers provide a service in many areas and some arrange advice sessions and take up campaigns locally.
- Local organisations for particular groups of claimants may offer help. For instance, there are Unemployed Centres, pensioners groups, centres for people with disabilities etc.
- Claimants Unions give advice in some areas. For details of your nearest group contact the Plymouth Claimants Union, PO Box 21, Plymouth PL1 1QS *or* The Swindon Unemployed Movement, Room 20, Pinehurst People's Centre, Beech Avenue, Pinehurst, Swindon, Wiltshire.
- Some social workers and probation officers (but not all) help with benefit problems especially if they are already working with you on another problem.
- Solicitors can give free legal advice under the green form scheme (pink form in Scotland). This does not cover the cost of representation at an appeal hearing but can cover the cost of preparing written submissions and obtaining evidence such as medical reports. However, few solicitors have a good working knowledge of the benefit rules and you may need to shop around until you find one who does.

If you cannot find any of these agencies in the telephone book your local library should have details.

Unfortunately, CPAG is unable to deal with enquiries directly from members of the public but if you are an adviser you can phone the advice line which is open from 2.00 to 4.00 pm on Monday to Thursday – 071 253 6569. This is a special phone line; do not ring the main CPAG number. Alternatively, you can write to us at Citizens' Rights Office, CPAG, 4th Floor, 1-5 Bath Street, London EC1V 9PY. We can also take up a limited number of complex cases including appeals to the Social Security Commissioners or courts if referred by an adviser.

Advice from the Benefits Agency

You can obtain free telephone advice on benefits on the following numbers. These are for general advice and not specific queries on individual claims.

Benefit Enquiry Line 0800 882 200
  (Minicom) 0800 243 355
Cantonese 0800 252 451
Disability Benefits 0800 882 200
English 0800 666 555

Family Credit Helpline 0800 500 222
Northern Ireland 0800 616 757
Punjabi 0800 521 360
Urdu 0800 289 188
Welsh 0800 289 011

Books, leaflets and periodicals

Many of the books listed here will be in your main public library. HMSO books are available from the six HMSO bookshops but also from many others. They may be ordered by post, telephone or fax from HMSO Books, PO Box 276, London SW8 5DT (tel: 071 873 9090, fax: 071 873 8463). Enquiries to PC51D, HMSO Books, 51 Nine Elms Lane, London SW8 5DR (tel: 071 873 0011).

I. Textbooks

Claim in Time by M. Partington (Legal Action Group, 2nd edn, 1989). Detailed study of the rules on the time limits for claiming benefits. Available from Legal Action Group, 242 Pentonville Road, London N1 9UN.

2. Case law and legislation

Social Security Case Law – Digest of Commissioners' Decisions by D. Neligan (HMSO, looseleaf in two volumes). Summaries of commissioners' decisions grouped together by subject.

The Law Relating to Child Support (HMSO, looseleaf in one volume).

The Law Relating to Social Security (HMSO, looseleaf in ten volumes). All the legislation but without any comment. Known as the 'Blue Book'. Volumes 6, 7 and 8 deal with means-tested benefits.

Child Support: The Legislation by E. Jacobs and G. Douglas (Sweet & Maxwell, 1st edn, £27.50 incl p&p from CPAG Ltd, 1-5 Bath Street, London EC1V 9PY – if you are a CPAG member). Contains the primary legislation with a detailed commentary. A supplement will be available from Autumn 1994, £7.95 (prov.). If this is ordered from CPAG before 31 May 1994, the price is reduced to £7.50. It will also be available in bookshops at full price later in the year.

CPAG's Income Related Benefits: The Legislation by J. Mesher and P. Wood (Sweet & Maxwell, 1994/5 edn available from August, £37.90 (incl Supplement) incl p&p from CPAG Ltd, 1-5 Bath Street, London EC1V 9PY – if you are a CPAG member). Contains the most useful legislation with a detailed commentary. Supplement available December. If the main work and supplement are both ordered from CPAG before 31 May 1994, the total price is reduced to £36.00.

CPAG's Housing Benefit and Council Tax Benefit Legislation by L. Findlay and M. Ward (CPAG Ltd, 1994/5 edn available June, £38.95 (incl Supplement) incl p&p from CPAG Ltd, 1-5 Bath Street, London EC1V 9PY). Contains the main legislation with a detailed commentary. Supplement available December. If the main work and supplement are both ordered from CPAG before 31 May 1994, the total price is reduced to £35.00. The reduced price of just the main volume if ordered on the same conditions is £27.50.

Medical and Disability Appeal Tribunals: The Legislation by M. Rowland (Sweet & Maxwell), 1st edn, 1993, available if you are a CPAG member, £29.95 incl p&p, from CPAG Ltd, 1-5 Bath Street, London EC1V 9PY. A supplement will be available from June 1994, £7.95. If this is ordered from CPAG before 31 May 1994, the price is reduced to £7.50.

3. Official guidance

Adjudication Officers' Guide (HMSO, looseleaf in ten volumes). Volumes 3 and 4 deal with means-tested benefits.

Benefits Agency Manual, *IS for 16/17-year-olds*, HMSO, March 1994.

Child Support Adjudication Guide (HMSO, looseleaf in one volume).

Child Support Manual (Child Support Agency, looseleaf in three volumes).

Field Officers' Guide (Child Support Agency, looseleaf in one volume).

Housing Benefit and Council Tax Benefit Guidance Manual (HMSO, looseleaf in one volume).

Income Support Manual (HMSO, looseleaf in one volume). Procedural guide issued to Benefits Agency staff.

The Social Fund Guide (HMSO, looseleaf, in two volumes).

The Social Fund Administration Guide (HMSO, looseleaf in one volume).

The Social Fund Maternity and Funeral Payments Guide (HMSO, looseleaf in one volume).

The Social Fund Cold Weather Payments Handbook (HMSO, looseleaf in one volume).

4. Tribunal handbooks

Social Security Appeal Tribunals: A Guide to Procedure (HMSO).

5. Leaflets

The Benefits Agency publishes many leaflets which cover particular benefits or particular groups of claimants or contributors. They have been greatly improved in recent years and the bigger ones extend to 48-page booklets. They are free from your local Benefits Agency office or on Freephone 0800 666 555. If you want to order larger numbers of leaflets, or receive information about new leaflets, you can join the Benefits Agency Publicity Register by writing to the Benefits Agency, 4th Floor East, 1 Trevelyan Square, Leeds LS1 6EB or by phoning 0645 540000 (local rate). Free leaflets on HB/CTB are available from the relevant department of your local council.

6. Periodicals

The *Welfare Rights Bulletin* is published every two months by CPAG. It covers developments in social security law and updates this *Handbook* between editions. The annual subscription is £15 but it is sent automatically to CPAG Rights and Comprehensive Members.

7. Other publications – general

Rights Guide to Non-Means-Tested Benefits, £6.95 (£2.45 for claimants).

Child Support Handbook, £6.95 (£2.45 for claimants).

Council Tax Handbook, £7.95.

Debt Advice Handbook, £7.95.

Ethnic Minorities' Benefits Handbook, £8.95.

Guide to Housing Benefit and Council Tax Benefit, £10.95.

Guide to Money Advice in Scotland, £7.95.

Disability Rights Handbook, £8.95.

Rights Guide for Homeowners, £7.95.

Fuel Rights Handbook, £7.95.

Most of these are available from CPAG Ltd, 4th Floor, 1-5 Bath Street, London EC1V 9PY. Prices include p&p.

Abbreviations used in the notes

AC	Appeal Cases	para	paragraph
All ER	All England Reports	QB	Queen's Bench
Art(s)	Article(s)	r	rule
CA	Court of Appeal	reg	regulation
CAO	Chief Adjudication Officer	RSC	Rules of the Supreme Court
CMLR	Common Market Law Reports	RVR	Rating & Valuation Reporter
CSBO	Chief Supplementary Benefit Officer	s(s)	Sections
		SBAT	Supplementary Benefit Appeal Tribunal
DC	Divisional Court		
ECJ	European Court of Justice	SBC	Supplementary Benefits Commission
ECR	European Court Reports		
HBRB	Housing Benefit Review Board	Sch	Schedule
HC	High Court	SCLR	Scottish Civil Law Reports
HL	House of Lords	SF Dir	Social Fund Direction
HLR	Housing Law Reports	SFI Dir	Social Fund Inspector's Direction
NAB	National Assistance Board	TLR	Times Law Reports
NIC	National Insurance Commissioner	WLR	Weekly Law Reports

Acts of Parliament

CA 1989	Children Act 1989	HSS&SSA Act 1983	Health and Social Services and Social Security Adjudication Act 1983
CSA 1991	The Child Support Act 1991		
CSDPA 1970	Chronically Sick and Disabled Persons Act 1976	LAA 1988	Legal Aid Act 1988
		LASSA 1970	Local Authority Social Services Act 1970
DP(SCR)A 1986	Disabled Persons (Services, Consultation and Representation) Act 1986	LGHA 1989	Local Government and Housing Act 1989
		NAA 1948	National Assistance Act 1948
DWAA 1991	Disability Living Allowance and Disability Working Allowance Act 1991	NHS Act 1977	National Health Service Act 1977
		RHA 1984	Registered Homes Act 1984
EA 1944	Education Act 1944		
EA 1962	Education Act 1962	SSA 1986	Social Security Act 1986
EA 1980	Education Act 1980	SSAA 1992	Social Security Administration Act 1992
E(MP)A 1948	Education (Miscellaneous Provisions) Act 1948	SSCBA 1992	Social Security Contributions and Benefits Act 1992
ERA 1988	Education Reform Act 1988		

Regulations

Each set of regulations has a statutory instrument (SI) number and a date. You ask for them by giving their date and number.

CB Regs   The Child Benefit (General) Regulations 1976 No.965

CC(DIS) Regs	The Community Charge (Deductions from Income Support) Regulations 1990 No.107
CS(AIAMA) Regs	The Child Support (Arrears, Interest and Adjustment of Maintenance Assessments) Regulations 1992 No.1816
CS(C&E) Regs	The Child Support (Collection and Enforcement) Regulations 1992 No.1989
CS(CEOFM) Regs	The Child Support (Collection and Enforcement) of Other Forms of Maintenance) Regulations 1992 No.2643
CS(IED) Regs	The Child Support (Information, Evidence and Disclosure) Regulations 1992 No.1812
CS(MAP) Regs	The Child Support (Maintenance Assessment Procedure) Regulations 1992 No.1813
CS(MASC) Regs	The Child Support (Maintenance Assessments and Special Cases) Regulations 1992 No.1815
CSAT(P) Regs	The Child Support Appeal Tribunals (Procedure) Regulations 1992 No.2641
CT(DIS) Regs	The Council Tax (Deductions from Income Support) Regulations 1993 No.494
CTB Regs	The Council Tax Benefit (General) Regulations 1992 No.1814
CTB(T)O	The Council Tax Benefit (Transitional) Order 1992 No.1909
DWA Regs	The Disability Working Allowance (General) Regulations 1991 No. 2887
F(DIS) Regs	The Fines (Deductions from Income Support) Regulations 1992 No.2182
FC Regs	The Family Credit (General) Regulations 1987 No.1973
HB Regs	The Housing Benefit (General) Regulations 1987 No.1971
HRG(RG) Regs	The Housing Renovation Grants (Reduction of Grant) Regulations 1990 No.1189
IS Regs	The Income Support (General) Regulations 1987 No.1967
IS(Amdt 3) Regs	The Income Support (General) Regulations Amendment No.3 1991 No.1033
IS(LR) Regs	The Income Support (Liable Relatives) Regulations 1990 No.1777
IS(Trans) Regs	The Income Support (Transitional) Regulations 1987 No.1969
NA(AR) Regs	The National Assistance (Assessment and Resources) Regulations 1992 No.2977
NHS(CDA) Regs	The National Health Service (Charges for Drugs and Appliances) Regulations 1980 No.1503
NHS(GOS) Regs	The National Health Service (General Ophthalmic Services) Regulations 1986 No.975
NHS(OCP) Regs	The National Health Service (Optical Charges and Payments) Regulations 1989 No.396
NHS(TERC) Regs	The National Health Service (Travelling Expenses and Remission of Charges) Regulations 1988 No.551
RA(RPORE) Regs	The Residential Accommodation (Relevant Premises, Ordinary Residence and Exemptions) Regulations 1993 No.477
RCH Regs	The Residential Care Homes Regulations 1984 No.1345
SF(App) Regs	The Social Fund (Applications) Regulations 1988 No.524
SF(AR) Regs	The Social Fund (Application for Review) Regulations 1988 No.34
SF(Misc) Regs	The Social Fund (Miscellaneous Provisions) Regulations 1990 No.1788
SF(RDB) Regs	The Social Fund (Recovery by Deductions from Benefits) Regulations 1988 No.35
SFCWP Regs	The Social Fund Cold Weather Payments (General) Regulations 1988 No.1724
SFM&FE Regs	The Social Fund Maternity and Funeral Expenses (General) Regulations 1987 No.481

SOB Regs	The Scholarship and Other Benefits Regulations 1977 No.1443
SS(AA) No 2 Regs	The Social Security (Attendance Allowance) (No.2) Regulations 1975 No.598
SS(Adj) Regs	The Social Security (Adjudication) Regulations 1986 No.2218
SS(C&P) Regs	The Social Security (Claims and Payments) Regulations 1987 No.1968
SS(Cr) Regs	The Social Security (Credits) Regulations 1975 No.556
SS(DLA) Regs	The Social Security (Disability Living Allowance) Regulations 1991 No.2890
SS(ICA) Regs	The Social Security (Invalid Care Allowance) Regulations 1976 No.409
SS(PAOR) Regs	The Social Security (Payments on Account, Overpayments and Recovery) Regulations 1988 No.664
SS(SDA) Regs	The Social Security (Severe Disablement Allowance) Regulations 1984 No.1303
SS(US&IB) Regs	The Social Security (Unemployment, Sickness and Invalidity Benefit) Regulations 1983 No.1598
SS(WB&RP) Regs	The Social Security (Widow's Benefit and Retirement Pensions) Regulations 1979 No.642
SSCP Regs	The Social Security Commissioners Procedure Regulations 1987 No.214
WF Regs	The Welfare Foods Regulations 1988 No.536

Other Information

AOG	*The Adjudication Officers' Guide* (see Appendix 3).
BA Manual	*IS for 16/17-years-olds*, (see Appendix 3).
CSAG	The *Child Support Adjudication Guide* (see Appendix 3).
CSM	The *Child Support Manual* (see Appendix 3).
CWPH	*The Social Fund Cold Weather Payments Handbook.*
FOG	*The Field Officers' Guide* (see Appendix 3).
GM	The *Housing Benefit and Council Tax Benefit Guidance Manual* (see Appendix 3).
IS Manual	This is a largely procedural guide to the implementation of income support, which is issued to adjudication officers/DSS staff (see Appendix 3).
LGOR	*Local Government Ombudsman's Report* (LGO's Office).
SF Dir/SFI Dir	Direction(s) on the discretionary social fund. They are printed in the *Social Fund Guide* and Mesher and Wood (see Appendix 3).
SFAG	*The Social Fund Administration Guide* (see Appendix 3).
SFG	*The Social Fund Guide* (see Appendix 3).
SFMFG	*The Social Fund Maternity and Funeral Payments Guide* (see Appendix 3).

References like CIS/142/1990 and R(SB) 3/89 are references to commissioners' decisions (see p176).

Notes

References are to the statutes and regulations as amended up to 18 March 1994. All regulations are (General) Regulations unless otherwise stated. There is a full list of abbreviations in Appendix 4.

44 Sch 3 para 7(1)(a) IS Regs
45 Sch 3 para 7(1)(b) IS Regs
46 CIS/705/1991
47 Sch 3 para 7(9) IS Regs
48 Sch 3 para 7(10) IS Regs
49 Reg 3A IS Regs
50 Sch 3 para 7(11) IS Regs
51 Sch 3 para 7(2) IS Regs
52 Sch 9 para 29 IS Regs
53 Sch 3 para 7(1)(b) IS Regs
54 Sch 3 para 7(6) IS Regs
55 Regs 42(4)(a)(ii) and 51(3)(a)(ii) IS Regs
56 Reg 54 IS Regs
57 Sch 9 para 29 IS Regs
58 Sch 3 para 8(1) IS Regs
59 Sch 3 para 5A(1) IS Regs
60 Sch 3 para 8(3) IS Regs
61 para 27787 AOG
62 CIS/278/1992
63 CIS/689/1991
64 CSB/420/1985
65 Sch 3 para 6 IS Regs
66 Sch 3 paras 7(6B)-(6E), 7A and 7B IS Regs
67 Reg 4 IS (Amdt 3) Regs
68 CIS/85/1992
69 Sch 10 para 26 IS Regs
70 Sch 9 para 22 IS Regs
71 Reg 3 IS Regs
72 CSB/1163/1988
73 Reg 3(4) and (5) IS Regs
74 Sch 3 para 11(1) and (7) IS Regs
75 Sch 3 para 11(6) IS Regs
76 Sch 3 para 11(1), (2) and (8) IS Regs
77 Reg 5(3) IS Regs
78 Sch 3 para 11(3) and (4) IS Regs
79 Sch 3 para 11(5) IS Regs
80 Sch 3 para 10(3) and (4) IS Regs
81 Sch 3 para 10(4) IS Regs
82 Sch 3 para 10(5) and (7) IS Regs
83 R(IS) 12/91
84 CSB/617/1988
85 R(SB) 7/89
86 Sch 3 para 10(6) IS Regs
87 R(IS) 9/91
88 Sch 3 paras 5A(5)(b) and 10(1) IS Regs
89 CIS/574/1992
90 Sch 3 para 6(2) IS Regs
91 CIS/275/1991; CIS/656/1992
92 Sch 3 paras 5A(2) and 10(2) IS Regs
93 Sch 3 para 10(2)(a) IS Regs
94 Sch 3 para 5A IS Regs

3. Transitional protection (pp43-44)

95 IS(Trans) Regs
96 Reg 17(2)-(7) IS Regs
97 Reg 17(1)(g) and Sch 3A IS Regs
98 Reg 17(1)(g) and Sch 3B IS Regs

4. Urgent cases payments (pp44-47)

99 Reg 70(2) IS Regs
100 Reg 70(4) IS Regs
101 Reg 8(3) IS Regs
102 Reg 71(1)(a) IS Regs
103 Reg 71(1)(b) and (c) IS Regs
104 Reg 72(1) IS Regs
105 Reg 72(1)(c) IS Regs
106 Reg 72(2) IS Regs

Chapter 4: The unemployed and people on government training schemes (pp48-66)

1 s124(1)(d)(i) SSCBA 1992
2 Reg 8 SS(C&P) Regs
3 Reg 11 IS Regs
4 Reg 7(1)(a) SS(US&IB) Regs; reg 10(1)(d) IS Regs
5 Reg 10(6) IS Regs
6 CSIS/13/1991
7 Reg 9(1)(a) IS Regs; reg 64(1) SS(Adj) Regs
8 para 25300 AOG
9 Reg 9(1) IS Regs; reg 7(1)(a) SS(US&IB) Regs
10 CSB/975/1989
11 Reg 7(1) IS Regs
12 Regs 9, 10, 11 and 12 SS(US&IB) Regs
13 Reg 10(1) IS Regs
14 R(U) 1/82
15 Reg 10(2) IS Regs
16 Reg 10(1)(d) IS Regs
17 Reg 10(4) and (5) IS Regs
18 Reg 10(1)(a) IS Regs
19 Reg 12E SS(US&IB) Regs
20 R(U) 20/60; R(U) 5/71; R(U) 2/77
21 R(U) 10/61; R(U) 15/62
22 Reg 9(1)(b) IS Regs
23 Reg 7(c) IS Regs
24 Reg 10A(3) IS Regs
25 Reg 12B SS(US&IB) Regs; reg 10A(3) IS Regs
26 Reg 10A(4) IS Regs; reg 12D SS(US&IB) Regs
27 Reg 7(2) IS Regs
28 Reg 10A(1) and (2) IS Regs
29 Reg 5(1) IS Regs
30 Reg 35(1) IS Regs
31 Reg 22(6) IS Regs; CIS/640/1993
32 Reg 22(4)(c)(iii) IS Regs
33 s28 SSCBA 1992
34 Reg 12G SS(US&IB) Regs
35 Reg 12E SS(US&IB) Regs
36 s28 SSCBA 1992; reg 22(4)(c) IS Regs
37 s28(1) SSCBA 1992; reg 22(4)(c) IS Regs
38 Reg 22(6) IS Regs
39 Reg 21A IS Regs
40 Reg 22(1)(a) and (b), (4)(c) and (6) IS Regs
41 Reg 22(2) IS Regs
42 Sch 1 para 11 IS Regs

43 Sch 1A para 1 and Sch 1 para 11 IS Regs
44 Sch 2 para 12(5) IS Regs
45 Sch 9 para 13(a) and (b) IS Regs
46 Sch 9 para 13(b) IS Regs
47 Sch 9 para 13(c) IS Regs; Sch 2 para 11 FC Regs; Sch 4 para 11 HB Regs; Sch 4 para 11 CTB Regs
48 Reg 36(2) and Sch 8 paras 1-13 IS Regs
49 Sch 9 para 13(a) and (b) IS Regs; Sch 2 para 11(c) FC Regs; Sch 4 para 11(c) HB Regs; Sch 4 para 11(c) CTB Regs
50 Sch 10 para 30 IS Regs

Chapter 5: Special rules for special groups (pp67-119)

1. 16/17-year-olds (pp67-76)
1 Sch 1A IS Regs
2 Sch 1A para 1 IS Regs
3 Sch 1A para 3 IS Regs
4 Sch 1A para 2 IS Regs
5 Sch 1A para 4 IS Regs
6 Reg 7D(2)(b) CB Regs
7 Reg 2(1) and Sch 1A Part II IS Regs
8 Reg 13A(4)-(6) IS Regs
9 s125(1) SSCBA 1992
10 paras 4041-42 BA Manual
11 paras 8005-14 BA Manual
12 para 8017 BA Manual
13 paras 4006-07 BA Manual
14 para 4051 and Appendix 3 BA Manual
15 paras 4069-74 BA Manual
16 para 4070 BA Manual
17 para 4067 BA Manual
18 paras 3017 and 4069 BA Manual

19 paras 4105-109 BA Manual
20 para 6011 BA Manual
21 para 6012 BA Manual
22 paras 4011 BA Manual
23 para 4012 and Appendix 2 BA Manual
24 para 4014 BA Manual
25 para 8002 BA Manual
26 para 4101 BA Manual
27 para 8016 BA Manual
28 para 4097 BA Manual
29 para 4117 BA Manual
30 para 4123 BA Manual
31 para 4112 BA Manual
32 para 9006 BA Manual
33 s125(3) SSCBA 1992
34 s72(1) SSAA 1992
35 Sch 2 para 1(1)(a), (b) and (c) and (2)(a), (b) and (c) IS Regs
36 Sch 2 para 1(1)(b) and (c) and (2)(b) and (c) IS Regs
37 Sch 2 para 1(3) IS Regs
38 s25(3) ERA 1988
39 sA3 Dept of Employment Guide 13 (M22 107/0488) YTS Bridging Allowances

2. People affected by a trade dispute (pp77-81)
40 ss27 and 126 SSCBA 1992
41 R(U) 1/87
42 Reg 5(4) IS Regs; para 90017 AOG
43 s27(3)(a) SSCBA 1992
44 CU/66/1986
45 s27(1)(a) SSCBA 1992; R(U) 1/84
46 s27(2)(b) SSCBA 1992
47 s126(1) and (2) SSCBA 1992
48 s126(2) SSCBA 1992
49 ss27 and 126(1) SSCBA 1992
50 Reg 64(1) SS(Adj) Regs
51 s126(3)(a) and (d) SSCBA 1992
52 Sch 1 para 19 IS Regs
53 Reg 5(4) IS Regs
54 para 33175 AOG

55 para 33191 AOG
56 s126(3) SSCBA 1992
57 Sch 3 para 3(2) IS Regs
58 s126(5)-(7) SSCBA 1992
59 Sch 9 para 34 IS Regs
60 s126(5)(a)(ii) SSCBA 1992; reg 41(4) IS Regs
61 Sch 9 para 28 and Sch 10 para 17 IS Regs
62 Reg 48(10)(a) and (c), Sch 9 paras 15 and 39 and Sch 10 para 22 IS Regs
63 Sch 9 para 21 IS Regs
64 Reg 35(1)(d) IS Regs
65 Reg 48(6) IS Regs
66 s126(5)(a)(i) SSCBA 1992
67 s127 SSCBA 1992
68 Reg 6(e) IS Regs
69 Sch 1 para 19 IS Regs
70 s127(b) SSCBA 1992
71 para 33191 AOG
72 Reg 26(4) SS(C&P) Regs
73 s127(c) SSCBA 1992; reg 20 SS(PAOR) Regs
74 Reg 26 SS(PAOR) Regs
75 Reg 19(1) SS(PAOR) Regs
76 Reg 19(3), (4) and (5) SS(PAOR) Regs
77 Reg 22(3) SS(PAOR) Regs
78 Reg 18(2) SS(PAOR) Regs
79 Reg 22(2) SS(PAOR) Regs
80 Reg 22(4) SS(PAOR) Regs
81 Reg 20(1) and (2) SS(PAOR) Regs
82 Reg 22(5)(a) SS(PAOR) Regs
83 Reg 22(6) SS(PAOR) Regs
84 Reg 21(1) SS(PAOR) Regs
85 Reg 25 SS(PAOR) Regs
86 Reg 28 SS(PAOR) Regs
87 Reg 29 SS(PAOR) Regs
88 Regs 27 and 29 SS(PAOR) Regs
89 Reg 27(5) SS(PAOR) Regs

90   SF Dir 26
91   SF Dir 17
92   SF Dir 8(c)

3. People from abroad
(pp81-97)
93   s124 SSCBA 1992; reg 21(3) IS Regs
94   s124 SSCBA 1992; reg 21(3) IS Regs
95   Reg 21(3) IS Regs
96   Sch 7 para 17 IS Regs; para 28831 AOG
97   Reg 70(3) IS Regs
98   Sch 7 para 17(c)(i) IS Regs
99   Reg 70(3) IS Regs
100 Reg 70(4) IS Regs as amended
101 s78(6)(c) SSCBA 1992
102 Unger (1964) CMLR 319 and Levin (1982) 2 CMLR; Directive 90/365/EEC
103 Art 1 Reg 1612/68 Treaty of Rome
104 CSB/1218/1988
105 Case 48/75 Jean Noel Royer; Case 118/75 Watson and Belmann; Case 8/77 Sagulo, Brenca and Bakhouche ECR 1495 and 1504
106 CSB/1218/1988
107 Lubbersen Immigration Appeal Tribunal 7; *R v Pieck* [1981] February 1984
108 Reg 21(3)(a) and (b) IS Regs
109 Treaty of Rome, Art 7 Reg 1612/68
110 Antonissen, Case C-292/88 [1991] ECR 1-745
111 Treaty of Rome, Arts 52-66
112 Directives 90/364/EEC and 90/366/EEC
113 Reg 21(3)(h) IS Regs
114 Reg 70(3)(i) IS Regs

115 Regs 21(3)(a) and 70(3)(b) IS Regs
116 Reg 70(3)(b) IS Regs
117 R(U) 1/82
118 Sch 1 para 20 IS Regs
119 para 51210 IS Manual
120 R(SB) 43/83
121 R(SB) 2/85 – A recent Court of Appeal decision on housing law *R v Secretary of State for the Environment ex parte London Borough of Tower Hamlets* [1993] 25 HLR 524 held that the local authority was entitled to investigate and decide on immigration status without reference to the Home Office.
122 R(SB) 11/88

4. Residential and nursing care
(pp97-113)
123 s17 HSS&SSA Act 1983
124 Sch 1 NA(AR) Regs
125 Reg 21(4) IS Regs
126 Reg 21(4A) IS Regs
127 s22 NAA 1948
128 Sch 7 para 10A IS Regs
129 Sch 7 para 10C IS Regs
130 Sch 7 para 10B(3) IS Regs
131 Sch 7 para 10B(1) IS Regs
132 Reg 17(f) and (g) IS Regs
133 Sch 7 para 13(1)(a) IS Regs
134 Sch 7 para 13(1)(c) IS Regs
135 Sch 7 para (13)2 IS Regs
136 Reg 16(3)(e) IS Regs
137 Sch 7 para 13(1)(d) IS Regs
138 Regs 7 and 8 SS(AA) No 2 Regs; regs 9 and

10 SS(DLA) Regs
139 Sch 7 paras 6(2A), 7(2) and (3)(c) SS(C&P) Regs
140 Sch 2 para 2A(3) IS Regs
141 ss1 and 19(4) RHA 1984
142 Reg 19 and Sch 2 para 2A(3) and (4) IS Regs
143 Sch 2 para 2A(4) IS Regs
144 Sch 2 para 2A(5) IS Regs
145 Reg 19(1ZB) and (1ZC) IS Regs
146 Reg 19(1ZE) IS Regs
147 Reg 19(1ZK) IS Regs
148 Reg 19(1ZF) IS Regs
149 Sch 4 para 13 IS Regs
150 Sch 4 para 1(1)(a) IS Regs
151 Sch 4 para 2(2) IS Regs
152 Sch 4 para 2(1) IS Regs; *Pearce v CAO* (CA) reported in R(SB) 11/91
153 Sch 4 para 3 IS Regs
154 Sch 4 para 5 IS Regs
155 Sch 4 paras 6 and 7 IS Regs
156 Sch 4 para 9 IS Regs
157 Sch 4 para 10 IS Regs
158 Sch 4 para 6(2) IS Regs
159 s55 RHA 1984
160 Reg 1(2) RCH Regs
161 CSB/1171/1986
162 s20(1) RHA 1984
163 Sch 4 paras 9(b) and 10(4) IS Regs
164 CIS/263/1991
165 Sch 4 para 11 IS Regs
166 CIS/515/1990
167 Sch 4 para 12(1) and (2) IS Regs
168 Reg 19 Sch 4 para 12(3) and (4) IS Regs
169 Department of Health Circular LAC(93) 6 para 17
170 s26A(1) NAA 1948
171 Regs 4-9 RA(RPORE) Regs

172 Sch 9 para 30(d) IS Regs
173 Department of Health Circular LAC(93) 6, paras 26-28
174 Sch 7 paras 6(2), 7(2) and (3)(c) SS(C&P) Regs
175 Reg 73(2)-(5) IS Regs
176 Reg 69(5) SS(Adj) Regs
177 Sch 4 para 1(c) IS Regs
178 Reg 19(1A) IS Regs
179 Sch 7 para 16 IS Regs
180 Sch 7 para 16 IS Regs
181 Reg 16(3)(e) IS Regs
182 Sch 4 para 14 IS Regs; R(IS) 2/91
183 Reg 2(1) IS Regs; R(SB) 22/87
184 R(SB) 22/87
185 R(SB) 9/89
186 Sch 4 para 14 IS Regs
187 para 28044 AOG
188 Sch 4 para 17 IS Regs
189 Sch 4 para 15 IS Regs
190 para 28016 AOG
191 Sch 4 para 16 IS Regs
192 Sch 4 para 18 IS Regs
193 Reg 21(3A) IS Regs
194 Regs 7 and 8 SS(AA) Regs; regs 9 and 10 SS(DLA) Regs
195 Memo AOG vol 7/17
196 Sch 9 para 30A IS Regs
197 s22(4) NAA 1948
198 Regs 20-28 NA(AR) Regs
199 Sch 4 para 18 NA(AR) Regs
200 s22 HSS&SSA Act 1983

5. People in hospital
(pp113-117)
201 CIS/192/1991
202 Sch 3 paras 2 and 4(8)(c) IS Regs
203 Reg 16(2) IS Regs
204 Sch 2 para 13 IS Regs
205 Sch 7 para 1 IS Regs
206 s70(2) SSCBA 1992; Sch 2 para 14ZA IS Regs
207 Sch 7 para 1(a) IS Regs
208 Sch 7 para 2(b) IS Regs
209 Sch 7 para 2(a) IS Regs
210 Sch 2 para 13 IS Regs
211 Sch 7 para 1 IS Regs
212 s70(2) SSCBA 1992; Sch 2 para 14ZA IS Regs
213 Sch 7 para 1(b) IS Regs
214 Sch 2 para 15(5) IS Regs
215 s70 SSCBA 1992; Sch 2 para 14ZA IS Regs
216 Reg 4(1) and (2) SS(ICA) Regs; Sch 2 para 14ZA IS Regs
217 Sch 7 para 1(c)(i) and Sch 2 para 12(1)(c)(ii) IS Regs
218 Reg 16(2) and Sch 3 para 4(8) IS Regs
219 Sch 7 para 2 IS Regs
220 Reg 16(2) and Sch 7 para 1(b) IS Regs
221 Sch 7 para 3 IS Regs
222 Sch 2 para 14(b) IS Regs
223 Sch 7 para 18(a) IS Regs
224 Sch 2 para 4A IS Regs
225 Sch 7 para 18(b) and (c) IS Regs
226 Sch 7 para 18(b)(i) and (iv) 1st case IS Regs
227 Sch 7 para 18(b)(ii) 2nd case and (b)(iv) 3rd case IS Regs
228 Sch 7 para 2A IS Regs
229 Sch 7 para 7(1) SS(C&P) Regs
230 Reg 21(2) IS Regs
231 Sch 7 para 7(3)(d) SS(C&P) Regs
232 Sch 7 para 7(2) SS(C&P) Regs; R(S) 4/84

6. Prisoners
(pp117-119)
233 Sch 7 para 8 IS Regs
234 Reg 21(3) IS Regs
235 Reg 16(3)(b) IS Regs
236 Reg 16 IS Regs
237 R(IS) 17/93
238 Reg 16(5)(f) IS Regs
239 Sch 7 para 8(b) IS Regs
240 See *R v HBRB ex parte Robertson* 1988
241 CIS/561/1992
242 Reg 48(7) IS Regs
243 Sch 1 para 18 IS Regs

7. People without accommodation
(p119)
244 Sch 7 para 6 IS Regs
245 para 5.404 IS Manual
246 para 28503 AOG
247 para 5.407 IS Manual

Chapter 6:
Maintenance payments
(pp120-141)
1 para 10611 CSM
2 s105(3) SSAA 1992
3 s108 SSAA 1992
4 s108(5) SSAA 1992; Reg 3 IS(LR) Regs
5 s106(4)(a) SSAA 1992
6 s30(1) CSA 1991; CS(CEOFM) Regs
7 s106 SSAA 1992
8 s8(3) CSA 1991
9 *NAB v Parkes* [1955] 2 QB 506
10 *NAB v Parkes* [1955] 2 QB 506; *Hulley v Thompson* [1981] 1 WLR 159
11 s106(2) SSAA 1992
12 s105(1) SSAA 1992
13 Reg 54 IS Regs
14 s6(1) and (2) CSA 1991; reg 34 CS(MAP) Regs
15 paras 10660-5 CSM
16 para 2553 CSAG; para 10660 CSM
17 s6(11) CSA 1991; para 10743 CSM
18 s46 CSA 1991
19 Reg 35 CS(MAP) Regs

20 s46(10) CSA 1991
21 R(SB) 33/85
22 s46(3) and (4) CSA 1991
23 s2 CSA 1991; para 2558 CSAG
24 s46(7) CSA 1991
25 s6(8) CSA 1991
26 Reg 40 CS(MAP) Regs
27 Reg 39 CS(MAP) Regs
28 Reg 36(8) CS(MAP) Regs
29 Reg 36(9) CS(MAP) Regs
30 Reg 47 CS(MAP) Regs
31 Reg 36 CS(MAP) Regs
32 Reg 36(4) CS(MAP) Regs
33 Reg 37 CS(MAP) Regs
34 Reg 36(7) CS(MAP) Regs
35 Reg 47 CS(MAP) Regs
36 Reg 41 CS(MAP) Regs
37 Reg 38 CS(MAP) Regs
38 Reg 48 CS(MAP) Regs
39 Reg 48 CS(MAP) Regs
40 Reg 40 CS(MAP) Regs
41 Regs 43 and 44 CS(MAP) Regs
42 Reg 49 CS(MAP) Regs
43 Reg 46 CS(MAP) Regs
44 Reg 47(4)-(7) CS(MAP) Regs
45 Reg 42 CS(MAP) Regs
46 s6(9) CSA 1991; reg 2 CS(IED) Regs
47 Reg 5 CS(IED) Regs
48 Reg 3 CS(IED) Regs
49 para 10631 CSM
50 para 3333 FOG
51 Reg 6 CS(IED) Regs
52 para 11012 CSM
53 Reg 6(1) CS(MAP) Regs
54 Reg 8 CS(MAP) Regs
55 Reg 30 CS(MAP) Regs
56 Appendix 9 FOG
57 para 3870 FOG
58 para 11161 CSM
59 para 11164 CSM
60 s26 CSA 1991
61 Sch 1 para 7 CSA 1991; reg 26 CS(MASC) Regs
62 s43 CSA 1991
63 Reg 28 CS(MASC)

64 s43 and Sch 1 para 5(4) CSA 1991; reg 28 and Sch 4 CS(MASC) Regs; Sch 9 para 7A SS(C&P) Regs
65 Reg 28(5) and Sch 5 CS(MASC) Regs
66 s16 CSA 1991; reg 17 CS(MAP) Regs
67 ss17 and 19 CSA 1991
68 Reg 20 CS(MAP) Regs
69 Reg 24 CS(MAP) Regs
70 s20 CSA 1991; reg 42(9)-(11) CS(MAP) Regs
71 Reg 3 CSAT(P) Regs
72 s29 CSA 1991; Reg 2 CS(C&E) Regs
73 Regs 3 and 4 CS(C&E) Regs
74 s29(3) CSA 1991; reg 2 CS(C&E) Regs
75 Reg 5 CS(C&E) Regs
76 Reg 60B IS Regs
77 Regs 60C and 60D(b) IS Regs
78 s74(1) SSAA 1992; Reg 7 SS(PAOR) Regs
79 s41(2) CSA 1991; Reg 8 CS(AIAMA) Regs
80 Reg 60D(a) IS Regs
81 Reg 25A IS Regs
82 Reg 54 IS Regs
83 Regs 54 and 55 and Sch 9 IS Regs
84 Reg 58 IS Regs
85 Reg 54 IS Regs
86 Reg 58(4) IS Regs
87 Reg 59(1) IS Regs
88 s74(1) SSAA 1992; reg 7(1) SS(PAOR) Regs
89 Reg 54 IS Regs
90 *Regina v West London Supplementary Benefit Appeal Tribunal ex parte Taylor* [1975] 1 WLR 1048 (DC); *McCorquodale v Chief Adjudication Officer* (CA) reported as an appendix to R(SB) 1/88
91 Regs 54, 55, 60(1) IS Regs
92 Reg 60(2) IS Regs
93 CSB/1160/1986; R(SB)

1/89
94 R(SB) 1/89
95 Reg 57(1) IS Regs
96 Reg 57(2) IS Regs
97 Reg 57(3) IS Regs
98 Regs 57(4) and 59(2) IS Regs

Chapter 7: Claims, reviews and getting paid
(pp142-169)

1. Claims
(pp142-147)

1 Reg 4(3) SS(C&P) Regs
2 Reg 4(4) SS(C&P) Regs
3 Reg 33 SS(C&P) Regs
4 R(SB) 5/90
5 CIS/379/1992
6 Reg 4(1) SS(C&P) Regs
7 Reg 4(5) SS(C&P) Regs
8 Reg 4(7) SS(C&P) Regs
9 Reg 4(7) SS(C&P) Regs
10 Reg 5(1) SS(C&P) Regs
11 Reg 5(2) SS(C&P) Regs
12 Reg 7(1) SS(C&P) Regs
13 R(SB) 29/83
14 Reg 7(2) SS(C&P) Regs
15 Reg 32(1) SS(C&P) Regs
16 Reg 6(1) SS(C&P) Regs
17 R(SB) 8/89
18 Reg 13(1) SS(C&P) Regs
19 Reg 19(1) and Sch 4 para 6 SS(C&P) Regs
20 Reg 19(3) SS(C&P) Regs
21 Reg 19(2) SS(C&P) Regs
22 Reg 19(4) SS(C&P) Regs
23 s2 SSAA 1992
24 R(SB) 9/84
25 CS/371/1949
26 R(P) 1/79
27 R(I) 28/54
28 R(SB) 6/83
29 CS/50/1950
30 R(U) 9/74
31 R(U) 35/56
32 R(S) 5/56
33 R(S) 14/54; R(G) 4/68; R(U) 9/74

34 R(S) 14/54
35 R(S) 11/59; R(G) 1/75
36 R(S) 10/59; R(S) 3/69;
     R(SB) 17/83
37 R(SB) 6/83
38 R(G) 2/74
39 R(SB) 17/83; R(IS)
     5/91
40 R(P) 2/85

2. Decisions and reviews
(pp147-151)
41 ss20 and 21 SSAA
     1992
42 Reg 64 SS(Adj) Regs
43 Reg 63(1) SS(Adj) Regs
44 Reg 63(7) SS(Adj) Regs
45 Reg 63(5) SS(Adj) Regs
46 s21(1) SSAA 1992
47 *R v Secretary of State*
     for Social Services ex
     parte CPAG and
     others, [1989] All ER
     1047 (HC) (CA)
48 s25(1) SSAA 1992
49 Sch 7 para 7 SS(C&P)
     Regs
50 *CAO v McKiernon* CA
     8 July 1993
51 Regs 69(5) and 69A
     SS(Adj) Regs
52 CIS/714/1991
53 R(IS) 15/93
54 Reg 69(1) SS(Adj) Regs
55 Reg 64A SS(Adj) Regs
56 *Saker v Secretary of*
     State for Social
     Services; R(I) 2/88
57 R(IS) 11/92
58 s69 SSAA 1992; reg
     64B SS(Adj) Regs

3. Payments of benefit
(pp151-161)
59 Reg 20 SS(C&P) Regs
60 Reg 21 SS(C&P) Regs
61 para 5030 IS Manual
62 Reg 38(1) SS(C&P)
     Regs
63 Reg 38(2A) SS(C&P)
     Regs
64 Reg 26(4) SS(C&P)
     Regs
65 Sch 7 para 5 SS(C&P)
     Regs

66 Reg 28 SS(C&P) Regs
67 Reg 26(1) and Sch 7
     SS(C&P) Regs
68 Sch 7 para 1 SS(C&P)
     Regs
69 Sch 7 para 6(1)
     SS(C&P) Regs
70 Sch 7 para 3 SS(C&P)
     Regs
71 Sch 7 para 3 SS(C&P)
     Regs
72 Reg 2 SS(PAOR) Regs
73 Regs 3 and 4
     SS(PAOR) Regs
74 Regs 37, 37A and 37B
     SS(C&P) Regs
75 *Walsh v DSS*, Bromley
     County Court, 12
     February 1990.
     Not reported – see
     Bulletin 96
76 R(IS) 7/91
77 *Hansard*, 4 May 1993
78 Reg 33 SS(C&P) Regs
79 Reg 34 SS(C&P) Regs
80 Sch 9A para 2
     SS(C&P) Regs
81 Sch 9A paras 8 and 9
     SS(C&P) Regs
82 Sch 9A paras 3 and 5
     SS(C&P) Regs
83 Sch 9A para 6
     SS(C&P) Regs
84 Reg 35 SS(C&P) Regs
85 Sch 9 para 2 SS(C&P)
     Regs
86 Sch 9 para 5(1)
     SS(C&P) Regs
87 Sch 9 para 5(2)
     SS(C&P) Regs
88 Sch 9 para 5(3)
     SS(C&P) Regs
89 Sch 9 para 5(4)
     SS(C&P) Regs
90 Sch 9 para 5(1)(c)
     SS(C&P) Regs
91 Sch 9 para 5(1)(c)(ii)
     SS(C&P) Regs
92 Sch 9 para 5(1)(c)(i)
     SS(C&P) Regs
93 Sch 9 para 5(7)
     SS(C&P) Regs
94 Sch 9 para 3 SS(C&P)
     Regs
95 Sch 9 para 3(5)
     SS(C&P) Regs

96 Sch 9 para 1 SS(C&P)
     Regs
97 Sch 9 para 3(4)
     SS(C&P) Regs
98 Sch 9 para 4 SS(C&P)
     Regs
99 Sch 9 para 4(1)
     SS(C&P) Regs
100 Sch 9 para 7 SS(C&P)
     Regs
101 Sch 9 para 1 SS(C&P)
     Regs
102 Sch 9 para 7(1)
     SS(C&P) Regs
103 Sch 9 para 7(2)
     SS(C&P) Regs
104 Sch 9 para 7(7)
     SS(C&P) Regs
105 Sch 9 para 6 SS(C&P)
     Regs
106 Sch 9 para 6(1)
     SS(C&P) Regs
107 Sch 9 para 6(4)
     SS(C&P) Regs
108 CC(DIS) Regs
109 Sch 9 para 4A
     SS(C&P) Regs
110 Regs 1-7 F(DIS) Regs
111 Sch 9 para 5(6)
     SS(C&P) Regs
112 Sch 9 para 3(2)
     SS(C&P) Regs
113 Sch 9 para 3(2A)
     SS(C&P) Regs
114 Sch 9 para 6(2)
     SS(C&P) Regs
115 Reg 2 CC(DIS) Regs
116 Sch 9 para 7(3)-(6)
     SS(C&P) Regs
117 Sch 9 para 8(1)
     SS(C&P) Regs
118 Sch 9 paras 6(6), 7(8)
     and 5(5) SS(C&P)
     Regs
119 Sch 9 para 4(2)
     SS(C&P) Regs
120 Sch 9 para 4A(3) and
     (4) SS(C&P) Regs
121 Sch 9 paras 1 and
     2(2) SS(C&P) Regs
122 Reg 2 CC(DIS) Regs
123 Sch 9 para 9 SS(C&P)
     Regs; reg 2 CC(DIS)
     Regs
124 Regs 15 and 16
     SS(PAOR) Regs; reg

3 SF(RDB) Regs
125 Reg 4 CC(DIS) Regs;
reg 8 CT(DIS) Regs

4. Overpayments and fraud
(pp161-168)

126 R(SB) 2/91
127 s74 SSAA 1992
128 CIS/457/1992
129 s71 SSAA 1992
130 s71(5) SSAA 1992
131 CSSB/621/1988 and CSB/316/1989
132 CSB/688/1982
133 *Page v CAO* (CA), *The Times*, 4 July 1991
134 *Jones/Sharples v CAO, The Times*, 22 July 1993; R(SB) 9/85
135 R(SB) 3/90
136 CIS/222/1991
137 R(SB) 21/82; R(SB) 28/83; R(SB) 54/83; CA/303/1992
138 Reg 32(1) SS(C&P) Regs
139 CSB/688/1982; R(SB) 12/84; R(SB) 20/84; R(SB) 40/84
140 R(SB) 18/85
141 CWSB/2/1985
142 CSB/347/1983
143 R(SB) 33/85
144 R(SB) 54/83
145 CSB/393/1985
146 R(SB) 36/84; R(SB) 54/83; R(SB) 2/91
147 *Jones/Sharples v CAO, The Times*, 22 July 1993
148 CIS/159/1990
149 R(SB) 20/84; R(SB) 24/87
150 Reg 13 SS(PAOR) Regs
151 *Commock v CAO* reported as appendix to R(SB) 6/90
152 R(IS) 5/92
153 Regs 15 and 16(3) SS(PAOR) Regs
154 Reg 14 SS(PAOR) Regs
155 Reg 15 SS(PAOR)

Regs
156 s74(2)(b) SSAA 1992
157 Reg 16(3) SS(PAOR) Regs
158 Reg 16(4), (5) and (6) SS(PAOR) Regs
159 Reg 16(6) SS(PAOR) Regs
160 Reg 17 SS(PAOR) Regs
161 *Secretary of State for Social Services v Solly* [1974] 3 All ER 922; R(SB) 21/82

Chapter 8: Appeals
(pp170-182)

1 s22 SSAA 1992; R(IS) 7/91
2 R(SB) 29/83; R(SB) 12/89; CIS/807/1992
3 Reg 63(7) SS(Adj) Regs
4 Reg 3 and Sch 2 SS(Adj) Regs; R(IS) 18/93
5 Reg 3(3) SS(Adj) Regs
6 R(IS) 18/93
7 R(SB) 24/82
8 R(SB) 18/83 para 10
9 Reg 6(2) SS(Adj) Regs
10 CIS/068/1991
11 Reg 2(1)(b) SS(Adj) Regs
12 para 38(1) *Social Security Appeal Tribunals: A guide to procedure*, HMSO
13 Reg 4(2) SS(Adj) Regs
14 CIS/544/1991; CS/99/1993
15 Reg 4(4) SS(Adj) Regs
16 s41 SSAA 1992
17 Regs 24(2) and 25(1) SS(Adj) Regs
18 Reg 25(2) SS(Adj) Regs
19 Practice Direction No 1 of 1993
20 Sch 2 para 7 SSAA 1992
21 CIS/643A/1992

22 Practice Direction No 3 of 1993
23 Reg 24(3) SS(Adj) Regs
24 Reg 25(2) SS(Adj) Regs
25 Reg 11 SS(Adj) Regs
26 R(SB) 4/90
27 CSB/172/1990
28 R(SB) 1/92
29 Reg 10 SS(Adj) Regs
30 R(SB) 33/85; R(SB) 12/89
31 R(SB) 10/86
32 R(IS) 6/91
33 R(SB) 1/81
34 R(SB) 6/82
35 s36 SSAA 1992; R(SB) 1/82; R(FIS) 1/82
36 Reg 5 SS(Adj) Regs
37 s123(2) SSCBA 1992
38 s39(2) SSAA 1992
39 s23 SSAA 1992
40 R(I) 12/75
41 s23 SSAA 1992
42 R(A) 1/72; R(SB) 11/83
43 s23(9) SSAA 1992
44 Reg 26(1) SS(Adj) Regs; reg 3(1) SSCP Regs
45 Regs 3(3), 26 and Sch 2, para 5 SS(Adj) Regs
46 Reg 3(1) and (3) SSCP Regs; R(IS) 18/93
47 Reg 3(2) and (5) SSCP Regs; R(IS) 18/93
48 Reg 7(1) SSCP Regs
49 Reg 5(2) SSCP Regs
50 Regs 10, 11 and 12 SSCP Regs
51 Reg 27(3) and (4) SSCP Regs
52 Reg 15 SSCP Regs
53 s57 SSAA 1992
54 Reg 17(4) SSCP Regs
55 Reg 22(2) SSCP Regs
56 s23(7)(b) SSAA 1992
57 s23(7)(a) SSAA 1992
58 *Innes v CAO* (unreported) (CA) 19 November 1986
59 Regs 24 and 25 SSCP Regs
60 s24 SSAA 1992
61 Regs 27(2) and 31(1) SSCP Regs
62 *White v CAO* [1986] 2 All ER 905 (CA), also

reported as an
appendix to R(S) 8/85
63 s24(2)(b) SSAA 1992
64 RSC 0.59 r.21(3)
65 RSC 0.3 r.5 and 0.59
r.14(2)
66 RSC 0.59 r.14(2),
(2A), (2B)
67 RSC 0.59 r.21(2)
68 RSC 0.59 r.4(3)
69 *Bland v CSBO* [1983]
1 WLR 262 (CA), also
reported as R(SB)
12/83
70 ss2(4)(a), 15(1) LAA
1988

PART THREE: FAMILY CREDIT
Chapter 9: Family credit
(pp184-195)
1 s128(1) SSCBA 1992
2 Reg 3(1) FC Regs
3 R(P) 1/78; R(M) 1/85
4 CFC/11/1992
5 Reg 3(2) FC Regs
6 para 39101 AOG
7 ss128(1)(b) and
129(1)(a) SSCBA 1992
8 R(FIS) 1/83
9 R(FIS) 1/86
10 See R(FIS) 6/83; R(FIS)
1/84; R(FIS) 1/86
11 Reg 4 FC Regs; reg 6
DWA Regs
12 R(IS) 1/93
13 para 39335 AOG
14 CSFC/4/1991
15 Reg 4(3) FC Regs; reg
6(3) DWA Regs
16 Reg 4(5) FC Regs; reg
6(5) DWA Regs
17 Reg 4(6) FC Regs; reg
6(6) DWA Regs
18 R(FIS) 2/83
19 R(FIS) 6/83; R(FIS)
1/84
20 R(FIS) 6/83
21 R(FIS) 1/85; *R v Ebbw
Vale & Merthyr Tydfil
SBAT ex parte Lewis*
[1982] 1 WLR 420
22 R(FIS) 2/81; R(FIS)
2/82

23 R(FC) 1/92
24 Reg 4(4)(a) FC Regs;
reg 6(6) DWA Regs
25 para 39381 AOG
26 R(FIS) 6/85; para
39372 AOG
27 Reg 4(4)(b) FC Regs;
reg 6(4)(b) DWA Regs
28 Reg 4(4)(c)(ii)(bb) FC
Regs
29 Reg 4(4)(c)(i) FC Regs;
reg 6(4)(c)(i) DWA
Regs; CIS/261/1990
30 Reg 4(4)(c)(ii)(aa) FC
Regs; reg 6(4)(c)(ii)
DWA Regs
31 CIS/748/1992
32 s128(1)(d) SSCBA
1992
33 Reg 52 FC Regs
34 s128(1)(a) SSCBA
1992; reg 47(1) FC
Regs
35 s128(2)(a) SSCBA
1992
36 s128(2)(b) SSCBA
1992; reg 48 FC Regs
37 Reg 46(1) FC Regs
38 Sch 4 FC Regs
39 Reg 46(4)-(6) FC Regs
40 Reg 46(2) and (3) FC
Regs
41 Reg 28 SS(C&P) Regs
42 Reg 27(2) SS(C&P)
Regs
43 Reg 14(3) FC Regs
44 s128(3) SSCBA 1992
45 Reg 6(1) SS(C&P)
Regs
46 Reg 4(7) SS(C&P)
Regs
47 Reg 19 SS(C&P) Regs
48 Reg 5 SS(C&P) Regs
49 Reg 19 and Sch 4 para
7 SS(C&P) Regs
50 Reg 16(1) and (3)
SS(C&P) Regs
51 s128(3) SSCBA 1992
52 Reg 16(1B) SS(C&P)
Regs
53 Reg 9 SS(C&P) Regs
54 Reg 7(3) SS(C&P)
Regs
55 s21(1) SSAA 1992
56 Reg 20 SS(Adj) Regs
57 Regs 20 and 27

SS(C&P) Regs
58 Reg 21 SS(C&P) Regs
59 Reg 27(1A) and (2)
(C&P) Regs
60 Reg 27(1) SS(C&P)
Regs
61 s128(3) SSCBA 1992
62 s128(4) SSCBA 1992;
reg 50 FC Regs
63 Reg 49 FC Regs
64 Reg 51 FC Regs
65 CFC/18/1989
66 Regs 15 and 16
SS(PAOR) Regs
67 s25 SSAA 1992
68 s128(3) SSCBA 1992
69 Reg 70 SS(Adj) Regs
70 s22 SSAA 1992

PART FOUR: DISABILITY WORKING ALLOWANCE
Chapter 10: Disability working allowance
(pp198-211)
1 Reg 7B SS(Cr) Regs
2 s129(1) SSCBA 1992
3 Reg 5 DWA Regs
4 s129(1)(b) SSCBA
1992
5 s11(2) SSAA 1992; reg
4 DWA Regs
6 Reg 3 and Sch 1 DWA
Regs
7 Sch 1 para 24 DWA
Regs
8 s129(1), (2) and (4)
SSCBA 1992; reg 7
DWA Regs
9 s11(3) SSAA 1992
10 s129(1)(d) SSCBA
1992
11 Reg 57 DWA Regs
12 Reg 31 DWA Regs
13 s129(5) SSCBA 1992;
reg 53 DWA Regs
14 Reg 51 and Sch 5
DWA Regs
15 Reg 4(1) SS(C&P)
Regs
16 Reg 4(3A) SS(C&P)
Regs
17 Reg 4(7) SS(C&P)
Regs

18 Reg 5 SS(C&P) Regs
19 Sch 1 Part 1 SS(C&P) Regs
20 Reg 6(1) SS(C&P) Regs
21 Reg 6(10) SS(C&P) Regs
22 s30(13) SSAA 1992
23 Reg 6(11) SS(C&P) Regs
24 Reg 19(4) SS(C&P) Regs
25 Reg 19(2) SS(C&P) Regs
26 Reg 19(1) and Sch 4 para 11 SS(C&P) Regs
27 Reg 19(3) SS(C&P) Regs
28 Reg 7(1) SS(C&P) Regs
29 Reg 7(3) SS(C&P) Regs
30 ss20 and 21 SSAA 1992
31 s54 SSAA 1992
32 Reg 20 SS(Adj) Regs
33 Reg 16(1) and (3) SS(C&P) Regs
34 Reg 16(1C) SS(C&P) Regs
35 Reg 16(1B) SS(C&P) Regs
36 Reg 27(2) SS(C&P) Regs
37 s129(6) SSCBA 1992
38 Regs 21 and 27 SS(C&P) Regs
39 Reg 36 SS(C&P) Regs
40 s129(6) SSCBA 1992
41 Reg 55 DWA Regs
42 Reg 54 DWA Regs
43 Reg 56 DWA Regs
44 s30(1) SSAA 1992; reg 26A SS(Adj) Regs
45 s30(5) SSAA 1992
46 s35 SSAA 1992
47 ss31 and 35(8) SSAA 1992
48 Reg 26B SS(Adj) Regs
49 Reg 70B SS(Adj) Regs
50 s71 SSAA 1992
51 s33 SSAA 1992
52 Reg 26C SS(Adj) Regs
53 ss42 and 43 SSAA 1992
54 Reg 26G SS(Adj) Regs

55 s55 SSAA 1992
56 ss33(7), 42 and 68(10) SSCBA 1992
57 s9(5) DWAA 1991

PART FIVE: HOUSING BENEFIT
Chapter 11: The basic rules
(pp214-238)

1. Introduction
(pp214-225)
1 s130 SSCBA 1992
2 Reg 6(1)(c)(i) HB Regs
3 Reg 6(1)(c)(ii) HB Regs
4 s134(2) SSCBA 1992; reg 71(1) HB Regs
5 Reg 10(5) HB Regs
6 Reg 10(3) HB Regs
7 Reg 6(2) HB Regs
8 Reg 6(1)(d) HB Regs
9 s130(1) SSCBA 1992; reg 5 HB Regs
10 para A3.15 GM
11 Reg 5(5)(c) HB Regs
12 Reg 5(8) HB Regs
13 *R v Penwith DC ex parte Burt*
14 Reg 5(3) and (9) HB Regs
15 Reg 5(1) HB Regs
16 Reg 5(5)(b) HB Regs
17 Reg 5(5)(a) and (7A) HB Regs
18 Reg 7A HB Regs
19 Reg 5(5)(d) HB Regs
20 Reg 7A HB Regs
21 Reg 5(5)(a)(ii) and (8)(a) HB Regs
22 Reg 5(4) HB Regs
23 Reg 5(5)(d) HB Regs
24 Reg 5(6) HB Regs
25 Reg 5(5)(e) HB Regs
26 Reg 48(A)(1) HB Regs
27 Reg 7(1)(e) HB Regs
28 Reg 10(2)(a) and (c) HB Regs
29 Reg 2(1) HB Regs
30 Reg 7(a) HB Regs
31 Reg 2(1) HB Regs
32 para A3.31 GM
33 Reg 7(b) HB Regs
34 *R v HBRB Sutton ex parte Keegan* [1992]

35 *R v Manchester City Council ex parte Baragrove Properties* [1991]
36 Reg 7(1)(c) HB Regs
37 Reg 8(3) HB Regs
38 Reg 10(2)(e) HB Regs; Part A8 GM
39 Reg 10(2)(b) HB Regs
40 Reg 10(2)(d) HB Regs
41 Reg 7(1)(d) HB Regs
42 Reg 7A HB Regs; reg 4A CTB Regs
43 HB/CTB Circular 94(13)

2. 'Eligible rent'
(pp225-231)
44 Reg 10(1) HB Regs
45 Reg 2(4)(a) HB Regs
46 Reg 10(3)(a) and (6) HB Regs
47 Reg 8(2)(a) HB Regs
48 Reg 10(2)(c) HB Regs
49 Reg 10(4) HB Regs
50 Reg 7(1)(e) HB Regs
51 Reg 10(2)(e) HB Regs
52 Part A8 GM
53 Reg 10(2)(a) HB Regs
54 Reg 10(2)(b) HB Regs
55 Reg 10(2)(d) HB Regs
56 Reg 8(2)(b) HB Regs
57 Sch 1 Part II para 4 HB Regs
58 Sch 1 para 5(1) HB Regs
59 Sch 1 para 5(1)(a) HB Regs
60 Sch 1 para 5(2) and (2A) HB Regs
61 Reg 10(1)(e) and (5) HB Regs
62 Sch 1 para 5(3) and Sch 6 para 9(c) HB Regs
63 para A4.76(ii) GM
64 Sch 1 paras 4 and 5(1)(b) HB Regs; para A4.81 GM
65 Sch 1 para 7 HB Regs
66 Sch 1 para 7 HB Regs
67 Reg 10(1)(e) HB Regs
68 Sch 1 para 1(a)(iii) HB Regs
69 Sch 1 para 1(a)(ii) HB Regs

70 Sch 1 para 1(b) HB
Regs
71 Sch 1 para 1(a)(iv) HB
Regs
72 Sch 1 para 1(a)(iv) HB
Regs
73 Sch 1 para 1(c) HB
Regs; para A4.67 GM
74 Sch 1 para 1(f) HB
Regs; para A4.69 GM
75 Sch 1 para 3 HB Regs
76 Sch 1 para 1 HB Regs
77 Reg 10(3)(c) and Sch 1
para 2(1A) HB Regs
78 Sch 1 para 2 HB Regs
79 Sch 1 para 1(a)(i) HB
Regs
80 Sch 1 para 1A(1) HB
Regs
81 Sch 1 para 1A(5) and
(6) HB Regs
82 Reg 7(1)(e) HB Regs
83 Reg 8(2ZA) and (2ZB)
HB Regs
84 Reg 7(2) HB Regs
85 Reg 7(4)-(12) HB Regs
86 Reg 7(3) HB Regs

3. 'Unreasonably high rents
(pp231-238)
87 para A4.88 GM
88 LGOR Ipswich
Borough Council,
March 1993
89 Reg 11(2) HB Regs
90 Reg 11(6)(a) HB Regs
91 para A4.105-6 GM
92 *Macleod v HBRB for
Banff and Buchan
District* [1988] SCLR
165; *Malcolm v HBRB
for Tweedale* [1991]
93 Reg 11(3) HB Regs
94 Reg 11(7) and (8) HB
Regs
95 Reg 2(1) HB Regs
96 *R v Sefton MBC ex
parte Cunningham*
97 para A4.108 GM
98 *Malcolm v HBRB for
Tweedale* [1991]; *R v
Devon DC ex parte
Gibson* [1993]
99 Reg 11(6)(b) HB
Regs

100 *R v London Borough
of Brent ex parte
Connery*, QB
23/10/89
101 Reg 11(3A) HB Regs
102 Reg 11(4) HB Regs
103 Reg 11(5) HB Regs
104 Reg 95(7) HB Regs
105 *R v London Borough
of Brent ex parte
Connery*; para A4.86
GM
106 Reg 12(b) HB Regs;
para A4.115 GM
107 Reg 12 HB Regs

Chapter 12: The amount of benefit
(pp239-248)
1 Reg 61 HB Regs
2 Reg 64 HB Regs
3 Reg 37 HB Regs
4 s130(3)(a) SSCBA
1992
5 Reg 62 HB Regs
6 Reg 2 HB Regs
7 Reg 69 HB Regs
8 Reg 69(2)(a) HB Regs
9 Reg 69(2)(b) HB
Regs
10 Reg 70(3) and Sch 1
para 6(2) HB Regs;
para A5.49-53 GM
11 Reg 70(3)(a) and Sch
1 para 6(2)(a) HB
Regs
12 Reg 70(3)(b) and Sch
1 para 6(2)(b) HB
Regs
13 Reg 63 HB Regs
14 Reg 3(2) HB Regs
15 Reg 3(4) and Sch 1
para 7 HB Regs
16 Reg 63(6) HB Regs;
reg 52(6) CTB Regs
17 Reg 63(7) HB Regs;
reg 52(7) CTB Regs
18 Reg 63(1) HB Regs;
reg 52(1) CTB Regs
19 Reg 63(8) HB Regs
20 Reg 63(1) and (2) HB
Regs
21 Reg 4(1) HB Regs;
reg 4(1) CTB Regs
22 Reg 4(4) HB Regs;
reg 4(4) CTB Regs

23 Reg 4(1) and (2) HB
Regs; reg 4(1) and (2)
CTB Regs
24 Reg 4(5) HB Regs; reg
4(5) CTB Regs
25 para A5.30-32 GM
26 para A5.16 GM
27 para A5.23 GM
28 Reg 63(3) HB Regs
29 Reg 63(5) HB Regs
30 Sch 4 para 19 HB Regs
31 Reg 20(1) HB Regs
32 Reg 20 HB Regs
33 Reg 77 and Sch 6 para
12 HB Regs
34 Reg 61(2) HB Regs
35 Reg 61(2) HB Regs
36 Reg 61(2) HB Regs
37 ss134(8) and 139(6)
SSAA 1992
38 s134(9) and (11) and
139(7) and (9) SSAA
1992
39 Reg 5(8) HB Regs
40 Reg 18(1)(a) HB Regs
41 Reg 18(1)(b) HB Regs
42 Reg 18(1)(c)(i) HB
Regs
43 Reg 18(1)(c)(ii) HB
Regs
44 Reg 18(1)(d)(i) HB
Regs
45 Reg 18(1)(d)(ii) HB
Regs
46 Reg 18(3) HB Regs

Chapter 13: Special rules for students
(pp249-256)
1 Reg 46 HB Regs; reg
38 CTB Regs
2 Reg 46 HB Regs; reg
38 CTB Regs
3 Reg 46 HB Regs; reg
38 CTB Regs
4 para C5.03 GM
5 Reg 46 HB Regs; reg
38 CTB Regs
6 Reg 46 HB Regs; reg
38 CTB Regs
7 Reg 48A(2) HB Regs;
reg 40(3) CTB Regs
8 s131 SSCBA 1992; reg
6(1)(e) HB Regs
9 Reg 48A(1) HB Regs;

reg 40(3) CTB Regs
10 Reg 48 HB Regs
11 para C5.33 GM
12 Reg 52 HB Regs; para C5.32 GM
13 Reg 5(8) HB Regs; paras A3.19-22 GM
14 Reg 50(1) HB Regs
15 Reg 50(2) HB Regs
16 Reg 50(3) HB Regs
17 Reg 52 HB Regs
18 Reg 50(1) HB Regs; para C5.37 GM
19 s131 SSCBA 1992; regs 6(1)(b) and 52 HB Regs
20 Reg 51(1) HB Regs
21 Reg 52 HB Regs
22 Reg 51(2) HB Regs
23 Reg 69(8) HB Regs
24 Reg 90 HB Regs

Chapter 14: Claims, payments and reviews (pp257-294)

1. Claims
(pp257-262)
1 Reg 71(1) HB Regs; reg 61(1) CTB Regs
2 Reg 71(2) HB Regs; reg 61(2) CTB Regs
3 Reg 71(3) and (5) HB Regs; reg 61(3) and (5) CTB Regs
4 Reg 71(6) HB Regs; reg 61(6) CTB Regs
5 Reg 71(4) HB Regs; reg 61(4) CTB Regs
6 Reg 72(1) HB Regs; reg 62(1) CTB Regs
7 Reg 72(2) HB Regs; reg 62(2) CTB Regs
8 para A2.09 GM
9 Reg 72(7)(b) and (8) HB Regs; reg 62(7)(b) and (8) CTB Regs
10 Reg 72(7)(a) and (8) HB Regs; para A2.24 GM; reg 62(7)(a) and (8) CTB Regs
11 Reg 74(1) HB Regs; reg 64(1) CTB Regs
12 Reg 74(2) HB Regs; reg 64(2) CTB Regs

13 Reg 72(4)(a) and (b) HB Regs; reg 62(4)(a) and (b) CTB Regs
14 s191 SSAA 1992
15 Reg 72(4)(a) and (b) HB Regs; reg 62(4)(a) and (b) CTB Regs
16 Reg 72(4)(c) HB Regs; reg 62(4)(c) CTB Regs
17 Reg 72(1) HB Regs; reg 62(1) CTB Regs
18 Reg 73(1) HB Regs; reg 63(1) CTB Regs
19 Reg 76(2)(b) HB Regs; reg 66(2)(b) CTB Regs
20 Reg 73(1) and (3) HB Regs; reg 63(1) and (3) CTB Regs
21 Reg 73(2) HB Regs; reg 63(2) CTB Regs
22 Reg 95(7) HB Regs
23 Reg 72(5)(c) HB Regs; reg 62(5)(d) CTB Regs
24 Reg 72(5)(a) HB Regs; reg 62(5)(a) CTB Regs
25 Reg 72(5)(b) HB Regs; reg 62(5)(b) CTB Regs
26 Reg 72(5)(bb) HB Regs; reg 62(5)(c) CTB Regs
27 Reg 65(1) HB Regs; reg 56(1) CTB Regs
28 Reg 72(15) HB Regs; paras A2.14-16 and B2.29 GM; reg 62(16) CTB Regs
29 paras A2.16 and B2.34 GM
30 Reg 72(15) HB Regs; reg 62(16) CTB Regs
31 Reg 5(6) HB Regs
32 Reg 72(11) HB Regs; reg 62(12) CTB Regs
33 Reg 66 HB Regs; paras A6.07 and B4.17 GM; reg 57 CTB Regs
34 Sch 6 paras 9(g) and (h); 10(a) HB Regs; Sch 6 paras 9(d), (e) and 10(a) CTB Regs
35 Reg 72(13) HB Regs; reg 62(14) CTB Regs
36 Reg 72(14) HB Regs; para A6.12 GM; reg 62(15) CTB Regs
37 Reg 67(a) and (b) HB

Regs; reg 58(a); (b) CTB Regs
38 Reg 72(13) HB Regs; paras A6.12 and B4.13 GM; reg 62(14) CTB Regs
39 para A6.13 GM

2. Decisions
(pp263-265)
40 Regs 76(3), 77(1)(a) and 88(3) HB Regs; regs 66(3), 67(1)(a) and 77(2)(b) and (c) CTB Regs
41 Reg 76(2) HB Regs; reg 66(2) CTB Regs
42 Reg 77(1) HB Regs; reg 67(1) CTB Regs
43 paras A6.17 and B6.4 GM
44 Reg 77 and Sch 6 HB Regs; reg 67 and Sch 6 CTB Regs
45 Sch 6 para 6 HB Regs; Sch 6 para 6 CTB Regs
46 Sch 6 para 2 HB Regs; Sch 6 para 2 CTB Regs
47 Sch 6 para 3 HB Regs; Sch 6 para 3 CTB Regs
48 Sch 6 paras 9-13 HB Regs; Sch 6 paras 9-13 CTB Regs
49 Reg 77(3)-(5) HB Regs; reg 67(2) and (3) CTB Regs
50 para C12.10 GM

3. Payment of benefit
(pp265-271)
51 Reg 66 HB Regs; reg 57 CTB Regs
52 Reg 65(1) HB Regs; reg 56(1) CTB Regs
53 Reg 65(1) HB Regs; reg 56(1) CTB Regs
54 Reg 2(1) HB Regs; reg 2(1) CTB Regs
55 Reg 65(2) HB Regs
56 Reg 69(4)(a) HB Regs
57 Reg 69(2)(b), (5)(a), and (6) HB Regs
58 Reg 66(3) HB Regs; reg 57(3) CTB Regs
59 Reg 66(2) HB Regs;

paras A6.07 GM; reg 57(2) CTB Regs

60 Reg 66(1)(a) HB Regs; reg 57(1) CTB Regs
61 Reg 66(1)(b) HB Regs; reg 57(1)(b) CTB Regs
62 Reg 72(13) HB Regs; reg 62(14) CTB Regs
63 Reg 66(4) HB Regs; reg 57(4) CTB Regs
64 Reg 67 HB Regs; reg 58 CTB Regs
65 Reg 67(c) HB Regs; reg 58(1)(c) CTB Regs
66 Reg 67(a) and (b) HB Regs; reg 58(1)(a) and (b) CTB Regs
67 Reg 72(14)(a) HB Regs; reg 62(15)(a) CTB Regs
68 Reg 67 HB Regs; reg 58 CTB Regs
69 s134(1)(b) SSAA 1992
70 s134(1)(c) SSAA 1992; reg 92(1) HB Regs
71 Reg 90(1) HB Regs
72 Reg 90(2) HB Regs
73 Reg 88(2) HB Regs
74 Reg 90(3) HB Regs
75 Reg 90(4) HB Regs; para A6.30 GM
76 Reg 88(1)(b) HB Regs; reg 77(1) and (3) CTB Regs
77 para A6.24 GM
78 para A6.34 GM and Circular HB/CTB (93)37
79 Reg 91(1) HB Regs; *R v London Borough of Haringey ex parte Azad Ayub*
80 Reg 91(2) HB Regs
81 Reg 91(3) HB Regs
82 para C9.223 GM
83 Reg 88(1) HB Regs; reg 77(1) CTB Regs
84 Reg 92(1) HB Regs; reg 78(1) CTB Regs
85 Reg 92(2) HB Regs; reg 78(2) CTB Regs
86 Reg 92(3) HB Regs; para A6.40 GM
87 Reg 96 HB Regs; reg 81 CTB Regs
88 *R v London Borough*

Haringey ex parte Azad Ayub
89 Reg 93(a) HB Regs
90 Reg 93(b) HB Regs
91 Reg 94(a) HB Regs
92 *R v London Borough Haringey ex parte Azad Ayub*
93 Reg 95(1) HB Regs
94 Reg 95(3)(a) and (b) HB Regs
95 Reg 95(2) HB Regs
96 Reg 95(7) HB Regs
97 Reg 95(4) HB Regs; reg 80(1) CTB Regs
98 Reg 95(5) HB Regs; reg 80(2) CTB Regs
99 Reg 95(3)(a) and (b) HB Regs
100 Reg 95(6) HB Regs; reg 80(3) CTB Regs

4. Changes in your circumstances (pp271-274)

101 Reg 75(1) HB Regs; reg 65(1) CTB Regs
102 Sch 6 paras 9(i) and 10(a) HB Regs; Sch 6 paras 9(f) and 10(a) CTB Regs
103 Reg 75(1), (2)(e) and (3) HB Regs; paras A6.50 and B4.10 GM; reg 65(1), (2)(d), (3) and (4) CTB Regs
104 Regs 73(2) and 75 HB Regs; regs 63(2) and 65 CTB Regs
105 Reg 75(1) HB Regs; reg 65(1) CTB Regs
106 Reg 75(2) HB Regs; reg 65(2) CTB Regs
107 Regs 2(1), 73(2) and 75(1) HB Regs; regs 2, 63(2) and 65(1) CTB Regs
108 Reg 68 HB Regs; reg 59 CTB Regs
109 Reg 68(1) HB Regs; reg 59(1) CTB Regs
110 Reg 68(1) HB Regs; reg 59(1) CTB Regs
111 Reg 67(a) and (b) HB Regs; reg 58(a) and

(b) CTB Regs
112 Reg 68(2) HB Regs
113 Regs 26 and 68(1) HB Regs; regs 18 and 59(1) CTB Regs
114 Reg 68(3) HB Regs; reg 59(4) CTB Regs
115 Reg 35(4) HB Regs; reg 26(4) CTB Regs
116 Reg 68(4) HB Regs; reg 59(7) CTB Regs
117 Reg 68(5) HB Regs
118 Reg 67(c) HB Regs; reg 58(c) CTB Regs
119 Reg 67(a) and (b) HB Regs; reg 58(a) and (b) CTB Regs
120 Reg 79(1)(a) and (3)(a) HB Regs; reg 69(1)(a) and (3)(a) CTB Regs
121 Reg 79(5)(b) HB Regs; reg 69(5)(b) CTB Regs
122 Reg 99 HB Regs; reg 84 CTB Regs

5. Overpayments (pp274-283)

123 Reg 98 HB Regs; reg 83 CTB Regs
124 s134(2) SSAA 1992
125 Sch 6 para 14(b) HB Regs; paras A7.44 and B5.6 GM; Sch 6 para 16(b) CTB Regs
126 para A7.48 GM
127 ss112 and 116 SSAA 1992
128 Reg 99(2) and (3) HB Regs; para A7.22 and B5.5 GM; reg 84(2) and (3) CTB Regs
129 Reg 99(2) HB Regs; reg 84(2) CTB Regs
130 *R v Liverpool City Council ex parte Griffiths* [1990]
131 Reg 91(3) HB Regs
132 Reg 100 HB Regs; reg 85 CTB Regs
133 paras C10.12-17 GM
134 Regs 79(2) and 100-102 HB Regs; regs 69(2), 85 and 86 CTB Regs

135 Sch 6 para 14(d) HB Regs; Sch 6 para 16(d) CTB Regs
136 Reg 104(a) HB Regs; reg 90(a) CTB Regs
137 Reg 104(b) HB Regs; para A7.29 GM; reg 90(b) CTB Regs
138 Reg 103(1) HB Regs; reg 89(1) CTB Regs
139 Reg 103(1)(a) and (b) HB Regs; paras A7.31-3 GM; reg 89(1)(a) and (b) CTB Regs
140 Reg 103(2) HB Regs; reg 89(2) CTB Regs
141 Reg 101 HB Regs; reg 86(1) CTB Regs
142 Reg 101(1)(a) HB Regs
143 Reg 101(2) HB Regs; reg 86(2) CTB Regs
144 paras A7.45-47 GM
145 *R v London Borough Haringey ex parte Azad Ayub*
146 Reg 102 HB Regs; reg 87 CTB Regs
147 Reg 88 CTB Regs; para A7.36(v) GM
148 paras A7.37-40 GM
149 *R v London Borough of Haringey ex parte Azad Ayub*
150 Reg 105 HB Regs; reg 91 CTB Regs
151 Reg 102 HB Regs; para A7.36(iv) GM
152 Regs 102 and 105 HB Regs; regs 87(3) and 91 CTB Regs
153 Reg 105(1) HB Regs; reg 91(1) CTB Regs
154 Reg 77(b) HB Regs; reg 67(1)(b) CTB Regs
155 Sch 6 paras 2, 3, 6 and 14 HB Regs; para A7.45 GM; Sch 6 paras 2, 3, 6 and 16 CTB Regs
156 Reg 77(4) and (5) HB Regs; reg 67(2) and (3) CTB Regs

6. Fraud
(pp283-286)
157 HB/CTB 93(11)
158 National Service level agreement defined in HB/CTB 93(20), as modified by local agreements
159 s112 SSAA 1992
160 s15 Theft Act 1968
161 HB/CTB 93(20)
162 s116 SSAA 1992
163 HB/CTB 93(20); para 17 National Service level agreement

7. Reviews
(pp286-292)
164 Reg 79(1) and (1A) HB Regs; reg 69(1) CTB Regs
165 Reg 79(6) HB Regs; reg 69(7) CTB Regs
166 Reg 79(3)(c) and (5) HB Regs; reg 69(3)(c) and (5) CTB Regs
167 Reg 79(2) HB Regs; reg 69(2) CTB Regs
168 Reg 79(2) HB Regs; reg 69(2) CTB Regs
169 Reg 78(3) and (4) HB Regs; reg 68(3) and (4) CTB Regs
170 Sch 6 para 3 HB Regs; Sch 6 para 3 CTB Regs
171 Reg 78(3), (4) and (5) HB Regs; reg 68(3), (4) and (5) CTB Regs
172 Reg 79(4) HB Regs; reg 69(4) CTB Regs
173 Reg 77(4) and (5) HB Regs; reg 67(2) and (3) CTB Regs
174 Sch 6 para 2 HB Regs; Sch 6 para 2 CTB Regs
175 Reg 79(2) and Sch 6 paras 4 and 5 HB Regs; reg 69(2) and Sch 6 paras 4 and 5 CTB Regs
176 Reg 79(3)(b) HB Regs; reg 69(3)(b) CTB Regs

177 Reg 79(3)(c) and (5)(a) HB Regs; reg 69(3)(c) and (5)(a) CTB Regs
178 Reg 81(1) and (2) HB Regs; reg 70(1) and (2) CTB Regs
179 Reg 78(3), (4) and (5) HB regs; reg 68(3)-(5) CTB Regs
180 Reg 82(1) HB Regs; reg 71(1) CTB Regs
181 Reg 82(2) and (1A) HB Regs
182 Reg 82(3) HB Regs; regs 70(5) and 71(3) CTB Regs
183 Reg 82(5) HB Regs; reg 71(5) CTB Regs
184 Sch 7 HB Regs; Sch 7 CTB Regs
185 Reg 82(7) HB Regs; reg 71(7) CTB Regs
186 paras A6.64 and B6.18 GM
187 Reg 81(4) HB Regs; reg 70(4) CTB Regs
188 Reg 82(2)(a) HB Regs; reg 71(2)(a) CTB Regs
189 Reg 82(2)(b) HB Regs; reg 71(2)(b) CTB Regs
190 Reg 82(2)(c) HB Regs; reg 71(2)(c) CTB Regs
191 Reg 82(9) HB Regs; paras A6.68 and B6.22 GM; reg 71(9) CTB Regs
192 Reg 82(2)(c)(ii) HB Regs; reg 71(2)(c)(ii) CTB Regs
193 Reg 82(4) HB Regs; reg 71(4) CTB Regs
194 Reg 82(5) and (6) HB Regs; reg 71(6) CTB Regs
195 Reg 83(1) HB Regs; paras A6.70 and B6.24 GM; reg 72(1) CTB Regs
196 Reg 82(8) HB Regs; reg 71(8) CTB Regs
197 Reg 83(4) HB Regs; reg 72(4) CTB Regs

198 Reg 83(2) HB Regs;
reg 72(2) CTB Regs
199 Reg 83(5) HB Regs;
reg 72(5) CTB Regs
200 *R v HBRB of Sefton
MBC ex parte
Cunningham,* 22
May 1991, QB
201 Reg 84 HB Regs; reg
73 CTB Regs
202 Regs 79(3)(c), (5) and
83(3) HB Regs; regs
69(3)(c) and 72(3)
CTB Regs
203 Regs 85(1) and 87(1)
HB Regs; regs 74(1)
and 76(1) CTB Regs
204 Reg 87(3) HB Regs;
reg 76(3) CTB Regs
205 Reg 86(1) HB Regs;
paras A6.79-82 and
B6.33-6 GM; reg
75(1) CTB Regs
206 Reg 86(1) HB Regs;
reg 75(1) CTB Regs
207 Reg 86(1) HB Regs;
reg 75(1) CTB Regs
208 Regs 78(2) and 86(2)
HB Regs; regs 68(2)
and 75(2) CTB Regs
209 Reg 87(2) HB Regs;
reg 76(2) CTB Regs
210 Reg 86(3) HB Regs;
reg 75(3) CTB Regs
211 Reg 86(4) HB Regs;
reg 75(4) CTB Regs
212 Reg 87(3) HB Regs;
reg 76(3) CTB Regs
213 Regs 78(2) and 87(2)
HB Regs; regs 68(2)
and 76(2) and (3)
CTB Regs

**PART SIX: COUNCIL
TAX BENEFIT
Chapter 15: Council
tax benefit
(pp296-325)**
1 s131(9) SSCBA 1992
2 Reg 51(1)(a) and
(2)(a) CTB Regs
3 Reg 51(2)(b) CTB
Regs
4 Reg 51(3) CTB Regs
5 Reg 51(4) CTB Regs

6 Reg 51(1) CTB Regs
7 para B3.26 GM
8 Sch 6 paras 9-10 CTB
Regs
9 s131(4) SSCBA 1992;
reg 51(1) CTB Regs
10 s131(8)(a) SSCBA
1992
11 s131(8)(b) SSCBA
1992
12 Reg 3 CTB Regs
13 Regs 51(1) and 52
CTB Regs
14 Reg 3(2)(d) CTB Regs
15 Reg 3(3)(b) CTB Regs
16 Reg 3(2)(e) CTB Regs
17 Reg 3(3)(a) CTB Regs
18 Reg 2 CTB Regs
19 Reg 3(3)(b) CTB Regs
20 Reg 3(2)(f) CTB Regs
21 Reg 52(3) CTB Regs
22 Reg 52(5) CTB Regs
23 Reg 52(6)-(8) CTB
Regs
24 Reg 52(1), (2) and (9)
CTB Regs
25 Reg 52(3) CTB Regs
26 Reg 12 CTB Regs
27 Reg 60(a) CTB Regs
28 s131(9) SSCBA 1992
29 s131(1)(b), (6) and
(8)(c) SSCBA 1992
30 s131(7)(a) SSCBA
1992
31 Reg 54, Schs 2 and 5
para 45(1) CTB Regs
32 Sch 5 para 45(2) CTB
Regs
33 Reg 55(b) and (d) CTB
Regs
34 s131(6) SSCBA 1992;
reg 54 CTB Regs
35 Reg 54 and Sch 2 para
1(2) CTB Regs
36 Reg 54 and Sch 2 para
2-3 CTB Regs
37 Reg 54 and Sch 2 para
1 CTB Regs
38 Reg 54 and Sch 2 para
1(2) CTB Regs
39 Reg 54 and Sch 2 para
1(1) CTB Regs
40 Reg 54 and Sch 2 para
2 CTB Regs
41 Reg 54 and Sch 2 para
3 CTB Regs

42 Reg 54(2) CTB Regs
43 Reg 54(3) CTB Regs
44 Reg 60(b) CTB Regs
45 s131(9) SSCBA 1992
46 Reg 62(10) CTB Regs
47 Reg 62(12) CTB Regs
48 Reg 62(11) CTB Regs
49 Reg 62(16) CTB Regs
50 Art 3 CTB(T)O
51 Art 4 CTB(T)O
52 s1(2)(b) SSAA 1992
53 Sch 6 paras 9(a) and
10(a) CTB Regs
54 Sch 6 paras 12(b),
14(b) and 15 CTB
Regs
55 Sch 6 para 13(c) and (f)
CTB Regs
56 Sch 6 paras 9, 10, 13
and 15 CTB Regs
57 Reg 56(2) CTB Regs
58 Reg 84(5) CTB Regs
59 Reg 77(1)(b) and (3)
CTB Regs
60 Reg 77(3)(a)(ii) CTB
Regs
61 Reg 77(3)(c) CTB
Regs
62 Reg 78 CTB Regs
63 Reg 80 CTB Regs
64 Reg 81 CTB Regs
65 Reg 83(1) CTB Regs
66 Reg 84(2) and (4) CTB
Regs
67 Reg 86(2) CTB Regs
68 Reg 91 CTB Regs
69 Reg 87(2)(b) CTB
Regs
70 Reg 87(2)(a) CTB
Regs
71 Reg 87(3) CTB Regs
72 Reg 91(1)(a) CTB Regs
73 Reg 91 CTB Regs
74 Reg 88 CTB Regs
75 Reg 65(1) CTB Regs
76 Reg 65(2) CTB Regs
77 Reg 65(4) CTB Regs
78 Reg 59(1) CTB Regs
79 Reg 59(2)-(6) CTB
Regs
80 Reg 59(7) CTB Regs
81 Reg 59(1) CTB Regs
82 Reg 70(4) CTB Regs
83 s131(3)(b) SSCBA
1992; reg 40 CTB Regs
84 Reg 40(3) CTB Regs

PART SEVEN: CALCULATING NEEDS AND RESOURCES
Chapter 16: Who counts as your family (pp328-338)

1 s137 SSCBA 1992
2 s134(2) SSCBA 1992
3 Reg 4(2) SS(C&P) Regs
4 s129(1) SSCBA 1992
5 Reg 4(3A) SS(C&P) Regs
6 **IS** Reg 16(1) IS Regs
 FC Reg 9 FC Regs
 DWA Reg 11 DWA Regs
 HB Reg 15(1) HB Regs
 CTB Reg 7(1) CTB Regs
7 *Santos v Santos* [1972] 2 All ER 246; CIS/671/1992
8 para 27732 AOG
9 R(SB) 4/83
10 R(SB) 8/85
11 R(SB) 13/82
12 CSB/463/1986
13 s137 SSCBA 1992 definition of 'married couple' and 'unmarried couple'
14 CFC/7/1992
15 **IS** Reg 2(1) IS Regs
 HB Reg 2(1) HB Regs
 CTB Reg 2(1) CTB Regs
16 **IS** Regs 18 and 23 IS Regs
 FC Reg 10 FC Regs
 DWA Reg 12 DWA Regs
 HB Regs 17 and 19 HB Regs
 CTB Regs 9 and 11 CTB Regs
17 R(SB) 17/81
18 R(G) 3/71
19 *R v Penwith District Council ex parte Menear, The Times,* 21 October 1991
20 R(SB) 8/85
21 *Crake & Butterworth*

v SBC [1980] quoted in R(SB) 35/85
22 R(SB) 35/85
23 para 15027 AOG
24 para 15042 AOG; para C1.04 GM
25 CSB/150/1985
26 CSSB/145/1983
27 **IS** Reg 16(1) IS Regs
 FC Reg 9 FC Regs
 DWA Reg 11 DWA Regs
 HB Reg 15(1) HB Regs
 CTB Reg 7(1) CTB Regs
28 **FC** Reg 9 FC Regs
 DWA Reg 11 DWA Regs
29 Reg 7(1) CTB Regs
30 **IS** Reg 16(1) and (2) IS Regs
 HB Reg 15(1) and (2) HB Regs
31 para 26047 AOG
32 Reg 16(3) IS Regs
33 Sch 7 paras 11 and 11A IS Regs
34 Sch 1 para 22 IS Regs
35 Sch 7 para 9 IS Regs
36 Sch 7 para 9 col (2) IS Regs
37 **All** s137 SSCBA 1992
 IS Reg 17(1)(b) IS Regs
 FC Reg 46(1)(b) FC Regs
 DWA Reg 51(1)(c) DWA Regs
 HB Reg 16(b) HB Regs
 CTB Reg 8(b) CTB Regs
38 **IS** Reg 14 IS Regs
 FC Reg 6 FC Regs
 DWA Reg 8 DWA Regs
 HB Reg 13 HB Regs
 CTB Reg 5 CTB Regs
39 **FC** Reg 7(1) FC Regs
 DWA Reg 9(1) DWA Regs
 HB Reg 14(1) HB Regs
 CTB Reg 6(1) CTB Regs
40 **FC** Reg 7(2) FC Regs
 DWA Reg 9(2) DWA Regs
 HB Reg 14(2) HB Regs

CTB Reg 6(2) CTB Regs
41 Reg 15(1) IS Regs
42 Reg 15(2) IS Regs
43 Reg 15(1A) IS Regs
44 **ALL** s134(2) SSCBA 1992
 IS Reg 15(4) IS Regs
 FC Reg 7(3) FC Regs
 DWA Reg 9(3) DWA Regs
 HB Reg 14(3) HB Regs
 CTB Reg 6(3) CTB Regs
45 **IS** Reg 16 IS Regs
 FC Reg 8 FC Regs
 DWA Reg 10 DWA Regs
 HB Reg 15 HB Regs
 CTB Reg 7 CTB Regs
46 Regs 15(3) and 16(6) IS Regs
47 **HB** Reg 15(5) HB Regs
 CTB Reg 7(4) CTB Regs
48 **FC** Reg 46(6) FC Regs
 DWA Reg 51(6) DWA Regs
49 Regs 15(3) and 16(6) IS Regs
50 Reg 16(5)(a), (aa) and (7) IS Regs
51 **IS** Reg 14 IS Regs
 HB Reg 13 HB Regs
 CTB Reg 5 CTB Regs
 All ss137(1) (definition of 'family') and 142 SSCBA 1992; regs 1(2) (definition of 'remunerative work') and 7 CB Regs
52 **All** Reg 7D(1) CB Regs
 IS Reg 14 IS Regs
 HB Reg 13 HB Regs
 CTB Reg 5 CTB Regs
53 s134(2) SSCBA 1992
54 **IS** Reg 14(2) IS Regs
 HB Reg 13(2) HB Regs
 CTB Reg 5 CTB Regs
55 **FC** Reg 6(2) FC Regs
 DWA Reg 8(2) DWA Regs
56 **FC** Reg 6(2) FC Regs
 DWA Reg 8(2) DWA Regs

Chapter 17:
Applicable amounts
(pp339-356)

1 IS Reg 18 IS Regs
HB Reg 17 HB Regs
CTB Reg 9 CTB Regs
2 Reg 18(2) IS Regs
3 IS Part I Sch 2 IS Regs
HB Part I Sch 2 HB
Regs
CTB Part I Sch 1 CTB
Regs
4 IS Reg 18(1)(b) IS Regs
HB Reg 17(b) HB
Regs;
CTB Reg 9(b) CTB
Regs
HB/CTB paras C4.05-
06 GM
5 IS Sch 2 para 5 IS Regs
HB Sch 2 para 5 HB
Regs
CTB Sch 1 para 5 CTB
Regs
6 IS Sch 2 para 7 IS Regs
HB Sch 2 para 7 HB
Regs
CTB Sch 1 para 7 CTB
Regs
7 IS Sch 2 para 3 IS Regs
HB Sch 2 para 3 HB
Regs
CTB Sch 1 para 3 CTB
Regs
8 Regs 15(3) and 16(6)
IS Regs
9 HB Reg 15(5) HB Regs
CTB Reg 7(4) CTB
Regs
10 IS Sch 2 paras 14 and
15(6) IS Regs
HB Sch 2 paras 14 and
15(6) HB Regs
CTB Sch 1 paras 15
and 19(7) CTB Regs
11 IS Sch 2 paras 14(c),
12(1)(a)(iii) and (2) IS
Regs
HB Sch 2 paras 14(c),
12(1)(a)(v) and (2) HB
Regs
CTB Sch 1 paras 15(c),
13(1)(a)(v) and (2)
CTB Regs
12 IS Sch 2 para 14(a) IS
Regs

HB Sch 2 para 14(a)
HB Regs
CTB Sch 1 para 15(a)
CTB Regs
13 IS Sch 2 para 14ZA IS
Regs
HB Sch 2 para 14ZA
HB Regs
CTB Sch 1 para 16
CTB Regs
14 s70(5) SSCBA 1992;
reg 10 SS(ICA) Regs
15 s70(6) SSCBA 1992;
reg 11 SS(ICA) Regs
16 *Secretary of State for
Social Security v
Thomas*, ECJ case
C-328/91, 30 March
1993
17 IS Sch 2 para 14A IS
Regs
HB Sch 2 para 14A HB
Regs
CTB Sch 1 para 17
CTB Regs
18 IS Sch 2 para 8 IS Regs
HB Sch 2 para 8 HB
Regs
CTB Sch 1 para 8 CTB
Regs
19 IS Regs 15(3) and
16(6) IS Regs
HB Reg 15(4) and (5)
HB Regs
CTB Reg 7(3) and (4)
CTB Regs
20 IS Sch 2 paras 11 and
15(4) IS Regs
HB Sch 2 paras 11 and
15(4) HB Regs
CTB Sch 1 paras 12
and 19(5) CTB Regs
21 IS Sch 2 para 12 IS
Regs
HB Sch 2 para 12 HB
Regs
CTB Sch 1 para 13
CTB Regs
22 IS Reg 2(1) IS Regs
HB Reg 2(1) HB Regs
CTB Reg 2(1) CTB
Regs
All Definition of
'attendance allowance'
23 IS Sch 2 para 14A IS
Regs

HB Sch 2 para 14A HB
Regs
CTB Sch 1 para 17
CTB Regs
24 IS Sch 2 para 14B IS
Regs
HB Sch 2 para 14B HB
Regs
CTB Sch 1 para 18
CTB Regs
See also CIS/144/1993
25 IS Schs 2 para
12(1)(c)(ii) and 7 para
1 and reg 21 IS Regs
HB Sch 2 para
12(1)(a)(iii) and reg 18
HB Regs
CTB Sch 1 para
13(1)(a)(iii) and reg 10
CTB Regs
26 IS Sch 2 para
12(1)(a)(iii) and (2) IS
Regs
HB Sch 2 para
12(1)(a)(v) and (2) HB
Regs
CTB Sch 1 para
13(1)(a)(v) and (2)
CTB Regs
27 IS Sch 2 para
12(1)(a)(ii) IS Regs
HB Sch 2 para
12(1)(a)(iv) HB Regs
CTB Sch 1 para
13(1)(a)(iv) CTB Regs
28 IS Schs 2 para 12(1)(b)
and 1 para 5 IS Regs
HB Sch 2 para 12(1)(b)
and (6) HB Regs
CTB Sch 1 para
13(1)(b) and (6) CTB
Regs
29 IS Sch 2 para 12(3) IS
Regs
HB Sch 2 para 12(3)
HB Regs
CTB Sch 1 para 13(3)
CTB Regs
30 R(S) 11/51(T)
31 IS Sch 2 paras 11(b)
and 12 IS Regs
HB Sch 2 paras 11(b)
and 12 HB Regs
CTB Sch 1 paras 12(b)
and 13 CTB Regs
32 IS Sch 2 paras 7(1)(b)

and 12(5) IS Regs
HB Sch 2 paras 7(1)(b)
and 12(5) HB Regs
CTB Sch 1 paras
7(1)(b) and 13(5) **CTB**
Regs
33 CSIS/65/1991
34 CSIS/66/1992
35 **IS** Sch 2 paras 9, 9A,
15(2) and (2A) IS Regs
HB Sch 2 paras 9, 9A
and 15(2) and (2A) HB
Regs
CTB Sch 1 paras 9, 10,
19(2) and (3) **CTB**
Regs
36 **IS** Sch 2 paras 10 and
15(3) IS Regs
HB Sch 2 paras 10 and
15(3) HB Regs
CTB Sch 1 paras 11
and 19(4) CTB Regs
37 IS Sch 2 para
10(1)(b)(ii) and (3) IS
Regs
HB Sch 2 para
10(1)(b)(ii) and (3) HB
Regs
CTB Sch 1 para
11(1)(b)(ii) and (3)
CTB Regs
38 **HB** Sch 2 para 10(3)(c)
HB Regs
CTB Sch 1 para
11(3)(c) CTB Regs
39 **IS** Sch 2 para
10(2)(b)(ii) IS Regs
HB Sch 2 para
10(2)(b)(ii) HB Regs
CTB Sch 1 para
11(2)(b)(ii) CTB Regs
40 Regs 5 and 20(3)
SS(SDA) Regs
41 **IS** Sch 2 para 7(1)(a) IS
Regs
HB Sch 2 para 7(1)(a)
HB Regs
CTB Sch 1 para 7(1)(a)
CTB Regs
42 **IS** Sch 2 para
12(1)(c)(i) IS Regs
HB Sch 2 para
12(1)(a)(ii) HB Regs
CTB Sch 1 para
13(1)(a)(ii) CTB Regs
43 **HB** Sch 2 para 10(3)(c)

HB Regs
CTB Sch 1 para
11(3)(c) CTB Regs
44 **IS** Sch 2 para
12(1)(c)(i) IS Regs
HB Sch 2 para
12(1)(a)(ii) HB Regs
CTB Sch 1 para
13(1)(a)(ii) CTB Regs
45 Sch 2 para 12(1)(c) IS
Regs
46 CIS/458/1992
47 s33(1)(b)(ii) SSCBA
1992
48 s57(1)(d) SSCBA 1992;
reg 13 SS(US&IB) Regs
49 para 29828 AOG
50 Reg 2(4) SS(WB&RP)
Regs; para 80615
AOG
51 Directive 79/7/EEC
52 *R v Secretary of State
for Social Security ex
parte Smithson*, ECJ
Case C-243/90
53 *Jackson* and *Cresswell
v CAO*, ECJ cases C-
63/91 and C-64/91, 16
July 1992
54 *Secretary of State for
Social Security v
Thomas, Cooze, Beard,
Murphy, Morley, Equal
Opportunities
Commission*, ECJ case
C-328/91, 30 March
1993
55 CS/27/1991 (*Graham*);
CS/92/1992 (*Connell*);
CS/79/1992 (*Nicholas*)
56 **IS** Sch 2 paras 13 and
15(5) IS Regs
HB Sch 2 paras 13 and
15(5) HB Regs
CTB Sch 1 paras 14
and 19(6) CTB Regs
57 **IS** Sch 2 para 14A IS
Regs
HB Sch 2 para 14A HB
Regs
CTB Sch 1 para 17
CTB Regs
58 **IS** Sch 2 para 13(2A) IS
Regs
HB Sch 2 para 13(2A)
HB Regs

CTB Sch 1 para
14(2A) CTB Regs
59 **IS** Sch 2 para 14B IS
Regs
HB Sch 2 para 14B HB
Regs
CTB Sch 1 para 18
CTB Regs
See also CIS/144/1993
60 **IS** Reg 3(4) and (5) IS
Regs
HB Reg 3(4) HB Regs
61 **IS** Reg 3 IS Regs
HB Reg 3 HB Regs
CTB Reg 3 CTB Regs
62 **IS** Sch 2 para 13(3)(a)
IS Regs
HB Sch 2 para 13(3)(a)
HB Regs
CTB Sch 1 para
14(3)(a) CTB Regs
63 **IS** Sch 2 para 13(3)(d)
IS Regs
HB Sch 2 para 13(3)(c)
HB Regs
CTB Sch 1 para
14(3)(c) CTB Regs
64 Sch 2 para 13(3)(c) and
(4) IS Regs
65 Sch 2 para 13(3A) IS
Regs
66 Regs 3 and 7(1) HB
Regs
67 *Fullwood v
Chesterfield BC*, TLR,
15 June 1993
68 CIS/180/1989
69 Reg 3 CTB Regs
70 **IS** Reg 2(1) IS Regs
HB Reg 2(1) HB Regs
CTB Reg 2(1) CTB
Regs
All Definition of 'close
relative'
71 CIS/180/1989
72 *Fullwood v
Chesterfield BC*, CA, 9
June 1993, *The Times*,
15 June 1993
73 CIS/195/1991;
CIS/754/1991
74 CIS/754/1991
75 CSIS/28/1992;
CSIS/40/1992
76 CIS/299/1990
77 C 14/91(IS) (N Ireland)

78 CIS/754/1991
79 CSIS/28/1992;
CSIS/40/1992
80 CIS/195/1991
81 **IS** Sch 2 paras
13(2)(a)(iii), (b) and
14ZA IS Regs
HB Sch 2 paras
13(2)(a)(iii), (b) and
14ZA HB Regs
CTB Sch 1 paras
14(2)(a)(iii), (b) and 16
CTB Regs
82 s74 SSAA;
CIS/457/1992
83 CIS/457/1992

Chapter 18: Income (*pp357-393*)

1. Introduction (*pp357-362*)

1 s136(1) SSCBA 1992
2 Reg 23(4) IS Regs
3 Reg 23(5) IS Regs
4 **IS** Reg 17(b) IS Regs
FC Reg 46(4) FC Regs
DWA Reg 51(4) DWA
Regs
HB Reg 16(b) HB Regs
CTB Reg 8(b) CTB
Regs
5 **IS** Regs 25 and 44(5) IS
Regs
FC Reg 27(3) FC Regs
DWA Reg 30(3) DWA
Regs
HB Reg 36(2) HB Regs
CTB Reg 27(2) CTB
Regs
6 s136(1) SSCBA 1992
7 **IS** Reg 44(4) IS Regs
FC Reg 27(2) FC Regs
DWA Reg 30(2) DWA
Regs
HB Reg 36(1) HB Regs
CTB Reg 27(1) CTB
Regs
8 **IS** Reg 25 IS Regs
FC Reg 27(2) FC Regs
DWA Reg 30(2) DWA
Regs
HB Reg 36(1) HB Regs
CTB Reg 27(1) CTB
Regs

9 **IS** Sch 8 para 14 IS
Regs
FC Sch 1 para 2 FC
Regs
DWA Sch 2 para 2
DWA Regs
HB Sch 3 para 13 HB
Regs
CTB Sch 3 para 13
CTB Regs
10 **IS** Sch 8 para 15(b) IS
Regs
HB Sch 3 para 14(b)
HB Regs
CTB Sch 2 para 14(b)
CTB Regs
11 **IS** Sch 8 para 15(a) IS
Regs
HB Sch 3 para 14(a)
HB Regs
CTB Sch 3 para 14(a)
CTB Regs
12 **IS** Reg 44(4) IS Regs
HB Reg 36(1) HB Regs
CTB Reg 27(1) CTB
Regs
13 **IS** Reg 14 IS Regs
HB Reg 13 HB Regs
CTB Reg 5 CTB Regs
All ss137(1) (definition
of 'family') and 142
SSCBA 1992; regs 1(2)
(definition of
'remunerative work')
and 7 CB Regs
14 Reg 42(4)(a)(ii) IS Regs
15 Reg 44(2)(a) IS Regs
16 Reg 44(2)(b) IS Regs
17 Reg 44(9) IS Regs
18 Reg 44(3) IS Regs
19 **HB** Reg 35(3)(a) and
Sch 4 para 13(1), (2)
and (5) HB Regs
CTB Reg 26(3)(a) and
Sch 4 para 13(1), (2)
and (5) CTB Regs
Both paras C3.107 and
C3.112 GM
20 **HB** Reg 35(3)(a) and
Sch 4 paras 13(3) and
47 HB Regs
CTB Reg 26(3)(a) and
Sch 4 paras 13(3) and
46 CTB Regs
Both paras C3.89,
C3.110 and C3.112

GM
21 **IS** Reg 32(1) IS Regs
FC Reg 18(1) FC Regs
DWA Reg 20(1) DWA
Regs
HB Reg 25 HB Regs
CTB Reg 17 CTB Regs
22 CIS/654/1991
(apparently to be
reported as R(IS) 3/93
23 Reg 32(6) IS Regs
24 Reg 32(2) and (3) IS
Regs
25 Reg 32(4) IS Regs
26 Reg 32(5) IS Regs
27 Reg 29(2)(a) IS Regs
28 Reg 29(2)(b) IS Regs
29 Reg 31(1)(a) IS Regs
30 Reg 31(1)(b) IS Regs
31 Reg 31(2) IS Regs
32 Reg 2(1) IS Regs
33 R(SB) 33/83
34 R(SB) 22/84; R(SB)
11/85

2. Earnings of employed earners (*pp362-371*)

35 **IS** Reg 36(3) IS Regs
FC Reg 20(3) FC Regs
DWA Reg 22(3) DWA
Regs
HB Reg 29(3) HB Regs
CTB Reg 20(3) CTB
Regs
36 CIS/521/1990
37 **FC** Regs 14(2) and
20(4) FC Regs
DWA Regs 16(7) and
22(4) DWA Regs
HB Regs 22(2) and
29(4) HB Regs
CTB Regs 14(2) and
20(4) CTB Regs
HB/CTB para C3.22
GM
38 **HB** Reg 26 HB Regs
CTB Reg 18 CTB Regs
HB/CTB paras C3.03-
04 GM
39 R(SB) 21/86
40 **IS** Reg 35(1) IS Regs
FC Reg 19(1) FC Regs
DWA Reg 21(1) DWA
Regs
HB Reg 28(1) HB Regs

CTB Reg 19(1) CTB Regs
41 IS Reg 35(1)(a) to (i) IS Regs
FC Reg 19(1)(a) to (h) FC Regs
DWA Reg 21(1)(a) to (i) DWA Regs
HB Reg 28(1)(a) to (i) HB Regs
CTB Reg 19(1)(a) to (i) CTB Regs
42 IS Reg 48(3) IS Regs
FC Reg 31(2) FC Regs
DWA Reg 34(2) DWA Regs
HB Reg 40(3) HB Regs
CTB Reg 31(3) CTB Regs
43 FC Reg 19(1)(g) and (h) FC Regs
DWA Reg 21(1)(g) and (h) DWA Regs
HB Reg 28(1)(i) and (j) HB Regs
CTB Reg 19(1)(i) and (j) CTB Regs
44 Regs 35(2)(b) and 40(4) and Sch 9 paras 1, 4 and 4A IS Regs
45 HB Reg 28(1)(i) and (j) HB Regs
CTB Reg 19(1)(i) and (j) CTB Regs
46 FC Sch 2 paras 27 and 31 FC Regs
DWA Sch 3 paras 27 and 31 DWA Regs
47 Regs 35(2)(b) and 40(4) and Sch 9 paras 1, 4 and 4A IS Regs
48 Reg 21(1)(i) DWA Regs
49 FC Reg 19(1) FC Regs
DWA Reg 21(1) DWA Regs
50 See *R v NIC ex parte Stratton* [1979] QB 361
51 IS Reg 35(2)(a) IS Regs
FC Reg 19(2)(a) FC Regs
DWA Reg 21(2)(a) DWA Regs
HB Reg 28(2)(a) HB Regs

CTB Reg 19(2)(a) CTB Regs
52 IS Sch 9 para 21 IS Regs
FC Sch 2 para 20 FC Regs
DWA Sch 3 para 20 DWA Regs
HB Sch 4 para 21 HB Regs
CTB Sch 4 para 22 CTB Regs
53 IS Reg 48(5) IS Regs
FC Reg 31(5) FC Regs
DWA Reg 34(5) DWA Regs
HB Reg 40(5) HB Regs
CTB Reg 31(5) CTB Regs
54 Reg 48(6) IS Regs
55 IS Sch 9 para 14 IS Regs
FC Sch 2 para 12 FC Regs
DWA Sch 3 para 45 DWA Regs
HB Sch 4 para 12 HB Regs
CTB Sch 4 para 12 CTB Regs
56 IS Reg 35(2)(c) IS Regs
FC Reg 19(2)(b) FC Regs
DWA Reg 21(2)(b) DWA Regs
HB Reg 28(2)(b) HB Regs
CTB Reg 19(2)(b) CTB Regs
57 CIS/89/1989; R(IS) 6/92
IS paras 29155-166 AOG
HB/CTB para C3.10 GM
58 IS Sch 8 para 11 IS Regs
FC Sch 1 para 1 FC Regs
DWA Sch 2 para 1 DWA Regs
HB Sch 3 para 11 HB Regs
CTB Sch 3 para 11 CTB Regs
59 IS Sch 8 para 12 IS

Regs
FC Sch 1 para 3 FC Regs
DWA Sch 2 para 3 DWA Regs
HB Sch 3 para 12 HB Regs
CTB Sch 3 para 12 CTB Regs
60 IS Reg 35(2)(d) IS Regs
FC Reg 19(2)(c) FC Regs
DWA Reg 21(2)(c) DWA Regs
HB Reg 28(2)(c) HB Regs
CTB Reg 19(2)(c) CTB Regs
61 IS Reg 40(4) and Sch 9 para 1 IS Regs
FC Reg 24(5) and Sch 2 para 1 FC Regs
DWA Reg 27(4) and Sch 3 para 1 DWA Regs
HB Reg 33(4) and Sch 4 para 1 HB Regs
CTB Reg 24(5) and Sch 4 para 1 CTB Regs
62 Reg 35(2)(a) IS Regs; para 29126 AOG
63 FC Reg 19(3) FC Regs
DWA Reg 21(3) DWA Regs
64 HB Reg 28(2)(a) HB Regs
CTB Reg 19(2)(a) CTB Regs
65 Reg 14(1) and (2) FC Regs
66 Reg 14(3) FC Regs
67 Reg 20(5) FC Regs
68 Regs 14(1), 14A, 17(b) and 18(3) FC Regs
69 Reg 16(2)-(4) DWA Regs
70 Reg 19(a) DWA Regs
71 R(FIS) 1/87; R(FIS) 2/87
72 Reg 16(5) DWA Regs
73 Reg 16(3), (4)(b) and (9)(b) DWA Regs; s27(3)(b) SSCBA 1992; R(U) 5/87
74 FC Regs 14(4) and 20A FC Regs

75 **FC** Reg 20A FC Regs
  DWA Reg 23 DWA
  Regs

76 **FC** Reg 14(5) and (6)
  FC Regs
  DWA Reg 16(7) and
  (8) DWA Regs

77 **HB** Reg 22(1)(a) HB
  Regs
  CTB Reg 14(1)(a) CTB
  Regs
  HB/CTB para C3.16
  GM

78 **HB** Reg 22(1)(b) HB
  Regs
  CTB Reg 14(1)(b)
  CTB Regs
  HB/CTB para C3.17
  GM

79 *R v HBRB of the
  London Borough of
  Ealing, ex parte
  Saville*, QB, 2/5/86

80 **HB** Reg 22(2)(a) HB
  Regs
  CTB Reg 14(2)(a) CTB
  Regs
  HB/CTB para C3.19
  GM

81 **HB** Reg 22(2)(b) HB
  Regs
  CTB Reg 14(2)(b)
  CTB Regs
  HB/CTB para C3.19
  GM

82 **HB** Reg 22(3) HB Regs
  CTB Reg 14(3) CTB
  Regs

83 **IS** Reg 45 IS Regs
  FC Reg 28 FC Regs
  DWA Reg 31 DWA
  Regs
  HB Reg 37 HB Regs
  CTB Reg 28 CTB Regs

84 **IS** Reg 53 IS Regs
  FC Reg 36 FC Regs
  DWA Reg 40 DWA
  Regs
  HB Reg 45 HB Regs
  CTB Reg 37 CTB Regs

85 **IS** Regs 35(1)(b) and
  40(1) IS Regs; para
  29189 AOG
  HB Regs 28(1)(b) and

  33(1) HB Regs
  CTB Regs 19(1)(b)
  and 24(1) CTB Regs

86 Sch 8 para 1(a)(i) IS
  Regs

87 Sch 8 para 1(a)(ii) IS
  Regs

88 Reg 29(4B) and
  (4D)(b) IS Regs

89 Reg 48(11) IS Regs

90 Regs 29(4C) and
  32(7) IS Regs

91 Regs 5(5) and
  29(3)(a) IS Regs

92 Reg 29(4) IS Regs

93 Reg 29(3)(b) IS Regs

94 Reg 5(5) and Sch 8
  para 1(b) IS Regs

95 Sch 8 para 2 IS Regs

96 Reg 29(4) and (4C) IS
  Regs

97 CIS/104/1989

98 **HB** Sch 3 para 1(a)(i)
  HB Regs
  CTB Sch 3 para
  1(a)(i) CTB Regs

99 **HB** Sch 3 para 1(a)(ii)
  HB Regs
  CTB Sch 3 para
  1(a)(ii) CTB Regs

100 **HB** Sch 3 para 2 HB
  Regs
  CTB Sch 3 para 2
  CTB Regs

101 **HB** Sch 3 para 4 HB
  Regs
  CTB Sch 3 para 4
  CTB Regs

102 Sch 8 para 5 IS Regs

103 **IS** Sch 8 para 4(2) IS
  Regs
  HB Sch 3 para 3(2)
  HB Regs
  CTB Sch 3 para 3(2)
  CTB Regs

104 **HB** Sch 3 para 3(2)
  HB Regs
  CTB Sch 3 para 3(2)
  CTB Regs

105 **IS** Sch 8 para 4(4) IS
  Regs
  HB Sch 3 para 3(4)
  HB Regs
  CTB Sch 3 para 3(4)
  CTB Regs

106 **IS** Sch 8 para 4(3) and

  (5) IS Regs
  HB Sch 3 para 3(3)
  and (5) HB Regs
  CTB Sch 3 para 3(3)
  and (5) CTB Regs

107 **IS** Sch 8 para 4(6) IS
  Regs
  HB Sch 3 para 3(6)
  HB Regs
  CTB Sch 3 para 3(6)
  CTB Regs

108 **IS** Sch 8 paras 6A and
  6B IS Regs
  HB Sch 3 paras 4A
  and 4B HB Regs
  CTB Sch 3 paras 4A
  and 4B CTB Regs

109 **IS** Sch 8 para 7(1) IS
  Regs
  HB Sch 3 para 6(1)
  HB Regs
  CTB Sch 3 para 6(1)
  CTB Regs

110 **IS** Sch 8 para 8 IS
  Regs
  HB Sch 3 para 7 HB
  Regs
  CTB Sch 3 para 7
  CTB Regs

111 **IS** Sch 8 para 7(2) IS
  Regs
  HB Sch 3 para 6(2)(b)
  HB Regs
  CTB Sch 3 para
  6(2)(b) CTB Regs

112 Sch 8 para 6 IS Regs

113 Reg 3A and Sch 8
  paras 4(7) and 6(2)-
  (2C) IS Regs

114 Sch 8 para 9 IS Regs

115 **HB** Sch 3 paras 5 and
  8 HB Regs
  CTB Sch 3 paras 5
  and 8 CTB Regs

3. Earnings from self-employment
(pp371-375)

116 **IS** Reg 37(1) IS Regs
  FC Reg 21(1) FC
  Regs
  DWA Reg 24(1)
  DWA Regs
  HB Reg 30 HB Regs
  CTB Reg 21 CTB
  Regs

117 IS Reg 38(3) IS Regs
FC Reg 22(3) FC
Regs
DWA Reg 25(3)
DWA Regs
HB Reg 31(3) HB
Regs
CTB Reg 22(3) CTB
Regs
118 IS Regs 2(1) and
38(12) IS Regs
FC Regs 2(1) and
22(12) and (13) FC
Regs
DWA Regs 2(1) and
25(14) and (15)
DWA Regs
119 FC Reg 21(1) FC
Regs
DWA Reg 24(1)
DWA Regs
120 CFC/24/1989
121 CFC/4/1991
(*Kostanczuk v CAO*)
122 CFC/23/1991
123 IS Reg 37(2) IS Regs
HB Reg 30(2) HB
Regs
CTB Reg 21(2) CTB
Regs
124 IS Sch 9 para 26 IS
Regs
HB Sch 4 para 24 HB
Regs
CTB Sch 4 para 25
CTB Regs
125 Reg 37(2)(a) IS Regs
126 FC Reg 21(2) FC
Regs
DWA Reg 24(2)
DWA Regs
127 IS Reg 38(3)(a), (4),
(7) and (8)(a) IS Regs
FC Reg 22(3)(a), (4),
(7) and (8)(a) FC
Regs
DWA Reg 25(3)(a),
(4)(a), (5), (6), (9)
and (10)(a) DWA
Regs
HB Reg 31(3)(a), (4),
(7) and (8)(a) HB
Regs
CTB Regs 22(3)(a),
(4), (7) and (8)(a)
CTB Regs

128 R(IS) 13/91; R(FC)
1/91; CFC/25/1989
129 IS Reg 38(6) and
(8)(b) IS Regs
FC Reg 22(6) and
(8)(b) FC Regs
DWA Reg 25(8) and
(10)(b) DWA Regs
HB Reg 31(6) and
(8)(b) HB Regs
CTB Reg 22(6) and
(8)(b) CTB Regs
130 IS Reg 38(5) IS Regs
FC Reg 22(5) FC
Regs
DWA Reg 25(7)
DWA Regs
HB Reg 31(5) HB
Regs
CTB Reg 22(5) CTB
Regs
131 IS Reg 38(11) IS Regs
FC Reg 22(11) FC
Regs
DWA Reg 25(13)
DWA Regs
HB Reg 31(10) HB
Regs
CTB Reg 22(10) CTB
Regs; R(FC) 1/93
132 Reg 30 IS Regs
133 FC Reg 15(1) FC
Regs
DWA Reg 17(1)
DWA Regs
134 FC Reg 18(2) FC
Regs
DWA Reg 20(2)
DWA Regs
135 FC Reg 17 FC Regs
DWA Reg 19(b)
DWA Regs
136 Regs 15(2) and (4)
and 17(a) FC Regs
137 Reg 17(3) DWA Regs
138 FC s128(3) SSCBA
1992
DWA s129(6) SSCBA
1992
139 CFC/24/1989;
CFC/14/1991
140 HB Regs 23(1) and
25(2) HB Regs
CTB Regs 15(1) and
17(2) CTB Regs
141 IS Reg 38(9) IS Regs

FC Reg 22(9) FC
Regs
DWA Reg 25(11)
DWA Regs
HB Reg 31(9) HB
Regs
CTB Reg 22(9) CTB
Regs
142 IS Reg 38(2) IS Regs
FC Reg 22(2) FC
Regs
DWA Reg 25(2)
DWA Regs
HB Reg 31(2) HB
Regs
CTB Reg 22(2) CTB
Regs
143 DSS press release No
93/214, 1 December
1993
144 CFC/19/1990
145 Directive
EEC/76/207

4. Other income
(pp375-391)

146 IS Reg 40 and Sch 9
para 1 IS Regs
FC Reg 24 and Sch 2
para 1 FC Regs
DWA Reg 27 and Sch
3 para 1 DWA Regs
HB Reg 33 and Sch 4
para 1 HB Regs
CTB Reg 24 and Sch
4 para 1 CTB Regs
147 HB Reg 26 HB Regs
CTB Reg 18 CTB
Regs
148 CIS/25/1989; R(FIS)
4/85
149 HB Reg 24 HB Regs
CTB Reg 16 CTB
Regs
150 FC Reg 16(1) FC
Regs
DWA Reg 18(1)
DWA Regs
151 Reg 35(2) and Sch 9
para 4 IS Regs
152 s74(2) SSAA 1992
153 para C3.100 GM
154 IS Sch 10 para 7(b) IS
Regs
FC Sch 3 para 8(b)
FC Regs

DWA Sch 4 para 8(b)
DWA Regs
HB Sch 5 para 8(b)
HB Regs; para
C3.103 GM
CTB Sch 5 para 8(b)
CTB Regs; para
C3.103 GM
155 IS Sch 9 para 9 IS
Regs
FC Sch 2 paras 4 and
7 FC Regs
DWA Sch 3 paras 4
and 7 DWA Regs
HB Sch 4 paras 5 and
8 HB Regs
CTB Sch 4 paras 5
and 8 CTB Regs
156 IS Sch 9 para 33 IS
Regs
FC Sch 2 para 28 FC
Regs
DWA Sch 3 para 28
DWA Regs
HB Sch 4 para 31 HB
Regs
CTB Sch 4 para 32
CTB Regs
157 IS Sch 9 para 6 IS
Regs
FC Sch 2 para 4 FC
Regs
DWA Sch 3 para 4
DWA Regs
HB Sch 4 para 5 HB
Regs
CTB Sch 4 para 5
CTB Regs
158 IS Sch 9 para 8 IS
Regs
FC Sch 2 para 6 FC
Regs
DWA Sch 3 para 6
DWA Regs
HB Sch 4 para 7 HB
Regs
CTB Sch 4 para 7
CTB Regs
159 IS Sch 9 paras 7 and 8
IS Regs
FC Sch 2 paras 5 and
6 FC Regs
DWA Sch 3 paras 5
and 6 DWA Regs
HB Sch 4 paras 6 and
7 HB Regs

CTB Sch 4 paras 6
and 7 CTB Regs
160 Sch 2 para 4 FC Regs
161 Sch 3 para 46 DWA
Regs
162 IS Sch 9 para 31 IS
Regs
HB Sch 4 para 30 HB
Regs
CTB Sch 4 para 31
CTB Regs
163 IS Sch 10 para 18 IS
Regs
FC Sch 3 para 19 FC
Regs
DWA Sch 4 para 19
DWA Regs
HB Sch 5 para 19 HB
Regs
CTB Sch 5 para 19
CTB Regs
164 IS Sch 9 para 38 IS
Regs
FC Sch 2 para 33 FC
Regs
HB Sch 4 para 37 HB
Regs
CTB Sch 4 para 39
CTB Regs
165 IS Sch 9 paras 40-42
IS Regs
FC Sch 2 paras 35-37
FC Regs
DWA Sch 2 paras 34-
36 DWA Regs
HB Sch 4 paras 35-36
and 48 HB Regs
CTB Sch 4 paras 37-
38 and 47 CTB Regs
166 IS Sch 9 paras 5, 45-
46 and 52 IS Regs
FC Sch 2 paras 3, 41-
42 and 49 FC Regs
DWA Sch 3 paras 3,
39-40 and 47 DWA
Regs
HB Sch 4 paras 40-41
and 51 HB Regs
CTB Sch 4 paras 36,
41 and 50 CTB Regs
167 FC Sch 2 para 3 FC
Regs
DWA Sch 3 para 3
DWA Regs
HB Sch 4 para 4 HB
Regs

CTB Sch 4 para 4
CTB Regs
168 IS Sch 9 para 11 IS
Regs
FC Sch 2 para 9 FC
Regs
DWA Sch 3 para 9
DWA Regs
HB Sch 4 para 10 HB
Regs
CTB Sch 4 para 10
CTB Regs
169 IS Sch 9 para 47 IS
Regs
FC Sch 2 para 43 FC
Regs
DWA Sch 3 para 41
DWA Regs
HB Sch 4 para 43 HB
Regs
CTB Sch 4 para 42
CTB Regs
170 FC Sch 2 para 50 FC
Regs
DWA Sch 3 para 48
DWA Regs
HB Sch 4 para 50 HB
Regs
CTB Sch 4 para 49
CTB Regs
171 FC Sch 2 para 15 FC
Regs
DWA Sch 3 para 15
DWA Regs
172 FC Sch 2 paras 27
and 31 FC Regs
DWA Sch 3 paras 27
and 31 DWA Regs
173 IS Sch 9 para 53 IS
Regs
FC Sch 2 para 51 FC
Regs
DWA Sch 3 para 49
DWA Regs
HB Sch 4 para 52 HB
Regs
CTB Sch 4 para 51
CTB Regs
174 IS Sch 9 para 16 IS
Regs
FC Sch 2 para 14 FC
Regs
DWA Sch 3 para 14
DWA Regs
HB Sch 4 para 14 HB
Regs

CTB Sch 4 para 14
CTB Regs
175 **IS** Sch 9 para 36 IS
Regs
FC Sch 2 para 29 FC
Regs
DWA Sch 3 para 29
DWA Regs
HB Sch 4 para 33 HB
Regs
CTB Sch 4 para 34
CTB Regs
176 ss134(8) and 139(6)
SSAA 1992
177 **FC** Reg 16(2)(a) and
(2A)(a) FC Regs
DWA Reg 18(2)(a)
and (2A)(a) **DWA**
Regs
178 **FC** Reg 16(2)(b) and
(2A)(b) FC Regs
DWA Reg 18(2)(b)
and (2A)(b) **DWA**
Regs
179 **FC** Reg 31(6) FC
Regs
DWA Reg 34(6)
DWA Regs
180 **HB** Reg 33(1) HB
Regs
CTB Reg 24(1) CTB
Regs
HB/CTB paras
C3.88-9 GM
181 s136(1) SSCBA 1992
182 **FC** Sch 2 paras 13(3)
and 47 FC Regs
DWA Sch 3 paras
12(3) and 13 **DWA**
Regs
HB Sch 4 paras 13(3)
and 47 HB Regs
CTB Sch 4 paras
13(3) and 46 CTB
Regs
183 **IS** Reg 61 IS Regs
FC Reg 37 FC Regs
DWA Reg 41 DWA
Regs
HB Reg 46 HB Regs
CTB Reg 38 CTB
Regs
All Definition of
'grant'
184 R(SB) 20/83
185 **IS** Reg 61 IS Regs

FC Reg 37 FC Regs
DWA Reg 41 DWA
Regs
HB Reg 46 HB Regs
CTB Reg 38 CTB
Regs
All Definition of
'grant income'
186 Reg 61 IS Regs
definition of 'grant
income' (c)
187 **IS** Reg 62(3) IS Regs
FC Reg 38(3) FC
Regs
DWA Reg 42(3)
DWA Regs
HB Reg 53(3) HB
Regs
CTB Reg 42(4) CTB
Regs
188 **IS** Reg 62(4) IS Regs
FC Reg 38(4) FC
Regs
DWA Reg 42(5)
DWA Regs
HB Reg 53(4) HB
Regs
CTB Reg 42(5) CTB
Regs
189 **IS** Reg 62(3A) IS Regs
FC Reg 38(3A) FC
Regs
DWA Reg 42(4)
DWA Regs
HB Reg 53(3)(b) HB
Regs
CTB Reg 42(4)(b)
CTB Regs
HB/CTB para
C5.47ii and Annex A
GM
190 CIS/109/1991
191 **IS** Reg 62(2) IS Regs
FC Reg 38(2) FC
Regs
DWA Reg 42(2)
DWA Regs
HB Reg 53(2) HB
Regs
CTB Reg 42(2) CTB
Regs
192 **IS** Regs 61 (definition
of 'covenant
income'), 62-66 and
68 IS Regs
FC Regs 37

(definition of
'covenant income'),
38-42 and 44 FC
Regs
DWA Regs 41
(definition of
'covenant income'),
42-46 and 49 DWA
Regs
HB Regs 46
(definition of
'covenant income'),
53-57 and 59 HB
Regs
CTB Regs 38
(definition of
'covenant income'),
42-46 and 49 CTB
Regs
193 Sch 2 Education
(Mandatory Awards)
Regulations 1987
194 **IS** Reg 65 and Sch 9
para 36 IS Regs
FC Reg 41 and Sch 2
para 29 FC Regs
DWA Reg 45 and Sch
3 para 29 **DWA** Regs
HB Reg 56 and Sch 4
para 33 HB Regs
CTB Reg 45 and Sch
4 para 34 CTB Regs
195 **IS** Reg 66(1) IS Regs
FC Reg 42 FC Regs
DWA Reg 46 DWA
Regs
HB Reg 57 HB Regs
CTB Reg 46 CTB
Regs
196 **IS** Reg 67 IS Regs
FC Reg 43 FC Regs
DWA Reg 48 DWA
Regs
HB Reg 58(1) HB
Regs
CTB Reg 48 CTB
Regs
197 Reg 58(2) HB Regs
198 **IS** Reg 66A IS Regs
FC Reg 42A FC Regs
DWA Reg 47 DWA
Regs
HB Reg 57A HB
Regs
CTB Reg 47 CTB
Regs

199 IS Reg 61 IS Regs
FC Reg 37 FC Regs
DWA Reg 41 DWA
Regs
HB Reg 46 HB Regs
CTB Reg 38 CTB
Regs
All Definition of 'last
day of the course'

200 IS Sch 9 para 36 IS
Regs
FC Sch 2 para 29 FC
Regs
DWA Sch 3 para 29
DWA Regs
HB Sch 4 para 33 HB
Regs
CTB Sch 4 para 34
CTB Regs

201 IS Reg 40(3A) IS Regs
FC Reg 24(4A) FC
Regs
DWA Reg 27(5)
DWA Regs
HB Reg 33(3A) HB
Regs
CTB Reg 24(4) CTB
Regs

202 IS Reg 66A(3) IS Regs
FC Reg 42A(3) FC
Regs
DWA Reg 47(3)
DWA Regs
HB Reg 57A(3) HB
Regs
CTB Reg 47(3) CTB
Regs

203 Excluded from
definition of 'grant'
in:
IS Reg 61 IS Regs
FC Reg 37 FC Regs
DWA Reg 41 DWA
Regs
HB Reg 46 HB Regs
CTB Reg 38 CTB
Regs

204 IS Sch 9 para 25(1)(a)
and (2)(b) IS Regs
HB Sch 4 para
23(1)(a) and (2)(b)
HB Regs
CTB Sch 4 para
24(1)(a) and (2)(b)
CTB Regs

205 FC Sch 2 para

22(1)(a) and (2)(b)
FC Regs
DWA Sch 3 para
22(1)(a) and (2)(b)
DWA Regs

206 IS Reg 17(1)(b) IS
Regs
FC Reg 46(4) FC
Regs
DWA Reg 51(4)
DWA Regs
HB Reg 16(b) HB
Regs
CTB Reg 8(b) CTB
Regs

207 IS Sch 9 para 25(2)(a)
IS Regs
FC Sch 2 para
22(2)(a) FC Regs
DWA Sch 3 para
22(2)(a) DWA Regs
HB Sch 4 para
23(2)(a) HB Regs
CTB Sch 4 para
24(2)(a) CTB Regs

208 IS Sch 9 para 26 IS
Regs
FC Sch 2 para 23 FC
Regs
DWA Sch 3 para 23
DWA Regs
HB Sch 4 para 24 HB
Regs
CTB Sch 4 para 25
CTB Regs

209 IS Sch 9 para 25(1)(b)
and (2) IS Regs
FC Sch 2 para
22(1)(b) and (2) FC
Regs
DWA Sch 3 para
22(1)(b) and (2)
DWA Regs
HB Sch 4 para
23(1)(b) and (2) HB
Regs
CTB Sch 4 para
24(1)(b) and (2) CTB
Regs

210 IS Reg 48(8) IS Regs
211 IS Sch 10 para 8(b) IS
Regs
FC Sch 3 para 9(b)
FC Regs
DWA Sch 4 para 9(b)
DWA Regs

HB Sch 5 para 9(b)
HB Regs
CTB Sch 5 para 9(b)
CTB Regs

212 IS Reg 48(10)(c) and
Sch 9 para 39 IS Regs
FC Sch 2 para 34 FC
Regs
DWA Sch 3 para 33
DWA Regs
HB Sch 4 para 34 HB
Regs
CTB Sch 4 para 35
CTB Regs

213 IS Sch 9 para 39 IS
Regs
FC Sch 2 para 34 FC
Regs
DWA Sch 3 para 33
DWA Regs
HB Sch 4 para 34 HB
Regs
CTB Sch 4 para 35
CTB Regs

214 IS Reg 48(9) IS Regs
FC Reg 31(3) FC
Regs
DWA Reg 34(3)
DWA Regs
HB/CTB There are
no specific provisions
for HB/CTB but such
payments are
obviously capital

215 Reg 48(10)(a) IS Regs
216 Reg 48(10)(b) IS Regs
217 IS Sch 10 para 8 IS
Regs
FC Sch 3 para 9 FC
Regs
DWA Sch 4 para 9
DWA Regs
HB Sch 5 para 9 HB
Regs
CTB Sch 5 para 9
CTB Regs

218 IS Sch 10 para 29 IS
Regs
FC Sch 3 para 31 FC
Regs
DWA Sch 4 para 31
DWA Regs
HB Sch 5 para 32 HB
Regs
CTB Sch 5 para 32
CTB Regs

219 IS Sch 9 para 15 IS
Regs
FC Sch 2 para 13 FC
Regs
DWA Sch 3 para 12
DWA Regs
HB Sch 4 para 13 HB
Regs
CTB Sch 4 para 13
CTB Regs

220 Sch 9 para 15A IS
Regs

221 IS Sch 9 para 36 IS
Regs
FC Sch 2 para 29 FC
Regs
DWA Sch 3 para 29
DWA Regs
HB Sch 4 para 33 HB
Regs
CTB Sch 4 para 34
CTB Regs

222 IS Sch 9 para 21 IS
Regs
FC Sch 2 para 20 FC
Regs
DWA Sch 3 para 20
DWA Regs
HB Sch 4 para 21 HB
Regs
CTB Sch 4 para 22
CTB Regs

223 *R v Doncaster MBC
ex parte Boulton*
[1992] QB, *The
Times*, 31 December
1992

224 IS para 29567 AOG
FC/DWA para 40147
AOG
HB/CTB para C3.90
GM

225 IS Sch 9 para 19 IS
Regs
FC Sch 2 para 19 FC
Regs
DWA Sch 3 para 19
DWA Regs
HB Sch 4 para 20 HB
Regs
CTB Sch 4 para 20
CTB Regs

226 IS Sch 9 para 20 IS
Regs
FC Sch 2 para 40 FC
Regs

DWA Sch 3 para 38
DWA Regs
HB Sch 4 para 42 HB
Regs
CTB Sch 4 para 21
CTB Regs

227 All Definition of
'board and lodging
accommodation'
IS Reg 2(1) IS Regs
HB Sch 4 para 42(2)
HB Regs
CTB Sch 4 para 21(2)
CTB Regs

228 IS Sch 9 para 18 IS
Regs
FC Sch 2 para 18 FC
Regs
DWA Sch 3 para 18
DWA Regs
HB Sch 4 para 19 HB
Regs
CTB Sch 4 para 19
CTB Regs

229 All CIS/85/1992
IS Reg 48(4) IS Regs
FC Reg 31(4) FC
Regs
DWA Reg 34(4)
DWA Regs
HB Reg 40(4) HB
Regs
CTB Reg 31(4) CTB
Regs

230 IS Sch 9 para 22(1) IS
Regs
FC Sch 2 para 16(1)
FC Regs
DWA Sch 3 para
16(1) DWA Regs
HB Sch 4 para 15(1)
HB Regs
CTB Sch 4 para 15(1)
CTB Regs

231 IS Reg 48(4) IS Regs
FC Reg 31(4) FC
Regs
DWA Reg 34(4)
DWA Regs
HB Reg 40(4) HB
Regs
CTB Reg 31(4) CTB
Regs

232 IS Sch 9 para 22(1) IS
Regs
FC Sch 2 para 16(1)

FC Regs
DWA Sch 3 para
16(1) DWA Regs
HB Sch 4 para 15(1)
HB Regs
CTB Sch 4 para 15(1)
CTB Regs

233 IS Sch 9 para 22(2) IS
Regs
FC Sch 2 para 16(2)
FC Regs
DWA Sch 3 para
16(2) DWA Regs
HB Sch 4 para 15(2)
HB Regs
CTB Sch 4 para 15(2)
CTB Regs

234 IS Reg 53 IS Regs
FC Reg 36 FC Regs
DWA Reg 40 DWA
Regs
HB Reg 45 HB Regs
CTB Reg 37 CTB
Regs

235 Reg 41(1) IS Regs

236 FC Reg 25(1) FC
Regs
DWA Reg 28(1)
DWA Regs

237 HB Reg 34(1) HB
Regs
CTB Reg 25(1) CTB
Regs

238 IS Reg 29(2)(a) IS
Regs
FC Reg 18 FC Regs
DWA Reg 20 DWA
Regs
HB Reg 25 HB Regs
CTB Reg 17 CTB
Regs

239 IS Reg 44(1) IS Regs
FC Reg 27(1) FC
Regs
DWA Reg 30(1)
DWA Regs
HB Reg 36(5) HB
Regs
CTB Reg 27(5) CTB
Regs

240 IS Reg 41(2) IS Regs
FC Reg 25(2) FC
Regs
DWA Reg 28(2)
DWA Regs
HB Reg 34(2) HB

Regs
CTB Reg 25(2) CTB
Regs
241 Regs 41(4) and 48(2)
IS Regs
242 Reg 41(3) IS Regs
243 *R v SBC ex parte
Singer* [1973] 1 All
ER 931; *R v Oxford
County Council ex
parte Jack* [1984] 17
HLR 419; *R v West
Dorset DC ex parte
Poupard* [1988] 28
RVR 40; para C3.117
GM
244 para C2.09(xix) GM
245 *R v West Dorset DC
ex parte Poupard*
[1988] 28 RVR 40
246 IS Sch 10 para 20 IS
Regs
FC Sch 3 para 21 FC
Regs
DWA Sch 4 para 21
DWA Regs
HB Sch 5 para 21 HB
Regs
CTB Sch 5 para 21
CTB Regs
247 IS Reg 48(2) IS Regs
FC Reg 31(1) FC
Regs
DWA Reg 34(1)
DWA Regs
HB Reg 40(2) HB
Regs
CTB Reg 31(2) CTB
Regs
248 IS Reg 48(2) IS Regs
FC Reg 31(1) FC
Regs
DWA Reg 34(1)
DWA Regs
HB Reg 40(2) HB
Regs
CTB Reg 31(2) CTB
Regs
249 Regs 41(4) and 48(2)
IS Regs
250 IS Reg 40(4) IS Regs
FC Reg 24(5) FC
Regs
DWA Reg 27(4)
DWA Regs
HB Reg 33(4) HB

Regs
CTB Reg 24(5) CTB
Regs
All Definition of
'occupational
pension' in reg 2(1) of
each of those regs
251 IS Reg 41(2) and Sch
9 para 17 IS Regs
FC Reg 25(2) and Sch
2 para 17 FC Regs
DWA Reg 28(2) and
Sch 3 para 17 DWA
Regs
HB Reg 34(2) and
Sch 4 para 16 HB
Regs
CTB Reg 25(2) and
Sch 4 para 16 CTB
Regs
252 Sch 9 para 29 IS
Regs; para 29666
AOG
253 Sch 9 para 30(a) IS
Regs
254 Sch 9 para 30(b) IS
Regs
255 Sch 9 para 30(c) IS
Regs
256 Sch 9 para 30(d) IS
Regs
257 Sch 9 para 30(d) IS
Regs
258 HB Sch 4 para 28 HB
Regs
CTB Sch 4 para 29
CTB Regs
259 IS Sch 9 para 11 IS
Regs
FC Sch 2 para 9 FC
Regs
DWA Sch 3 para 9
DWA Regs
HB Sch 4 para 10 HB
Regs
CTB Sch 4 para 10
CTB Regs
260 IS Sch 9 para 2 IS
Regs
FC Sch 2 para 2 FC
Regs
DWA Sch 3 para 2
DWA Regs
HB Sch 4 para 2 HB
Regs
CTB Sch 4 para 2

CTB Regs
261 IS Sch 9 para 21 IS
Regs
FC Sch 2 para 20 FC
Regs
DWA Sch 3 para 20
DWA Regs
HB Sch 4 para 21 HB
Regs
CTB Sch 4 para 22
CTB Regs
262 IS Sch 9 paras 14 and
51 IS Regs
FC Sch 2 paras 12
and 48 FC Regs
DWA Sch 3 para 45
DWA Regs
HB Sch 4 paras 12
and 49 HB Regs
CTB Sch 4 paras 12
and 48 CTB Regs
263 IS Sch 9 para 43 IS
Regs
FC Sch 2 para 38 FC
Regs
DWA Sch 3 para 37
DWA Regs
HB Sch 4 para 38 HB
Regs
CTB Sch 4 para 40
CTB Regs
264 IS Sch 9 para 28 IS
Regs
FC Sch 2 para 25 FC
Regs
DWA Sch 3 para 25
DWA Regs
HB Sch 4 para 26 HB
Regs
CTB Sch 4 para 27
CTB Regs
265 IS Sch 9 para 27 IS
Regs
FC Sch 2 para 24 FC
Regs
DWA Sch 3 para 24
DWA Regs
HB Sch 4 para 25 HB
Regs
CTB Sch 4 para 26
CTB Regs
266 IS Sch 9 para 10 IS
Regs
FC Sch 2 para 8 FC
Regs
DWA Sch 3 para 8

DWA Regs
HB Sch 4 para 9 HB Regs
CTB Sch 4 para 9 CTB Regs
267 IS Sch 9 para 23 IS Regs
FC Sch 2 para 21 FC Regs
DWA Sch 3 para 21 DWA Regs
HB Sch 4 para 22 HB Regs
CTB Sch 4 para 23 CTB Regs
268 IS Sch 9 para 24 IS Regs
FC Sch 2 para 30 FC Regs
DWA Sch 3 para 30 DWA Regs
HB Sch 4 para 32 HB Regs
CTB Sch 4 para 33 CTB Regs
269 IS Sch 9 para 48 IS Regs
FC Sch 2 para 44 FC Regs
DWA Sch 3 para 42 DWA Regs
HB Sch 4 para 44 HB Regs
CTB Sch 4 para 43 CTB Regs
270 IS Sch 9 para 49 IS Regs
FC Sch 2 para 45 FC Regs
DWA Sch 3 para 43 DWA Regs
HB Sch 4 para 45 HB Regs
CTB Sch 4 para 44 CTB Regs
271 IS Sch 9 para 50 IS Regs
FC Sch 2 para 46 FC Regs
DWA Sch 3 para 44 DWA Regs
HB Sch 4 para 46 HB Regs
CTB Sch 4 para 45 CTB Regs
272 HB Sch 4 para 17 HB

Regs
CTB Sch 4 para 17 CTB Regs
273 HB Sch 3 para 9 HB Regs
CTB Sch 3 para 9 CTB Regs
274 HB Sch 4 para 18 HB Regs
CTB Sch 4 para 18 CTB Regs
275 HB Sch 3 para 9 HB Regs
CTB Sch 3 para 9 CTB Regs

5. Notional income (pp391-393)
276 IS Reg 42(1) IS Regs
FC Reg 26(1) FC Regs
DWA Reg 29(1) DWA Regs
HB Reg 35(1) HB Regs
CTB Reg 26(1) CTB Regs
277 IS Reg 42(2) IS Regs
FC Reg 26(2) FC Regs
DWA Reg 29(2) DWA Regs
HB Reg 35(2) HB Regs
CTB Reg 26(2) CTB Regs
278 paras C3.98-102 GM
279 IS Sch 10 para 7(b) IS Regs
FC Sch 3 para 8(b) FC Regs
DWA Sch 4 para 8(b) DWA Regs
HB Sch 5 para 8(b) HB Regs
CTB Sch 5 para 8(b) CTB Regs
280 Reg 42(3) IS Regs
281 Reg 42(3A) and (3B) IS Regs
282 Reg 70(2)(b) IS Regs
283 Reg 42(5) IS Regs
284 Reg 2 SS(PAOR) Regs
285 IS Reg 42(4)(a)(ii), (4A) and (9) IS Regs

FC Reg 26(3)(a) FC Regs
DWA Reg 29(3)(a) DWA Regs
HB Reg 35(3)(a) and (8) HB Regs
CTB Reg 26(3)(a) and (8) CTB Regs
286 Reg 42(4) IS Regs
287 IS Reg 42(4)(b) IS Regs
FC Reg 26(3)(b) FC Regs
DWA Reg 29(3)(b) DWA Regs
HB Reg 35(3)(b) HB Regs
CTB Reg 26(3)(b) CTB Regs
288 IS Reg 42(6) IS Regs; CIS/191/1991
FC Reg 26(4) FC Regs
DWA Reg 29(4) DWA Regs
HB Reg 35(5) HB Regs
CTB Reg 26(5) CTB Regs
289 R(SB) 13/86
290 R(SB) 13/86
291 IS Reg 42(6) IS Regs
FC Reg 26(4) FC Regs
DWA Reg 29(4) DWA Regs
HB Reg 35(5) HB Regs
CTB Reg 26(5) CTB Regs
292 *Sharrock v CAO* (CA) 26 March 1991; CIS/93/1991
293 CIS/93/1991

Chapter 19: Capital (pp394-413)

1. Introduction (pp394-395)
1 HB Sch 5 para 5 HB Regs
CTB Sch 5 para 5 CTB Regs
2 IS Reg 45 IS Regs

FC Reg 28 FC Regs
3 DWA Reg 31 DWA
Regs
HB Reg 37 HB Regs
CTB Reg 28 CTB Regs
4 IS Reg 53(1) IS Regs
FC Reg 36(1) FC Regs
DWA Reg 40(1) DWA
Regs
HB Reg 45(1) HB Regs
CTB Reg 37(1) CTB
Regs
5 IS Reg 53 IS Regs
FC Reg 36 FC Regs
DWA Reg 40 DWA
Regs
HB Reg 45 HB Regs
CTB Reg 37 CTB Regs
6 s136(1) SSCBA 1992
7 IS Reg 47 IS Regs
FC Reg 30 FC Regs
DWA Reg 33 DWA
Regs
HB Reg 39 HB Regs
CTB Reg 30 CTB Regs
8 IS Reg 17(1)(b) IS Regs
FC Reg 46(4) FC Regs
DWA Reg 51(4) DWA
Regs
HB Reg 16(b) HB Regs
CTB Reg 8(b) CTB
Regs
9 IS Reg 44(5) IS Regs
FC Reg 27(3) FC Regs
DWA Reg 30(3) DWA
Regs
HB Reg 36(2) HB Regs
CTB Reg 27(2) CTB
Regs
10 IS Regs 25 and 44(5) IS
Regs
FC Reg 27(3) FC Regs
DWA Reg 30(3) DWA
Regs
HB Reg 36(2) HB Regs
CTB Reg 27(2) CTB
Regs
11 IS Reg 17(1)(b) IS Regs
FC Reg 46(4) FC Regs
DWA Reg 51(4) DWA
Regs
HB Reg 16(b) HB Regs
CTB Reg 8(b) CTB
Regs

2. What counts as capital (pp395-398)

12 para C2.09 GM; paras
30011 and 42011
AOG
13 IS paras 30010 and
42010 AOG
HB/CTB para C2.08
GM
14 R(SB) 35/83
15 CIS/654/1991
16 IS/FC/DWA Reg 2
SS(PAOR) Regs
HB Reg 91(1) HB Regs
17 R(SB) 12/86
18 R(SB) 53/83; R(SB)
1/85
19 R(SB) 49/83
20 R(SB) 23/85; para
30027 AOG
21 IS Sch 10 para 13 IS
Regs
FC Sch 3 para 14 FC
Regs
DWA Sch 4 para 14
DWA Regs
HB Sch 5 para 14 HB
Regs
CTB Sch 5 para 14
CTB Regs
22 R(SB) 3/89
23 R(IS) 1/90
24 R(SB)23/85
25 *Barclays Bank v
Quistclose Investments
Ltd* [1970] AC 567;
R(SB) 49/83;
CFC/21/1989
26 IS Reg 48 IS Regs
FC Reg 31 FC Regs
DWA Reg 34 DWA
Regs
HB Reg 40 HB Regs
CTB Reg 31 CTB Regs
27 paras 40145, 40152-3
AOG
28 FC Reg 31(6) FC Regs
DWA Reg 34(6) DWA
Regs
29 IS Sch 9 para 32 IS Regs
FC Sch 2 para 26 FC
Regs
DWA Sch 3 para 26
DWA Regs
HB Sch 4 para 29 HB
Regs

CTB Sch 4 para 30
CTB Regs

3. Disregarded capital (pp398-404)

30 IS Sch 10 para 1 IS
Regs
FC Sch 3 para 1 FC
Regs
DWA Sch 4 para 1
DWA Regs
HB Sch 5 para 1 HB
Regs
CTB Sch 5 para 1 CTB
Regs
31 IS Reg 2(1) IS Regs
meaning of 'dwelling
occupied as the home';
R(SB) 13/84;
CIS/427/1991
FC Sch 3 para 1 FC
Regs
DWA Sch 4 para 1
DWA Regs
HB Sch 5 para 1 HB
Regs
CTB Sch 5 para 1 CTB
Regs
32 IS Sch 10 para 1 IS
Regs
FC Sch 3 para 1 FC
Regs
DWA Sch 4 para 1
DWA Regs
HB Sch 5 para 1 HB
Regs
CTB Sch 5 para 1 CTB
Regs
33 R(SB) 1/85
34 IS Sch 10 para 25 IS
Regs
FC Sch 3 para 26 FC
Regs
DWA Sch 4 para 26
DWA Regs
HB Sch 5 para 24 HB
Regs
CTB Sch 5 para 24
CTB Regs
35 IS Sch 10 para 27 IS
Regs
FC Sch 3 para 28 FC
Regs
DWA Sch 4 para 28
DWA Regs
HB Sch 5 para 26 HB

Regs
CTB Sch 5 para 26
CTB Regs
36 **IS** Sch 10 para 26 IS
Regs
FC Sch 3 para 27 FC
Regs
DWA Sch 4 para 27
DWA Regs
HB Sch 5 para 25 HB
Regs
CTB Sch 5 para 25
CTB Regs
37 R(SB) 32/83
38 para 30211 AOG
39 **IS** Sch 10 para 28 IS
Regs
FC Sch 3 para 29 FC
Regs
DWA Sch 4 para 29
DWA Regs
HB Sch 5 para 27 HB
Regs
40 Sch 5 para 27 CTB
Regs
41 **IS** Sch 10 para 3 IS Regs
FC Sch 3 para 3 FC
Regs
DWA Sch 4 para 3
DWA Regs
HB Sch 5 para 3 HB
Regs
CTB Sch 5 para 3 CTB
Regs
42 CIS/685/1992
43 R(SB) 14/85
44 **IS** Sch 10 para 2 IS Regs
FC Sch 3 para 2 FC
Regs
DWA Sch 4 para 2
DWA Regs
HB Sch 5 para 2 HB
Regs
CTB Sch 5 para 2 CTB
Regs
45 **IS** Sch 10 para 8(a) IS
Regs
FC Sch 3 para 9(a) FC
Regs
DWA Sch 4 para 9(a)
DWA Regs
HB Sch 5 para 9(a) HB
Regs
CTB Sch 5 para 9(a)
CTB Regs
46 **IS** Sch 10 para 8(b) IS

Regs
FC Sch 3 para 9(b) FC
Regs
DWA Sch 4 para 9(b)
DWA Regs
HB Sch 5 para 9(b) HB
Regs
CTB Sch 5 para 9(b)
CTB Regs
47 *Barclays Bank v
Quistclose Investments
Ltd* [1970] AC 567;
CSB/975/1985
48 **IS** Sch 10 para 9(a) IS
Regs
FC Sch 3 para 10(a) FC
Regs
DWA Sch 4 para 10(a)
DWA Regs
HB Sch 5 para 10(a)
HB Regs
CTB Sch 5 para 10(a)
CTB Regs
49 **IS** Sch 10 para 9(b) IS
Regs
FC Sch 3 para 10(b)
FC Regs
DWA Sch 4 para 10(b)
DWA Regs
HB Sch 5 para 10(b)
HB Regs
CTB Sch 5 para 10(b)
CTB Regs
50 **IS** Sch 10 para 37 IS
Regs
FC Sch 3 para 39 FC
Regs
DWA Sch 4 para 38
DWA Regs
HB Sch 5 para 37 HB
Regs
CTB Sch 5 para 36
CTB Regs
51 para 30208 AOG
52 **IS** Sch 10 para 4 IS Regs
FC Sch 3 paras 4 and
30 FC Regs
DWA Sch 4 paras 4
and 30 DWA Regs
HB Sch 5 para 4 HB
Regs
CTB Sch 5 para 4 CTB
Regs
53 **IS** Reg 2(1) IS Regs
definition of 'partner'
FC Reg 2(1) FC Regs

definition of 'partner'
DWA Reg 2(1) DWA
Regs definition of
'partner'
HB Reg 2(1) HB Regs
definition of 'partner'
CTB Reg 2(1) CTB
Regs definition of
'partner'
All s137(1) SSCBA
1992; definition of
'married couple' and
'unmarried couple'
54 **HB** Sch 5 para 24 HB
Regs
CTB Sch 5 para 24
CTB Regs
55 **IS** para 30237 AOG
FC/DWA para 42237
AOG
HB/CTB para
C2.12.ii.a and b GM
56 **FC** Sch 3 para 4 FC
Regs
DWA Sch 4 para 4
DWA Regs
57 **IS** Reg 2(1) IS Regs
definition of 'relative'
FC Reg 2(1) definition
of 'close relative' and
Sch 3 para 4 FC Regs
DWA Reg 2(1)
definition of 'close
relative' and Sch 4 para
4 DWA Regs
HB Reg 2(1) HB Regs
definition of 'relative'
CTB This is not
defined for CTB but
presumably the same
definition will apply
58 CSB/209/1986;
CSB/1149/1986; R(SB)
22/87
59 **IS** Sch 10 para 10 IS
Regs
FC Sch 3 para 11 FC
Regs
DWA Sch 4 para 11
DWA Regs
HB Sch 5 para 11 HB
Regs
CTB Sch 5 para 11
CTB Regs
60 CIS/494/1990
61 **IS** Sch 10 para 8(a) IS

Regs
FC Sch 3 para 9(a) FC
Regs
DWA Sch 4 para 9(a)
DWA Regs
HB Sch 5 para 9(a) HB
Regs
CTB Sch 5 para 9(a)
CTB Regs
62 IS para 30271 AOG
FC para 42271 AOG
63 IS Sch 10 para 6 IS
Regs
FC Sch 3 para 6 FC
Regs
DWA Sch 4 para 6
DWA Regs
HB Sch 5 para 7 HB
Regs
CTB Sch 5 para 7 CTB
Regs
64 FC Sch 3 para 7 FC
Regs
DWA Sch 4 para 7
DWA Regs
65 R(SB) 4/85
66 CFC/15/1990
67 IS Sch 10 para 19 IS
Regs
FC Sch 3 para 20 FC
Regs
DWA Sch 4 para 20
DWA Regs
HB Sch 5 para 20 HB
Regs
CTB Sch 5 para 20
CTB Regs
68 IS Sch 10 para 15 IS
Regs
FC Sch 3 para 16 FC
Regs
DWA Sch 4 para 16
DWA Regs
HB Sch 5 para 16 HB
Regs
CTB Sch 5 para 16
CTB Regs
69 IS Sch 10 para 11 IS
Regs
FC Sch 3 para 12 FC
Regs
DWA Sch 4 para 12
DWA Regs
HB Sch 5 para 12 HB
Regs
CTB Sch 5 para 12

CTB Regs
70 IS Reg 41(2) IS Regs
FC Reg 25(2) FC Regs
DWA Reg 28(2) DWA
Regs
HB Reg 34(2) HB Regs
CTB Reg 25(2) CTB
Regs
71 IS Sch 10 para 5 IS
Regs
FC Sch 3 para 5 FC
Regs
DWA Sch 4 para 5
DWA Regs
HB Sch 5 para 6 HB
Regs
CTB Sch 5 para 6 CTB
Regs
72 CIS/85/1992
73 IS Reg 48(4) IS Regs
FC Reg 31(4) FC Regs
DWA Reg 34(4) DWA
Regs
HB Reg 40(4) HB Regs
CTB Reg 31(4) CTB
Regs
All CIS/85/1992
74 IS Sch 10 para 12 IS
Regs
FC Sch 3 para 13 FC
Regs
DWA Sch 4 para 13
DWA Regs
HB Sch 5 para 13 HB
Regs
CTB Sch 5 para 13
CTB Regs
75 R(SB) 2/89
76 IS Regs 40 and 46 IS
Regs
FC Regs 24 and 29 FC
Regs
DWA Regs 27 and 32
DWA Regs
HB Regs 33 and 38 HB
Regs
CTB Regs 24 and 29
CTB Regs
All CIS/559/1991
77 *Thomas v CAO*
(appendix to R(SB)
17/87)
78 IS Sch 10 para 13 IS
Regs
FC Sch 3 para 14 FC
Regs

DWA Sch 4 para 14
DWA Regs
HB Sch 5 para 14 HB
Regs
CTB Sch 5 para 14
CTB Regs
79 IS Sch 10 para 14 IS
Regs
FC Sch 3 para 15 FC
Regs
DWA Sch 4 para 15
DWA Regs
HB Sch 5 para 15 HB
Regs
CTB Sch 5 para 15
CTB Regs
80 IS Sch 10 para 16 IS
Regs
FC Sch 3 para 17 FC
Regs
DWA Sch 4 para 17
DWA Regs
HB Sch 5 para 17 HB
Regs
CTB Sch 5 para 17
CTB Regs
81 IS Sch 10 para 23 IS
Regs
FC Sch 3 para 24 FC
Regs
DWA Sch 4 para 24
DWA Regs
HB Sch 5 para 30 HB
Regs
CTB Sch 5 para 30
CTB Regs
82 IS Sch 10 para 23 IS
Regs
FC Sch 3 para 24 FC
Regs
DWA Sch 4 para 24
DWA Regs
HB Sch 5 para 30 HB
Regs
CTB Sch 5 para 30
CTB Regs
83 IS Sch 10 para 24 IS
Regs
FC Sch 3 para 25 FC
Regs
DWA Sch 4 para 25
DWA Regs
HB Sch 5 para 31 HB
Regs
CTB Sch 5 para 31
CTB Regs

84 **IS** Sch 10 para 11 **IS**
Regs
FC Sch 3 para 12 **FC**
Regs
DWA Sch 4 para 12
DWA Regs
HB Sch 5 para 12 **HB**
Regs
CTB Sch 5 para 12
CTB Regs
85 **IS** Sch 10 para 12 **IS**
Regs
FC Sch 3 para 13 **FC**
Regs
DWA Sch 4 para 13
DWA Regs
HB Sch 5 para 13 **HB**
Regs
CTB Sch 5 para 13
CTB Regs
86 **IS** Sch 10 para 7 **IS**
Regs
FC Sch 3 para 8 **FC**
Regs
DWA Sch 4 para 8
DWA Regs
HB Sch 5 para 8 **HB**
Regs
CTB Sch 5 para 8 CTB
Regs
87 **IS** Sch 10 para 41 **IS**
Regs
FC Sch 3 para 43 **FC**
Regs
DWA Sch 4 para 42
DWA Regs
HB Sch 5 para 38 **HB**
Regs
CTB Sch 5 para 37
CTB Regs
88 **IS** Sch 10 para 36 **IS**
Regs
FC Sch 3 para 38 **FC**
Regs
DWA Sch 4 para 37
DWA Regs
HB Sch 5 para 36 **HB**
Regs
CTB Sch 5 para 35
CTB Regs
89 **IS** Sch 10 paras 31, 32
and 33 IS Regs
FC Sch 3 paras 33, 34
and 35 FC Regs
DWA Sch 4 paras 33,
34 and 35 DWA Regs

HB Sch 5 paras 28-29,
35, 42 and 45 **HB** Regs
CTB Sch 5 paras 28-
29, 34, 41 and 44 **CTB**
Regs
90 **IS** Sch 10 para 38 **IS**
Regs
FC Sch 3 para 40 **FC**
Regs
DWA Sch 4 para 39
DWA Regs
HB Sch 5 para 39 **HB**
Regs
CTB Sch 5 para 38
CTB Regs
91 **IS** Sch 10 para 39 **IS**
Regs
FC Sch 3 para 41 **FC**
Regs
DWA Sch 4 para 40
DWA Regs
HB Sch 5 para 40 **HB**
Regs
CTB Sch 5 para 39
CTB Regs
92 **IS** Sch 10 para 40 **IS**
Regs
FC Sch 3 para 42 **FC**
Regs
DWA Sch 4 para 41
DWA Regs
HB Sch 5 para 41 **HB**
Regs
CTB Sch 5 para 40
CTB Regs
93 **IS** Sch 10 para 18 **IS**
Regs
FC Sch 3 para 19 **FC**
Regs
DWA Sch 4 para 19
DWA Regs
HB Sch 5 para 19 **HB**
Regs
CTB Sch 5 para 19
CTB Regs
94 **IS** Sch 10 paras 42-43
IS Regs
FC Sch 3 paras 44-45
FC Regs
DWA Sch 4 paras 43-
44 DWA Regs
HB Sch 5 paras 43-44
HB Regs
CTB Sch 5 paras 42-43
CTB Regs
95 **IS** Sch 10 para 17 **IS**

Regs
FC Sch 3 para 18 **FC**
Regs
DWA Sch 4 para 18
DWA Regs
HB Sch 5 para 18 **HB**
Regs
CTB Sch 5 para 18
CTB Regs
96 **IS** Sch 10 para 29 **IS**
Regs
FC Sch 3 para 31 **FC**
Regs
DWA Sch 4 para 31
DWA Regs
HB Sch 5 para 32 **HB**
Regs
CTB Sch 5 para 32
CTB Regs
97 **IS** Sch 10 para 22 **IS**
Regs
FC Sch 3 para 23 **FC**
Regs
DWA Sch 4 para 23
DWA Regs
HB Sch 5 para 23 **HB**
Regs
CTB Sch 5 para 23
CTB Regs
98 **IS** para 30476 AOG
FC/DWA para 42464
AOG
HB Reg 73(1) and (3)
HB Regs
CTB Reg 63(1) and
(3) CTB Regs
99 **IS** Sch 10 para 34 **IS**
Regs
FC Sch 3 para 36 **FC**
Regs
DWA Sch 4 para 36
DWA Regs
HB Sch 4 para 38 **HB**
regs
CTB Sch 4 para 40
CTB Regs
100 **IS** Sch 10 para 30 **IS**
Regs
FC Sch 3 para 32 **FC**
Regs
DWA Sch 4 para 32
DWA Regs
HB Sch 5 para 33 **HB**
Regs
CTB Sch 5 para 33
CTB Regs

101 **IS** Sch 10 para 21 IS Regs
FC Sch 3 para 22 FC Regs
DWA Sch 4 para 22 DWA Regs
HB Sch 5 para 22 HB Regs
CTB Sch 5 para 22 CTB Regs

102 **IS** Sch 10 para 20 IS Regs
FC Sch 3 para 21 FC Regs
DWA Sch 4 para 21 DWA Regs
HB Sch 5 para 21 HB Regs
CTB Sch 5 para 21 CTB Regs

4. Notional capital (*pp404-410*)

103 **IS** Reg 51(6) IS Regs
FC Reg 34(6) FC Regs
DWA Reg 37(6) DWA Regs
HB Reg 43(6) HB Regs
CTB Reg 34(6) CTB Regs

104 **IS** Reg 51(1) IS Regs
FC Reg 34(1) FC Regs
DWA Reg 37(1) DWA Regs
HB Reg 43(1) HB Regs
CTB Reg 34(1) CTB Regs

105 CIS/124/1990; CSB/1198/1989
106 R(SB) 9/91
107 CIS/124/1990
108 CIS/40/1989
109 CIS/621/1991
110 CIS/264/1989
111 R(SB) 38/85
112 **IS** para 30323 AOG
FC para 42323 AOG
HB/CTB para C2.67 GM
113 **IS** Reg 51(1) IS Regs
FC Reg 34(1) FC Regs

DWA Reg 37(1) DWA Regs
114 CIS/236/1991
115 **IS** Reg 51(7) IS Regs
FC Reg 34(7) FC Regs
DWA Reg 37(7) DWA Regs
116 CIS/634/1992
117 **IS** Reg 51(6) IS Regs
FC Reg 34(6) FC Regs
DWA Reg 37(6) DWA Regs
HB Reg 43(6) HB Regs
CTB Reg 34(6) CTB Regs
118 R(SB) 9/91; CIS/25/1990; Contrast R 1/92 (IS) (Northern Ireland decision)
119 CIS/18/1990 (apparently to be reported as R(IS) 14/93)
120 para C2.69 GM
121 para C2.97 GM
122 para C2.92 GM
123 **IS** Reg 51A IS Regs
FC Reg 34A FC Regs
DWA Reg 38 DWA Regs
HB Reg 43A HB Regs
CTB Reg 35 CTB Regs
124 **IS/FC/DWA** s25(1)(c) SSAA 1992
IS para 30391 AOG
HB Reg 66(2) HB Regs
CTB Reg 57(2) CTB Regs
125 para C2.84 GM
126 para 30382 AOG
127 R(IS) 9/92
128 R(IS) 1/91; R(IS) 9/92
129 R(IS) 9/92
130 **IS** Reg 51(2) IS Regs
FC Reg 34(2) FC Regs
DWA Reg 37(2) DWA Regs
HB Reg 43(2) HB

Regs
CTB Reg 34(2) CTB Regs
131 **IS** Reg 51(3)(a)(ii) and (8) IS Regs
FC Reg 34(3)(a) FC Regs
DWA Reg 37(3)(a) DWA Regs
HB Reg 43(3)(a) and (7) HB Regs
CTB Reg 34(3)(a) and (7) CTB Regs
132 **IS** Reg 51(8) IS Regs
FC Reg 34(3)(a) FC Regs
DWA Reg 37(3)(a) DWA Regs
HB Reg 43(7)(b) HB Regs
CTB Reg 34(7) CTB Regs
133 **IS** para 30356 AOG
FC/DWA para 42352 AOG
134 **IS** Reg 51(3)(b) IS Regs
FC Reg 34(3)(b) FC Regs
DWA Reg 37(3)(b) DWA Regs
HB Reg 43(3)(b) HB Regs
CTB Reg 34(3)(b) CTB Regs
135 **IS** Reg 51(4) IS Regs
FC Reg 34(4) FC Regs
DWA Reg 37(4) DWA Regs
HB Reg 43(4) HB Regs
CTB Reg 34(4) CTB Regs
136 **IS** Reg 51(5) IS Regs
FC Reg 34(5) FC Regs
DWA Reg 37(5) DWA Regs
HB Reg 43(5) HB Regs
CTB Reg 34(5) CTB Regs
137 **IS** para 30371 AOG. See also CIS/184/1991.

apparently to be reported as R(IS) 13/93
FC/DWA para 42372 AOG

138 para 42372 AOG

5. How capital is valued (pp410-413)

139 IS Reg 49(a) IS Regs
FC Reg 32(a) FC Regs
DWA Reg 35(a) DWA Regs
HB Reg 41(a) HB Regs
CTB Reg 32(a) CTB Regs

140 R(SB) 57/83; R(SB) 6/84

141 R(SB) 18/83

142 R(SB) 6/84

143 CIS/24/1990

144 IS Reg 49(a)(ii) IS Regs
FC Reg 32(a)(ii) FC Regs
DWA Reg 35(a)(ii) DWA Regs
HB Reg 41(a)(ii) HB Regs
CTB Reg 32(a)(ii) CTB Regs

145 CIS/255/1989

146 R(SB) 27/84

147 R(SB) 2/83; R(SB) 31/83

148 CSB/1198/1989

149 IS Reg 49(a)(i) IS Regs
FC Reg 32(a)(i) FC Regs
DWA Reg 35(a)(i) DWA Regs
HB Reg 41(a)(i) HB Regs
CTB Reg 32(a)(i) CTB Regs

150 IS Reg 49(b) IS Regs
FC Reg 32(b) FC Regs
DWA Reg 35(b) DWA Regs
HB Reg 41(b) HB Regs
CTB Reg 32(b) CTB

Regs

151 IS Part 30 Appendix 2 AOG
FC/DWA Part 42 Appendix 2 AOG
HB/CTB C2: Annex B GM

152 IS Reg 52 IS Regs
FC Reg 35 FC Regs
DWA Reg 39 DWA Regs
HB Reg 44 HB Regs
CTB Reg 36 CTB Regs

153 CIS/391/1992; CIS/417/1992

154 *CAO v Palfrey; CAO v Dowell; CAO v McDonnell*

155 IS Reg 52 IS Regs
FC Reg 35 FC Regs
DWA Reg 39 DWA Regs
HB Reg 44 HB Regs
CTB Reg 36 CTB Regs

156 IS para 30057 AOG
FC/DWA para 42056 AOG
HB/CTB para 2.42 GM

157 CIS/449/1990

158 CIS/553/1991

159 IS Reg 49(a) IS Regs
FC Reg 32(a) FC Regs
DWA Reg 35(a) DWA Regs
HB Reg 41(a) HB Regs
CTB Reg 32(a) CTB Regs

160 R(SB) 18/83; R(IS) 2/90

161 IS para 30131 AOG
FC/DWA para 42132 AOG
HB/CTB para C2.34 GM

162 *Peters v CAO* (appendix to R(SB) 3/89)

163 IS Reg 50(a) IS Regs
FC Reg 33(a) FC Regs
DWA Reg 36(a)

DWA Regs
HB Reg 42(a) HB Regs
CTB Reg 33(a) CTB Regs

164 IS Reg 50(b) IS Regs
FC Reg 33(b) FC Regs
DWA Reg 36(b) DWA Regs
HB Reg 42(b) HB Regs
CTB Reg 33(b) CTB Regs

165 IS Sch 10 para 21 IS Regs
FC Sch 3 para 22 FC Regs
DWA Sch 4 para 22 DWA Regs
HB Sch 5 para 22 HB Regs
CTB Sch 5 para 22 CTB Regs

PART EIGHT: THE REGULATED SOCIAL FUND
Chapter 20: The regulated social fund (pp416-422)

1 Reg 5(1) SFM&FE Regs

2 Reg 6 SFM&FE Regs

3 Reg 5(2) SFM&FE Regs

4 Reg 9(1) SFM&FE Regs

5 Reg 9(2) SFM&FE Regs

6 Reg 9(3)(b) SFM&FE Regs

7 Reg 3(1) SFM&FE Regs meaning of 'confinement'

8 Reg 5(1)(b)(ii) SFM&FE Regs

9 Reg 4(2) SFM&FE Regs

10 Reg 6(1) SS(C&P) Regs

11 Reg 19 and Sch 4 para 8 SS(C&P) Regs

12 Reg 7(1) SFM&FE Regs

36   paras 5005 and 5026 SFG
37   para 5281 SFG
38   para 5283 SFG
39   para 5280 SFG
40   paras 5284-5364 SFG
41   paras 5284-5308 SFG
42   paras 5286-5287 SFG
43   para 5120 SFG
44   paras 5300-5302 SFG
45   para 5301 SFG
46   para 5302 SFG
47   para 5303 SFG
48   paras 5304-5306 SFG
49   paras 5307-5308 SFG
50   paras 5321-5329 SFG
51   paras 5343-5346 SFG
52   paras 5340-5342 SFG
53   paras 5360-5362 SFG

4. Easing exceptional pressures on families
(pp441-443)
54   SF Dir 4(a)(iii)
55   paras 5005, 5026 and 5392 SFG
56   para 5380 SFG
57   para 5381 SFG
58   *R v Secretary of State for Social Security ex parte Healey, The Times*, 22 April 1991
59   CIS/104/1991
60   paras 5400-5420 SFG
61   paras 5421-5423 SFG
62   paras 5424-5429 SFG
63   paras 5440-5443 SFG
64   paras 5469-5470 SFG
65   paras 5465-5468 SFG
66   paras 5460-5464 SFG
67   paras 5483-5484 SFG
68   paras 5480-5482 SFG

5. Travelling expenses
(pp443-445)
69   SF Dir 4(b)
70   SF Dir 4(b)(i)
71   paras 5520-5524 SFG
72   para 5544 SFG
73   paras 5526-5528 SFG
74   para 5529 SFG
75   para 5544 SFG
76   paras 5542-5548 SFG

Chapter 23: Loans
(pp446-457)

1. Budgeting loans
(pp446-449)
1   SF Dir 5
2   SF Dir 8(1)(a)
3   SF Dir 8(1)(c)
4   SF Dir 8(2)
5   para 3124 SFG
6   SF Dir 2
7   SF Dir 10
8   SF Dir 11
9   para 3060 SFG
10   para 3043 SFG
11   para 3080 SFG
12   para 3061 SFG
13   para 3062 SFG
14   para 3063 SFG
15   SF Dir 10
16   para 3163 SFG
17   para 3163 SFG
18   para 3003 SFG

2. Crisis loans
(pp449-454)
19   SF Dir 14(a)
20   SF Dirs 15, 16 and 17
21   SF Dir 22
22   SF Dir 21; para 4183 SFG
23   SF Dir 14(b)
24   SF Dir 3(a)
25   SF Dir 3(b)
26   SF Dir 15
27   SF Dir 16
28   SF Dir 16
29   paras 4040 and 4063 SFG
30   para 4042 SFG
31   para 4007 SFG
32   para 4402 SFG
33   R(SB) 1/83
34   para 4402 SFG
35   para 4101 SFG
36   para 4101 SFG
37   para 4102 SFG
38   paras 4103-28 SFG
39   para 4126 SFG
40   para 4127 SFG
41   para 4128 SFG
42   para 4103 SFG
43   para 4124 SFG
44   paras 4062 and 4400 SFG

45   paras 4440-42 SFG
46   para 4443 SFG
47   paras 4422-23 SFG
48   paras 4444-45 SFG
49   paras 4463-67 SFG
50   paras 4424-26 SFG
51   para 4420 SFG
52   para 4421 SFG
53   paras 4460-61 SFG
54   paras 4480-81 SFG
55   para 4481 SFG
56   para 4462 SFG
57   SF Dirs 18, 20 and 21
58   SF Dir 22
59   SF Dir 21
60   SF Dir 18
61   SF Dir 20
62   para 4181 SFG
63   para 4225 SFG

3. Repayments
(pp454-457)
64   s78(1) and (2) SSAA 1992
65   Part 3 SFAG
66   paras 3002-03 SFAG
67   para 3004 SFAG
68   para 3007 SFAG
69   para 3008 SFAG
70   para 3009 SFAG
71   para 3010 SFAG
72   para 3011 SFAG
73   para 3012 SFAG
74   para 3013 SFAG
75   para 3014 SFAG
76   Reg 2 SF(Misc) Regs
77   Reg 2(2) SF(Misc) Regs
78   paras 3125-26 SFAG
79   Reg 3 SF(RDB) Regs
80   s78(3)(a) SSAA 1992
81   s78(3)(b) SSAA 1992
82   s78(3)(c) SSAA 1992; para 3051 SFAG
83   para 3051 SFAG
84   para 3501 SFAG
85   App 2 SFAG
86   para 3502 SFAG
87   para 3503 SFAG
88   para 3040(1) SFAG
89   para 3040(2) SFAG
90   para 3040(3) SFAG

Chapter 24: Applications, payments and reviews (pp458-468)

1 Reg 2(1) and (2) SF(App) Regs
2 Reg 2(5) SF(App) Regs
3 Reg 2(4) SF(App) Regs
4 Reg 3(a) SF(App) Regs
5 Reg 3(b) SF(App) Regs
6 para 2100 SFG
7 para 2101 SFG
8 paras 2080-86 SFAG
9 paras 2103-05 SFG
10 para 2002 SFAG
11 para 1043 SFG
12 para 1043 SFG
13 paras 4081-82 SFG
14 SF Dir 7
15 paras 3100, 4080 and 5060 SFG
16 para 2062 SFG
17 para 2061 SFG
18 para 2068 SFAG
19 s138(3) SSCBA 1992
20 para 7022 SFG
21 s66(1)(a) SSAA 1992
22 Reg 2(1) and (2)(a) SF(AR) Regs
23 Reg 2(4) SF(AR) Regs
24 Reg 2(6) SF(AR) Regs
25 Reg 2(3) SF(AR) Regs
26 Reg 2(5) SF(AR) Regs
27 SF Dir 37
28 s66(1)(b) SSAA 1992
29 SF Dir 31
30 s66 SSAA 1992
31 para 7050 SFG
32 para 4005 SFAG
33 s66(6) SSAA 1992
34 s66(7) SSAA 1992
35 SF Dir 39(a)
36 SF Dir 39(b) and (c)
37 SF Dir 32
38 SF Dir 33
39 SF Dir 33
40 SF Dir 34
41 para 7140 SFG
42 para 7140 SFG
43 para 7141 SFG
44 SF Dir 35
45 SF Dir 36
46 para 7242 SFG
47 para 7129 SFG
48 s66(3) SSAA 1992
49 Reg 2(1) and (2)(b) SF(AR) Regs
50 Reg 2(4) SF(AR) Regs
51 Reg 2(6) SF(AR) Regs
52 Reg 2(3) SF(AR) Regs
53 para 4046 SFAG
54 s66(6) and (7) SSAA 1992; SFI Dirs 1 and 2
55 para 8013 SFG
56 s66(4) SSAA 1992
57 s66(5) SSAA 1992
58 SF Dir 38
59 para 7224 SFG

PART TEN: OTHER BENEFITS
Chapter 25: Health benefits (pp470-483)

1 Reg 6(2) NHS(TERC) Regs
2 Sch 1 para 3 and Table B NHS(TERC) Regs
3 Reg 4(e) NHS(TERC) Regs
4 Sch 1 para 1 and Table A NHS(TERC) Regs
5 Reg 6(5) NHS(TERC) Regs
6 Regs 3, 4, 5, 6 and 7 NHS(CDA) Regs
7 Reg 10 NHS(CDA) Regs
8 Reg 8(2) NHS(TERC) Regs
9 Reg 8(5) NHS(CDA) Regs
10 Regs 3 and 4 NHS(TERC) Regs
11 Sch 12 paras 2(4) and 3(4) NHS Act 1977
12 Reg 8 NHS(TERC) Regs
13 Reg 5(3) NHS(TERC) Regs
14 Reg 13 NHS(GOS) Regs
15 Reg 4 NHS(OCP) Regs
16 Reg 8(2) NHS(OCP) Regs
17 Regs 9(4) and 17 NHS(OCP) Regs
18 Reg 12(1) NHS(OCP) Regs
19 Sch 1 NHS(OCP) Regs
20 Reg 5 NHS(TERC) Regs
21 Reg 3 NHS(TERC) Regs
22 Regs 3 and 5 WF Regs
23 Reg 12 WF Regs
24 Reg 12(2A) WF Regs
25 Reg 9A WF Regs
26 Reg 16(2) WF Regs
27 Reg 9 WF Regs
28 Reg 12 WF Regs
29 Reg 4 WF Regs
30 Reg 5 WF Regs
31 Regs 10 and 11 WF Regs
32 Reg 3 WF Regs
33 Reg 3 and Sch 2 WF Regs

Chapter 26: Local authority benefits and services (pp484-492)

1 s77(2) SSA 1986
2 ss22(1)(b) and 23(1)(b) EA 1980
3 s77(1) SSA 1986
4 s77(2) SSA 1986
5 Reg 4(a) SOB Regs as amended
6 s5(2) and (3) E(MP)A 1948 as amended by s29(1) EA 1980
7 Regs 4(e)(i) and 6 SOB Regs
8 Sch 9 para 11 IS Regs; Sch 2 para 9 FC Regs; Sch 3 para 9 DWA Regs; Sch 4 para 10 HB Regs
9 s2 EA 1962
10 s17 EA 1980
11 ss55 and 39 EA 1944
12 s39(5) EA 1944
13 s39(5) EA 1944
14 *Rogers v Essex CC* [1986] 3 WLR 689 (HL)
15 s53 Education (No.2) Act 1986
16 *R v Essex Council Council ex parte C*, CA, *The Guardian*, 26 November 1993
17 s55(2) EA 1944
18 Administrative

Memorandum 6/66
19   Sch 2 para 16 CA 1989
20   s106 ERA 1988
21   s106 ERA 1988
22   s107 ERA 1988
23   s106 ERA 1988
24   s108 ERA 1988
25   s110 ERA 1988
26   s18(5) CA 1989
27   s18(6) CA 1989
28   s29(3) CA 1989
29   s29(2) CA 1989
30   s111 ERA 1988
31   s101 LGHA 1989
32   ss103-4 LGHA 1989
33   ss103-4 LGHA 1989
34   ss104-105 and 136
      LGHA 1989
35   s107 LGHA 1989
36   s131 LGHA 1989
37   s102 LGHA 1989

38   Reg 3 HRG(RG) Regs
39   Regs 8 and 12
      HRG(RG) Regs
40   Reg 8(2) HRG(RG)
      Regs
41   Regs 17, 18 and 19
      HRG(RG) Regs
42   Sch 3 para 4 HRG(RG)
      Regs
43   Reg 37 HRG(RG) Regs
44   Reg 12(b) HRG(RG)
      Regs
45   Reg 10 HRG(RG) Regs
46   s17(6) CA 1989
47   s17(10) CA 1989
48   s24(7), (8) and (9) CA
      1989
49   s26(3) CA 1989
50   Sch 2 para 1(2)(a) and
      (b) CA 1989
51   s17(9) CA 1989

52   s2 CSDPA 1970
53   s2 CSDPA 1970; s4
      DP(SCR)A 1986
54   s17 HSS&SSA Act
      1983
55   s73(14) SSCBA 1992
56   *R v Hereford and
      Worcester CC ex parte
      Chandler,*
      CO/1759/91; *R v Kent
      CC ex parte Bruce*
      [1986], *The Times,* 8
      February 1986
57   s7(D) LASSA 1970
58   s7(B) LASSA 1970

Chapter 27: Other sources of help *(pp493-497)*

1   s3 NHS Act 1977

Index

How to use this index

Because the *Handbook* is divided into separate sections covering the different benefits, many entries in the index have several references, each to a different section. Where this occurs, we use the following abbreviations to show which benefit each reference relates to:

(IS)	Income support	(CCB)	Community charge benefit
(FC)	Family credit	(CTB)	Council tax benefit
(DWA)	Disability working allowance	(RSF)	Regulated social fund
(HB)	Housing benefit	(SF)	Social fund

References to common provisions appear first in the sequence. We list individual references in the order above, which reflects the order of the sections of the *Handbook*.

Entries against the bold headings direct you to the general information on the subject, or where the subject is covered most fully. Sub-entries are listed alphabetically and direct you to specific aspects of the subject.

C

caecostomy
  free prescriptions 473
calculation
  council tax benefit 309-18
  disability working allowance 203-4
  family credit 189-91
  housing benefit 239-42
  income support 27-9
campsite fees (IS) 29; (HB) 226
capital 394-413
  abroad (FC) 191
  budgeting loans 447
  capital treated as income 387-8, 403
  child's 358, 387, 394-5, 410; (IS) 13; (FC)
    189; (DWA) 204; (HB) 215; (CTB)
    298, 313
  community care grants 435
  council tax benefit 297, 313
  couple living apart (IS) 335
  crisis loans 451, 453
  definition 395-8
  deprivation of capital 404-9
  diminishing capital rule 407-9; (IS) 166;
    (HB) 279
  disability working allowance 203
  disregards 398-404
  expenses of sale 411
  family credit 184, 189
  fixed term investments 395
  health service benefits 470, 471
  housing benefit 221, 239, 240
  housing renovation grants 490
  income from capital 385-7
  income treated as capital 397-8
  instalments 387-8, 402
  jointly owned 411
  limit for claiming xi, 394
  loans 396
  maintenance payments 135-41
  matrimonial assets 411-12
  non-dependant's (HB) 245-6
  notional capital 403-9
  overpayments arising from (IS) 165; (HB)
    277
  partner's 394; (IS) 13; (HB) 215; (CTB)
    298
  property 395-6
  savings 395
  tariff income 385-7; (HB) 240
  third party payments 408-9
  trade dispute (IS) 79
  trusts 396-7
  urgent cases payments 46
  valuation 410-13
  withdrawals 387
capital mortgage repayments (IS) 32, 35
caravan
  see: mobile home

care
  claiming for young person in care
    (IS/HB/CTB) 336, 337
  community care grants 434-45
  social services payments 490-2
  treatment of payments to young people
    leaving care 390, 402; (IS) 388
  see also: residential care
carers
  claiming (IS) 16, 22-3, 50, 68; (FC) 186;
    (CTB) 307
  not treated as a non-dependant (IS) 38-9;
    (HB) 243
  Restart, failure to attend 60
  treatment of wages 393
  see also: Independent Living Fund
carer's premium (IS/HB/CTB) 342, 343-4
  and severe disability premium 355-6
  while person cared for in hospital 114
caretakers
  see: service charges
**certificates for free or partial remission of
  health charges** 472-3
changing your claim (IS) 144; (FC) 192;
  (DWA) 205; (HB) 258
  see also: overpayments
changing which partners claim (IS) 54, 143;
  (HB) 262
charitable payments 382-4, 403-4
  deduction from funeral payments (SF)
    419
  payment direct to mortgagor (IS) 35
  payments in kind 403
  trade dispute (IS) 79, 383
  urgent cases payments (IS) 46
charities 496-7
  unpaid work 390; (IS) 16, 46; (FC) 186
cheque
  lost or missing (HB) 268
  see also: giro
child
  abroad (IS) 337; (FC) 186
  absence from home 329, 336
  capital 358, 387, 394-5, 410; (IS) 13; (FC)
    189; (DWA) 204; (HB) 215; (CTB)
    297
  claim by person from abroad (IS) 85-6, 93
  claiming for a child 335-8; (IS) 13; (FC)
    185, 188, 189-90; (DWA) 199, 203-4,
    205-6; (HB) 215; (CTB) 298
  disabled child premium (IS/HB/CTB) 342,
    343
  earnings 358-9
  family premium (IS/HB/CTB) 342, 343
  hospital/residential care (IS) 115-16, 337;
    (FC) 189, 337; (DWA) 204, 337; (HB)
    248
  income 258-9; (FC) 189; (DWA) 204;
    (HB) 215; (CTB) 298

clothing
  budgeting loans 448
  community care grants 438
  grants from education authorities 484-5
coastguard 370, 397; (IS) 46
cohabitation rule 330
  challenging decision that cohabiting 332-3
  withdrawal of benefit 332-3
  see also: couples, separation
cold weather payments xi, 3, 9, 421-2
college
  leaving (IS/HB/CTB) 338; (FC/DWA) 338
  see also: students
colostomy
  free prescriptions 473
commission, counted as paid work 362; (FC) 186, 366
commissioner for local administration
  see: Ombudsman
commissioners' decisions (IS/FC) 171, 178, 181
communal areas
  housing renovation grants 488
  service charges (HB) 228-9
community care grants 3, 10, 434-45
  amount payable 436
  application 458-60
  excluded items 430-2
  notification 460
  payment 461
  reviews 461-8
  time limit on giving decision 460
  withdrawing application 460
  see also: budgeting loans
community charge
  arrears deducted from IS 159, 160
company
  see: self-employment
compensation
  loss of employment/unfair dismissal 363, 397-8; (IS) 367; (FC/DWA) 368; (HB/CTB) 369
  for official errors 154-5
  for underpayments (IS) 147, 151, 169; (HB) 261
  personal injuries 385, 391, 392, 397, 401, 404
  see also: *ex gratia* payments
complaints
  about BA administration (IS) 168-9; (FC) 195; (SF) 461
  about local authority administration (HB/CTB) 292-4; (CTB) 323
  to councillor (HB/CTB) 263, 267, 293
  to MP (IS) 147, 169; (FC) 195; (HB/CTB) 267; (SF) 465
  to Ombudsman (IS) 147, 169; (HB/CTB) 263, 267, 293

  see also: appeals; reviews
compulsory purchase order
  removal expenses excluded from social fund (SF) 430
conditional sale agreement (HB) 223, 227
connections/disconnections
  see: fuel costs
constant attendance allowance 376, 377
contract for house purchase
  tenant buying own home (IS) 42
contrived tenancies (HB) 222
co-ownership scheme (IS) 29; (HB) 223, 227
council tax 298-309
  disability reductions 304-5
  discounts 305-8
  exempt properties 299-300
  joint and several liability 302-3
  owner's liability 301-2
  resident's liability 301-2
  transitional reduction 308-9
council tax benefit 296-8, 309-325
  advance claims 318
  amount of benefit 309-18
  applicable amount x, 339
  backdating a claim 318-19
  benefit period 320
  benefit week 320
  calculating benefit 311
  capital 297, 313
  carers 307
  change of circumstance 322-3
  claiming CTB and other benefits (HB) 259
  claiming for child 335-8; (CTB) 298
  claiming for family 328-9
  claiming for partner 330-5; (CTB) 298
  claims 297-8, 318
  community charge transitional arrangements 319
  complaints 323
  couples 298, 312
  date of claim 318
  death of claimant 321
  decisions 319-20
  deductions from IS for arrears 158-9
  disability reductions 304-5
  discounts 305-8
  gay and lesbian couples 312
  hospital 306, 324-5
  houses in multiple occupation, liability of owners 301
  hostels, liability of owners 301
  income 297, 313
  joint liability 302-3
  liability to pay council tax 300-3
  non-dependant deductions 312-13
  overpayment 321-2
  payment 320-1
  person from abroad 296, 324
  prison 306

hospital (*cont.*)
  claiming in advance of leaving hospital (IS) 145
  crisis loans not available 449
  earnings disregard (IS) 370
  fares to hospital 390, 403, 480-1; (SF) 444, 453
  free wigs and fabric supports 479-80
  going in and out of hospital (IS) 117
  moving into new home from hospital (HB) 221
  partner in hospital (IS) 115, 334; (FC/DWA) 333; (HB) 247-8; (CTB) 324-5
  resettlement benefit 377
  social fund payments for furniture and clothing 117
  students (HB) 252
hostel
  liability of owners for council tax 301
  moving out – community care grants 347-9
  payments counted as rent (HB) 214-15
  transitional protection (IS) 44
hot water
  see: fuel charges
hours of work (IS) 14-17; (FC/DWA) 186-8
  non-dependants (HB) 244
  short-time work (IS) 16, 57; (FC) 187
house sale
  capital 385, 398-400; (IS) 46
  proceeds on separation (IS) 139-40
houseboat (HB) 226
household 328-9; (SF) 442
  see also: absence from home; child; couples
household equipment
  budgeting loans 447
  community care grants 438
houses in multiple occupation
  housing renovation grants 487-90
  liability of owners for council tax 301
housing association deposits 399
housing benefit 214-294
  absence from home 218, 247-8
  amount of benefit 239-48
  applicable amounts x, 239, 339
  benefit period 262, 265-7
  benefit week 241
  capital 214, 240
  capital of non-dependant 245-6
  claims 214-16, 257-62
  claiming for a child 214, 335-8
  claiming for family 328-9
  claiming for partner 214-15, 257, 330-5
  claiming with CTB 258 (CTB) 318
  claiming when on IS 14; (HB) 258
  date of claim 258, 260
  decisions 263-5

deductions from eligible rent 226-7
delays in payment 259, 263
earnings 358-9, 362-75
eligible rent 225-31
eligibility 214-15, 221-5
extra benefit for exceptional circumstances 239, 246-7, 261
fuel charges 227-8
income 214, 215, 239
income disregards 245-6
information to support a claim 259-60
in hospital 247-8
joint occupiers 216-17, 242-3
moving home 220-1, 262
non-dependants (HB) 223, 239, 242-6
nursing homes/residential care 230-1
overpayments 274-83
passport to social fund funeral payments 7, 419
payments 265-71
payments on account 267-8
personal allowances 340-1
persons from abroad 223-5
premiums 342-56
recourse to public funds 83-5
renewing a claim 262
rent 214-15, 241-2
rent increases 238
rent-free periods 241-2
rent in advance 267
repairs 220
residential care 280-1
reviews 286-92
service charges 228-30
shared accommodation 216-17, 243
sheltered accommodation 243
social fund loans cannot be deducted 456
students 218-19, 221, 244, 249-56
subsidy arrangements 237, 261, 277-8
sub-tenants 243
tapers 240
tariff income 240
trainees (HB) 218-19
transfer of tenancy 246
transitional payments (HB) 248
treatment as income 377; (IS) 46; (SF) 451
two homes 217-18, 218-19, 220
unreasonably high rent 231-8
violence 219-20
waiver of rent during repairs 217, 242, 270
withholding benefit 260, 270-1
Housing Benefit Review Board 288-91
housing costs met by IS 29-43; (HB) 223
  deductions from IS 157-8
  deductions of fuel and other costs if included (IS) 30
  excessive costs (IS) 40-42
  in hospital 114

housing costs met by IS (*cont.*)
   mortgage interest payments (IS) 32-5
   prisoners 118
   tenants who buy their own homes (IS) 42
housing renovation grants 487-90
husband
   see: couples
hypoadrenalism
   free prescriptions 474
hypoparathyroidism
   free prescriptions 474
hypopituitarism
   free prescriptions 474

I

ignorance of rights
   good cause for late claim (HB) 261
ileostomy
   free prescriptions 473
illegal entrant
   claiming benefits (IS) 85-86
   crisis loans 450
   urgent cases payments 87-88
immigration
   see: person from abroad
immigration authorities
   see: Home Office
improvements, house
   deduction if included in housing costs met
     by IS 30
   housing renovation grants 487-90
   loan interest (IS) 30, 33, 36, 389, 399
incapable of work
   claiming when under 18 (IS) 68
   disability premium (IS/HB/CTB) 345-7
   higher pensioner premium (IS/HB/CTB)
     348-50
   signing on exemptions (IS) 22
   temporary absence from GB for medical
     treatment (IS) 25
   (during) trade dispute (IS) 77
   voluntary unemployment 60
income 357-93
   calculating weekly amount 359-60; (IS) 28
   capital treated as income 386-8, 404
   child's 358-9; (FC) 190; (DWA) 204
   council tax benefit (CTB) 297
   deprivation of income 391
   disability working allowance (DWA) 199
   earnings 362-75; (FC) 364-6; (DWA) 365-6; (HB/CTB) 366
   failure to apply for income 391
   family credit (FC) 184-5, 193
   health benefits 471-2
   housing benefit (HB) 214, 239
   housing renovation grants 489-90
   income from capital 385-7, 397-8
   income other than earnings 375-91
   income treated as capital 397-8

   maintenance (IS) 135-141; (FC/DWA) 378-9
   non-dependants (HB) 215, 246
   notional income 391-3
   part-weeks (IS) 359-60
   partner's 357-8; (IS) 13; (HB) 215; (CTB) 298
   period covered by income (IS) 360-1
   students (HB) 255; (CTB) 323
   student rent deductions 381; (HB) 254-5
   trade dispute (IS) 79, 363, 383, 388, 403, 404
   urgent cases payments 45-6
income support 12-182
   appeals 170-82
   applicable amounts 8-9, 27-8, 339-56
   backdating 145-7, 150-1
   benefit week 361
   Business Start-Up Allowance 65
   calculation 27-46
   capital 394-413
   claiming CTB 14, 297, 318-19
   claims 13-14, 142-7
   claims for child 335-8
   claims for family 328-9
   claims for partner 330-5
   Community Action 63-4
   complaints 168
   decisions 147-51
   direct payments of benefit to other people 155-61
   entitlement 12-26
   European Social Fund training 65-6
   fraud 167-8
   hardship payments 13, 24-5, 70-4
   homeless 119
   hospital in-patients 113-16
   housing benefit claims when receiving IS
     (IS) 14; (HB) 258, 259
   housing costs met 29-43
   income 357-93
   interim payments 148-9, 152-3
   late claims 145-7
   Learning for Work 63-4
   lost and missing payments 154
   maintenance 120-41
   non-dependant 38-40
   overpayments 161-7
   passport to other benefits 12
   payment of benefit 151-61
   person from abroad 81-97
   personal allowances 340-1
   premiums 342-56
   prisoners 117-9
   recourse to public funds 83
   relationship with HB 223, 240-1
   residential care, local authority 97-100
   residential care, private/voluntary 100-13
   reviews 149-150

lay-off (*cont.*)
   non-dependants (HB) 244
   see also: short-time work
learning difficulties (IS) 106-7
   community care grant – priority group
     436
Learning for Work 63
leaseholders
   rent/ground rent (IS) 29
   service charges (IS) 29
leaving a job
   payments (IS) 15, 361, 363, 366-71;
     (FC/DWA) 368; (HB/CTB) 368-9
   redundancy payments 366
legal aid
   judicial review (IS/FC/DWA) 182; (HB)
     292
legal fees
   excluded from SF help 430
lesbian couple
   claims 330; (IS) 143; (HB) 215, 257
liability to pay council tax (CTB) 298-303
liability to pay housing costs (IS) 31-2
liability to pay rent (HB) 216-17
liable relative
   maintenance payments 124-5
   payments from – effect on health benefit
     entitlement 398-9
   recovery of SF loan 455-7
licensee
   definition of non-dependant (IS) 38
   payments, counted as rent (HB) 215,
     226
life insurance 401
lifeboat crew
   actively seeking work 57
   Restart – failure to attend 61
   treatment of payments 370-1, 397
   urgent cases payments 46
life interest 401-2
life-rent (Scotland) 402
lighting
   see: fuel charges
living together as husband and wife
   see: cohabitation rule
loans
   educational 381-2
   from employer 363, 396
   repair/improvement loans (IS) 29, 33, 36,
     389, 399
   SF loans 446-57
   Trade dispute ends – IS loan (IS) 79-81
   see also: capital
local authority
   mortgage – negotiating interest only
     payments (IS) 35
   see also: complaints
local scheme (HB) 246-7
lodgers 384

lone parent
   see: single parent
lone parent premium (IS) 121; (IS/HB/CTB)
     342, 344-5
   earnings disregard (IS) 369
   whilst in hospital (IS) 114
long lease
   exclusion from HB 221, 227
lost payments (IS) 154; (FC) 194;
    (DWA) 207; (HB) 268; (SF) 452
low income
   entitlement to health benefits 471-3
   setting of maintenance payment level
     133
low-paid work 392-3
lump-sum payments of maintenance (IS) 139-
    41
   health benefit entitlement 471-2

M

Macfarlane Trust 494
   treatment of 382, 392, 403-4, 410; (IS) 79;
    (HB) 259; (SF) 452
maintenance 120-41
   absent parent required to pay 122-23
   arrears of periodical payments 137-9
   assessment of child support 133
   benefit penalty 127-30
   Child Support Agency 125
   child support scheme 125-35
   effect on benefits (IS) 135-41;
    (FC/DWA/HB/CTB) 378-9
   fear of violence 125, 126
   information to Child Support Agency 130-
    2
   liability for maintenance 122-25
   liable relatives 124
   lump sums 139-41
   payments to Child Support Agency 135
   periodical payments 136-9
   required to apply 125-8
market rent (HB) 233-4, 237, 260
market value (assessing capital) 410
maternity
   free dental treatment 475
   free milk tokens 482
   free prescriptions 473
   free vitamins for nursing mothers 483
   (during) trade dispute (IS) 77
maternity allowance 376
   SF loan repayments 456
maternity expenses payment (SF) xi, 2, 9,
    417-18
maternity leave (IS) 15; (FC) 187
   non-dependants (HB) 245
maternity pay (FC/DWA/HB/CTB) 363
maximum amount of benefit (FC) 189-90;
    (DWA) 203-4; (HB) 239; (CTB) 311

part-time work (IS) 15-16, 360-1, 368;
    (HB/CTB) 368-9
  claiming (IS/FC) 184
part weeks (IS) 359-60
partially sighted
  free sight tests 476-7
partner
  see: couples
partner outside GB (IS) 96-7, 340
  recent arrival in GB (IS) 24
  signing on (IS) 24
  sponsorship of 88-9
  urgent cases payment 87-8
  see also: overseas students; refugees
paternity disputes
  child support 132-3
pay day for benefit (IS) 151-2; (FC) 194;
    (DWA) 206
pay in lieu of notice 362, 363; (IS) 15, 367;
    (FC/DWA) 368; (HB/CTB) 368-9
payment of benefit (IS) 151-61; (FC) 194;
    (DWA) 206-7; (HB) 265-71; (CTB)
    320-1
  (in) advance/arrears (IS) 151-2; (FC) 194;
    (DWA) 177; (HB) 267
  (to) appointee (IS) 155; (HB) 257-8, 269
  benefit period (FC) 194; (DWA) 206; (HB)
    241, 262, 265-7; (CTB) 320
  benefit week (HB) 241; (CTB) 311, 320
  change of circumstances (FC) 194-5;
    (DWA) 207; (HB) 271-4
  compensation payments (IS) 154-5
  delays in payment 155 (HB) 260, 263
  extra benefit for exceptional
    circumstances (HB) 246-7
  frequency of payment (IS) 152; (FC) 194;
    (DWA) 206-7; (HB) 206-7, 265-6;
    (CTB) 320
  interim payments (IS) 148-9, 152-3; (FC)
    193-4; (HB) 260, 263, 267-8
  (to) landlord (IS) 157; (HB) 214, 267,
    269-70
  method of payment (IS) 151-2; (FC) 194;
    (DWA) 206-7; (HB) 214, 267; (CTB)
    320-1; (SF) 460
  rounding up of benefit (IS) 151; (FC) 190;
    (HB) 240; (CTB) 311
  (to) someone else (IS) 155-161; (HB) 269-
    70,
  students (HB) 255-6
  suspension of payment (IS/FC) 153, 166
  (to) third party (IS) 155-61
  withholding benefit (IS/FC) 153, 166; (IS)
    74; (FC) 194; (HB) 270-1; (CTB) 321
  see also: deductions from benefits
payments in kind 363, 390
  counted as paid work (FC) 186
  tied accommodation 364
pensioner premium (IS/HB/CTB) 348

amount 342
  temporary absence from GB (IS) 25
pensioners
  free prescriptions 473
period of study 379-80; (HB) 250-1
person from abroad (IS) 25-6, 73-85; (FC)
    191; (HB) 223-5
  applicable amount (IS) 340
  available for work (IS) 94-6
  children (IS) 93
  couples (IS) 86-7
  crisis loans 450
  good cause for late claim (HB) 225
  investigation of entry status when
    claiming 95-6
personal allowances
  definition (IS/HB/CTB) 340-1
  rates (IS/HB/CTB) ix, 340-1
personal injury compensation 385, 391, 397,
    402, 409
personal pension 362, 372
personal possessions 400-1
Polish resettlement accommodation (IS) 334
poll tax
  see: community charge
polygamous marriages 330; (FC) 190; (HB)
    257
  non-dependants (HB) 245
post-graduate student 379
power of attorney (HB) 257
pregnancy
  claiming when under 18 (IS) 68
  free dental treatment 475
  free milk tokens 482
  free prescriptions 473
  free vitamins 483
  maternity expenses payment (RSF) 416-
    18
  (during) trade dispute (IS) 77
premium bonds 395
  see also: capital
premiums (IS/HB/CTB) 342-56
  amounts ix-x , 342
  carer's premium 343-4, 355-6
  disability premium 345-6
  disabled child premium 343
  family premium 343
  higher pensioner premium 348-50
  lone parent premium 344-5
  pensioner premium 348
  severe disability premium 351-6
  when in hospital 113-17
premiums for retirement annuity contract 372
prescriptions
  free 473-5
  pre-payment certificates 474-5
presenting officer (IS/FC) 173
preserved right
  residential care (IS) 101-5

S

savings 395
  see also: capital
scholarship
  see: grant, student
school exams
  returning to take exams and effect on
    benefit (IS) 18
school fees 358, 383, 487
school field trips 485
school-leavers
  16/17-year-olds (IS) 67-8
  exams, returning to take (IS) 18
  leaving before official date (IS) 18
  terminal dates/child benefit extension
    period (IS) 18, 68-70
school meals
  free 10, 484
  SF help not available 430
school pupils
  claiming (IS) 17-19
  educational benefits 484-7
  educational needs excluded from SF 430
  health benefits 473-479
  signing on exemptions (IS) 23
  transport 485; (SF) 430
  young mothers (IS) 122
school uniforms 384; (SF) 430
Scottish Special Housing Association (HB)
  259
self-employment
  benefit period (HB) 266
  business assets 385, 397, 401
  calculation of weekly earnings 360, 373-4
  claiming FC 187
sole owners/partners of companies 410
selling capital 410-1
selling a home
  proceeds on separation (IS) 140-1
  urgent cases payments 46
  value disregarded 385, 398-400
senility
  see: Alzheimers disease
separation (IS) 333-5
  continuing to live under same roof 329;
    (IS) 120
  house sale, proceeds 385, 398-400; (IS)
    139-40
  liability for housing costs previously paid
    by ex-partner (IS) 30
  mortgage payments (IS) 32-5
  review of benefit when partner fails to pay
    mortgage (IS) 34
  see also: maintenance
service charges (IS) 29; (HB) 228-30
  paid by rent direct (IS) 156, 157
setting aside
  tribunal decision (IS) 174-5
  review decision (HB) 291-2

severe disability premium (IS/HB/CTB) 342,
  351-6
  earnings disregard (HB/CTB) 370
  hospital in-patient 114, 115
  temporary absence from GB (IS) 25-6
severe disablement allowance
  disability working allowance 202
  evidence of incapacity for work (IS) 22
  qualifying for premiums 343, 344, 348
  SF loan repayments 456
  treatment of 377
sewerage
  see: water charges
sexual harassment/abuse
  complaints about BA behaviour (IS/FC)
    169
  leaving work and the voluntary
    unemployment deduction 59
sexually transmitted diseases
  help with fares to hospital 480
shared accommodation
  apportionment of rent (IS) 30; (HB) 216-
    17
  with landlord 221-2
  see also: communal areas; joint occupiers
shared ownership scheme (HB) 221, 227
shares 395, 413
  see also: capital
sheltered accommodation (HB) 243
  claiming HB 215
  charges for communal areas (HB) 228
short-time work (IS) 16, 57; (FC) 187; (DWA)
  365
sick pay (FC/HB/CTB) 363
sickness
  absence from work (IS) 15, 360; (FC)
    187
  disability premium (IS/HB/CTB) 342, 345-
    6
  extra HB for exceptional circumstances
    246-7
  failure to attend Restart 60
  health authorities – provision of facilities
    496
  higher pensioner premium (IS/HB/CTB)
    342, 348-50
  non-dependants (HB) 245
  signing on and evidence of incapacity for
    work (IS) 22
  16/17-year-olds 67
  Social Services help 491-2
  temporary absence from GB for medical
    treatment (IS) 25-6, 334, 337
sickness benefit 376; (IS) 360
  claiming sickness benefit instead of
    retirement pension 349
  evidence of incapacity for work (IS) 22
  SF loan repayments 456
signing on (IS) 21-4, 48-9

students (*cont.*)
　free wigs and fabric supports for under
　　19s 480
　grants 379-81
　hospital (HB) 252
　liability for rent (HB) 218-19
　loans 379-81
　non-dependant deduction for students (IS)
　　39; (HB) 244
　nurses (CCB) 306
　part-time student (IS) 20-1; (HB) 250,
　　252; (CTB) 306
　period of study (HB) 250
　sandwich courses 379; (HB) 250, 251,
　　255
　single parents (IS) 17, 23
　student rent deduction 380; (HB) 254-5
　summer vacations (IS) 19, 32; (HB) 249,
　　250-1, 252, 256
　tax refunds 380
　two homes (IS) 32; (HB) 253
　see also: disabled students; overseas
　　students
subsidy arrangements
　backdating (HB) 261
　unreasonably high rent (HB) 232, 237
sub-tenants (IS) 38
　claiming HB 215, 243
　how paid HB 267
suing the DSS
　lost or missing payments (IS) 154; (FC)
　　194; (DWA) 207; (HB) 268
suitable alternative accommodation (IS) 41;
　(HB) 235-6
supplementary benefit 43-4, 143
supported housing
　transitional protection for boarders (IS) 44
surrender value 400, 410
suspension from work (IS) 368; (FC) 187
suspension of benefit (IS/FC) 153, 166; (HB)
　271
swapping claimant role for couples (IS) 24,
　34, 54, 143; (IS/HB/CTB) 347; (HB)
　262

T
tapers (HB) 240, 247
tariff income 386-7; (HB) 240
　diminishing capital rule 407-9
tax
　see: income tax
telephone claims (HB) 258
temporary accommodation
　benefit paid for two homes during repairs
　　(IS) 31; (HB) 220
tenants
　right to buy (IS) 42-3
　treatment of payments from 384
tent (IS) 29, 119; (HB) 226

terminal date (IS/HB/CTB) 338; (IS) 18, 69;
　(FC) 338
term-time accommodation (IS) 32; (HB) 253
Territorial Army (IS) 370-1
third party payments (IS) 35, 155
　capital 409-10
　income 391-2
tied accommodation 364
time limit (for)
　appealing to court 181
　appealing to social security appeal
　　tribunal 149, 170-1
　appealing to Social Security
　　Commissioners 179
　applying for further review (HB) 264; (SF)
　　462, 466
　asking for explanation of decision (IS)
　　148; (HB) 265
　asking for review (DWA) 207-8; (HB)
　　287; (SF) 462
　BA to send information to local authority
　　(HB) 259
　backdating of benefit (IS) 145, 150-1; (FC)
　　192; (DWA) 205
　correcting claim (IS) 143-4; (FC) 191-2;
　　(HB) 258
　deciding claim (IS) 148; (FC) 193; (DWA)
　　206; (HB/CTB) 263; (SF) 460
　hearing of further review (HB) 288-90
　making a claim (RSF) 417-18, 420
　notification of overpayment (HB) 283
　renewing claim (FC) 192; (DWA) 205;
　　(HB) 266
　repayment to next of kin (HB) 269
　review of decision to recover overpayment
　　(HB) 280
　supplying information in support of a
　　claim (HB) 259
trade dispute 77-81
　amount of (IS) 77-9
　calculation of capital/income 79
　can claim FC 191
　earnings (FC) 364; (DWA) 364; (HB/CTB)
　　366
　funeral expenses payment 418
　health benefits 471
　loan of IS at end of dispute 79-81
　maternity expenses payment 417
　non-dependant (HB) 244
　signing on 24
　SF budgeting loans – ineligibility 81, 433
　SF community care grants 432-3, 435
　SF crisis loans 81, 433, 450
training allowance
　claiming IS 21, 62-4
　Training for Work 63-5
training bonus 47, 65, 404
Training for Work 63-5
　mortgage interest payments 64

Family Premium — zoar one child - Payable with any other premium.

Loan Parent - Single Parent- one child -, + family premium / Disable child premium / carars premium.

Pensiar " - claimant / Partner - 60-74 - " " family Premium " " " " " " "

enhanced pensiar premium - 75-9 - / / " / " " " "

Higher pensiar premium , 80+ OR 60+ if satisfy disability Premium - if under 60 .

or - Claimant / Partner was entitled to disability premium within 8 weeks of 60th Birthday and has remained entitled to IS Since. NB - Couple rate pensiar / Higher pensiar premium - only satisfy conditions Payable with family - Disabled child - SDP - CP.

DP= Claimant / Partner under 60 + receives Mobility Supplement / DLA / Invalidity Pensen allowance
SDA - one registered blind - under 60 + uncapable of work for 28 weeks - Payable with family Premium, Disable child premium, SDP - CP.

SDP Severe disability - Single Claimant must be getting AA, or higher / middle rate of DLA
Care comp - Carar not getting ICA, or higher-middle rate DLA Care no - Non-dep over 18.

Non-dep getting AA - Couple - Both must get AA or higher /middle of DLA Care - no none
then one Carar receiving ICA - Payable with family Premium, Disability Premium, higher pensiar
couple - both - disabled child . - Disabled child premium - where child YP gets DLA or IS
registered blind - Capital Less then 3000 - Payable with any other premium.
Carars Premium - Carar in receipt of ICA or would be if not receiving overlapping - any other premium.

Welfare Rights Bulletin

The *Bulletin* is essential reading for welfare rights advisers, lawyers and anyone else needing to keep up to date with social security issues. One of its unique roles is to provide a bi-monthly update to the National Welfare Benefits Handbook and Rights Guide, as well as to CPAG's Child Support Handbook and Ethnic Minorities' Benefits Handbook.

In 1994 the *Bulletin* expands in size — consolidating its position as the journal with the most detailed and comprehensive coverage of social security developments available.

Contents will include the fullest coverage of:
- the new incapacity benefit and job seekers allowance
- new regulations, guidance and procedure, with comment, analysis and practical advice
- Social Security Commissioners' decisions — these will appear sooner and in greater quantity than before
- Court decisions, including appeals to the European Court
- reports on benefit law and service delivery issues, eg National Audit Office, Parliamentary and advisory committees, ombudsmen
- news from welfare rights workers — campaigns, issues and tactics

There will also be expanded coverage of such issues as housing benefit, benefits for people with disabilities, people from abroad.

Like the CPAG benefit guides, the *Welfare Rights Bulletin* is the best value in the field — and compulsory reading for any adviser needing the very latest benefits information.

ISSN 0263 2098

£15.00 for a full year's subscription (6 issues)

Sent automatically to CPAG Rights and Comprehensive members, and Bulletin subscribers.

Debt Advice Handbook

1st edition

Mike Wolfe and Jill Ivison
edited by John Seargeant

The *Debt Advice Handbook* is the only comprehensive practitioner's guide to the practice and processes of money advice in England and Wales. Accessible and authoritative, this Handbook draws together all the essential information needed for successful debt work, as well as offering advisers an armoury of tried and tested strategies and tactical advice, accompanied by practical examples.

All the stages and key issues of money advice are explained clearly. For example, there is guidance on Court procedures, tackling time orders and insolvency.

The text is fully indexed and cross-referenced to the Consumer Credit Act and other legislation, and to County and High Court rules. In addition, sections of the Consumer Credit Act are reproduced, along with other legislation, sample Court forms, standard letters and money advice forms.

The *Debt Advice Handbook* provides an approachable introduction to money advice for those new to debt work, and for generalist advisers. It is also an invaluable reference source for the more experienced adviser. Money advisers, welfare rights workers, social workers, solicitors, housing officers, consumer advisers, banks and building societies are amongst those who will find this Handbook an essential tool in their day-to-day work.

March 1993   0 946744 46 7   £7.95

"An invaluable guide to negotiating with creditors, dealing with bailiffs and Court procedures" — *The Observer*

"Aimed principally at counsellors ... but people in debt may also find it a useful self-help guide" — *The Times*

"For advisers ... this handbook will undoubtedly become an invaluable source of practical information and guidance" — *Ann Abraham, Chief Executive, National Association of CABx*

"Covers almost every aspect of debt law, with practical advice ... it is a gem for trainees and unqualified consumer advisers" — *The Law Society's Gazette*

"This book has been needed for a long time ... add it to your library" — *New Law Journal*

"Arguably the most lucid and probably the most definitive on the subject" — *Credit Management*

"Comprehensive ... (the authors) are to be congratulated on their achievement" — *Roof*

"CPAG are to be congratulated on producing such a useful and invaluable guide" — *Money Advice Association*

Rights Guide for Home Owners, 1994-95

10th edition

This edition is completely revised and updated and includes coverage of housing law in England, Wales and Scotland, as well as social security issues. New features include: council tax, CTB and problems over transitional relief; changes to County Court rules over possession proceedings; changes with housing costs if you are on income support.

Also covered are: types of mortgages, information for leaseholders, cutting mortgage costs and increasing income, repairs and improvements, arrears and avoiding repossession, Court action, shared arrangements and partnership breakdown, consumer credit and secured loans, mortgage rescue schemes, how to find another home.

The *Rights Guide for Home Owners* is widely used by mortgage holders, CABx, local authority departments, housing and debt advisers, consumer advisers and building societies.

"This very practical guide provides valuable step-by-step advice" — *Daily Telegraph*

"Invest in Rights Guide for Home Owners ... It is full of invaluable information and careful study should answer most of your questions" — *Daily Mirror*

"Covers everything you need to know about home ownership" — *The Independent*

"Running into mortgage arrears? Spending a few pounds on a book may save your home" — *Bella Magazine*

"For excellent advice turn to Rights Guide for Home Owners" — *Good Housekeeping*

"An extremely practical, step-by-step guide" — *NACAB Booklist*

Autumn 1994   **£7.95**

0 946744 58 0   Publ.CPAG/SHAC

CPAG's Housing Benefit and Council Tax Benefit Legislation, 1994/95

7th edition

Lorna Findlay and Martin Ward

This definitive, annual publication is invaluable for anyone dealing with the ever-changing complexities of housing benefit or council tax benefit legislation. Coverage includes Scotland, Wales and England.

All the relevant statutory material is collected together and accompanied by an expert commentary. Information is fully indexed and cross referenced.

It is completely revised and updated to contain the legislation in force as at April 1, 1994, as well as official guidance and case law. A particular emphasis is placed on identifying and commenting on the latest case law. This edition is particularly important as it appears after a year's practical experience of the council tax and CTB in operation. Amongst other key changes covered are new rules for benefits for people from abroad.

For advisers, lawyers, local authority administrators, students, review board members and their clerks.

"Packed with relevant information in an easily portable form. The title remains a work which no one concerned with housing benefits can be without" — *Family Law*

"An important tool for anyone advising about housing benefit" — *The Law Society's Gazette*

"A most valuable addition to social security law" — *New Law Journal*

"An indispensable guide for all those advising claimants in whatever capacity" — *Scots Law Times*

June 1994   £31.00 (main volume)

0 946744 62 9

Updating **Supplement:** December 1994, **£7.95**

> **SPECIAL OFFER: Findlay/Ward and its Supplement are £38.95 at full price, but are reduced to £35.00 per set if we get your order before 31 May 1994.**
> Main volume only — reduced to £27.50 before 31 May.